RIFLES

A
MODERN
ENCYCLOPEDIA

Rifles

A MODERN ENCYCLOPEDIA

Henry M. Stebbins

THE STACKPOLE COMPANY
HARRISBURG, PENNSYLVANIA

PREFACE

IN 1947 Harry Stebbins' book *Small Game and Varmint Rifles* was published. It was followed in 1952 by *How to Select and Use Your Big Game Rifle*.

The introductions to each, to which the reader of this volume is referred, could well be combined for this book and be apt, with one condition.

The twelve years which have passed since the end of World War II have marked a development without parallel in the field of arms and ammunition. The ordnance departments of the world powers used the lessons which that bitter strife had uncovered, and they revised previous concepts of both the rifle and cartridge which should arm the riflemen of their future tactical infantry units.

The fact that advances in ordnance designs in rifles and cartridges are followed quickly by application in the commercial channels that cater to riflemen in the target and hunting segments of the shooting public has resulted in so many changes in what the buyers may select from that this volume becomes essential to intelligent choice from the varied fare that is offered over the counter or at the gunshop.

Being a rifle crank of the most advanced type, Harry found in each new rifle or cartridge another opportunity for study and evaluation from the viewpoint of his experience on the range and in the game field. His life work of teaching English literature assures his ability to give his readers a clear as well as an impartial, advanced gun crank's opinion of rifles from black powder days through the most recent developments.

Harry is human and has his preferences in arms and ammunition, as all we shooters have, but in my wide acquaintance with riflemen he is almost unique in that he has no prejudices! Out of our long friendship I've gathered the impression that according to his philosophy all rifles are good, but some are better suited to specific needs than others; and in this book he has set forth clearly the why and wherefore of currently available arms and cartridges, for the information of the novice and the oldtimer, in concise, complete and fair-minded form.

THOMAS C. FLORICH

White Plains, New York.

v

FOREWORD

WRITING this book was an humbling experience because it proved the loyalty of old friends and brought me some new ones. Always the doubt comes up of whether I have made a pest of myself and am deserving of such kindness. But Robert Louis Stevenson said—and he was like you and me in loving the wild places where the wind blows free instead of ricochetting off architecture—"There is a deal more kindness than is ever spoken." Usually it doesn't need to be spoken; it shows.

Tom Florich, Tom Florich, Jr., and Bert Shay wrote long, carefully expressed contributions and illustrated them with photographs. Parker Ackley, Jules La Bantchni, and Roy Weatherby stuck out their necks and discussed that controversial subject, the custom-built American sporting rifle. I think they wrote as men who love the rifle as well as craftsmen who make a living at the business. Judge Roy S. Tinney gave immeasurable help in the effort to publicize the fact that we must "make America, once again, a Nation of riflemen," and that it *can* be done. Henry Way-Silvers, Paul Matthews, Charlie Tait, and others helped with sympathetic photographs. I can't count all the help.

Many friends gave me the benefit of their experience, and the sharpening of shared knowledge that comes in long, leisurely discussions. Let me add the names of Jerry Fuller, Brad Upton, Francis Clarke, Charlie Canoll, Earnie Lamb, Lewie Dunbar, Bert Armstrong, John Austin, Warren Sherwood, Jim White. The list stretches back, incomplete, of course, and maybe it will reach forward. I hope so.

The American Rifleman, Combat Forces Press, *Gun Digest, Guns,* and *Precision Shooting* were kind, too. They would be; they're for the free but safe use of firearms in America. They know about that underpinning of national strength.

Arms and ammunition companies, gunsmiths, engravers, and importers gave me photographs, many taken especially for this book. When I needed technical information on their products, they supplied it.

But most of all I thank my wife. For one thing, she put up with the hundreds of hours of withdrawn, remote silence broken only by the rustle of papers, the rattle of the typewriter, and my harried grunts and mutterings. Hardly a living companionship!

For another thing, there was her direct help. Often we'd prove the maxim, "Two heads are better than one," in straightening out and simplifying some flinty, obstinate passage or in discussing "what is and what ain't" about rifles and riflemen. And sometimes she'd tone things down a bit: "I don't really think I'd say that, if I were you."

I'll write three more words and sign off.

Dedication
To Glen.

HENRY M. STEBBINS

Winchester, Virginia.

CONTENTS

IN THE historical sense the "modern" age can start at the date of Columbus' first voyage to the New World. Studying the modern American sporting rifle we do well to begin at the time of the Civil War. Then our modern arms began, and our modern demands, too.

CIVIL WAR LEGACIES

The Spencer and Henry lever action repeaters served in that war, and so did a bolt action, the .52 rimfire single shot Palmer carbine. The Henry started a type of action that still is enormously popular, and it didn't take long in becoming so.

Bullet weight for the .44 Henry was standard at 200 grains, and both flat and pointed forms went into the tubular magazine under the barrel. Black powder doses in this cartridge, which went into revolvers too, varied from 26 to 28 grains in weight.

Closely similar proportions of powder and lead went into the bigbore Spencer loads, and all of these rounds developed the low rifle velocity of some 1100 feet per second. The .56-.56 case was practically straight, and it carried a bullet of about .56 inch diameter. Tapered, sometimes gently bottle-necked, and usually lengthened, it became the .56-.52, and a still longer, more tapered case was known as the .56-.50.

Note the decimal points. The first figure referred to the basic caliber, the second to its final form. These bullet calibers were more nominal than exact. In wartime service there was some interchanging, the .56-.50 having been used in the larger caliber arms. The sudden, sharp blow of black powder upsets considerably undersized soft lead bullets to seal a bore, and the exceptionally heavy crimp of the .56-.50 case mouth would have helped the expansion by its delaying action.

Spencer charges varied. Winchester, at least in the later years, poured in 45 grains of black for all of them. Bullets weighed 350 grains, except the .56-.52, which was a pumpkin of 386. Not to be outdone, Remington issued rations of 45 and 350, 45 and 400, and 42 and 362 for the three calibers, .50, .52, and .56.

In carbine form, Spencers were handy for hunting. True, that mule-ear hammer had to be cocked by hand for each shot—operating the lever didn't do it—and the tubular magazine in the buttstock held only about half as many rounds as the Henry did. But the Spencer was solid and heavy, with heft enough to hold steadily in spite of its shortness; and the big bullets plunked into game with considerable authority.

It was a short-range arm, and you had to really stalk when using it on the plains of the fast-opening West. Attempting to remedy this, the company brought out a special sporting caliber, the decidedly bottle-necked .56-.46, with the usual 45 grains of powder and a longer, slimmer 330-grain bullet. Perhaps it was the first factory "wildcat." Strictly speaking, that term refers to gunsmithed alterations of standard case forms—rarely to a completely new cartridge—the most common being a neckdown to smaller caliber in order to increase velocity.

CHAPTER 1

SOME MODERN HISTORY

The Henry rounds, and most of the Spencers, were marketed up to and past World War I. Not only collectors bought them. All over the world they were used for killing game, and for grimmer purposes. The old carbines and rifles went to far places, and to rough places.

The Henry, later as the Winchester 1866 with wood forestock and a loading gate in the side of its receiver, was manufactured for years after the 1873 Winchester had outmoded it. That '66 came in at least two centerfire sizes, too, the .44 Smith & Wesson American revolver load and a special .44 Henry.

WINCHESTER 1873

But our modern repeaters as we know them—and still meet them in "outlandish, desolate places" of absolutely unspoiled beauty—began with the Winchester 1873. It had the toggle-lock action of the Henry, and the long, heavy receiver with only the firing pin, not the breechblock, sliding out back to cock the hammer. Its .44-40-200 (40 grains of black powder and 200 of gray lead) was a much deadlier cartridge than the little rimfire .44, more reliable in its priming system and stronger in construction. Centerfire ignition let you reload your fired cases, and inside lubrication made the cartridge waterproof.

The rifleman came into his own. It takes thousands of practice shots to get and keep the mastery of your rifle. Reloading cuts the costs until you almost blush.

That same year of 1873 saw the coming of the Government .45-70 Springfield single shot, superseding the .50-70. Today you find more .45 Springfields than 73s in use, by far.

Marketing of the 73 kept up until 1924. It had been popular in .32-20-115 and .38-40-180 also, and reasonably so in .22 short and .22 long versions which came out in 1897 and continued for six or seven years. It was a clumsy, crooked-stocked old gun, much too heavy for the power it carried. Even the standard 20-inch-barreled carbine went to 7½ pounds, and the rifles added another pound, sometimes about two, of sag. But by and large it was the favorite of the American hunter. There was fast repeating if you wanted it, quick, sure cocking for the first shot, and great reliability if the rounds were of fairly normal length. Too short or too long, they'd tie up the action. Reloaders learned this.

Magnified, it became the 1876 or Centennial big-game rifle. The .44-40 had been a terrible wounder of game. But the .40-60-210 and .45-60-300 were respectable deer cartridges. (Sometimes a couple of extra grains' weight of powder went into these loads, and much later Remington offered safe, low-pressure smokeless rounds for the .40.) For really big American game there were the steeply bottle-necked .45-75-350 with solid bullet and the gently necked .50-95-300 with copper-tubed, hollow-point "Express" lead. The .50 also had a 312-grain solid and, like so many other Winchester black powder loadings on special order, full patch and soft-point, jacketed bullets. And there was a curious soft, hollow point, jacketed, with only a narrow cavity and no express tube to add the expansive quality of trapped air compressed on impact. These special bullets were all of standard 300-grain weight. It mustn't be supposed that all these loadings or even all these calibers came out in the model year. Ballistics engineers worked out theories and hunters' requirements were sounded, just as they are today. No more 1876 rounds are being made, though the .45-60 case is easy to form: you shorten .45-70 brass.

SINGLE-SHOT TENACITY

In 1876 and for years afterward people still depended on the single shots for power and for accuracy. During the last 25 years or so of the old century, Remington, Sharps, Maynard, Ballard, Bullard, Stevens, Winchester and some others made these "britch-loaders," as an old guide used to call them. They handled practically all the repeating-rifle rounds and many special jobs of their own.

Probably the biggest long-range buffalo cartridge was the .50-170-700 Sharps in a 3¼-inch straight case, though the .45 Sharps, used in some Winchesters too, was pretty formidable. Its case lengths ran from 2.1 and 2.4 inches (.45-70 and .45-90 Winchester lengths) to 3¼, powder charges from 70 and 75 to 120 grains of black, and lead from 420 to 550 grains.

A favorite in "smallbores" on the plains was the .40-90-370 prescription, in bottle-necked and "Sharps Straight" brass, and in a straight-tapered Ballard version. The Ballard came in powerful .44 and .45 calibers, too.

Whittling down and sometimes practically wiping out our wealth of magnificent big game in those days wasn't enough. Cheap shotguns and cheap .22 single shots slaughtered the small stuff and the term "game-hog" was practically meaningless—then. Yet even that far back there were artists in small-game hunting who took pride in clean one-shot kills, and not too many of them, either, or too easy kills. A great variety of small-game cartridges came out for their single-shot rifles—loads that are still fascinating to use when you can get or make the empty brass for handloading.

The .22-8-45 Maynard and .22-13-45 Winchester fitted many makes of rifles; and for the perfectionist who wanted—and usually got—more accuracy, punch, and ranging power, there was the long, straight .22-15-60 Stevens. Also of Stevens design were the straight .25-21-86 and .25-25-86, popular up to World War I, and the .28-30-120 and .32-25-150 Ideal. This lineup is only a sampling. Varieties of handloads and special bullets were nearly if not quite as liberal as in our most favored modern case forms. For that matter, buffalo hunters too were handloaders. The lonely prairies were big and the job involved a lot of shooting.

Single shots attained great popularity in three main action types, and Remington made specimens of all. The famous rolling block, used in thousands of military Rems, was one of the earliest and simplest. One model, the little Number 4 rimfire, hung on until 1933. Cock the hammer, which swings on a big pivot, then thumb back the breechblock, which rolls on a similar pivot up front. Load, shove the breechblock forward, and fire. The interlocking of the huge hammer base and the breechblock take the backthrust of the explosion. This is the famous Rider pattern.

The Remington-Hepburn is a straight-falling block action. Most specimens are operated by a thumbpiece on the right side of the receiver, but a few Heps are opened and closed by a finger-lever extension of the trigger guard, like the Winchester or the usual Stevens.

The tiny Number 6 Remington, another survival up to 1933, is perhaps the only rocking-block Remington. The breechblock does not roll, nor does it fall straight. In a Stevens Model 44 you see the perfect specimen: the breechblock rocks back in a smooth curve as you throw the finger-lever forward. The later 44½ first drops, then rocks, and it's a stronger action.

The tip-up barrel breech action was another type that the fine Maynard rifle—and early Stevens rifles, too—made fairly popular for a time. One still in good shooting shape might be hard to separate from its owner. In light, inexpensive design Stevens kept the type alive in its Maynard Junior and its later Marksman, both under-lever actuated.

Remington-Rider single shot rolling block action. Some breechblocks had a higher and more upright spur ahead of the hammer, but this is a fine, typical specimen in the Remington museum.

Although the Winchester single shot was not made by that company until the 1880's, the Browning patent date of Oct. 7, 1879, is stamped on Winchester top tangs. This specimen of the beveled High Wall, a .30-40, was stocked by Thomas C. Florich. *Courtesy* Combat Forces Press.

Great varieties of styling and caliber were made in single shot. The Winchester range of choice seems about average, though none of their single-shot lever guns was inexpensive.

There were solid frame and later takedowns, rifle, shotgun, and carbine or musket buttstocks, straight and pistol grips. At least four sizes of receiver were made: the common high-wall with beveled sides; the heavy, unbeveled high-wall or "Express;" the smooth-sided low-wall sporter for calibers up to .44-40; and the beveled low-wall, a little heavier, which was used in the last years on the .22 musket or training-rifle style. And some beveled high-walls for light barrels seem to have been thinned down.

At least eight barrel sizes were marketed regularly, from the small Number 1 to the Number 5, a .35 and .405 Number 3½, a carbine and a musket. The latter became the standard-weight Model 52 bolt action .22 target rifle barrel and was used practically unchanged until about 1955, when the muzzle was made flat instead of rounded, and the front sight lug came off, being replaced with a pair of screw holes for the base of a target front. Most of the old barrel sizes came in round, octagon, or half-octagon shapes, the latter stepped down to round just ahead of the forearm tip. There were regular and special lengths from 15 to 36 inches.

THE 1880s

This was an active decade for the American sporting rifle.

Marlins

The 1881 repeater took its special .40-60-260 and .45-85-285 cartridges, the latter really a .45-70 express, though its speeded-up bullet was solid, not hollow pointed. The 1883 handled the target-famous .32-40 and .38-55, and the 1888 the .32-20, .38-40 and .44-40 Winchester 1873 line. These were top-ejecting lever actions. In 1889 Marlin featured a side ejector for the small cartridges.

Colts

The year 1885 saw the first of the Colt slide-action rifles. Their earlier metallic-cartridge repeater, the .44-40 Burgess lever gun of 1883, was made for only a year or so. The new pump action gave hunters what they wanted, fast magazine fire; and the exposed hammer was quick to cock for the first shot. No one with sense laughed at the trade name "Lightning."

Calibers were the familiar .32-20, .38-40 and .44-40, and there was a neat little .22 rimfire for short or long cartridges, as desired. The big Express model of 1886 came in some Winchester 1876 calibers, .45-60, .45-75 and .50-95, and for the Winchester Model 1886 rifle's little deer load, the bottle-necked .38-56-255 brought out in 1887. Then there were special Colt sizes. The .40-60-260 was in fact almost a duplicate of the Marlin caliber under that name, which closely resembled the Winchester .40-65-260 in case shape, though some were made with thinner rims. The Colt Lightning's .45-85-285 was a solid-bullet express load that took the Marlin .45-85 prescription in a longer case, 2⅛ inches instead of the 2.1 which was Government .45-70 standard.

The Colts were strong and reasonably reliable black powder rifles. I never heard of one jamming, nor had I ever any difficulty whatever in using one that I got to know fairly well. However, you'll notice that none of them took really heavy bullets for their caliber, and the extracting power of all the early slide actions seems to have been weaker than the pully-hauly of good lever guns. Colts worked well with factory loads, but some gave trouble with thin, much-reloaded brass like that of the .50-95, for example.

Engraved, inlaid, and carved, this fine '86 from the Winchester collection represents the best of the old-time work. The curved "rifle" buttplate, octagon barrel, and takedown frame reflect the tastes of the early 1900's. You can see the magazine lever, for unscrewing the mag tube preparatory to taking down, just below the muzzle.

Winchester 1886

The Colt Express hadn't much chance, for the Winchester 1886 lever-throw was so short and easy that hunters took to it—and still do. Probably it's the earliest action still popular, for it was changed only in minor details—including strength of materials—to become the Model 71.

The '86 was chambered originally, it seems, for the .45-70 Government, .40-82-260 and .45-90-300. These three could be had later in hollow-point as well as solid-lead, like the .50-110-300 which followed. Other black powder '86 loads that rated birth announcements in the rifleman's world right up to 1894 or '95 were the .38-56-255, .38-70-255, .40-65-260, .40-70-330 and .50-100-450. The .33 high-power smokeless, smaller than today's .348 in all but rim dimensions, was a 1903 arrival.

The old action has been famous for reliability and handiness. It's convenient, too. Being one of the first rifles with a cartridge stop at the exit of its magazine, it "permits the use of cartridges of different lengths, having the same length of shell," as catalogues explained. For instance, the .45-70 took loads that were as short in overall as the .45-70 Short-Range, and as long as the .45-70-500. You could mix them up, for as a cartridge left the magazine the stop went into action and prevented crowding a lot more effectively than the door of a New York subway car! Roughly, two general overall lengths were accommodated by the action: the long .38-70, .40-70, .40-82, .45-70-500, .45-90, the big .50s—and the others. Every single one had its admirers, and plenty of them.

The gun represented a great and successful effort by the factory to please its customers. You can trace the ebb and flow, the changes of taste, in its history. The beautifully colored old case-hardened receivers of early times were right enough in black powder days; but with the coming of smokeless powder, and with special High Velocity rounds in .45-70, .45-90, .50-110 and .40-65 (by Remington) some doubts arose. The later blued receivers left no doubt. With rifle number 126,000 still tougher steel was used, and handloaders check that matter before going much beyond old factory velocities. (Or they'd better.) The 71 action backs up wildcat .45's of great power. Usually they're formed from .348 brass.

The early rifles were heavy, from about 8½ to a good 9 pounds, and the 22-inch carbine of 1889-1919 was listed at 8, and feels it. It was handy in a saddle holster, however. So were the later Extra Light Weight rifles, catalogued in .45-70 only. The solid frame weighed 6¾, the takedown 7¼. With 22-inch, nicely tapered, nickel steel barrels, hollowed-out shotgun stocks with light, hard rubber buttplates, and usually half magazines holding four rounds, they are a delight to carry and to handle. They shorten long woods miles. Recoil? With heavy-bullet loads, 405 grains and more, they do come back. As I remember the kick, it was noticeably less than that of the old 1895 model in .405, and much less than the shove of the .375 Model 70. Any of them can be mastered, particularly by the grace of handloading: then we step up the loads gradually. And this anyone should do with his first heavy-recoiling rifle. It's a mistake to think we shan't flinch in the game fields if we've been kicked into it by practice rounds.

The standard .33 rifle carried on the modern idea of shotgun butt, smooth lines and moderate weight. With a 2-inch-longer barrel than the featherweight and less nickel steel bored out of it, weight went up about a half pound. An odd thing is that none of these rifles seems muzzle-light for quick offhand work, and you need weight out front for that, too. In 1935 the .33 bowed out and the Model 71 came in.

Those were obliging times. Back in '34 I ordered a .33 with special barrel having no rear sight cut. I had no idea that the 86 was quite so close to its last days, but after a few weeks the factory came through with what I wanted.

Bolt Guns

In the 1880s there were a few American bolt-action rifles. The Remington-Keene with tubular magazine under its barrel was patented, in fact, in 1874. Its calibers include the .44-40, a .40-60-260 that apparently was the Marlin round, and the .45-70 with 405-grain bullet. As a bolt action it looks odd with that hammer stuck on the rear of the bolt as a sort of afterthought, but as W. H. B. Smith has remarked in his *Small Arms of the World,* the military mind couldn't accept as normal any rifle without a thumb-operated hammer. You don't see many Keenes out from under collectors' glass; but my friend Charlie Canoll, gunsmith in Waverly, N. Y., does occasionally use his for hunting, and he has plenty of rifles to choose from. It's a kindly revival, for he treats a gun with respect.

The Remington-Lee of 1886-1906 came in many calibers during its life-span: .30-30, .30-40, .32-40, .32 Special, .35 and .405 Winchester, .38-55, .38-72,

Winchester-Hotchkiss bolt-action repeating sporter, a special job. Note the folding leaf rear sight with sliding bar for elevation, so well liked then, and the graceful curve of the snobble at the tip of the forestock.

.43 Spanish, .44-77, .45-70, .45-90, 6, 7, and 7.65 mm, and probably more. Most of them were military arms. Lever actions and most slide actions were rugged and reliable enough for the American hunter. At that time most game could be approached more closely than today, and such advantage in accuracy as early bolt guns possessed was less known and. much less generally demanded. The rifles seemed slow to operate, and techniques of rapid-bolt-action fire as we now know them hadn't been developed.

As a military rifle the Remington-Lee was fast. Its bolt handle lay well to the rear, and the big, single-column box magazine was a smooth feeder. At first these magazines were detachable, and a well supplied soldier could keep up a continuous and rapid fusillade. In 1888 the British incorporated Lee's system into their Lee-Metford .303, a smallbore that originally used a cake of compressed black powder as propellant. Modified into various patterns of Lee-Enfield, the essential idea served Britain well in two world wars.

From about 1879 to 1887 the Hotchkiss was part of the Winchester line. Some sporters were made in the .45-70 caliber, and the late Ned Roberts, designer of cartridge forms that led to our factory-made .257 Roberts, once recorded having used a Hotchkiss .38-70. His choice was discriminating; he knew rifles from the caplock muzzle-loader through the old black-powder cartridge guns right down to the modern high-intensity type.

THE 1890s

This decade was gay enough for riflemen. It saw the flowering of three of the five basic types* of high-power lever actions that in cartons and cases hurry across the nation in those breathless weeks before big-game seasons open. It saw, too, the beginning of the enormous popularity of the .22 rimfire and its use by men as well as by youngsters. Lots of rifles made or at least designed in those ten years are still useful, and still bought for service and not as relics. This is true of the 1886 Winchester, but few others as old as that get out to American game country any more. Those that do are prized highly, as a rule, and if used within their limitations they aren't disappointing.

The Winchester 1890

It came at the right time for the popularity a good .22 rifle deserved. There had been good ones already,

---

*Marlin 336, Savage 99, Winchester 94. The others are the Winchester 71 and the recent 88.

notably the Colt 1887 for shorts or longs (and both in the same repeating action) and a fine variety of Stevens single shots in .22, .32 and the new .25 rimfire. Some of the imported Floberts—once so popular that the name became and long remained a synonym for ".22 rifle"—in the better grades were fine little rifles. Remington and other makes of .22 were in at least limited use, but the Colt had been almost if not quite the only .22 repeater for American riflemen.

The general impression in the sporting world and outside of it, too, rated a .22 as not much more than a toy, impractical for hunting and not much good as a target arm; though Carver, Lyman and others were setting up great long-run records. They fired at glass balls or wooden blocks and on one rather comic occasion at lumps of coal sailing through the air.

Too many thought that a .22 was next door to harmless—and for that matter, too many still do! It wasn't, though black powder rimfire velocities of the time were almost all below 1000 feet per second. And the little .22 slugs could kill.

But they weren't really effective on small game. Many cripples got away, and some hunters, even when game was so plentiful, were decent enough to feel bad about it. The .22 earned and deserved a bad reputation as a hunting rifle.

To a definite extent the Model 1890 Winchester changed this. Being produced to sell, it naturally was made for .22 shorts only, or for .22 longs. But with it appeared also a special cartridge, made for its own bigger, longer chamber. This was the .22 Winchester Rim Fire, .22 WRF, .22 Special or .22-7-45.

Shorts had been loaded with 3 or sometimes 4 grains of black powder and a 29- or 30-grain bullet. Longs took 5 grains of powder and from 29 to 35 of lead. Their bullets were outside lubricated, smeared with grease; and they were of the "heel" type so general among rimfires, stepped down at the rear to seat in the copper case. Lots of rifles were ruined, and some still are, by grit that the grease picked up from dirty pockets.

The .22 WRF, like the .25 Stevens rimfire that came out at about the same time, had only the front taper of its bullet exposed. Grease grooves lay within the cartridge case like those of centerfire Winchester repeating-rifle loads. To add to this similarity to a big-game hull, the taper of the bullet nose ended in a flat point, safer than a rounded nose in a centerfire rifle's tubular magazine—and a better killer, too. So general was the use of the flat point that even some of the

Sharps and Remington bigbore target bullets had it, though usually not so wide, caliber for caliber.

Some early .22 WRF loadings had 50% more powder than the .22 longs, 7½ grains, though a 7-grain charge became the standard. Bullet weight was 45 grains, even in most of the hollow points that Winchester introduced later and continued until about 1947. Remington did adopt a 39-grain standard for the hollow point, and for some years Peters solid bullets were listed at a grain or two over 45.

Even in early days, and with no cavity to increase mushrooming, WRF bullets were noticeably better stoppers than those in other .22 rimfire sizes. Here was a squirrel rifle that a sportsman needn't be ashamed to take into the woods. It was businesslike. Velocities over 1100 f. s. were standard for black powder and for the later Peters semi-smokeless and Du Pont Lesmok. The report was still moderate, didn't spread the alarm through seven acres.

In 1892 the rifle came out in takedown form, handier for packing into camp and for cleaning the action, though you still had to clean the barrel from its muzzle or bend your wiping-rod. When the 90 went out in 1932, 849,000 had been made, a good record for a fairly expensive .22 back when there were much fewer hunters and plinkers to enjoy it.

About 1908 or a bit earlier the action was strengthened. The receiver was slotted clear across, up front, to give a wider base for the locking shoulders on the bolt. You still see the older type in the field, occasionally. In time a 90 action loosens a little, but almost never enough to produce dangerous headspace between breechblock and the face of the barrel.

Its great relative durability helped to account for its amazing popularity in .22 short caliber as a shooting-gallery arm. Then, too, because it's so easy to make sure by a glance at the big hammer whether or not the gun is cocked, the 90 is much more reassuring to the men behind the green counter than any hammerless or even bolt action pea-shooter. Those fellows *know* the .22 is no pea-shooter. Their vigilance keeps them alive.

Short, long, and WRF Model 90 rifles all have been chosen by hunters. By noting the selection you could judge pretty well how serious and considerate a hunter a man was, or at least how well informed.

The 90 was reliable as well as durable. I've never seen or heard of a jam with a .22 short gun, and never happened to use the long, or the type for .22 long-rifles which was introduced so tardily in 1920. I've seen jams with the .22 WRF, though none that took more than five seconds to reduce. The loaded round simply has to go from the carrier into the chamber; it's headed straight that way and there's not the slightest scraping or shaving as it enters. But sometimes the long WRF empty would be tipped sidewise by the extractor and lodge between carrier and receiver instead of flying up and out. Only one of three WRF 90 rifles I knew rather well gave this trouble.

With different woodwork, a shorter round barrel instead of the old 24-inch octagon, a coil main or hammer spring replacing the flat one, and a slightly altered breech lock, the present Model 62 is really an 1890. The newer arm handles the familiar "short, long and long-rifle" trilogy. A trip in the carrier regulates the flow from the magazine. You can mix 'em up but you can't louse 'em up.

Some Marlins

Even in its earliest days the Model 90 Winchester had set a standard, and the Marlin Firearms Company took up the challenge quickly.

Their 1891 lever action was a finely engineered, advanced job. In the 1892 .32 caliber it was convertible from rim- to centerfire by simply changing the firing pin, as some single shots were. Its centerfire rounds were the short and long Colt, practically centerfire duplicates of the .32 short and long rimfire. The gun also handled the inside lubricated .32 long-rifle rimfire and .32 Colt centerfire improvements which came out in 1901. The Colt pattern finally became the standard in that now odd centerfire size, and it still hangs on in factory load lists—fortunately. These cartridges used .32 long black powder charges, but their deeply seated bullets were eight grains lighter than the longs' usual 90 grain standard. Can't you hear the oldtimers saying "They're clean to pack in your pocket, and they shoot faster, too"?

These Marlins are solid-frame rifles and by that virtue more accurate than the takedown in .22 rimfire that appeared as the Model 1897. For only a couple of years or so had the 90 Winchester been made in solid. By removing the Marlin sideplates you can get in to clean gummed lubricant and powder ash from the action parts. Some of these parts, at least in .22, were smaller and apparently more subject to wear than those of the 1890 Winchester. Yet some of these rifles have had decent care and give service even today.

The lever action was quick and easy. In usual Marlin fashion the cartridge carrier lifts the loaded round on the home stroke of the lever, not on the outward trip as in Winchester fashion. Marlins used to have a rather serious reputation for jamming. I think it was built on the carelessness or ignorance of the shooter, in most cases. I've had or seen but little of it. When the lever is thrown out and drawn back positively and fully there's seldom any trouble, though some of the old ones definitely were surer with long and long-rifle rounds than with shorts.

The 91 Marlin was in advance of its time in having a shotgun butt just rounded enough to stay on your shoulder in rapid fire. This rifle and the 97 were made in more different grades of checkering and high finish of the wood than the Winchester 90, the company going to considerable effort to please its public.

Like the rarely seen 1889 Marlin, these rifles were side ejectors. Empties were flipped out to the right, away from the line of sight—a good advertising point and a fine thing today, when short, low-power hunting scopes are extra equipment on so many lever guns. But truly, the sight of fired cases hopping out of the top of a receiver, or even the spectacle of the 90 Winchester's breechblock humping up as it's unlocked, isn't particularly disturbing. If you work the action with the smooth speed of second-nature—and you do, after a reasonable acquaintance—you don't notice such things. Oh yes, they may be registered by some sort of subconscious observance, but they don't take your mind off the business of getting ready for the next carefully aimed and squeezed-off shot, if you need one.

That Marlin lever action of 1891, once so well known, like all the succeeding ones through the recent 36 high-power, was about as snow- and dust-proof as a repeater could be. The breechblock was flat-sided. Closed, it fitted into the smooth contour of the receiver. The ejector slot was narrow, making single-loading a little difficult for some; but except in a training rifle for youngsters, that means little. The long, full-length magazine held much more than enough cartridges, and like the Winchester 1890 and all later tube-under-barrel mags for .22s, it was easy to load. Draw up the inner tube (or in some rifles the outer) and drop the cartridges in. Push down and lock the tube and it's done.

It is a highly sensible practice to do this when the chamber is empty, and you know it's empty!

Marlin made a great deal of the "solid top, side ejection" features, and with good reason. But in implying that the solid top receiver was safer in the event of a blowback from a burst case, they were a bit off the beam. Gas is too fond of going back through a firing pin channel or alongside a breechblock, and who except the bull-pup* user fires with his face on top of the action?

The solid top does keep out snow and rain. So in bad weather it lets you focus your attention on hunting, not on the rifle.

Some Used-Gun Bargains

Yes, they are, or they can be if you know what you want and use your wits when you buy or trade. The three outstanding makes of lever-action, centerfire repeaters came close to their highest development in the 1890s. Lots of the Savage, Marlin and Winchester hunting rifles actually made back then are in service. Two of the patterns, Winchester 1894 and Savage 1899, are still manufactured with few basic changes. People keep wanting them. These healthy survivals seem a bit strange when you remember that only the 1895 Winchester, no longer made, and the 1899 Savage, were originally meant for smokeless powders.

Winchester 1892

The 1892 rifle got a good start as being a small 1886, though the twin locking bolts close to the rear of

*A rifle stocked in bull-pup style has its action, usually of turn-bolt design, at the rear of the stock. A long rod puts the second trigger (the business trigger, really) up where you can reach it.

the breechblock slant back instead of being nearly upright. The spring cover through which you load the 92's magazine is shorter and neater, and the whole rifle, compared to the 86, is almost of junior size. That hasn't kept it from doing a great deal of big-game hunting. In .44-40 caliber it went all over the world, like its 1873 predecessor, and it is nearly two pounds lighter. A handy gun.

It's a trifle faster to operate, with the short and easy lever throw that helped make the 86 so well liked, and its smaller hammer seems just as convenient to thumb back as the high-spurred type of the Henrys and the 66, 73 and 76 Winchesters. Most 92s balance well, and the .44 carbines with half magazines weigh only 5½ pounds—less than a good many little .22 repeaters.

Other calibers were the .32-20 and .38-40, with the .25-20 coming along in 1895, about five years after the full establishment of the longer, slimmer .25-20 Single Shot round. In .25 and .32 some really good shooting has been done with the 92. These are better balanced loads than the .38 and .44, and though pressures all run about the same with equivalent loadings (standard or high velocity) the small inside diameter of the little cases, down at the bottom, cuts the rearward thrust on the bolthead. The last version of the 92, the 65 that was dropped from the line after World War II, gave almost bolt action accuracy in .218 Bee caliber. Five-shot groups at 50 yards went under an inch, measured from center to center of the holes farthest apart, or the rifleman was at fault. Two-inch 100-yard groups of five shots were common on still, windless days.

The Model 53, which preceded the 65, took the same .25-20 and .32-20 calibers, also the .44-40. All these later rifles were modernized with light, nicely tapered barrels, 22-inch except for the 24-inch Bee. At first only a small barrel lug was used to bring the front sight up to level, but later and by degrees the 65 sprouted a full-length matted ramp, in keeping with the change of taste. Most 53s have a straight grip, shotgun buttstock with steel buttplate grooved in the middle to prevent slipping. The 65 plate is like that of today's Model 70 or 71, deeply checkered and with enough curve at the middle and swell at the heel, or upper part, to give security. The 65 is standard with rather close and full pistol grip, and a swelled, semi-beaver-tail forestock came in with the .218 Bee caliber rifle.

Winchester 1894

The new Winchester was entirely different from the 1886 and the 1892. It handled rather long cartridges—the .30-30 and most of its cousins—but its receiver was kept slim and easily grasped by a dropping link which increased the reach of its leverage. This link is the bottom part of the receiver, and it is hinged up front. As the lever goes forward the link falls, giving a sort of dropped-pants appearance to the action and a chance for any serious guncrank to criticize the whole arrangement rather bitterly.

An 1894 in the Winchester collection, engraved, inlaid, and carved. This rifle has the shotgun butt with hard rubber buttplate, a more "modern" touch than the crescent shape so popular right up to the 1920's. The magazine's takedown lever lies on the left side of this rifle. After unscrewing the magazine about an inch you opened the breech and twisted the barrel and forearm a quarter turn to the left, counterclock-wise. Then the gun came apart. You may be able to see the joint just behind the inlays at the front of the receiver.

There's no question of the action's strength for the backthrust of loads meant for it. The locking bolt covers nearly the full rear surface of the breechblock, and it locks into sturdy slots in the receiver. Really old actions with droopy finger-levers that seem to start opening when discharge occurs usually can be corrected by a new little "friction stud" installed at the rear of the link.

But rigidity of the 94 action is a different subject for debate. After all, the receiver has only sides, no solid top or bottom, so accuracy seldom is good with full power modern loads. The black powder .32-40 and .38-55 for which the rifle was designed have given winning turkey-shoot accuracy time and again, and so have their low-pressure smokeless loadings similar to the stuff we can buy now. The little .25-35, which came out, like the .30-30, in 1895, delivered useful and really interesting precision at least in the days of 2000 f. s. velocities.

The .32 Special cartridge of 1902 was a sort of compromise for shooters who wanted to reload their fired cases. Rifling twist in this caliber and in the long-established .32-40 is a slow one-turn-in-16-inches. You can use plain lead bullets, cast from almost any soft lead scrap you get hold of, and not have to worry about the metal piling up fast over the rifling grooves, destroying accuracy temporarily and letting you in for a tiresome, long job with a brass cleaning-brush. You could use black powder, too, in the .32 Special, and the company wanted you to. As late as World War I it strongly advised against the reloading of any rifle ammunition with any smokeless powder. The company sold not only reloading tools and molds for the Special, but also lead bullets for the handloader. The recommended charge was 40 grains of black, advertised as giving 1385 f. s. velocity.

A 94 action is probably as rigid as the old Stevens 44 made for .32-40 and .38-55, and it's considerably stronger. Moderate pressures and good ammunition can give you good accuracy. With the increased power of modern .30-30 and .32 Special factory loads your 100 yard groups may open to four or five inches, depending on many variables. Such accuracy serves well for most white-tail deer hunting in the woods. The rifles and their ammunition were designed, maintained and constantly improved for just that purpose.

Factories Were Obliging

Winchester 1894 rifles, like the 1886, 1892 and the 1895 in black powder models, came in many styles. So did Marlins and Savages of parallel types. The factories aimed to please, and streamlining of production apparently hadn't been thought up.

There were solid and takedown frames, round, octagon and half-octagon barrels, straight or pistol-grip stocks, usually, and curved rifle, flat shotgun, or curved but comfortably flat carbine-type buttplates. Several models came with extra light barrels on special order, and 50 years or so ago you could get a heavy barrel for a Winchester 1873 or 1886 that would increase gun weight from one to two pounds. Factory stuff.

Carbines were an important and standard sort of production. Except for 22-inch 1886 and 1895 Winchesters, the usual barrel length was and still is 20 inches. Rifles had 24-, 26-, or 28-inch barrels as standard, but some special jobs went up to 36 inches. On the other hand there were both rifle and carbine barrels, at least in Winchester 1892 and 1894 models, as short as 14 inches. South America and the West Indies, as well as our own West, took a good many of these shorties.

In the 1894 Winchester and in Savage rifles too there was the solid frame or takedown premium priced light-weight barrel, round, and in the 94 octagon or half-octagon too. For some reason the .32 Special was an exception. In its early days that caliber was considered a pretty powerful size: it had the highest velocity of any of the .30-30 class loadings. This may have been an excuse. The 26-inch barrel then popular would have been definitely more whippy and less consistent in maintaining elevation than a .30-30, or perhaps even a .38-55 with low-powered rounds. There seems to have been no featherweight .32 Special until the Model 55 superseded the 94 *rifle*—the 94 still comes out in its thousands as a carbine.

The 55 had the original extra light weight barrel, but in 24 inch instead of 26 or about what you pleased on a special order. It was stocked like the Model 53 that succeeded the 92—interchangeably stocked, in fact—and it also came normally in half magazine and shotgun butt style. The 55 carried on the .25-35, .30-30 and .32 Special until the present Model 65 replaced it.

It was an easy rifle to carry, being as light as seven pounds in solid frame .30 or .32 caliber, and yet it always seemed to have enough weight out front to balance as well as any 26-inch Model 94 streamliner, round or octagon.

Winchester 1895

As regularly made, the 95 was a straight-gripped rifle only. Some were custom stocked with pistol grip even farther back and of less real use than those on other rifles of the time, but apparently the factory wasn't interested.

There was a reason. Although the 95 at first came out with soft steel barrels, 26 inches long, for its special .38-72-275 and .40-72-330 black powder loads as well as with nickel steel tubes for the .30-40 Krag and the semi-rimless 6 mm. or .236 Navy, the pressures and possibilities of rather high intensity smokeless rounds were considered. The long steel tangs that, with a single screw through the small of the stock, held stock and receiver together, were meant to give rigidity. They succeeded rather well.

With early .30-06 loadings, comparable in 150- and 180-grain weights to the .300 Savage and—almost—the .308, the 95 rifles and carbines gave long range hunting accuracy that served well in the more open big-game fields of the world. There were several musket types, too, in the .30 calibers, for the military style of target shooting.

The action was strong, more rugged than that of the bolt-action .30-40 Krag. Most older shooters know that the 95 went off the market only after a number of the uninformed had been made suddenly wiser by firing a 7.92 or "8 mm." Mauser round in one of the old Winchesters chambered for the .30-06 or for the longer necked .30 1903 Springfield. Even not many bolt-action rifles could be expected to take such terrific pressure.

The single locking bolt of the 95 is good-sized, of fine quality steel, elastic, not brittle. It moves straight up and down, not at a slant, to cover most of the rear face of the long breechblock. The continued use of excessive loads could set it back gradually, but it is not at all liable to let go suddenly, as Krag bolts have done. When a Krag bolt blows completely out of the receiver it usually flies off to the side, not back at the shooter. This is a rare occurrence indeed. With sensible loads Krags continue to give faithful service. They probably will do that for at least another generation of humans.

Ammunition for the Winchester 95 came from careful, painstaking development. Of course the service rounds were labored over scientifically, the 6 mm. Navy, .30-40 Krag, .30-03 and .30-06, .303 British, and the 7.62 mm. Russian which perhaps shows an Oriental touch of architecture in its curiously rounded base. Many 95s were made for it during World War I. But the .38-72 and .40-72, brought out for the large body of shooters who in 1895 were not convinced of the advantages of smokeless powder, were among the finest as well as the last of black powder designs.

The long, slim 275-grain bullet of the .38 was meant to give ranging power and penetration. It had them; in fact its penetration equalled that of the big .40-90-370 Sharps. Yet its temper of one part tin to 20 of lead was the same as that of the .38-56 and .38-70 Winchester 1886 slugs, and you could count on mushrooming. Length and weight gave it penetration, and they helped in the brush, too. It could be deflected—any bullet can—but it should have got through as well as the lighter 1886 .38s with their woods-popular form of wide, flat points. None of the black-powder loads for big game gave velocities high enough to disqualify them for reliable behavior in the brush, just on that basis. Reliable behavior? That's relatively speaking, and the search for good brush-bucking bullets goes on.

The .40-72 was practically a revival of the once-popular Sharps .40-70-330. It kept that favored bullet weight except in some 300-grain jacketed bullets made for it later. Its bullet's point was rounded, for the 95's box magazine held cartridges one above the other, not head to tail, and flat noses weren't necessary for safety. But the old 330 grain had one of the stubbiest rounded points ever designed for an American rifle. This added to killing power even though the tin-lead temper was one to sixteen and it expanded rather fast. Most other Winchester .40s were one to twenty.

The straight-cased .40-72 was fairly deadly on any American big game, and the beautifully bottle-necked .38-72 became known as a super deer load by those who wanted complete, through-and-through penetration, at any angle, to let out a blood trail. But the strong 95 action could take more and never blink; so out came the .35 in 1903, and the famous .405 in 1904. With 250- and 300-grain bullets respectively they shot a little flatter up to 300 yards than the .30-30-170 and .30-40-220 of those days. Since iron sights were almost universally looked through at that time, 300 yards was a mighty long shot under wilderness conditions. It takes skill to kill *cleanly* that far with any modern rifle and scope.

But long-range stuff was incidental in designing these loads. Velocity did help sell the rifles, for we were getting into the first generation of speed, but the main and well proved point was power. The .35 had more authority than any of the .30 calibers then in use, and the .405 made a great African reputation. Perhaps the designers' dream was of a Winchester "big enough for anything in the world." It is no elephant, rhino or buffalo rifle, though it managed to kill a few. Now we have the .458 Winchester with its tough 500-grain bullet—and much less plentiful great game to try it on.

This has been a long discussion of Winchester 95 ammunition. Still, that rifle came at perhaps the most decisive year of the break between old and new, rifle-wise, in America. The .30-30 and .30-40 cartridges proved the efficiency of smokeless powder and jacketed, soft-point bullets. Then the other sporting cartridges came along. We still have the argument over big and small bores and probably shall until every old or greenhorn hunter gives unbiased thought as to what's best, where. And even then there will have to be compromises.

You see the Model 95 most often today, and perhaps think of buying one, in any of three different forms. There's the .30-40 rifle with long, slim 28-inch barrel that weighs about 8¼ pounds. In 22-inch carbine, .30-40 or .30-06, it's a bit lighter. The rather heavy but nicely tapered barrel of the 24-inch rifle puts a .30-06 close to nine pounds, though in .35 or .405 the gun is noticeably lighter. Unless you're a handloader and can find brass to work with, you don't buy a .35 or .405. They quit manufacturing these, but still put out the .22 *long* rimfire and a host of small-gauge shotshells with pellets too coarse to give any sort of killing pattern beyond 20 yards. Demand creates supply, you bet!

If you get a chance to look over a 95, do so. Many go hunting and are prized because of the competent loads they fire and their swift, easy action. Throw the lever and see how its forward extension carries the long bolt back, and how the trigger is disconnected during the process.

The magazine is a straight single-column type like that of the 1888 Mauser, but not open at the bottom. Rimless cartridges are easy to load into it: you push them straight down between the magazine lips. But rimmed cases must lie in progressive order, each one with its flange just ahead of the one below it. The simplest way to stuff them in and to be sure your loading is jam-proof is to hold each round by its bullet and push the base straight down, just ahead of the lips. Then swing the bullet forward, letting the base of the cartridge go down and back under the lips. Feeding is smooth, straight off the top of the magazine, not right-left-right as in typical Mauser fashion.

The 95 lever throw is practically as short and easy as that of the 86. Since the cartridge carrier (magazine follower we'd call it in a bolt action) is spring-actuated to bring the rounds up in line for chambering, there's no special effort necessary to insure full lever throw. The three preceding lever action Winchesters, especially the 94, do require a last little forward hitch to kick up the carrier. After a couple of practice firing sessions or even of dry firing without ammunition, this effort ought to blend into an easy, natural throw.

The great difficulty is to convince some new hunters that they need any sort of practice before they take off for game country. Grandfather—or Uncle Punk, maybe —got his share of deer, didn't he? And those things are inherited, aren't they?

Marlin Centerfire Actions

Through the 1890s and later, these lever actions, made in the same friendly little city as the Winchesters, ran in steady competition without being at all imitative. They still do.

The 1893 Marlin was actually the first truly modern lever action for the medium-power deer cartridges, .32-40 and .38-55. In those times a .32-40 *was* a satisfactory load for white-tails, easy and economical to shoot. For more than a generation it remained a favorite with farmers who liked to have a rifle of some consequence handy beside the door.

To many the Marlin seemed a little special. Case-hardening of receivers was standard, not only in the beginning, and the colors were beautiful. No one questioned their strength, or needed to. General finish was as good as any.

Marlins too had a safety provision that prevented discharge before the action was closed and locked. The company just had the good sense to publicize it more fully, and "Marlin Safety" became a familiar trademark printed on paper or stamped into steel. The arrangement is still there without much change in the current Model 336. The short rear section of the divided firing pin cannot be aligned with the front part before the breech is closed and locked. This system of two-piece firing pins shows more obviously in Winchester 1894 and 1895 rifles, though the others cannot be fired with an unlocked breech. In the 86 and 92 models the forward spur of the finger lever holds the firing fin back until the action has been closed.

Marlin 1893

Popular at the start in .32-40 and .38-55 calibers, the 93 Marlin soon was adapted to the .30-30 and its own special cartridge, the .25-36. The .32 Special came in due time.

The .25-36, for which no other rifles seem to have been made, had the luck of considerable advertising. It was developed as an accurate, flat-shooting cartridge for antelope, though actually its trajectory curve arched higher than the .30-30's. There was no doubt of its accuracy, and the light recoil made good shooting possible for almost anyone.

Perhaps it was the first caliber to be promoted as a varminter. There were many more woodchucks or groundhogs out East then than now, and the little Marlins often carried long target scopes of Malcolm, Stevens or Winchester make. Side ejection of empties let them ride directly over receiver and barrel. The soft- or full-metal patched (hard point) bullets normally weighed 117 grains and were like the .25-35 Winchesters except for the location of the crimping cannelure. That was set farther forward to give standard .30-30 overall length of almost exactly two and one-half inches in spite of the extra long .25-36 case.

A soft-point 86-grain load also was listed for a while. Evidently shooters—and manufacturers too— weren't so slow in recognizing the value of a faster, flatter-shooting varmint bullet, one that was more likely to break up on hitting stone or hard-packed earth than to ricochet and squeal away over a peaceful countryside—and be quite capable of doing serious harm.

Marlin Model 36, shown here in carbine form, had practically the same action as the 1893, though it was not made for the old .25-36, .32-40, and .38-55 cartridges. Note the tight, flush fit of the breech-block in the ejector cutout along the side of the receiver.

A .25-36 rifle or carbine in good shape is a useful collector's item that deserves to get out under the sky occasionally. The last factory rating for the 117-grain bullet was only 1855 f. s. velocity. But just before the .220 Swift got well underway*, a Du Pont booklet advised maximum loads of 19.5 grains of 4198 or 23.5 of 3031 Military Rifle Powders. Muzzle velocities for a 26-inch barrel were 2055 and 2105 f. s. The strength of modern primers was considered, and those loads should be safe in sound Marlins. However, it's always best to start handloading at least 10% below any recommended top load. Rifles and cartridge components have their variations. They do indeed!

Old brass may have become brittle. With a full length .25-36 case-resizing die and .25-35 Winchester or .32-40 brass the handloader can make his own empties. The .32 is longer, just right for this purpose, but the brass should be fresh, of good strong head construction. You can judge that fairly well by sectioning and comparing cases. The .25-35 has been fired, unaltered, in .25-36 arms.

Among the discerning, the .25-36 was quite a favorite. Although Theodore Roosevelt believed in owning a few rifles and knowing them well he was a gun-lover too, who liked a decently wide firsthand acquaintance. Not long after the return from the African trip he gave his .25-36 to one of the three naturalists who had shared his campfires and worked so hard at preserving specimens. J. Alden Loring, who lived in Owego, N. Y., must have found plenty of use for that rifle in the rolling fields near his home until age brought, as it does to some well seasoned outdoorsmen, the feeling that most animals are more interesting alive than dead.

The Loring .25-36, now in a museum, was made in a special style much approved at the time: takedown frame, shotgun buttstock with pistol grip, half magazine and half octagon barrel. The woodwork is checkered nicely, and of plain walnut: fancy grades cost more and almost always increase rifle weight. Apparently this gun never carried a scope, but the sights are of that woods-hunting style so long popular, a Lyman folding peep on the tang and a small ivory bead up front.

The 93s were respected deer rifles, and as deer rifles do, at times they killed bigger game. In .32-40 and .38-55, like the rival Winchesters, they often figured at turkey shoots. A Westerner I knew even used his .38-55 Marlin in stiff bench rest competition against heavy barreled single shots. For steadiness he had poured the long magazine full of lead. As he was a careful hunter, a single shot rifle suited him afield.

Marlin 1894

This smaller, lighter Marlin took the four old favorite low-power cartridges that the Winchester 1892 handled, .25-20, .32-20, .38-40 and .44-40, and it used the factory High Velocity loadings too, of course. In black powder there were two special lead bullet weights, the .32 with 100, not 115, grains, and the .44 with 17 grains more than the 200-grain Winchester standard. Similar loadings were marketed for the Colt lightning magazine rifle, the pump gun, and the headstamps interest collectors.†

You still see Marlin 94s in use. As with 92 Winchesters, new barrels often are sadly needed. Most people insisted on using smokeless powder when it became available, and the old potassium chlorate primers were almost sure death to steel in connection with small cases using "nitro" powders. (Many of them did contain nitro-glycerine then.) The big bores got away with it much longer under equally good care, and a few old .38-40 and .44-40 barrels are free from pitting or even a little "roughness," a kindly term for what is really pitting, after all. The .25-20 and .32-20 seldom kept what is called "hunting accuracy" for long. As few as 300 nitro rounds could start the ruination of a carefully cleaned barrel.

Marlin 1895

Here was the answer to the 1886 Winchester, and in a way to the 1895. This big Marlin was chambered for all of the cartridges used in the 86 except the .38-70 and the two big .50s. Consequently, Marlin admirers were well served: the .45-70 and .45-90 were much respected short-range piledrivers and the .33 was rated as a long-range cartridge almost until the outbreak of World War I.

In the black-powder sizes 26- and 28-inch barrels were common, but the Marlin .33 was streamlined. Its 24-inch barrel was prettily tapered, and rifle weight was as low as the Winchester's or even lower. There was no question of the strength of the action for the loads the 95 handled, and most of the aspersions that used to be cast on Marlin lever-action reliability came from people who owned some other make and preferred the tear-down to the build-up attack in advancing an argument.

---

*At about that time the powder factories ceased publishing load recommendations.

†.25-20 Marlin or Mar., and a simple .32-20, .38-40 or .44-40; .32, .38 and .44 C. L. M. R.

Savage 1899

As far back as 1895 there were Savage repeaters, a 30-inch military style of rifle, a 26-inch sporter, and a 22-inch carbine. This 1895 model, at least some of which were made by Marlin though marked "Savage," is for collectors. The 1899 Savage, now called the 99, is one of the most frequently seen American big-game rifles.

Early 1899s can be distinguished by the square rather than rounded rear face of the breechblock and by the indicator that sticks up at the front of that block when a cartridge lies in the chamber. In good condition, they are safe with their original calibers. Rebarreling to .250, .300, or .22 Hi-Power undoubtedly has been done, but it doesn't appear to be good medicine.

The famous .303, a special Savage size, seems to have been the earliest caliber. There were also the black-powder .32-40 and .38-55 and the smokeless .25-35 and .30-30.

The .22 Hi-Power, a necked-down .25-35, came in 1912 and made some startling history, based chiefly on what its 70-grain bullet at 2800 f. s. could and couldn't do. "One hundred feet per second faster than the Army Springfield" was good advertising copy and sold a lot of rifles. After all, the so-called Imp was the first purely sporting high-velocity cartridge for a rifle made by one of our large factories.

Charles Newton designed it, also the .250-3000 which followed in 1915—though 1914 had seen the use of a pilot model .250 on Mexican deer. Newton had his own rifles too, with much superior ballistics. Their cartridges were not skimped in case size, and bullet weight was respectable. But the Savage 99 takes rounds of only about 2½ inches overall, and the publicity value of 3000 f. s. velocity was so inviting that it just had to be substantiated. It was ten years or so before 100-grain bullet loads were offered for the .250, though Newton had wanted them from the first.

When World War I ended, the .30-06 burst into general popularity as a hunting caliber, and the .300 Savage appeared, giving practically the same ballistics as the wartime Springfield.

So many types of 99 have been made—and still carry price tags as used guns—that we ought to take a look at them. They reflect the changes of taste, too, which sometimes move in pendulum fashion.

The early rifles were like the 1895 Savages in having 26-inch, round, octagon or half octagon barrels. Later 25 inches became standard, and then 24. The Savage is hammerless and its receiver is pretty long. Old Featherweight barrels were 20 inches long, and this weight went on the first .22 Hi-Powers. Early .250s and .300s were 22 and 24 inches respectively, and they were tapered to be light. Heavier barrels, and others as short as 20 inches, appeared from time to time.

The carbines were reasonably popular. A late 20-incher was the 99-T, a rifle, not a carbine in its styling, with a fairly stiff barrel. It was worked up by people who liked a short gun for woods hunting but found the usual carbine too muzzle-light for good shooting on either standing or moving game. Today's 99-F closely resembles the old Featherweight except for its fuller forestock. A newer generation has to learn the delights and drawbacks of extremely short, light rifles. Willingness to learn makes the type profitable to manufacture, not only in Savage brand or in factory output. Certainly a featherweight has its proper and useful place.

Most early 99s had an extremely curved, sharp-pronged steel buttplate, the "rifle" type. The Savage people seem to have been quick to learn that the flat shotgun shape is preferable, and to put enough hollow into it to make it stick to the shoulder. There's more resistance to the rearward throw of a 99 lever than to those of hammer guns, for the mainspring is compressed as the action goes shut. Savage carbines had the usual double-curved but flat and comfortable steel buttplates.

The 99 action and rifle helped educate us Americans. It took time. The prejudice against hammerless rifles was deep-seated. You couldn't tell whether they were cocked or not—until late 99s had that little indicator pin that sticks up at the rear of the receiver to warn you. Even so, you have to look or feel rather attentively to be sure; and perhaps after all it's just as well that no firearm can appear to be foolproof, for none is.

The Savage set high standards for lever-action accuracy. It is one of the few that compare favorably with good bolt-action sporters. To learn marksmanship you must have the tools that give accuracy.

Then too, the Savage holds only six rounds. Enough? Contemporary rifles with full length tubular magazines held from 8 or 9 to 14 or even more. A fast, generous magazine reservoir had to become recognized as the illusion it is. The Savage was fast to operate but maybe its lower capacity helped to teach a needed lesson.

Bolt Actions of the 1890s

They seemed slow in the 1890s and few hunters wanted one. The Krag-Jorgensen .30-40 of 1892, 1896 and 1898 models was a service arm and not all National Guard or volunteer units could latch on to this bolt action for duty in the war of 1898, in which Spain used mostly 7 mm. Mausers of practically modern design. It wasn't easy for a civilian to get hold of a Krag.

The commercially made Blake never was well known. This beautifully made rifle took a rimmed version of the 6 mm. Lee, or the .30-40, or its own .400, the .40-72 Winchester case heavily loaded with smokeless powder and a 300-grain jacketed bullet, practically a .405. The seven-shot revolving magazine took cartridges in packet assembly.

As so many shooters realize, the Navy's 6 mm Winchester-Lee was "too early seen unknown, and known too late," though a few sporters were made. Ammunition was discontinued long ago and the case is hard to duplicate for handloading.

This early clip-loader is fast in bolt-throw. "Straight pull," it needs only a back and forth flick of the hand to send the bolt rearward, up a little, then forward and locked. Its bullet was fast—too fast and light, some thought. Even the early 135-grain left at 2460 f. s. With full jacket it needled through 62 dry pine boards of ⅞-inch thickness. The later 112-grain standard, furnished in soft point too, went at 2562 or 2571, according to loading companies' varied claims, and naturally greater variations than this could be expected from a single box of ammunition. It punched through 60 boards, or a deer-killing 12 in soft point style.

Handloaders were fascinated, still more so after the ammunition went off the market. The .220 Swift case can be formed to chamber and fire in the Lee, although it's decidedly different in both body taper and rim from the almost rimless 6 mm. Brass comes out a little short.

My friend Olmstead Peet is one of those who do not demand the last foot-second of velocity from a case, and he has reported no chamber-neck erosion from the short brass he has to use. (Only a few original rounds came with his gun.) But he does want accuracy and killing power at the distances he shoots over.

He hunts. He learned to do it on deer and small game, and he's patient and skillful enough to get up reasonably close on varmints, too. Though not a light-bullet admirer, he finds the 90-grain rather nice in his 6 mm., and the report of his conservative loadings doesn't seem to get him into trouble with land-owners.

"Did I write you that I shot a chuck with it and finally discovered where the bullet entered and found one very small hole where a fragment came out? The chuck was jelly inside. That same day I had a very lucky freak shot." (Most of these freaks come from a pretty fair degree of marksmanship, I've noticed.) "As I was examining the chuck a crow flew overhead and I took a pot shot at him. Down he came, the 6 mm. bullet blowing up on contact with his neck. Needless to say, I am very fond of that old Lee 6 mm."

EDGING INTO THE MODERN

The first two decades of the twentieth century brought a great variety of new or revamped rifles in big and small calibers, and the development of semi-automatics for the general market. A lot of shooters liked their "fire power."

Of course that term includes accuracy of fire as well as volume of fire, but the former is still liable to be forgotten in the enthusiasm of either discussion or use! But the "automatics," as most of us called them right from the start, were bound to appear. Progress demanded them. Learning to use them effectively is

difficult, but the ability once gained does add to a rifleman's deadliness.

In these twenty years, too, the long-range accuracy of the American rifle and the technique of its use advanced to the doorstep of a new era, our own. But appreciation and sharing of this progress were mostly for the few.

Theodore Roosevelt's 1909 safari in Africa helped popularize the 1903 Springfield and the .30-06 cartridge. The combination was a good start and it still is fine equipment. Teddy was particular about stock fit and sights, insisting on what seemed to him the best for his purposes and the most helpful to his limitations. Though he stated that he was a fair shot only at moderate ranges, his African records show long kills with a moderate expenditure of the full-jacketed, sharp-point service loads he used.

During these years a few gun writers—such as Townsend Whelen, Edward C. Crossman and Charles Askins—were busy in developing and in trying to popularize a new and more efficient type of rifle for the hunter-marksman, one that would help him to almost sharper accuracy than he'd even dreamed of. It was an uphill fight.

The European bolt actions, Mauser and Mannlicher-Schoenauer mostly, did get to this country in the years from 1900 to 1920. Fine wood, neat checkering and the high polish of steel prettified them, made them costly, too. Though their rigid bolt lockup and high velocity ammunition gave them accuracy and power for long shooting above that of almost all the familiar lever actions, few of them had the right answer.

Ludwig Wundhammer, Fred Adolph and a few other gunsmiths and riflemen had it. It was mostly stock fit and assembly. A specimen of the early but efficient long-range American sporter looks about like this: medium weight, 24-inch barrel for the .30-06 or the 7 mm. Mauser cartridge; Springfield or Mauser bolt action, rarely with a set trigger but instead with the military pull, a long, soft takeup and then a clean, brittle release; two-way adjustable aperture rear sight and ivory, gold or black steel front; leather gunsling for shooting as well as carrying; half-length forestock tapered to feel good in the hand and yet be light; buttstock with pistol grip and high comb, and buttplate of thin, slightly curved, checkered steel. Now we have a heavier forestock, and the pistol grip is more sharply curved and, like the comb, farther forward.

Those early custom rifles were tailored. Stocks were inletted for barrel and receiver with great care, and their outside dimensions were for the man who ordered them and patiently waited for their delivery. One little touch has lasted, among others that may have been forgotten, to perpetuate an old gunsmith's name. The "Wundhammer swell" can yet be ordered on your custom stock. Gently rounded, it comes to a height of about 3/8 inch above the surrounding surface of the grip. If you have been careful in measurements it fills

A Springfield custom sporter with big-game scope in a precisely fitted set of ring mounts, custom made by Tilden. Attaching the front sling swivel to the barrel, not the fore-stock, is rather on the European plan. It is a rather neat and attractive method, and with the good barrel weight of this particular rifle there may be no liability of considerable elevation changes when the piece is fired with, and without, the tension of a sling.

that empty hollow of your palm. But you might not want it: you may be one of those who grip much farther back in prone than in offhand, and then it could be as much of a nuisance as if you'd ordered carelessly. A really good gunsmith could remove the swell, and what's more, restore the checkering to correspond with the surrounding diamonds.

Some men who were not gun experts could appreciate those few fine early rifles. Stewart Edward White was too busy and happy writing fiction and fact about the outdoor life he loved to contribute heavily to arms literature, but his custom Springfield did amazing work in Africa and less publicized game fields. As Crossman admitted, White was the impossible, a natural-born rifle shot, or as near it as ever was. Yet White appreciated top-flight equipment and shot better with it, too.

Never to be forgotten are Adolph O. Niedner and Dr. Franklin W. Mann, one a gunsmith, the other an investigator. They studied accuracy. Niedner developed many special calibers, "wildcats" that came before the name was coined. With the powders available he reached high velocities, with accuracy, in .22 and .25 calibers that were ten or twenty years ahead of their time.

SMALL RIFLES

The first twenty years of this century brought improvements in rimfire rifles—.22s mostly, though the .25 and .32 still were popular—and introduced new models and three practically unheard-of types. These were the autoloader, the inexpensive bolt action single shot, and the bolt gun for serious target competition.

This couldn't have happened if the .22 rimfire cartridge hadn't grown up. It became much more accurate and reliable, and—far more important—the average shooter acquired almost as healthy a respect for it as for the bigger and obviously more deadly fellows in rim- or centerfire.

There is of course a long way yet to go. Contemporary education is doing its part, sometimes as part of the public schools' offering.

Single Shots

The Winchester Model 1900 was probably the first generally available American bolt action .22 single shot, now so well known and literally beloved. Shorts, longs, and BB and CB caps were its rations. Though it had a tiny bolt handle and the striker or firing pin had to be cocked by finger and thumb against a stiff spring, it became popular as a boy's rifle. A non-adjustable open sight on the barrel was standard, and there was no pistol grip. The trigger guard was of stamped steel.

The 1902 carried the same 18-inch barrel and non-adjustable sight equipment, though a fixed rear peep sight was available and for a while was standard. Its trigger pull was shorter and less draggy, often rather good. The trigger guard was carried back to form an odd but useful pistol grip with a fancy little curl at the end. For a quarter century or so this was common form on most .22s of the type. Early 02s had a nicely curved shotgun buttplate of steel. Later the hard rubber or composition plates went on.

A rather heavy 21-inch barrel and screw-adjustable open rear sight stolen from the 1903 .22 automatic featured the 1904 rifle. At first the gun had the standard heavy steel rifle buttplate exactly the same as those that made you rub your shoulder and look miserable after firing a shot from a .405 or .50-100 so equipped. A flat black rubber plate improved later types of this rifle.

There was also the Thumb Trigger rifle, like the 02 but with no guard to give you a grip. You laid your thumb on a plunger behind the firing pin and pressed off the shot. The theory was interesting and the rifle was the least expensive of old Winchesters. Of course you still see all of these models around.

In the last years the chambers were reamed out for the .22 extra long cartridge as well as smaller fry. When you could buy .22s with 40-grain long-rifle bullets and 7-grain black powder charge instead of the five of the long or long-rifle they were worthwhile for important hunting. After high velocity long-rifles came, the extra long was headed for collectors' exhibits.

These Winchesters were by no means the only popular .22s of the time. There were the Stevens Little Krag and the Savage 1904, in general like the 02 Winchester. In the 1905 model Savage went farther. It had a 22-inch barrel and came in various grades. For instance, one type carried a finely adjustable two-way open rear sight and a long-pronged Schuetzen style buttplate like those on the costly offhand target rifles. Adults as well as kids bought these rifles for their own use. Even the 18-inch 1904 models weren't exclusively for youngsters. They were handy on the trapline, in a fishing boat, and in a big-game hunting outfit.

The .22 was becoming more appreciated all the time.

Those who had learned rifle shooting and hunting with the muzzle-loader, starting on squirrels, crows and rats, often did frown on the .22, and too often they were right. Cartridges were cheap and loading the rifle was fast; so there was much more shooting than hitting. The curse stays with us.

Some of us remember the Hamilton .22. There was a pump repeater, but it's the tip-down barrel single shot you're likely to unearth. Bronze barrel with more grooves than you could easily count, and a steel jacket folded around it for looks, a plank stock, a tiny, sometimes hard to cock hammer. You could buy a Hamilton, but it was easier to sell packages of blueing to your parents' friends and get one free.

Naturally these rifles saw the country. At one time they were popular grouse guns in the Canadian northwest. Hack off the stock to pistol size, bore a hole in it and run a line through. Sling it over your back and the two or three pounds of weight didn't bother you on the trail—or off trail, following compass sights through any kind of stuff they led you into. A trial we made in the late 1920s convinced us that the Hamilton isn't right for modern ammunition!

And some far better .22s of those times aren't, either. We owe a debt to the little old Stevens, Remington, Hopkins & Allen and other single shots that a kid of those times could buy. Rifle shooting belongs to America. Start 'em early and safely and pretty often it sticks.

But the small-frame single shots are best not used with any modern ammunition except perhaps the low speed .22 shorts. Our brass cases of today are strong: they seldom rupture when backed by a sound breech lockup. But modern pressures are nearly double those of early black powder or the much-underloaded smokeless .22s, and little actions do wear loose. Breechblocks of many small rifles barely cover the case-heads. Even some early bolt guns were poorly designed, the bolt cylinder tapering down, up front, instead of being left at full width to provide a good cover. Bolt-action firing pins, like those of hammer guns, frequently are loose enough to open an easy rear exit for gas from a burst case. When that happens, your face takes it.

It's true that many of the single shots of small proportions were made in .25 and .32 rimfire as well as .22, and that some handled light centerfire rounds. But the guns were engineered before smokeless powder with hot non-mercuric, non-corrosive rim- and centerfire priming came in. Little rolling, falling or rocking block actions like the Remington Numbers 4 and 6, the Stevens Favorite, Crack Shot, Little Scout, and their Maynard Junior and later Marksman with tip-down barrels, the Hopkins & Allen and the British Page-Lewis—they're doubtful enough to be retired and museumized, though they were fascinating in their day.

There were some odd but popular rifles, such as the Quackenbush with long, square breechblock rounded at the ends. To load, you thrust it to the side with your thumb, picked out the empty, and inserted a live round, then snicked the block back into place. You cocked the striker by pulling back a little knob at the right. The striker was rebounding, drawn back from contact with the cartridge when you lowered it gently. There wasn't any forestock; the long, narrow steel frame took its place. Good trigger pull and barrel weight made the gun easy to shoot and the breeching was tight and safe for cartridges made then.

The heavier, more expensive single shots were in their great day all through this period. Not many boys owned one. Many fine old Stevens models were yet available, and the Winchester, some Remingtons, and others.

Smallbore Target Rifles

In the 1900-1920 years there were two distinct types of .22 rimfire target rifles, one going out, the other coming in. Most Stevens and Winchester models were stocked definitely either for hunting or for offhand Schuetzen-style target shooting. It was exacting competition. You used no sling, but stood there and balanced the weight of the heavy rifle on a palm rest, a more or less hand-filling knob attached to a rod that depended from the forestock. You shot the rifle, usually, off the arm, not off the shoulder. The long, curved prongs of the Schuetzen buttplate made a half circle around your upper arm.

It was an art. For calibers like .32-40, the bored-up .33-40, and the .38-55, the regulation distance was 200 yards. But you needed plenty of 25 yard indoor practice and competition with .22 short or long-rifle ammunition, as you chose. About the lightest load used much at 200 yards was the .25 rimfire, which did rather well on a calm day.

The other sort of target work has been leaping ahead in popularity and achievement ever since 1919. Not many except servicemen had done it before. It was precision work in prone. You learn that well, then get up off the ground, higher and higher into difficulty—sit, kneel, and stand. You need a gunsling and a flat buttplate that's comfortable well in between shoulder and collarbone.

Stevens made a couple of eight-pounders for this four-position shooting, the 414 with almost military length forestock and a short beavertail swell for the forward hand, and the more fancy 404 with long beavertail on a sporter length forestock and, unfortunately, the front sling swivel attachment on the barrel itself. The 8½-pound Winchester single-shot "musket" lasted in various forms from 1905 to 1920. There were some custom-made or home-adapted target .22s, but not many.

Bolt Action Repeaters

They were few during these twenty years. Hopkins & Allen made one with tubular magazine under the barrel, and the Savage Model 1911 was produced until 1915. It handled shorts only and was advertised as a 20-shot repeater. So it was, in a fashion. Two buttstock tubes held 10 rounds each. You fired off

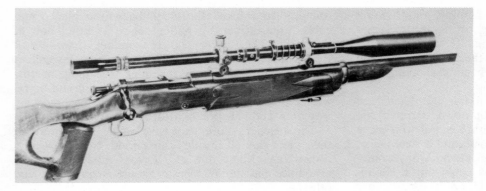

A Fecker "Champion" 1⅝-inch target scope, one of the best, was not too good to mount on this old "slow-lock" 52 Winchester with standard-weight barrel. The custom-made stock has the hand-hole style of grip, and a high comb above it for target work with the glass. The coil spring brings the scope back into battery after recoil has carried it forward. The rifle's firing pin or striker is cocked, and you can see the hole the factory drilled in it for lightness. It was customary for shooters to cork this hole, just in case a cartridge rim might burst!

the first allotment, then depressed the gun muzzle, pulled out the spring-loaded tube and let the second ten slide in. The rifle was nit-sized, and the bolt handle, too. It was accurate, for it was well made, with a one-piece stock; and shorts shoot well with correct chambering and a slow rifling twist.

The National Matches included smallbore events in 1919, and the Savage N. R. A. Match Rifle came out in that year. It had its own design of receiver peep sight, a one-piece stock with pistol grip and long, military fore-end, and it weighed about eight pounds. Later models of this basic Savage appeared, some with shorter and rather wide beavertail fore-ends, sometimes heavier barrels, too, and there were similar semi-target styles in .22 Hornet centerfire. You still see the match .22s doing well, though they don't show up at many important competitions.

You still see some pretty early Model 52 Winchesters, too, quite a little different from and quite a lot like the pilot model that went to the Nationals at Sea Girt, N. J., that year of 1919. The early ones weighed about 8¾ pounds, and scope blocks on the barrel were *not* standard equipment. For gallery use you could have the 52 in .22 short.

The factory took pride in making this rifle handle and feel like the Type S service 1903 Springfield, the one that had been used in the war. The 52 did have a pistol grip, though small, well back, and rounded at the bottom. But its rear sight, which went on the receiver instead of 'way out over the chamber, was a ladder affair, flopping down out of the way like the one on the 03. Stock length and drop were listed with great satisfaction as "same as Springfield." That was no joyful news to the few highly informed riflemen we had in those times.

Still, the Winchester 52 and the Savage 19 between them got us off to a head start on precision shooting with light ammunition that could be fired conveniently all the year 'round, indoors or out where the wind blows powder fumes away, and with no long trek to some barely accessible back-of-beyond where other people will tolerate the sound of heavy rifle fire. We needed such sharpening of skill, we still need it, we shall need it through the foreseeable future.

Slowly the single shots disappeared from the firing

lines. A few survive, and I for one am thankful that they do. But Ballard, Stevens, and Winchester lever actions find it hard to compete against the best of our modern bolts—or even some quite early 52s—and the old British Vickers with one-piece stock, and the Birmingham Small Arms .22, also with falling Martini-type action, are rare sights now. The new B. S. A., however, seems well worth its price to some of our best shots.

Slide Actions

In various forms the Marlin lever action .22s have been popular all through this century, and probably more are sold right now than ever before. The 39 succeeded the 97, and the 39-A is modern with its high-comb stock, large pistol grip, and semi-beavertail forearm. The 56 Levermatic is new in a revolutionary way.

But when school kids talked wistfully or confidently among themselves about owning a ".22 repeater" pretty soon, they almost always meant the slide or trombone action, the pump gun. It was the best known, and it came in a wide price range.

Savages

When the 1903 Savage came out it was something new and different to them in two distinct ways. The gun was hammerless; that is, its hammer lay concealed under the smooth lines of the receiver. No breechblock thrust out into the open when you drew back the slide handle. At the rear of the receiver was the safety, double-shotgun style, as quick and easy to slide forward with your thumb as it always had been to cock a well spurred hammer.

The magazine was different, too, detachable box type, a "clip" as it promptly though incorrectly was called. It stood out just ahead of the trigger guard, far enough back to be out of the way when you carried the rifle at your side, trail fashion. Seven rounds went into it, and it snicked into its bed with the reassuring snugness and ease that quality gives. The Savage had that, all right. As a rule it handled long-rifles and longs more surely than shorts, and so do most magazines of the sort. Though it wasn't milled out of solid steel it was rugged enough to stand a generation or more of service—and some abuse. Bent magazine lips can cause jams, but you seldom see them in that old Savage.

The 1903 had a 24-inch octagon barrel, rifle butt, and a neatly rounded pistol grip, its swell too far back to offer much except attractive looks. Seeing the importance of the junior trade, Savage brought out the 1909 in a style that most of us would prefer today, except perhaps for its weight of just under five pounds. The barrel was round, 20 inch, and the stock though straight gripped had a shotgun butt.

In those days the hammerless feature came in for criticism. But progress demanded it and it had to come. Some time later, shooters realized that these Savages were safe for a reasonably careful user. The hammerless breech was more nearly gas-proof than most exposed-hammer actions, and the clip magazines made unloading easy. (Of course you had to remember to jack out the chambered round!) Occasionally a cartridge will hang in a tubular magazine, waiting to make trouble after you think you've unloaded the gun.

Those clips were handy in another way. Back in those times there was nothing illegal about taking a surrey or buggy ride over back roads, looking for crows, woodchucks or red squirrels in the fields and woods you rumbled gently past. With a clip beside you on the seat there was no excuse for having the rifle loaded.

The tubular magazine 1914 eventually displaced the 03 and 09. It had the usual large magazine capacity of the type, also the 24-inch octagon barrel that was still correct on senior grade .22s. But its stock was the first nearly modern one on a factory rifle of this class. Comb and heel were high, and the comb well up forward. So was the pistol grip, close enough to the trigger guard to give some help in steady holding. And the buttplate was of shotgun form, with corrugated metal gripping your shoulder. The 1914 kept the good tang safety, but the Model 25 that followed had the common cross-bolt trigger lock in the trigger guard, easy to make but less convenient for the shooter.

Marlins

During these years the Marlin people produced .22 pump guns with exposed hammer and with neatly closed and snug side-ejection ports like those in their big-game rifles. Round and octagon barrel lengths ran through more than the usual variety—Marlin as a rule has been generous in style choice—and one type of buttplate was unusual and good. It was a sort of modified steel rifle plate, flat and wide like the shotgun style, but curved to hold to the shoulder and with heel and toe rounded in pleasant lines.

Most of these Marlins were takedown, and like the old Savage in split or two-piece receiver construction. This makes it easy to clean and oil the working parts, and to clean the bore from the breech, a feature which was coming into demand. But unless the fitting is close there's less rigidity than the one-piece Remington or Winchester receiver gives, theoretically at least.

Marlins had reasonable sales: you saw a good many around. Their hammerless .22, in which stock tang and receiver were hooked as well as thumb-screwed together, was less successful in the race, though it was a good, reliable rifle. It had a one-piece receiver.

For a long time the Marlin pump gun in more effective small-game calibers was well liked and the only thing of the sort available. In .25 rimfire it mounted a 24-inch round barrel, and in .25-20 and .32-20 a 24-inch octagon. It was similar in appearance to the .22s and not much heavier. A takedown, it couldn't equal the precision of solid frame Marlin and Winchester lever actions, or that of the good single shots, some of which were takedown, too.

Winchesters

In these years the Winchester 1906 was the only new entrant from that part of New Haven. True, in 1920 the company produced the 1890 in .22 long-rifle caliber, handling that cartridge only, just as the other 90s took just one length.

The 06 was a junior rifle and until 1908 it accepted only shorts. This chambering of the rifle was popular for years and years in the shooting galleries. The later style of carrier has a cartridge stop that lets you use all three lengths. Straight grip, 20-inch round barrel, and shotgun stock with rubber buttplate make the rifle up into a five-pounder. Occasionally you see an early 06 with smooth, ungrooved slide handle, and most of them still work, a little loose in breeching, maybe, and almost always with completely shot-out or rusted-out barrels. These rifles have quite a bit more stock drop than later 06s. Times were changing.

Remingtons

The Company wasn't a bit too soon in making the 06 rifle take all three popular .22 lengths. In 1909 Remington brought out the hammerless Model 12, a beautiful arm and a formidable contestant against the other makes. It took all three cartridge lengths, though the .22 short gallery gun soon appeared, and later the .22 Remington Special—a .22 WRF.

The junior rifle, not normally made for the WRF, was the prettiest little pump gun ever, and good balance made it effective. The round 22-inch barrel was longer than the recognized junior type, and a good thing, too. Total weight was under five pounds. Straight-grip shotgun stock with rubber buttplate, and the grip was higher than on hammer guns—too high, it did seem on first acquaintance. The heavier 12 had a 24-inch octagon barrel and rifle butt, with weight going to 5½ pounds. About the time when the .22 Remington Special appeared the stock was given a pistol grip, small and not much good, so far back it was.

Remingtons were different from other .22s in having a sliding magazine. The tube comes back with the

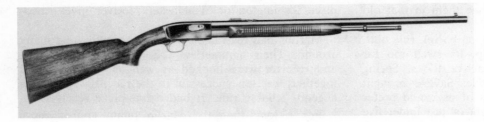

The action of the 121 Remington was almost, not quite, identical with that of the long-popular little Model 12. The stock was modernized with a higher comb to rest your cheek on, and the barrel was made only in round, 24-inch style, with good weight.

forearm when you open the rifle. As you start to close the action the carrier lifts the cartridge out of the magazine and gives it to the breechblock, all ready to go straight into the chamber. When the action goes shut the carrier falls back into position below the breechblock, which is locked, up front, into a cut in the top undersurface of the receiver. This action and the Winchester are among the safest of the old-timers to use with any modern ammunition that fits.

Both Remington and Savage hammerless .22s seemed smoother in action than Winchester hammer guns, but no faster. Any of them works much too fast in game country for a shooter who lacks coolness. The Remington was the first and probably the only side-ejector .22 pump that is easy to single-load with thumb and finger starting a cartridge into the chamber. The ejector slot was carved out big with this detail in mind.

In 1936 the Model 12 became the Model 121. The 24-inch round barrel is fairly heavy, the pistol grip and shotgun buttstock good-sized, and the slide handle long enough to serve as a real forearm. It was in current production, or at least easy to find, until the entirely different Model 572 replaced it in 1955.

Remington made a medium-caliber slide action, the Model 25, from 1923 to 1936. Calibers were .25-20 and .32-20, and magazine capacity was 10 rounds. Following the lines of the Model 12, it was a pretty rifle, and not much heavier than the .22. Both 24-inch rifle and 18-inch carbine barrels were made. Any good new rifle gets a sale, but the competition of existing lever guns was rough on the Model 25, and after the .22 Hornet cartridge came out in the early 1930s it hadn't much chance.

Stevens

The Stevens people had their .22 pump gun, the inexpensive Visible Loader that used a short single-shot rifle frame as its receiver. Those people always have had in mind a fact that's almost unbearable to some contemporary advertisers, the hard fact that some of us just don't have it! Always the Stevens outfit has offered some guns that were cheap, but not shoddy. It produced fine, expensive single-shot rifles and pistols but never forgot the kid and the poor man.

Maybe the best proof of this is their having designed a supersized .32 rifle cartridge, the straight-cased Ideal, expressly for shooters whose .32 rimfires and .32-20s had been shot out. Rebarreling was more expensive than reboring and even firing-pin relocation, too. The Ideal was so good a cartridge in its own right that many Stevens and Winchester single shots were made for it in the first place.

The Visible Loader .22 repeater was a solid-frame, non-takedown rifle, maybe a little more accurate for that reason, and cheaper to build. The whole breechblock slid back out of the receiver to pick up a cartridge from the tubular magazine under the 20-inch round barrel. As far as I recall, the gun never was made as a senior size .22, but everyone knew it and a lot of folks bought it. It isn't to be recommended for use with high velocity ammunition, but in its time it made many people happy.

Automatics

Until fairly recent times most kids despaired of owning a .22 automatic, and all in all that was just as well. They did read and talk and wonder about them, and some bought them soon after getting their first good job. A few had had the chance to tickle an auto's trigger, and then the disease was liable to have got a firm hold. Although many grown men aren't mature enough to rate an autoloader, ready or not, a lot of shooters feel its fascination. Some do fine work with it even in difficult hunting.

The Winchester. The Winchester 1903 was announced and illustrated on the inside front cover of E. K. Tryon's Philadelphia catalogue of October, 1903, and the rifles got out pretty soon. From the New Haven plant they went all over the world for just-out-of-town shooting and for fill-the-pot contributions in the least known backwaters, forests and mountains. The round-pointed 45-grain bullets slew big game, too, just because the little 5¾-pound gun was so handy to take along—and rather fascinating, as implied before.

This rifle has a 10-shot tube magazine in its buttstock, and it is side-ejecting and hammerless like the Savage pump guns. Its simple blowback action set the general fashion for .22 automatics that followed it.

In those days no light alloys were considered proper for breechblocks. Designers used steel. A semi-automatic was built around just one loading: too little back-thrust on firing and the gun jammed, too much and action parts were punished. The L-shaped Winchester breechblock is guided and slowed in its recoil through the receiver by the long, light forward section that reaches part way up inside the fore-end. The hammer spring is heavy, too.

The .22 Winchester Automatic cartridge was a masterpiece in architecture for the job it had to do. The case was one of the strongest used for any rimfire, with unusually thick rim. That was reassuring to people who first saw the hustle and slam of automatic reloading. A compact smokeless powder charge was confined, usually, by a thick cardboard wad at the bullet's base, and the oversize ".22" bullet was heavy—45 grains—to develop recoil. It was hard, too, which gave still more resistance, and totally without lubrication. The crimp of the case was abnormally heavy: the cartridge has even been called bottlenecked! The rifle's 20-inch barrel was just about long enough to burn and use the powder charge without letting gas energy go to waste in shoving a no longer accelerated bullet through more barrel!

Early loads were rated at 1125 f.s. velocity. (Major Payne down on South Broad found and gave me some, and I certainly noticed the difference!) They may have been rough on some actions, for later the speed went down, for a while, to about 900. Today's 1055 f. s. level does nicely in guns that have had decent care.

There were other changes, to a soft lead, lubricated hollow point, then a solid bullet of that kind, both 45 grains. The short-lived Spotlight was a hollow point with contact-flash powder in the cave. It made a big wink on an iron target and quite naturally the type was produced in .22 short also.

Now the .22 Auto has a brass case. It always has been among the most oil- and waterproof of all rounds, like the .22 Remington Autoloading, .22 WRF or Special, .25 Stevens short and long, and .32 longrifle rimfires. All are or were inside lubricated, except the early solid, hard lead for the Winchester auto.

With fresh, strong ammunition and a clean action the 03 was more than fairly reliable, and raising the velocity above 1000 f. s. seemed an improvement in the two rifles I had at different times and used for many years. But too often the patronizing of hometown stores was a self-sacrificing policy if you lived in a small place. The high price of both ammunition and rifle kept the gun an item for either the well-to-do shooter or the hopelessly involved guncrank, though second-hand jobs seldom stayed long in the stores. Ammunition got stale. The other fellow in town who used one of these rifles never seemed to buy and shoot up his share fast enough. Though it wasn't fair, sometimes you'd buy a few boxes in the big city and keep 'em for serious work in the field! With hollow points the gun was a good killer up to 40 or 50 yards, and that was enough.

The 03 became the 63 we have today. It's the last of the oldline, high quality .22 auto-rifles of elaborately engineered design.

The Savage. In 1912 Savage put out an inexpensive automatic that would fire standard .22 longrifle ammunition. A little earlier, as I recall, had come the announcement of the Batavia, made by the old Baker Gun Company of Batavia, N. Y., famous for sturdy though rather heavy double shotguns that were far superior to cheap imported jobs. This longbarreled little rifle used .22 shorts only and it never became at all well known.

The Savage had advertising and essentially it was a good rifle. The receiver and clip magazine were similar to those of 1903 and 1909 pump guns, though sprouting out the right side was the operating handle. It shot back and forth as you fired, but it was out of your way—and a doggoned interesting thing to watch, too!

The gun had a 20-inch barrel, like the Winchester, a nicely rounded forearm, and straight grip, shotgun buttstock. It was about a pound lighter than the Winchester, but it handled well. However, it was doomed.

The priming of small-capacity smokeless rounds corroded rifle barrels fast and surely, almost always. The few partly burned powder kernels spilled through the action gave no trouble if you cleaned the works occasionally, as any auto-rifle user should. But if you fired black or even semi-smokeless ammo to save your barrel, the autoloading action was fouled and gummed, and you got too many jams unless you took painstaking care of the rifle. Not many shooters do this for any gun; so a nice little rifle went off the market. It should have been safe and pleasant to use with modern low velocity long-rifles, though the powerful loadings could be risky. Their back-thrust is too much for a balanced recoil system made so long ago.

It was possible to keep these rifles in perfect condition through many years of use—at least the Winchesters and Remingtons with their stiffer powder charges and heavier bullets. The method was elaborate. First you cleaned the barrel with Winchester Crystal Cleaner, an ammonia solution meant to dissolve the fouling left by copper jacketed bullets. (Water would have done as well for the .22s, had we known it, for potassium chlorate primer fouling is just a salt.) Then you cleaned with gun oil, which helped remove any of the faint leading left in a good barrel, and after wiping it out you smeared the bore liberally with Safeti-Paste. This grease, then made by Birmingham Small Arms and regularly imported for the big gun houses, was of about the consistency of apple-sauce. It was a fore-runner of RIG, meant to protect bores that hadn't been properly cleaned.

This triple lineup of dope went in canoe duffle with me. A nuisance? Of course it was.

Remingtons. That Remington Model 16 of 1914 is one of the few things that make me hark back to the past with longing. Durn thing looked like a rifle.

It followed the lines of the Model 8 high-power autoloader, though it was less angular. It had the same sort of operating handle on the side, though it was attached to a sliding coverplate that kept the weather out. The receiver was rather long, housing the light action spring in the bolt—the heavy hammer spring lay in the stock. The gun weighed 5¾ pounds and had a 22-inch barrel.

When you take the rifle down—easiest takedown I know of; just pull back the button on the port side of the receiver and twist the barrel a quarter turn—the barrel and forearm are in one hand, the stock and action parts in the other. You clean the barrel from the breech and you can dismount the action for cleaning and oiling, though the job is a little more complicated than with the 1903 Winchester.

The Remington balances well and its trigger pull is one of the cleanest and lightest any automatic ever had. The gun was easy to shoot, though it seemed to me that its takedown system was less durable in long use than the Winchester's. The only objection I had to the 16's handling was its stock length: the buttstock magazine holds 15 shots against the Winchester's 10. That stock might not have bothered a long-armed man, but it did me. Even though the curved buttplate was rounded at the toe, it caught on my hunting coat too often.

The special cartridge was longer and thinner than the Winchester's. Velocity of solid or hollow point 45-grain bullets, always inside lubricated, was listed at from 920 to 950 f. s. This was more than some 40-grain .22 long-rifle bullets of the time developed, but it was feeble. Evidently the action couldn't take much more and still function well, as the more simple Winchester could.

Today the .22 Remington Autoloading rounds are hard to find, and they might be dropped from production at almost any time, so few are sold. It is possible to use .22 *longs* in the rifle. Their cases are much under-size for the chamber, but the little 29-grain bullets fit the bore pretty well. The special cartridge will chamber in .22 WRF rifles and revolvers, and it makes a useful subload for them. The M16 receiver, like the Winchesters', is about as gas-proof as any you find.

These three .22 automatics may seem important only as a part of firearms history. Some who still use and love them would feel differently, but they're mostly back-country boys who live where the game is and know how to hunt—that's all!

Yet it is important that these rifles appeared and were more than reasonably successful. Now we have .22 autos that are within reach of the average shooter. That's not so good for conservation of game, for so much is wounded and lost by sloppy shooting. However, in time a fellow changes places with his automatic and becomes the boss. From a military or security viewpoint the popularity of the automatics is a national asset.

BIGBORE RIFLES

The time from 1900 to 1920-plus saw the fervid development of the autoloader, the beginning of bolt-action popularity, and some modernization of existing lever actions, which held their own in spite of innovations. Probably in most hunting camp sessions the automatics got the most discussion, pro and con.

Winchester Self-Loaders

That was the name the factory gave its centerfire "automatics," a correct name, too. They reload automatically but they don't fire in that way unless something goes awfully wrong.

The 1905 rifle was sensational. A lot of people bought it in the .32 or .35 caliber, and some were satisfied with the approximate .32-40 or .38-40 ballistics even after the .351 of 1907 brought an extra 450 f. s. of speed and much better killing power. To most deer hunters the Model 1910 .401 seemed too much gun, though it's the only sure, quick deer-slayer in the lot.

In action they are much alike, simple blowbacks like the 1903 .22, with long breechblocks and heavy recoil springs designed to take their respective back-thrusts of recoil. The .351 is now the Model 07, with heavy, high-comb modern stock and a fuller forearm. In operation they were all—except some of the earliest 1905s and 1907s—extremely reliable and durable. A police gun must take some abuse or neglect in line of duty, and many departments rely on the 07.

The detachable five-shot magazine (four in .401) in front of the trigger guard bothers little if any in the trail carry, but the stiff spring makes it hard to fill when your fingers are also stiff, with cold. Unloading is easy and an extra mag, fully loaded, doesn't weigh much. For the smaller calibers there are 10-shot magazines and the .351 saw aircraft service in the early years of World War I. The special cartridge held a sharp pointed, full jacketed bullet of slightly smaller diameter.

The 1905 has a 22-inch plain steel barrel for its low pressure ammunition, and the barrel band at its forearm tip doesn't completely encircle the barrel. It's a rather graceful gun. The .351 and .401 have 20-inch nickel steel or Proof Steel barrels, and these guns are really of carbine length. They came out when short, handy rifles—like the Savage 99 Featherweight—were popular. This preference is common now, with emphasis on light weight. The .401 would have been much more popular with a 22-inch barrel, for even that extra length would have reduced its muzzle blast noticeably. "Just a big roar," one guide said of the .401.

Pistol grips, too far back except for a heavily gloved hand, were standard except on early 05s, and a comfortably flat and big shotgun buttplate of hard rubber. Gun weight ran from 7½ to 8¼ pounds with standard American walnut used for woodwork. "Fancy" grades were heavier, and some of this walnut was as black as your hat, but grainy.

The cartridges are straight-cased, with just enough microscopical tapers to assure easy extraction, and they are semi-rimless. The extracting groove or can-nelure is almost unique in form, tapered and shallow, somewhat like that of the Japanese 6.5 mm. service round, or the 7.7 as made for the Model 99 machine gun. Not much brass is machined out to form the groove, and a good strong, thick case-head is left.

A blowback automatic can't use high pressure bottle-necked cartridges. Gas pushing forward against the shoulder and back against the base tends to tear the brass apart. So these early Winchester rounds are short-ranged. For killing power they depend more on bullet diameter than on velocity. With almost any weight of bullet, .40 caliber long had been respected as a deer-hunting size. No one with experience sneers at the .401's deadliness in the deer forests.

Only the .351 is loaded now. The .35 will fire .38 Long Colt and .38 Special rounds as a single loader, and .351 empties can be cut to 1⅛ inches for hand-loading. The .32 was used as a starting point to develop the .30 M-1 carbine cartridge, and these empties perhaps could be formed into .32 S. L., though they are truly rimless, haven't the wide extracting flange of the .32. Factory soft point .351 and .32-40 bullets fit these two calibers closely, and the weights are correct. Molds have been made by Ideal for all four Winchester Self-Loading calibers. Sometimes you can work up an accurate cast bullet load fast enough to operate the action, and yet of low enough velocity to avoid leading the bore.

This would be nice in .401, converting it into prac-tically a .40-65—famous deer caliber—if you use a bullet at least as heavy as the 250-grain Ideal now listed as 240. The .401 case is hard to duplicate: 2½ inches long and almost straight, about .4555 inch at the rim and .4285 at the critical point, just above the cannelure. The .30-30 etc. are too small, the .35 Rem and even the little .276 Pedersen experimental Army round too large. But .303 Savage runs about .438 above the rim, .220 Swift .441 above the cannelure. Both have possibilities.

Rims will have to be trimmed and cannelures deepened. After doing any kind of this work it's wise to section your product, also an original case, and compare the brass thickness. Winchester self-loaders normally handle any ruptured brass safely, but no one wants that sort of thing to happen. In the self-loader it's pretty sure to mean a jam, and in any gun it could mean much worse. Go easy in working up your loads.

Remington Autoloaders

Remington production didn't lag in getting the Model 8 into the swim. This Browning-designed auto-loader came out in 1906, a year after the Winchester .32 and .35, and it handled what were then long range cartridges. The .25, .30 (at first a ".30-30 Rem") and .32 were like the .25-35, .30-30 and .32 Special in power, though the .32 should *not* be used with peak .32 Special handloads. The .35, resembling a shortened and big-mouthed .30-06, but actually slimmer, is similar to the .33 Winchester in ballistics. All are bottle-necked, and all but the .25 are still factory loaded. The .32 may have begun to wobble, but form-ing .25 or .32 cases from the .30 isn't difficult. About as many different bullet weights were loaded as in the rimmed .25, .30-30 and .32, and the .35 at various times has come up in 150, 170, 200 and 210 grain.

The Remington is a locked-breech automatic with turning bolt: the barrel shoots backward through its jacket and is returned in time to receive the cartridge that the delayed bolt picks out of the magazine. It's a complicated action but, like the Winchester, almost completely reliable. The gun is no more difficult to keep in order except that when assembling it from takedown you sometimes must guide the bolt lugs into the slots in the barrel extension. You do this with a screwdriver or a bullet point, holding the bolt handle back with your thumb until the parts line up. You clean the gun from the breech, as with most Remington automatics.

Some liked the balance of this 22-inch-barreled rifle better than that of the Winchesters, and with its small, tapered fore-end it was more streamlined. Weight ran from 7½ to 8 pounds. Like the Win-chester, it was muzzle-heavy and steady, and it was a bit longer.

The magazine is built in, though custom-made detachable mags have shown up from time to time. The bolt stays open after the last round is fired, and you can reload with a clip—special clips came with the new rifles—or by hand. Both the magazine spring and the trigger pull are light and easy.

Its takedown system is not much different from those used on some old black-powder single shots, one big screw holding the flat surfaces together. This screw takes up wear pretty well, but accuracy seldom is big news. As with the Winchesters it runs from about 3- to 5-inch 10-shot groups at 100 yards. For woods shooting that's plenty unless you have to slide a bullet between a couple of big limbs or tree-trunks. The Remington was used a lot in the woods and it still is. The .35s have been to Africa and proved acceptable even on buffalo—with great luck. This gun has been enormously popular and good used specimens bring a high price. In the old days some guides waited patiently for years until they could buy one. For the wonderful work they did, those men weren't paid much—certainly not a specialist's wage.

The Rem is handy, even though you have to jack the cartridges out one at a time in unloading. For a gloved hand the safety is convenient; it's a big lever on the right side of the receiver. With bare hand you can strain it away from the receiver and ease it down noiselessly.

Of course this rifle kicks in the heavier calibers, .35, and the .300 Savage that was taken up in the last few years of its life. A soft rubber recoil pad helps, and

Model 81 Remington was and is a popular woods rifle. Except for the modernized woodwork and the adoption of one new caliber, the .300 Savage, it was practically the same as the old Model 8.

so does cutting the stock to put the toe or lower end a little farther forward. This gives it the down-pitch that'll be needed on either the Model 8 or the later 81 if you ever do any prone shooting. Except for stock and forearm styling these models are essentially the same.

The 81 stock has a high, fat comb and big, close-up pistol grip. Except perhaps in earliest production it wasn't made in .25 caliber. The trade to the .300 suited most people, though some remembered the .25 for its really quite good accuracy and light recoil that let you get in follow-up shots, if you needed them, so very fast. There wasn't much upchuck to its muzzle. The 81 went out in 1951 to let dealers have plenty of time to sell off their stock before the entirely different Model 740 appeared.

Remington Slide Actions

These were the interesting new and popular big-game repeaters of the period. Many old lever-action models were continued, or somewhat modernized in style, but only one fine, completely new one came out, the Stevens.

It handled the four Remington autoloading sizes and was a side-ejector like the Marlin. With fairly heavy 22-inch round barrel it went to about 7¾ pounds. It was no shorty, for the long, smooth receiver covered the breechblock during all of its rearward travel. The exposed hammer was cocked by leverage, in this respect resembling the covered hammer of the rather new Marlin 56 Levermatic .22. Barrel weight kept the gun from feeling breech-heavy, and this Stevens deserved much more popularity than it got. Even during the years of its manufacture few hunters seemed to have heard of it.

Neither were the Standard rifles popular, though they were chambered for the same well established cartridges, Remington rimless. For one thing, the slide handle of the pump gun was pretty far out, a long reach, and both this model and the autoloader were rather ungainly. The auto was gas operated, not recoil operated like the Remington and Winchester, and it was notoriously unreliable. Back then, few riflemen had any realization of the care that's necessary to keep this type of action in good working order. The gas port can be sealed off purposely, converting the gun into a manually operated repeater. Both types of Standard rifle seem to have given trouble. Perhaps if the company had had the capital to put their product through years of development and tests, they would have made the ripple.

Since the time of the Colt pump gun there had been considerable prejudice against a slide-action rifle for big game. In general, the Colts were a little less capable than Winchester and Marlin lever guns in extracting battered or swollen, much-reloaded brass, and in black powder days the percentage of reloaders must have been at least as high as now. Remington took a chance in producing the Model 14 high power in 1912.

Any doubts in shop or office were laid to rest. This streamlined, hammerless rifle was an early and lasting success. You see lots of them in the woods, a few in saddle scabbards, but not a whale of a lot of them in dealers' used-gun racks. Prying one loose from an individual owner might be difficult.

In takedown, barrel and receiver come off from stock and trigger tang, but removing the breechblock (by hand) gives a clear view through the bore and affords a clean thrust for the wiping-rod. The takedown seems at least as rigid as that of lever guns of this tribe, and the front-locking of the Remington breechblock is an assist to accuracy. Even the original slide handles were long and comfortable, long enough for most woods hunters though too far out for a shooter trained in the Army offhand. He holds his forward hand in closer, almost to the point of balance, unless a cross-wind pulls and jerks at the rifle.

With 22-inch barrel the Model 14 weighs about seven pounds in .35 caliber, which in this pump gun came out a bit later than the .25, .30 and .32. Balance is excellent, and handling too, the grip seeming less high than the Model 12 .22 repeater. The 18½-inch carbines are noisy, but their shortness and considerably lighter *feel* have attracted quite a few brush-buckers. Both models hold six cartridges when fully loaded.

In 1913 the .38-40 and .44-40 Model 14½ rifles appeared, with 22½-inch soft steel barrels and usually with full-length 11-shot magazines. The "half" magazines, and the tube of the 18½-inch carbine, hold nine of these stubby rounds. The 14½ is practically the same as the 14 except for barreling, slight action changes, and the straight-tube magazine. The spiral mag of the 14 keeps the bullet points away from primers ahead, a safety measure unnecessary with the flat-nosed .38 and .44 loads. Both magazines move back and forth with the slide handle's motion.

The 14½ went off the market in 1931 but the 14

The Remington 141 slide action carried a fairly heavy 24-inch barrel, as compared to the 14's 22-incher. The stock and forearm were heavier, too.

became the heavier, modernized 141 in 1937. That old favorite varmint load for bolt-action rifles, the .25 Rem, was dropped from the line perhaps a little earlier. In 1950 this slide action went out, and the current 760 came along a couple of years later.

Bolt Actions

After World War I the bolt action began to be popular as a sporter in the United States. Before then it was unfamiliar. A few experienced long-range shots liked it and possibly as many Americans of German or Austrian descent bought it for old times' sake. Mausers and Mannlicher-Schoenauers were attractive in line and finish, and until just after the war there were no shoddy ones among them. Calibers fairly popular here ran from 6.5 to 9.5 mm. And there were the Jeffery rifles, imported from England by Abercrombie & Fitch of New York. Most were in perhaps unnecessarily heavy calibers, .333 and .404, but there were also the .333-.280 and the .256. Some got around.

Various old military bolt guns did, too. They seldom cost much, those .41 rimfire Swiss Vetterlis, 7 mm. 1892 single- and 1893 double-column box magazine Spanish Mausers, the 8 mm. German '88s, and the 11 mm. black powder type Mausers.

The Canadian Ross Model 10 straight-pull sporter got a lot of advertising and its .280 was perhaps the first magnum cartridge built on this continent. Today most people who know rifles are quick to advise a shooter never to have anything to do with any model or caliber of Ross, though some are trickier than others, it's admitted. Bolts have been wrongly assembled and have blown out with disastrous, sometimes fatal results. A few who know and love the Ross get by without harm.

The Newtons were made for a while during these years. Projected long-range calibers were and are fascinating: .22, .256, .276, .280, .30, .33 and .35. Only the .256, .30 and .35 rounds had much factory production, by Western and to some extent by Remington.

The Newton was an advanced design, Mauser type, and essentially sound. It was stocked in shootable style, though its tiny bolt handle certainly wasn't meant for military rapid fire. Boring was often so oversize that accuracy was poor with the available bullets. Some Newtons were quite accurate, even in takedown style. For some of his rifles Newton used imported Mauser actions, and there was his own design of straight-pull bolt, now a collector's item.

The takedown was ingenious. The magazine floorplate catch is a button in the front of the trigger guard, as in the modern Winchester Model 70. Pressing in this catch releases the hinged floor-plate, which you use as a lever to turn out the big assembly screw. Then you tip barrel and action down and they come away from the stock, magazine, and trigger guard. But all in all the Newton was just a little too early and made by just a little too unfamiliar a firm to take hold. The company had its financial troubles, too.

Remington and Savage got into the bolt-action field at the right time, a game season or two after the war had ended. The Winchester 54 came later, profiting somewhat by the others' experiences.

Savage 1920. This is a rifle of about seven pounds' weight, with steeply tapered 22-inch barrel for the .250-3000. Later it came in 24 inch .300. Its action is much like the short or *kurz* Mauser in length and weight, safe and reliable for cartridges made for it.

In weight and balance the 20 is amazingly like a popular type of rifle made today, light to carry and quick to mount to the shoulder. There was even an aluminum buttplate to save ounces—no nylon then, of course! For its heft it was an accurate rifle, though one of my friends had his fitted with a special, heavier Model 99 .250 barrel before he was satisfied with it as a varmint gun.

The factory made a real effort to stock it well. You see the beginning of modernity in the at least fairly sharp curve of its pistol grip, which is still too far back to suit most of us. The comb is fairly high, though the heel drop is considerable, in the early fashion. With irons it fits rather well, though you need a buildup of the comb for practically any scope on the 20.

A later model, never well known, has an action so long that the .30-06 was added to the line. The succeeding 40 and 45 Savage rifles aren't of Mauser type at all. Magazines are detachable, and the bolt lugs are far back, not up front, close to the cartridge head. They were inexpensive but really sound little guns for the .250, 30-30, .300 and .30-06. The 45 has a Lyman peep sight and checkered wood.

Remington 30. This Enfield conversion appeared soon after the war, chambered for the rimless Autoloading series, and in .30-06 it had an early and satisfactory test in Alaska. For it, new .30-06 loadings

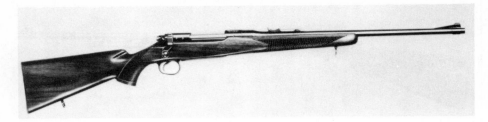

Remington 720 with 22-inch barrel. Other lengths regularly offered were 20 and 24 inches.

came out with modern high velocities and bronze-point 150- and 180-grain pointed bullets.

It is a light rifle, about 7¼ pounds, with slim 22-inch barrel and spindly buttstock and forearm. The weight is in the big receiver. Like the 1917 Enfield, early models were cocked by the closing shove of the bolt. Trigger pulls at first were creepy, and National Rifle Association members made quite a run on the Army's Director of Civilian Marksmanship, buying Enfield parts to install. Though the Enfield has the two-stage military pull—which some Rem 30s had, too—the final release can be made crisp if it isn't so already.

Almost everyone likes the side thumb safety, similar to the Enfield's, and it was to prove ideal for use with low mounted scope sights, which weren't well known then. The comb of the stock is too low and thin, and too far back, and the stock is a bruiser when you fire loads much above .30-30 power. It seemed that the factory couldn't quite unstick itself from nineteenth-century ideas, for the steel buttplate is narrow and curved, and sharp at heel and toe. It prods.

But the action has great locking strength and the barrels are well bored and rifled. Always the gun had possibilities. Belding & Mull of Philipsburg, Pa., established loading tool makers, were persuaded to furnish the N. R. A.-type stocks designed by experts—and to fit them to the steel with great exactness. The wood was generous, high comb, sizable pistol grip, and plenty of forearm for the anchorage of the front sling swivel. At this time B&M were producing advanced models of big-lensed scope sights, a hunting and a target model with fine adjustments, and most of their Remingtons carried one, it seems. In .25 Rem the job became a favorite varmint rifle for those who knew their stuff. There were no .22 Hornets to compete, and many of us wanted something less noisy than a .250 or .30-06. These rifles had about the same inherent accuracy as the 9½-pound Winchester single shot .25-35 which hadn't been made since the war, at least as standard factory issue.

The 30-S or Special rifle was Remington's improvement, a heavy 8½-pound gun made at different times for .25 Remington, .257 Roberts, 7 mm. Mauser and .30-06. It was modernized, at least in late models, to the extent of cocking on closing, and its woodwork was for most purposes entirely modern. It is still among the best of bolt actions, nearly as desirable as

the more streamlined Model 720 that gave way to the present 721 and 722. It has the military type trigger.

Winchester 54. Like the Savage 1920, this is in no sense a revised army rifle. Back in, you still find a few who speak disparagingly of bolt actions as "army guns," and if that back country is thick forest, pondering may lead you to conclude that they aren't entirely wrong. Or it may not.

The 54's receiver is smooth and sleek, its bolt handle raked back for easy grasp from the shoulder. Before we were educated to modern firing techniques the original stock lines looked pretty. As would have been expected in 1925, the comb and heel were low, pistol grip too far to the rear, buttplate almost without down-pitch, and forestock tapered slim and ending in a snobble or fancy little curl—which is coming back into style on some custom and factory stocks. But the .30-06 and brand new .270 in a rifle of some eight pounds' weight marked a step almost as far forward as the Newtons had, a decade before. And most 54s are accurate in any caliber if you feed them good ammunition.

Other calibers were the .22 Hornet, .220 Swift, .250 Savage, .257 Roberts, .30-30, .300 Magnum, and 7, 7.65 and 9 mm. Mauser. They came, and they went. At about the time of the Hornet the stock was modernized to N. R. A. style, much like that of today's Model 70 though noticeably lighter up front. Still, the N. R. A. forestock gives you a fairly comfortable hold in target sessions.

The 54 has few faults. You have to remember to flop the wing safety at the rear of the bolt to the right, not left in Springfield or Mauser fashion, or you may lose a quick shot. You could have a gunsmithed side safety. The stamped steel trigger guard and magazine floor-plate may not look pretty, though they're nicely inletted, not tacked on, and plenty rugged. A few years after the rifle's birth the company made a serious effort to improve accuracy by careful bedding of barrel and action into the stock, though many of the old rifles had done right well. At various times there were fancy grades, carbines, 20-inch rifles, and heavy sniper rifles in addition to the standard sporter with 24-inch barrel, or 26 in .220 Swift and .300 Magnum. The 54 was a great favorite for custom remodeling. Unaltered, it is still a favorite of lots of hunters. In the first few years even some gun writers complained of the weight, from 8 to 8¾ pounds, according to how big a hole had been bored through the barrel and how dense the stock wood happened to be. Going out in 1936, it wasn't in production long enough to be made as a featherweight. It was about 16 years before the Model 70 got the treatment.

WHERE ARE THEY NOW?

Do you wonder what became of the millions of old American metallic-cartridge rifles? I do.

Attics, ponds, scrap heaps, museums and private collections took some. So did fires and floods, and some were destined to become children's toys. Export, legitimate and otherwise, must have accounted for thousands, and perhaps every day a few become "junkers," providing gunsmiths with replacement parts for rifles still in use.

It's surprising, though, how many are still giving service, with a fair percentage never having needed a lick of repair work. A few people must have loved those rifles, in manufacture and in use. The wild places—"desolate" country, "submarginal" lands, where always it's beautiful—still give the old ones a chance to do their work. People get sentimental about rifles—some rifles, anyway. "I use it because it's the best I've got" may be a cryptic explanation.

MAYBE these little .22 rimfires are the most important of all sporting firearms.

Kids deserve a good start. "Sooner than you think," as we all find out, they come of age. Voting citizens can resist the infiltration of unwise anti-gun laws, innocent enough sometimes in intention but still hurtful to national security. "Nation of riflemen": yes, that's the ideal, and a nation grows from its youth as a body grows from its new cells.

Even before voting age comes service in the armed forces. Long familiarity with firearms is a G. I. asset of value. Sometimes it makes the difference in combat.

Most boys and a rather surprising number of girls want to shoot a rifle and will do it, too, without guidance or supervision if they must. You read the accounts in the paper, and you feel bad.

The first and most significant lesson in the start towards becoming a rifleman is gun-safety. It's being publicized widely now, and high time! For a generation or more the National Rifle Association has been plugging away with its junior rifle clubs. They number in the thousands and there'd be more if there were more adults who knew how much downright fun it is to coach a group of youngsters. The Sporting Arms and Ammunition Manufacturers' Institute has given wide publicity to the Ten Commandments of Safety, and passing the N. R. A.-developed Junior Hunter Course is required by law, in some states, before a kid can take out his first license to go afield with a gun in his hands.

The rifles featured in this chapter are believed to be safe, just like all cars put on the market. They are infinitely preferable to most of the black-powder-design .22s still offered as second-hand goods. They are made for modern ammunition just as the ammunition is made for them, with those strong brass cases that seldom burst unless they're fired in a relic built to corral pressures about half as potent.

However, the rifles aren't foolproof. We still have to watch that muzzle, whether the gun's loaded or not, for habit is a powerful thing and can be made to work for our good. And we still have to assume responsibility for the final resting place of shot or bullet. Once they're gone we can't whistle them back like a bird dog.

Another part of the good start is marksmanship, and we can be thankful for the accuracy of modern .22 rifles. Naturally they vary a great deal in absolute accuracy, the precision that's built into them, and it's easier to get that accuracy out of some than out of others. Still, they all have the stuff that makes the first stages of N. R. A. Junior qualification—Pro-Marksman, Marksman and Sharpshooter—entirely possible. Put on a gunsling and a peep sight and a kid can go to the top of the ladder with any of them. A few models come from the factories ready to serve as both hunting and junior target arms.

And what other factor is there in the start? It's sportsmanship, I think, and maybe that depends least

CHAPTER 2

KIDS' RIFLES

of all upon the gun. We should give our game a fair chance, sure, and not be hoggish, and there's the humane side of it, too. A clean one-shot kill takes ability—and the restraint that makes you wait and be sure. Marksmanship comes partly from good equipment, partly from skill, and partly too from a well based confidence—knowing your gun and loving it.

So never *choose* a kid's first gun. Help him to choose, steer him as straight as you can, but remember he's got to love it because it has what he needs for the shooting he's going to do.

* * *

For convenience, the specifications of barrel length, rifle weight, sighting equipment, magazine capacity of repeaters, and the type of safety that locks against accidental discharge are tabulated at the head of each rifle's section of text. Weight and magazine capacity need a little explanation.

As for weight, I've seldom known a manufacturer to over-estimate it! No need to, for we do that ourselves at the end of a long day afield. But catalogue weights are pretty close to the mark. Stock wood, walnut or not, varies in density, and the outside contours of barrel and receiver infrequently are shaved to the exact thousandth of an inch. Not every gun goes to the Bureau of Standards at Washington for a definitive check-up!

Magazine capacity varies a trifle, too. My wife's beautiful little Shelhamer stocked Model 63 .22 Winchester automatic holds the advertised 10 .22 long-rifles in its magazine, but you can slip in 11 hollow-points if you have any earthly use for such capacity in a hunting rifle. Lots of other tubular magazine repeaters hold an extra round or two. Box or clip

Harrington & Richardson 750 Pioneer.

J. C. Higgins 204.

magazines of long-rifle length may *hold* the same complement of .22 shorts, though a loading of more than three or four of these little fellows may jam the action. What of it? We choose our best ammunition for .22 hunting, and that isn't the short. It's the .22 long-rifle with hollow point.

Some safeties lock the bolt shut, too, as on the Winchesters. That prevents a scuff against the pants-leg or a withy sapling from raising the bolt handle and deactivating the rifle when we might want to use it. It also requires us to unload the chamber with the safety unlocked—usually. Pro or con matters little to a careful rifleman. He keeps his wits awake when loading or unloading, and he glances at his rifle now and then, just to make sure that everything's all right.

SINGLE SHOTS

These are the least expensive rifles, but hardly anything equals the thrill of that first gun. For this they're tops. Remove one cartridge and the rifle's empty; there's no magazine to forget about.

They are good little rifles, so good that they shouldn't be spoken of in a patronizing manner. For the youngest N. R. A. shooters they're fine: magazine fire isn't permitted on those ranges, for obvious safety reasons. And when you have just one shot to get your game, you're careful—or at least you're encouraged to be!

Not only kids use these rifles. They go to all the wild parts of the earth, fill the blackened cooking pots and skillets with small game, kill big stuff too, when it's tame and easy to stalk. Forests, mountains, jungles and unnamed little rivers—they know the single shot .22s.

Harrington & Richardson 750 Plainsman
Barrel: 24 inches.
Sights: open rear and bead front.
Safety: non-automatic, at right rear of receiver. Striker is cocked by operation of bolt, but safety must be set on by hand.
Weight: 5 pounds.

The earlier Model 365 was heavier, about 6½ pounds, and regularly fitted with a Lyman adjustable receiver peep sight. Along with the still heavier H&R 65 and 165 autoloaders and the 265 and 465 bolt repeaters, this single shot was one of the first rifles whose publicity material invited us to snap its striker on an empty chamber, just as often as we pleased. The firing pin was so positioned that it couldn't thrust out far enough to hit the edge of the chamber and mar it. The good material used was in a practical sense almost unbreakable, not at all like the soft or brittle-tempered stuff in so many inexpensive .22s of the first fifty years or so of small bore popularity.

As a matter of fact, most modern arms can be dry-snapped almost unrestrainedly without harm, and the same is true of many oldtimers, the Winchester 1890, Remington 12, etc. It was usually the inexpensive rifles that gave trouble. But when a firing pin breaks, the shooter is generally the one to pay the bill. So some of us pad that striker with an empty case, stuffed with paper to prevent grit from being kicked into the bore. Few modern rimfire firing pins are long enough to reach and mar the breech-face.

The 365 was one of the most expensive .22 single-shot bolt guns ever made for hunting and all-round use. The present Model 750 aims at a different market, though it isn't in the lowest price class. In its stock lines it is much better looking than the earlier H&Rs just mentioned; it's a compact, neat little arm. The safety is handier than those on earlier bolt guns of this make, being at the side, not at the rear of the receiver. The pistol grip comes down close to the trigger guard, but not too close, as on some sporters that have fallen more under the influence of the target rifle trend. It's far enough back, and small enough, to help and not hinder in snapshooting. The rearward sweep of the bolt handle is attractive and practical, though it's a little different from that of any other rifle. This rather long handle lies close to the stock,

Iver Johnson 2 X.

isn't liable to snag in brush or to grab the breeches. It looks businesslike, and so does the whole rifle.

J. C. Higgins 204

Barrel: 24 inches.
Sights: open and bead.
Safety: none; see below.
Weight: 4½ pounds.

This rifle, made for Sears, Roebuck and Co., is not self-cocking. You pull the striker back with finger and thumb—or by thumb alone—to cock it. Down, the striker is prevented by an automatic safety device from going forward and touching the cartridge rim. No one with sense roams the fields and woods with his finger on the trigger, and unless the trigger is held back, a blow on the striker can't move it. This familiar rebounding lock system has been used for years on single- and double-barrel hammer shotguns and on many .22s. It's all right. The only liability is that the backed-up striker doesn't cover that part of the case-head.

The head or cocking piece of this Higgins striker is big and well knurled, easy to grip even with gloves on. A light mainspring makes cocking and lowering easy, but the striker's weight and length of travel are good insurance against misfires. This rifle, like some others, is fairly short-barreled and a kid should be warned to keep the muzzle away from his feet when he lowers the striker.

It has the reliability of its class, the modern single shot that gives so much for what it costs. Forty or even thirty years ago, misfires were quite common, sometimes more than one or two in a hundred. Bolt action strikers of today hit a heavier and usually much faster blow than did the little hammers of lots of the inexpensive falling, rocking, or rolling block .22s of the past. Speed as well as weight of blow makes for sure and even ignition, good for both accuracy and reliability. And the striker's mark is usually clear across the rim, as it should be. After the shot is fired, there's seldom any difficulty in extracting the empty from a well kept modern .22. It wasn't always so with the old ones, in cold weather.

Iver Johnson 2 X

Barrel: 24 inches.
Sights: open rear and flat-topped Patridge-style front.
Safety: automatic.
Weight: 4 pounds, 6 ounces.

The 1871-established "I. J." firm always has given good value for value received, from the lightest solid-frame pocket revolvers to the fine skeet-style shotguns it once made. It is about the only old American arms firm still on deck that never went in for magazine repeaters—at least as far as I know.

The 2 X rifle succeeded the Model X, which came on the market in 1931. It is a self-cocker, and the striker knob turns up and locks on safe as it goes back. There is no separate safety catch, nor is one needed. Lowering the knob releases the safety, and one should glance at it now and then, as at any safety or hammer.

The 2 X is one of our lightest rifles, lean and stream-lined and good-looking. Although its pistol grip slopes back too gently to suit a target man, it is of good size, and comfortable and handy even if you wear gloves. Many a young shooter is handicapped in trying to use a stock that's too long for him, and an abruptly curved pistol grip adds to his troubles. This rifle is unusual in its class in having a steel buttplate. Hard rubber or composition is the general thing.

The 2 X has, to my mind, one of the neatest trigger guards ever put on a .22 of this type. The shape and hang of the trigger are good, too. The fact that the bolt handle is far forward, halfway up the long, slim receiver, is no great handicap in a single shot. We use this sort of rifle to learn to make our first shot count, not to depend on speed of fire. Or when we're older perhaps we use a single shot because we have learned—and take some pride in the fact.

This Iver Johnson is so light—and yet so well balanced for its weight—that it deserves to be kept for a lifetime. On the big-game trip that a youngster dreams of it'd be handy as a pot-filler.

Marlin 100

Barrel: 24 inches.
Sights: open and bead.
Safety: none. Same system as Higgins 204.
Weight: 4½ pounds.

Here's another light .22, stocked more in target style than the Iver Johnson. Comb and pistol grip are shoved farther forward. It too is made by an old firm, like Iver Johnson and Harrington & Richardson, though this fact shouldn't be emphasized. New outfits must be on their toes, or perish. Sometimes they play the jig tune for the older chaps to follow as fast as they can—Mossberg and Ruger and Weaver being good examples.

In general, quite new is the micro-groove system now used on all Marlin .22s, including the centerfire .218 Bee and .222 Remington calibers. It consists of

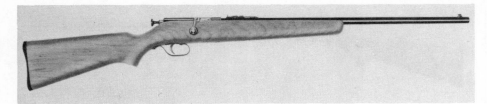

Marlin 100.

Noble 10.

Remington 514.

16 shallow grooves instead of the 4, 5, 6 or 7 deeper cuts usually rifled into a barrel. Some of us remember the bewildering array of furrows in the bronze barrels of Hamilton .22s, or think of cannon rifling or some other example. But Marlin has something new in Micro-Groove and tests have proved the claim: it does give somewhat better accuracy than the commoner system, in the same class and quality of rifle.

For junior target training this Marlin is one of the best in its price class, well stocked for prone shooting and right for sling attachment. It needs to have a peep sight mounted on its receiver. The fact that the well-forward bolt handle and hand-cocked striker make it slow to reload is no drawback.* Juniors tend to fire too fast, as a rule, until they get well into their Sharpshooter bars.

Noble 10

Barrel: 22 inches.
Sights: open rear, blade front.
Safety: none; see below.
Weight: 4½ pounds.

A good little rifle, one of the least expensive to be had, the Noble deserves to be more widely known. Although it's designed for boys, many adults would find use for it, so light and short it is.

This shortness calls for extra care when you lower the striker on a loaded round after having decided

---

*Properly, a target shooter should keep the butt at his shoulder during single-cartridge reloading except in standing offhand position. For a small kid this is impossible in prone unless the stock has been shortened to fit him. This calls for effort and is frequently neglected.

not to fire. Its head is knurled and it's of good size. When it is cocked, the gun is locked against opening.

Remington 514

Barrel: 24¾ inches.
Sights: open and bead.
Safety: rotary, at rear of bolt.
Weight: 5¼ pounds.

This is Remington's inexpensive .22, with the self-cocking feature in which they believe. The rotary safety must be deliberately pushed in to turn, and a red indicator shows when it's in the "off" position.

In price this gun parallels the Winchester 67, another big-name brand. Advertising, availability, the romance of legend, and quality sell them both by the thousands.

The 514 has a full, well curved pistol grip and a sloped bolt handle that add to looks and easy handling. It's a good junior target rifle and a good hunting rifle, too, one of the best of its class. From time to time little improvements come to all these guns, such as the wider trigger face and wider trigger-guard on late 514s. All these currently made single shots offer good value. You choose by price, your personal regard for a brand name, and the build and hang. You don't go seriously wrong on any of them unless you get a lemon. That's rare, and the factories stand by their stuff and make wrongs right. They have to.

The following caution in regard to the 514 may sound silly to those who haven't put in much time with juniors on an indoor range. But there this little gun will bear watching. It heaves its empties out with such enthusiasm that they arch high up to the right and

Remington 510-P with rear peep sight and ramped front.

Stevens 15.

come down, according to the law of gravity, with considerable poop maybe two positions over. So No. 1 shooter may hit No. 3 in the eye, and that isn't 100 per cent of the time funny. Naturally the kid with the semi-automatic (fired as a single-loader; rules require it) takes his position on the extreme right, but the 514 is something of a hazard, too. So the cheap rifles and the automatics have no place in a junior club? Kids love their own rifles, and until better ones can be had for them they want to use their own. It'd be the height of stupidity, or a slick excuse, to put off organizing a junior outfit until the best of material could be had for it.

Remington 510 Targetmaster

Barrel: 25 inches.
Sights: open and bead, or peep and ramped post front.
Safety: automatic, at right rear of receiver; red dot shows in the firing position.
Weight: 5½ pounds.

In the more expensive bracket of single shot .22s, nicely styled and reliable, this Remington ranks among the best of its class. Its stock is shootable, its barrel long and of good weight, its bolt handle raked back handily though ending in a small, rather peculiarly shaped knob, not like those of rifles of other make. The action is quite similar to that of the fairly heavy 513 target gun, with double extractors, double locking lugs, and a fast, short-throw striker with red end that, when cocked, sticks out at the pointy rear of the bolt.

Those three last features help to sell the rifle. Let's be critical. Double locking lugs add strength and give assurance of safety. When properly aligned they stiffen an action and increase rifle accuracy. However, well fitted single lugs stand up for thousands upon thousands of practice or hunting rounds, and I for one never heard of their giving way or even being set back by .22 rimfire pressures except after *many* thousands of shots. As for accuracy, the Winchester 75 and Remington 513 target models seem to be on an absolute par for precision of a high order. Yet the Winchester has but one strong-rooted lug.

Double extractors might help when arctic cold freezes a greasy cartridge case in the chamber. Yet a strong single extractor, as on most centerfire rifles, and most .22s as well, can do all right—usually does.

The red warning at the tip of the Remington .22's striker is a good thing. The only apparent objection—and somewhat farfetched—is that it leaves an opening at the rear of the bolt through which gas might rush if a case-head bursts. The solid rear of the competitive Winchester Model 47's bolt is more comforting! However, when you get a really bad burst, gas is as liable to travel back along the outside of a bolt as through it.

The Remington's thumb safety lies at the now so popular location, right rear of the receiver, and it goes on automatically. Even on a .22 for junior target training this is a good feature, and properly sighted and equipped with a 1¼-inch Army-type sling the 511 is a sensible choice for a beginner at the game. Right away he'll appreciate the loading platform below the breech opening. Drop a cartridge on it, slide the bolt forward and down, and the round is cleanly chambered. There should be no shaving of lead, though it's necessary to remark that some of the most expensive target arms with loading trays do fail to feed perfectly, do shave a little lead. Then you go back to the deliberate way of starting the hull into the chamber by hand, and the little extra time required to do it doesn't hurt your score a bit! In hunting, you'd best not depend on the tray—too easy for the round to roll off into the grass if you're in the slightest hurry, which of course you shouldn't be, anyway.

This rifle, like quite a few other .22s, can be had smooth-bored for shot cartridges, long-rifles with crimped end (no top wad) and a feeble dose of Number 12s. Nothing new: .32s used to come bored for shot, too. It's no end of fun to break midget clay birds with .22 shot-shells, and the practice at least teaches us to keep the gun swinging as we aim and press trigger. These loads shouldn't be used on any kind of game, ever. Against rats they're deadly and clean-killing at hardly more than 15 feet. A rifled barrel opens the

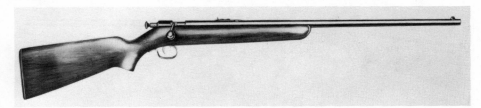

Winchester 67.

Winchester 67 Boy's Rifle.

pattern much too quickly, but oddly enough the shot don't foul the grooves of a well-kept barrel as badly as we'd expect. A few swipes with a brass brush generally take out the leading.

Stevens 15

Barrel: 24 inches.
Safety: none; see below.
Sights: open and bead.
Weight: 5 pounds.

From the start the Stevens people had the young boy and the poor man in view. Though they made some of the finest single-shot target rifles and pistols, they included low-priced arms in their line: pistols, rifles, shotguns. Here is their bid for the low priced, junior market, and I advise you to wipe out the barrel and take a look at Stevens rifling if you're unfamiliar with it. It bears inspection.

This rifle must be cocked by hand. Its striker is of the safe rebounding type, and the cocking piece is well shaped for a good grasp, though it projects less far to the rear than those of some other guns in its class.

The stock is "walnut finish" but well shaped for shooting and not at all bad looking. Some of the late issues have the black-tipped forestock (a paint job, but neatly done) that was typical of the Stevens Buckhorn .22s when the less expensive product— single shot and repeating—was sold under the "Stevens-Springfield" brand name.

The action of the 15 is shorter than those of most other single-shot bolt guns, and its receiver is in fact integral with the barrel, milled out of the same piece of steel. There's nothing objectionable about this. Actually, if you need a new barrel, the complete barrel-plus-receiver costs less than a barrel for a slightly higher grade of rifle. For a good bit more than a half-century this system has worked nicely in small-bores.

When fitted with a sling, the 15 can be carried about as easily as a Navy binocular, and with the leather

it can be held steadily on the mark. Of course it needs a peep sight, but don't they all, nearly?

Winchester 67

Barrel: 27 inches, and 20 inches as "Boy's Rifle."
Sights: open and bead.
Safety: wing type, behind receiver.
Weight: 5 and 4¼ pounds.

The 67 has been on the market for about a quarter of a century, and its woodwork has changed in that time to meet changing demands. Even the earliest 67s had come a long way from the 1900, 1902, 1904, and the later 58, 59, 60 and 60-A models.

The stock of the 67 always was well shaped, straight enough to make good shooting easier than with old-timers that had lots of drop at comb and heel. Comb and pistol grip are full and close enough for off-hand work with iron sights, and yet they're good-looking, too. The modern forestock is full and wide, semi-beavertail. Early ones were narrow and had deep grooves along the sides for "handgrasp." You don't squeeze a rifle's forestock unless you're shooting in a cross-wind, or maybe have adopted that hold for your snapshooting.

As on earlier Winchesters of the type, the barrel and receiver are all-same-one-piece, and the bolt is short and compact. You cock the striker by hand and set the safe by shoving that bright-finished wing of metal straight up. It gets in your line of view when you aim, and it's meant to. If you're a Springfield or Mauser fan you have to remember to shove it to the right to release it; you don't get anywhere trying to stab it to the left. The 54 Winchester big game rifle saved the lives of a few deer because it worked the same way as the 67 in this respect. Of course a hunter who doesn't know his gun deserves no particular sympathy.

I've still to meet a 67 owner who knows how easy it is to unload this rifle safely. (No doubt thousands do.) No need to throw off the safe and lower the striker by hand: just hold back the trigger and pull

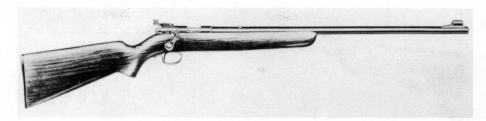

The 47 Win with peep rear and hooded, ramped front sights.

up and back on the bolt handle. Keep pulling and the bolt comes clear out, exactly as if the rifle were un-cocked.

You often see Model 68s, and it's a pity they ever dropped that model. True, the· peep sight is 'way up on the barrel and pretty slow for snapshots, but at least it is a peep sight. The front is a bead over a thin, stamped-out ramp that clips on to the front sight. It is rugged, but if you want to hunt without the front sight hood you'd best take off the ramp too, or risk losing it in the brush. In other ways this model is like the 67.

The Boy's Rifle needs a peep and a sling, which can be fitted, and its 12³⁄₁₆-inch stock fits a small youngster and lets him or her do the best possible work. About 13½ is the standard length even for kid's rifles, and why, please? You measure stock length from the front curve of the trigger to the middle of the buttplate, and sometimes it's quite revealing to do so.

Bundle up in an old-fashioned wool hunting coat— no sleek, down-filled affair—sling this Boy's Rifle over your shoulder, and take off to the winter woods. If you see no game you should be just as happy, for the country is even more beautiful and more revealing in its snow signs, than you'd remembered. If you do shoot you may be surprised to find how well that rifle fits, even though it seems to have been made for Snow-White's tiny friends. I can't help liking the little runt.

Winchester 47

Barrel: 25 inches.
Sights: open and bead, or peep and hooded, ramped bead
     front.
Safety: automatic, at right rear of receiver.
Weight: 5½ pounds.

The barrel is screwed into the short, compact re-ceiver and the action is much like that of the Model 75 target and sporting rifles. A loading trough or tray is built in, and makes this rifle still more useful in junior marksmanship training. In weight, stocking and appearance it is much like the Model 69 clip re-peater, which has seen a lot of service in indoor gal-leries as well as afield. The 47 is just ¼ inch shorter overall than the long-barreled 67. Except to a Model 54 user its safety is handier. You get a little more workmanship and finish than in the 67, but not neces-sarily superior accuracy. Both are far more accurate than any open-sight system deserves.

The 47 entered a hard market, almost in the same price range as repeaters of the same make, and it ap-pears to have been dropped from production. Used 47s in good shape are, however, sensible buys. You'll notice that Winchester and Remington bolt action rifles of the junior class usually run neck and neck in price—not even a nickel's difference. The reason is obvious. But as mentioned before, you can't go wrong on any of the rifles described in this chapter. There is more than dollar value. There's name appeal, also such truly important matters as stock fit, barrel length, weight, styling, and safety locks. The offering is wide enough to make decision difficult, but the choosing is fun as well as perhaps somewhat agonizing. During it you learn more about rifles, and that's to the good.

BOLT ACTIONS WITH BOX MAGAZINES

With detachable box or clip magazines and simple though rugged bolt actions, these are the least ex-pensive .22 repeaters. When the speed of a slide or lever action isn't considered necessary they are also among the best of the class.

The close lockup of the bolt, the one-piece stock, and the usually fast striker fall are aids to accurate shooting. Almost always the barrel and receiver are bedded at least fairly well in the stock, and refine-ment of bedding by the slow, careful sand-and-try method is easier than on the more expensive tubular magazine bolt guns. On either type it is usually pos-sible to install a second stock screw through wood into steel, farther back toward the receiver, if the job seems desirable. Or the steel can be glass-bedded into the wood; the Herter formula being quite a favorite.

Much handier for single loading than most of the tube mag bolt guns, these rifles are as well suited to the junior marksman as the single shots are. Sling attachment is easy and good adjustable peep sights are available.

Most of them, like the tube guns, are coming out with their receivers grooved for the Weaver Tip-Off, Mossberg, or other quick-detachable mounts for in-expensive, good little hunting scopes. More will be made so, to fill the demand. On most of them, bolt lift is kept so low that the quick up-back-forward-down wrench and thrust are still pretty easy under a low-mounted scope. The magazines hold more than enough cartridges for a hunter, and they make com-plete, safe unloading simple. Click out the clip, then empty the chamber, and the rifle is positively empty.

Harrington & Richardson 865 Plainsman.

J. C. Higgins 228 with scope.

Harrington & Richardson 865 Plainsman

Barrel: 24 inches.
Sights: open and bead; receiver grooved for Tip-Off mounts.
Magazine capacity: 5.
Safety: thumbpiece behind bolt handle.
Weight: 5 pounds.

This is a light, easy-to-carry rifle, with its clip almost flush with the forestock where your hand grips it at the trail carry. For its quality it is not expensive. Naturally all the manufacturers watch every nickel in figuring costs, for the .22 rifle market is as competitive as any other in the firearms world.

Soon after World War II Harrington and Richardson produced much more expensive clip repeaters, the 265 and the 465, weighing about 6½ and 9 pounds, with long 10-shot magazines and Lyman receiver peeps. They had quality, all right, and they shot well, but they were neither handy to carry nor easy to look at. Though you'd grip them ahead of the long magazine in trail carry, the dingbat did occasionally get in your way, and the stocks of these rifles were downright ugly. Their lower line, running up from the toe, would if projected forward come out well up on the forestock instead of at the rear of the trigger guard. In simpler words, they were pot-bellied.

About the only good looks they had were in their nicely tapered barrels and rakish bolt handles, features which the new model has, too. And the 865 is light and inexpensive enough to fall into a quite different class, the boy's, trapper's or woods-wanderer's .22. It stands up well in this competitive market.

J. C. Higgins 228

Barrel: 24 inches.
Sights: open and bead; 4 and 6 power scopes offered as extras.
Magazine capacity: 8.
Safety: thumbpiece behind bolt handle.
Weight: 6 pounds.

Sears, Roebuck gun-racks hold sound little repeaters in this model, and the price is highly competitive. Scoped, they cost some 50 percent more—about as

a high-quality big-game rifle would. Plastic caps, taped together so that they're less liable to vanish under leaves or grass, come on the scopes and protect the lenses when you're not using them.

The unnecessarily long and large-capacity magazine makes the gun a bit unhandy to carry, for some of us, but most kids wouldn't care. They'd be happy enough to tote a rifle of their very own, a safe, reliable arm that they'd been able to afford. There is plenty of room for a gunsling, and plenty of accuracy for qualifying in early stages of the N. R. A. Junior rifleman ladder. These rungs are hard enough for many adult shooters firing an expensive match rifle.

The buttplate is worth noticing. It's thick and strong at toe and heel where the wear comes in rough wilderness country, and in the middle it's hollowed, and grooved too, so that it will stick to the shoulder. This makes off-the-shoulder bolt operation possible in spite of the fact that the bolt handle is pretty far forward.

Marlin 80

Barrel: 24 inches.
Sights: 80-C has open and bead; 80-DL (de luxe) has peep rear and hooded, ramped front, also swivels for gunsling. Receivers are grooved for Tip-Off mounts.
Magazine capacity: 8.
Safety: thumbpiece behind bolt handle.
Weight: 6½ pounds.

As bare specifications go, this rifle is much like the Higgins 228. Actually it is a good deal different, costs about 10 percent more, and is a little heavier.

At this writing, at least, a good deal of attention is being paid to accuracy: Marlin has to prove the worth of Micro-Groove rifling and seems to be doing it, though rifling alone is only one of the many details that add up to precision.

The stock of the 80 has beautiful, clean lines, though some might choose to round off the blunt forearm tip. The sling swivels on the DL model are still rather unusual equipment on a rifle of this class. They are sturdy and good-looking, though a long-armed shooter might have to set the front one farther forward.

This rifle is well balanced for junior target work—which means that it's easy to shoot from any standard position—and it's light enough for all but the youngest. For hunting, the rear peep sight on the DL is one of the neatest and best located put on a sporting rifle.

Mossberg 140

Barrel: 24½ inches.

Sights: 140-K has open rear and flat-topped front sight; 140-B has hinged receiver peep with ½ minute-of-angle click adjustments, open rear sight on barrel, and ramp front with four interchangeable inserts. Receiver of 140-K is tapped for peep sight, and both styles have the receiver grooved for scope mount.

Magazine capacity: 7.

Safety: lever behind bolt, with red and green indicators.

Weight: 5¾ pounds.

Back in depression days the Mossbergs kept on selling lots of .22 rifles by regularly furnishing custom-gun features like detachable sling swivels (you could buy a used Army sling for about half a dollar), Monte Carlo and cheekpiece stocks, and pretty fair peep sights with both windage and elevation adjustments. They still sell a good rifle for the money.

These 140s are in sporter style, with cheekpiece, the Monte Carlo lift that rises a little ahead of the buttstock's heel, large pistol grip, and the snobble or swell at the forestock tip, popular long ago on custom and factory high-powers, and back in society again. Like so many Mossbergs of the past, these rifles have a trigger pull that's adjustable for weight of let-off. Also in common Mossberg fashion the plastic trigger guard extends down the face of the pistol grip. It is nicely inletted and it has finger grooves. These corru-

gations may not add to beauty, but they do position the hand the same for each shot, and evidently most buyers OK them. They could of course be sanded out.

Like so many rifles, including a few custom or near-custom jobs, the 140s do have stock lines that cry out for trimming away just behind the pistol grip, to make that handful of wood stand out distinctively. The swell ahead of the trigger guard is too big for looks or for easy grasp, and the size of the snobble is overdone.

All these objections come from the angle of the perfectionist, who dislikes also the protuberant clip. People keep on buying Mossbergs because of the still remarkable durability and good service built into them for the price asked. The extra features have plenty of appeal, too.

Mossberg 142

Barrel: 18 inches.

Sights: peep rear and front sight with guard; open rear and bead front on 142-K. Receivers are grooved for Mossberg scope mounts.

Magazine capacity: 7.

Safety: similar to that on Mossberg 140 models.

Weight: 5 pounds.

This little fellow is built somewhat in M-1 .30 carbine style. Short and light, it's a favorite of many grownups—trappers and woods-cruisers—who like an easily packed but effective .22. It comes with a carrying strap attached to the left side of the stock in Army carbine fashion. The trigger pull is adjustable, and you usually get a pretty clean one on a Mossberg, maybe good enough not to need refinement with a file and a polishing stone.

The pistol grip is rounded, good-looking, and both

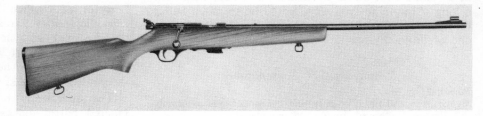

Marlin 80-DL.

Mossberg 140-B.

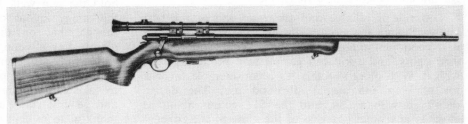

The 140-K with Mossberg 4M4 four-power scope.

Mossberg 142-K with open sights. Rear sight has fine screw adjustment for elevation. Forestock tip, now made of black plastic, swings down for submachine-gun type of handhold.

Mossberg 142 with peep rear and guarded front sight.

buttstock and forestock are well proportioned for a light gun of this sort. At the tip of the forestock is a black, molded, five-inch plastic extension which can be swung down nearly at a right angle, and this is advertised as an advantage for practical shooting. On a sub-machine gun, fired full-automatic, it would be; it would help you to control the climb of the muzzle as the shots rattled out. The sportsman trained in modern rifle marksmanship seldom would have use for it. Rest it on the ground in prone shooting and the shots almost certainly would go wild. The padding of a folded coat under the extension would help, but a long, Army-type loop sling would be so much better that you're forced to conclude that this feature is just one of those things.

Remington 511 Scoremaster

Barrel: 25 inches.
Sights: open and bead, or peep and flat-topped post on ramp. Receivers grooved for Tip-Off mounts.
Magazine capacity: 6.
Safety: thumbpiece behind bolt handle.
Weight: 5½ pounds.

The clip repeater version of the basic Model 510 single shot, the Scoremaster has the same features of double extractors, twin locking bolts, fast striker fall, and safety indicator. It is of similar weight and feel and the styling is identical. You pay a little more and get the convenience of a magazine.

This rifle is reliable and accurate, one of the best known though not necessarily the best of its class. It is a good junior target rifle, being finely stocked for iron sights, and a kid can get off to a promising start with it. With older shooters it's a considerable favorite for plinking and casual all-round use. The design didn't grow in a day, and the 511 comes about as close as any other .22 rifle of the class to the concep-

tion of what makes an efficient and still good-looking sporter.

Remington 513-S Sporter

Barrel: 27 inches, double countersunk at muzzle.
Sights: open rear and ramped post front; receiver tapped for peep sights and grooved for Tip-Off scope mounts.
Magazine capacity: 6.
Safety: thumbpiece behind bolt handle.
Weight: 6¾ pounds.

This is the sporting version of the 513 target gun, so familiar on the range both as private property and as out on loan to N. R. A. clubs from the Army's Director of Civilian Marksmanship. Like the target rifle, the sporter is really a takedown, only one screw holding stock and steel together. But the Remington does splendid target work both indoors and out, and too much attention needn't be paid to this somewhat theoretical drawback.

The sporter is reasonably heavy and its long, tapered barrel makes it balance steadily. Really, it serves well for both snapshooting and deliberate work afield, for it isn't as muzzle-light as many sporters are. Its buttplate is of checkered steel, not rubber, nylon or Bakelite.

The action is of the light Remington type, with adjustable trigger pull, and the let-off is usually clean and sharp as it comes from the factory. Stock lines are both pretty and designed for efficiency: you can hold the gun well. Perfectionists could well object to the stingy layout of checkering on the pistol grip, though that on the wide, comfortable forearm is plenty. For a young boy this sporter is a bit heavy, and it may also seem too long. But for a first gun it's almost too good, too expensive. A kid learns slowly to take care of fine equipment. But that is a broad and general statement, and the exceptions to it, I'm thankful to remember, are many.

Remington 521-TL

Barrel: 25 inches.
Sights: Lyman 57 peep and flat-topped front.
Magazine capacity: 6.
Safety: thumbpiece behind bolt handle.
Weight: 7 pounds.

This came out originally as a target rifle for the forgotten man, the junior trying for his qualification medals. Edwards Brown, Jr., then an N. R. A. staffman, had labored hard in trying to convince the factories that a little kid can't do his best with a rifle stocked to fit a grownup. "Pete" Brown found it a discouraging enterprise, I'm afraid, but the 521 seems to have been one of the goals he reached.

Weight, balance, equipment—all are about right for the lower- and middle-teen shooter, and I've seen them do good work with it. That was with the early models, which had unusually short stocks. The present stock is about as long as that of the bigger 513-T target rifle, though its Bakelite buttplate is put on at a more conservative angle than the steel plate of the larger rifle. There is less down-pitch, a feature that makes the 521 more of an all-purpose rifle, and this general usefulness is emphasized in current advertising.

The comb of the 521 stock is thick and well rounded, undercut or fluted to let the shooter cross the grip with his thumb, and it is of just about the ideal height for a youngster using iron sights, which are required in Junior qualifications. Remember that a kid is, for his size, rather long-necked. The fore-stock has enough beavertail swell, not so much as to feel like a 4x4 in a small hand. A one-inch sling comes on the rifle and the front swivel is adjustable for position: you can plug it in at the hole that gives the

correct reach. An aperture front sight can be bought as an extra, and it would help in target work.

But the 521 is being pushed as a hunting rifle too, and the standard Patridge front sight is good for such use, except in dark woods where a red or an ivory bead would show up much better. The advice that you merely have to screw out the small-aperture target peep disc to convert the gun into a sporter is a little amusing. Of course that's all you need to do! Will Lyman had the idea about 75 years ago and did his best to publicize it. Yet since that time each new generation has had to learn.

Savage 4

Barrel: 24 inches.
Sights: open and bead; 4-S has peep rear and hooded, ramped front. Receivers are grooved for Tip-Off mounts.
Magazine capacity: 5.
Safety: thumbpiece behind bolt handle.
Weight: 6 pounds.

This Savage is an old, proved model, now refined with Monte Carlo comb and cheekpiece stock, and a beavertail forearm. The extra walnut went on without spoiling the clean, fine lines of the rifle.

There is only a few cents' difference in price between this gun and corresponding Winchester and Remington models, and it's a little heavier, bigger-feeling arm. It ranks right up in quality.

The slightly protruding magazine and its spring-steel release might bother some folks in trail carrying, though not very much. Unfortunately, the action is not designed for quick bolt-throw from the shoulder, for the handle, though raked back a bit, is still pretty far out. However, many other .22's have this Mannlicher-Schoenauer sort of reach, and perhaps bolt

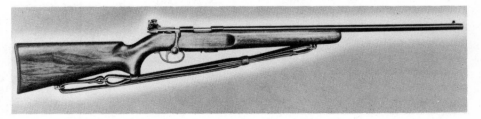

The 511-P has peep rear and ramped front sights.

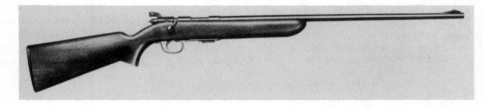

Remington 513-S sporter. A well balanced and reasonably light little rifle.

Remington 521-TL junior match and sporting rifle.

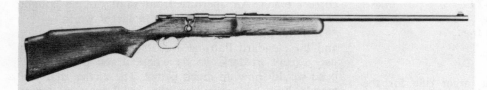

Savage 4 De Luxe.

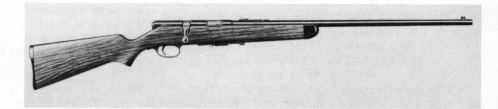

Stevens 84.

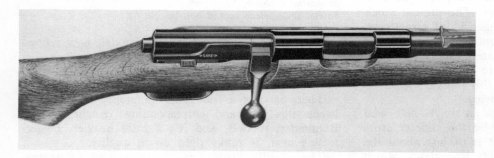

Like most other rifles of its class, as now made, the 84 has the grooved receiver top for the Weaver Tip-Off and similar scope mounts.

guns shouldn't be chosen for the sort of frenzied hunting that calls for rapid repeat shots. Perhaps too, no rifle should! The first shot ought to count, and bolt action accuracy helps in the attempt.

The safety of the Savage 4 is well located, close and handy to the thumb. There's never the least temptation to hunt with it in the "off" position.

Stevens 84

Barrel: 24 inches.
Sights: open and bead; receiver is grooved for Tip-Off scope
  mounts—formerly tapped for Savage 150 Micro Peep.
Magazine capacity: 5.
Safety: thumbpiece behind bolt handle.
Weight: 6 pounds.

This is essentially a less expensive counterpart of the Savage Model 4. The walnut finished birch stock * usually has the black forearm tip made to look like the plastic, ebony or buffalo horn tips that decorate many high-power sporters without adding a bit to their efficiency. Some of us, in fact, dislike them, for unless they're freed from barrel contact they may affect the rifle's shooting, and they are—or at least some are—vulnerable in extreme cold. This tip on the Stevens is of course part of the wood. It is a really good-looking job. Chipping it off by careless handling leaves the light wood showing and calls for a refinishing job. Some dislike a blonde stock, even though nicely oil-finished, and others don't give a hoot about the looks—their guns show it!

---

*Such stock woods have been used, may have given way to walnut in late production.

You get a thoroughly good rifle in the 84 and it's an almost sure bet that the rifling will be beautifully done, easy to clean and giving fine accuracy. The Stevens reputation was built long ago and it's worth keeping.

Ten-shot magazines can be had for this rifle and the corresponding Savage, but they're useful only in plinking. You don't use magazine fire in precision .22 target work—aren't permitted to as an NRA Junior or on many ranges for grownups—and the long clip is a nuisance when you hunt.

Winchester 69

Barrel: 25 inches.
Sights: open and bead, or peep and hooded, ramped front.
  Receiver grooved for Tip-Off mount.
Magazine capacity: 5. Ten-shot clip and single-loading adapter
  are available.
Safety: thumbpiece behind bolt handle.
Weight: 5½ pounds.

It wasn't built in a day, but in a long human generation. Early 69s have a narrow forestock and a different rear peep sight. Their striker fall was long and slow by comparison and the cocking piece itself was the safety—pull back and twist to right to lock, reverse for ready. The latter wasn't unhandy for a right-hander, but the southpaw was out of luck. These old-timers were cocked on the closing, not the opening, of the bolt. It took considerable force.

Now the 69 has a speed lock and a trigger pull adjustable for weight like the 75 target and game rifles. The rocker safety catch lies handily to the rear, just above the knob of the raked-back bolt handle. Trigger, safe, and bolt handle are in ideal position for most of us. Not all these improvements came at one time.

For a while the 69 was made in Target and Match grades, the first with the factory peep sight, the second with Lyman 57 E peep. Front sights were flat-topped posts and both guns had 1¼-inch Army-type slings attached. For better fit in prone position the buttstocks were altered, shortened at the toe to give the three-inch down-pitch so generally liked for target shooting. Set upright on the butt, the rifle had its muzzle slanted three inches down from the vertical, just as on the Model 70 bigbore target arm. These were excellent all-round .22s of the class.

The regular sporting model of the 69 is popular. You see both new and early versions of it afield quite commonly. Lots of them crack away on the 50 foot junior ranges, too.

Winchester 75 Sporting

Barrel: 24 inches.
Sights: open rear and hooded, ramped front, or Lyman 57 E peep and hooded, ramped front. Grooved for Tip-Off mounts.
Magazine capacity: 5. Ten-shot clip and single-loading adapter are available.
Safety: thumbpiece behind bolt handle.
Weight: 5½ pounds.

The 75 sporter is a rather expensive rifle for a kid to start with, but it's been done, and with no cluck-clucks over neglect or abuse having been called for. It's such a pretty little gun that almost anyone handles it carefully. In late models it's still prettier, with forearm tip rounded instead of left rather square, and with bolt handle slanted back rakishly.

There seem to be just two possible objections to its use as a youngster's training rifle: the almost complete lack of down-pitch of its buttplate (though this may have been remedied lately), and the extremely thin, light barrel. The kids I watched over didn't seem

The glass goes on like this. Not a really low, snug mounting, but durable and convenient. A cheek-pad would bring the shooter's face up in line with the scope for quick, sure aim, or deliberate, sure aim.

Winchester 69.

The 69 with peep rear and ramped, hooded front sights.

Sling and scope this M-75, and you have a a fine little rifle. Front sight cover or hood has been removed to show the lines of this sight and its solid steel ramp.

The Winchester 75 with rear peep sight.

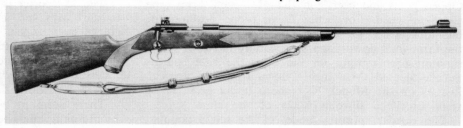

Winchester 52 Sporter.

to mind. That buttplate is steel, checkered to stick to your shoulder, and the one-inch sling threaded through the swivels that come on the rifle was based far enough forward to suit most of them. Perhaps the checkering on pistol grip and forestock seemed helpful, and it was on just the right places. They were mad about that rifle, and the little early-teen girl who owned it was generous in letting them use it. The rifle was accurate enough to keep its shots punching or nicking the 10-ring at 50 feet if we did what we were supposed to.

Offhand, it's a hard rifle to shoot; it's so muzzle-light. Or maybe we should say it's a longer job to get good with it. For woods carrying and for snapshooting it's almost ideal; at least it's the ideal of many who are saving their money to buy it. A grownup likes it as a companionable little arm, out under the sky, and at home it's satisfying to show or to look at. You'd hardly think that a neat little black cap on a pistol grip could do so much for a rifle's looks. Of course the 75 sporter has the lines for this embellishment to work on. Some haven't! Comparison to human good looks will be spared.

Comparison of the 75-S to the Remington 513 sporter might be odious, certainly would be unfair. The Remington's extra pound of weight goes out where it helps in both snapshooting and slow fire, though absolute accuracy of the two should be about on a par. The Winchester too is a takedown; only one screw goes through stock into steel. So a sensible choice between the two is based on the purposes in mind. Light and medium-heavy rifles both have their special field of service.

Winchester 52 Sporting

Barrel: 24 inches.
Sights: Lyman 48-F receiver peep and hooded, ramped Redfield full length gold bead front. Target scope blocks available.
Magazine capacity: 5. Ten-shot magazine and single loading adapter can be had as extras.
Safety: thumbpiece *in front of* bolt handle.
Weight: 7¼ pounds.

These specifications need a bit of explanation.

Weight with the one-inch Army-type sling that is regular equipment sometimes goes to eight pounds if the stock is of selected, fancy grade walnut that comes at an increased price. Then the rifle is muzzle-light for offhand work unless you have the buttstock hollowed inside and fit an aluminum or nylon buttplate as made by the factory for the 70 and 88 featherweight high-powers.

Sight choice is wide. You can order the rifle without sights, at a considerable saving, and fit irons or a scope of your choice. Target scope blocks mounted on the barrel at the standard 7.2 inches center-to-center distance apart put most scopes too far forward to let us get our eye close enough for the full field of view when we shoot offhand. The front block can be set back to "six inches on centers," converting quarter-minute scope mount clicks to about third-minute, no serious disadvantage. A third of an inch at one hundred yards is close shooting for a sporting rifle. A hawk's eye might resolve that space at that distance.

The five-shot magazine lies flush with the forearm and never gets in the way as we carry the 52. This is a bit uncommon in clip-magazine .22s. Some of these Winchester magazines give trouble after they've been carried, loaded, in the rifle for long hours on end. When you try to reload you'll eject the empty case all right, but the round on top of the magazine may tilt downward and fail to feed into the chamber. Ernie Lamb, an old rifleman and an old friend, showed me how to fix that. With a narrow-jawed pair of pliers bend the rear wall of the magazine slightly back— just a little. If you still have trouble, give it some more. Late magazine-follower plates are humped up to avoid that. They do.

Yes, the safety does lie ahead of the bolt handle, unusual in any rifle. But that handle is unusually far back. It's right over the trigger, couldn't be raked back without liability of the web of the hand lifting it and thus preventing discharge when we toss up the rifle for a snapshot. I hunted a lot with my 52 Sporter, sometimes having to wear heavy gloves, and the safety was always right under my thumb when needed.

This rifle has been on the market since 1934, and as a rule much in the current style of the factory's fancy grade of highpower sporter, the 54, and the 70 of 1936. Grip and forestock are checkered nicely. The grip is capped (with steel now) and the forestock is finished with a black plastic tip. There's a cheekpiece on the left side of the stock, and a Monte Carlo comb has become standard, well liked for scopesight use. Late receivers come tapped for hunting scope mounts, thanks to someone's thoughtfulness.

It was 14 years before the factory offered the 52 as a sporter, and folks at the New Haven plant had been urged to bring out such a rifle. They took their time in designing it and they had the advantage of studying certain custom-made sporter .22s owned by shooters who just couldn't wait. The Niedner Rifle Corporation of Dowagiac, Mich., Griffin & Howe of New York, and probably others had made some, with 52 or U. S. Springfield M-1 or M-2 actions as starting points. The factory's problem was to strike a pleasing average in styling, at a price a good bit lower than the finest custom work. Except for some criticism of the barrel's extreme lightness and considerably varied comments on stock design, the impossible task came near to being accomplished.

The sporter is practically as accurate as the heavier-barreled target 52s. One-inch 10-shot groups at 50 yards are easy for it—for the rifle, that is—and even with high velocity ammo of a good run of production. Prone with sling and scope, you generally get the idea that the rifle has much more than you can bring out of it—twice as much, maybe. That's good: you feel it's worthwhile to keep trying.

This model might seem far too costly for the average kid to hope to own. That's relative. Some of them earn enough in a summer to buy several 52 sporters. But many more don't. At any rate, a kid can dream, can't he?

BOLT ACTIONS WITH TUBULAR MAGAZINES

Most of these are more expensive counterparts of clip magazine rifles made by the same factories. Some people choose them for definite reasons; some select them because they think that a higher price tag indicates higher quality.

As for workmanship there's no difference, make for make. The tube mag rifle normally weighs a few ounces more, and the extra heft lies out front where it helps to damp the muzzle-weave as we hold on a mark.

These guns handle short and long .22s with considerable reliability, in addition to the long-rifles for which they're chambered and rifled. And they hold a lot of cartridges. Such matters appeal to the plinker who shoots for fun, shoots fast, and accepts hits as so much gravy. Unless you hunt in your BVDs and own no cartridge belt the big ammunition warehouse under the barrel is seldom of the slightest advantage afield. Usually it's quite the opposite, for psychological reasons. You're liable to depend more on lots of bullets than on a single well-directed one.

Many of these rifles are difficult to single-load as you would in serious target practice. Any of them could, by ill chance, have a bent or clogged magazine in which a cartridge would hang up after you think you've completely unloaded the gun. That's dangerous. It pays to squint carefully into the open breech and make sure that you see the tip of the magazine follower showing before you put that rifle away. A nuisance, of course, but nuisances do save lives.

J. C. Higgins 229

Barrel: 24 inches.
Sights: open and bead. Receiver grooved for scope mount.
Magazine capacity: 25 short, 18 long-rifle.
Safety: thumbpiece behind bolt handle.
Weight: 6¼ pounds.

This model is companion to the Higgins clip repeater, at less than the usual increase of price for this style of action. Scopes of four and six power are offered at moderate extra cost, just as with the clip guns.

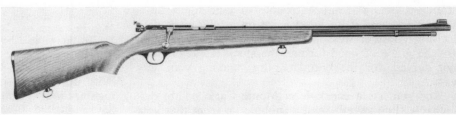

J. C. Higgins 229 with scope.

Marlin 81-DL.

Mossberg 146-B.

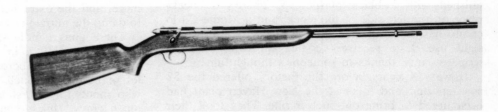

Remington 512-A Sportmaster.

Savage 5 De Luxe.

Marlin 81

Barrel: 24 inches.
Sights: 81-C has open rear and bead front sights; 81-DL has peep rear and hooded, ramped front, also sling swivels. Receivers are grooved for Tip-Off scope mounts.
Magazine capacity: 26 short, 18 long-rifle.
Safety: thumbpiece behind bolt handle.
Weight: 6½ pounds.

Here is the tubular magazine version of the Marlin Model 80, an arm of good weight and efficiently stocked for use with iron sights. The woodwork is of generous size, well suited to a grownup but not too big for the average middle-teener.

Mossberg 146-B

Barrel: 26 inches.
Sights: swing-out peep on receiver, open rear sight on barrel, and hooded, ramped front with four sidewise-folding inserts (post, bead and apertures) permanently attached. Receiver grooved for scope mount.
Magazine capacity: 30 short, 20 long-rifle.
Safety: behind bolt-head, swinging, with red and green dot indicators.
Weight: 7 pounds.

It's a man-sized .22; a small boy or girl would have to grow up to it unless you shortened the stock. You could put in fillers later as the youngster's arms stretched out. Too much trouble to take for a kid? I think not, and if his heart is set on a tube mag rifle, let him consider this one as carefully as any others. By the grace of good fortune the stock is cut off flat, not curved, for the buttplate, thus making your job easy.

The gun has a cheekpiece, Monte Carlo comb, detachable sling swivels, and a snobble up front that you

might elect to sand off. Balance is good, and a trigger pull I tried recently was clean, with no more than the average backlash—rearward motion after the striker had fallen. Only the particular are annoyed by this "give." Winchester 75s have it; yet people keep right on turning in good scores with those little match rifles.

This Mossberg's full length magazine reminds you of old Marlin and Winchester lever guns with the same barrel length. Its capacity helps to sell rifles to the plinkers, and that tribe does more than its share in keeping the gun and ammunition makers in business.

Remington 512 Sportmaster

Barrel: 25 inches.
Sights: open and bead, or peep and ramped, flat-topped post front. Receivers are grooved for Tip-Off scope mounts.
Magazine capacity: 22 short, 15 long-rifle.
Safety: thumbpiece behind bolt handle.
Weight: 5¾ pounds.

Here you get the same quality as in the Model 511 clip rifle, and slightly more muzzle-weight, of course. Despite its price the rifle is a good seller in its class, and it deserves to be.

Savage 5

Barrel: 24 inches.
Sights: open and bead, or peep rear and hooded front. Receivers grooved for scope mounts.
Magazine capacity: 22 short, 15 long-rifle.
Safety: thumbpiece behind bolt handle.
Weight: 6 pounds.

Like the Model 4 Savage, this is a high quality arm. With open sights it is priced a bit lower than Remingtons and Winchesters of the same type; with the Savage Micro Peep sight, as Model 5-S, it costs at this moment a few cents more than its Rem-Win rivals. The buttstock with Monte Carlo and cheekpiece, and the forestock of semi-beavertail design, are 1955 innovations.

Stevens 86

Barrel: 24 inches.
Sights: open and bead. Receiver is grooved for scope mounts.
Magazine capacity: 22 short, 15 long-rifle.
Safety: thumbpiece behind bolt handle.
Weight: 6 pounds.

Stevens Model 84 clip magazine repeater features are duplicated in this rifle, and both of them sell at lower prices than their Savage cousins, the 86 being one of the least expensive old-line .22s of its type. They are not to be considered as "seconds" of Savage arms.

Winchester 72

Barrel: 25 inches.
Sights: open and bead, or peep rear and hooded, ramped front. Receiver is grooved for Tip-Off scope mounts.
Magazine capacity: 20 short, 14 long-rifle.
Safety: thumbpiece behind bolt handle.
Weight: 5¾ pounds.

To fill demand, this was brought out as a companion piece to the long-established Model 69 clip repeater. Some shooters consider it the handsomest of all the tubular magazine bolt guns, and the chief reason for such an impression could be the rather short magazine tube. It doesn't look quite so lean and lonesome, sticking out there. The semi-beavertail forearm is nicely rounded at the tip, much like that of a big-game rifle, and this little detail helps, too.

LEVER-ACTION REPEATERS

Two models are made, both by Marlin. At present there are no single-shot lever guns coming out, like the old Stevens, Hopkins & Allen, the rather expensive Winchester, the British Page-Lewis, and the Mossberg. Only one company has capitalized on .22s as understudies for bigbore lever-action repeaters since the heavy Winchester 1873 went out.

Marlin 39-A

Barrel: 20 and 24 inches.
Sights: open rear and hooded, ramped front. Receivers are tapped for peep sights and tapped, also, on top, for a grooved adapter base to take Tip-Off scope mounts.
Magazine capacity: 20 short, 14 long-rifle; 26 short, 19 long-rifle.
Safety: half-cock hammer notch.
Weight: 6 and 6½ pounds.

This highly modernized revision of the Model 39 comes in 20-inch Mountie carbine and 24-inch rifle styles. Both are stocked well for iron sights, the

Stevens 86.

Winchester 72 with peep rear and ramped, hooded front sights.

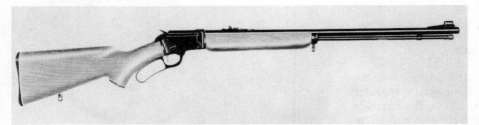

Marlin's "Golden" 39-A of early 1957 has the added though standard features of pistol grip cap, sling swivels, and gold trigger.

Marlin 39-A Mountie.

Marlin 56 Levermatic with the 22-inch barrel made standard early in 1957.

Mountie with straight, not pistol grip and usually with a less pronounced beavertail fore-end. Stock combs are set well back in early lever action fashion, not bad at all when you wear gloves. Slings have been fitted and have given reasonable satisfaction.

In spite of the takedown construction, and split receiver too, accuracy has been surprisingly good, at times pretty close to match quality. For almost any .22 rimfire hunting it's entirely adequate. The action is slick and smooth, fast enough to have been chosen by some exhibition shots, and the trigger pull is clean and easy to lighten if you want it that way. It's easier and faster to cock an exposed hammer for that so important first shot at running game than it is to throw off almost any sort of bolt action or hammerless rifle's safety lock. In snow or rainstorm this gun asks no special favors: its breechblock is machined to fit the receiver contour and shut tightly.

Keeping the action clean of bullet lubricant and half-burned powder grains is a cinch: the works are exposed when you turn out the takedown screw and pull stock and barrel apart. Bore cleaning is easier than on earlier Marlin .22 lever guns, and it should be! A special screw locks the ejector back into the receiver wall, out of the way of the cleaning rod.

The 39-A costs more than any of the slide or trombone action .22s, and only one semi-automatic, the Winchester 63, is more expensive. Many people like it enough to buy it, and then they generally hang on to it.

Marlin 56 Levermatic

Barrel: 24 inches.
Sights: open rear and hooded, ramped front. Receiver tapped for peep sight and tapped, on top, for a grooved adapter base for Tip-Off scope mounts.
Magazine capacity: 7, 10 and 12 shot clips available. The 7-shot is standard issue.
Safety: underneath, on trigger guard plate.
Weight: 6½ to 7 pounds.

Like the Winchester high-powered Model 88, the Marlin 56 is unusual in being a lever-action repeater with one-piece stock for accuracy, and with extremely short lever throw for speed. An attractive combination, this, and tagging the 56 down in the slide-action price class doesn't hurt its circulation!

The travel of the lever is so short that a big hand needn't completely let go of its grip on the small of the stock. Naturally the arc of the little .22's lever is shorter than that of the big rifle. If they weren't rugged, some of the oldtimers might snap them off in the field! The Marlin lever actuates an accelerator that cams the

breechblock out of its locking shoulder and then sends it back with *increasing* speed. Rollers ease the job, and an anti-friction washer in the lever engages the hammer's cocking surface and sends it back; breechblock or firing pin needn't do it, as in all the exposed-hammer lever guns except the old Stevens high-power. The hammer can touch the breechblock and firing pin only when the action is closed and locked—a good

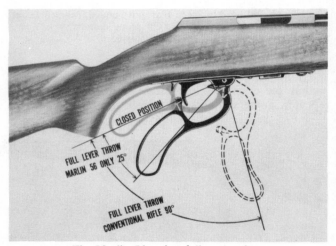

The Marlin 56 action fully opened.

How the fingers, not the whole hand, work the 56 action.

sales point, though the conventional type of lever action is safe, too.

A devotee of the 56 might well prove it as fast as a pump gun with a safety feature like those of the Noble or the new Remington, which make it necessary to release the trigger and let it go forward before each succeeding shot. The fellow who can simply hold back the trigger as he works the slide would win the race, literally hands down. None of the competitors could expect to hit the proverbial bull—anywhere!

The 56 is heavy enough, and rigid enough in stock and action, to do excellent shooting, and actually it is a solid-frame gun. It is stocked well for iron-sight use, and to attach a sling is easy. For scope use the stock comb is pretty low. The angle of the pistol grip is great enough to anchor a lift-up cheek pad of Monte Carlo type like the Jostam or Stam, and one should go on for glass sight shooting.

The action is well engineered—has to be to keep the cost of the rifle ās low as it is. To dismount, take out the clip magazine, open the lever, and loosen front and rear guard screws. Then lift barrel and action out of the stock as you would with a bolt gun. If you need to disassemble the action for cleaning, remove the front and rear sideplate screws and studs, but don't take out the screw on the right sideplate, above the lever hinge, for this permits the action to let go all holds. And then assembly is plenty difficult.

The sliding safety of this rifle is a little reminiscent of the Savage 99 in its location. It does all that such a jigger should—locks the sear into engagement with the hammer so that the latter can't fall and strike the firing pin, and locks the lever shut, too. Of course you have to remember to lock the safety after you've released it and haven't fired, or have fired and reloaded! And out in the hunting field you have to watch *any* safety, or *any* hammer, just so that the day will go happily for everyone.

Like practically all .22 rimfire repeaters except the .22 short gallery models, this Marlin is meant to do its best with long-rifle ammunition. Loading its magazine to full capacity with the short cartridges might cause feeding troubles, just as with a bolt-action box magazine repeater.

SLIDE ACTIONS

With the present-day accent on bolt actions, and with the auto-loaders growing ever more popular, once again, you sometimes wonder why the .22 pump guns stay on the market. Well, half a dozen models are still made, and you'd have to take off for another planet to avoid meeting them out where the game is. Why is this so?

They were the first well known type of .22 repeater, widely known, and much wanted by the youngster who had started with a single shot. Hardly anyone spoke disparagingly of their accuracy, back then. It was as good as that of any others in the four- to six-pound weight, wasn't it, and what more would you want? Slick, fast repeating action delighted the plinker as much then as it does now, and *occasionally* it helped in the game fields instead of piling up wild shooting's common score of misses and crippling hits. The pump was the weapon of the commercial shooting gallery and of the exhibition shot, amateur or professional, who drew envious admiration and pure wonder from the crowd.

So its traditional desirability persists, and for good reasons. The little guns are attractive to carry, operate and fire.

They aren't for junior marksmanship training. Many have far more than enough accuracy, but they're hard to fit with a shooting gunsling of the Army type and most of them are slow and bothersome in single loading. Adequate target sights are available, of course, and few rifles can carry a low-power hunting scope so snugly down close to the barrel.

Since more rounds out of the annual millions are fired in plinking or in hunting than are expended in formal target shooting, the pump guns still stand in the racks of almost every firearms dealer, big or little. They move, too; people buy them and become fond of them. With an easy assist from imagination they become the youngsters' lever action deer rifles!

Harrington & Richardson 422.

J. C. Higgins 33 with quick-detachable scope.

Noble 235.

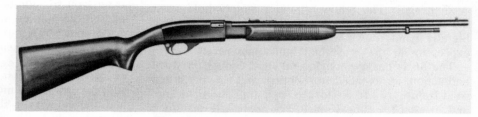

Remington 572 Fieldmaster.

Tip-Off scope mount on 572 Rem.

Harrington & Richardson 422

This rifle is practically identical to the Noble 235, which, following alphabetical dictation, steps into place just a bit farther along in this discussion of slide action .22s. Except in the woodwork there is little difference between the two rifles. Both of them are surprisingly good values, and they are to be bought with confidence.

J. C. Higgins 33

Barrel: 23¼ inches.
Sights: open rear and ramped bead front. Receiver has mount bar built in for scope mount, and a four-power scope is offered.
Magazine capacity: 25 short, 17 long-rifle.
Safety: cross-bolt button at *front* of trigger guard.
Weight: 5½ pounds.

The 33 is still unusual in its type. Like the Remington 572 it is practically a solid frame, not takedown. As a matter of fact, its barrel *is* screwed solidly into the receiver, but you can remove the breech parts for cleaning.

The action is as easy and slick as most, and on the opening stroke its cartridge carrier snaps up with fairly terrifying eagerness. Most people like its long forearm in spite of the fact that it has more depth than width, the opposite of the target-popularized beavertail. It suits almost any reach, even the close-in hold of a shooter trained in Army offhand, and to see it slide back over the receiver in skeet or trap pump-shotgun style is fascinating!

For its moderate price this rifle is well finished, with nicely shaped and capped pistol grip, unusually thick and apparently durable buttplate, and ramped front sight. Details that more costly .22 pumps have may be missing, such as a smoother trigger pull. It must be safe, and that involves heaviness and a spongy drag, on some specimens. Carefully cost-estimated production can't always avoid this condition, but the buyer can correct it out of his own time or out of his pocket to a gunsmith. It isn't only the less expensive models that occasionally need this or other sorts of tuning to bring out their best.

The four-power scope is normally kept in the store and ready to go on the 33. Wisely, the 6X offered for Higgins bolt-action .22 repeaters isn't listed for the pump gun. The beginner, firing offhand as he usually would with a slide action, finds it hard enough to get a reasonably stay-put sight picture with the 4. The customer must be satisfied, and that's that.

Noble 235

Barrel: 24 inches.
Sights: open rear and ramped front. Receiver grooved for scope mounts.
Magazine capacity: 21 short, 15 long-rifle.
Safety: sliding thumbpiece.
Weight: 6 pounds.

This inexpensive slide-action rifle, which deserves to be better known, is a revised Noble Model 33. It is interesting and efficient in design. The open-top receiver makes it look at first glance somewhat like a bolt action, but it is entirely different, though it too has few working parts.

The breechblock locks against the top face of the receiver, up front, as close to the cartridge head as it possibly can, and the engaging surface is wide. This is unusual in a .22 rimfire repeater. The gun is visible-loading; you see the cartridges being fed into the chamber, just as with a bolt action. Empties pop out of the top of the receiver.

Evidently safety was the designers' great concern. The gun is hammerless and the breechblock does not come back out of the receiver on the opening stroke of the slide handle—a short stroke, by the way, and the system is planned to give smoothness. Of course the Noble can't be fired until the breechblock is closed and locked; we'd expect that of any modern arm. Neither can it be fired in rippity-poop fashion by holding back on the trigger while you saw the slide handle back and forth, for the action isn't unlocked by the fall of the firing pin. You have to let the trigger go forward before you can open the breech again.

The rifle is well balanced for good shooting, with plenty of weight out front, and the pistol grip curves up close to the trigger guard. The forearm is conventional in size, rather small, and it tapers down at the front to give good looks and a comfortable grasp. The stock of the 235 is carried farther forward than that of the earlier model, making the gap between it and the slide handle much shorter. This results in more handy carrying at the trail position, and the front of that stock is rounded off in pleasing style—altogether a good-looking rifle. Economy of production made the trigger guard of stamped steel like those of most bolt-action .22s. There is certainly no serious objection to this detail. And since the Savage 1914 went out, this is the first .22 pump to have a convenient safety catch, easy to become familiar with.

Like the Higgins and the Remington, the Noble is a solid frame, non-takedown gun. The buttstocks can be removed from any of them if packing space is limited, as it might be in a blanket roll, for instance.

Remington 572

Barrel: 23 inches.
Sights: open and bead; receiver is grooved for Tip-Off scope mount.
Magazine capacity: 20 short, 15 long-rifle.
Safety: large cross-bolt at rear of trigger guard.
Weight: 5½ pounds.

For some 45 years the Model 12 and 121 action design came out of the factory and satisfied almost every purchaser. The 572 lined up for inspection with current Remington slide and semi-automatic shotguns and high-power rifles, and it shows the squad's traits in its appearance, even to the heavy, streamlined front of the trigger guard. Some people like that shape, finding it comfortable in the over-arm, muzzle-straight-ahead carry; some feel that the gun is liable to slip forward and land muzzle-down in the mud.

The 572 is less expensive than the 121 that it dis-placed, and in some respects it's a better rifle. The tight assembly improves accuracy and is inconvenient only in packing for travel and in cleaning. Barrel removal is a home job but replacement must be done with care.

The safety button is larger than that of the older rifle, and the action-release plunger that lets you open the closed and cocked rifle is handier. Single-loading is easy: drop the cartridge, bullet forward, in through the ejection port and close the action. The safety can be put on before doing this, and it should be, except on the firing line of a target range.

This pump gun is comfortable to carry at trail, for its large steel action slide fills most of the gap between slide handle and receiver. The handle is of just about ideal size, a bit short for prone, but most pump gun firing is from offhand. Although the pistol grip is large and looks comfortable, it is too far back. A small hand, moved up to squeeze the trigger with the first joint of the forefinger, would get almost no advantage from the swell: the actual curve of the grip starts too far back. "Distance from trigger to point of pistol grip" means little if the grip is straight for the first two inches or so.

The rather dull finish of 572 steel is less reflective than the fine old blues. It's less liable to give away your presence on a sunny day, and less good-looking on the gun rack.

Ruggedness, accuracy and reliability ought to assure this rifle's long-lasting popularity. Whether it is the last design of .22 slide action to be brought out by any factory is worth a moment's wonder. Less expensive bolt actions, autoloaders, and lever guns in time may displace the pump, which at present does seem to be enjoying a pretty substantial comeback.

Savage 29-G

Barrel: 24 inches.
Sights: open and bead; receiver is grooved for Tip-Off mounts.
Magazine capacity: 20 short, 14 long-rifle.
Safety: cross-bolt at rear of trigger guard.
Weight: 5¾ pounds.

It's a little less expensive than the new Remington but an old, established model that sells regularly and gives long service. The gun is a takedown, like most pumps you see. Not having the two-piece receiver of earlier Savage pumps, it should be more accurate, and 100% gas-proof, too. One I know went to the Canadian Northwest to do the little skillet-filling jobs that are pretty far from a .375 Magnum's line of duty. Taken down, it was no trouble to stow away in camp duffle.

The Savage is hammerless, like all but one of the others in this roundup, and its receiver is short and compact. The stroke of the action is short and quick.

There's nothing in the least extreme about this rifle's styling, which in fact is rather conventional. The pistol grip is small, a bit neater than the one on the earlier Model 29, I think, and fairly close-up. It feels good in offhand hold. Compared to the others in

Savage 29-G.

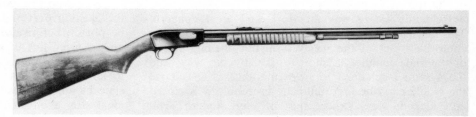

Winchester 61.

Winchester 62.

this class, its forearm seems unusually long and slim, not much taper or rounding off. But it makes an easy grasp and it's long enough to help in such prone shooting as you'd be likely to do with a slide action rifle.

Winchester 61

Barrel: 24 inches.
Sights: open and bead. Receiver grooved for Tip-Off mounts.
Magazine capacity: 20 short, 14 long-rifle.
Safety: cross-bolt at *front* of trigger guard.
Weight: 5½ to 5¾ pounds.

Since almost all shooters know the 1912 or Model 12 Winchester hammerless repeating shotgun, the company did well in following its pattern closely in the 61 action. The short breechblock locks at the rear but is so finely fitted that looseness from wear, common in lots of old .22 pump guns, seldom develops in this rifle. This lockup, with the tight fitting of the trigger tang into the bottom of the one-piece receiver, helps to produce the accuracy for which this rifle is rather famous —excellent precision for a light takedown. The 61 is well worth fitting with a hunting scope.

Back in the 1930s, when burst cases were fairly common in the non-corrosive but mercuric primed rimfire ammo of the time, the 61 was known as one of the rather few rifles—even among hammerless designs —that was absolutely safe from blowbacks. The repeating action is trustworthy, too, the carrier sliding the cartridges up the face of the breechblock into the grasp of the extractor, ready to go straight into the chamber as the forward motion of the slide handle is continued. Jams are rare in this rifle, and for that matter, in most .22 repeaters made now. The extractors pull almost any case, even in mighty cold weather.

For many years a more expensive sort of 61 styling was made with the old-fashioned octagon barrel that brought gun weight up to nearly six pounds. It came in .22 short, .22 long-rifle, and .22 Winchester Rim Fire calibers, chambered and rifled for just one load. The short rifle, incidentally, handled CB caps perfectly but balked at a full loading of the stubby BB's. For a while the .22 WRF was continued in round-barrel style.

The 61 action is unusually smooth. This means little, for any of them can be fired fast enough to send our shooting haywire. Trigger pull is almost always excellent for a hammerless rifle, and the safety is unusual, among .22 slide actions, in being located in the front, not the rear part of the trigger guard. Some of us find it easier for our forefinger to punch it off and slide back to the trigger than to punch a rear safe and then reach forward. Familiarity with the chosen type is the great thing, and a slice of a second counts when we get ready for that first carefully let-off shot at game on the run.

The gun could be improved in looks and in handling. Its forearm is good, long enough for most of us, rounded at front and rear, and beavertailed flat at the bottom. The pistol grip, though neatly formed, is a little too far back. The lower line of the stock is not brought up as it should be for looks, though an amateur can alter it to point straight at the root of the trigger guard and still leave enough wood for strength. I did it, and I'm certainly no wood wizard.

Though the buttplate is of checkered steel, shatterproof, and anxious to stick to your shoulder as it should, it has too little down-pitch for quick use on ground game. In the workshop of his New Mexico ranch Bradley Upton and his gunsmith cousin, Mert Hueber, cut nearly one-half inch off the toe of the stock, none at all off the heel, and replaced the buttplate neatly. Then, in the aerial snapshooting we'd been enjoying, we began to hit more regularly. You could notice the improvement in any shooting you did with the little gun.

The 61 is the most expensive .22 corn-sheller now made; nothing cheap about it. In spite of its rather sad stock design, as issued, it is worth consideration by a shooter who likes this type of .22 repeater. And a lot of us do, you can bet.

Winchester 62

Barrel: 23 inches.
Sights: open and bead.
Magazine capacity: 20 short, 14 long-rifle. Also made for .22 short only.
Safety: half cock notch on hammer.
Weight: 5½ pounds.

Marlins came in a great variety of styles and finish in slide action .22 with exposed hammer, Winchester made the 1890 in fancy as well as plain finish, and there were two or three regular stylings of the short 1906 model. The 62 is left.

It's popular because of its moderate price and also because so many shooters feel that a gun with a hammer in plain sight is safer than a hammerless or even a bolt action. There is good sense in this opinion. A cocked hammer looks as foreboding as a cat's ears laid back for battle—and it is!

Even the Noble repeater isn't quite as quick to make ready for the first shot as this Winchester is— not for most of us, at least. There should never be any temptation to thumb back the hammer in the mere hopeful expectation of a shot, and that's a point for safety. A kid that starts with a .22 hammer gun will be ready for a bigger rifle of that type later, or for a revolver, though he'll need the special reminder to be extra careful of the muzzle of the small and so easily handled short-gun.

The 62 action isn't gas-proof. A severe case-burst sends gas and dirty oil back towards the shooter's face. However, ordinary spectacles give protection against most .22 rimfire liabilities, and ruptured brass is rare today in .22s as closely breeched as this one. Worn-out rolling, rocking or falling block single shots are the ones to look out for.

The action has been changed but little from the 90 and 06 designs. A coil mainspring replaces the flat one and possibly it speeds the hammer fall. Cartridge handling is reliable, a straight-line run from the secure enclosure of the carrier into the chamber, and the single extractor works reliably. The breechblock is still milled out, front and center, so that you can peek in to see if there's a cartridge in the chamber. Since the firing pin strikes the rim at the top, this open slot carries off at least some of the gas from the usual sort of case-head burst.

Most 62s have a clean, brittle trigger pull. If you want to refine it, or to lighten it to, say 2½ pounds, the job is easier than it is on most hammerless rifles.

Today a straight grip stock looks odd on a sporting or even a military rifle. The 62 stock has its comb well back, not offering any support to a small hand, and in general it resembles one on an old Winchester lever gun fitted with a nice flat shotgun butt. But the comb is higher and thicker, and with iron sights this rifle fits well. Top ejection of empties makes the 62 unsuited to most scopes. A prismatic hunting scope like the Boone probably could be based on the flat receiver, or a conventional glass could be offset, preferably to the right. Any top-ejecting repeater can use a high-mounted target glass for slow fire; you just hope the empties won't fall back into the action, and if they do, you pick 'em out.

Formerly the top tang was tapped for the front base screw of a Marble or Lyman peep sight, the best for a 62, 90 or 06. The rear base screw replaces the buttstock screw. Now you may have to get a gunsmith to drill and tap for you, and this is true of many contemporary rifles on which you'd like a tang peep.

The 62 handles well because its weight is nicely distributed, and the pitch of the buttplate is right for most shooters. Though its slide action may seem stiff compared to those of the best hammerless pumps, you'll never notice it in the hunting field. The heavy hammer spring you compress on the back-pull is pretty fair insurance against misfires, too.

Most hammerless rifles have a bolt through the stock to bind wood and receiver tightly together. This is good for accuracy—just one of many details, of course. The 62, like most lever-action hammer guns, gets by with long, snugly inletted tangs held by a single screw.

SEMI-AUTOMATICS

After a kid has found out the facts he wants to make *hits,* not make like a bunch of firecrackers. Too many youngsters get an automatic for a first gun, and that's bad for marksmanship, conservation of game, and human life expectancy, too. The old head on young shoulders is a rare apple, and maybe, when you think it over, that seems quite as it should be.

You and the youngster both need patience when he's learning gun-safety, and the riveting rattle of the autoloader is an invitation to impatience. Usually it's a long road to absolutely safe gun-handling, with occasional switchbacks to forgetfulness.

But the self-loader has its place, and its popularity is growing as fast as it did in the 1905-1915 decade. As an *inexpensive* .22 rifle or pistol it's still fairly new. The former seems to have gone back to its original light-weight form, not too heavy for youngsters, and liked by many older shooters because of its handiness.

For some years after World War II, Harrington & Richardson put out a couple of man-sized .22 auto-

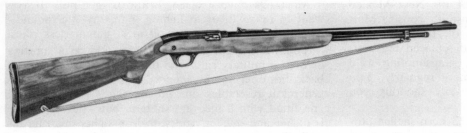

J. C. Higgins 31 with Roll-Away carrying sling.

Marlin 88-DL.

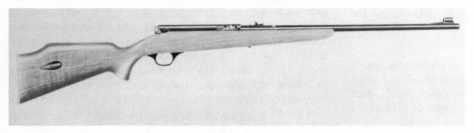

The Marlin 98 of early 1957 replaced the 88-C and 88-DL in the line.

matics, the Leatherneck 165 weighing from 7 to 7½ pounds and the Reising 65 going close to nine. Redfield receiver peep sights were standard equipment, also web gunslings and long, cumbersome 10-shot magazines. The later Leatherneck 150, lighter and less expensive, was regularly supplied with open sights and no sling. Its magazine held five rounds and was nearly flush with the bottom of the forestock.

J. C. Higgins 30 and 31

Barrel: 23¼ inches.
Sights: open rear, ramped bead front; receiver grooved for scope mounts. Four-power scope with plastic end-caps is an extra that is readily available.
Magazine capacity: 25 short, 17 long-rifle.
Safety: cross-bolt at front of trigger guard.
Weight: 5½ pounds.

These models are much alike. The 30 operates as an autoloader only with .22 long-rifles; the 31, a bit more expensive, takes the short and the inferior long as well as the long-rifle. Balanced breechblock weight and recoil spring made this possible.

The Higgins is a nice-handling .22 auto, with well-shaped pistol grip, capped for appearance, and a semi-beavertail, slightly grooved forestock. Solid frame construction increases its accuracy, but makes frequent bore-cleaning a bit troublesome. The action parts attached to the trigger plate can be had out for cleaning, and the bolt, too, by following the simple directions that are printed for the gun.

Sold at a moderate price, it can't have all the extras—even the *useful* ones!—a shooter would expect on a custom-made gun. The bolt handle needs checkering or grooving to provide a better hold for a half-frozen

finger. The trigger pull is long and spongy even for an autoloader, some of which do have excellent pulls—like the old Remington 16 for its special .22 cartridge, to cite one example.

One extra that would be appreciated when you're skiing, snow-shoeing, or just tramping across unproductive country is the Roll-Away nylon sling. It is housed down near the toe of the butt and can be drawn out and hooked up front on the magazine ring. It's a carrying sling, too short and maybe too frail to be a good shooting-sling. But I don't remember any other autoloader that has come from the factory with standard equipment like this.

Marlin 88

Barrel: 24 inches.
Sights: 88-C has open rear and hooded, ramped bead front. Special back plug for the receiver, containing a peep, can be added as a wise after-thought. 88-DL has the peep as regular equipment, along with sling swivels and checkering on stock and forearm. Both models are grooved for Weaver Tip-Off scope mounts.
Magazine capacity: 14 long-rifles in buttstock tube magazine with funnel loading.
Safety: at rear of receiver. Locks sear.
Weight: 6¾ pounds.

This rifle has good weight and balance, and its pistol grip is large and close enough to the trigger guard to be helpful to the hunter. The fluted comb is an extra touch of neat appearance, and it feels good to that large class of riflemen who always lay their thumb across the stock for secure grasp—except of course when firing one of the old Type S 1903 Springfields with that awfully short, straight grip stock!

Like several other modern .22 automatics, the Marlin has plenty of forestock length for sling attachment, though this reach isn't taken full advantage of in the DL or de luxe model. A long-armed man probably would want that front swivel farther front, and he could place it so. This would be worth doing for shooting in either prone or sitting, and there is considerable accuracy built into .22 auto-rifles of such weight and quality. It is worth bringing out with the aid of the leather.

Marlin 98

Barrel: 22 inches.
Sights: hooded, ramped front; receiver rear peep, though this specimen shown here has an open rear sight. Receiver grooved for Tip-Off scope mounts.
Magazine capacity: 15 long-rifles in buttstock tube magazine with loading port on right side of stock.
Safety: at rear of receiver. Locks sear.
Weight: 6½ pounds.

This early 1957 model is designed to replace the 88 Marlins, of which so many are in use that they deserve a place in this book. The most apparent changes in the new rifle's styling are the Monte Carlo comb, the slimmed-down forestock, and the barrel shortened from the old standard 24 to 22 inches. Other 1957 Marlin .22 rimfires, bolt action and autoloading, carry 22-inch barrels, and since their receivers are long, they can stand it. The report of firing is not much louder— it might be impossible to notice the difference—and an overall of about 40 to 42 inches is enough to suit the average plinker or small game hunter who threads his way through brush.

The 98 styling is interesting because it reflects present-day popular taste, though how soon tomorrow will arrive with something quite different is anyone's guess. It's a sure bet that it'll get here, and it wouldn't be surprising to see it towing a taste for longer barrels once again.

The 98's rather sharply sloped but not over-full or cramped-up-close pistol grip is typical of many of today's factory and custom-made sporters. So are the Monte, the slim forestock, and the at least fairly short barrel. The rifle is trim, looks lighter than it is, and has

the appearance of being headed for the woods or mountains rather than the target range. From the strictly practical angle, the side loading port is a joyful lot handier than a buttplate fodder door! There's no need to hold the magazine tube in your teeth, like a squirrel, while you drop in the hulls. The "special new finish" on the receiver certainly does no harm, and you can see from the accompanying portrait that it looks good.

All 1957 Marlins have a new sort of stock finish to resist weather, and to one sort of hunter, for sure, that means a lot. He can take mighty little care of the stock and it'll still look presentable. Another sort, the real guncrank and rifle-lover, isn't beglamored by any finish that comes ready made on a stock. He scrapes it off and applies his own. Underneath this Marlin's skin— and underneath those of most American rifles now sent out—he'd find walnut, a comforting sight to his devoted eyes. Time was, you might unearth birch, gumwood, or some mystery tree.

Marlin 89-C

In general specifications this model is similar to the 88-C. Being a clip-loader, it costs quite a bit less to produce, or to buy. Seven shots are the capacity of the standard magazine, which protrudes only a short distance from the bottom of the forestock. The plinker or exhibition fancy shot can get 10 or 12 shot clips as extras.

The cleverly engineered, serviceable little "peep sight back plug" can be ordered for this rifle, as for the 88-C, and it's easy to install. You get both windage (side to side) and elevation adjustments in it, and it's about as neat and unobtrusive as any receiver sight could be.

The 89 isn't in any way to be regarded as a "second" quality Marlin. The clip mag simplifies manufacture and assembly at the factory, and with many riflemen it's the first choice. Unloading the rifle is much faster and simpler when you have only to remove the clip and eject the barrel load. You can also, if you wish, carry the gun completely empty and load it without much loss of time.

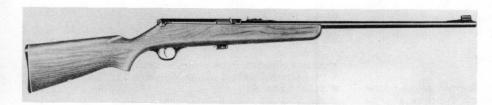

Marlin 89-C.

Mossberg 151-K.

Mossberg 151-M with swing-out peep and open rear sights, ramped, hooded front.

Mossberg 152.

Mossberg 151-K

Barrel: 24 inches.
Sights: open and blade; receiver grooved for Mossberg scope mounts.
Magazine capacity: 15 long-rifles in buttstock tube.
Safety: knob on receiver goes back, opening action about ¼ inch and is pushed in to lock. Cartridge in chamber can be seen, and pulling out on the knob lets it go forward under spring propulsion.
Weight: 6 pounds.

Much like the Mossberg 140-K bolt-action in its styling, this rifle is advertised as "a beautiful little automatic especially for open-sight shooting." The stock has Monte Carlo comb, cheekpiece, and a full, close-up pistol grip with the usual Mossberg finger grooves, an extension of the plastic trigger guard. In general build it is designed more for snapshooting than for deliberate precision work, and that suits most buyers of semi-automatics. It's accurate, however, and there's enough weight, properly located, to make good shooting not too difficult.

The stock wood is real walnut, not stained to resemble walnut, as some woods were in some Mossbergs of the past. The substitutes formerly used generally did have attractive grain and would refinish into nice-looking stocks—unless you were one of those who always preferred brunettes, the natural kind.

For a full sized autoloader this is one of the least expensive on the market. It is sound, though, and a guncrank could buy it with confidence and then refine and equip it to suit his ideas.

Mossberg 151-M

Barrel: 20 inches.
Sights: Micro-Click swing-out peep and hooded, ramped front with 4 inserts permanently attached. Receiver grooved for Mossberg scope mounts.
Magazine capacity: 15 long-rifles in buttstock tube.
Safety: same as on 151-K.
Weight: 7 pounds.

A sturdy little rifle—a carbine, really—this Mossberg is convenient for sling or hand carrying in the woods, and its good weight makes it steady to hold in spite of its short barrel. We must remember that this type of .22 automatic does have a good bit of

length in the tubular receiver. It costs more than the 151-K, having some extra features that are worth while, and in appearance it's entirely different. You just choose the style you happen to prefer.

The sling swivels are quick-detachable, but they should be taken off only when there's still-hunting to be done and the faintest tick or rattle can spook the game. They are—must be at the price—less rugged and wear-resistant than the finely machined q. d.s of an expensive sporter. In sensible use they stand up for years—I don't know how many. Mine did well.

Model 151's stock has the usual cheekpiece, but no Monte, which isn't needed on such a straight job. Its pistol grip is shoved up close to the guard, and gives excellent support to the firing hand. The forestock is of the usual full length Mannlicher-Schoenauer type, but the last hand-span or so is a separate piece. The joint lies hidden under the metal band that carries the front sling swivel. This is OK; the rifle's moderate price depends on the closest figuring of materials as well as labor. To finish the stock and make an entry for the magazine tube the buttplate is steel, not hard rubber or plastic that are so liable to be chipped or broken in rock climbing. In such exercise, by the way, it pays to be extra careful with a short rifle. You don't want its muzzle to tickle you under the chin.

Mossberg 152 and 152-K

Barrel: 18 inches.
Sights: 152 has peep rear and front with guard; 152-K has open sights. Receivers are grooved for Mossberg scope mounts.
Magazine capacity: 7 long-rifles in detachable clip.
Safety: positive locking as on Mossberg 151 autoloaders.
Weight: 5 pounds.

Glamor sells these rifles.

Like the bolt action 142 Mossbergs, they resemble the Army's M-1 .30 caliber carbine. They are of sub-junior size, evidently pointed at the juvenile market; yet they are better arms for the trapper, woods-cruiser, or canoe explorer than for the average kid. This is not only for the good reason that nearly all young marksmen are handicapped by an autoloader, which invites fast and careless shooting. The short

Mossberg 152-K, showing sling attachment.

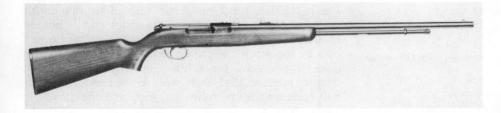

Remington 550-A.

barrel is no help in steady holding, and the U. S. carbine-type sling is a better carrying strap than a muzzle stabilizer. It's attached to the left side of the stock.

The adult who goes in for fast and fancy shooting, a real art in showmanship, might find that the hinged plastic forearm tip, turned down, would dampen the upchuck of the muzzle in rapid fire. The little gun has its purposes and fills them well, but it definitely isn't a junior training rifle or a proper hunting rifle for any beginner. Sorry, but I've seen what happened, and such at any rate are the basic principles of rifle work that harvests hits.

Remington 550-A

Barrel: 24 inches. 550-2G for .22 shorts only has 22-inch barrel.
Sights: open and bead; receiver grooved for Tip-Off scope mounts.
Magazine capacity: 22 short, 15 long-rifle.
Safety: thumbpiece at right rear of receiver.
Weight: 6¼ pounds.

The Remington 24 autoloader of 1922-35 and the heavier 241 that outlived World War II production drop-outs were expensive, old-line rifles that competed against the best in the class in appearance, workmanship and finish. They couldn't compete against inexpensive autoloaders with tubular receivers, not the flat and elaborately machined-out receivers that cost so much to produce. These Remingtons were made for .22 short only or for .22 long-rifle only.

The 550 did what had been dreamed of, what no other autoloader had been able to accomplish. It handled all three popular lengths of .22 rimfire ammo *as a self-loader.* This means a lot to the plinker, and, by golly, a lot to any serious rifleman-hunter who can't afford the thousands of shots a year he needs to keep in trim if his weapon handles only the more expensive .22 long-rifle loads. Playing the scale up and down from pipping low-speed shorts to cracking high-speed long-rifles, all in the same magazineful, doesn't mean

much to him except in some zany interlude. The practice in short and longer range, in slow and rapid fire, certainly does.

The "power piston" makes possible the automatic loading of cartridges as different in length and in backthrust as those standard velocity shorts and high velocity long-rifles. The piston is a short, supplementary chamber that fits inside the breech of the barrel proper. Just a little longer than the short case, it lets powder gases from that tiny round get in and muscle back the breechblock in recoil. The second version of the Colt Ace .22 automatic pistol on the .45 frame (now known as the Conversion Unit and made for the .38 Super Auto also) used a similar principle to make the recoil of a .22 long-rifle appear nearly as heavy as that of, say a .30 Luger. This was a big help in training for .45 timed- and rapid-fire matches. It seemed more like the real thing!

Though it's the most expensive of the tubular-*receiver* type of semi-automatic .22 rifle, the Remington is extremely popular. About the only criticism that can be made by one who has no prejudices against autoloaders is that the open rear sight is set pretty far out, farther than necessary. A far-sighted shooter wouldn't mind that a bit.

You see many of these rifles in use where automatics are acceptable, and you wonder if Remington plans to bring out a new version simply to muster it in with the streamlined 572 .22 pump, 740 and 760 high-powers, and 48 and 870 shotguns. They have a good rifle in the 550 just as it is.

Any semi-automatic arm needs care if it is to keep on functioning reliably. The action should be clean and its moving parts lightly lubricated to ease their work. In bore cleaning the chamber should get particular attention, and especially so when cartridges of different length are run through the works. The floating chamber or power piston of the 550 calls for more attention than we'd give a conventional rifle chamber in the best of care. We must keep it clean and free-moving

Remington 552.

if we want to enjoy the reliability and the convenience that were built into the rifle's clever design.

Remington 552

Barrel: 23 inches. *Weight:* 5½ pounds.
Sights: Open and bead. Receiver grooved for Tip-Off scope mounts.
Magazine capacity: 22 short, 15 long-rifle.
Safety: Cross button at rear of trigger guard.

The 552 was formally announced early in 1957 and in a sense it was no surprise. It was logical to bring out a smallbore companion to the streamlined Remington autoloading shotguns and the Model 740 high-power rifle. Resemblance alone will sell a lot of 552s, but let's study this .22 in its own right.

The first glance says that it's good-looking, and this impression could be lasting. It's a little more expensive than the 550, which it is not designed to replace, either as an all-round .22 sporter or as a special .22 short gallery gun. It looks like money; it almost reminds you of fine old-line .22 automatics, of which the Winchester 63 and the Browning survive in current production. About all the smoothing it needs is at the square forestock tip.

Engineering is clever, permitting relatively low-cost manufacture. It is ingenious, it is scarcely complicated, but this gun is a devil to keep clean! That final statement comes from a fellow who likes to have his guns bright and slick inside as well as out. A lot of us don't, and the 552 will, ordinarily, keep on shooting when it's as foul as a medieval slum.

Yes, the gun is a cinch to dismount. A screwdriver for the forestock, a drift or even a whittled hardwood twig for the receiver pins—they do it. You can slush out the receiver and its insides with solvent and a tooth-brush, or you can peck and pry with an oiled rag and a stick. When the gun is apart its two-piece stock lets it fit a Victoria-style case for travel or storage, and the breech-block with its tiny head just drops out, allowing you to clean the bore from the breech. Since the patch must go through a slum to get there, it's simpler to swab from the muzzle, and the well bored and rifled barrel comes clean fast. You notice that the barrel is a fairly loose push fit in the receiver; yet you find the rifle's accuracy to be pretty darn fair, of good plinking grade or better.

When it comes to hitting offhand—that difficult position for most of us, especially with a light rifle—the 552 is fine. That beautifully blued receiver is of light alloy, shoving the balance well forward, and the trigger pull is good, for an automatic. At least my sample was. Between shots, the gun carries nicely at trail.

The stock comb is plenty high for iron sights, and I'm particular, for I need one high. This rifle is for both kids and grownups, and its pistol grip is no-end smart. The swell comes far back and therefore doesn't add to the stock's apparent length as a close-up one does. That's good for a little guy who tries to shoot with a standard 13½-inch pull. A big hand gets some pull-back advantage from the grip, and the family is happy. Yes, I recall my page 47 words!

In modern styling, the forestock is semi-beavertail, a nice moderate size. It's big enough to pretty well shield the operating handle. That gadget needs comment.

It lies at the left, under the rear sight notch, much like the one on the Winchester 77 automatic. Both of them come back, on firing, with commendable if perhaps frightening vigor. Painful, and no perhaps, if the forward hand gets in the way. Could it? No salesman would admit that liability, I suppose, and naturally. But an uncoached beginner takes some odd holds, and so might an oldtimer under the thrust of emergency. In hip-rest offhand it's barely possible that a thumb or finger might get belted. All this adds up to liability as thin as a ghost, but calling for mention.

The gun has possibilities as a trainer, if properly sighted. It could wear a sling, it balances steadily, and the pull is decent, much like that of the 740 big-game rifle's in design. With magazine removed (or left in) it's easily single-loaded, like the Winchester 63. Hold the breech open and drop a cartridge in through the ejection port. The shell deflector, screwed on the right side of the receiver, doesn't get in the way, and just reasonable care is needed to prevent the bullet end of the round from dropping into the magazine trough. With the deflector left on, empties go right-forward and down, away from the next-door shooter on the firing line. They come out so fast that the long-rifle high-smacks—not the shorts—have their mouths battered, but the noise is swallowed up by the report; it wouldn't give away your location when you're hunting.

Handling shorts, longs and long-rifles as they come, the 552 is one of those that can be played like a banjo, plink, plonk, *plunk*. For getting and keeping in trim it's nice to be able to use whatever's available, or to vary power and noise as need dictates. The light breech-block and the built-in loading ramp that leads from the magazine let this rifle handle all three lengths without resort to a floating chamber. That's to the good when a gun is to be used with greased ammunition, used a lot, and cleaned only when a sluggard spirit moves!

Savage 6 De Luxe.

Stevens 85.

I like the safety button, similar to that of the Winchester 63. It is *not* a hammer indicator: it can be set "on" whether the gun is cocked or not. This system makes for safe loading and unloading, and it'd be good, perhaps, if all kids' rifles had it.

There was some trouble with the specimen 552 sent me for trial. With shorts it worked beautifully. Some lots of long-rifle, as it happened, gave frequent misfires, for though the coiled mainspring is strong, the hammer is light. There were jams, too, not of the empties, but of loaded long-rifles. Both the rounded Western bullet-nose and the semi-pointed Remington were able to catch, just above the barrel breech, and stop the firing. These rounds could be pried into the chamber with a knife-blade—no healthy diversion—or removed by taking the gun apart—certainly a brief operation. By the time full production is under way, it seems likely, these troubles will have been corrected. There is no reason to think they couldn't be, or wouldn't, for the 552 is attractive, and it seems headed for considerable popularity.

Savage 6

Barrel: 24 inches.
Sights: open and bead. Model 6-S has peep rear and hooded, ramped bead front. Receivers are grooved for Tip-Off scope mounts.
Magazine capacity: 22 short (as hand-operated repeater), 15 long-rifle.
Safety: thumbpiece at right rear of receiver.
Weight: 6 pounds.

Savage and Stevens .22 automatics are of the modern tubular-receiver type. They can be converted instantly into non-automatic repeaters of the straight-pull bolt-action type: you have only to push the cross-bolt to the left to cut out the self-loading feature. Then you pull back on the cross-bolt to cock and load for each separate shot, and the action functions with shorts, longs or long-rifles.

This means a lot when you're training a youngster, even though these arms weren't designed with that purpose—pleasure, really—in mind. In states where semi-automatic rifles are illegal for hunting it wouldn't mean a thing, as the rifle is issued, for a mere pull-out on the bolt handle makes the arm a self-loader

once more. To legalize the gun as a hand-operated repeater the alteration would have to be permanent. Most state laws still let us use our semi-automatics for hunting.

The walnut stock of the Savage has a cheekpiece and a Monte Carlo comb, and its pistol grip is well shaped for sporting use—and not badly for target, too. The bottom line of the stock, from toe to trigger guard, is unusually pleasing, and the semi-beavertail forearm up front blends well into the fine lines of the rifle.

At first view the openwork, gills or ventilation cuts along the left side of the receivers of these rifles may look odd. They serve a sensible purpose, for they let a fair amount of the fouling gas and powder residue escape where they do no harm—not even to a left-handed shooter. Advertising once claimed that a thousand shots could be fired before cleaning was necessary. That is a bit optimistic. A rifleman who takes pride in his arm—and expects reliability in return—would treat it more considerately, especially when it's a semi-automatic.

Savage 7

This is the clip or box magazine Savage auto, and it appears to have been dropped from production. However, a good many 7s are still around, and before this writing quite a few discontinued guns and cartridges have enjoyed a return engagement. Most people like a lot of magazine capacity in an automatic, though a few remark that there can be too much, for a hunter. They may go further and observe rather acidly that the sight of a long magazine tube under a barrel isn't exactly breath-taking in its beauty.

Stevens 85

Barrel: 24 inches.
Sights: open and bead. Receiver is grooved for Tip-Off scope mounts.
Magazine capacity: 5 long-rifle; 10-shot clips are available.
Safety: thumbpiece at right rear of receiver.
Weight: 6 pounds.

A relatively inexpensive autoloader—or straight-pull repeater—with the serviceable and safe box or

Stevens 87.

Winchester 63 in original 20-inch
barrel length.

clip magazine, the 85 can be recommended for
quality and reliability. The walnut finish stock with
blacked forearm tip has good lines and fits well in
iron sight shooting.

This rifle, like the Stevens 87 and the Savages, has
been on the market a long time. Only a few minor
changes have been made or have seemed necessary.
It is well established as a satisfactory hunting and
plinking arm with the weight and length that help so
much in both slow and rapid fire, at still or moving
targets.

Stevens 87

This is the tubular-magazine counterpart of the
Stevens 85, and in most details it is similar to the
Savage Model 6. It's a little more expensive than the
clip-magazine Stevens 85.

Used as repeaters, some tubular magazine rifles
handle .22 shorts and even .22 longs much more
reliably than clip rifles made for the long-rifle do.
Special blocked-off clips have been made for Winchester 56, 57 and 69 bolt actions and for some of
the earliest 52 target rifles that were chambered and
bored for the short cartridge. The usual .22 long-
rifle clip—not all—may accept only three or possibly
four shots and feed them reliably. The longs usually
do better, but in other respects they're no great bargain.

The Stevens 87 has made for itself a pretty strongly
held place in the .22 rifle world, and for about four
good reasons. It's man-sized and it has good weight
that's distributed well to give steadiness. It has plenty
of magazine capacity and behaves well as a repeater
with the economical .22 shorts, then goes back to
handling long-rifles without a murmur if the chamber
is reasonably clean. And it's inexpensive, for an automatic, without being the least bit cheap or shoddy.
A highly respected firm makes it.

Winchester 63

Barrel: originally 20 inches; now offered only in 23-inch
length.
Sights: open and bead; rifle takes various models of tang
and receiver peep sights, or scope mounts, after drilling
and tapping.

Magazine capacity: 10 long-rifles in buttstock tube, or 11,
usually, in hollow-point style.
Safety: small cross-bolt trigger lock at rear of trigger guard;
can be set on whether hammer is cocked or not, and
during loading and unloading.
Weight: 5½ to 5¾ pounds.

A 20-year service hitch with no time out for repairs is not a bit unusual with this simple, sturdy
automatic. One small and one large screwdriver, and
a nail to push out the firing pin stop, are all the tools
needed to dismount the action for cleaning and oiling—and for the chance to admire its beautiful simplicity.

In assembling, the receiver goes over the trigger
tang tightly, making an absolutely gas-proof joint.
The hookup is rigid, resulting in good takedown rifle
accuracy. For a mere plinking rifle, this one has it!
Ten shots in an inch at 50 yards is nice grouping for
a light .22 automatic, and this one sometimes can do
it with low-speed ammunition that it happens to like.
Guns are individuals and have their preferences. Although the high-velocity stuff is recommended in catalogue literature, most 63s operate reliably with the
gentle loads, too, except in really cold weather.

In 23-inch length the rifle is well balanced for
quick offhand shooting. The old 20-inch barrel was
slightly handier in brush so thick and so noisy that
most of us would have little success in hunting any
wary game there. It made the gun muzzle-light as
well as noticeably sharper in report.

The 63 has its faults. In trigger pull it is different
from almost all other good rifles except the much
bigger companion models in centerfire, and of course
the old 1903 .22 automatic. You have to learn that
trigger pull before you can do good work with the
rifle in either slow fire or snapshooting. It's heavy,
six pounds or so, and apparently it has a great deal
of drag and creep. Actually it has the fairly light
takeup or slack of a military bolt action; then comes
a pretty clean but awfully heavy final pull.

You must clean this rifle from the muzzle, like
many .others that continue to be popular. If you're

careful, and if you use a smooth rod, this theoretically dreadful method does little if any harm.

The gun is good-looking (and usually downright beautiful in finish) except for the takedown screw sticking out at the rear of the receiver. "What's *that* thing?" is a standard question. Well, it holds the assembly tight in a simple, effective way, although after years of steady use you may have to watch it. Then, under the stress of lots of shooting, there's a tendency for the ratchet to slip. The system used in the 1903 .22 and the centerfires of this type and make—including the Model 07 .351 until rather lately—was a whole lot better. You had to depress a little thumb-operated spring lock before you could turn out the takedown screw.

After long use, too, the firing-pin retractor spring may weaken enough to let the pin go forward during the slam of reloading. No, not enough to cause the rifle to double or to go full-automatic, but just to leave the faintest pin-prick on the rim of the unfired round. This isn't dangerous in any way, nor is it a phenomenon peculiar to this semi-automatic. It's just interesting enough to rate mention.

The 63 isn't suitable as a junior training rifle. It has accuracy, and the trigger pull can be mastered, but how are you going to mount a sling? The fore-arm is too short, and if you slot or band the barrel for a swivel, the direct pull-down on that barrel will cause bullet impact to vary with the degree of strain and to be entirely different from what you get when you fire without the sling. This is sad, for the 63 is one of the easiest of all rifles to single-load. Drop a round into the open breech and let the action go shut. The bullet will nose its way right into the chamber—unless the cartridge has to do an end-over-end flip to put the lead up front.

This is the last of the old-line .22 automatics of absolutely top quality and workmanship, short, simple and compact in its action. If its high price forces it off the market some of us will feel pretty bad. Enough have been made and sold to give it a rather wide reputation, and a favorable one. But maybe not enough are in circulation to avoid something of the crazy, wild-eyed scramble for used specimens that followed the temporary discontinuance of the Single Action Army Colt sixgun.

Winchester 77

Barrel: 22 inches.
Sights: open and bead; receiver grooved for Tip-Off scope mount.
Magazine capacity: 8 long-rifles in clip style; 15 in tube-under-barrel magazine type.
Safety: rotary thumbpiece at right rear of receiver.
Weight: 5½ pounds.

Only rarely do the Winchester people enter the low-priced competitive field. However, the Model 77 with detachable clip magazine is among the least expensive of .22 self-loaders.

The 77 replaced the Model 74, a heavier rifle with tubular magazine in its buttstock, and incidentally a well balanced arm for steadiness in offhand. The 74 came at first in .22 short caliber, later in .22 long-rifle, with 24-inch barrels, a length finally cut to 22. Towards the last, the short chambering was discontinued. Early 74s could be had with a peep sight somewhat like that now offered for Marlin automatics, but without windage adjustment.

The 77 receiver has fine, flowing lines instead of being a straight tube with a bung at the end of it. It's a fairly short receiver, and that contributes to the rifle's compact appearance.

With clip magazine the gun looks a bit like that true thirteen-day wonder, the U. S. M-1 carbine. Yes, it took just that long for Winchester engineers to design that .30-caliber under the stress of wartime need. The clip magazine sits back against the trigger guard, looks better than some that are 'way out near the rear sight, and is less noticeable when you carry the gun at trail. In clip style this rifle is popular for lots of hard, practical service, and the tubemag model holds the average rations for plinking. No rifle with this type of magazine is the right choice for the roughest service unless the tube is rugged like those of centerfire lever or slide actions (or a bolt gun like the old Swiss .41), or else enclosed in wood like that of the 151 Mossberg and some others. The half-

Winchester 77, clip magazine.

Winchester 77 with tubular mag.

magazine lever guns have little of the tube showing beyond the forestock. Sometimes even a careful, deliberate hunter will fall, and a good lick across the trunk of a down tree or over a rock can put a thin magazine tube out of commission.

The 77 stock has beautiful lines, though at the expense of having its pistol grip rather far back, the target-trained shooter might say. The forestock is a beavertail, not so large that the average youngster doesn't like it. Somehow it goes well with the rest of the stock job, for it's only a little cub beaver, after all.

In several ways this rifle is rather unusual. Certain parts are made of nylon, not steel, which gives lightness and the strength actually required. Its safety catch is different in location and in operation from the usual thing, but it's convenient and not hard to "learn." But any shooter unfamiliar with this model might wonder where in this or any world the operating handle is hiding. Well, it sticks out unobtrusively from the left side of the forestock, away up by the rear open sight. Handy when you learn it, and not liable to snag your hand, either.

The 77 is really a solid-frame design: a forearm screw and one behind the trigger guard hold steel and wood together. For the inveterate bore-cleaner the 77 is, maybe, a total loss. Dismounting to detach the barrel and take apart the action seems complicated at first, and assembly calls for somewhat more than the usual care. After a while you get on to it and have no trouble. Apparently the Winchester Avenue people, when designing it, figured that the average user of a .22 automatic relies on the relatively clean-burning and completely non-corrosive qualities of modern smokeless rimfire ammunition, and rarely swabs out action or bore except a week or so before hunting season and again on a rainy day in March or April. They probably were right.

Some Foreign Autoloaders

European arms makers have cashed in on our national prosperity, and as they're our allies, why not? Most recent exports to us have been small automatic pistols, shotguns, and bolt-action high-powers. There are also .22 auto-rifles. Those attracting most attention right now are the Belgian Browning, Italian Beretta, and French Gévarm.

The Browning, an old, proved system, is familiar to most shooters, except the youngsters, in the Remington 24 and later 241, both discontinued and sometimes mourned for their passing. Its buttstock magazine's follower shunts the cartridges chamberward in unusual fashion, *over the top* of the breechblock; yet they arrive with the reliability of a crack transcontinental. Empties are flung straight down from the bottom of the streamlined receiver, and they can sting and scorch a bare arm or elbow! Remingtons, some at least, came with a stamped steel deflector that added

nothing to looks or carrying ease but sent the brass tinkling off to the right. All in all, so many shooters like the old Rems that the Browning imports were sure of a welcome.

Takedown is quick and easy and a barrel-breech adjustment can keep it rigid. I didn't care for this feature on my 24; it tended to shift without telling me. But you couldn't lever Bert Shay loose from his 24, and there is intelligent approval of a rifle model that didn't suit me in all respects. Bert's not the inveterate bore-swabber that I am.

In the .22 autoloading class the Browning-Rem has produced fine accuracy and reliability. I can't recall mine ever having jammed, or even misfired, and rimfire ammo of the late 1920's wasn't as sure-pop as the stuff we buy now. These rifles took high-speeds in stride; they aren't antiquated.

The Beretta comes from an old firm and is quality arm. Most foreign gunmakers have learned that we Americans have at least outward sophistication and can judge between junk and acceptable trade muskets. With 4-round clip magazine it is a neat, trim gun, less so with the optional 8-shotter. Its breech is neither smooth and flowing in line like the Browning's nor as uncompromisingly abrupt as those of some other .22 autos. The six-pound weight is good, and rather well distributed.

Externally the action resembles that of a bolt gun. When the handle is turned down the action is no longer semi-automatic, but hand-operated, and all three lengths of cartridges can be used.

The Gévarm operates from an open bolt that slams forward to seat and immediately fire the cartridge. Some find this heavy striker-fall, if we can call it that, a decided nuisance, disconcerting to any try at marksmanship. The Marlin 50-E .22 used that system and partly for that reason won few popularity awards. All right for a machine or sub-machine gun, perhaps, but a .22 hardly needs those intervals of cooling off.

The firing pin is an integral ridge across the bolt-face, striking the rim in two places and giving claim to better ignition—and higher velocity, too. Reminds me of a story I read as a kid, "Cougar Sam's Hard Trigger Pull." Sam swore he got more zoop from his rifle by holding it hard against his shoulder and giving the trigger a terrific yank.

Maybe the Gévarm's 17½-inch rifling twist would give extra velocity, more than that of the possibly antiquated 16-inch .22 long-rifle standard. Less resistance wouldn't burn the powder too fast and expend energy in pushing the bullet through the last half-foot or so of bore. And for accuracy it may be better for high-velocity long-rifles, or others, all so much faster than the original. As speed goes up, twist can be slower and still stabilize a bullet. But the .22 rimfire automatic rifle, unlike some pistols of the type, isn't yet a match gun by any sensible standard. Most of them just do quite a lot better than we might expect.

PHWITT! says the little .22 long-rifle cartridge, and there can be as much eagerness to find out the result of the shot as if a .300 Magnun had blasted.

Thouands of us find smallbore practice and competition as fascinating as any form of rifle shooting. Those who follow this sport are a dedicated clan. They're living fully: the game grips them not only during those exacting minutes when their relay is on the firing line, but before and after, too. There's the constant study to improve, the listening to the advice of experts, always ready to share the best they know, and the position drill and dry snapping at home. Sometimes the last blurry thought at night returns to the padded or sodded firing point. Win or lose, they're a happy lot.

But maybe they're a clan apart?

TIME OF FLUX

Like almost everything else in this critical epoch—except a few unchanging human values—the smallbore rifle game is in a state of flux. It is much more than a game, though, for its contribution to national security is and has been immense. No need to go on about that: accurate rifle shooting starts with slow fire, learning to hit small, stationary marks at known distances by means of correct holding, aiming and trigger squeeze.

Snapping in a successful shot at running game or dodging enemy gets its groundwork in patient, slow-fire target shooting. We go back to the essentials—hold, sight picture, and squeeze—and we find that none can be frantic or slurred if our bullet is to do what we tell it to.

There are two sensible criticisms of the smallbore target sport—they apply to bigbore, too—which outline serious threats to the very life of this truly beloved game. It costs too much; it lacks spectator appeal. For the same two reasons the old Schuetzen 200-yard offhand competition died. No, it didn't die, for some still follow it. But how would you like to see thousands and thousands of our smallbore following cut down to a few hundred?

SCHUETZEN OFFHAND

This was considered a German sport, though many others besides German-Americans enjoyed it. You know how they fired, "on their hind legs," the weight of the heavy single shot balanced on a palm rest that hung from the forestock, long enough to let the elbow cradle in above the hipbone. It took years of practice to become really good, and even then the rifle was "impractical" in the hunting field except for deliberate shots at game like woodchucks or crows. But the sport held most of its followers and for a generation or more attracted enough new blood to stay alive.

It was expensive. Harry Pope, master barrel-maker, *guaranteed* his rifles from .28-30 to .39 (a recut

CHAPTER 3

SMALLBORE TARGET RIFLES

.38-55) to group in from 2½ to 3 inches at 200 yards.* That's good shooting for cast bullets even when they're loaded from the muzzle as Pope recommended. But the old gentleman couldn't make and assemble a barrel on a Ballard, Stevens or Winchester action, travel to the range and test it in his machine rest in an eight-hour day! Sometimes he had to take several trips to make connection with weather that would let his product do anywhere near its best. He had to charge for his work and he was justified in charging for his skill. It took an enthusiast to buy an expensive rifle and give it the most faithful care, for target shooting only.

The firing and the scoring on the small-ringed "German" target were exacting. Sure, there was relaxation, and no hurry at all. A keg of beer was trundled out at most Schuetzenfests—and they *were* festivals in a manner of speaking—and German *Hausfraus* were noted for their cooking. They were noted for their patience, too, these ladies. They stood or sat around watching the game—maybe with half an eye, through boredom—and they constituted the greater part of the gallery at most shoots except the really important ones. Paper-punching isn't sensational to many except those who do it.

---

*He believed that most of them would go under two inches when weather conditions were right.

PICTURE COULD BE BLACKER

But there's good reason to hope and work for wide-spread basic training in marksmanship. Anything beats the casual rattling-out of .22-automatic shots at tin cans, which teaches little and soon looses the grip of its interest. If plinking goes on to lots of firing at moving and tossed targets, where it's safe to do it, the casual shooter in time becomes a fine, deadly snapshot. Even so, he needs the incentive of organized, competitive and publicized shooting.

Yet for effective slow-fire work on difficult and fairly distant targets, sometimes moving, I do think that basic marksmanship training simply can't be dodged. We need to make it more available and more interesting to keep the spur of competition and at the same time to encourage the beginner. Already much is being done. After World War I the Schuetzen game was pretty well out. But lots of veterans and others too became interested in .22 caliber rifle shooting and joined the hard core of enthusiasts. Rifles were made for them, the 52 Winchester, 19 Savage, and others. Remington even fitted the Model 12 slide action with gunsling, Lyman No. 1 rear peep sight adjustable only for elevation, and a "globe" or hooded front with key adjustment for windage. It sold, too, in spite of its takedown construction, curved rifle buttplate, and six-pound weight. Competition then was mostly in the prone position.

The Winchester Junior Rifle Corps went after the youngsters and taught so many that the company was glad to turn the program over to the National Rifle Association, which now has nearly 4,000 active junior clubs. In WJRC we provided the kids with almost anything available, even single shots chambered and bored for .22 extra longs being used with .22 shorts. Now the NRA clubs have some of the finest light and medium weight .22s, and to reach Distinguished rating a kid has to fire 40 targets that would tax the abilities of a good many competent adults.

Four-position shooting came in for adults, and that is practical—and more fun for most people. When you can fire from either sitting, kneeling or standing as the roll of land or the screening of brush demands, you're on the way to becoming an effective rifle-shot. One adult club in Cleveland does nothing but offhand. They're post-graduates. Give them a well balanced hunting or military rifle and make them fire without using the hip-rest position and they'd do all right because they've learned trigger control.

But as time went on, equipment necessary to win or even place in big matches became more expensive. The training needed to learn to get the best out of it became longer and more exacting. That's how we stand today.

Not quite, though. Up in Canada the "sporting rifle" program grew popular several years ago, and it's taking hold here. Rifle weight was limited to seven pounds,* and the exclusion of scopes (of slings, too, at least in the beginning) kept equipment cost democratically low.

Of course you can spend tinkering hours or gunsmith's fees in improving your .22, but the weight limit, even eight pounds in some organizations, makes competition pretty fair. Kids and their mothers take part, and when a sport gets to family level it's based rather solidly.

Most NRA affiliated clubs and nearly all the junior outfits, of course, take advantage of the Army's Office of the Director of Civilian Marksmanship to borrow or purchase supplies, frequently drawing smallbore target rifles, Springfield M-2 (or M-II), Remington 513, Stevens 416, or Winchester 75. To keep these rifles they must fire an annual course which includes rapid fire—"sustained fire," as it's called now. Good psychology, too!

The junior clubs' DCM course is slow fire only, four positions, with a new one for 12- and 13-year-old boys, 40 shots prone. Girls and women don't rate in qualifications the Army sets up, and that is the only General Braddock thought process I can see in the whole fine DCM setup.

Course E for the mature shots takes in rapid, five shots in 40 seconds, a prone and a sitting string, both started from standing. You plump down into position, shove off the safety lock, and commence firing that long after the command or the whistle. Some clubs shoot that part of Course E several times in practice, and most of them need to! It's fun; it's practical; we need more of the same to keep the game alive.

There's no reason why skirmish runs can't be fired with the .22 on safe ranges, and learning to estimate distances and correct our sighting quickly for them is of value too obvious to rate the use of breath or paper.

There could be more interesting targets. Some of us remember the old iron targets with a generous-sized bullseye cut out and backed with a plate that rang cheerfully when smacked by a .22 bullet. Not only shooting gallery operators owned them. There were ringing targets for bigbore black powder rifles, too, with their slow lead bullets that did little harm to thick steel. The running deer plywood silhouettes are splendid, the rising bear also. Bustible and knockdown targets make folks sit up and look. American ingenuity ought to produce if we shooters make the demand, a definite concerted demand.

Yet no matter how appealing the game to contestants and spectators, the shooter still has to start by learning the basics: holding, aiming, and squeezing. If he can't hold steadily he never really knows what a good sight picture is. If he can't squeeze—or press—the trigger correctly he never knows the thrill of making target after target with closely grouped shots. That kind of shooting makes good technique second nature. Then

---

*In 1957 the NRA announced its Light Rifle program: 7-pound rifle (originally not over 8), peep sight allowed, but no sling, palm rest or curved Schuetzen buttplate. Special targets were designed for 50-foot ranges, and qualification scores set up for Marksman, Sharpshooter, and Expert. With club cooperation this program will do a great deal for the shooting game and for national preparedness.

he's ready to become a first-class shot under field conditions, and what he's mastered shouldn't forsake him under stress.

So we come to the question,

WHAT MAKES A GOOD TARGET RIFLE?

In the second chapter we couldn't help saying a good deal about the possibilities of various light .22s in Junior Rifleman marksmanship. We believe in this program, take it altogether seriously in spite of the fact that both quiet amusement and audible, shared laughter season every club meeting. Kids live merrily when they're free to do so, and you give and take with them without relaxing your vigilance, and imparting vigilance to them. So it's a safe program.

Perhaps we'd best revise that question. What makes a good target rifle for what purposes? Classifying target smallbores as light or heavy simplifies matters. The light rifles are the best for most junior training, and they serve well for squirrel or crow hunting. The .22 rimfire's lack of smash, of abundant killing power, isn't so serious when a good shot uses it, provided he's sportsman enough to pass up too difficult chances.

These light rifles are not terribly expensive and there are many of them, both old and new models, that are suitable to use and a pride to own. When we get into the heavy rifle class we pay more, except sometimes for old models or used current types, and unfortunately we are exceptional smallboresmen if we carry one afield more than two or three times a year. Lots of them never see grass or branches bend in the wind, except on a rifle range.

Trigger pull. Even though the range officer or other official weighs trigger pulls only infrequently, perhaps, at matches your club takes part in, no one wants to be disqualified because his rifle's pull is lighter than the three-pound limit set up in the American style of competition. And no one who plays the game like a sportsman wants to get by with an illegal pull.

Most modern target .22s have adjustable pulls, quite easy to set at a safe 3¼ pounds, and others can be gunsmithed to let go at this weight, and the parts hardened against wear. You weigh a trigger pull with one of the officially approved testers, though lacking one you can do well by wiring a holder to the trigger and putting in weights until you hear the click. Be sure that the supporting wires have free play even if you have to remove the stock and trigger guard. The pull should be straight down from the middle of the trigger's curve, from the natural point of finger contact.

A smooth pull that doesn't change its weight from shot to shot, and that stops as soon as the hammer or striker has been released, is the ideal. That unwanted "give" called backlash is practically absent from our best pulls, such as those of the new Remington 40X and the later issues of the Winchester 52 and the discontinued Rem 37. Custom triggers like the Thomas and the Canjar might be called a spur to factory production. All such triggers are a big help to lots of us.

However, perfect release isn't essential to really fine smallbore work. The main thing is to have the pull brittle and clean, without creep. The double-stage pull of a good Springfield, for instance, isn't a serious handicap except in shooting at game. Then, unless we're familiar with it, we tend to pull straight through on a snapshot, and to overshoot. "Take up the slack," as non-coms by the thousand have advised; then go to work on the entirely distinct and clean final pull that a good trigger of this sort gives you.

I really think that too much attention is paid to backlash. We can do *poor* work with any rifle if we divide our attention between looking for trouble and trying to get off a well-pulled shot. I've seen too much good work with clean triggers that had backlash to worry about that detail when I fire a score myself. Your top-flight smallboresman, your arrived or coming champion, usually insists on a perfect trigger—if ever one was made— but this book is written for beginners, too. Actually, your hot-shot could do pretty well with almost any pull: he got up the ladder partly by learning to disregard minor irritations.

Still, if you want to smooth the path to Distinguished Rifleman, and if your present pull doesn't suit you, it might be well to build or buy a trigger stop. A trigger shoe, which widens the area for finger contact, makes a pull seem lighter. Some of us think it gives better command of that tiny curve of steel, almost the most important part of any rifle worth an ammunition bill.

Gun weight and balance. For prone shooting only, the heaviest rifle you can hold steadily through, say, a 40-shot string (plus the sighters) is the thing. You can handle nearly as much weight in sitting, and only a little less in kneeling.

But if you go in for four-position shooting, the kind that helps to make an all-round rifleman, you'll have to learn to hold well in prone with a rifle that seems just a *little* light. Four-position matches usually are won by the best offhand scores, for that position separates the skilled from the pretty darn good. How much weight can you hold steadily for at least 10 shots offhand, and will you use a scope for some matches? If so, figure on another 1 to 2¼ pounds.

Most target rifles balance from about seven to nine inches ahead of the trigger. That is a wide latitude; yet a little either way isn't important. One that teeters at five or six inches ahead of the trigger is muzzle-light for target, though it could be the ideal of a rifleman who went in particularly for running deer matches, snapshooting. You can add muzzle weight by hollowing the buttstock. The forearm or the barrel can be shortened if the gun's too muzzle-heavy to suit you. Some shooters who use very heavy barrels load the hollowed buttstock with lead to get the balance they want. In a way this seems like defeating yourself, though a heavy barrel can and should have slightly more inherent accuracy than a lighter one, other qualities being equal. Certainly it has more practical accuracy, for it's less sensitive to slight changes you might make in your position as you fire a string—even though you know right well you shouldn't—and there's less liability of different firing positions calling for little changes in sight adjustment.

Stocking. The word reminds one of Santa Claus, though an ill-fitting stock is no Christmas present. You want to go to work on it or get a new one.

Target stock length is rather well standardized at about 13¼ inches from the front curve of the trigger to the middle of the buttplate. Sporter length goes about ¼ inch more because a hunting rifle's buttplate is usually much narrower and few of us wear a padded shooting coat afield. Stocks can be as short as 12¾ inches for an adult of small, stocky build, or as long as 15 inches. There's scarcely a limit except the sensible one of good feel. A big pistol grip set close to the trigger makes a stock seem longer, even if the comb is deeply undercut or fluted to let you cross your thumb comfortably over the stock. We need to experiment and do quite a bit of shooting before we settle on stock length. Much can be said for the M-2 Springfield type of buttplate.* It makes shortening the stock easy, or lengthening it with wood or plastic inserts. For that buttplate is flat on the inner side; the shoulder-hugging curve is on the outer side. That rifle has a pretty long stock, and a big stock, too, because the Armory people knew that a rifleman likes to alter an arm to suit him.

I wish I could remember the comment on the wide, flat beavertail forestock that came from an Army officer lecturing at the rifle school at Camp Perry. It was acid. Certainly the b. t. has no place on a rifle for hunting or for war, and if you carry a heavy-barreled piece at trail through rough country you'll want an easily grasped forestock of medium or even small size. Such a rifle balances on that forestock. The beavertail is just one more of those features that distinguish a target arm from a rifle meant for more serious business. Looked at in a hard, practical way, the less difference there is, the better.

But most of us play the target game to win, and win, place, or lose, we learn from it details of mastering the rifle that pay off when or if we have to shoot for keeps. The beavertail makes it easier to avoid rolling or canting the rifle, and it does help remind us to keep that forward hold loose—just cradling the forestock in the relaxed hand. We should hold any rifle like that, except in snapshooting or when we fire offhand without a sling and a crosswind pulls or jabs at the rifle.

Scope blocks. These come ready attached to the barrels of the top grade of target rifles, and the usual positioning is 7.2 inches apart, center to center. Most target scope mounts then give us a minute of angle correction, an inch at 100 yards, a quarter inch at 25, and so on, for each four clicks of windage or

elevation. The new Remington 40X blocks are spaced 10.6 inches on centers, giving one-sixth minute for each click, instead of one-quarter.

It is a regrettable fact that many of us can't bring a scope far enough back on a bolt action with long receiver to let us use the full field of the glass in offhand. Good offhand shooting is done despite this condition. But an additional front block set at six inches on centers gives us almost exactly a minute of correction if we crank off three clicks instead of four. (Windage adjustment may have to be changed, too, from the 7.2 spacing of blocks.)

Maybe a better way, if you need this shorter block distance, is to order one of those 2 1/16 inch-length blocks such as come on Winchester Model 70 .30-06 and .300 Magnum Bull Guns, which give both 7.2 and six-inch spacing. You may need one lower than the block from even the thick-barreled Bull Gun, as a high front block makes us put on more elevation. It raises the sight line, too. Only one new hole, the rear one, needs to be drilled and tapped into the barrel for this long block.

Iron sights. These, like scopes, come in a great variety of choice. On the target .22 it's a great advantage to have them quick-detachable, and of the same height above the axis of the bore as the scope—not just said to be of scope height. You pick the size of aperture in the rear peep and in the front sight too, according to your needs. Your vision matters, of course, and so does the lighting of the target. Not many would dispute the statement that a selection of different-sized apertures for the front sight is more necessary than for the rear. Or maybe most of us are optimists, for the choice of rear apertures runs into a lot more money. Let's not forget, however, that much good shooting is done with a non-aperture front target sight, a plain flat-topped post. You must use it in Army qualifications sponsored by the Director of Civilian Marksmanship. Service shooters stick pretty close to the practical. That doesn't mean that they scorn target aids: remember the Marine sergeant that took his padded shooting coat to Guadalcanal. Such a coat isn't to ease recoil, really; it's to help hold the buttplate in place.

Accuracy. This takes us almost into the realm of the intangible; it's so elusive in even the best rifles. A smallbore or a bigbore may shoot beautifully with a certain make and lot or factory run of ammunition and be durned indifferent to your wishes if you switch to another. Any of the rifles discussed in this chapter should give accuracy that puts 'em in the 10-ring of the Standard American targets at ranges up to 100 yards if everything works right—wind, visibility, ammo, and yourself. About the least inconstant of the lot is ammo; so it pays to try the different kinds and find out. Then we like to stock up on the good lot we've found. Most cartridge cartons, not all, carry a hodge-podge of letters and numerals stamped on them. Except for army lot stuff such as we get from the DCM, that's the factory lot number.

---

*This refers to the NRA type M-2. The type B (service) stock is shorter, has more drop, and is fitted with a thin steel buttplate.

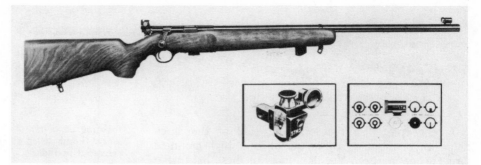

Mossberg 144-LS, showing details of iron sights.

The 144-LS with four-power 4M4 Mossberg scope. Lyman 57 peep has been slid off, out of the way of the scope.

We'll be talking about accuracy throughout this book because that topic goes with any discussion of the rifle.

LIGHT RIFLES

These aren't featherweights, which no serious target shooter wants, anyway, when he's after scores. I've seen girls and boys as young as 14—and a few even younger—do fine prone shooting with nearly all of them. The kids had learned to get that front elbow under the rifle, not offside, and to relax and let gravity steady the gun. For most adults these rifles have the weight needed in offhand, at least when a 1- or 1½-pound scope rides the barrel.

More than any other .22s they are family rifles. There are only about two or three years when a youngster starting to hunt needs a lighter arm. A husky kid in his late teens can use one effectively even for snapshooting: the weight slows the swing, makes him more certain than with a light rifle that bobs around in the excitement of trying to make a difficult shot. This is no endorsement of the .22 rimfire cartridge as a game load except for the most expert. But the sad fact is that .22s outnumber heavier calibers at least 100 to 1 in the small game field. There'll be less crippling, more clean killing, with a reasonably heavy weapon than with a pinweight.

Mossberg 144-LS

Barrel: 26 inches.
Sights: Lyman 57MS micrometer rear and non-detachable 17A front.
Magazine capacity: 7.
Safety: swinging lever at rear of and below the receiver.
Weight: 8 pounds.

Kindly let met get the following paragraph off my chest because so many people think that a good target rifle can't be produced to sell at such a low price as this Mossberg commands.

For two or three years I owned an earlier model of this rifle—just plain 44—and used it steadily on the target range. We had a club in town that met every week for indoor firing, and on the farm I had a 50-yard range about five minutes' walk from the back porch. Nearly every make and style of .22 long-rifle cartridge went through that barrel, and stuff that it liked would shoot well enough to make possibles on the 50-yard target with .89-inch 10-ring. Not many X's, and to clip a .39-inch ring right along needed a better rifle and a much better rifleman. The gun stood up perfectly, and did a little hunting on the side; while the trigger pull never seemed to change weight in all that use.

Since those depression days some changes have been made and today's 144 is a better sighted and more shootable rifle. It still has the reasonably heavy, untapered barrel, the adjustable trigger pull, the Mossberg detachable sling swivels that I, personally, like to leave on and never monkey with, and the big, comfortable grip—not too big, either.

But no longer does it have the slabsided forestock, with much more depth than width, which reduced material costs when every nickel counted. Instead, the stock is a semi-beavertail, about as large as that of the Winchester 75, and there's a hand-stop behind the front sling swivel that you can move back and forth until it butts snugly against your hand. The gun is still a solid frame, with big forestock screw and a barrel band holding wood and steel together.

I do not care for the finger grooves in the lower tang, an extension of the trigger guard, but they fit almost any hand and certainly never bothered me when I was concentrating on a shot let-off. For a while the later rifles were made with a cylindrical bolt handle knob which I thought was pretty ghastly, but the return was made to a round knob, and the rifle is once more a fine one for the smallbore rapid-fire courses we have and hope to have.

Remington 513-T.

A cheekpiece on the left-hand side of the stock helps anyone but a southpaw when a high-mounted target scope goes on. Yet like many of these light rifles it has a stock not really ideal for scope shooting. The comb needs to be raised, not necessarily the heel too, and a Jostam or Stam pad slipped into place will do wonders. A shooter with a full face might not need this buildup. But if our face grows thin and our back teeth drop out, we pretty near surely do! Older models came drilled for scope blocks, which was right. Now there's only receiver grooving for a Tip-Off mount.

As you'd expect in a target arm, the stock is real walnut, and mine worked up into a nice-looking oil-finished job. The grain ran right for accuracy, the forestock wood slanting up diagonally toward the muzzle, though I doubt that this detail is highly important when you're shooting a cartridge of such low pressure as the .22 rimfire.

The Lyman sights issued on the 144-LS aren't of telescope height, and they'd cost more if they were. The 57 rear peep has the usual quarter-minute click adjustments, which are stiff and sharp, unlikely, in fact impossible to be moved except when you or some meddler does so deliberately. Our junior club president and his father came down to the range last night with a brand new 144 rifle, and I looked at the elevation scale plate to see if times had changed. It was just the same: yardage marks were inscribed on the plate, but no minute scale was there. This is a serious omission on a target sight, for it's inconvenient to figure minutes from the yard marks. Target shooters aren't necessarily a lazy tribe—though a certain type of citizen thinks we are—but we do have feelings, too, and like a bit of help along the way. The elevation knob has the three minutes that you get from a complete turn clearly marked, the quarter-minutes, too. Some of the 57 series do carry a minute scale.

I'm glad to report that Bob Wolfe, one of our instructors and the hardest working man in the outfit, fired a five-shot sighting group that would have been a possible if it'd been dropped over the 10-ring. Naturally, we did *not* comment on any drawbacks we found in the rifle—and there was none of importance. The boy and his dad went home happy, and there you have a pair of good Americans.

Remington 513-T

Barrel: 27 inches.
Sights: Redfield extension micrometer peep and target front with 7 interchangeable inserts. Also furnished without sights.

Magazine capacity: 6.
Safety: thumb lever at right rear of bolt handle.
Weight: 9 pounds.

This is one of the latest rifles of its class, although it has been on the market for well over a decade. It was used in military basic training during World War II, and so were the Mossberg 44 U. S., Stevens 416 and Winchester 75. Practically all rifle models that have been available for many years have had various changes made in their styling, equipment or even mechanism. Advertising doesn't always announce these alterations, for obvious reasons.

The 513 is one of the rifles issued to junior and senior cubs by the DCM, altered with a low, ramped front sight of flat-topped post type, and without a hood. The comb is lowered a trifle, too, to bring the shooter's eye down to the sight line. For use with the sights that are standard commercial equipment the factory issue stock is splendid, and only a few of us would find it too low for scope use.

Why this deservedly popular rifle has a six-shot magazine is a mystery. Only five-shot strings are called for in the present rapid-fire courses, and most adult clubs and all NRA Junior clubs insist on single-loading for slow fire. A five-shot mag in this gun would seat completely flush with the lower line of the stock. The magazine release lever is handy, though less so than the side button of the Winchester, it seems to me.

Oddly enough, this rifle is a takedown. One big screw holds stock and steel together; there's no barrel band, which, of course, *could* interfere with barrel vibrations. The gun averages as fine accuracy as others of the class. My friend Frank Sheary used one for years, doing well in state and regional matches with it. Sometimes he considered installing another stock screw, but he never got around to it—bought a Model 37 Remington instead. He might not have gained by such gunsmithing. Remington calls the barrel "semi-floating," as good a description as any.

It's a good barrel. The weight helps a shooter who can handle it, and I remember seeing a little thirteen-year-old girl show all the boys how to shoot it in a junior match one evening. The firing was in prone, and she put her elbow under the big, wide beavertail forestock and let the 513's own weight steady it.

This barrel, like the Mossberg's, appears to be absolutely without taper. With the long forestocks the general effect isn't at all bad-looking. The pistol grip's curve comes close to the trigger guard, as so many shooters like it. Stock lines are far from beautiful, but for most people the stock is a shootable one.

Ignition is fast and the trigger pull good, with little backlash. For rapid fire the rake-back of the bolt handle is excellent: you find the knob just where you expect it, and fast.

Only in offhand is the weight of this rifle, balanced so far forward, excessive for lots of junior shooters. For that position I've seen many of them shift to a Winchester 75, though some were rash enough to try a 5½- or 6-pound sporter. Big, husky youngsters handle the 513 well. It's a good rifle for the adult beginner who isn't yet sold on target punching as a lifetime hobby. So our job is to encourage him to make the most of what he has, let him use our own when he wants to, and bring him along so fast that in a year or so he'll be asking us seriously, "What do the best match rifles cost, and what do you think's the best one?" By that time we've almost snared him as a lifer.

The front sling swivel is adjustable for position, and like that of the Winchester 75 it hangs down far enough to let you shoot the rifle prone with considerable comfort even if you don't use a glove or a handstop. Most champion shooters use both, of course.

The barrel is a little unusual in having a countersunk muzzle, one of the things that Remington believes in for a target rifle. This offers some protection and may improve accuracy. Winchester designers like the flat, not counterbored muzzle for bullseye guns. This has been standard on the heavier Model 52 barrels, and lately the lighter weight has come out in this style. For some 30 years it had the gentle counterbore or crown of the old and respected .22 single-shot musket barrel, which it parallels in weight and contour.

Remington's 521-TL target rifle for the early-teeners is described in the chapter preceding this one. It is not the arm for the serious target shot who can handle a heavier one, though it makes a good supplement to a family battery since it has so many uses. If our rifle-shooting game is pepped up and popularized as it ought to be, it should take care of still more needs.

Springfield M-2

Barrel: 24 inches.

Sights: Lyman 48 micrometer peep mounted on *right-hand* rear of receiver; narrow, flat-topped post front without hood, although a front sight cover can be used as hood.

Magazine capacity: 5.

Safety: Mauser wing type at rear of bolt.

Weight: about 9 pounds, 6 ounces without Army sling, which adds approximately ½ pound.

Try to make a hot competitor fire a match with an M-2 Springfield and most likely he'll raise hell and drag it across the grass. "It's muzzle-light. The gun isn't stocked for a scope. Its trigger pull stinks. Why, the thing isn't even accurate!"

The guy may be a high-scorer in the modern smallbore game, but he doesn't know the score about rifles. The M-2 (or M-II) is a *practical* rifle.*

Ordnance developed it from the M-1, many of which are still around and justly prized by their owners, to whet up marksmanship in the Service and among civilians, too, who were wise and willing enough to learn battlefield—and game field—techniques. And Ordnance was smart in making it an attractive-looking rifle. It resembles the NRA Springfield Sporter, caliber .30-06, that with slightly heavier barrel than the Service rifle, a higher comb, bigger buttstock and larger buttplate, was made for civilians to buy through the DCM—when it was still available.

So the M-2 is a perfect understudy .22 for heavy, bigbore custom sporters of about its weight and balance. True, its bolt has a short throw, much like that of the 52 Winchester, and seemingly that wouldn't be so good in an understudy to a .30-06, say, or maybe a magnum Mauser with really long bolt travel. But the hardest things to master—so at least it seems to me—are the first upward wrench and final slap-down of the bolt handle. The straight back-and-forth slide is easy, even from the shoulder.

These M-2s aren't outdated. Many are still out on loan to rifle clubs, and many are privately owned—and not easy to buy. They give excellent training as well as satisfaction that is hard to measure. The M-2 was the Army's final development of a bolt-action .22 training rifle; it came a long way.

Back in 1915 our school formed a rifle club, and the sergeant who coached us each week would bring along two or three Springfield .22s. They looked like the Type S .30 unless you took a cautious sidelong glance at the muzzle. The barrel of this model was bored and rifled for .22 short, chambered for a steel cartridge holder of .30-06 length, which could be clip-loaded like a caliber .30 round. It took some time to pull empties and reload five holders, but we had time then: our entry into the war was two years away. Lots of time, oh sure!

In ejecting those holders you had to be careful not to dent their muzzles. The .22 short bullet took a long jump through the smoothbored tube before it hit the rifling, and the best accuracy wasn't tackhole. Still, I wonder if any of us knew the difference, for organized smallbore shooting was a scarce thing. The sergeant did teach us position, sling, aim, squeeze, everything in the basics. One day we even went to a National Guard range and were given .30-40 Krag firing. That was the first and only time I ever saw a Krag with a cracked bolt lug, and even now they are not common.

Let's consider those objections to a much better .22 trainer, the M-2. Muzzle-light. Yes, it is, for prone specialists. But four-position shooters average well with it in iron-sight matches, and they *can* fire in the

---

*The M-II is a modernized M-I, with M-2 bolt and magazine assembly. Stock may be either Service or NRA type.

practical Army offhand, elbow clear of the ribs, without the long training needed to shoot a heavy barreled rifle in that way.

Stock? It fits most people well for iron-sight work, wasn't made for scope. If it's too long, no great skill is needed to shorten it. The face of the buttplate that touches the wood is straight, not curved for grace and charm. The shoulder-hugging curve is on the other face. Yes, it's a thick, heavy steel buttplate, takes a lot of grinding and filing to dress it down. What's wrong with a Mershon plate for target shooting, though? That thin rubber pad is easy to fit down with a file.

Pull? Durn few M-2s left the Armory with a poor one. There's the military takeup or slack, but then comes a clean release, not adjustable for weight by turning a simple screw, but usable and practical as it is.

Accuracy? I doubt that enough smallboresmen have tried to really find out. It just isn't styled as a match rifle. Of course it'll shoot possibles right along. Tom Florich's NRA or DCM .30-06 sporter came with a 200-meter test target showing five shots in one and five-sixteenth inches. No doubt Frankford Arsenal ammo of match grade was used. The .22 barrel is heavier—less steel is bored out of it—but modern rimfire ammunition won't shoot with the best of centerfires. Still, the Armory knows how to make rifles, don't you think? Pressed for an opinion, driven down to hard facts, I'd say I felt sure that the M-2 is the most accurate arm described in this section on "light rifles."*

There's quality throughout, at least in all I've used or seen. The slide of the bolt is a dream of smoothness, to mention just one item. The gun was a bargain because it *had* to be good, or else, and because no advertising costs went into the figure of what you paid for it. Now you look hard to find one, in the personal ads in *The American Rifleman, Precision Shooting, Shotgun News,* and so forth. Just to see one and fire a string with it is a privilege.

It was one of the earliest .22s to have a speed lock. The striker fall is much shorter than those of the Service .30 and the M-1 smallbore. Furthermore, safety was considered in designing that lock. The head of the cocking piece is so wide that it acts as a shield in the event of a case-burst.

Picture a late summer day in the North Carolina mountains, a jewel of a day, and a crowd of kids who'd been patient all through six weeks of dry train-

ing in the gym while waiting for a range to be made available to them. And on the first relay, too, I think it happened. The twelve-year-old girl with the M-2 was startled, not really scared, and best of all, not hurt. When the war-surplus case let go, the magazine was blown out and her forearm was singed. But no brass fragments, powder grains or oil came back into her freckled face. She went right along and made some good scores that day. After this the kids had to wear long sleeves—they'd been wearing shooting specs already—though as it happened we never had another case rupture during the time I stayed in that part of the country.

Winchester 75

Barrel: 28 inches.
Sights: Redfield extension 75 micrometer rear peep; Winchester 105-A hooded front with 1 post and 3 apertures. Also available without sights.
Magazine capacity: 5. A 10-shot magaine is offered and a single-loading adapter now comes regularly with the rifle.
Safety: thumb lever at right rear of receiver. When on, it locks action shut.
Weight: 8 pounds, 10 ounces.

Having been around for some 20 years, the 75 has gone through changes. The first sights were Winchester-made, though Lyman and Redfield designs came along soon. The new Winchester front is much sturdier and a whole lot better looking than the original pressed steel issue; perfectly adequate, I think.

The DCM issues of 75 generally have the stock comb lowered for use with the low, unhooded post front sight supplied on these special jobs. On late commercial 75s the bolt handle slants back rakishly, handier for rapid fire or even single loading, and easier to look at, some would say. In early years an inexpensive little Winchester eight-power scope was available for this model and others, but stock dimensions listed in the first folder are the same as those of today.

The stock fits most shooters well, and the iron sights are so high that when you detach them and put on a target scope you notice little difference in the fit. In curve of pistol grip the stock hits a useful medium, neither too abrupt for offhand target work or even snapshooting afield, nor too far back for control in prone.

It seems to me that the weight distribution of the 75 is a bit unusual, for the gun feels lighter than it is and yet balances well ahead of the trigger. Barrel taper was neatly worked out. In prone most shooters do better with a Remington 513. The 75 is more strictly a junior's gun (middle teen-age) and a hunting rifle too, within the limits of the power of the cartridge. These are personal opinions. If you see more 75s than 513s around this doesn't mean that the former are superior. They had a running start, were on hand several years earlier.

The 75's forestock is narrower than the 513's, its

---

*Sample accuracy. An M-II with the Type B service stock and a slight bulge in the bore, about a foot from the chamber, and that chamber had been lengthened (I don't know why) so much that it would actually take a .22 extra long without marring the bullet. From rest it made 5-shot, 50-yard verticals under ½ inch. Wind spread some horizontals, but we got some 17/32-inch overall groups. Springfield people understand bedding steel into wood. Ammo was fresh long-rifle standard and some stale long-rifle match.

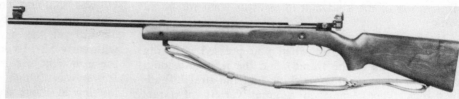

Winchester 75 target rifle.

pistol grip smaller, and the lower line of its buttstock is more in sporter than in target style. Wood is attached firmly to steel by a stock screw and by a barrel band up near the forestock tip. Tension of the barrel band is adjustable, but most shooters turn it tight and leave it so. This was the original factory recommendation, though it does no harm to experiment. The placement of the front sling swivel is adjustable to a shooter's reach, and the swivel hangs low enough to prevent pinching the hand.

Like nearly all target .22s now made, the 75 has adjustable trigger pull—adjustable for weight, that is. There is no adjustment for over-travel—backlash after the sear has tripped the striker—as on the late 52s.

Here we have the only serious fault of the 75. True, late models don't have quite as long over-travel as early ones had, but the matter hasn't been corrected. If a shooter is looking for trouble he can be obliged by this trigger. A stop could be built in, but it should be easily removable or thrown out of gear if the owner wants to clean his rifle occasionally. It is certainly best to clean from the breech, and the 75 trigger, like so many others, acts as the bolt stop. You pull it back to remove the bolt.

The bolt of this rifle is closed at the rear, unlike those of the Remington 513, Winchester 52 and many others. No striker tip protrudes when it's cocked, giving us warning. However, unless the 75 striker is cocked we can't draw the safety back to locked position. In a target rifle this matter is not important, for on the range all bolts must be open except on the firing line, and then too, before "Load" has sounded, and after "Cease Firing." If the "hammerless" bolt of the 75 looks reassuring against possible blowbacks from burst cartridge brass, don't put too much faith in it. Almost any bolt action or hammer rifle, and some of true hammerless design, can fail to save you from a plastering if brass lets go. Wear shooting glasses.

Many of our .22s have but one locking lug, the root of the bolt handle, and the 75 is one of them. Although there's no worry as to the safety of such an arm, thoroughly tested before it leaves a reputable factory, there could be a theoretical objection when the rifle is for target use. Is the breech-up snug enough to help deliver fine accuracy? Snugness means lack of end-play as well as breech-up, and the extremely short, compact 75 bolt, adding not much more to the gun's overall length than a single shot action would,

is well known for its relative freedom from such play. Double locking lugs are fine, but to contribute to *supreme* accuracy they should approach perfection in alignment. This takes time, and time costs money.

The two strong survivals in .22s of this class and weight are moderately priced, though they certainly may not seem so to a youngster, who is our shooting game's hope of survival. Slight differences in accuracy lie more in individual rifles than in the makes. You base your choice on weight, balance, fit, action, and brand name appeal.

Old Rifles

Many are available as used guns in excellent shape. Time and again a good-sized section of the shooting public has been annoyed when a favorite model went off the market because not enough thousands could be sold per year. You will find plenty of admiration for these orphans, and good service in many of them. Stock fit as issued may be hopeless for scope shooting, but quite all right for the use of irons. Inside and out, the quality of finish may astonish you unless you're a sophisticated antiquarian!

Stevens. First place goes to the Stevens 416 because it was discontinued only rather lately and hundreds of them are still serving junior and senior clubs. A rather heavy 26-inch barrel, long action, and husky semi-beavertail stock bring weight to nine pounds, or 9½ including the sling furnished with the rifle. Adjustable trigger pull and low lift of bolt handle to clear a target scope are modern features. The only criticisms point to the closeness of the front sling swivel to forestock wood, making a shooting glove almost essential to 'way-out-front holding, and the location of the bolt handle far ahead of the trigger guard, unhandy in rapid fire and even in slow. Like other rifles in this class, it had screwholes ready drilled and tapped into its barrel, and the target scope blocks themselves were standard issue on some 416s, it seems.

Perhaps if the handy Savage Model 23-AA action had been used on a revised 416 we'd now have more than two competitive rifle makes in this particular corral. Savage did make several models of target .22s, most of them, however, with barrels less heavy than that of this Stevens. Only a few other alterations would be required in modernizing the 416, such as raising the stock comb for use with a scope, mounting irons higher than the Stevens 106 peep and hooded 25 front, and tacking on a better front sling swivel. The heel of the 416 is already high, making a nice straight job of the kind that most of us want for target work.

Heavy Stevens single shots with breakdown action (the barrel tipped down when you pressed a button on the left side of the frame) and the later and long-continued Ideal actions (rocking and fall-straight-and-then-rock types) came in a great variety of target styles, and a lot of them were for the .22 long-rifle cartridge. Harry Pope, the great offhand shooter and supreme barrel-maker, worked at the plant for a time and helped make the Schuetzen-style Stevens with palm rest a famous contender. There was a .22 Stevens-Pope Armory load, the .22 long-rifle with bullet of special contour.

Later, when four-position shooting had begun to replace the Schuetzen game, came the 414 and 404 rifles, .22 short or .22 l-r, of about eight pounds' weight with sling. Both had shotgun butts, flat, not curved and arm-gripping like the Schuetzen, the 404 carrying a buttplate of hard rubber instead of steel, though styling was less rigid then than now. The 404 was a fancy model. It had a large, English-style fore-stock just a foot long and nicely checkered, though the straight-grip stock was smooth. So the front sling swivel—no rear one was attached, as a rule—had to be set into the barrel ahead of the forestock, which would give contemporary shooters some reasons for vast contempt. The 414 somewhat resembled the much heavier Winchester .22 musket, as its forestock reached nearly to the muzzle. Just behind the front swivel, though, it swelled into a semi-beavertail, and no doubt street-corner loafers often asked, "Is that a pump gun you got there?" A rear swivel made the 414 useful in the hunting field. In its day it was a rather sharp little all-round .22. The action was the rocking-block 44, whereas the 404 employed the 44½ type—sometimes, anyway. That breechblock falls straight for a short distance before it rocks back to open.

The Stevens single-shot lever gun hung on until about the outbreak of World War II, and some fine, useful specimens were made in modern style. The boys'-size 418 and 418½ were well stocked for iron sights, well sighted, too, and an Army style sling and semi-beavertail forearm were standard equipment. With two-way adjustable Lyman peep on the tang the 418 was a splendid training rifle of about 6½ pounds. The 418½ was for hunting. It carried a Lyman peep without windage, a gold bead front, and it came in .22 W. R. F. and .25 Stevens rimfire as well as .22 long-rifle. The eight-pound 417½ was perhaps the best standard factory rifle ever offered for small game hunting. It offered the 418½ calibers, had a similar front sight and a two-way 103 rear, and of course a sling. Though the stock is low for a target scope, it was a good match rifle in other respects, of light weight for an adult.

Savage. From 1919 until the 1930s, Savage .22s were keen contenders in match rifle production. The 19 was the first commonly seen bolt action of the type because it cost so much less than the Winchester 52 and yet was a pretty darn good score-maker. As with early 52s, its stock comb was barely high enough for iron-sight use in the techniques we follow today. But it was a businesslike target arm, rather unusual looking in those days, with long, military-style fore-stock, high, sharply cut post front sight, and a tall, two-way rear peep of Savage design.

Savages went through several model variations, one much liked being the 19-NRA that began with serial number 25,000. Barrels got heavier, stock combs rose and grew fat. Many of these late rifles do well today with either iron or glass sights. A special heavy model went over nine pounds, and on the Model 1923 action there was built a target or varmint shooting .22 Hornet centerfire of about that weight. None of them was expensive, and that fact was favorable to rifle shooting in America.

Winchester. Winchester lever-action single shots came in target styles, from the 12- and 13-pound Schuetzen models in .22 caliber and up, to the popular 8½-pound .22 short or .22 long-rifle muskets. Most Schuetzen rifles used the heavy high-wall action, and early muskets did, too. Later a *special* low-wall action went on the musket, beveled like the common high-wall but cut away to make loading small, greasy cartridges much easier.

It would be hard to estimate how many Winchesters, including the light, perfectly flat receivered, true low walls, have been made into smallbore target rifles by professional and amateur gunsmiths. Range of weight and styling even of factory pieces was enormous. Despite minor drawbacks the action has been—and by some of us still is—extremely well thought of. If the hammer fall is slow for match use it can be speeded up by lightening it, cutting a new full cock notch to shorten its travel, and by grinding away the lower section where the half-cock notch belongs. The narrow upper and lower tangs of the receiver grip the stock less securely—some chance for vibration—than the long, heavy rear extension of the Ballard, and there's some liability of their splitting the stock unless you keep the two receiver screws tight to hold the lower tang in place. So what? Free the contact where it's necessary and run a bolt up through the stock into a steel block set between the two tangs. As a matter of fact, most Winchesters as issued give no trouble if the shooter gives them normally good care.

Muskets are scarce now. Some have been shot out, many more ruined by neglect, and lots of the good barrels left have been rechambered to Hornet, even the .22 shorts, which can do fairly well with a 35-grain Hornet pill in spite of their slow rifling twist. The soft steel barrels weren't meant to take such velocities, but the Hornet cartridge simply bowled over the rifle-man's world when it appeared, and we're human. Most of us wanted one of those new .22 centerfires mighty bad, and a slew of us were short of cash in depression days.

Muskets have low combs, their hammer fall is slow, and some find it awkward to throw the lever down when they shoot in prone. But one in good condition makes a fine medium-weight rifle if you build up the comb and fit good adjustable sights. If it's somewhat of a museum piece it's still safe to use provided you treat it right. A strong selling point of the early 52 bolt action was that its barrel was the same as that of the musket. Right there was a ready-made reputation for accuracy, you know.

Harrington & Richardson. For some time after World War II the Harrington & Richardson match rifles were available. The nine-pound 465 mounted a heavy 23-inch barrel and presumably was made for junior shooters, although the long 10-shot clip magazine would have been ruled out in the NRA program. A two-way adjustable Lyman 57 E receiver sight and a ramped post or "blade" front were aiming equipment; and the thick stock comb, though a bit low for scope use, wouldn't have been by any means hopeless for such shooting. It was a mistake, though not a serious one, to issue a web instead of a leather sling with the rifle. A spring type bolt release was handier than that of the H. & R. Medalist model. To prepare to clean that one from the breech you have to loosen a coin-slotted bolt stop screw.

In other ways the Medalist is a better match rifle. A 26-inch barrel gives steadier balance, and a nearly flush magazine makes for attractive appearance. One I used had a Lyman 524 extension receiver peep, adjustable for distance from the eye, and a hooded front sight to give choice of post and aperture inserts. This rifle balanced well, and the rather low position of its pistol grip under a sharply cut-away comb didn't bother me at all. It was a good iron-sight rifle, but neither of those H. & R.s was able to compete in price and ready availability with Remington 513 and Winchester 75 match .22s.

A .22 Short Training Rifle?

In this weight of about nine pounds or a bit less, or in six- to seven-pound trainers, it seems to my unsophisticated mind that there's need for a .22 short weapon. With short chamber and rifling twist of from 20 to 24 inches' complete turn it would give accuracy enough to make 10s on the 50-foot target more than accidental, and the 9-ring couldn't take out any life insurance at all. In match rifles chambered and bored with the usual 16-inch long-rifle twist you can generally keep all shots at least nipping the 8-ring, though the quality of short ammunition, *as now made,* does vary a little. It's used almost entirely for plinking and commercial shooting-gallery supply—though some kids who think they can't afford better hunt with it—and there's no popular demand to make it accurate.

In heavy-barrel Schuetzen rifles it used to be popular for indoor use, to keep your hand in, and good work was done with it up to 75 feet. As far as I know, there was no premium-priced match ammunition. The old U. S. Cartridge Company's "Boy Scout" designation was a trade name. I've seen this make of short with flat-pointed bullet but presume it was for hunting more than for target. It wasn't a wadcutter point, full enough to punch clean round roles in the target.

Modern shorts, especially the low velocity kind, shoot well in a rifle made for them, but what have we left to choose from? About the only rifles made for shorts are the Winchester 62 hammer repeater and the Remington 550-2G autoloader, both on special order and neither one a target arm.

This editorial merely suggests: the writer did not take his shirt off and sweat while composing it. Its point is that too many of our little guys and little girls are having their firing rationed by the cost of .22 long-rifle ammo. Yes, even when it comes from the DCM. To get more shooting, many of them right now are firing over-stabilized short bullets that spin madly from a 16-inch twist.

Gun companies make money from .22 rifles, and chambering and rifling nearly all of them for the 1-r cartridge cuts production costs. A dividend of low- and moderately-priced .22 short target rifles would be appreciated. If the objection is that not one young shooter in a hundred fires in NRA programs the answer is obvious. The kids are available; why aren't we? Organizers and instructors are scarce, the reason being indifference.

HEAVY RIFLES

It's a common saying that only the Winchester and Remington heavy models have a look-in when adult shooters gather for hot competition. That isn't quite true, but it's near enough to the truth to be a bit discouraging. Still, these two companies are right on the ball when incorporating alterations and improvements, and in struggling to perfect match ammunition. In both respects, notably in the matter of ammunition, they are handicapped by limitations of retail price.

It seems possible that .22 long-rifle cartridges could be fashioned to compete almost with centerfire bench-rest loads up to 100 yards on a windless day. This would require substitution of many hand- for machine-performed operations, exacting tests and inspections of components and of the final, marketable product. What it would cost I don't know; more than a nickel a round, I'd guess. Meanwhile, this matter is in the day-dream stage and likely to stay there a while. At least one factory has tried it experimentally. Results: "You can't get out of the X-ring," one rifleman told me.

The big rifles have to be expensive, so much care is spent on their manufacture and testing before they leave the factories. Little niceties go into their completion at the plants—excellent triggers, scope blocks ready installed, actions smoothed, stocks carefully bedded, and so on. Usually they're equipped with iron sights that cost more than a rather nice plinking rifle, complete. The ambitious target shot wants a rifle of this quality much sooner than later, but he may be somewhat appalled at the price. If he buys a new rifle, not a used one, he can cut cost by ordering it without iron sights and use a scope if he has it. Or he can buy a good target front sight with inserts and an inexpensive but serviceable receiver peep—for some of these rifles, at least—at less than half the price of the most expensive and of course helpful combinations regularly listed by the maker of the rifle. An extension peep would come nearer his eye and give some advantage, especially in prone, and a shaded front is good indoors as well as out under the sun. Yet he can wait for these aids without having to wait to get into the game with a mighty good rifle.

Remington 37 Rangemaster

Barrel: 28 inches.
Sights: various combinations. Rifle also came without sights.
Magazine capacity: 5. Single loading platform also was furnished.
Safety: wing type at rear of bolt cylinder.
Weight: 12 pounds.

Though discontinued in 1955, the 37 has been so popular that thousands are in active service, and once in a while you get a chance to buy a used one. In its long history there have been slight modifications from time to time, such as the "miracle trigger" that seems to have no rearward motion after the striker has been released. Any Model 37 is essentially modern and efficient for target shooting. In the last variant of all, the "small" of the stock is so big and high that if you're a thumb-crosser the extended rear sight practically scrapes that digit. For a time this was a popular form of stocking for prone, and some shooters like it in any position. Others never did, but we can buy sandpaper and linseed oil, and a home-finished stock gives a lot of satisfaction to many of us. Sure, a lacquered factory stock is more damp-proof than an oiled one, but we take care of our rifles and watch for any shift in bullet impact. Most well stocked guns hold their zero, anyway.

The 37 never was offered—regularly, at least—in anything except the standard heavy weight, which most shooters want, even for offhand, after some training and conditioning. The long action is heavy, smooth to operate, and fast enough for rapid fire interludes because its bolt handle is slanted back correctly.

Remington at first put on their own sights, and the receiver peep with six-hole eyepiece was a good one. Then extension sights with adjustable positioning became popular, and Lyman, Redfield, Marble-Goss, and other makes went on, and long, shaded-aperture front sights, too. Scope blocks on the barrel were standard issue, and always the 37 was stocked for scope use. Its detachable iron sights were of scope height, or practically so.

Ignition by the speed lock is fast and the trigger pull is adjustable. It wears well. So does the specially heat-treated bolt action. This rifle was built, like all of its class, to give faithful service through many, many thousands of rounds.

Even the box magazine is of heavy construction, not made of thin stampings. As far as I know, the 37 was the rifle that introduced the single-loading adapter. Now the use of this convenience is almost universal on the target range. Not quite, though. A few of us still prefer to start each round carefully into the chamber. Time is not of the essence in slow fire unless there's a plaguy wind which lets down now and then. At such intervals there's good sense in stepping up the firing rate a little.

You seldom see a shooter kissing the bullets, nowadays. That moistening with saliva was considered a good thing when Lesmok and other semi-smokeless powders were used, though they did burn cleanly except on hot, dry days. However, a little devotional exercise of this sort helped to keep us calm in sharp competition, even if we felt it was next door to useless in a practical way.

Remington 40X Rangemaster

Barrel: 28 inches.
Weight: heavy barrel rifle, 12 pounds, 12 ounces with Redfield Olympic front and rear sights; standard barrel rifle with Redfields, 10 pounds, 12 ounces. These sights weigh 12 ounces, and rifles may be ordered without sights. Scope blocks are 10.6 inches apart, on centers, instead of the standard 7.2 inches, and each click of the usual scope mounts gives 1/6 inch correction at 100 yards instead of the usual 1/4 inch. Receiver ring is drilled for a block to give 7.2-inch spacing.
Magazine capacity: none. This is a single shot rifle with built-in single-loading cartridge tray.
Safety: thumb lever at right rear of receiver.

Many Model 37 owners must wonder why Remington ditched that rifle in 1955 and brought out an entirely different top-grade target .22. It was, of course, expensive to manufacture. For some time the company has been giving a certain similarity to its line, the "matched set" idea. In smallbore and high-power sporting rifles, in shotguns too, Remington finally brought out by mid-1957 *generally* similar appearing models in both pump and autoloading styles. This makes for more economical manufacture. The 40X receiver is much like that of the 722 bolt-action high power, some action parts are similar, and others so much alike as to simplify production.

But there are new features in the 40X. The bedding device, "tuning screws" near the forestock tip, are called new. They are different, of course, though the Winchester 52 heavy-barrel rifle had opposing forestock screws, adjustable, before the "straight pull-down barrel band" was latched on to all 52s except the little sporter. Pull or push, the idea is to be able to adjust contact up front.

On the 40X these bedding screws click as you turn them in making adjustments of wood-and-steel contact. You can record the settings and it really pays to ex-

Remington 40X Rangemaster
with heavy barrel.

The 40X with standard-weight
barrel.

periment and find the best for each lot of match ammunition you use. To get the first contact with the barrel you use a flashlight circuit to inform you, to "say when"—the electric bedding system that is so carefully gunsmithed into many custom-grade match rifles. Or you can use cellophane to note the first contact. And some shooters prefer to have no contact at all.

Three stock screws (or "bolts") give secure anchorage of steel and wood. Then, to avoid possibility of long-continued recoil, tapping away for thousands of shots, setting the steel back into the stock, there's a wide, square recoil lug plate held between barrel and receiver, and inletted into the stock wood.

The positioning of 40X scope blocks is new on an American factory rifle, and it should please a lot of the best shots. The single-shot action is an idea taken from the bench-rest shooters, whose custom rifles often have no magazine-well to detract from the rigidity of even the heavy stocks they favor.

Who wants a magazine in a .22 match rifle, anyway, except the folks who think that an occasional string of rapid fire is sensible recreation? It's practical, you know, though the slow-fire belly-shooter who pegs away constantly in prone isn't interested in it unless he happens to be a bigbore shooter, too, or a hunter, or a potential minute-man in national defense.

In fairness to the prone purist I must admit that he keeps the rifle and ammunition manufacturers on their tiptoes, that he appreciates making every shot count, and that if there were serious need he'd be a most deadly sniper under almost any conditions. He's learned self-control, and he could do all right with any good rifle.

But that no-magazine feature will help to sell 40X rifles, and why not? All of us know that it takes all of us, specialists as well as all-round shots, to keep civilian firearms banging away in America. "Nation of riflemen?" You bet we work for it.

The front sling swivel is adjustable for hand-reach, and there's more yet. You can move the angle of the swivel to make the pull-direction of your sling comfortable—to left or right—and it stays put. There's no rear swivel issued at present. For prone, sit and kneel you use the loop sling, and the tail-piece of the sling is a nuisance. Why have one, or a swivel to thread it through? "Why" is right, for most small-boresmen who used to wrap up in the hasty sling for offhand, if they used leather at all in that position, now prefer the loop, and it's allowed under present ruling when we shoot in NRA offhand position. The hasty sling is practical, for it's the sling in handy shoulder-carry length, and within its limits of comfort and security it's helpful in steady holding. But this 40X rifle is for target purists.

The action is of hardened alloy steel, as we'd expect, and the barrel is of ordnance steel, like that used in high-power rifles. It is button-rifled, the grooves pressed in rather than cut out, a process perfected (or darn near made perfect) in wartime production. On this rifle it's no economy measure.

Of course there's nothing soft or punky about Winchester Proof Steel barrels that go on modern 52s. In the past the New Haven company offered nickel steel and also rust-resistant Staynless steel at extra cost in 52 barrels—and in others, too. There was some difficulty in rifling the old-time Staynless as accurately as is desirable, and it was not regularly on the market for long.

The trigger pull is adjustable for weight, like that of the Remington 722 high power, except that the screw you turn is in plain sight—no need to remove the stock to get at it. It clicks, and you're told to figure on getting about ¼-pound change each time it sounds off. Trigger movement is adjustable as on the new 52 Winchesters, though to get at this screw you must remove the Remington stock. Then, to avoid loosening, you should seal the screw with cement. It's stated that you can get a minimum of five to seven thousandths of an inch travel. Striker fall is short in rifles of this class, about .225 inch on the new Remington.

The lugs of the two-piece 40X bolt—the front section doesn't turn, of course—are located at the middle of the receiver, not 'way back, and this is an improvement in smallbore target-punchers, though the Spring-

Standard-weight-barrel 52 Winchester with Redfield Olympic rear and front sights.

field .22 doesn't lock clear back where your trigger finger lies. Front locking is out, for loading across the lug-well in the receiver ring would be too difficult with a .22 rimfire. Adding to stiffness is the high left-hand wall of the receiver.

Something else new in a modern match rifle is the look of the stock. It really isn't homely! Though the pistol grip is close-up and the comb is high and full, the cutting away of some unnecessary wood has produced almost sporter streamlining. The Mershon butt-plate of soft rubber is welcome equipment. It makes stock shortening or lengthening a down-cellar job, whereas a steel plate, curved on the inner surface, sometimes calls for a trip to the gunsmith.

Quite a lot is made of the "new barrel profile," and the 40X does shoot well. The theory and no doubt the practice of this contouring are fine, but I'm reminded of a medium power .22 hot-shot, Hornet or Lovell probably, that was one of the favorite groupers of a rifleman and experimenter you've all heard of. The little black hole at its muzzle was decidedly off-center, and not by intent, either. In theory that was pretty sad; in practice it shot where it looked, time after time, and it could be relied on!

Winchester 52

Barrel: 28 inches.
Weight: standard, 9¾ pounds; heavy, 11 pounds; Bull Gun, 12 pounds. Weights of gunsling and sights are not included.
Sights: various combinations offered, available in telescope height. Rifle can be ordered without sights.
Magazine capacity: 5 Single-loading adapter is furnished and 10-shot magazine is offered as an extra.
Safety: thumb lever at right of receiver, just ahead of bolt handle, locks trigger and sear and holds bolt shut.

Since 1920 the 52 has gone through many changes. It was wise never to change the model number, for in the minds of most marksmen the name *52* rings a bell, just as the name *48* does when iron sights are mentioned.

The earliest 52s had Winchester-made sights—at least no other name went on them—and they were a post front and a Springfield-type "ladder" peep that folded down on the receiver. There were no scope blocks. Both .22 short and .22 long-rifle calibers were offered, for the little fellow was still popular for 50- and 75-foot shooting. A special blocked-off, five-shot magazine fed the shorts. By modern and correct marksmanship standards the comb of the stock was excessively low, even for iron-sight work. The forestock was rather narrow, about like that of the 1903 Springfield service rifle.

This rifle had the "slow lock." Its striker travel was long, and a good-sized cocking piece for thumb and finger grip delayed ignition enough to be hacksawed off by some shooters whose thinking was in advance of the time. The wing safety was like that of the 03 rifle except that it had no intermediate position. Straight up, it locked striker and bolt; turned to the left, it let go both holds. After a few years the speed lock came along, also the adjustable trigger pull, and meanwhile the stock approached modern standards— maybe helped to develop them.

Although lots of these early 52s are doing good work, and many of them with their original barrels, a word of caution is needed. When trigger pulls have been worn or set below the three-pound minimum allowed in matches where our Standard American targets are official, there is sometimes danger of the rifle's firing if the safety is snapped off suddenly.

The 52B model can be recognized by the thumb-lever safety on the right of the receiver, as on the current 52C, and by the speed-lock, adjustable trigger pull, and the *B* at the end of the serial number. It should be a long time before 52Bs are scarce at important tournaments.

Many consider the 52C's "micro-motion" trigger as good as any, factory or custom made. The face of it is wide, like that of the new Remington 40X, and few shooters would feel that they needed to put a metal shoe on it to give better control and make the pull seem lighter. It has a slight lateral motion which might, I should guess, annoy some of the most punctilious smallboresmen. Being only a rather punk shot, I've decided to turn to plinking if and when this gentle seesaw throws me. I can't notice it when I fire, and I can't notice any backlash in this trigger, either. If I cared to turn the adjusting screw to put a bit of "overtravel" in the trigger, I'd get busy with a screwdriver. This screw, and the one that regulates weight of pull, show on the bottom of what we'd call the magazine floor-plate of a Mauser-type high power.

The adjustment screw that lies ahead of these two (toward the muzzle) regulates the trigger lever and rocker, and it is hidden away under the floorplate or trigger guard extension. It is set as it should be at the factory, and only a person with real gunsmithing ability should try to change it. The trigger mechanism is protected by a metal housing and never should be lubricated. The parts are machined and honed precisely, and hard chrome plated. When you clean the bore there's no need for special care to prevent oil getting down in there.

Standard-weight 52 without iron sights. Later models of this 52C have no front sight lug on the barrel, as shown here, which was practically identical with the barrel of the old single-shot Musket, the lever gun that did so much to make Winchester's early reputation for smallbore rifle accuracy. All 52 target rifles are drilled and tapped for a target front-sight base.

Heavy-barrel 52 with Lyman 524 and 77H target sights.

To remove the bolt of this new 52C you lower the striker and push the trigger forward instead of pulling it back as on previous models, then open the action. Out she comes as slick as an icicle. This method avoids wear on the trigger, which after long use sometimes develops if a trigger is used as a bolt stop and must be held back to get the bolt out. To clear the high and close-up stock comb the bolt rises just before it's out of the receiver. If there's trouble in replacing the bolt (you hold back the trigger to do this) you simply shove your little finger into the front of the receiver channel and press down.

The pull-down barrel band on my C—the fifth 52 I've had—gave its boost to such splendid accuracy that I left it alone until I took time to remodel and oil-finish the stock. Then I was surprised at the bedding, for I'd thought that the rubber pad system had gone down the stream. These pads, at the rear of the receiver, the breech of the barrel, and behind the barrel band, float the steel in the stock. Most target shots, I suppose, have their way with the bedding of any rifle they use a great deal, but this one suits me as it is. Bench-rest shooting proves it more accurate than I can hold in prone without rest: so it's plain that the gun has more than I have, and therein lies the incentive for me to keep on trying.

Bolt and receiver of the 52C are carburized, given a hard skin to resist wear, keep the headspace tight. This should provide the "lifetime of service" that's so much-used a term in advertising almost anything today, when so many goods are made to wear out fast. According to claims, this skin resists a file, and you may not be able to expect the new 52 ever to have the smoothness of bolt operation that so many old rifles have. The other action parts are carburized, too, a fact that helps to explain why the trigger pull, for instance, is so uniform and unchanging. It is smooth, too. If the bolt operation seems rough—and it may, on some specimens, and to some shooters—we should pay that price gladly to get the long-time service.

Choice of three barrel weights on a target rifle is unusual, or it would be if the 52 hadn't had them for so many years, twenty or so. The standard barrel has a decided taper, and a pretty one, from an inch at the breech to .715 inch at the muzzle. This taper, just as much as the lighter weight, I think, adapts the rifle to four-position shooting for more riflemen than choose it: it is easier to hold, without tremor, through strings of offhand fire. Easier for most of us, that is, for only a few have the physique or training, or both, to handle the heavier weights without a struggle.

To the average pretty good shot, who enjoys the game tremendously although he's properly serious about wanting to improve, it naturally seems that the equipment used by the top-flight competitors must be the best. That's a heavy-barrel rifle, and for them it is the best; they're hardened. So too many of us spend more, or save longer, and get the heavy. It just may not be the best for us, ever, even after years of practice. This comment is entirely apart from the thought of using a standard 52, or a standard 40X, as a hunting rifle. Within their ballistic limits, which are narrow, they are OK in the hunting field unless the going is difficult. They provide a lot of fun, and perhaps unguessed-at satisfaction because of their precision, but that's a different story. With iron sights they have about the weight that some of us like in a .375 Magnum.

The heavy barrel measures an inch at the breech and ⅞ inch at the muzzle; the Bull is more tapered, from 1⅛ to ⅞. Not only because of price is the first one more popular. The Bull Gun is really that, patterned and named after custom, armory and factory .30-06, .300 Magnum and other long-reaching calibers built for the thousand-yard Wimbledon Match, the most gruelling prone regularly fired, though there used to be 1200 yard events. It takes a really powerful individual to use the Bull Gun in four-position and do his best.

The woodwork of the 52C is generous, made so to

The 52 Bull Gun without sights. This specimen has its barrel slotted for a front sight base, and the slot filled with a blank. Later 52C production used the drilled, tapped and plug-screw filled method, more generally popular.

satisfy, if possible, the kind of shooter who's always slapping inletted or plastic wood on a stock to build it up. As on the DCM .30 sporter and the M-2 smallbore, this perhaps excess wood fulfills another need, a satisfying leeway to the whittler. Honestly and according to my lights, the pistol grip and the comb are too far forward for a little guy like me. So back they came, and the fluting of the comb had to be deepened, too. A short-armed person notices this cramping—*if* he notices it, being generally seasoned to the too-bigness of things—particularly in offhand. The minds of most of us are least at peace in that position and little details, good or bad, can grow big. We like 'em good.

Other Rifles

You find a few other heavy rifles on the range alongside the 37s, 52s and 40Xs. Some are old-timers, like Stevens, Ballard or Winchester lever-action single shots, and possibly you'll see a barrel with the honored name of Peterson, Pope, Niedner or Schoyen, for the old masters made a good many and such artistry deserved the best of care. Don't think that these rifles won't shoot because of their two-piece, fore-and-aft stocking.

Bert Shay shoved the bright, flat muzzle of my Winchester high wall through an open window of his gun-room and sent five not very new, fresh Remington Targetmaster long-rifle bullets 100 yards up the line. They made a 5/16 inch group—I think he'd called one out—and four of them grouped into 5/32 inch. That was from his own design of bench rest, easiest I ever shot from. Since you fire uphill, the butt sinks back firmly against your shoulder without tension. He used a hooded post front and a tang peep rear sight, but he's a Navy man, retired a few years ago. This wasn't a selected group, but the only one he fired at 100 with that rifle. I did think it was a good time to stop!

Maybe the breeching of good single shots balances off the wicked vibration of two-piece stocks. You don't get much disturbance from a .22 rimfire load, and single shots can do beautiful work with some pretty ructious calibers, Hornet, 2-R Lovell (just below the .222), .25-35, and for that matter, stuff like the .277 Elliott Express, a wildcat 7 mm. made from .405 Winchester brass and much like the .30-06 in power.

For the breeching is close-up, you realize. It's only about ¾ inch from barrel to locking wall of the Winchester, for instance. The camming action of the Ballard makes a strong lock-up for .22 rimfire backthrust,

and the Stevens 44½ is a straight-falling action like the Winchester, during the first part of its opening, which is important when a .22 is to be snugged into place.

The Stevens 417 was put out by the factory in modern dress and was avilable as a new gun until about 15 years ago. With a standard 1¼-inch Army sling it weighed some 10½ pounds with its 28-inch barrel. For $40 extra, putting the price well over $100, you could get it with a special heavy 29-inch barrel. The big Stevens action supported these barrels well, and the lock-up was secure, too, though perhaps not adequate for the .22 Hornet cartridge used in some of the rifles of this type. The .22 rimfire accuracy was about on a par with that of good bolt guns. The only weakness lay in the attachment of the buttstock. Like other heavy-barrel lever guns with abrupt pistol grip and no long through-bolt anchoring the stock to the frame, it needed more rigid stock support than the tang screws could give it. This doesn't mean that the stock shot loose or wore loose: it just couldn't take the abuse that some beginners thoughtlessly give a rifle, even their own. As a "club rifle" for the instruction of new members, a sturdy bolt action rifle is better.

The 417 was well stocked for iron sights, and good ones were offered, the non-detachable, non-scope-height Lyman 17A front, and a choice between Lyman 48 receiver and 144 tang peep sights, both with micrometer windage and elevation clicks.

Also lever action single shots are the *British BSA* and *Vickers,* the former quite popular in America some 30 years ago and now in revised form a wanted rifle. Early BSAs came in a choice of weight, and most shooters took the heavy one. This rifle and the Vickers, which is distinguished by having a rigid, one-piece stock, used the Martini hammerless, falling-block action, hinged at the rear. A short flick-down of the lever drops the front of the block below the barrel breech, and loading a cartridge down the slant of the breechblock is easy. The BSA, so well known, was celebrated for its crisp trigger and the fast ignition that a Martini striker gives.

The modern BSA as we know it in America took its form largely as a result of the thought and planning of the man who imports it, Al Freeland, 3737 14th Ave., Rock Island, Ill. Slightly redesigned by Birmingham Small Arms, it's representative of the best imported rifles of its kind.

Its Mark II action features a trigger that acts on the *hammer,* not on a sear connecting hammer, or striker, and trigger. The fall of the hammer knocks the sear out of engagement with the tumbler that holds the firing pin or striker in cocked position. This easing of the load on contact faces reduces wear and makes for even, consistent weight of pull. Pull weight is adjustable from two to four pounds, and the amount of the trigger's overtravel or backlash after striker release is adjustable, too. The control screws are where you can get at them, in the front of the trigger guard, and locking screws hold what you ask for and get.

In the best British fashion, the action parts are machined and hand-fitted—no pressed parts are used— and the action can be taken from the bottom of the receiver as a unit, unaccompanied by the tinkle and drop of separate pieces. Lever throw is short, making it possible to reload without shifting your elbows in prone, and empties pop out, it's stated, no matter how vigorously or gently you work the lever. The side of the receiver is cut away, as ordered, for right- or left-hand loading.

Some of us still believe in cleaning a match .22, occasionally at least. So the high stock comb is grooved and the rear of the receiver is drilled to make way for a wiping rod. The rod bends a little, but a smooth one like the Parker-Hale of celluloid-covered steel could do little if any harm in moderate use.

Two barrel weights are offered. The 29 incher on the 14-pound rifle is much like the Winchester 52 Bull Gun barrel in contour. The 11-pound BSA carries a 26-inch tube a bit lighter than that of the 52 Heavy Barrel model. Rifle lengths are 44.4 and 41.4 inches as compared to the 52's 45¾; the short, single-shot action accounts for that, in spite of the long BSA stock.

That stock measures 13¾ inches from middle of trigger to buttplate, whereas the usual American standard is 13⅛ or 13¼. It would be easy to shorten the BSA because the inner surface of the buttplate is flat.

Stock and forearm are of matched walnut of the type known to the trade as "French," regardless of geography. It's hard, dense, and able to hold fine-spaced checkering. The stock has a heavy cheek-piece and a high comb, carried well forward, and the pistol grip is large and steep. The forearm is a wide beavertail, and its sling swivel and hand-stop are adjustable for position.

The Parker-Hale front and rear sights are precision jobs, as would be expected on a rifle of this grade. The aptly named "tunnel" front comes with six inserts and somewhat resembles the Vaver or the Redfield Olympic. The receiver sight, with 2½-inch leeway in eye relief, has the well-proved Parker-Hale six-hole eyepiece to give you almost any aperture opening that changing light conditions would make you want. American-style target scope blocks are on the barrel.

That barrel is up to competitive target standard, must fire on factory tests three consecutive 10-shot

Closeup of BSA Mark II action opened. Notice the short throw of the lever.

strings cutting a one-inch circle at 100 yards. It is lapped to one-half thousandth inch tolerance, just like our best American factory-made match .22s.

The German JGA Model 54 is a fairly recent importation by the Stoeger Arms Corporation. This single shot bolt action has the speed lock, adjustable trigger, loading platform, and shrouded bolt-head that we'd expect in a competitive rifle, and a wing safety at the rear of the bolt sleeve locks the bolt shut and disengages the sear. Its striker fall is about as short as that of the BSA, Remington 40X or Winchester 52. When the striker is cocked a pin sticks out the back of the bolt. I don't know why this is thought desirable on a target rifle. "Bolts open" is the rule except right on the firing line.

The established J. G. Anschutz firm makes this rifle, putting in quite a bit of hand work, such as checkering the bottom of the trigger guard to secure the thumb when we shoot in NRA offhand, the hip-rest position. The guard is of milled steel, not stamped, unimportant to scores, for sure, but a point-with-pride detail for some shooters. As you might expect,

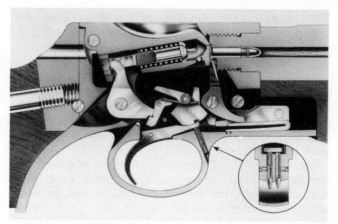

Cutaway of BSA action. Inset shows trigger adjustment screws.

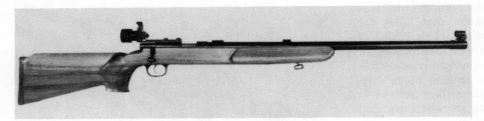

Anschutz Model 54. Note thumb groove on stock, just below rear sight overhang.

Anschutz Model 54 Super Match.

the German iron sights are imposing, competent and hefty. Detached, they clear the deck for a scope, and that goes on American style scope blocks.

Some of us would object to the Monte Carlo comb on a target rifle, wanting the heel good and high, as well as the comb, and more than just some of us would find the 14-inch stock nearly an inch too long. It would be easy to remove the soft rubber buttplate and shorten the wood. The stock is well finished, has some nice checkering, and provides a thumb rest for a right-hander. Barrel length is 27½ inches, gun weight 10 pounds, 13 ounces.

The Super Match JGA is designed about as much for Olympic style shooting as for our American four-position or (too often) strictly prone courses. Its forestock just ahead of the trigger is built deep, to help in hip-rest offhand, and the big, heavy stock has a thumb-hole. This brings your whole hand, nearly upright, close to the trigger, and it's a familiar pattern in bull-pup style stocks made by many of our hobbyists and some gunsmiths. The pup, though, is a shorty, as its name suggests. Its action is brought back to lie under your face as you fire. The thumb-hole of this JGA Super is much smaller: it *is* a thumb-hole, not big enough to shove your fist through. For good grip, some of us might need to open it a bit.

The Morgan-Johnson match .22 is representative of the best American custom jobs. It is truly custom, built to order, at present in Eric Johnson's shop at Hamden, Conn. Eric, of course, is a famous barrel-maker. The Morgan action is custom, too, and can be described as having both Winchester and Remington characteristics.

Mrs. Viola E. Pollum, up in the Master class though with only eight years' shooting experience behind her, was the first woman to become national smallbore champion. That was at the 1955 Camp Perry matches, and she used a Morgan-Johnson. For the record, because it's interesting, her iron sights

were a Unertl tube rear (like a small telescope tube but containing an aperture sight rather than magnifying lenses) and a Vaver front. Her scope sight was a Unertl 16 power. Two other Masters, also high in the 1955 ranking, used M-J rifles. They were Arthur Cook and Roy Oster.

Roy Dunlap's left-hand action is another of the custom jobs of top quality, and some outstanding shots are southpaws. His design somewhat resembles the 52 but has the interior touches that mark custom work, and the exterior, too, some as obvious as the machined, not stamped-out trigger guard. Dunlap's address is 2319 Ft. Lowell Road, Tucson, Arizona.

What's the advantage, if any, in using a custom .22? Lots of people do well without them, and not all winners use them.

A top-flight gunsmith gave me a good answer. I'd like to name him, but I shouldn't. "When you get one of those," he said, "you're sure to get a good rifle. With a Winchester or Remington you might not; you *might* get a poor one."

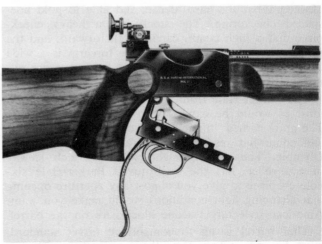

BSA action comes out one-piece for cleaning.

That's a good answer, but I think it needs a bit of blowing out—not blowing up. With competition between factories and between riflemen so keen, the liability of getting a poor one grows thinner all the time. It is true that some factory specimens are better than others, seldom by much, though sometimes you win—or lose—by only a little difference, and most rifles respond to expert tuning-up.

Most high-ranking smallboresmen tinker with their rifles: stock alterations, custom stocks by themselves or by other hands, bedding refinements, custom barrels, special trigger mechanisms, and so on. They don't do these things for fun or to have something to look wise about. They are after better scores, from the rifle, the ammunition, and their own human potentialities.

Comparatively few of these shooters, it's safe to say, have the highest designing ability and mechanical skill. The best gunsmiths have, and they execute the customer's ideas. With his permission, usually eager, they also help to perfect those ideas. "Two heads are better than one," provided, that is, both are sound. Stupid ones don't get to the top, in the shop or on the range.

THEY don't make 'em any more.

Such a comment on small-game rifles wouldn't necessarily come from a homesick feeling for what has gone. It could be sense.

All our small-game rifles now made are chambered for the .22 long-rifle cartridge, which has its limitations in the field. It's true that some of our good small-game *cartridges* still come off the loading machines, though a few of them seem to be living a bit precariously. In rimfire there are the .22 Winchester, .25 Stevens and .32 short and long. In the more or less long-ago the first two were available with hollow point lead. The life-grip of the .25-20 and .32-20 centerfires is fairly strong. They're reloadable, and lots of rifles—expensive enough to rate good care—were made for them rather recently. The latest was the Winchester Model 43 bolt gun, offered for some years after World War I, and still popular in Hornet and Bee. Many Colt and Smith & Wesson .32-20 revolvers were made, and some long-barreled H&R single-shot pistols.

So in small-game rifle choice we have no fill-in between .22 long-rifle and .22 Hornet calibers, though manufacturers haven't dismissed this lack from their minds—not quite. Some ten or fifteen years ago, factory lots of .25 Stevens rimfire were made up in high velocity style, and they shot well. Two factors kept them from being made in marketable quantity. One was the serious matter of breech pressure. Many old, small-frame rifles like the Stevens Favorite were still in use—and are today—and the majority had served their time. They no longer breeched up tightly. Another drawback, serious in a different way, was that .25 rimfire ammunition cost, and sometimes the difficulty of finding the stuff, had destroyed the once great popularity of this size. Mass production had come in and had made mass sales essential. A person has to know something about hunting-field ballistics to choose the .25, and it's an effort to acquire knowledge!

There was the thought, too, of designing an entirely different rimfire small game special. This could be a bottle-necked .25 that wouldn't enter the old chambers unless they were reformed to take it—and even then a relocation of the firing pin would be necessary. Or it could be a larger or slightly smaller caliber that could use higher pressures, thanks to modern brass cases and non-mercuric priming that even in long storage can't weaken cartridge brass. The idea lives on, though that old risk of insufficient demand persists. It's a formidable risk.

WHAT CARTRIDGES DO WE WANT?

Small game is to eat, not to waste. In two ways we want clean killing: humane execution and no cripples with any fairly well-placed shot; no excessive destruction, either.

Our opportunities, and consequently our needs,

CHAPTER 4

SMALL-GAME RIFLES

overlap to some extent. Year by year wild turkeys are coming back to many of our states, in shootable quantity, and on the average they're far harder to kill than squirrels, cottontail rabbits, grouse, or the little quail that in some woods are just too tame to snipe with a rifle. Individual specimens of any game are harder to kill than others, and there are geographical differences, too. Some species of Deep South squirrels, for instance, are just plain whoppers.

Still more obvious to the experienced is the toughness of the woodchuck or groundhog, though he can be stalked. Such skill, added to fine marksmanship, would let us use a rather low-power caliber in hunting him. Game? Of course he is. You can eat him, even "an old tough one" if you know how to cook him, and woodchuck liver is the choicest of any I know. Western jack-rabbits also are classed as varmints, but their meat has fed many a homestead family.

Crows and hawks are outright varmints. I've tasted both. Even a hawk is sometimes hard to get close to; so the matter of range may enter our choice of a small-game caliber, unless we specialize. To include a really destructive hawk or owl, or a crow, in our small game "bag" can improve the hunting, and then there are the weasel, coyote and bobcat, the last two requiring quite a lot of killing. The problem of power

79

gets curiouser and curiouser, as I think Alice re-marked of the Wonderland world.

For the kid it's easy. He hunts with a .22 rimfire because the gun and its ammo are cheap. Usually he has the advantages of sharp eyesight and hearing, and single-mindedness of purpose. He isn't thinking about his income tax or some foul-up at the office. Already he may possess patience. If not, he learns it, along with knowledge of game, skill in stalking, self-control in sitting still, and—let us fervently hope—marksmanship. In several ways, you see, he resembles the Indian hunter, and he finds the sport completely absorbing. He gets good at it, maybe too good.

Few grownups do, today, at least with the rifle. Most of them want results. With seasons short, and less game and more hunters in the woods, they use the shotgun, which they can afford to buy and shoot. There's also the competitive spirit. The average man isn't man enough to be skunked and face the consequences when he gets back home. He's a meat hunter who doesn't need the meat. All he needs is the guts to say, "I had a swell day and don't give a hoot that I didn't get any game."

But some men aren't average, and even more than a kid they can savor the rewards of hunting small game with a rifle. As training for big game hunting or as a sport in itself it gives us what we want. There's the utter absorption, the occasional excitement, and the ever-present, underlying satisfaction of being where we want to be and doing what we want to do. It's enough. The woods, the fields, the swamps, hills, mountains, mesas, prairies, all have their charm. There's never anything ugly or spoiled to look at, and no matter how well we know our country there's never the sameness of two days alike.

The rifle is our companion and we choose its caliber carefully.

The Rimfires

The .22 long-rifle isn't to be condemned. For some uses it's the best; for some it just gets by.

In hollow point, high velocity loading it kills cotton-tails with fair regularity. Since its bullet expansion is unreliable—sometimes too much, sometimes almost non-existent when it strikes no great resistance—it's not ideal for the average squirrel hunter. For the rifleman who takes only head shots on this game it's accurate, particularly in a good, fairly heavy rifle and in the low velocity, target type of loading, with solid point.

The .22 WRF was a much better killing size when it came in hollow point. Even yet, with its faster, heavier, flat-nosed bullet it sometimes kills as well as the long-rifle hollow point, or better. Solid bullets as tightly crimped in as this Winchester .22 sometimes can be drilled successfully to the hollow, mushrooming form.

The same bullet shape, at much lower velocity,

makes up the .25 Stevens, long considered one of the best, if not *the* best, for small game hunting at woods ranges. It kills reliably, with moderate destruction. Bullet weight and width do it. Actually in the .25 class, and in some combinations just as accurate, are the rimfire .32s. Their heavier, larger bullets are slower, and not so bluff-pointed.

None of these rimfires should be considered as powerful enough for turkey hunting. And none of them is at all reliable in brush shooting. Their bullets are too light and short to cut through a maze of twigs without being deflected, though they do have the low velocities that help in this chancy sort of firing.

Modern Centerfires

Only the .25-20 and .32-20 are left, but good rifles for them aren't hard to find in used-gun offerings. True, most of them made before the non-corrosive mixtures of the latter 1920s show ruined bores, and not all factories can provide replacements. Reboring the .25 to .32 is still done occasionally, and it can be worth while.

Bullets of both calibers are too short and light to be good brush-cutters, but this is true of practically any small-game load, factory- or hand-assembled. They behave better than the rimfires now made, and their killing power is about twice as great.

In this respect they're excessive for most small game except turkeys, but handloading can give the right answer. The .25 can duplicate the rimfire of that size, a 65- to 67-grain flat-nosed bullet at 1130 f. s., and give good accuracy even though the usual .25-20 rifling twist of one turn in 14 inches is three inches faster than the .25 rimfire standard. The bullet is over-stabilized, but not much.

Normal or lighter .32-20 bullet weights can do all right at reduced velocities. The 20-inch twist isn't choosy. Such a leisurely spin makes this caliber well suited to round bullets seated in the case-mouth over a wad of Ipco grease, or smeared with lubricant outside. With a mold we can cast good round bullets; most buckshot vary so much in size and in degree of true-roundness that they must be culled over heartlessly!

These two calibers are fairly satisfactory for varmint shooting at close ranges. Even so, their bullets must strike a vital part, and they are impractical and inhumane for use beyond 100 yards or so. They do have the merit of low, not-too-sharp report in any loading. Of course the .32-20 in a revolver is noisy and sharp in pitch. It sounds a little like a .30 Luger automatic, though each is distinctive.

Older Calibers

A few of us use older calibers, or at least more thoroughly "outmoded" ones, for small game hunting. The .22-13-45 Winchester and .22-15-60 Stevens single shots had plenty of admirers in the smallbore following, and with good reason. Even the lighter one is more powerful than the modern .22 WRF. Handloading let us vary the power to the need, and there were molds for hollow points in nearly all centerfire rifle sizes of the old school.

Yes, a school. Then as now, handloaders knew the score, and they led commercial production on to useful offerings.

Most of these old calibers are hard but not impossible to supply with reloadable brass. In the .25s, the long, gently bottle-necked .25-20 Single Shot is becoming a rarity. Lots of the brass was necked down to form the fine, high-velocity .22 Lovell forms, which later were made for Griffin & Howe of New York and may still be available—and possible to expand to .25. The Straight .25-21 and .25-25 are scarce. So is the .32-25-150 Ideal, for which many Stevens and Winchester single shots were made or rebored, and on meeting the .32-30-125 Remington or .32-35-153 Stevens you should take off your hat.

Calibers go up to and past the still current, always useful .32-40, and they all had their devotees because each filled a certain need—or many needs, for most rifles of these calibers had the benefit of a guardian who understood handloading. In variety these factory sizes didn't begin to equal the wide, sometimes bewildering choice of later wildcat calibers, and for that reason there was less overlapping or duplication. Their reign of popularity was longer than that of all but the most thoroughly proved cats, and some folks still use them because they do exactly what's wanted in a certain sort of hunting.

The .28, .30, and .32 sizes could be loaded with a sharp-pointed, cast lead bullet for squirrel shooting. Then for somewhat larger game you could change to a blunt or hollow-nosed bullet and, without adjusting sights and *at the same range,* go ahead and fire with confidence. This required fitting the loads to the individual rifle, but it was fun to do it.

All these calibers will use either black or low pressure smokeless powders, and the former makes them independent as to what sort of primer you seat in the brass. Scrap lead is generally to be found, and except in the matter of cases these rifles are hard for a supply bottleneck to put out of action. In most barrels the rifling twists were obligingly slow.

High-Intensity Calibers

We could classify the Hornet as such even though its pressure is below those of most big game or long range varmint calibers. It's hot. But it's useful in mild loadings, too, and practically made to order to duplicate the .22-13-45 Winchester single shot from which it came. Handloading dope is published for it, at squirrel hunting levels—you can even use the fine-grained FFFG black powder in it—and for the .218 Bee, .219 Zipper, .222 Remington, .220 Swift, and many wildcat .22s. You choose between a cast lead and a full-jacketed bullet, sending the latter a good bit faster to be sure of killing power with the small

caliber. The quicker burning powders like Hercules Unique and 2400 and du Pont 4227 and 4759 let us cut cast-bullet velocity lower than most lists advise, and still get accuracy. Or we use pistol powders. Jacketed stuff, even when thin-coated, must go fairly fast to be sure of getting *through* a long rifle barrel!

Bigger calibers up to at least .375 Magnum can be handloaded for small game. The 6 mm. varmint sizes, the .243 Winchester, .244 Remington, and the wildcats that helped to develop them, have an Ideal cast bullet of 65 grains, plain base, that was designed for the 6 mm. Lee Navy of the 1890s. In that small case five grains of Unique give 1200 f. s. velocity—just right. Wide bearing bands made this bullet usable in the 7½-inch twist of the Lee. Modern 6 mms. use a 10- to 12-inch twist generally, and should handle this bullet even better. New molds for heavier gas-check bullets began to appear in the spring of 1956.

The .25s are famous for cast-bullet use, with any amount of weights and shapes to choose from. Except perhaps with the most large-bodied wildcats, accuracy shouldn't be hard to develop with a good rifle, though most twists are fast compared to that of the sedate little .25-20.

With the .270 and the .275s or 7 mms. we begin to get into large calibers for little game. For mild destruction we have to keep velocities low, or use sharp bullets. Molds are available, and the old .28-30 Stevens was also a 7 mm., or nearly so. Manufacturers' standards and tolerances differ a bit, more so overseas than here.

The .30s have countless lead bullets to choose from, and jacketed stuff, too, like the .32 Auto Colt and the .30 Luger and Mauser. Cast lead .32 revolver bullets do well in some .30 caliber barrels or can be sized to suit them. The .35s aren't hard to fit with .38 revolver lead, and the .375 has an old bullet design ready for it, the 149-grain Ideal .38-55 "short range." It's flat-pointed for safety in a tubular magazine, though more for reassurance, since recoil is so light. The flat is narrow, smaller than the face of a large primer, to make it not too destructive.

Reason 1001· for Handloading

We have to, for the factories no longer provide the little meat-in-the-pot rounds for our high powers. They used to load "short range" cartridges for us in .25-35, .25-36 Marlin, .30-30, .30-40, .303 Savage, .32-40, .38-55 and .45-70, right along. There were somewhat reduced loads also for .38-40 and .44-40, 28-grain doses of black. Old catalogues tell us of short-range accommodations in 6 mm. Lee and .30-03, that earlier, longer-necked edition of our .30-06. Both flat- and round-nosed lead bullets were used, and there were some with full metal jackets, the .30-30, .303, .32-40 and perhaps others. These hard-points were called "miniature" cartridges, following British nomenclature.

Bullet weights were low. Here are some standards: 86-grains in .25, 100 and 117 in .30, 98 and 100 in

.32, 150 in .38, and 140-grain round ball or 230-grain conical in .45. With the light powder charges these bullet weights kept report low. A long-barreled Krag, for instance, sounded about like a .32 rimfire. Killing power on small game, close up, was usually adequate, seldom excessive except with .38, or of course .45, and the latter loads were meant more for armory practice with the Springfield than for hunting.

All these cartridges, however, were rather well proved afield, and their bullet weights are at least suggestive when we work up small-game rounds for our big-game rifle. There won't be much expansion of lead, and even the .25s did not need it, for as a rule they were flat-pointed like the .25-20.

A SMALL-GAME RIFLE'S ANATOMY

The type of action doesn't matter, provided it pleases us and lets us do our best work. If a person gets out a good deal with a rifle all through the year, as most enthusiastic small-game hunters do, there's no great need for it to resemble his big-game arm in action type. He can choose what he likes for each sport. In the years I've hunted I can remember only one or two occasions when I forgot what rifle I was using. Lots of my friends call me absent-minded, too, and I'm uncomfortably sure that they're right. Trained reflexes are mighty dependable, and no hunter has any business in the field with an unfamiliar gun.

Speed of action is a sword that cuts two ways. It helps the seasoned hunter at those rare times when he needs it, and just as certainly it handicaps the hunter who's unsure of his ability. The easily rattled, over-anxious type does best with one cartridge to depend on. Many boys have to start hunting with a single-shot rifle—or shotgun—and nearly all of them ought to. When game appears, lots of us older people shed the self-control that maturity is supposed to bring. It takes wing faster than a grouse or woodcock or quail!

Some actions and some rifle accessories are noisy. The slide handles of many pump guns give a slight rattle or click as we shift the weapon from hand to hand, and game has acute hearing. Too many sling swivels become loose, give a slight tick as gun position is changed, and the quick-detachable swivels often are bad offenders when the weight of the leather hangs from them. As it pendulums from side to side, the swivels chatter. This can be stopped by little leather washers around the holding pins.

The rifle's balance and weight can be right, and help us in the particular sort of small-game hunting we do, or they can be dead wrong. A pretty safe rule should be a little more weight than we *think* we can handle well and comfortably in the line of country we plan to hunt. Pretty soon we get seasoned to it; then we do a better job and are thankful for having chosen as we did. Balance makes a hunting rifle feel right, either alive and responsive for fast work (not rapid fire!) or steady and equally cooperative in deliberate firing. You take your choice, or maybe you hope to find a compromise, an all-rounder. Balance is hard to define but easy to appreciate after a fair amount of hunting experience.

The fit of a rifle—whether or not it's built correctly for us—takes still more background to judge. We want it to be right for us, though the human frame is more adaptable than we might think. It's well known that many of the best shots have fitted themselves to the gun they've used for so many seasons, and quite likely they'd do poor work with an unfamiliar one that had been tailored to them by an expert stocker.

How good they'd have been if such a craftsman had helped them in the beginning is for speculation. That sort of story is seldom told. Most hobbyists drift into their big interest; few enter it scientifically. Then too, many of us change our shooting habits slightly as time goes on. *We* change, too—physically.

Correct sighting equipment depends on the country, the game, and the manner of hunting that game. More than ever before, rifles are being made to offer a choice between glass and iron sights. In a single day we might use both, with advantage.

Long before this, the reader has become impatient. "Small-game rifles" is just too complex a subject. We simplify it by deciding whether we want the gun primarily for snapshooting or for deliberate use when we hunt quietly and do a good deal of sitting around, watching.

Snapshooting Rifles

These rifles should feel light and lively, up to a point. We cover more ground than we would in still-hunting, though in the woods a two-mile-an-hour gait, with numerous stops to look and listen, is quite fast enough to suit most good hunters. Since we go a long way to get to promising country we want to do justice to it after we've got there. More than half of good hunting is the relishing of the outdoors and the unconscious storing up of memory pictures. They come in handy during shut-in times and we don't get those rewards, or learn much about wildlife's habits, by stepping on the gas.

But there's some walking to do, and lots of it out in the west; so we don't carry a crowbar. Yet when the chance at a jack or cottontail rabbit comes we don't want a gaspipe, either. Pin-weight barrels are too responsive in the swing and follow-through on moving game, and even on straightaway shots they don't settle down fast enough. Weight out front steadies us and helps the muzzle to swing accurately instead of bobbing around. This is as true in the woods as out on the prairie.

Balance. We can tell a good deal by the way the rifle balances. A teeter point four or five inches ahead of the trigger means a muzzle-light rifle, or a butt-heavy one, which add up to the same thing. Let the balance point go forward an inch or even two and we have a better arm for accurate, quick shooting.

A heavy action on an overall light rifle puts too much weight between our hands, where it does no good. Few rifles are built that way, though you can find the breech-heavy sort exemplified in an old Remington Model 8 autoloader (the 81 was an improvement in this respect) or a light-barreled Winchester 1895.

If we wisely choose a snapshooting rifle that feels just a little heavy after a long day afield, a gunsling can help in the carry across unproductive country. Then if the chance comes for a long, deliberate shot, with plenty of time to take it, we are thankful to have that sling in our pocket and easy and noiseless to hook on.

Gun Fit. Since good snapshooting becomes partly instinctive—it has to!—we want the rifle to fit us. Stock length should be comfortable, responsive, in fact. Too-short is better than too-long, and when we wear thick, heavy clothes summer's too-short is just right.

A stock comb full and high enough to let us rest our cheek firmly (though relaxed) against it helps us steady down fast for that first and so important quick shot, just as it helps us in a rapid-fire target course, in steadying down from the recoil of a semi-automatic or from the interlude of working a bolt. If a pistol grip isn't so close to the trigger as to cramp our hand in the standing position it can give added control of the snapshooting rifle. However, at the risk of being hound-dogged out of camp I'll say that some of the best snapshooting I've seen done was with rifles having low, thin combs, pistol grips bashful or absent, and even the curved old "rifle" buttplates that are becoming uncommon sights no matter how far back in from the gun-store your hunting takes you.

You rested your jawbone more than your cheek on the comb, and you fitted yourself to the gun. At least the sights stood up high and prominent, and tang peeps were close to your eye. Since I learned with that sort of rifle and knew no better for the first ten years or so, the little I did learn evidently stuck. Many years later I got a single-shot .25-20 in that unspeakable style and found that the knack came right back to me. The curved buttplate hopped into place—more or less on the arm, I'll admit—and the sights were where I expected to find them. I certainly hadn't expected all this, for I'd read and found out too much since. Such experiences sort of over-stabilize the mind, if you see what I mean, just as .30-06 rifling makes a short .32 pistol bullet go somewhat giddy!

I think we can conclude this discussion of snapshooting stock fit by saying that practice is the great thing and we can get it by dry firing in a hall bedroom and be happy as a clam. A stock that feels right, a modern stock, shortens the learning process. In fitting it for perfection don't hesitate to shorten or lengthen, carve away or build up. When you get what you want, a custom stock for appearance's sake is all right. Don't let it weigh more or less than the guineapig stock, for that could change the rifle's balance.

Killing Power. Snapshooting at small game is usually done at fairly close range where we don't need flat trajectory, and a fast bullet is liable to be entirely too destructive. At long ranges, high remaining velocity certainly does make the estimate of how far to hold ahead a lot less critical.

But even on small game we need more killing power than we do in slow, deliberate sniper fire, as it's so much harder to hit an instantly fatal spot. So when time is short and aim less certain, the .22 rimfire may not do well on game harder to kill than a cottontail rabbit. Most squirrels need much more instantly-stopping power. Freak shots don't count in sensible thinking. For reliable, sportsmanlike killing we need a bigger and more deadly bullet.

Sights. Small game is fast, and it doesn't offer a big vital target. We need good sights. Even in the brush the common open-sight system is poor, for in haste we fail to pull the front bead clear down into the rear sight notch, and thus overshoot. A wide, flat-topped post front that fits loosely, we might say, into a wider and pretty deep square rear notch does good work for some shooters whose eyesight is keen. They can see enough light on each side of the front sight to help them center it in the notch. Only a few rifles, such as some of the Mossbergs, are commonly sighted in anything like this manner, so popular on pistols and revolvers. Contrasting colors of rear and front sight are helpful to most eyes, and here we get into the department of special jobs.

A wide-apertured rear sight, close to the eye, and a good-sized front—bead or post as you prefer—are the best snapshooting irons for most of us who hunt the brushy places. The few hours spent in mastering them buy a bargain.

If we use a scope it should be low-powered, 3x or three magnifications being quite enough, with 2½ being still a great favorite. A post reticle in the scope shows up fast, but it must be flat on top, not sharp-pointed, or in trying to catch it fast we'll fail to see that little spearhead distinctly and consequently overshoot. For most of us, coarse crosshairs do all right in snapshooting.

Sometimes we get a chance for a deliberate shot, and then the rear peep is much to be thankful for, the scope still more welcome. Never think that because the professional exhibition shot uses open sights they are the big medicine for *us*. We take our targets under all sorts of conditions of weather, light, and background and at all sorts of angles—provided they're safe. There's no uniformity to simplify matters for us, not even in range. Therefore, our long practice at inanimate targets should come under conditions as varied as we can find. Since we don't shoot for a company that manufactures rifles and equips the vast majority of them with open sights, we're free to choose the best. For us, notch sights are a poor sort of economy when we consider the much longer time and the many thousand more rounds it takes to become even reasonably proficient with them.

Sniping Rifles

Weight is what we want here. They need to be as heavy as we think we can carry comfortably, maybe a bit heavier. The small game sniper gets most of his favorable opportunities when he's sitting and waiting for them. Yet weight can be excessive, for to get to good country and move now and then from place to place usually calls for some climbing of hills and stooping under brush.

Weight steadies a rifle for accurate shooting on the target range where we fire from familiar positions we've trained ourselves to use. In the hunting field our shots often must be taken from decidedly unorthodox, even contorted positions, to left or right, up or down, as the chances come. Dry-land shooting may then be nearly as difficult as that from a canoe in still water or even in the easy slide of a gentle current. And as always in small-game hunting with a rifle, our marksmanship simply must be of high grade. The 7s and 8s can cripple; the 9s and center 10s become necessary for clean killing. Sniping, we have a reasonable time limit in which to fire—it isn't snapshooting—but we've got to be good.

This means a heavy rifle. It will feel so in the carrying, but it will hang right when the shot is offered.

Balance. The gun should feel muzzle-heavy. This sort of small-game rifle should balance at 7, 7½ or 8 inches ahead of the trigger, or even farther out.

If we want to reduce rifle weight and still have the rock-like steadiness we need—and actually can get under good conditions—we choose a light action and buttstock. Or we lighten the buttstock and attach a buttplate of aluminum, hard rubber, plastic or nylon in place of steel.

Actions. Few actions except the bolt and the carefully chosen single shot contribute to the accuracy we want. There are exceptions, such as the lightly handloaded big-game or varmint rifle of almost·any type, especially the lever.

A solid-frame lever-action arm can be made to give splendid small-game accuracy, as a rule, in the .22, .243. .25, .30, and .32 calibers and still not be too destructive with the light lead or full-jacketed bullets we use. This takes rather competent handloading and probably some careful experimenting with different rations of powder, primer, and bullet. A recommended load may not do at all well in our rifle; yet slight changes in its makeup perhaps will work wonders.

The Sling. A gunsling belongs on the sniping rifle. It helps in the toting of any heavy arm, and much more important, it helps in the holding. You may have to fire from a windswept hillside where you'd be helpless without it.

A carrying strap isn't enough, though you *can* use it, like the loop or Army-style sling, in the well-named "hasty" style. The hasty sling is always a substitute for the loop, used when time is short. But our small-game sniping is going to be deliberate work except for those unexpected chances that come to even a seasoned hunter who knows so well when, where, and what to expect.

We must fit the hasty sling as carefully to us as the loop style. Also we need to memorize the correct setting, and to remember that heavier clothes aren't accommodating in the matter of sling fit.

We're built differently and we have different ideas as to where our forward hand should close lightly around the forestock, but here is the general rule for fitting the hasty sling.

Hold the rifle horizontal and adjust the leather to hang about 10 inches below the gun at its lowest point, which might be under the curve of the trigger guard— or might not, of course, for that depends on the location of the sling swivels. Now we have a nice length of sling for over-shoulder carrying that in open country lets us step out with our hands free, as unconcerned as a mountain daisy.

Well, maybe it will be our right length for hasty, too. The left hand—reverse for a southpaw, poor soul, who's used to following directions in looking-glass-world fashion—the left mitt shoots through that wide space between sling and forestock, whirls up to the left, around the sling, clamps on to the forestock, and slides back to tighten the rig. If there's time, you turn the right-hand edge of the sling up and around to the left, and hold it so, while your left hand is performing the dive and whirl and grasp just described. There seldom is time, though; and if it does, your refined hasty sling isn't so hasty, is it?

Plenty of sit-and-watch hunters, out for either small or big game, adjust the loop sling on their arm, pull down the leather keepers to hold it in place, and leave it there before the long, patient wait has even begun. If they fire a shot at an extreme or in any way awkward angle from sitting, or high up or 'way down, shifting the left hand or foot takes care of it without noise or fuss. Usually it does! Hunting isn't a sport of mathematical certainties, and it wouldn't be a sport if it were.

Iron Sights. They need not always be chosen especially for small-game sniping, though often they are. The open rear sight is definitely out for precision shooting, and that's what we're planning to do. Since there's no particular hurry, the aperture of the rear peep sight can be smaller than we'd use in snapshooting, and therefore a bit more precise, shapening the vision slightly in good light, too. Yet if our shooting is to be in shady woods or in dark, overcast weather, so productive in lots of small-game hunting, an aperture that would be just right in a well lighted indoor gallery or on a sunny outdoor range can be pretty hopeless. So too, a wide black steel disc around an aperture can be a nuisance, and it seldom is necessary. The thing shuts off the wide view we need (with both eyes) to find our game and follow it easily if it moves. It can louse up even the shooter who keeps both eyes open when firing, as he should. It's true that some of us must close or partly close the non-aiming eye.

These are the main objections to target discs in the field. You'll find plenty of hunters who use them and do well, but you notice that these things are detachable! Turn 'em out and you have the wide, thin-rimmed style of peep to use.

It takes excellent light and eyesight to do well on small game with the hooded, aperture target front sight that frames a round black bullseye for execution. The narrow post insert, or the wide one if you won't have to hold-over for distance, is a rather good hunting front except in dim light. Then it would be better to whiten the tip of the bead insert that came with the others in the little tin can, for unless the hood of your target front is a long one the bead will show up fairly well. Since it stands up higher than the post, you're going to have to resight to use it.

Hunting front sights with red or ivory beads or posts are bright in some awfully dark woods, and a shooter with good eyesight can see a gold bead rather clearly in such places. It is better to use a good-sized bead and hold just under the exact spot you want to hit than it is to use a tiny bead and tag it over that spot. Here we refer to slow, deliberate work under poor light conditions. I think that most good snapshooters lay the tip of the front sight on (or of course ahead of) the spot they want their bullet to strike. But long-trained target shooters who have used the post front a lot generally operate in a different fashion with a bead— laying it just *under* the desired point of impact— when they're hunting.

Scopes. For the best work the sniper wants a scope, quite naturally. There are so many models made, in different powers, widths of field, and degrees of illumination, that if he has the ideal glass for one shot out of five in a day's hunt he's most fortunate! That is looking at it from the super-critical and therefore plumb dumb silly viewpoint.

We don't need to be so particular. Even a varied-power glass isn't essential, though this kind is fun to play with and undeniably most useful when distances and visibility vary a great deal in the kind of small- or big-game hunting, or target shooting that we have the chance to enjoy.

In the woods, most glasses of six-power or above usually have too little light and field to let us pick up a squirrel or a turkey fast enough to be able to settle down for a sure aim. The three- or four- or even 2½-power generally let us see what we need to, and their fields are big. Moving the rifle barrel slowly and cautiously, we can even do some scanning with them. With these powers, light is almost always good enough to let us use a crosshair reticle, though not an extremely fine one. Beyond about 100 yards the 2½ seldom shows small game with the clarity we'd want.

There are many exceptions to these general statements, just as there are differences in unaided vision and in woodsmanship and huntercraft. A general rule is that most of us tend to use too much magnification. This has become even truer since manufacturers began giving us four-power scopes with the field of view that old 2½s afforded. There's still tremor. Only in prone and sitting, or over a rest, can we hold like a rock. The target shooter who does fine offhand work with the 10-, 12-, or 15-power scope he finds so useful in prone, sit and kneel has different holding problems in the woods. And just what limb was it that squirrel was on, anyway? We need a wide field of view.

In reasonably open country there's the opportunity, or the need, to do really long range shooting at small game. A turkey may look like a fairly big mark, away off there in the open, but his vital parts are small. A too powerful bullet will ruin him for the table. It's almost criminal to wound one of these fine birds—or any game or varmint at all—and let him get away to die. So the six- or eight-power varmint glass could be exactly right for some kinds of small game sniping. Then the scope's light-gathering power and width of field would only rarely be critical.

Ammunition. Without accuracy the sniping rifle is worse than useless, and we must have the skill to use its accuracy. Add ammunition quality and suitability to the factors of rifle, sighting equipment, and the rifleman himself, and you have the four wheels on which accuracy navigates. There may be a spare or two, such as knowing better than to fire in a 20-mile cross-wind, but we aren't concerned with the spares now.

Some really expert squirrel hunters do choose the .22 long-rifle with solid-point bullet, and preferably of match grade or a fine DCM issue of standard stuff. They make head shots.

For body shots on squirrel or almost any other small game the solid-point .22 l-r simply hasn't reliable killing power, even in high velocity loadings. Almost always it meets too little resistance to expand and make a quickly killing wound. Entirely too much game is crippled and lost, usually to die later—much later, and miserably. On the small bodies of squirrel the hollow point too can fail to mushroom. At other times it's entirely too destructive. A squirrel raked lengthwise can be almost ruined for eating.

The essentials to hunting with the .22 rimfire are accurate shooting and vital placement of hits. The cartridge's killing power gives little or no leeway to the bungler.

For that reason the smart small-game sniper of today often uses a handloaded centerfire size. Caliber limits are wide, for he can take his pick along the line from .22 Hornet to .36-06—or even beyond. He insists on accuracy, and on killing power suited to his game. Cast bullets of the proper shape and weight give him what he wants in woods shooting.

When ranges lengthen he's apt to go to jacketed stuff. Sent at low velocity, an expanding bullet doesn't mushroom; its destructive power can be moderate enough for small game. But a full-jacketed bullet can go faster, shoot flatter, and still do the right job on arrival.

Some thirty years ago practically every smokeless, centerfire American rifle cartridge could be had in a choice of "full metal patch" or expanding. Only a few are left, as loaded cartridges or as "bullets only" to be ordered for handloading. Some custom bullet makers furnish them, too, from .22 Hornet on up, and skilled amateurs make their own.

For long-range turkey sniping, blunt small or medium bore metal-cased bullets are still available in .25-35 and .30-30. Most high-power rifles in these bore diameters handle them well, except for those .250 Savages that have a slow 12- or 14-inch twist. The pointed .30 caliber military bullet of 150 to 154 grains has been used a lot. Sent too fast it's unduly destructive; too slow, it slips through without killing promptly. Blunt points perhaps give us a little more leeway as to the nearly ideal velocity and consequent killing power at different ranges and on different animals or birds. Again, the meaningful factors are good shooting and knowing where to place the shots, and the long-range sniper frequently has time to wait for the chance to place his bullet just right.

Thinking of, or doing, this sort of shooting makes some of us regret what has gone. The full-jacketed 87- and 100-grain .250 Savage bullets were good handloading timber for the small-game hunter, and the .25 Remington autoloader with somewhat more abruptly pointed 101-grain full jacketed was a pretty good turkey cartridge just as it came out of the cardboard box. Its muzzle velocity was 2330 f. s., down at the lower edge of the so-called "explosive" bracket of speed.

All-Rounders

In the matter of *caliber* it's probably as hard to choose an all-round small-game rifle as an all-round big-game arm. Always there must be compromises in velocity and power, and even in trajectory. So too, the makeup of the rifle must be a matter of give-and-take.

Whether we like it or not, a plump, full-bodied 99 per cent of the rifles that go small-game hunting are .22 rimfires. Immediately the limit of sure, quick killing power comes in and in a way simplifies our choice. That limit is 65 yards, I believe, and it is to be reached only after long practice and study in both target range and field shooting at inanimate marks.

With the latter, if not before, comes in the art of judging distance, judging it under all sorts of light conditions and across different sorts of terrain. Actually, 40 yards should be our limit for a long time. The flight of the .22 long-rifle bullet is a rainbow, and the tiny slug offers little resistance to cross-winds. It gets pushed around. So our field practice, before we do any game shooting beyond 35 or 40 yards, should include plenty of wind study. This doping isn't easy with the .22, but what we learn there will help us with the bigbores.

Choosing a centerfire caliber for all-round small-game hunting isn't dificult. All we need in power is enough for the hardest-to-kill small game we'll hunt, though range may enter as a consideration, too. For instance, if turkey is the big prize—and legal to hunt with a rifle in our state—the factory-loaded .22 Hornet or .218 Bee would give us all the swat we needed at reasonable ranges, and maybe too much on some close-up shots. But as distance stretches out, say beyond 150 yards, we'd probably want more power, flatter trajectory, and certainly less sensitivity to wind. Then we might go to the .219 Zipper, .222 Remington, or .220 Swift, or even a 6 mm. or a .25, in all probability using none of them in full power loadings, since we like to eat roast turkey better than turkey hash.

Rifle Weight. The rifle itself is to be as happy a medium as we can get between snapshooting responsiveness and a certain sluggishness of weight that helps us to hold steadily when we have time for a difficult long-range shot. We can come rather close to this ideal.

Many of us have the strength to handle an unaltered Mossberg 144 or Winchester 75 target .22 in the brush and make quick, sure shots with it. Both weigh well under nine pounds. They have small, semi-beavertail forestocks that make trail carrying not too hard and that don't seem awkward for the quickest sort of snapshot—after we're used to them. Some of us could use a heavier smallbore target rifle in the same places. A gunsling fouls up in brush, and by removing it we take about one-half pound off the rifle. Put a four- or six-power target or "target and small game" scope on the gun, hook on the sling, and we have about two extra pounds' weight for the days when we go sniping. Of course there are light game scopes, too, and some pretty heavy, and there's a choice in iron sights.

Lighter .22s than the 75 and 144 can be made up into all-round small-game rifles. Interchangeable stocks could be fitted, light and heavy, though there's some danger of the off-duty stock's warping. Wood can be hollowed and filled with removable weights.

Some adjustments are so simple that they look silly. In the old Lynchburg, Virginia, rifle club a thin-barreled 52 Winchester sporter had been giving some of the members plenty of trouble when they got up higher than prone. A split section of heavy garden hose—not plastic stuff—clamped on the barrel added about a half pound just where it helped, and scores improved. It converted a snapshooting rifle into a pretty fair precision arm: you could get out more of the beautiful accuracy that had been built into the gun.

Fit. There's no great compromise here. The snapshooting rifle must feel just right, and for some of us that rules out an abrupt, full, close-up pistol grip and a comb pretty thick and high for iron sights. A too-long stock is bad for both snap and precision work. We fit the stock for fast mounting to the shoulder and learn to do good slow fire with it. That isn't hard.

Balance. Here we use about the same compromise—if it is a compromise—as we apply in the matter of fit. Too many think, I really believe, that we want a muzzle-light rifle for snapshooting. It feels good in the gun-store, "comes up like a shotgun," as we say. But our rifle shooting has to be far more precise than our scattergun work.

We still have the problem of leading game that's moving fast—and only one pellet to do the work. Time is short, and we must settle down quickly to the swing—and not overlead. The more experience we have in fast rifle shooting, the more we tend to appreciate extra weight out front in the barrel.

There's individual leeway here, the factors of reaction time and muscular development enter, and usually some ingrained habits insist on a hearing. But I do think that the barrel of the all-rounder we're considering should run no risk of being condemned

as a fly-weight when deliberate sniping happens to be in the order of the day's sport.

Sights. Not much more need be said about them here. Perhaps a good way to choose an all-purpose set is to select the iron or glass, or combination of both, that best suits us for the quick, usually close-up work, then have a target or small game scope of higher power handy for our slow precise shooting. If the rifle is stocked for snapshooting with irons, then a standard high-mounted target glass is going to ride so high that we lose the benefit of firm cheek-to-comb contact we need so badly in either slow or fast rifle work.

Putting on a cheek-pad brings comb height up where it belongs, though the heel stays low. This is no great disadvantage, though it certainly doesn't help! Be careful in choosing the height of the cheek-pad, for a tall one can scuff or even block the bolt of a long-throw bolt action. A short throw like those of the Model 70 Hornet and M-2 .22 Springfield isn't bothered.

A good combination of iron sights came as a rear peep with detachable pinhole target disc and one of those folding fronts that gave the choice between a bright, unshaded bead or post and a black post with a little protective ring of steel around it. This type of front seems to be off the market now.

If we keep out of shady woods—and how I'd hate to!—there'd be little need for a gold, red or ivory-tipped front sight. Out west you will find some of the best hunters doing well with a black steel front, and they keep it black to avoid any liability of glitter. Such a shine can absolutely crunch our hope of doing accurate shooting: it makes us see the center of the sight where it isn't.

BACKWOODS people have some pleasant ways of expressing themselves, usually including brevity. Their word for "vermin" is "varmints." It's a prettier term, though still unfamiliar to lots of nice people who'd blow their bolt at the thought of any close personal contact with vermin.

It seems that the British started using the itchy, crawly word "vermin" to include birds and four-footers that preyed on their preserved game. Here, our varmints are any creatures that are a general nuisance, or even a nuisance to a few. Leaving out the human types, we can list some of them as running in size from panther, wolf and coyote to woodchuck or groundhog, some hawks, the crow, and the all-too-common rat, whether or not he's of Norwegian background, with much of the Vikings' ruthlessness and courage in his make-up. These varmints can be harmful—perhaps they usually are—and so can such pests as bobcats, porcupines and snakes.

Today's varmint hunting ordinarily involves long-range shooting. Sometimes the bobcat is seen far off, but as a rule he's met close-up, as the other two are. He can be vicious, even dangerous, and so can a snake. But Porky is harmless unless you lower the range to the reach of his sweeping tail, and he isn't "sporting." He's not much warier than a stump, and not much faster in getaway than a caterpillar, which he resembles in gait.

Varmint hunting, on this continent, has come a long way in the last half-century. Supplying the varminter is a good-sized industry; it runs from mass production to art.

OLD TIMES

Back in the early 1900s varminting was a sport for kids, out east, and an occupation for men, out west. (Apply the usual discount needed to make common sense out of any sweeping statement.) The woodchuck was alive and therefore could be killed. In the days of horse-drawn farm machinery his burrows were hazardous to the legs of horses, or of cows, and he ate rich clover and raided gardens. Kill him and it was OK, though to the average landowner his eradication was a chore, and days were too full of work already. The same reasoning went for the crow and for many species of actually useful hawks.

Killing off wolves in the West was more of a business than a sport, and after a while there weren't many left to hunt. The coyote had his turn and—bless his hardy little soul—he hung on even through Government-backed poisoning campaigns. (Good grief, those employes had votes, hadn't they, and had to be looked after?) So it went, even though to competent and numerous riflemen he'd become as *desirable* a varmint as had the eastern woodchuck before him. The 10-80 poison, they tell me, kills slowly; it isn't like a well placed high velocity bullet. Birds, including eagles, ate the dead coyotes, and the damned stuff killed them. Some of the finest country became almost a lifeless desert.

CHAPTER 5

VARMINT RIFLES

As a sport, varmint hunting at first was casual. Now and then a deer rifle had the between-seasons dust blown out of it in the summer meadows and stubble fields, and lots of youngsters would take one or two trips a summer with a .22. Few of these part-time chuck, crow or coyote rifles were accurate as we know accuracy, and the rimfires crippled more often than they killed outright. Most people were harder then than now—I don't mean grittier or more enduring—and the thought of a gut-shot animal waiting hours or days for final release wasn't particularly harrowing, if it occurred at all.

Yet there were sportsmen in those days, a small proportion as always, and some of them liked varmint hunting and became artists through skill and good equipment. Even in the 1800s there were riflemen who used black powder and soft, gray lead in that sport. Some carried their bigbore hunting rifles and some toted heavy, superbly accurate single shots, many of them in Schuetzen 200-yard offhand style, with long-pronged buttplates, high, comfortable combs, palm rests attached to the forestocks, and sharply adjustable peep or glass sights. In calibers of .40, .45 and .50 the express bullets were common, hollow pointed and capped with a thin copper tube to increase bust-up when impact compressed the trapped air. Open hollow points were cast in calibers as small as the centerfire .22s, and some shooters used longer, heavier solid bullets for accuracy at greater ranges.

World War I Impetus

We Americans became bolt-action conscious after our part in the war that we entered on April 6, 1917. Springfields, Enfields and Mausers were converted to the uses of peace. The .30-06 started to become a popular cartridge, even displacing the .30-30 to some extent. Its 150-grain expanding bullet at a mere 2700 f. s. muzzle velocity was a killer on small stuff as well as on deer and black bear. Along with other loads it gave good accuracy, *and American riflemen began to make hits more regularly and at greater distances than ever before.*

Some did, that is, and some had been doing it for a long time. Custom rifles and wildcat cartridges weren't new, though both were almost unknown to the average shooter. Adolph O. Niedner's tight chambers that would accept only specially turned cartridge cases had been available to a few who knew about them, and special case forms had been tried with success. An efficient extreme was Niedner's "Hamburg" .25 that sent a 104-grain bullet at 3400 f. s. The case had a head of .30-40 Krag size and was over three inches long. The name came from the bullet's effect on chucks. Both Niedner and Dr. Mann had special single-shot bolt actions in this caliber.

Other varminting wildcats came along and some are still in use. They include Niedner's .22 Baby High Power, a long-bodied .218 Bee on .32-20 brass, his .22 Magnum, much like the factory Zipper that came years later, his .25s formed from .30-40 and .30-06 cases, and several trial .25s based on the 7x57 mm, made up for Major Ned Roberts. Two of the latter went into custom production, a Niedner shape, and a Griffin & Howe.

The Savage .22 High Power came out in 1912 and the .250 in 1915, Charles Newton designs. Newton had his own .256, a 6.5 mm, practically, on shortened 06 brass. In his catalogue he said of the .256 that "As a woodchuck rifle it is unexcelled." Its 123-grain soft point, wire reinforced against damage in magazine or upsetting from inertia when fired, left the muzzle of a 24-inch sporter at some 3000 f. s. A Western Cartridge Company load was available up to the 1930s, 129-grain open point at 2770, and many .256 Newton barrels, original and of later make, still get warmed up from firing.

And there were handloaders, busy as never before since black powder days. Some had to economize to get the shooting they wanted. In the 1930s a young chap told me of his pet woodchuck rifle, a sporterized Springfield, and of how he fed it. Jacketed stuff was fine, sure, but those bullets cost nearly three cents apiece (back then) and he liked his own pretty well. He cast the Ideal 311413 gas-check, so accurate as a 169-grain solid, and good enough even for chuck shooting in the hollow-point style he used. No doubt he spent time at it, but he'd hit a bullet temper that gave good breakup on stone and expansion on game, yet didn't lead his barrel. He was typical of thousands.

Single-shot enthusiasts had their fun, as always, and often got fine accuracy, too. Winchester, Remington-Hepburn and Stevens actions served with new or original barrels, and there were importations, such as the British Westley-Richards, Gibbs, and Farquharson.

In 1930 the first factory experimental lot of .22 Hornet cartridges was made. Pretty soon the tall, square, blue boxes of the first public issue, by Winchester, had shooters standing slack-jawed before store windows, then pleased or pretty durn doubtful, inside the shops. The velocity of those early rounds, non-corrosive but mercuric primed, was listed at 2350 —150 f. s. ahead of the 60-grain .25-20 high speed of that time. It was good velocity but not amazing. With the advent of non-mercuric and reloadable stuff, the figure went to 2400. Now it's climbed to 2690.

Unfortunately perhaps, many fine old single shots were rebarreled or relined for the new cartridge. It was certainly unfortunate when poor workmanship made the change. For years the Hornet was under a cloud as a result. "It just isn't accurate." "It keeps shifting its windage and elevation zeros." So do the others, in poorly assembled rifles.

Those who wanted bullet weight continued to get it in old reliable part-time varmint calibers that doubled as deer rifles, the .25-35 Winchester and Savage, .25-36 Marlin and .25 Remington. For the first and last a number of fine bolt actions were custom-made, and a heavy .25-35 single shot still is highly regarded as a varmint rifle, within its limit of range, and where people know rifles.

Factory and custom bolt guns in .250 Savage, .257 Roberts, .270, and .30-06 have done a lot of varmint hunting. Some became single-purpose arms for the sport, though the first two calibers weren't factory-loaded purely for varmint hunting until several years after World War II.

Between the two great wars the gunsmiths and designers and some who might not deserve either name brought out hundreds of wildcat cartridges, experimenting with case shape and capacity. The majority came in calibers of .25 or under, and most of these were of varmint hunting types. One of the finest, the Gebby .22 on .250 Savage brass, actually had the copyrighted name of "Varminter."

Special custom rifles for this sport became common, and in great variety of design. Among them was the Bull-pup type, short, heavy, chunky, and easy to pack, with its action, usually bolt, back along the high-comb stock, and its sights, almost always telescopic, riding high above the barrel. Bull-pups serve a number of purposes, but a lot of them specialize in varminting.

Later Days

So do more and more riflemen! The Second World War, like the First, was followed by a greatly increased interest in hunting—and to an encouraging extent in target shooting, too. The end of the flood of new, often one-season hunters is not in sight, and if some of us can't be altogether glad of it, we can at least do our part in making hunting safer.

That we can discuss later, but for one phenomenon we can be especially thankful. That is the increased popularity of the rifle-scope. It began, really, in depression days, when Weaver, Mossberg and others put them out at prices so low that even the kids could afford them. Cheap though they had to be, they were better than irons for hitting, and they let anyone with sense *know what he was shooting at.*

Depression days made available, too, improved American and foreign hunting scopes and mounts in the higher price brackets. Improvement has been steady, with varied-power scopes now becoming so general that failure to own one begins to look grim. It threatens social ostracism! The higher powers, and the bigger· objective lenses that carry a flood of light back to the eye, aren't only for the varminter, but he can use them as appreciatively as the bench-rester or the prone target shooter. They aren't essential. Skill is, and precision of equipment.

How About Hunting Skill?

Have varmints become more wary, necessitating us to take longer shots? Not much—in the east, that is. Out west the coyote has had to sharpen his wits or become extinct, and we must admire him for having partially succeeded—so far. Out east the crow, fox and chuck are much the same. Their situation as of now isn't so desperate.

I can't say that either woodchuck or hawk is wary game, can you? Short shots come along pretty regularly. I admire these varmints, all of them, the hawk especially for his wild, free living, the chuck for his grit and persistence in survival. But rarely can I admire one of either species as an artful dodger. Yes, some chucks that have been shot over do acquire wariness. But at that point one becomes a well known local challenge, and he seldom lives through the summer.

Usually a long-range shooter gets him, but sometimes a real hunter, a *stalker,* fires the fatal shot. Most of us with our flat-trajectory rifles are throwing away chances to learn to hunt, to use cover, to advance through it and fire from it. In open country, patience can make stalking possible, and that's a hunter's virtue, or a sniper's.

We respect the woodchucker or the western rock-chucker when skill lets him turn down all shots under 100 yards, or 150, or still more. Personally, I do *not* respect the shooter who makes 500- and 600-yard kills. Mostly he's lucky, and always the game killed outright at such distances is damned lucky. Too often a nose is blown off, a leg or foot shattered, or an abdomen opened just enough to insure death—after a while. To a civilized man, happenings like these "don't ·bear thinking of." Nor would they be easy to

bear, if we were on the wrong end of the incident.

Our varmint supply isn't inexhaustible, and these animals and birds. deserve as much consideration as game, for really they are game, too. Each of us has his sure, effective ·range on certain sorts of target, and we can lengthen that range by choosing the right equipment and *learning how to use it.* You bet we'd want to learn if we were wartime snipers and the target could return our fire. We'd study marksmanship techniques, wind and range estimation, sight adjustment, bullet trajectory and all the rest that adds up to hitting when the muzzle lifts in recoil. We'd learn our limitations, put a fence out behind them, and stay where we belonged.

Varmints are seldom protected by law, though they need it more and more as equipment is bettered—and general American rifle-shooting skill too, thank Heaven! I think it was Charles Landis who first spoke up in print against the springtime shooting of woodchucks. Give them till July 1 to raise their families, he said, and he was right. Kill the mother, and the helpless pups will starve. Self-imposed closed seasons apply to other game too. (I mean varmints, which are game to me and to lots of the other fellows.)

As a matter of hard fact, sometimes effective when other considerations go flat, nothing except poisoning and trapping is as hard on good chuck country as spring shooting is.

Varmint Calibers

Simply for convenience, we consider varmint calibers in this chapter as ending with the .257 Roberts. In its experimental and final forms it was designed for this sort of hunting. When Remington standardized the wildcat .25 of Major Roberts they necked the 7x57 Mauser case to hold .257-inch bullets. The Major had reformed the shoulder, giving it a gentle slope to burn the powders he'd been using with 87-, 100-, and 117-grain bullets, all of which did well with correct rifling spin. The more abrupt Remington shoulder eased case manufacture and gave greater powder capacity. High velocity sells rifles, and the factory case has capacity enough to let the handloader use it, unaltered, for heavier, longer custom bullets, really more big-game than varmint loads.

The .270 and .30-06 hang on to their old popularity as useful varmint sizes when appropriately loaded. Many other powerful sizes go varmint hunting. One of my friends used his .375 Magnum for a while; it was accurate and he was careful to avoid ricochets. In my early days I was as bad, probably worse, for I carried my·father's .50-95 black-powder express many a mile in woodchuck and crow country. I loved that 1876 Winchester, though it made me sweat on the hills. Its action was reliable, its trigger pull perfect, and I don't remember any of its bullets' glancing. The lead I cast was soft, and as a rule I slid the hollow-pointing plunger into the mold before I reached for the ladle.

J. C. Higgins 52.

Marlin 322.

FULL-TIME VARMINT RIFLES

At this writing we have three American factory-made rifles intended for that sport and nothing else. They aren't deer rifles, although with proper loading—which means more than just using full-metal patched bullets at standard velocity—they are excellent small-game guns. They get some use on bench rests, too.

J. C. Higgins 52

Barrel: 26 inches. At least some of these Higgins barrels have been chrome plated to resist erosion.
Weight: about 7½ pounds.
Sights: receiver peep and ramped gold-post front. Dovetails on receiver take regular Sako rings or loops for Weaver K-6 scope.
Magazine capacity: 5-shot detachable clip.
Safety: at right rear of bolt. Red indicator shows when it's off, regardless of whether striker is cocked or not.

Sears-Roebuck has given no "dusty answer" to the call for .222 Remington caliber sporters. Right now the report is that barrel and stock are made by High Standard, a capable, experienced firm.

My impression is that big mail-order houses award contracts where and when they get what they need in that nice balance of quality, price, and availability in quantity. It would be good business sense to do so, and they have it. It seems obvious that mail-order .22 rimfire ammo is made, from time to time, by different loading companies. Bullet design suggests that. There are several specially packaged brands besides the big five—Federal, Peters, Remington, Western and Winchester. Nearly all of them do what each particular type of cartridge should. I remember a 10-shot possible with "American Ammunition Company" long-rifles that none of us at the club had heard of before. High-speed stuff, which is *not* match ammunition.

The Higgins 52 action is the Finnish Sako, a tiny Mauser with two rear locking lugs and an extra or "safety" lug on the bolt handle. It started as the works for a Finnish small-game and varmint rifle using a short 7 mm. cartridge of no obvious value in America, it seems, though wildcatters may get around to little

.275s yet. It is a light action, but strong enough to mount guard over the pretty high .222 pressure, and it's stiff enough to bring out much of the fine bench-rest accuracy of that cartridge. The magazine capacity is enough for almost any varmint shooting—maybe not for coyotes, where packs still exist. Today, some of us would be inclined to marvel, not fire, at such a sight.

Good iron sights come on the rifle, and a six-power hunting scope is as appropriate on a .222 sporter as a four-power is on a Hornet or Bee. Each shows what you need to see within effective, sportsmanlike ranges. A glass with objective lens much bigger than the K-6's would have to ride higher to clear the barrel, though the 3/16-inch Firearms International adapter blocks would help. In final analysis that help would have doubtful value. The three factory rifles described in this section have only moderately high combs, and 3/16-inch extra drop is noticeable even when a comb is good and thick, as on this Higgins stock.

The rifle is neat and racy and its quick-detachable sling adds a custom look. Accuracy is good, around one-inch five-shot grouping at 100 yards, which is expected of a .222 Sporter.

Marlin 322

Barrel: 24 inches, Micro-groove rifling, 16 lands.
Weight: about 7½ pounds.
Sights: two-position receiver peep, giving approximately 100- or 200-yard zero selection instantly, as on the Higgins. Ramped, hooded front sight. Scope bases integral with receiver.
Magazine capacity: 3 .222's in detachable clip.
Safety: at right rear of receiver.

Like the Higgins, this Marlin is built on the Sako action with adjustable trigger pull and an indicator on the rear of the bolt to tell the locked or ready position of the safety. There's little difference in the appearance of the two rifles, and at this writing the Marlin costs only a few dollars more.

Marlin has gone to a fairly heavy barrel, without much taper, a good feature in a varmint rifle. Just

Winchester 43. Discontinued.

Winchester 43 Special. Gone!

ahead of the receiver, this barrel has an abrupt little step-down, more in the West European style than the gradual over-chamber taper of the Higgins. White spacers separate buttplate and grip cap from the walnut, but that decorative touch has appeared on and then vanished from some other Marlin models. The stock is of good American walnut, oil finished, the quality in keeping with the rest of the rifle. Oil is not the stuff to hide poor grain or color of walnut. Varnish does pretty well! It often hides real beauty, too.

Winchester 43

Barrel: 24 inches.
Weight: 6 pounds.
Sights: open rear and ramped, hooded front. Receiver is drilled and tapped, fore and aft, for scope mounts. Receiver peep sights have been available for the 43 since it came out. in late 1948 or early '49.
Magazine capacity: 3 in detachable clip.
Safety: at right rear of receiver.

The 43 is a less expensive, less powerful varminter than the Higgins or Marlin. The standard grade costs little less than half as much, though you can get it in the "Special," with pistol grip cap and checkering that add to its appearance. Its .22 Hornet and .218 Bee cartridges are effective up to, say 150 yards, and the .222 handled by the other two rifles adds some 50 or 75 yards' reliability. These ranges are named without any particular attention to smack or even to flatness of shooting, but with deep and rather somber reflection on what wind does to light little bullets that are far below the 4000 f. s. velocity class, for ultra speed does help a bit.

At first the .25-20 and .32-20 were in the line, the latter carrying only two rounds in its magazine—enough, at that, for a .32-20 is a hunter's rifle. It was wise to keep magazine capacity low and the bottom line of the stock so clean, for the protruding clip had been almost the only objection to the handling qualities of the enormously popular Savage 23 that once was made in all these calibers except the Bee.

But that .218 had made a reputation for accuracy in custom single shot and bolt guns, and in the Model 65 lever gun, too; so it was smart to carry it over to the new bolt action. This is a light bolt action, with locking lugs back amidships, and it is not for souped-up handloads. It has safe, adequate strength for doses of factory power, but here is a good place to remark that many of our little cases, post-war, are thicker at the base than originally made, and for that reason show reduced capacity. Handloads *must* run below pre-war maximum, for the extra brass doesn't add proportional strength to hold the increased pressures that old-time recipes would whip up in the new cases.

The 43 action somewhat resembles that of the Model 75 .22, though it has an extra locking lug and is about two inches longer. Like the Sako, it is a short bolt action for small centerfires. The bolt handle slants to the rear, nice-looking and handy. Early 43 and 75 handles are straight, not streamlined, though I never heard any practical objection to them. Probably we riflemen aren't as exacting as we should be, though arms manufacturers and some gunsmiths might call that the year's silliest statement.

HEAVY-FRAME VARMINT RIFLES

In breech action these are big-game rifles, so designed originally, and usually they are still barreled for such cartridges. Some make up into long range target or bench-rest rifles. Yet more and more of the sporters are being used as at least part-time varmint rifles; a few are frankly full-time.

Because they are primarily big-game rifles it seems best to describe their action details in later chapters. Here we consider them as varminters, and they've more than earned their right to such consideration.

Marlin 336 Zipper

Barrel: 20 inches, .219 Zipper, Micro-groove with 16 lands.
Weight: about 6¼ or 6½ pounds.
Sights: open rear and ramped, hooded front. Receiver drilled and tapped on top for Weaver and other scope mounts, and on the left side for receiver peep sight.
Magazine capacity: 5.
Safety: half cock notch in exposed hammer.

Marlin .219 Zipper carbine.

Remington 722-A, .222 caliber.

Winchester worked up the .219 Zipper cartridge for a varminting version of their Model 64 deer gun, fitting a long 26-inch barrel contoured like that of the old Extra Light Weight 1894 that was a special job, pretty much, and now seldom seen. Although the .218 Bee cartridge, which followed for the 65 Winchester, gave amazing lever-gun accuracy, the .219 64s were quite often disappointing. Almost any lever gun of this rear-locking type, handling a load of .219 power and intensity, fails to give consistent five- or ten-shot group accuracy on targets. Shots string up and down as the barrel gets hot. Immediately the Savage 99 comes to mind as an exception; its breech-up is snugger than that of most exposed-hammer repeaters. The little 65 Bee also did shoot good five- and even ten-shot groups, but more ambitious calibers usually start to wobble after three or four shots. Naturally a good varmint hunter seldom needs to use a magazineful.

So the little Marlin has its uses, as a flat, short saddle gun or as a light-weight for the dismounted varmint hunter. A sling comes on the SD or De Luxe Carbine 336, and it has quick-detachable swivels that wouldn't be hard to install on the less expensive standard carbine.

The 336 Zipper reminds me of a rather similar Winchester carbine I used for years, and liked. It was a good short range woodchuck gun, and all right for close-up deer if you took your time and were extremely careful, for its long 117-grain .25-35 bullet gave reasonable penetration. Yet that bullet expanded promptly on chucks and I have the decent memory of none ever wounded and lost by it. The longest shot I ever made with this gun was 133 paces, perhaps 120 yards, and the majority was below forty.

Almost every single chuck was dead when I got up to him; the old bullets were jacketed rather lightly. The now obsolete 87-grain hollow point at about 2700 f. s. (from a 26-inch rifle barrel) didn't appeal to me, but the frail 86-grain .25-20 soft point made up into a delightful low-power handload for practice

—not for chuck hunting. I had too much respect for those animals, I reckon.

The hollow-point Zipper jacket is so tough, comparatively, that I shouldn't expect good expansion much beyond 150 yards. That is probably well over the limit of .219 lever-repeater accuracy, such precision, anyway, as we ought to demand when we hunt small varmints. A .219 loaded to Hornet power shoots well, usually. That caliber is about through at 150 yards when the wind blows, and wind tempers a varmint-hunting day to our enjoyment. "The wind blows free" is a simple line of poetry, not the least bit intellectual, but to me it stirs priceless memory, and anticipation, too. I'm one of those fools who hunt for pleasure, not to boost my ego with long or difficult shots. A different sort of fool would pick a lever-action carbine for distance work.

Remington 722

Barrel: 26 inches in .222 and .244, 24 inches in .257 Roberts.
Weight: 8 pounds in .222 and .244, 7 to 7¼ in .257.
Sights: open rear and ramped bead front. Receiver is drilled and tapped for scope mounts and peep sight.
Magazine capacity: 4 in .244 and .257, 5 in .222.
Safety: at right rear of receiver.

This rifle, like the Model 721 for the longer .270, .30-06 and .300 Magnum cartridges, lost little time in gaining the respect of both varmint and big-game hunters. Several distinct advantages appeal to the varminter: high comb stock optional for the scope user; reasonable width of forestock and close-up location of pistol grip; adjustable weight of trigger pull and little if any rearward motion after the striker has been released; great action strength. Let's draw breath and then check over these details.

Both iron and scope sight stocks are of conventional hunting-rifle design, in no way extreme. The lines are good, though some forestock tips might need a bit of rounding off to please a critical eye. For most scopes and most shooters the scope stock is high enough. Since the pistol grip is located normally, it's no trouble to lace on a leather-covered comb pad, like the Jostam, if a thin-faced person using a tall-mounted scope needs it—and it'll fit where it's supposed to. On a rifle to really hunt with, moving about on our own two legs, the width of forestock is just about right. A full beavertail carries like a brick.

Precision shooting makes a varminter want a clean trigger pull, not too heavy. Only the experienced shooter wants and uses effectively a set trigger of "hair" weight. The plain trigger of this Remington is one of the good ones. Any factory rifle *may* get through inspections when it shouldn't, and then corrections are in order. The statement also applies to custom rifles, some of which are only so-called custom.

The action is strong, though that matter can best be discussed in a later chapter. This strength of lockup and the practically gas-proof enclosure of brass mean something to some varmint hunters—unfortunately. More than other hunters, I think, quite too many are tempted to use excessive charges in handloading, perhaps not realizing that what is a "maximum" load for one rifle may be dynamite in another of the same make, model and caliber. This action is no guarantee that folly's price won't have to be paid, but it's a help.

If you get a standard 721 or 722 you'll have the job of installing sling swivels. Leaving them off is one of the ways by which Remington keeps the price low, like the use of some steel stampings instead of machined parts. Fair enough: you can locate those swivels to please yourself. For woods hunting of deer and bigger game you might not want a sling. Even swivels catch in brush.

Both .222 and .244 in the Model 722 are popular. They are accurate, and you choose between them according to details of ammunition cost, the amount of racket you can make in your hunting grounds, and the ranges at which you'll shoot, and—let's hope—learn your rifle and yourself and thus kill cleanly. Barrel life comes in, too, and we'd expect much longer tenure from the .222, although .244 barrels are made of selected Ordnance steel. Time will tell their value, but

two practically identical barrels *may* enjoy quite different life-spans even when treated alike.

The light .257 is mentioned as a varmint rifle because so many like this caliber for both deer and varmint hunting, in appropriate seasons. A light rifle gets around when a heavy one often stays home. Familiarity sharpens our skill with a rifle. The .257 with the 117-grain bullet is fairly useful in brush, which the 95 grain .244 or any bullet so light and fast is not. If this Remington .257 had a long magazine or one that could easily be lengthened safely (to the rear, not up front near the seat of the locking lugs), we could handload 125- and 140-grain bullets for it. We do this with some other .257s, perhaps having the rifling throat reamed to give a safe, proper fit for long bullets.

That high-comb stock deserves study. Comb drop is 1⅜ inches, heel 2-3/16, from the line of iron sights. Figures for the Winchester Model 70 with Monte Carlo are 1-5/16 and 2-5/16, with 1-11/16 at the rear of the Monte. All these are approximate, wood not being turned and finished with the precision spent on even the outside of a fine rifle barrel. For most shooting in prone I don't like a Monte as well as a straight-top stock. Though I'm particular, either of these stocks would suit me and soon become familiar. On a rifle of heavy recoil, like the .375, or the Featherweight .358, I'd want a high comb to slant away forward so that it wouldn't rise up and crack me. But hardly anyone chooses a varmint rifle that kicks. For most hunting of this type there's no need to.

Remington 760

Barrel: 22 inches.
Weight: about 7¾ pounds in .257, .222 added, 1957.
Sights: open rear and ramped front. Receiver is ready for better sights, iron or glass.
Magazine capacity: 4.
Safety: cross button at rear of trigger guard.

Why isn't this a varminter in .257? Even the heavier calibers give rather good accuracy in this tightly breeched and rigid rifle that revised our opinions of what to expect from pump guns, now that the old

The 722-A in .244.

Remington 722-B "Special" grade comes with sling swivels and checkering, and this .222 has a quick-detachable type of swivels and sling and is fitted with Koilmorgen Bear Cub 6-power scope on a Stith mount.

solid frame Colt black-powder arm is little more than
a memory.

Although the 760 barrel can be removed, the factory people state that this is a gunsmith's job and
shouldn't be done except when necessary. They call
the 760 a solid-frame rifle, and essentially they're
correct. Since the action tube is not hog-tied to the
barrel like the magazine tubes of pump action .22s,
the barrel is practically free-floating, and that feature
makes for accuracy in a rifle of this type. Rather moderate handloads would increase accuracy, just as they
do in a bolt action .220 Swift, for example, or a .219
lever gun.

Speed of pump-action fire would mean little to an
experienced varminter, and he might call the method
of sling attachment, out at the end of the action tube,
neither convenient nor comfortable. Still, he could use
this .257 effectively in his woodchuck or coyote hunting, and then have a handy deer rifle familiar and
ready for the fall season.

Perhaps I'd best confess that I included the 760
in this chapter partly because of a certain bullhead-
ness that plagues my soul at times, and partly because of my respect for the .257 Roberts, which lately
has been treated like a stepchild with halitosis. But
really it belongs here, if only to settle into its place
with a somewhat disturbing jolt. Probably 997 varmint hunters in 1000 would prefer a bolt, and two
a single shot. That leaves one, who'll take the 760
and be happy. Late-comers I'd forgotten would be
carrying lever guns, or a 740 Remington Auto in .244.
I can't swear to these ratios.

Savage 99

Barrel: 22 inches on 99-F Featherweight, 24 inches on EG,
   R and RS.
Weight: F, about 6½ pounds; EG, 7¼; R and RS, 7½.
Sights: open rear, ramped gold bead front. Receivers are
   drilled and tapped for peep sights and top-mounted
   scopes. Factory fits Weaver scopes on special order.
   99-RS has Redfield 70 LH receiver peep with micrometer elevation and windage knobs, and a blank piece
   in rear sight slot on barrel.
Magazine capacity: 5 in revolving spool magazine.
Safety: sliding fingerpiece at right rear of trigger guard.

For many years the 99 has been doing nicely as a
varmint rifle, though it was designed as a big-game
arm. True, a 1900 ad called it "one rifle for large and
small game," in the .303 caliber.

The rigid stock-bolt, the solid abutment of the
breechblock against the rear wall of the receiver, and
the absence of a tubular magazine under its barrel
produced better than usual lever-action accuracy. The
.25-35, .303 and .32-40 Savages shot well and got
lots of off-season use on varmints. The .250 carried
on as a modern high-intensity caliber, and even the
unfortunate .22 Hi-Power cartridge developed good
accuracy when fired from a solid-frame 99 with heavy
barrel of standard or special issue.

In 1956 the .243 Winchester went into the line, a
sensible addition. The strength of the action, an early

smokeless powder design, was at, or close to, the top
of lever-operated repeaters, and *modern* steel increases it.

Savage uses chrome-molybdenum steel in currently
made barrels for this model. This is a great favorite for
strength and wearing qualities—though the strength
of modern barrels is taken for granted.

Contemporary 99 stocks have typical iron-sight dimensions. The drop in inches at comb and heel, and
the length, are as follows: F, 1⅝, 2⅝, 13; EG, 1⅞,
2⅝, 13; R and RS, 1⅝, 2⅞, 13½. But the hammerless, side-ejecting Savage is ideal for low scope mounting, and a comb pad can be laced on, for no open-air
bolt slides back to scuff against it. Forestocks look
short for sling anchorage, but we must remember
that the Savage action and receiver are nearly two
inches longer than those of most lever guns with exposed hammers.

The buttplates of the F and EG are smaller than
those of the R and RS, which are designed more as
precision rifles for target or long-range field shooting,
with bigger stocks and semi-beavertail forearms. In
considering the .243 or .250, as the lever-fancying
varminter certainly would, this detail would mean little. These cartridges have light recoil, and the modern
99 buttplates are so well shaped that positioning any
of them securely between shoulder and collarbone is
no trouble at all.

But it's certainly true that a high velocity 6 mm.—
wildcat or .243 or .244 factory standard—is downright unpleasant for some of us to shoot if we've
chosen a 22-inch barrel. Thing cracks like a Swift, or
worse! Two more inches of barrel add little if any
velocity, but some comfort. Many shooters don't mind
noise, just as some don't mind recoil. A cotton plug
in the left ear, if you're right-handed, takes the end-
of-all-that's-lovely blast out of most rifle reports, and
it's no great handicap in open-country hunting of varmints. Recoil? We can learn to ride it out. You get
little of it from these small calibers.

The .250 Savage 99 with solid frame and reasonably
heavy barrel has a long-established reputation as the
best of lever-action varminters. At moderate ranges
the discontinued .218 Bee Winchester Model 65 shot
as accurately, but its light bullet at medium velocity
was not satisfactory at much over 100 yards if the
wind whipped up, just like the Hornet. The .243 flattens 99 trajectory—plenty. If its full power loads give
less accuracy than that of the 99 .250, slightly reduced
handloads should bring it into line.

Savage 340

Barrel: 22 inches in .22 Hornet; 24 in .222 Remington.
Weight: about 6¾ pounds in these calibers.
Sights: disc elevator open rear with click adjustments, ramped
   front with gold insert. Receiver ready for Savage 175
   Micro Peep and, in these calibers, for Weaver detachable
   side-mounted scopes.
Magazine capacity: 4 Hornets or .222s in detachable clip.
Safety: at right rear of receiver.

Winchester 70 .243 Varmint Rifle, heavy-weight barrel. Front scope block, on barrel, gives two positions, 7.2 or 6 inches on centers, when rear block is on receiver ring. But this one has its rear block back on the receiver bridge, just behind the loading opening, to give longer radius and finer adjustments.

This is the least expensive of American-made varmint rifles, and of .30-30 deer rifles too, now that the Savage 219 single shot is out. The latter was a breakdown of single-barrel shotgun-action type, and something of a surprise in good accuracy, especially perhaps in its light calibers, Hornet, .25-20 and .32-20. Most of us had forgotten how foreign sporters of the type—much more expensive of course—would shoot.

The 340 gives choice of standard or the special 340-S grade. The latter has grip and forestock checkering, a peep and hooded gold-bead front, and screw eyes for a carrying strap. These we'd turn out and replace with swivels for an Army-type gunsling.

The 340s aren't cheap. They represent a refinement through many years, starting with the 325 Stevens, which was serviceable but pretty clubby in appearance. The present 340 is stream-lined, as the advertising says, except for a certain chunkiness through the mid-section, which would annoy few people, and please others, for it stiffens the stock where the magazine inlet comes, and thus improves accuracy. The pistol grip is a little far back, maybe, but it might not seem so if you think of a *hunting* rifle and forget all the target arms you ever saw.

That stock is long, 13¾ inches from trigger through buttplate, but it has the standard 1⅝ and 2⅝ drop for iron sights. Side ejection and low bolt-lift let a scope ride low, and we charge the magazine when it's out of the rifle: we don't feed the rounds in through the top of the receiver. That is, we don't have to.

Shortening the stock would make the comb feel higher, for our face would move up on the stock. This would be easy to do, and it should be done if a short-armed shooter is to get much benefit from the pistol grip. A long trigger-reach makes the swell seem more of a nuisance than a help. This grip is close-up enough to help any hand but an extremely small one.

Action refinements provide a fast striker fall, and the crispness of trigger release is stressed. The Savage plant adjusts the headspace of this rifle snugly and precisely. This makes for safety and is one of the built-in factors of accuracy.

For the shooter who wants a rugged, inexpensive varmint rifle the 340 is a logical choice. It retails for less than most used guns that might look—and prove —satisfactory for the purpose, and in buying it you get a new barrel, not one that quite likely has had the peak of accuracy shot out of it. If the buyer is not well enough informed to select a second-hand rifle with complete, well-founded confidence—and perhaps isn't

sure that he's going to be a lifetime varmint hunter— he should find this 340 a good one to pick. Maybe he'll go on and refine it in little ways, and never let it go. For rough country and tough going it'll always be good to have.

Winchster 70

Barrel: 22 inches in Featherweight, 24 in most standard rifles, except 26 in .220 Swift, .300 Magnum, and heavy weight .243.

Weight: from about 6¾ or 7 pounds in small caliber Featherweights to about 10½ or 11 pounds in Heavy Weight .243.

Sights: open rear and ramped, hooded front are standard. Target models now come without iron sights, but muzzle is ramped and slotted, or smooth and drilled, for attaching a target-type front sight. Receivers are ready for peep sights or top-mounted hunting-type scopes, and any 70 not regularly equipped with blocks for target scope mounts can be so fitted. The screw holes for the rear block are already drilled, then filled with plug screws.

Magazine capacity: 5 in all calibers except the Magnums.

Safety: at right rear, on the bolt sleeve.

Varmint hunters were interested in the 70 as soon as it came out, in 1937. The preceding Model 54 had been made in four calibers useful in this sport: .22 Hornet, .220 Swift, .250 Savage and .257 Roberts. Its heavier calibers were also of value in the meadows and mountains and on the plains, such sizes as .270, 7 mm., .30-06 and .300 Magnum.

The 70 has changed a bit through its near-generation of use—a full generation, maybe, in old times, or at present. Now you might be even more sure of "getting a good one." Few have needed barrel-and-action bedding refinements at all badly, and wood-working techniques in factory production have improved. Barrel accuracy is of a high order. Trigger pulls are almost invariably good, and they're adjustable for weight.

Any Mauser-type bolt action handling rimmed or semi-rimless rounds through the staggered, double-column magazine can give a little difficulty in feeding, but there's been almost no trouble with the Hornet cartridge, a single-shot rifle descendant that is heavily rimmed, and not much with the Swift, a typical semi-. Most magazines let us handload bullets a *little* farther out than standard, and blocked-off mags like those of the .243 and .257 can be converted into full-length .30-06 style. Just knocking out the front spacer of the .220 lets us load about as long as we'd wish with 55- or even 60-grain bullets. These three calibers and the Hornet (much too good a little baby never to be considered) are those of interest to most varmint hunters who like a 70. It now appears that the Hornet is to be streamlined out of M70 production.

But for a super long range rifle there's the Bull Gun, which I mention in spite of two serious drawbacks. First, it weighs about thirteen pounds, and we'd want a sling to tote as well as to steady it, and a couple of pounds or so of good scope. Second, for long range varminting with the .30-06 or .300 Maggie for which this rifle is regularly made, most of us would demand at least a 150-grain bullet, which would have to be built lightly enough to expand promptly on small animals 'way out beyond, and to break up and not ricochet over settled country. The Win-Western 150 with long-exposed soft point is for varmints, all right, but it's a bit blunt at the nose. Some custom makers, such as Barnes, are obliging in jacketing bullets for special needs. Perhaps we could swage a 170-grain .30-30 soft-nosed to pointed form and not have so much lead sticking out that it'd upset from inertia when launched at high speed. Niedner, I think, and some others, made sharp-points from 117-grain .25-35s, but shed some of the lead weight in doing so.

A Magnum rifle built like this one isn't uncomfortable to shoot, compared, say, to a nine-pound .270 or 06 sporter. The heavy 28-inch barrel and the target stock of the Bull Gun lighten the jolt of recoil, and the barrel length cuts muzzle blast.

The standard heavy target rifle of about 10½ to 11 pounds formerly came in most 70 calibers except the .375. Now it's offered in 24-inch .30-06 and 26-inch .243. The latter barrel is made of stainless steel and it seems that this metal is used for all 70 .220s and .243s now put out. It is similar to the "Staynless" Winchester steel of 20 to 30 years ago, but by no means precisely the same, for then the stuff was in its infancy, as far as most American barrel-makers were concerned. Boehler Anti-Nit and Poldi Anti-Corro were old-timers by comparison, having been used in Europe about 1910. Early Winchester Staynless couldn't be blued, for blueing is a rust process; so it was lacquered. Modern Winchester stainless is iron-plated, then browned a nice dark finish. At this writing the factory estimates that it will triple barrel life with high-intensity loads.

Swift .220 barrels of Proof Steel have been noted for their outside finish, so much more glareproof than the standard. That sand-blasting now is applied to the stainless barrels, a good thing, for a varmint rifle usually goes hunting on sunny days. The bright gleam of polished, blued steel sends out the alarm; it's a sort of heliograph like those used to wink out signals during the Boer War. Then of course it was intentional; and "they did it with mirrors."

This target rifle is stocked perfectly for use with target scopes, which come in almost any magnification or light-gathering power we'd want—choosing in line with our needs—and with sharp, precise windage and elevation adjustments in the mounts. Some are spe-

cifically named "varmint scopes," and almost any of them *are* that.

Winchester christened the G 7012 CN the "Varmint Rifle," the first time they'd used the name so formally, to my knowledge. It's properly designated: .243 caliber, 26-inch heavy barrel, scope blocks instead of iron sights, though it's ready for irons, and a sporting-style high comb Monte Carlo stock. It's handsome, as varmint rifles usually go, except for its pistol grip. That cries out for a rubber cap, or for the refining trim-out that goes with a capped 70 grip. Admittedly, the cry is so faint that most shooters wouldn't hear it.

Scope blocks on this model need some comment. As standard, the rear block is screwed to the receiver ring, and the 70 match front block on the barrel, giving two inter-block distances, six and 7.2 inches, center to center. With the usual quarter-minute-click mount the 7.2 distance gives ¼-inch correction at 100 yards, and more or less in proportion to range. With 6-inch spacing we get about 1/3 minute per click. But some of these Varmint Rifles evidently carry the rear block on the receiver bridge, giving about 11 and 12.2 inches between centers. The 10.6-inch spacing on the Remington 40X .22 match rifle results in 1/6-inch clicks (or 1/6 minute of angle, for all practical purposes), and we'd get maybe 1/7 minute with the 12.2 basing. A shooter must prove out the finest details for himself, despite the beautifully exact work of both mount makers and rifle makers. Some of us find that in offhand even the short .6-inch setting on 70s does put the scope eyepiece too far ahead for a full view of the field. Then the front mount can be set back, a common custom adjustment, like the bridge locating of a rear mount.

The standard 70 sporters usually weigh at least 8½ pounds in the small varminting calibers, and for scope use they're available with the high Monte comb. These rifles do lots of varmint hunting and serve well. Accuracy and general performance are as a rule superb. The 70 is one of the most expensive American factory rifles, and if its makers, and others, can maintain quality in the face of higher labor and material costs, those of us who buy new rifles will be happy. Some of us have older rifles we shouldn't sell except under necessity, and quite often, it seems, these are 70s.

Winchester 88

Barrel: 22 inches.
Sights: Lyman folding 16 A open rear and ramped, hooded front. Receiver ready for peep sight or top-mounted hunting scope.
Magazine capacity: detachable box magazine holds 5 rounds and is inserted from below when breech is open.
Safety: cross button at front of trigger guard.
Weight: about 6¾ pounds in .243 caliber.

The three locking lugs of the bolt are right up front, and the extractor is built into the bolt face in Remington 721-722 style—or like those of earlier Win-

Sako Sporter.

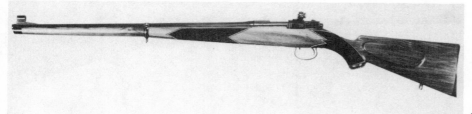

Sako Mannlicher.

Sako Heavy Barrel Rifle.

Sako barreled action.

chester lever action repeaters with exposed hammers. There's no cut-out of the receiver ring to let the extractor pass through. The results are rigid support of the cartridge's head, and great strength.

Many varminters have liked a light, short-barreled 6 mm., and perhaps almost as many have liked the handiness of a lever action. Here they get both, in a lever action design with tight breeching and one-piece stock that give accuracy on a par with that of bolt guns of similar caliber, weight and build.

The hammerless action, reasonably convenient forefinger safety up front, and side ejection are points they'd generally approve. This rifle is stocked like the standard 70 except that it's a bit higher at the heel, and the folding rear sight on the barrel indicates that the 88 is rather expected to wear a scope. A thinfaced shooter might want to lace a pad over the comb to raise it for a hunting glass. Few light-weight high velocity varmint rifles are fitted with a high-riding target scope. That usually goes on a heavier arm,

which is easier to shoot with fine precision and as a rule has finer inherent accuracy built into it. Yet more than ever before, it does seem, featherweight varmint rifles are popular. Some of us enjoy plenty of walking, even over rough ground, and have no consuming desire to make long, hard shots. We like the outdoors and want to visit plenty of it under the power of our own legs. So a good many .243 rounds will be fired from 88s, from Savage 99s too, as well as from the handy little bolt guns that are established so firmly.

SOME FOREIGN VARMINTERS

A few years after World War II a new type of foreign rifle began coming over, a light-weight varminter for medium-power smallbore cartridges. The short or *kurz* Mauser action had been pretty familiar for years. Made originally for cartridges like the 6.5x54 and 8x51, it was just right for our .250 Savage, or for the .35 Remington deer and black bear load.

Another short-action varminter,
the BSA with American-style stock.

BSA varmint rifle stocked in the
British style.

Fine, light custom varminters were made up in .250 caliber.

Here are a few representatives of the new crop.

The Finish Sako is light all-round, with small receiver and bolt, slim but adequate stocking, and thin, nicely tapered barrel. This 6½-pound varminter has become popular, especially in .222 Remington caliber, though the Hornet and Bee are still offered. It's accurate, often *averaging* one-inch 10-shot groups at 100 yards, for quality has been built into it. Foreign labor costs are Death Valley low, compared to ours.

Even so, the actions, with or without barrels fitted, are commonly imported by the agents, Firearms International Corporation, 1526 Connecticut Ave., Washington 22, D. C. Our best gunsmiths can build super-accurate rifles—there's no doubt of that—and some excellent amateur work is turned out, top grade "do it yourself" activity. When time and skill are available the work can be first-rate, wherever it is done.

Sako rifles are nice-looking. The current stocks are of French walnut instead of the light wood formerly used, and cheekpiece and checkering are in good proportions, well planned and executed. The action has an adjustable trigger and a detachable three-round magazine which show the results of careful workmanship.

Three styles are offered, the light-barreled sporter with average length, rounded-tip forestock, or with the full-length Mannlicher-Schoenauer style forestock, and the heavy-barreled eight-pound sporter or bench rifle that comes in .222 only, with higher, thicker stock comb. About the only way in which these arms look or feel different from most contemporary high-grade American sporters becomes apparent when you pick one up and mount it at your shoulder. Pistol grip and stock comb are a little far back. But these are hunting rifles, the sort you may have to fire from almost any inconvenient position, and after one has grown familiar with this type that seems rather old-fashioned, he's apt to approve it and be satisfied. It's

true that a small hand gets little support from such a grip and comb face.

The JGA or J. G. Anchutz is imported by the Thalson Company, 682 Mission St., San Francisco 5, and it's an established make. It has a small Mauser-type action, with double set triggers available for easing off a long, difficult shot, and with its little but adequate cheekpiece it resembles high-power Mausers that were imported a generation and more ago. Some

Bolt lift of the BSA gives plenty of room for a low-mounted scope.

But most varmint scopes now chosen have big objective and ocular lenses. Their wide, brilliant field is preferred to the snugness of a smaller, low-mounted scope such as the big-game hunter would select for use in the woods, where he might have to take a quick shot. The BSA bolt handle is planned to take care of low mounting for whoever might want it to get a good, high comb fit without having the stock built up.

JGAs have been made in .22 rimfire, and the popular little varmint trio, Hornet, Bee and .222, is planned for import.

The BSA short action varmint rifle comes from England to Al Freeland, 3737 14th Ave., Rock Island, Illinois. Calibers are Hornet and .222, the latter greatly favored, and there's thought of making the medium action Birmingham rifle—for mid-length rounds like the 7x57 mm., .257, .300 Savage and .308—in .243 and .244. Both actions can be had as single shots, with no magazine cut-out to detract from the stock's stiffness, a bench-rest rifle feature that went into common use some years ago and even then was far from new.

Two types of stock have come in. The British has a snobble-tipped forearm which is slim out front but will take a sling. Its cheekpiece is blended more into the top line of the stock than that of the American type, which has a heavier forearm with rounded tip. Both look good, and both are similar in lines to custom stocks that are made right along. Our earliest custom bolt-action rifles usually had that little curling

wave of a snobble (schnobble, schnauble: take your choice or construct your own variant), that swell out front, and so did many rifles from factories all over the world. It adds a touch that some shooters like and it does no harm unless it's so big that it's ugly.

The receiver is dovetailed for quick-detachable hunting scope mounts, and the irons regularly supplied are of an accepted American type for a rifle of this kind, bead front and two-leaf folding open rear. British Parker-Hale and American Stith scope mounts are offered, both good, established types. If a receiver peep sight is used, a full-faced man might have to sand down the American comb a bit, for it's as close to adequate "telescope height" for even a thin-faced individual as almost any that aren't specially custom made.

The built-in magazine has a hinged floorplate for emptying or cleaning, and holds four .222 rounds. Its familiar Mauser (or Japanese) type of release lies at the front of the trigger guard. The safety is a new one, handy to the thumb, at the rear of the action.

CUSTOM RIFLES

Used to be, about all you could get in a fine bolt action varmint rifle was made to order. Most of them took custom cartridges. The factories hadn't caught up with wildcatter's progress, because of mass-production costs and the resultant conservatism. They never can, at least in variety of cartridge shapes.

Years ago the Niedner Rifle Corporation listed for me some of their high-velocity .22s: .22 WCF, .25-20 Single Shot, .25-21, .25-25, .25-35, .25 and .30 Remington rimless, .28-30, .32-20 and .32-40. The latter two of these neck-downs were the most popular with the discriminating clientele. In weight, the jacketed bullets ran from 40 to 60 grains, and the specimen I still have is a beauty. Today's bench-resters could use that sort of stuff. Some of these bullets had the base band designed by Dr. Mann—or at least it seems original in the jacketed form. That 1/16-inch band fitted rifling diameter, and the bore-bearing section above it rode on the rifling lands.

An Ackley 6 mm. sporter on Mauser action. Weight 9 pounds, 1 ounce.

Left side view of the Ackley 6 mm. Stock is fancy American walnut. Some rather nice wood grows here, don't you think?

A .228 Ackley, Mauser action, stocked in koa wood.

An Anthony Guymon stream-lined sporter. It is typical of the "Western school" of stocking, planned for fit and comfort in long-range shooting. Most shooters either definitely like it or definitely don't.

And Niedner made well-known .25s on 7x57 mm., .30-40 and .30-06 brass, the first being one form of .25 Roberts. Griffin & Howe of New York made a .25 Roberts of slightly different case shape, and they were prompt in putting the factory .257 chambering into their production. There were other special Niedner cartridges, and their chambering for standard rounds left out little that was desirable then.

In rimfire barrels they made .22 and .25, in varminting sizes the Hornet, .25-35, and .250-3000 Savage. For the big-game hunter there were the .270, 7x57, .275 Holland & Holland Magnum as well as the .300 and .375, also the .300 Savage, .30-06— I'm not sure about the .30-40—.35 and .405 Winchester, .35 Whelen (a wildcat), .45-70 and .45-90. The .32-20 was included, and those old target sizes, .32-40 and .38-55. Niedner revolver barrels came in .38 and .44 Smith & Wesson calibers. This list isn't complete, probably; I wish it were.

A few high-intensity varmint calibers were imported. The .240 Holland & Holland Apex fires a 100-grain bullet at just under 3000 f. s. muzzle velocity, and the German Halger, of lurid memory, didn't know when to stop staking out claims to super-velocity. Nominally a .244, it used .252-inch bullets in the necked-down 6.5x57 case.

We mustn't forget the American .256 Newton, still in use by some who know and appreciate it. Western and Remington both made this ammunition—cases, at least—and the Western loaded ammunition was commonly available. Not now.

Paul Jaeger, Jenkintown, Penna., has been making special varmint rifles for some years. His calibers include .220, .243, .244 and .257, and the long-proved wildcat .22-.250. For these he generally uses Mauser actions, and for the .222, the Sako. His standard varmint rifle has a long, heavy barrel, no iron sights, just scope-blocks, a Monte Carlo that's high and full enough to give good support, and a pistol grip not too close-up to allow some flexibility when you fire

from impromptu positions. The forestock is semi-beavertail and the butt pad is thin, soft rubber, not to take up recoil but to position the stock securely against your shoulder. He can furnish his Model 50 adjustable trigger for Mauser, Springfield or Enfield actions; and for Mauser, Springfield, Krag and Winchester 54 rifles he has a long, wing-type safety that you can reach at the side of a low-mounted scope.

Anthony Guymon, 203-R Shore Drive, Bremerton, Wash., includes in his calibers the .220, .243, .244 and .250 Savage, and the wildcat .22-.250, .220 Swift Improved, .243 Rock-Chucker (a rock-chuck is a western woodchuck that offers long shots in safer country to take them from than is common out east), and .25-06 Improved. Pretty typical lineup, though some would condemn a cask of .25-06 Improved size, saying that the merely necked-down .30-06 case is quite large enough for any .25 caliber bullet's powerhouse, and that it's uneconomical to go bigger. You can get rifles from him, or from practically any custom gunsmith, in single-shot style if you want a solid, stiff mid-section in your stock. Like many others, he classifies his work as either semi-custom or built to order. He uses solid wood, or laminated, and many find the latter less subject to warpage and actually prefer the appearance, on a good job, naturally. Neat contrast of dark and light strips of wood does have its beauty.

His "stream-lined" stock looks odd to some, to state it mildly. Its large pistol grip flows back into the stock lines, forward to curl out toward the trigger guard. The Monte Carlo comb rises toward the rear like a wave, slants away forward almost into the grip, and the "roll-over" cheekpiece, though massive, is built for comfort. The forestock is a wide but tapered beavertail. An old custom trick, especially on rifles and shotguns built for ladies' use, is the cast-off of the buttstock's toe, only about one-half inch on the Guymon, but enough to prevent toe jab when you shoot prone.

This 5-pound, 14-ounce .22-.250 by Ackley, stocked in fancy American walnut, was built to combine extreme lightness with varmint-hunting accuracy.

Unquestionably this stock gives secure, comfortable grasp in most firing positions, and big magnum loads would be tamed by it because (1) the pistol grip is large enough to afford a real hold, (2) the full roll-over comb hasn't the least suggestion of abrupt, bruising lines, and (3) that comb slants downward at the front, so that it can't rise up and crack you one.

Any "extreme" stock styling gets some criticism; it's far from the streamlining of a Kentucky muzzle-loader, which was practical for the uses of its time. But between the Kentucky and the more conventional of today's best custom work there was no smooth and even progress. A few of the early custom bolt-action rifles are by no means as beautiful as some made today. You can't shoot them as well, either. Naturally I have my own preferences and tastes, but they're immaterial to the question we're grappling with here. That question is: can efficiency and beauty meet without fighting in a rifle stock? A sub-question, though a much tougher one, is: what constitutes beauty? We agree rather closely, according to our physical build, on what makes a stock so comfortable and easy to shoot that sometimes we do better than our former best with it. That's a rifleman's dream, sometimes realized.

.We don't agree about beauty, and tastes change with times. Today, some might say that Venus de Milo badly needs a dieting regimen, or that Mona Lisa has a prissy little face.

The Ace Varmint Rifle comes from Flaig's Lodge, Millvale, Penna. Caliber choice is .22-.250, .220, .250, .257 and .270, regular stock just now. This rifle is reasonably light, rather graceful in outline, and stocked well enough except possibly for the use of heavy loads in prone. But it's a varmint rifle.

Checkering is fine. The pistol grip cap is of real buffalo horn, and it flares out at the bottom, moderately. A Pachmayr rubber recoil pad or one of the beautifully made old Niedner checkered steel butt-plates finishes the stock.

Barrels are made by Ackley or Douglas (both excellent) and are 26-inchers of moderate weight. The action is the Fabrique Nationale Belgian Mauser, with Jaeger or Mashburn adjustable trigger. Regular issue, at extra cost, is the Ajack 7½-power scope with huge objective glass that gathers light if any is to be had. The side mounts are of Leupold or Jaeger make.

Parker O. Ackley (mailing address, Box 185, Murray, Utah) is one of the custom makers who have seen and applied changes in stock design in their time, but not merely to produce something new, a Friday morning special. I am afraid that some have done so, and I also fear that others have been accused of doing so when they were applying features which their reason and shooting experience told them were helpful.

Custom stocks for high-power bolt action rifles began in this country, we could say, at about the time when a few knowledgeable experts (and they deserved the name) took up the 1903 Springfield in .30-06 caliber as a sporting rifle. Much, not all, of the work was beautiful, wouldn't have offended even an artist by its line and proportion. Down through the years we've had such stocks. They're still made. Although some of us think they are ultra-conservative and even impractical for accurate shooting, some others don't. I quote from Mr. Ackley, with his permission, of course.

"We try to be flexible enough to furnish something the customer wants so that when he gets it, it will look like something he had in mind instead of something that the stockmaker thinks it should look like. This is a very common fault with many inflexible stockmakers because all of their stocks look like they have been cast in a mold regardless of whether some are light or some large and heavy. One of the best stockmakers in the United States is Jules La Bantchni, and he always says that a stock can be beautiful and useful at the same time."

Later: "I am still at a loss to understand why the American stockmakers get the club 'accent.' They seem to think it necessary to have a pistol grip close enough to the trigger so that you have to turn yourself inside out to get a hold on it. This might be all right for the Bench Rest profession, but on a sporting rifle it is completely out of place.

"We also have the Monte Carlo complex, or sort of a monstrous creation with the comb slanting down or up or crosswise or what have you.

"I think that if some of these guys would try it out, they would find that a straight stock without a Monte Carlo would not whip so much as these radical ones, thus making it more pleasant to shoot."

The Ackley range of caliber choice is wide, and some of his wildcats are to be discussed in the chapter on custom rifles.

Quote again. "There are no Wildcat cartridges which are actually revolutionary. There are a few which fill the gaps between existing commercial cartridges. There are many more which are no better and perhaps not as good as their commercial counterparts.

"There is no evidence which substantiates the claim that one cartridge design is more accurate than another. It certainly cannot be demonstrated that in-accurate barrels can be made more accurate by simply rechambering them to some so-called 'improved' cartridge of Wildcat caliber. This term applies to a Wildcat cartridge which consists of a redesigned commercial cartridge, the chamber for which will still accept factory ammunition.

"One well known gunsmith has made the statement that he has never seen an inaccurate cartridge when put in an accurate barrel."

———

Selecting any sort of custom work for mention in a general coverage of rifles and ammunition could be ticklish. I don't find it so, for I refer to a few good men and their products, purely as representative. There are lots of other good ones that you and I know.

OUR hypothetical rifleman—who isn't the average, though we could wish that he were!—now has a first-name acquaintance with the weapon type of his choice. Since childhood he's heard about rifles, from his father, his father's friends, and his own buddies. Even then he absorbed some background of the rifle's history, and time has brought him a bit of the discrimination that sorts out fact from fancy.

He's had the thrill that's never quite paralleled, though it can be equalled, that first ecstatic handling of that first rifle of his own. The little .22 gave him his mastery of basic marksmanship. It was a good teacher, for it showed him his limitations and how to start overcoming them. Because "it shot true" it gave him an understanding of precision. From the rifle, with luck, he'll get lifelong appreciation of precision in thought, speech and action. To the ancients, Truth was a goddess. Some worshiped her from close by!

A gunsling, a peep sight, and perhaps a special target front sight went on that .22. Competition among the kids in his club was keen, and all of them could see, far away, the gleam of the mountain peak, Junior Expert. Still more distant rose the loftier spire of Distinguished Junior Rifleman. Few of them thought much about *that,* at first.

But the competition within their club and outside taught them to shoot under pressure. It gave them much of the self-mastery and rifle-confidence that prevent "blowing up." Qualifying scores came along in practice and in matches, and several of these youngsters made Expert. Perhaps a persistent few reached Distinguished. When they'd turned nineteen they were ready for senior smallbore.

But before that birthday, most likely, our boy had acquired his first match .22. He was almost pledged and delivered to the fraternity as a lifetime rifleman. The certainty would depend largely on older, more experienced members of the senior club.

In his teens, he probably had done some hunting. But maybe he hadn't, and never would, for it's surprising how many kids tell their junior club instructor that they "aren't interested in killing things." They just love the rifle, and what more could we ask?

But if he's done much small-game hunting with the rifle—because he wants to use it, not simply because he can't afford a shotgun—he'll have developed some ideas ·from his experience. By this time, it's altogether probable, he'll have become a handloader.

As a varmint hunter he almost surely will have. And this sport will introduce him to wind, to long and unknown ranges, and to the necessity of rock-steady hold. Yes, he's learned much about· holding in his smallbore shooting, and a good bit about wind, too, after they'd fired occasionally at 50- and 100-yard outdoor ranges. If they'd shot at 200 he'd perhaps have learned too much—enough to scare him.

CHAPTER 6

CENTERFIRE TARGET RIFLES

Centerfire Rifle Target Shooting

Now he's ready for this, and let's hope it's ready for him. Even 200-yard ranges aren't available in every county. He and some others may have to lease or beg a strip of waste land and build their own. Construction may or may not be easy. It *must* be safe, and the NRA is ready with advice and blueprints. Perhaps he'll even have to go it alone.

In any event, it must be specified that only those responsible, including the landowner, who certainly isn't liable to take any fool chances, may fire on that range. Crazy irresponsibility has lost range sites. Even if no actual harm is done it gives us shooters a bad name. Locally, that's hard to live down, perhaps impossible.

But the rewards of bigbore are worth the effort, and worth any amount of precaution. Skill, the whetstone of competition, and plain fun, yes. The fellowship too, for bigbore shooters are a devoted band, still too few. We learn our rifles under practical conditions and become worth more to our Country.

"Bench-resters too?" you ask. "What good is a man with a 20-pound rifle that he can't carry anywhere, and fast?"

I will ask you this: how would an enemy, or a platoon of them, like to face a shooter who's dug in with a dead-accurate 300-meter rifle he knows like the face of his watch? A rifle that's as precise as his watch, too. Some of them would die. The bencher might die, too. "And so what?" he'd say. No good American who loves a rifle would want to survive as a slave. It just doesn't make sense that he would.

What Is a Bigbore?

In the 1880s and even in the 1890s a bigbore was .40 caliber and up. Lots of the ups were used in both hunting and target work. With the .35 Winchester cartridge of 1903, we might say, the dividing line went down to that caliber. The .405 that came the following year certainly wasn't a medium-bore over here; it was big. African and Indian hunters would have called the .405 medium or even small.

Within less than 20 years, bigbore competitive target shooting, military style, had gained a small but tenacious grip on civilian riflemen. They used the .30 caliber and called it a bigbore to distinguish it from the .22 rimfire, which also was blossoming as the arm of a great sport. Few American big-game hunters now would call the .30 a smallbore, although they'd give the .270 and the 7mm. or .275 that name.

Strictly speaking, only the military style of target shooting is called "bigbore." Most of the other common forms above .22 rimfire could be called "centerfire," but they aren't always. International, yes, that has its small- and bigbore, or its rim- and centerfire. High accuracy requirements keep bench-rest shooters confined to handloaded centerfires, almost exclusively. They haven't done all that can be done with their centerfire .22s, but for practical reasons they're working on the 6 mms. Call these calibers .240, .243, .244 or what you will: the old Navy designation was a modest .236. That was about the bore diameter; the opposite grooves were some .242 or .244 inch apart.

We'd certainly call the muzzle-loaders bigbores. True, in old days some were made as small as .25 or less, for lucky children. But large bullet holes edge into scoring rings that a .22 wouldn't cause to shiver from fear, and weight of lead helps fight wind when you can't have super velocity. It helps even when you can!

So this chapter is headed "Centerfire," though even so the title doesn't take care of everything. A muzzle-loader isn't a centerfire, is it? Or a rimfire? But it fires, and when we load and handle it right it gives with what we deserve.

MILITARY TARGET RIFLES

Even this heading isn't inclusive. After World War II we had the sporting-rifle classification for some military-type courses of fire, and the good sense of it is plain.

Well back, "any .30-caliber rifle" was permitted in some qualification courses. That let in sizes from standard or blown-out .300 Magnums down to the .32-20, for that little "pistol cartridge" takes .311-inch bullets. Sometimes we must go to that diameter of jacketed bullet to make certain over-bored .30-40.

Krags, for instance, give the target accuracy we want. Over the 200-yard course a good .32-20 could stay in the 10-inch bull we used then, unless there was an appreciable breeze. Most people shot Springfields or commercial .30-06 sporters that had the receiver slotted for clip loading in rapid fire.

Even then it was noticeable that bigbore target rifles were few in factory production—not much choice. There were Winchester 54 and 70 arms, and they were about all. Yet in smallbore you had enough to look over and decide between Remington 37 and Winchester 52 in the expensive brackets, and at moderate or low prices those two makes, and Harrington & Richardson, Mossberg, Savage, Stevens, and the fine old Springfield M-1 and M-2 as well.

Of course there were custom target .22s. One of the finest I ever saw for iron-sight intercollegiate shooting is easy to remember. That beauty had the M-2 action and about a 28-inch heavy but well tapered Niedner barrel.

The Garand

Always there have been, it seems, events open only to shooters of the contemporary Service rifle, with few if any alterations permitted. For such competition with the M-1 Garand the rules now specify a trigger pull no lighter than 4½ pounds. The stock can be altered only on the inside, to improve bedding for accuracy. (A Garand properly tuned up in that way is a considerably better shooting piece than the average standard M-1.) No special gunsling may be used, only the standard webbing or leather. Even the choice of rear sight aperture size is narrowed to the three manufactured by Ordnance for competitive shooting. The idea behind this apparent rigidity is to keep the game practical. When and if we shoot for keeps we may or may not have the chance to grab up our own pet iron.

The Garand is neither beautiful to gloat over nor handy to carry unless you have long fingers. It took me over a year of frequent use and conscientious caring for it to learn to love it. (How much percentage we should deduct for natural stupidity and a fondness for more familiar actions we needn't bother to compute.) But that short and chunky little gun is reliable, fits almost anyone pretty well, hands out amazingly soft recoil that helps in kneeling rapid fire, and has practical accuracy for its job. You can make fast hits with it at reasonable ranges; so it's a business rifle, and a good one.

Ordnance supplies a special hard grease for lubricating the bolt lugs and some other moving parts—and of course the printed dope that tells what we need to know about the care of the M-1. This lube is meant to make the rifle keep on operating as a self-loader in heavy rainstorms, and it does. Even in the tropics I've seldom seen rain as heavy as the barrage that came down on us one day at the range. We wanted to finish a certain course, and we did.

Garands have been legally available to some civilians for quite a while. Early in 1956 it was announced that an NRA member might buy one without having to be also a member of a club affiliated with the Director of Civilian Marksmanship, the office that does all that Congress will let it to keep us shooting military courses. The price is reasonable: a lot of skilled fitting is required to produce an M-1. Few of us would want one for hunting, but for competition, or just to be able to keep in trim with our Country's service rifle, it's good to be able to own one.

To get the practice we need to sharpen us and keep us sharp requires a lot of shooting with any rifle, even this gentle bigbore. The DCM's military rounds are a bargain, but enough of them could run into plenty of cost. There's handloading, and usually that office can sell us the components—powder, non-corrosive primers, and gilding metal-coated, steel-jacketed bullets. I've seen the 172-grain custom hollow points, too, work beautifully through the Garand. Bullets needn't be needle-sharp to feed.

Now, with bolt guns on the range we can do well up to 200 and even 300 yards using fairly heavy cast bullets at about 2100 or maybe 2200 f. s. They are economical loads to put up and they don't wear barrels out fast in rapid fire. Sure, we have to figure out and take more windage than we'd need to with service rounds. But you remember the old International Match load for the Springfield, the 173-grain M-1 jacketed bullet, boat-tailed at the stern, and leaving at about 2200 f. s. Practically a .30-30 start in life, but it was good at 300 meters, or just under 329 yards.

The semi-automatic needs a certain amount of recoil to function its works. Cast bullet loads that shoot cleanly, without leading the bore, may not function the Garand for rapid fire. A reduced handload that won't tease the action by trying and just failing to operate it makes the M-1 into a straight-pull repeater. Most matches are won or lost in offhand stages, and they're slow fire. Need that practice, don't we?

Caring properly for the Garand seems laborious, at first. The chamber mustn't be neglected, even with non-corrosive ammunition, and you'll like the chamber brush that is part of the "combination tool." Oiled patches wrapped around it make a good chamber job easy. The carbon has to be kept out of the works, but then, the M-1 *deserves* the care that the handbook prescribes for it.

The rear sight as now made seems to be the best that any military rifle ever carried. To record in your scorebook the different elevation and wind adjustments that you find you need is easy, and that sight is close to the eye, a great help in rapid fire.

Springfield 1903

Quality varies. Two World Wars caused that, and naturally. In the distant years before 1941 or so you could take the rifle marksmanship course at Camp Perry, Ohio, then buy your issued 03 to carry home if you wanted it (with the sight records for it) and had enough money left. It's for sure you hadn't spent it on food. The mess hall prices were extremely reasonable and the helpings were large.

Those National Match rifles were superb. They were stocked with a high comb for iron-sight shooting, and a good-sized pistol grip. The stock was long enough for almost anyone. Only a few little short folks, like me, shot the old Service rifle with great comfort. Ordnance had figured out a combination infantry rifle and cavalry carbine; so they'd put a saw to the stock as well as the barrel. That was one reason why so many people liked Krags. A lot of us still do, for many reasons.

Some wartime 03s couldn't equal the good ones of "the years between." Most of them shoot well or can be made to, and some have a pretty usable peep sight on the receiver, where it belongs. The old ladder sight out on the barrel can be adjusted finely, with the aid of an O'Hare or other good micrometer hung on to it. But for those of us with poor vision it was 'way too far out—not much inter-sight radius, either, and that magnifies alignment errors—and its pinhole peep was too small, even in slow fire under a good light. The largest size of Marine Corps aperture helped, a little.

Springfields aren't being made now, though some Arsenal replacement parts are available. Used '03s may or may not be good, and a few parts are breakage hazards. We can take these matters up in the military rifle chapter. In spite of any drawbacks the Springfield is still a favorite of lots of bigbore target shooters, and of hunters. Those owners are apt to want to keep those rifles.

Enfield 1917

This sturdy action often is converted to take a .300 Magnum barrel for long-range shooting. Rechambering the original isn't always wise. As issued, it's a reliable .30-06 with good weight and balance for target shooting, and its 26-inch barrel is slightly less noisy than the 24-inch of recent Springfields. Early 03s were 23.79, for they'd been cut off at the breech and rechambered for the 1906 cartridge, shorter necked than the original .30 1903.

A rear sight with windage adjustment and with closer elevation adjustment is needed for competition, though you can have a lot of fun and learn practical things with the issue sights. One of these is holding off for wind, "using Kentucky windage." It's obvious that it could be life-saving practical on some grim occasion. You zero the issue sights for windage by driving the post front sight to right or left.

The combless Enfield stock was designed for bayonet fighting, not for marksmanship. We need a reasonably high comb for comfort in slow fire and for quick steadying-down of the rifle after operating the bolt in rapid. Cheek and hand pressure do this.

The standard Model 70 target rifle in .30-06. Fitted with scope blocks and ready for irons, this arm comes close to being an all-round rifle—for some of us—when sighted for the particular job. Trimming the stock can take off about ½ pound of weight, if it's decided on. With sling and irons it goes (as unaltered) about 10 pounds, and few shooters would find it too heavy to handle when dropping into the sit, kneel, or prone positions for rapid fire.

The Heavy Weight 70 is popular for four-position shooting, too, by those who can handle it—and many can. It has been chosen as a hunting rifle for open country, the most popular calibers for such use having been .220 Swift and .270, .30-06, and .300 Magnum.

Adding a comb to the 1917 could well be one of the first amateur gunsmithing jobs.

Krag-Jorgensen 1898

There were earlier U. S. .30-40 Krags, 1892 and 1896, and the 1899 was a carbine with '98 action. In the hunting field the Krags still get around by the thousand, and some go to the target range.

Accuracy from a good one is a lot more than just interesting, and a 30-inch barrel is soft-spoken. Most of them have been cut since the Government transferred ownership. With 180-grain target bullets, velocities have to be about 200 f. s. or more below those of the .30-06, for pressures should be limited to little if any over 40,000 pounds per square inch—the rifle is an old one. With proper loads, the single front locking lug seldom if ever lets go. When it does, the rear lock of the bolt handle usually sends the bolt flying off to the right. Let's hope that the shooter is at the extreme right of the firing line, and let's not suppose that he'll find the experience delightful.

To fill a Krag magazine in rapid fire certainly would take some doing! You roll the hulls in at the right of the receiver, and the rims must be in the order of a flight of steps. I'm afraid I couldn't do it in the time limit. Learning to thumb home a clipful of Springfield rounds was easy, and the Garand wasn't hard, either, although I have a short hand.

As an offhand military rifle the 30-inch Krag is hard to equal. It's steady, for it has the right weight in the right places. Since the top cartridge in the magazine doesn't press itself mightily against the bolt, the action is one of the smoothest in rapid, or "sustained fire," as it's called now. It's like a Mannlicher-Schoenauer, which has a different sort of magazine, revolving. Only the follower of the Krag goes chasing around a corner. That magazine is simply a corral, not a spool.

Winchesters

Both the old 54 and the modern 70 are seen with extremely heavy barrels for long-range target shooting. The later rifle comes in three target weights, about 9½, 10½ and 13 pounds. Now they're called Standard, Heavy Weight and Bull Gun, and all can be had in .30-06. The Heavy comes also in .243, and the Bull in .300 Magnum. The 06 receivers are slotted for clip loading, like the early 70 sporters.

Not much need be said about the quality and desirability of the rifles. We could enlarge upon and regret the fact that they are the only over-the-counter, factory arms made for the military target shot. There just aren't enough of us bigbore shooters to induce other factories to get into the picture.

The Standard or former National Match rifle is something of an all-rounder in build as well as caliber. All three are stocked correctly for target scopes or high receiver peep and target front sights. An ivory or gold bead front, if wanted for hunting, can be bought in the proper height and driven into the slot in the ramp of the Standard. With its sporter weight .30-06 barrel, this rifle balances far enough back to let us carry it pretty comfortably at trail without having fingers eight inches long. It weighs a shade less than a standard Model 52 smallbore and its teeter point is a lot farther back. Those beavertail forestocks are wide.

The Heavy Weight, once called "Target Grade," used to come in .300 Magnum, and it was quite a favorite of husky big-game hunters who knew the score about long range marksmanship, as well as with target shots who wanted a .300—or some lighter caliber—but didn't care for the weight of the Bull.

That gun, with the extra heavy 28-inch barrel, was made with the 1,000-yard Wimbledon Match in mind. For this the .300 is still the logical choice among American factory rounds, and the Bull Gun tames its

At 500, 600, or 1,000 yards the 70 Bull Gun comes into its kingdom. Pistol grips of these bigbore match rifles have their swell located much farther back than those of .22 rimfire target rifles so that the trigger guard can't bruise the second finger when recoil gives its shove. Some shooters find this backed-up grip much handier in rapid fire, too. The Bull Gun's recoil in either 06 or .300 is comparatively light, and the long barrel reduces muzzle blast.

report and recoil. The .30-06 Bull Gun would be easy to shoot well from prone, but Maggie bucks the wind much better.

Custom Rifles and Others

A capable gunsmith who knows military marksmanship can build a rifle for this sport which is more than a sport—it's a paid insurance premium on the life of our Country. Such an arm needn't be expensive, though barrel and action bedding must be right for the conditions involved. These include rapid fire as well as slow, and a "walker" isn't to be tolerated. The barrel must not shift the point of bullet impact seriously as it warms up. "Warms up?" You could fry steak on it!

An "as issued" match of course means just that, the practically unaltered military rifle. But some special equipment is permitted in many events. Let's look briefly at the report of what 1955 National Match winners used at Perry. The full tabulation was given in the March, 1955, *American Rifleman*.

Besides the Garand and the Springfield, which we'd expect, there was a great number of Winchester 70s, and one 54 of that make. One of the few unmodified rifles was the M-1. Nearly all the others had either Redfield or Lyman sights, though there were three Griffin & Howe target fronts. There were Douglas barrels, including one with 11 and one with 12-inch twist instead of the usual 10, that direct descendant of .30-40 Krag and .30 *Model 1903* barrels that used long, round-nosed 220-grain bullets —and some of 230 grains in the Krag. One trigger was custom, a Canjar, and a Springfield was fitted with an Apex firing pin. One or two of the 70 rifles had Herter's glass bedding.

That year, Western Super-Match ammunition was a favorite, with Remington Palma and Frankford Arsenal prominent, too. There were handloads, with the 180-grain Sierra being well liked.

Special military target ammunition isn't new. A rather heavy-barreled Springfield .45-70 single-shot modification took its own cartridge. The case was about 2.4 inches long instead of the usual 2.1, and 10 extra grains' weight of black powder boosted the velocity of the 500-grain bullet, a help at long range, which then went as far as 1200 yards, sometimes. Long, sharp 200-grain .30 bullets have been made

for target, almost equaling the 180-grain Ross .280 in sectional density. Oldtimers, they were jacketed in cupro-nickel, the copper-nick alloy. that made bore cleaning difficult except at pretty low velocities, which this .30-06 loading might have had.

Over in England a .303 Magnum was made, with rimless case larger than the rimmed service brass. The Kynoch division of Imperial Chemical Industries credited it with sending a 175-grain spitzer bullet at 3050 f. s., with a mild 48,160 p. s. i. pressure.

What It Takes

Our present National Match Course isn't short range stuff, in spite of current emphasis on battle ranges, which it seems rarely exceed 300 yards, visibility being liable to be so poor. The N. M. is a practical course, calling for 50 shots, not too many for a fairly seasoned beginner to run through in an afternoon. Ten are slow fire, "one minute per shot," at 200 yards standing, and even the new 12-inch bull is elusive enough to many of us. The old 10 and 8 were hard for those with poor eyesight.

There are 10 more shots at that range, rapid fire, sitting or kneeling "from standing." That means you stand, maybe with a slight tremble at the knees, until the time signal sounds. At that, down you go, and there's a science in getting down fast without resembling a falling chimney. You have to be in shape to do some exact, fast sighting and fast but controlled trigger squeeze (or *press,* really) to rap out a decent score. At 300 yards it's still rapid, but you get 10 seconds extra—a full minute, that makes it—for the 10 shots. It's prone from standing. At 500 or 600 yards—whichever is available, and such ranges are hard to find as the land around us gets built up— you fire 20 shots from prone and have 20 minutes for that string.

Military matches that call for rapid fire with the ".30 caliber" distinguish between the M-1 and the bolt actions. Nine shots are fired, with one in the rifle, or four if it's a bolt gun, and a full clip in a pocket of the Service belt. With the M-1 you're allowed 50 seconds, and with the bolt action, 60.

It becomes "plainer than the sun at noonday" that a gilt-edged barrel is hardly necessary or even sensible for such courses. Barrels wear out much faster in rapid than in slow, and in slow much faster than in hunting. Good hunting rifle accuracy is fully adequate, in .30-06 or the equivalent, for even the V-rings of military targets, half the diameter of the 5-ring. That Roman numeral V is there to decide numerical ties, just as we have the heritage of ancient Roman law to decide what most people would call more serious matters.

But in long-range slow fire a cartridge like the .300 Magnum helps. Its fast bullet doesn't dally around so long for wind to play with it. Then too, the sharp point and boat-tailed base of this 180-grain (or other good weight of the type) haven't much "lag." The bullet doesn't drop an abnormally high percentage of speed during the trip. At rimfire ranges, for example, the .22 long-rifle high speed has so much more lag than the standard or slightly slower than standard round that wind affects it more. Odd, but true.

Other cartridges than the .300 pay off at 1,000 or even 500 or 600 yards. Maybe a .275, a bit slimmer than the famous old Ross .280, is the answer to the Wimbledon's challenge. There are wildcat 7 mms., and we may have factory rounds in that caliber, more powerful than the old .275 Holland & Holland Mag of about .30-06 length. The not-much-different 7x61 mm. Sharpe & Hart has done well already, and no one was much surprised that it did.

Some idea of the difficulties of the game is brought out in a brilliantly written article by Major General A. D. Mead, USA, in the May, 1956 *Rifleman*. "Can the 'Expert' Win?" the title asks. More than an Army Expert qualification is needed, by far, General Mead points out. The new Expert and the military (or civilian) winner both know how to hold, breathe, aim and squeeze. But the latter knows that he must combine *all* these techniques on *every* shot, and he has the "will to win." He also knows that sight alignment is more important than sight picture (holding the post front at 6 o'clock, at the bottom of the bull). And he's experienced with wind, can "read" it, and knows that he must make the correct allowances for each shot, not simply at the beginning of a slow fire string. He's on his toes, and his long range scores beat the Expert's. And he lives with his rifle, takes lots of dry practice in aiming and trigger squeeze, and keeps a complete score book, studying its records of light, temperature, wind, range, ammunition, and the sight adjustments that produced 5s and Vs.

The General concludes that the Expert can win if he does these things, which go far beyond basic training!

Sporting Rifle

For years there'd been some latitude of choice in the arms we could use in certain military events, and after World War II the Sporting Rifle classification was set up. Under the 1956 ruling it is liberal enough to invite a great many high power rifle users to try this game.

The minimum caliber allowed under this rule is .240, which takes in the wildcat and factory 6 mms. but bars the hot-shot .22s. In the most serious sense, few of them would be "practical" at the long ranges that could come up in home defense, guerrilla fighting. "Guerrilla" means "little war," but we could promise a big one to an invader. He'd learn about American long-range marksmanship. This calls for bullet weight. Maybe a cartridge like the old .22 Newton with 90-grain bullet would qualify, but few .22s of the present handle much over two-thirds of that weight.

To keep Sporting Rifle practical, the rule forbids palm rests and pronged buttplates, which serve well in slow, precise offhand shooting, with the elbow of the forward arm resting on the hip. For the same reason a three-pound trigger pull is minimum.

The rifle must be portable, not over 12 pounds with its sights. The extra half-pound of the sling isn't included in this limit. Iron sights are pretty much standard, though a scope of not over four power may be permitted. That's for the individual tournament managers to decide.

Sounds practical, doesn't it? For some of us a 12-pound rifle would be a little too much in offhand. We'd shoot better with a lighter arm, and really it's balance that does it. If the point of balance is about seven or eight inches ahead of the trigger we generally have a nice hanging rifle for offhand, and for other positions too, provided it isn't a pinweight. Custom or home-gunsmithed rifles aren't hard to plan within these weight limits, and for a readymade there's the Winchester 70 Heavy. The Bull 70 is out.

INTERNATIONAL MATCH RIFLES

Not so long ago, we American riflemen were desperate about our lack of equipment and the skill to use it in the international game. Our team members deserve great respect for taking the beatings that they did in the spirit of hang on, do your best, and learn. They were sportsmen, and no mistake!

In working toward our ideal of an international match or "free" rifle—so called because most of the restrictions laid on the small- or bigbore arms used for punching Standard American targets are removed—we have had the benefit of generous publicity. *The American Rifleman*, the old *Shooters' News* and the new *Precision Shooting* have acted as clearing-houses for ideas and for the results of ideas under proof. This goes on steadily.

At present there are no American factory rifles ready-made for high scoring on the difficult metric targets. There scarcely could be, for each shooter must fit his rifle to himself. The reverse of that process can do pretty well—after long acquaintance—in big game hunting. Even the upland bird hunter can, after many years, shoot like a true artist with a shotgun that's a horrible misfit. Such things happen continually, always have. "Always will?" Let's hope not.

But for International the shooter must be and have the best. The greatest honor and the highest responsibility in the sporting world are to compete for your country. In a practical way, too, our showing is important. To a ridiculous but real extent our country is judged by her showing at the Olympics. Human nature is what it is, rarely sophisticated, rarely intelligent.

Some of our best grade American rifles do well as the foundation of free rifles. In smallbore there have been the 52 Winchester and 37 Remington, and the newer 40X Rem would qualify, also. The Morgan-Johnson custom action is of course splendid. Bigbores can stem from Remington 721 and 722 actions, from Winchester 70s, and from custom jobs like the heavy Weber with tube-reinforced receiver, or the Mike Allen with three front-locking lugs and enclosed cocking piece or striker head. The imported Schultz & Larsen action is rigid in spite of its bolt lugs' being located at the rear. There are four of them, and the bolt is so finely fitted into the receiver, and shrouded at front under the receiver ring, that the lockup is both tight and smooth. We'd call it a hand-made action.

Comment from Arthur Cook

Arthur E. Cook's suggestions in the April, 1956, *Rifleman* are friendly and intelligent, as always. He had had five years' experience in shooting on our national teams.

He advises having two rifles. (The International Shooting Union rules allow any number, provided that they're of the same caliber.) This is not simply because he himself needs more stock drop in kneeling and standing than in prone. It's also to have a spare, and to be able to favor one barrel so as not to have to shoot the most exacting stages with one that's lost its gilt edge. The smallbore should be built as much like the bigbore as possible. Weight the stock, if necessary, to make balance the same in spite of its shorter, lighter action. You get your basic practice with the .22 rimfire, and much of your following practice, too.

Cook says that most of his free rifles don't resemble the usual type in stock design. He doesn't care for the thumbhole grip because it doesn't suit his off-hand stance, and he doesn't need a palm rest because his arms are rather long. Some shooters, he points out, have put a piece of wood under the trigger guard, to use instead of a palm rest, and "this insures rigidity."

In foreign calibers, he mentions the 6.5x55 Swedish Mauser, 7.5 Swiss and 7.62 Russian. He likes the 6.5x.257 Roberts, 57 mm. long, and reduced loads in the .30-06. Of course he handloads, and American primers are easier to punch out than the foreign Berdan, a simple cup primer, for the anvil is formed in the case's primer pocket. Accuracy of the 6.5x55 and 6.5x.257 is about the same, he finds. The .30-06

lets him use a 180-instead of a 140-grain bullet, and at that writing he admitted that he didn't know which he preferred, 6.5x.257 or 06. His light load of about 38.5 grains of 4895 ("Government" powder that's practically commercial, since so many handloaders get it from the DCM) evidently burns well behind the 180-grain bullet in the 06, though one might think that the half-inch shorter and straighter-bodied T-65 or .308 Winchester brass is of more appropriate size for 300-meter loadings. But we *know* the 06 much better.

He has used the imported Norma match bullets with soft steel jackets and thinks they may give less barrel wear than our gilding metal-jacketed Sierras and Hornadys. This is an important consideration in loading any match rifle. But as a rule he gets better accuracy with the latter two makes. The high velocity varmint .22s wear out too fast, often losing the required accuracy in from one thousand to two thousand rounds. "This is not enough even to permit working up a good load," he remarks, and how right he is! Even the comparatively small 6.5 calibers give free rifle life as long as six thousand rounds, and he's heard of some that went as much as seven thousand five hundred.

A heavy free rifle action looks good to him because it's rigid enough to suspend a free-floating barrel over the forestock. Most of the centerfires in International, he's observed, have that kind of bedding.

Things Are on the Move

The following letter in the May, 1956, *Precision Shooting* (Vol. 1, No. 1) was written by Master Sergeant Frank Conway at Fort Benning. It shows that something is being done on an official scale to produce American victories in the future.

"In regard to rumors to the effect that the Army has new Free rifles. I had the great pleasure of writing up the specifications on those rifles we had made up by Roy Dunlap. The rifles are not to supply an International squad, but rather to have appropriate equipment for the shooters of the Army rifle squad who have desires to compete as individuals in International-type competition.

"We ordered thirty in .22 rimfire and an equal number in .30-06. Same stocks, sights, and accessories for both, and approximately the same weight, with twenty-five of each weighing about 15½ lbs. and five each of 17½ lbs. The .22s have Douglas barrels and the .30s Titus barrels. Sights are Redfield, Olympic front and International rear. All the .22s and twenty of the .30s have Canjar light-weight triggers, the other ten .30s having Timney light-weight triggers.

"We were criticized for getting our 300-meter guns in .30-06. Some people can talk only 6.5, but we have found that the .30s stand up rather well and that the nations shooting the 6.5 do so because it is their *service cartridge*. The Russians and the Swiss use a .30 cal. and no one could complain about the

Two views of an Al Freeland International Match smallbore stock for 52 Winchester (this one), Remington 37, or Remington 40X rifles. Laminated or regular walnut can be provided. Electric bedder shows above forestock tip, and to the rear and below it is the hand-stop. Thumb-hole behind pistol grip is made large for comfort in any shooting position, and the standard aluminum buttplate is adjustable for height of the stock's heel—this specimen doesn't have the pronged buttplate toe that some choose for offhand. Sights are Freeland longshaded front and Parker-Hale rear.

results that they are getting! We feel that it is a matter of national pride to shoot *our* service cartridge.

"The ammo that Frankford Arsenal has made up for us in an international load is the finest ammo that I have ever shot. I really believe that with a proper rest and barrel it would shoot into the X-ring at 300 meters. I have fired only a couple of groups at 300 meters from the bench and in both cases had three or four bullets cutting into each other. This shooting was done with my own 300-meter gun which has a Douglas No. 8 barrel with 12-inch twist. In this shooting I have had less than a two-inch vertical, with the wind opening the horizontal to just over four inches, and that is rather good for hand-loads, not to talk of *production run ammo!* The components were selected but it was still run off on automatic machinery."

We Americans can move as a nation, and we will in this matter. We are lively as individuals, too, and there's the second half of our material strength.

Free rifle has gunsmiths and shooters going, and we're hardly started yet. We learn by trial, sometimes by error. So far, we haven't any American *type* of free rifle; probably shan't want it, either. Smallbore and centerfire trial and test go on. The special targets aren't new. For the convenience of those who have access to 50- and 100-yard smallbore ranges, easy to build safely almost anywhere, there are 50- and 100-yard reductions of 50- and 100-meter ISU targets. Thus we can size up our ability closely as we go along. The problem of trajectory when we move to the full meterage isn't difficult to solve with sight clicks. The 300-meter ISU has been reduced to 200- and 300-yard target paper. At least the former distance is fairly available and more than fairly simple to set up, in most country.

We aren't subsidized shooters. The men who represent us in competition are amateurs, not pros.

Expense comes in, but it has to face American ingenuity, and that's a formidable foe. Yet some of us will try costly foreign rifles and probably do well with them, too.

Examples are the Haemmerli bolt actions—Stoeger imports them—a 15½ pound .22 and a 17-odd pound bigbore. Stocks are heavy, of thumbhole type, pistol grips angling back right off the trigger guard, and adjustable buttplates with long lower prong to help in offhand support. The wooden palm rest on its adjustable rod is large, shaped for a hand of at least average size. Sights are elaborate but efficient. Though these are turn-bolt rifles, the bigbore has a lever sticking out to the right, to convert the action into a straight-pull.

Some of our people make their own free rifles. Adjustable palm rests and buttplates aren't hard to find, and they needn't be expensive. The Llanerch Gun Shop of Upper Darby, Pa., has a good variety, and cheekpieces, too, ready for the Winchester 52 and 70, and the Remington 37, 721 or 722.

Stock designs have taken various forms and they'll continue to do so. Even the short Bull-pup has been made as a free rifle for those who don't like the hang of a long barrel out front. No doubt many stockers will use the thumbhole design because it seems the proper thing for a free rifle. So it is, for some shooters. We'll feel our way along toward independence. We'll have to, or lose.

We make excellent sights in this country, and we have for many years. A new one, early 1956, is the Redfield International Match rear peep, an improvement on the time-tested Redfield Olympic. Windage and elevation knobs are big, and they click distinctly. They're spring-loaded ball clicks, to wear long under the frequent turns a shooter will give them to keep his sights up to date with wind and mirage. A latitude of 60, minutes of elevation is provided, and 48 of windage, in quarters. Back-and-forth eye relief is 1½ inches—enough for most of us. Like some other receiver peeps, this one can go on several rifles, each fitted with a base for it. The Sure-X aperture disc, ⅞-inch wide, fits this sight and some others. Its eyepiece turns to give choice of eight different sizes of aperture; ought to take care of most shooting-light conditions.

This sight is described here not as the last word, but to indicate that that word won't be spoken for some time yet. In a couple of years it might be "out of date," but it'd still be a good one.

BENCH-REST RIFLES

This sport is the development lab and proving ground of accuracy. Records at 100 and 200 yards and at 300 meters are broken so fast, comparatively speaking, that publication of winning groups can only comfortably keep up with the making of new ones. For a long time, it's true, the old C. W. Rowland group of 10 .32-40s in a .725-inch center-to-center cluster at 200 yards stayed unbeaten. He'd used a Ballard with one of the fine Pope barrels, and it was a practice group. The .5276 that Sam Clark of Waterville, Maine, shot was in competition. It stood for a long time, as records live today.

The National Bench Rest Shooters' Association, Lyndonville, Vermont, publishes at intervals a book on *The Ultimate in Rifle Precision,* with Colonel Townsend Whelen editing it. It is helpful, and so are frequent bench-rest stories in *The American Rifleman* and the old *Shooters' News,* now *Precision Shooting,* of which Phil Teachout of Lyndonville is editor. I never knew of any writer more devoted than Phil to the cause of rifle marksmanship.

Bench-Rest Popularity

Bench looks easy. "All you have to do is aim and pull the trigger." That so? Well, it may be disillusionment, but the skilled prone shot who is entirely new to bench often discovers that for some time it's hard for him even to *equal* his best prone groups unless the bench rest is formal, not extemporized. Even then he needs coaching, and who except the very best doesn't?

In formal bench-rest the rifle is heavy and steady, 20 pounds being only a fair average, if that. It carries a scope of say, 20 to 30 power, and its big forestock, four inches or so in width, and flat, rests on a padded pedestal, and the heel of the stock is usually rested, too. Ralph Pride, Gene Beecher and Ted Holmes are some of the men who make these cradles for benchers, and their work isn't sloppy!

But to use all these aids requires a special technique—or techniques. Sitting on the stool and aiming and squeezing without disturbing the scope crosshairs on the target seems awkward at first. The beginner must learn to take his time and never be satisfied with any letoff but the best of which he's capable.

It's tough competition. The rifles are giving nearly all the accuracy that's built into them and into their ammunition. Improvement in this equipment does *not* stand still. Nor does it in the shooters.

Yet the game is fascinating as well as challenging. At back-lot or at fully equipped range sessions the benchers gather, and only their absorption in the sport and their enjoyment and helpful goodfellowship are typical. Age, sex, physical vigor and fitness—they don't seem to matter. This old American game is having a revival that might have astonished the frontiersmen in buckskins. It certainly would have delighted them.

The Rifle

At this point let's look at a typical bench-rest rifle, if there is one. Hardly anything except ingenuity limits its form, and there are scarcely two alike. They aren't assembly-line jobs! Still, there are some details that are typical of winning rifles.

The barrel is heavy. "Crowbar" would be an inadequate term for it. Some have no taper; none is streamlined for looks. A few of the favorite makes are Douglas, Pride, Buhmiller, May, Pfeiffer, Apex, Hart, Johnson-Gartman, and Gregoire, all custom. Chrome-molybdenum, carbon-manganese, and chrome-vanadium are some of the steels. Lately the stainless steels have been favored. They do well and aren't to be confused with non-rusting steels of 30 years ago.

Many barrels are lapped with a lead plug carrying 125-150 granulation emery in lard oil. Muzzle and breech are then cut off the unchambered blank to get rid of any belling. Some barrels are honed, another way of removing tool-marks that might pick up bullet-jacket fouling and cause a change in point of impact on the target. Most bench barrels are of the almost standard six-groove sort. Some have eight. M. G. Watts, 5627 Euclid, Kansas City 30, Mo., makes these two and multigroove barrels also. With the latter type, grooving need not be so deep, and theoretically at least there's less harmful working of bullet jackets.

Stocks are heavy, often flat on the underside of forearm and heel. The grip is usually close-up, and it may have a thumb-hole behind it. Cheek-pieces, or heavy combs, or stocks that run straight toward the bolt, with no "small" at the grip, can be easy to relax on when we're wishing off a shot, and relax we must! Laminated wood, the grains running against each other, gives stiffness and much protection against warping. The contrast of light and dark strips can be beautiful, and some would say that a bench-rest rifle should be thankful for any good looks at all. Its beauty lies in precision.

Bedding is commonly free: no pressure of forestock against barrel. A heavy, stiff receiver can support a heavy, stiff barrel, but a light action, like some Mausers and others, can't. Then the barrel seems to need some forestock pressure, of wood, of shims, maybe of devices adjusted precisely by the aid of electric contacts. In the spring of 1956 Lou Landwehr, 305 Ash St., Jefferson City, Mo., announced his

Fabrique Nationale single-shot bench-rest action.

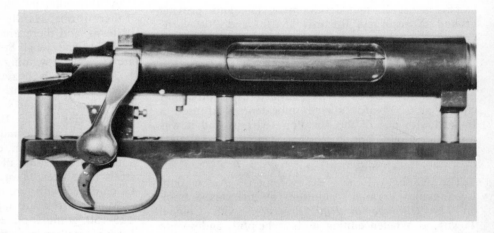

Weber bench-rest action.

hydraulic bedder. Using it, Barney Auston of Tulsa broke the National Match Course record.

It seems certain that the recoil lug up front at the bottom of the receiver should touch the inletted stock wood only at the rear, not at the sides and bottom.

Some bench-rest rifles are fully bedded, not floating. The work must be excellent, and Taylor & Robbins, Rixford, Pa., have become specialists in it.

Actions may be standard or altered American, imported, or special. Remington 721 and 722, Winchester 70, Springfield 1903 and Enfield 1917 are in use, commonly as single shots to permit greater stock stiffness. The Fabrique Nationale Mauser from Firearms International came along in 1956 in special bench-rest form and in three general sizes to take care of everything from .222 Rem to .300 Mag, the latter not often a bench-rest caliber because it's hardly necessary at 300 meters! (That needn't be the limit of range, forever, though.) Its one-piece guard lets us put in extra stock screws if we want to, and the receiver, flat on the bottom, is channeled on top to serve as a loading tray, a typical refinement on a bench action. Although its standard trigger is the Sako single-stage, others can be fitted. The Canjar, for example, sets nicely for a three-ounce release.

The Schultz & Larsen is Phil Sharpe's importation. A heavy action with four locking lugs back under the receiver bridge, it weighs about 4½ pounds. Precise fitting makes it rigid.

Cartridges, in general, are comparatively small. Even from a heavy rifle, recoil can be disturbing. At present the bencher's problem is to beat wind up to 300 meters, not a long target range. Of course we never can beat it, but these riflemen balance recoil against the bullet's wind-bucking ability.

The .219 Donaldson Wasp still is popular. It's the Zipper case (or .30-30 brass, if handier) shortened to about 1.76 inches and given a fairly abrupt 30° shoulder. Later the .222 Remington did fine work, and many shooters believe that high loading density burns powder most uniformly. They think it makes the bullets' time up the barrel more even, and the muzzles of thick, heavy barrels vibrate up and down too, though not in the buggy-whip fashion of some sporters that are a dream to carry and a nightmare to try to shoot well.

Western bench-resters more often—in fact, just about always—contend with strong winds, and the capacity of the .22-.250 gives them about 300 feet more velocity, with 55-grain bullets, than the Wasp does. It gives good velocity to 60-grain bullets, too. Top loads aren't always favored, by any means, but case capacity gives room for experiment, which benchers must have. They enjoy it, but they also need it,

Some special American actions are the Taylor & Robbins, Forster, King, Weber, and the Remington 722 reinforced by Hart. It is becoming quite usual for a receiver to be enclosed in a stiff outer tube with only a small port for ejection. Deep shrouding of the bolt-face that holds the case-head adds rigidity as well as really more strength than the usual bench loads come anywhere near to requiring.

Ready-Made Rifles

At present these are few, and not made by the big factories, of course. An example is the Johnson-Gartman from the firm by that name, Box 234, Providence, R. I. It's the successor to Johnson Automatics, which has made fine heavy-barrel target arms.

This seventeen-pound rifle has a twenty-nine-inch bull gun barrel, Enfield 1917 action, and a custom stock that is flattish on the bottom at front and rear. However, it has a distinct pistol grip and "small of the stock" ahead of the comb, and a heavy cheekpiece without Monte Carlo. The scope is the Unertl with two-inch objective. There's nothing "extreme" about this bench rifle, and it is only one of several styles at J-G, or at other places.

The Ammunition

About this the rest shooter is as particular as about his rifle, and he'd better be. Nearly all of it is handloaded, and constant testing of different combinations in a rifle leads eventually to some degree of the accuracy and stability he wants.

At long 300-meter range a muzzle velocity of 3200 f. s. can be mighty helpful, and a .22-.250 can impart this to a 60-grain bullet without a grunt. The .220 Swift in factory or altered shape is used, but not so frequently. And there's the .219 Zipper wildcat, more or less blown out, for high velocities. There are others, and there's no reason to quit experimenting with the friendly .22s, including that amazing .222.

At this writing the 6-mm. bench rifles have a good start, the wildcats and the .243 and .244 factory cases. A 100-grain bullet is a far better wind-bucker than a 60- or 65-grain one about .02 inch smaller in diameter. It has sectional density. The standard .250 Savage and .257 Roberts cases have been used a little, but for further bench development the .25s may need to wait for the 6 mms. to have their turn. That seems logical, for recoil as well as perfection of bullet manufacture is a factor that has great meaning.

Bullets from .22 (usually .224 inch) to .25 (nearly always .257 inch) get used right along. The .22s cost less than .24 and .25 calibers, to buy or to make, and even if in time they're superseded we can be thankful for the start they've given us. It was magnificent, and it isn't through yet.

Some of the popular commercial bullets ordered especially for bench are Baldwin, Holmes, Hornady, Jordan, Kenru, Sierra, Sisk, and Speer Products Co. All the well known makes play this game, and hard. Although one or two usually get to the top, shooters try several makes, weights and forms: a bench barrel must be *fitted,* to do its best. Hollow as well as soft

points get some use, and old shooters aren't surprised if they show good accuracy. This form *can* shoot well; witness the boat-tailed open-point expanding 180-grain .30 and some lots of .22 long-rifle low-speed hollow points that used to come off the machines. Frequently they had Standard American target accuracy, though hardly the precision the bencher demands.

Probably most advanced benchers make their own jacketed bullets. Among the favorite makes of equipment are Biehler & Astles, Brown, C-H, Gibbs, Hollywood, Pearson, and RCBS. Some benchers make part or most of their equipment, and new commercial machines or dies may come along at any time.

Jacket cups purchased for home manufacture of bullets must be even in thickness and in temper or anneal. An inside micrometer will check their thickness. In the December, 1955, *Shooters' News* Kent Bellah told how to fashion one from an old outside mike. He cut the end off the frame and soldered on a No. 6 nail for an anvil. Some jackets he miked with it were as thick as .020 inch on one side and as thin as .008 on the other!

The lead core must be pre-swaged in a die, aged before assembling and before shooting, and expanded *up* to approach perfect balance and concentricity. So, at least, some of the most exacting shooters seem to have discovered.

There are semi-custom makers who can take time to make bullets for an individual barrel. This is more than we could expect from most of the big makers, or from the large ammunition manufacturers. The best seem to come from slow, careful, practically continuous experimentation.

What we have learned about bullets from bench shooters is hard to exaggerate. Bullets are the cartridge components on which the final degree of accuracy depends. It is difficult to manufacture perfectly balanced bullets, and barrels of the same caliber are *not* alike, inside.

Primers and powders the bencher must more or less take for granted. We believe that they are good. Most shooters except .222 converts use the large rifle primer. The big commercial brands, including Federal, have quality. So do some new arrivals like Cascade Cartridge, Inc., formerly called Speer Cartridge Works. Competition is keen.

Powder is chosen for the case and the bullet weight. Standard over-the-counter numbers are supplemented by Government stuff like 4895. Most of our benchrest shooters use American bullets, primers and powders, though Norma and a few other foreign cases or bullets appear on the firing lines.

Handloading is done carefully, at home or on the range. The same make and lot number of cases, and the same number of firings, too, help us approach uniformity. Cases, like any cartridge components, need and get sharp inspection.

Scopes

The most powerful scope now commonly used is the Lyman 30X, with the Unertl 24 sharing about fifty-fifty in popularity. The 20X is well liked, and a dot reticle gains favor. A sunshade at the objective end helps in definition.

Possibly a multi-power scope like the Bausch & Lomb 6 to 24X will win top popularity. Some followers of the game, by no means all, find that great power gives trouble under mirage, or even late in an afternoon when light is dimming. An easy shift to a lower magnification could help them.

Hold-Off

This problem is mentioned here only to illustrate *one* of those that the bencher must tangle with. Holding off for wind is one technique; holding off to defeat the illusion of mirage is another.

An unsigned article in *Shooters' News* of December, 1955, discussed it ably. The writer was one of the top ten in that year's National Bench Rifle Championships.

The hold-off can be as fine as 1/16 inch at 100 yards, and quite understandably so. Your first look through a spotting scope that shows bulletholes cutting deeply into the first one at that range is illuminating. If you're firing, it's intoxicating, but in good bench shooting it's expected.

The best training for hold-off without wearing out your barrel, the writer says, is for one shooter to coach another. The coach centers his crosshairs on a target and tells the other when mirage drifts the target off—out from under the crosshairs. Wind drift, it's explained, usually is less serious than mirage drift. To correct for mirage effect the hold-off may be as much as 1½ inches at 100 yards, or four inches at 200, where a two-inch square above the rings is the aiming point. Alone, if he must be, the "shooter" can pencil-dot a target 10 times, at about 40-second intervals. This too gives him an idea of what mirage does.

Sporting Rifle

This is a smart step forward, and hardly to be the final one. We rifle, pistol, and shotgun shooters want more people to share our hobbies, and one way to it is economy in competitive equipment. Americans like competition, but hardly anyone wants to lose all the time, be it ever so gracefully done.

The National Bench Rest Shooters' Association defines the official sporting or varmint class of bench-rest rifle within liberal limits. Commercial rifles with scopes and accessories must not go over 13 pounds. This would let in the Heavy 70 but not the Bull 70. Barrels of *custom* rifles may be no more than 1.25 inches at breech, .90 at muzzle, and at no point between may the diameter be greater than that of a straight-taper barrel within these limits. Stocks must be of conventional varmint hunting type, not skeletonized to cut weight, for instance, and no wider than three inches at any point. There are no limits on the rifle's caliber or the power of its scope.

With these rifles eligible for 5- and 10-shot group contests at both 100 and 200 yards the not-so-wealthy shooter can use one for bench competition and hunting. Without sacrificing a great deal he could get into the military bigbore "sporting rifle" game, too. Already some bench-rest and bigbore clubs have been intelligent enough to let hunters use their ranges for sighting-in on certain days, under supervision, and with help if it's wanted. The new classifications give members a better chance to bring some of the unconverted into club affiliation.

It's hardly too much to hope that bench classifications will be lowered still further, and drastically. The game is too inviting to be kept as the private preserve of a few. Of course it isn't that, by any means, but a good democratic shot in the arm could do amazing things for our American game of the rifle—in all its branches. The time to get millions more into it is when they're interested, as they are now, but may not be for long. You've seen the evening rise of trout? Sometimes it's over and gone very soon.

BLACK POWDER RIFLES

The National Muzzle Loading Rifle Association was founded in 1932 on an appropriate day, February 22. Now it has over 6,000 members and holds four matches a year at the Friendship, Indiana, range named for the late Walter Cline. He was the author of *The Muzzle-Loading Rifle—Then and Now,* and he and E. M. ("Red") Farris were among the early ones who worked so hard to revive this early American sport.

NMLRA competitions are now among the scheduled events at Camp Perry. along with those in which modern rifles and handguns speak out across those broad, green levels. The Association holds its own National Matches, and there's an Annie Oakley competition for the ladies. Like bench-rest, big- and small-bore, pistol, skeet and trap, shooting the muzzle-loader is for everyone, kids included.

The rifle and pistol ranges for competition run from 25 to 200 yards. To even things up there is classification of rifles: offhand match, including hunting weapons; military, with "Civil War" skirmishes often featured on newsprint or on slick paper; and bench-rest, in which rifle weight goes as high as 25 pounds or more. In this last we often find such refinements as set triggers, false muzzles (removed before firing!) to let the loader start his bullet down the bore without deforming it, and really long "slug" bullets to be spun by fast twists.

Matches aren't too grim; hardly any rifle matches are. But the MLs are like the Schuetzen offhand riflemen of the late 1800s—and of today, for some still cherish that sport. They lighten things with their square dances and barbecues, and if you think they can't talk rifles and ammunition along with the most pixilated smallbore and military shooters you should hear them and rejoice. Getting the best out of muzzle-loaders is like teaching a class of sharp, independent-minded students: each one rates individual treatment.

The Association publishes a monthly magazine, *Muzzle Blasts*—headquarters address is Box 1150, Portsmouth, Ohio—and there's a library of the sport for study, quotation and application. Besides Walter Cline's book there are Ned Roberts' *The Muzzle-Loading Cap Lock Rifle,* Captain John G. W. Dillin's *The Kentucky Rifle,* and Dr. Franklin W. Mann's *The Bullet's Flight from Powder to Target.* Old *Shooters' News* and present *Precision Shooting* files, and those of *The American Rifleman,* let us turn up bits and chunks of useful information, and the den, range house, and ready line behind the firing line give first-hand help. Shooting enthusiasts are friendly.

The camp's another place, for muzzle-loading rifles probably do much more hunting now than ever before since the handy rim- and centerfire ammunition and repeating mechanisms "displaced" them. Light calibers are still "squirrel rifles," though good stalking lets them get other small game. The .40s and up are deer rifles, sometimes used on game that's even harder to kill with one shot.

As far as I know, muzzle-loading rifle hunters have no special open seasons, as archers have—and certainly deserve—in some states. They compete against hunters with modern equipment, and on their side there must be patience, woods-wisdom, and the durn sure realization that the first shot must make good. They do rack up high, sportsmanlike percentages of clean kills, as printed reports confirm.

Loading

As always in target shooting, the idea is to get the bullets there as accurately as possible. Velocity doesn't matter except as it helps to beat the wind. Bullet weight helps too, at 200 yards and even at 100, where some of the best target rifles have grouped into an inch or slightly less. Long, heavy bullets from fast twists, such as some of the old Norman Brockway rifles have, give stability at muzzle-loading target ranges. Rifling pitch runs from 16 inches for really long bullets to as slow as 100 inches for a complete turn in a barrel made for round bullets only.

There were gain twists, too, the pitch increasing toward the muzzle. Sometimes this form was used in barrels for breech-loading rifles like the .32-40 and .38-55. Whether the bullet was loaded from the front (a common practice with old cartridge rifles) or from the breech (in the case or pushed ahead of the case) there was always some criticism of the gain twist. It deformed the lead, some remarked. Some others used it and liked it, and they must have been just as hard to please. They all *demanded* accuracy.

For round bullets a good target velocity limit of 1400 f. s. has been named. Flatter trajectory and more power for hunting required the higher speed given by a stiffer powder charge, and 40 percent of the bullet weight should produce about 1700 f. s. Sometimes the figures went to about 2000 f. s.

Powder charges for long, conical bullets had to be kept down, for the bore resistance to the weight and bearing surface naturally increased pressures. Your true muzzle-loading rifleman is cautious.

It was common to test charges over fresh snow or even over bedsheets. They showed the unburned powder, if any, just as we fire over snow to see if the non-crimp-on variety of copper gaschecks drop off the bases of our cast bullets from modern cartridge rifles, as this kind should. But really the great length of so many muzzle-loading rifle barrels was for accuracy and handling qualities, not for velocity. Black powder burns fast. Many of the fine old target rifles are as tall as their owners, but the 26- and 28-inch barrels are popular for hunting.

Ignition of the powder is by flint or cap, usually the latter. By modern standards it's as slow as molasses up on the cold summit of Tug Hill, and this teaches us to follow through on the hold and not to flinch. Now that King's semi-smokeless is gone, it's black powder only. To avoid the risk of cap fragments piercing the skin of the hand, some shooters wear a glove, and wisely. A few hammer mechanisms prevent such spray, and rifles have been modernized to take a Berdan cup rifle cartridge primer, or an American Boxer cup-and-anvil primer, in a tube. Then a plunger, not the hammer itself, does the striking.

A mild flash will ignite black powder, and with fair uniformity, too, but it was common form to use a finer grain in flintlock priming pans, and many shooters thought that combustion was improved by a duplex loading in the barrel. This could be a 1/3 charge of FFFG (very fine) under the 2/3 measure of coarse FG.

Soft lead is the stuff for bullets, though some target bullets are duplex, a hard lead front section swaged on to the soft, bore-bearing part. This was done to prevent upsettage of the forward part from the quick blow of burning black powder, and from loading with a rod that might not fit the bullet nose perfectly.

Target bullet points are generally of serviceable hunting shape, flat or rounded up front. These shapes were used in the bullets of Sharps and Remington centerfire rifle cartridges that did so well at the long ranges on the Creedmoor, Long Island range in the late 1800s. When centerfire rounds went into tubular magazine repeaters the flats were almost always made much wider than the typical Sharps design. So they earned a reputation for brush-bucking and for short range killing.

The round bullet has diameter, doesn't stretch out to length and sectional density. Yet at moderate range it's a suitable target shape, and under the same limitation it's about as deadly as any form that can be dreamed up, weight and speed considered.

Sprue-scars of round bullets, where the tail of lead from the mold has been cut off, must be trimmed evenly. For uniform shooting the scar should be loaded up or down: the shooter takes his choice and is consistent. Conical bullets are often swaged to even the distribution of metal.

Bullets must be patched, and the patch cut off neatly at the muzzle. Greased linen and less expensive cloths are used. Buckskin really brings back the old days, but it varies in thickness. Varying the patch thickness, intentionally and consistently, is one of the ways to experiment for bullet fit and accuracy.

SINGLE SHOT RIFLES

"It is well argued that a return to single shot rifles with medium penetrating power and range, of large enough caliber to insure the killing of deer within ordinary distance, will work out very much protection to men in the woods." The quotation is from an article by my father in the February, 1908, number of *Stoddard's Northern Monthly,* a magazine that was published "for the saving of the Adirondacks." He used a single shot, and he still-hunted, although even then the Winchester and Remington autoloaders were appearing on drive stations, and a few guides may have been carrying them, too.

We still see this type of rifle afield and on the range in modern calibers and in black powder sizes. The latter get a lot of formal target use, though probably far less than the muzzle-loaders.

Even in the low power calibers smokeless is used commonly for its velocity, trajectory, and ease of maintaining accuracy without cleaning during a string of shots. Smokeless priming of black powder main charges is an old favorite method, too, which lately has been overdone in generosity. A bore need not be left *perfectly* clean after firing to prevent the build-up of sludge that sends bullets wild. There's the matter of pressure to consider when we use old-timers designed for some 20,000 pounds per square inch ruction, or even considerably less. Then too, those stiff boosters of pistol or mid-range rifle powders can swell cases. Although the old and perhaps hard-to-get brass can be full-length resized, such working shortens its life. I've found a 10 percent (bulk measure, not weight) dose of Du Pont 4759 too much in an old, thin-walled black powder case—safe to fire in that particular rifle and loading, but tough on brass. And 4759 is a mild-burning smokeless of the low pressure class, too. Du Pont *bulk* shotgun powder, for light field and trap loads, seems less prone to swell the bases of cartridges loaded in this duplex fashion. It's soft, though, and crumbles when compressed and stored for a few weeks or less. This runs up pressures. It is positively NOT to be loaded bulk-for-bulk, full-up, in old black-powder recommendations, as the old No. 1 Du Pont could be. In small cartridges like the .25-20 Single Shot, or the .25-20 Repeater, we might go as far as 20 percent black

powder boosting with 4759 or Du Pont Shotgun. But first we'd start low and watch for pressure signs.

A properly balanced duplex load of this kind is simply delightful to use. Unless the cases are really scarce we don't bother to wash them after firing. And somehow this sensible modernizing of an old-timer is so satisfying—and, I might as well out with it, flattering to the rifleman—that it gives a pleasure that the reloader who sticks to his big modern bench tools and strictly up-to-the-minute handloads and rifles never even knows about. He thinks we're nuts. So let him.

In some matches, like those of the "pioneer" type, black powder only is allowed. The minimum caliber may be .40, or even .44 or .45. Then most of us would be using a buffalo rifle, for the long, heavy bigbore cartridges had power: the .44-77-470, .44-90-520, .45-120-550, and that old Government load for which brass is still made, the .45-70-500. Most shooters, not all, would find the .50-170-700 too rough for target competition.

A few matches let us fire any centerfire caliber so long as we use a lead or lead-alloy bullet. Then the fine single shot stands about as good a chance as the modern bolt action. Pressures are low, with the breech-up of almost any sound old rifle snug enough for accuracy with them, and barrel vibration is scarcely a problem. A rifle with separate stock and forearm is no great handicap then.

There is a great deal of unorganized shooting of the single shot. Some of us find it as much fun as formal competition, and in certain moods, more fun. The single shot went along with many a lone wanderer when there was plenty of room in our country to be alone in!

Like nearly all the other rifles discussed in this chapter the single shot is individual. A specimen in mint condition, unaltered, is for the collector, though let's hope that he takes the pleasure of shooting it. Factory variations in styling the single shots were so numerous that a forgotten one may come to light at almost any time.

Many have been changed to suit an individual's needs or fancies. They may use the original cartridges, or they may be rebarreled, or relined, or rechambered for a longer or differently shaped case. You seldom find two alike, and those made originally for high-power smokeless rounds are rare. Even in the middle 1890s the single shot had become the arm of the specialist. Lots of old actions are unsafe with 40,000 pounds pressure, and never made up for such cartridges.

The enthusiast will want James J. Grant's book, *Single-Shot Rifles.* He'll read it through, later refer to it, and at odd free times con over a page or a picture for the relish of it. Grant knows his subject well. Although his enthusiasm seems to be restrained, it just has to bust out now and a while. It's like spring sun on thin snow. He should be an interesting man.

LONG-RANGE rifles used to stay where they belonged! Woods hunting seemed to call for a handy rifle, not necessarily a light one, that fired a cartridge with close-up smack. Its bullet was heavy and blunt enough to chop a little brush when it had to.

If there's anything wrong with those ideas about a woods rifle I don't see it. But even in the supposedly conventional East, times have changed. So have ways and means of deer hunting, which is far more popular and widely available than it was in the decade or two preceding World War II. Now our hunting may be in someone's pasture, orchard or open field. The deer work those places, have to because there are too many of them for woodlot browse to support.

Even in real forests, whose depths so few hunters ever see or even appear to want to see, there's sometimes need of a high-velocity rifle. It makes kills quicker and surer if the shot is poorly placed, and trailing up wounded game is an art that's rusting out from disuse. Too often a skilled follow-up does no good: some other hunter will have cut in before you, and by modern etiquette that deer is his. By and large, this reversal of the old rule that the game belonged to the fellow who'd put the first bullet into it means that fewer deer are lost and wasted.

However, this logical consideration didn't spark the popularity of the mountain and plains rifle in the woods. Before World War I it generally stayed outside. Only a few bolt actions went into the timber—Mausers, Mannlichers, Krags and Springfields, mostly. And they were scarce enough to draw a second look, to excite some wonder and maybe a little amusement.

But after the war the .30-06 cartridge began its long and steady climb toward the top of the heap. Springfields and Enfields came into civilian hands. They were more amenable to home-gunsmithing refinements than the rather heavy-barrelled Winchester '95 lever gun which had been almost the only .30-06 that was easy to find and not expensive to buy. Bolt-action accuracy, seldom needed in the woods, proved valuable in the enthusiastically revived sport of varmint hunting, and target shooting for plain fun or in competition made this rifle type familiar, no longer clumsy or slow.

The Savage 1920 and Remington 30 were light bolt actions aimed at the woods-hunting class of rifle buyers, and so was the later, inexpensive Savage 40 with its detachable box magazine and its locking lugs back at the rear. In between, in 1924, the Winchester 54 appeared, a heavier 06, for it weighed eight pounds in that caliber. With it came a new caliber, the .270, which was designed for mesa and canyon and prairie, not for the woods. It's a splendid long range load, which has become enormously popular for nearly all kinds of big-game hunting on this continent. So it is inevitably something of a woods favorite, too, and is

CHAPTER 7

BIG GAME RIFLES FOR THE WOODS

bought for such hunting although it's out of place in the brush. The round-nosed .30-06 180-grain soft point is better there, though even the Easterner might find the .270 a superior all-round cartridge if he does much varmint hunting.

But we still have woods rifles, lots of them. Although the bolt action is established in such use and serves well in appropriate loadings, we'll discuss only one of that type in this chapter. That is the Savage 340, limited in effective range by the .30-30 cartridge it handles. Here we consider the lever, slide and autoloading rifles, though it's true that some of them qualify for long range shooting. Overlappings of rifle actions or of cartridges needn't worry any shooter. Instead we should be thankful for them. They bring us closer to realizing the impossible or near-impossible, the all-round centerfire rifle.

Marlin 336

Barrel: 20-inch carbine; 24-inch rifle. Micro-Groove rifling.
Sights: open rear; bead front, which is ramped and hooded in rifle style and in the De Luxe and Sporting carbines. Receivers are ready for Weaver and other top-mount scope bases, and tang or receiver peep sights can be fitted.
Magazine capacity: 5. Carbines with full-length magazines take 6.
Safety: half cock notch on exposed hammer.
Weight: about 6¼ to 6½ pounds as a carbine and about 6¾ to 7¼ pounds or more as a rifle.

119

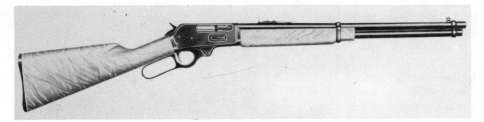

Marlin 336 Texan carbine is handy in a saddle boot or slanted against the bow decking of a canoe. Straight grip stock makes lever throw seem a little shorter than that of the pistol-gripped carbine.

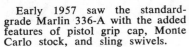

Early 1957 saw the standard-grade Marlin 336-A with the added features of pistol grip cap, Monte Carlo stock, and sling swivels.

The 336 De Luxe rifle, like the carbine, has quick-detachable swivels and one-inch gunsling.

This is a short-range arm for the woods, since it comes in .30-30, .32 Winchester Special and .35 Remington calibers. The .219 Zipper is for varmints, not deer or black bear. About the only long-range big-game rifle ever made by Marlin is the present Model 455 bolt action, unless we go gack to the 1895 lever gun. Its calibers included the .40-82-260 and .45-90-300 Winchesters, plains and mountain loads of their day, and available with copper-tubed hollow point express bullets of the same weights, with seven and five grains less of black powder behind those longer than standard slugs. Later, the '95 in .33 Winchester caliber was for a time considered a long range gun.

Design makes the 336 a handy rifle for the timber. Forefinger and thumb fall naturally on trigger and hammer, the firing hand sends the lever out and back readily if the stock is short enough for the woods-hunter who uses it, and grip and forestock are big enough to make shooting comfortable and to give sure command of the rifle. If the forestock seems too wide to a short-fingered shooter—and it might, even on the slimmed-down Texan carbine with straight grip and full magazine—he could taper it just ahead of the receiver. Then it would suit him in carrying. The comb and pistol grip stand well back, and if you wear heavy gloves against the cold you'll be glad that they do.

Lever-, pump-, auto- and most single-shot actions are proverbially hard ·to dismount and dry in camp after a wetting, and some of them must be bore-cleaned from the muzzle. Taking out the finger lever screw of the 336 lets us remove lever, bolt and ejector. That helps.

There's wide choice in styling. Carbines come with long or short magazines, the latter style available in De Luxe Sporting with checkered walnut and a quick-detachable one-inch gunsling. The rifle can also be had in De Luxe, much like the Winchester 64 Deer except that at present it comes without pistol grip cap. Light but strong composition buttplates take the place of steel on nearly all the Marlin rifles, saving weight, and any of these arms except the butt-loading .22 self-loaders can be fitted with a soft rubber recoil pad. In rock climbing this material stands the wear about as well as steel does and is just as useful except on ice. But the 336 was not planned as a mountain rifle.

Adding the .35 Rem to its lineup made it one of the best-liked rifles for those who want considerably more than .30-30 power, but not high velocity or flat trajectory. The bolt-face is specially machined to fit the .35's rimless case-head. Similar to the old .33 Winchester in deadliness, this bigbore is an easier load for the unseasoned shot to master than the .348 and .358, which to some hunters seem excessive for deer or even black bear. Years ago, it seems that there was a plan to include the .300 Savage in the 36 line—the model superseded by the 336. The modern Marlin is stronger, for its receiver is only slotted for ejection, not cut clear back to the breech. But the Remington Bronze Point .300 round is still a sobering thought! Its bullet is sharp, and bronze is harder than primer cup metal. Not so good in a tube mag, under the jolt of recoil.

Using a round instead of a square and elaborately machined breech-bolt cut production costs on the

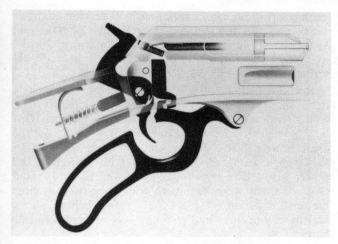

Marlin Safety action: the rear section of the firing pin is not aligned until the locking block has secured the breech closure.

With the Marlin lever fully closed and locking block in place, the rear section of the firing pin is lined up with the forward section.

336 and gave it an easy back-and-forth slide through the receiver. Some of the post-war 36s didn't have that, though most of the older rifles did. But those rifles, and the still current 39-A .22 lever gun, were about as snow-proof as any hammer gun could be, along with single shots and Colt, Burgess and Winchester repeaters. The double hammerless rifle is really proof, and so was the Remington Model 16 .22 autoloader, with the cover plate over its ejection port. Of course there really isn't much liability of snow getting into the receiver of a 336, a modern Remington auto or pump, or a Winchester 88 or 07.

Side ejection has brought about the scoping of lots of Marlins, including this one. So the hammer is made with a low spur that you can get at unless the glass is also pretty low, or far back. Then you'd want a side extension on the hammer, such as the Williams, for the 336 is a woods rifle, meant for snapshooting.

Remington 740

Barrel: 22 inches.
Sights: open rear, ramped bead front. Receiver ready for scope mounts.

Magazine capacity: 4 in detachable box.
Safety: cross button at rear of trigger guard.
Weight: about 7½ pounds.

A number of hunters had wanted a semi-automatic .30-06 sporter, and for many years. One or two models had been imported, but they were neither clean-lined nor priced within the average shooter's reach. After World War II there were a good many Remington 81s for the .300 Savage, a shorty 06, and then a few years later that model went off the market and Remington wasn't making any big-game autoloaders at all. The 1955 740 rifle came out about three or four years after the 760 pump, and it had been looked forward to by the informed for a long time. July, 1956, brought the first additional caliber, .308. The .244 and .280 followed.

Any self-loading rifle, shotgun or pistol needs special care in the matter of safety. The thing is ready to fire again before you could start to release your held breath—if you don't believe in follow-through—and the novice has to remember that fact. Most automatics need care in maintenance, too, more than a hand-operated repeater does. Folks began to wonder

Remington 740-A. This specimen has the low comb stock for iron-sight use.

A 740-ADL Remington with four-power scope.

when it became known that the 740 was gas-operated, Garand fashion, not a simple blowback like the old Winchesters or a locked-breech like the Model 81 it replaced. That one had a moving barrel that slid back into the receiver, hitched temporarily to the breechblock. "Shoot any of the old corrosive Service rounds in the new Rem and she'll be a mess of rust inside, won't she, loused up from one end to the other? And even with the clean ammunition she'll be a headache to keep in shape."

It isn't that bad. Firing chlorate-primer stuff in the 740 would hardly be a good idea, though the factory doesn't rule against it. The fire control mechanism can be removed with only a punch and a hammer to drive out the two trigger-plate screws. It can be washed in a petroleum solvent, dried, and oiled. While it's drying you can get into the receiver and brush the bolt and the bolt carrier with solvent, drain and dry 'em, and re-oil. Leave them in the receiver, and don't leave a fingertip inside where the bolt can mash it when it's released.

Turning out the fore-end screw, up at the front, lets you slide the wood forward and off. Then you can clean the exposed parts, including the metal liner of the fore-end. The gas-jet is self-cleaning, the instructions say; so leave it alone. Of course you clean the barrel of this rifle from the muzzle, for the gun is a solid frame—or should be so considered. A pistol brush—soft bristles and wire handle—can be bent to carry cleaning patches into the chamber, and this should be done once in a while. The bolt-face should be looked after, too.

All this sounds more laborious than it is. For a self-loader, the 740 isn't extremely complicated, though it's far less simple in its workings than the Winchester centerfires, the first of which came up in 1905, a year ahead of the Remington 8. The factory does advise us to remove excess oil from the 740 and to use dry graphite in its place when the temperature goes below freezing. Winchester blowbacks, rim- and centerfire, have perked well down to about zero, with no special favoring. We don't pick .22s with the gooiest lubricant to use in a self-loader when it's *that* cold.

Semi-automatic sporting rifles aren't designed for accuracy, but for quick work in the woods. With one, a cool, skilled marksman can stop wounded game that might conceivably get away if he were using a bolt action, or even a lever or pump. This Remington, however, was meant to revise our ideas of auto-rifle accuracy, just as the 760 had given previous concepts of pump-gun precision a working-over.

And though theoretically overloaded a 7½-pound .30-06 may be, it does shoot well. The barrel doesn't recoil backward into the receiver, like those of the former 8s and 81s. It's stationary. Also it's assembled tightly into the receiver. But it is a comparatively light barrel, and it *can* change its zero as it warns up in target use. This isn't surprising. The forearm re-

taining screw can cause variation if its tension changes. To correct this the Williams Gun Sight Co., Davison, Mich., has designed an inexpensive "accuracy block" to fit between fore-end tip and barrel boss. It's described in the April, '56, *Rifleman*.

Recoil of the 740 .30-06 is almost surprisingly light, thanks to its gas-operated autoloading system, which in general is like that of the M-1 Garand. One late November afternoon Bob Wolfe and I coached eight of our NRA Junior club shooters on a 100-yard range, using this Remington with 150-grain full power loads. The boys' ages ran from 12 to 14, and most of them were beginners with only two or three months' experience at the .22 game behind them. Hardly any of them had shot any sort of centerfire rifle before.

We had them fire from sitting, which next to offhand is about the most comfortable position, recoilwise, and as it was a pretty cold day they were well bundled up. Only two of them, the smallest though not the youngest, seemed to be at all bothered after the first shot, and none was hurt in any way. Six of them did creditable shooting, and all of them had a great time. Time and again I have seen grown men do much worse with a rifle of 06 power, and you've seen it, too.

In .30 caliber the 740 balances about seven inches ahead of the trigger, and for this reason it is pretty steady to hold offhand in spite of its light weight. Fine balance makes it seem lighter on the hoof than it really is, and this balance is made possible by the lightness of the receiver and the working parts it covers. The only discomfort in trail carry is the rather mild prod of the operating handle on the palm of the right hand. Scoping the rifle naturally changes its balance and feel, but the gun is accurate enough at moderate ranges to profit by a scope. And I certainly think that any unseasoned hunter who uses a semi-automatic should have a glass on it, at least if he's the least bit liable to become excited. In heavy cover, in deep shade, the bright lenses of a 2½, 3 or 4 power hunting scope tell him what's what. It's a gray stub, it's a granite boulder, it's a deer— or it's a man.

High-comb stocks are available for this rifle, as for the 760 pump, and both deserve a glass if the owner wants one. A thin-faced shooter might find the high comb just the right height for iron sights, and almost anyone could use it with them, comfortably.

Most of us need months or even years of rather frequent rifle or shotgun airings to become so familiar with a cross button safety in the trigger guard that we can punch it off instantly, as we mount the gun to our shoulder. Often a shooter can't find it until after the chance to fire has turned into something sour on his stomach! The top tang safe, double shotgun style, is about as quick to "learn" as a handy exposed hammer. The J. Dewey Gun Co., East Hampton, Conn., installs a tang safety on this rifle, the 760, and other Remington rifles and shotguns. Triangle Gun Co.,

Standard-grade 760 stocked for use with iron sights.

De Luxe 760, high comb stock.

A 760-BDL Remington with four-power hunting scope, quick-detachable swivels, and fine walnut stock and slide handle.

Baldwin, Mich., has a slightly less expensive do-it-yourself kit that gives similar results.

Remington 760

Barrel: 22 inches.
Sights: open rear and ramped bead front. Receiver drilled and tapped for scope mounts.
Magazine capacity: 4 in detachable box.
Safety: cross button at rear of trigger guard.
Weight: about 7½ pounds.

At present this model is offered in the .222, .244, .257, .270, .300 Savage, .30-06 and .35 Remington calibers. In outline it is much like the 740 autoloader— or the Remington shotguns. Both of these highpower rifles have multiple locking lugs up front, rigid and strong. Even though the 760 didn't appear in .270 for some time after the .300, 06 and .35 had become well known in this model, there is no doubt of the action's strength to handle properly loaded ammunition of this high-intensity class—as much as 55,000 pounds per square inch of pressure in the .270.

The tight breech-up, the free-floating barrel, and the semi-permanent assembly of that barrel to the receiver tot up to amazingly good shooting, compared to the work of earlier takedown slide actions in the high power class. Many of the 760 rifles do well in open-country hunting.

The double action bars (as on the 740) help to smooth the back-and-forth operation of the breech-block, and the case extraction, for a slide-action rifle, is strong. Many handloaders do use the 760. The receiver, a solid-breech hammerless with no takedown joint at the rear, is about as gas-proof as any could be,

though in that respect the hammerless Winchester autos and others are just as safe. Some old rifles of other makes were not. Both this rifle and the 740 support the case-heads snugly when the action is closed, much in the manner of the 721 and 722 Remington bolt guns.

Bore cleaning is done from the muzzle, just as with the 740, and the care to be taken of the chamber and action parts is similar, although a pump gun's insides need less frequent attention. Gun care doesn't worry many shooters today—the casual ones, at least—before something goes a bit wrong. It can go wrong at the wrong time.

The 760 isn't, to my mind, a beauty. Its fore-end or slide handle looks too much like a porch pillar, at least in standard grade. But so much rifle use is of the wear-it-out-and-throw-it-away sort that the factory people were wise in leaving a good thickness of walnut in that handle. Neither a careful hunter nor his rifle takes many tumbles, although they may travel rough country, and that kind of hunter often isn't a bit interested in the speed of fire of a pump or lever gun. A guide's job may require him to cover ground pretty fast now and then, and you rarely see him carrying a fine, delicate rifle when he's at work. He's apt to reserve it for his own trips, alone.

The pump action is fast: few lever-gun artists can quite equal the speed of a reasonably skilled trombone operator. But even with the autoloader, mechanical speed of action means little if your ammunition is powerful. It takes time to pull down and to steady

Savage 99 Featherweight.

The 99-EG. Damascening is now
applied to all of the 99 breechbolts.

Savage 99-R. Note the high, full
stock comb, set well forward.

down from the recoil of any rifle with more back-thrust than that of, say a seven pound .30-30. For this reason the .257 is the logical choice of the deer hunter who wants a 760 and (without much logic) all the rapidity of fire it can give him. Later—and let's hope it's a soonish sort of later—he may learn to try to make his shots count. Then he'll forget the hurry. In practical use the slow-ups from auto to pump to lever are trivial to an experienced big-game hunter. Or usually they are. Also nearly always, he can be fast enough with a bolt action, provided he needs a second shot at all.

The 760 balances at about six to six and a half inches ahead of the trigger. That gives almost exactly the extra muzzle-steadiness a seasoned upland game bird hunter would want in switching from his short, light 16- or 20-gauge pump shotgun (two shells in its magazine) to this rifle. It isn't entirely for appearance's sake, or even for economy, that Remington makes shotguns and high-power rifles so similar in lines and in functioning parts, too. Familiarity breeds content, and content breeds another sale.

This policy is nothing new with that company. It's merely been advanced in a logical way. In the preceding output there was much resemblance in line and in general appearance between .22, high power and shotgun—streamlined pumps and square-shouldered autoloaders. The first to drop out and be forgotten was the Model 16 .22 auto. It required a special smokeless cartridge that was low in power and pretty high in barrel-corroding ability. The 24 and 241 that followed had the flowing receiver lines of the already established pump action trio.

Savage 99

Barrel: 22 inches on 99-F Featherweight; 24 on the EG, R and RS.
Sights: open rear and ramped gold bead front. Receivers ready for peep rear sights or top-mounted scopes. The RS has a Redfield 70 LH micrometer peep, and a blank piece fills the rear sight slot on the barrel.
Magazine capacity: 5 in revolving brass spool.
Safety: sliding fingerpiece at right rear of trigger guard.
Weight: 99-F, about 6½ pounds; EG, 7¼; R and RS, 7½. These are close to minimum weights, with dense stock wood sometimes adding about ¼ pound.

This 1899 Savage is one of quite a few rifles I had looked forward to writing up in this book with a special sort of anticipation. A fellow has to respect it, and here's the brief of its story: lever action designed about 1895, when smokeless powder ammunition was new on the American market; thousands of old ones still doing well with appropriate ammunition; modern steel not only safely corraling the pressures of high-intensity cartridges, but so snugly, too, that they give good accuracy. So much for the pathetic old lever actions! The Winchester 88 is modern; in fact, it's about the first completely new lever-gun repeating system since 1895.

Originally the 99 was made for low-pressure cartridges, the black and smokeless powder .32-40 and .38-55, and the .25-35, .30-30 and .303. Early specimens in these calibers are identified by the loaded-or-empty chamber indicator at the front of the breechblock. Later 99s carry a striker indicator on the upper tang; it sticks up when the striker is in firing position.

The whole width of the rear of the breechblock abuts against the wall of the receiver when the action

Savage proprietary cartridges in the order of their development. From left: .303, .22 High Power, .250, .300. The last three originally appeared with sharp-pointed bullets, but they have been such popular calibers that they have been made in several styles. Only the .303 was confined almost entirely to Savage rifles.

is closed and locked, a strong and entirely safe breech-up but less rigid than those of front-locking lugs of the 1898 Mauser type, or of the 88 Winchester and modern Remington sort. With the coming of the 99's first high-intensity cartridge, the .22 High Power of 1912, reloaders began to notice the stretch of fired brass. Sometimes the used cases were hard to insert unless they'd been full-length resized, and that was a job for powerful tools. The brass had lengthened as well as expanded sidewise in the fashion that had been familiar when breech-up was snug enough for lower pressures.

That .22 had a chamber pressure of some 48- to 50,000 pounds per square inch, and the 99 loads that followed it sometimes go a bit over 50,000. These rounds are still offered in 99 choice, the .250 and .300 Savage. In 1955 and '56 the short-cased Winchester .243, .308 and .358 were added. The last was a late but hearty answer to those who throughout the years had asked why Savage didn't take up the .35 Remington load. It was hard to see why the Corporation didn't.

Now we have quite a large class of hunters who demand light but plenty powerful rifles. They explain, truthfully, that there's a lot more carrying than shooting, and they want wallop for big game, including deer. They don't mind recoil or muzzle blast, and they certainly get them! Some of these fellows do good shooting; so they're properly gunned with a featherweight that hits hard two ways.

To many of us the thought of firing the modern equivalent of the .35 Winchester '95 cartridges in a 6½-pound rifle is hardly inviting. The oldtimer weighed about 8¾ pounds and still handed out a free recoil of 20 foot-pounds, a pound more than the .30-06 220-grain delivers from a gun of approximately the same weight. The .405 in the '95 model came back with 28; the 300-grain .375 in the Model 70 is credited with 33½. A heavy old 12-bore double or repeater loaded with 3¼ drams of black powder and 1¼ ounces of shot kicked back with 31½, or with 28 when the prescription substituted smokeless powder. All of these figures are approximate and none of them represents unbearable recoil, to a seasoned shooter. A well shaped modern stock like

the Savage's does minimize recoil. I doubt that any of us would want a high, forward-rising Monte Carlo on any light .358, and I'm sure that most of us would appreciate a fat rubber recoil pad. Even the .300 and .308 have considerable kick when they're fired in a light rifle, though stock design unquestionably can be a comfort—or a curse—under the belting of heavy charges.

The Savage rotary magazine is easy to load even when your fingers are cold, and holding back the top round when closing the action on a loaded chamber is no trouble. Feeding and ejection are reliable, and as the empties fly out to the side and down, and there's no exposed hammer to reach for with the thumb, a scope can be mounted low on the Savage. It can sit well back for a full view of its field, too.

But we could wish for a hammer when a quick shot is offered. The safety at the rear of the trigger guard is hard to reach and pull back in a hurry, even though some have been made good-sized. It's a reliable safety and part of its work is to lock the action shut. This is necessary, for the down-fling of the lever is so easy that the unlocked action could come unstuck when we're hunting. Top tang, shotgun type safeties for the 99 have been offered by H. B. Anderson, 1203 Broadway, Yakima, Wash., Ellwood Epps, Clinton, Ontario, and the Sports Equipment Co., 345 Pine St., Lockport, N. Y. Under almost any scope mounting they are handy to the thumb.

The Savage does open easily; the hitch comes when the lever is on the return trip, for that is the time when the striker is cocked. A Marlin or Winchester hammer is thrust back on the out trip. If this slight resistance pulls the buttplate down on your shoulder, the closing action returns it—all a very smooth job. With the Savage we learn to pull the butt hard against our shoulder with the forward hand as we draw the lever back; then we relax into a normal hold, only the firing hand snugging the butt into place. It is true that some lever-gun shooters tense up with both hands throughout a burst of fire. Usually this technique makes for crackling fast fire and ten-quart-bucket-at-thirty-yards accuracy. But talk about rifles and riflemen always must provide the loophole of exceptions.

The standard Savage 340.

The 340-S De Luxe, Discontinued.

The 99s are no longer made as plain, undecorated rifles or carbines. The 20-inch carbine was only an insignificant 1½ inch longer than the old pet Winchester .30-30, and it was only a trifle thicker cross-lots in spite of the magazine housed in its receiver. But for continuous saddle-boot carrying a hammer gun is pretty well liked, logically or not. As now made, the 99s have fore-and-aft checkering, capped pistol grips, and damascened breechbolts.

The through-bolt attachment of the stock and the tight breech-up make for accuracy. In .250 the Savage has a long-earned reputation for shooting nearly as well as a bolt-action sporter. It gives light recoil and even with a 22-inch barrel the report is not extremely sharp. At least it isn't with the 100-grain bullet, which when jacketed for the job is good for game from woodchucks to deer. Even yet, it is a fine little all-around rifle and a good one for a lady to use if she shoots it well enough to place the bullet right. Perhaps it is one of the very best *first* high-powers she could have.

Far ahead of its time was the 99 ignition system. The throw of the striker or firing pin is as short as most of us would demand in a match rifle. This speed does help us to beat the wobble in offhand shooting. It's a nice point, though not essential in a woods rifle.

Some 99s have a rather heavy trigger pull, and the work-over is a gunsmith's job. Shortening the arm of the sear is dangerous, could cause the rifle to fire as the action is closed. But pulls are usually clean, and we can become familiar with any pull of that sort. Only a careful, experienced hunter needs a light one in cold weather. At that time the Savage comes into its own, for it's a popular woods rifle. Most of us would choose a bolt action for open country, usually but not always with good reason.

Savage 340

Barrel: 22 inches in .30-30 caliber.
Sights: click elevating open rear and ramped front with gold insert. Receiver is ready for Savage No. 175 Micro Peep. The 340-S De Luxe rifle has the 175 in place, and the front is hooded.

Magazine capacity: 3 .30-30s in detachable clip.
Safety: thumb lever at right rear of receiver locks sear and bolt.
Weight: about 6½ pounds.

Probably few well-to-do sportsmen would be interested in this little rifle, though they might be if they tried it. The 325 Stevens, of which it is a refinement, was the first factory-made bolt action .30-30 to follow the discontinued Winchester 54 in that never fully investigated caliber. Although the 340 is a featherweight it should develop interesting .30-30 accuracy with the right handloads. The action is plenty strong for its ammunition, and as a rule the finest precision does *not* come from super loadings. Correct headspace is practically assured by the method used in assembling the barrel to this action.

The gun is made as an inexpensive but reliable deer rifle. It's a sensible buy for the hunter who can't afford the best bolt, lever, pump or automatic, and who isn't sure of his ability to pick a used gun wisely. It's also for the hunter who wants a rugged little brush rifle that can take hard going and not show a heavy depreciation as a result. Above all, it's *only* for the deer hunter who is cool and steady enough to do good work with a load that is classed quite justly as having only marginal power. There are thousands of such hunters, praise be!

But for a second shot, if one is needed, this 340 isn't bad, as a bolt gun. Its bolt throw is short, and if the knob on the bolt handle should seem at all hard to get at, a little sanding-away of the walnut will correct that. The full capacity of only four shots would be a healthy deterrent to one kind of hunter. The other kind, just described, wouldn't be concerned about the supply.

For looks and for snapshooting this Savage is much improved by the new style forestock, slim and tapered. On shotgun or rifle a deep forestock is a handicap to most hunters when the time of opportunity is short: it tends to cause over-shooting. But we're of all sorts, some of us perhaps too tolerant,

Winchester 07 .351-caliber self-loader. Discontinued in 1957.

and too persistent in struggling along under handicaps that we could correct with a little effort.

Striker fall is fast, and trigger pull unusually good, as a rule, for a rifle in this price class. Since it's a bolt action, refining the pull shouldn't be too hard for folks who are handylike—provided any such attention is found necessary.

About the only real objection to the 340 is the size of its mid-section, a bit fat for such a small gun, and a stretch for very short fingers. It is possible to shave it a little, something we'd hesitate to do to a heavy arm of precision. For woods use the location of pistol grip and comb are just about right. The 340-S stock has checkering, and there are eyes for attaching a carrying strap. Although these are properly located for most of us, we'd prefer swivels for a shooting gun-sling, and the kitten could have the eyes to play with.

This is probably one .30-30 bolt gun that'll be on the market for quite a spell. It fills a definite need.

Winchester 07

Barrel: 20 inches.
Sights: open rear, bead front mounted on barrel lug. Tang and receiver sights have been made for it, and scopes have been used successfully.
Magazine capacity: 5 or 10; detachable box type. The ten-shotter is a snag-all in the woods.
Safety: cross button at front of trigger guard.
Weight: 8¼ pounds. About ½ pound heavier than the more streamlined Model 1907 it replaced.

The 07 is a police rifle as well as a sporter. This is probably the big reason for its survival, though the now defunct Remington 81 also was made for law enforcement officers. In this style, its magazine was long and curved, detachable, and it held 15 .35s.

The .351 caliber 07 is short, only 38 inches overall, nominally one-quarter inch longer than the .30-30 carbine of the same make. It's handy in boat, brush, or prowl wagon, and in spite of its stubbiness it holds steadily. The simple blowback action requires a heavy breechblock. It's a long block, extending up inside the hollow forearm; so the balance is well out front. This comparative muzzle-heaviness and the light recoil of the load reduce the upchuck in rapid fire. You can send aimed shots out fast if you need to.

Of the three old models of Winchester automatics we can hardly say that the fittest survived. Only 29,113 1905s were made, in .32 and .35 calibers, and the end came in 1920. The 1910 .401 wasn't dropped until 1936, when a mere 20,786 had been put out.

The 05 was weak: it had about .32-40 and 38-40 power. But the 10 was a buster—200- and 250-grain .40 caliber bullets at 2140 and 1875 f. s.—as good a short-range deer and black bear gun as those handling .33 Winchester or .35 Remington cartridges, so well proved. It kicked, though a seasoned shot wouldn't mind it, and the .351 always was gentle. So it stayed.

Perhaps the wrong kind of people would buy the .351, the twitchy kind. Fast follow-up shots are easy with this rifle, but hitting moving game with any rifle is hard for everyone but the trained expert. The .351 is, without any doubt, an easy short-range snapshooting rifle to master. Recoil and report are light, balance and stock fit fine. Unfortunately we aren't always allowed a second well-pulled shot when game is on the run; so we do need killing power under our finger for the first one. For that reason, many experienced hunters carry a high velocity rifle in the woods, and want reasonable bullet weight, too. Then a hit placed a little too far back may still be instantly fatal, or at least slow down the animal.

The 07 action is almost 100 percent reliable under the toughest conditions. It ranks with the best levers, pumps and bolts. This gun needs only a little favoring, and it's an oldtimer with more than human lifetime durability built into it. Oiling the top and sides of the receiver and working the breech block back and forth while we hold the front half of this takedown rifle upside down is sensible, maybe not mandatory. In extreme cold the gun will perk for a long time, anyway, with no oil at all in the works.

Accuracy is OK for a woods rifle, about three- or four-inch grouping at 100 yards on a good, comfortable range. Don't laugh: any deer shooting I'd do with it would be at less than 60 yards, a long shot in the woods. Though I've used this rifle only for prospecting around summer meadows I'd not hesitate to carry it in the fall. I'd pass up the hard shots just as I should with a .25-35. If I simply had to have deer-meat and got only a few days to hunt in good country, I'd want about the equivalent of .401 power, or more if the woods were crowded and I still *had* to get a deer for the winter.

Winchester 64 and 94

Barrel: 24 inches; 20 on 94 carbine.
Sights: open rear and hooded, ramped bead front. Receivers ready for peep sights. Offset scope mounts can be had, such as the Echo 18 D which puts the glass to the right, correctly for a right-handed shooter.

Winchester 94 carbine.

Standard-grade Winchester 64 rifle. This one and the 64 Deer used to come in 20-inch barreling, too, for .30-30 or .32 Special, but the little .25-35 wasn't regular issue in Deer rifle form. All 64 models, but not the 94 carbine, you can be sure, were discontinued in 1957.

Model 64 Deer rifle.

Magazine capacity: 5 in rifle, 6 (sometimes 7) in carbine.
Safety: half cock notch on exposed hammer.
Weight: 94, 6¼ pounds; 64, 7; 64 Deer, 7¼. All are approximate, and not overstated.

This 1894 action was built for the black-powder .32-40 and .38-55 Ballard and Marlin cartridges, and in 1895 the .30-30* went into the line. The .25-35, .32 Special and .219 Zipper followed, none of them giving more than about 40,000 pounds pressure in factory loadings, and often less. For such ammunition and for sensible handloads the lockup is certainly strong enough.

Probably a more powerful factory cartridge could be designed for it, such as a rimmed .35 with about .35 Remington ballistics. From a certain viewpoint there's no need for it. Carbine and rifle continue to sell fast in .30-30 and .32 Special calibers. They have a great reputation, are still the most widely known and generally accepted deer guns. Just how solidly based is this reputation?

It isn't built on accuracy, though the shooting is good enough for the job, bullets well placed in the neck or shoulder of a woods deer. The range is seldom as long as 100 yards, and often less than half of that. With *light* and carefully worked-up handloads the accuracy can come close to that of a good bolt action bigbore of similar weight. The 1894 shot well with the .32 and .38 black powder cartridges it was made

for, and with the smokeless powder, jacketed bullet loads of similar power. With considerably heavier charges, not including all of the .25-35 offerings, the weak point in design opened the groups.

There is much more backward slant to its single-locking block than there is to that of the big 1895 action that handled the .30-06, .35 and .405 rounds with quite fair accuracy. And like the '95 it has a receiver with no integral bottom to add stiffness to the assembly. The big rifle needed an opening for its box magazine to fit into; the '94 required a dropping link, a sort of false bottom, to give the necessary leverage to the long breech-bolt and still keep the receiver a slim, easy handful. The Marlins achieved this result by pivoting the lever well ahead of the trigger guard.

So the '94 lockup and openwork receivers haven't the rigidity and stiffness that bring out target accuracy. For all that, the action wears wonderfully well. About the only correction that long, long use with standard loads can make necessary is the insertion of a new pin or stud at the rear of the link. A badly worn one may let the lever drop down a very short distance when the gun is fired or even when it's being carried. This is not a matter of danger, but it's certainly inconvenient. Rare, too.

The carbine is so small and handy that it will almost fit into a pack-basket, and in a saddle boot or shoved under the forward decking of a canoe it's right at home. In .25-35 it was a pleasant little gun to shoot, fine for a beginner, and lots of oldtimers

---

*There was a 30-30-165 black powder cartridge of entirely different shape and characteristics, for the Wesson single shot, I think.

Standard 71 with Lyman 66A receiver peep sight. 1957 saw the 71 discontinued.

The special (and original) grade of 71 with checkered wood, pistol grip cap, and quick-detachable one-inch gunsling.

liked it because its accuracy and trifling recoil let them make sure hits up to about 150 yards. The .30-30 and .32 Special are noisy in this short barrel, the muzzle blast causing the recoil to seem heavier than it is. A little shooting experience makes them less unpleasant, and to those who hunt with a short-barreled featherweight magnum the sound and shove are trivial.

At least three stock designs have been used on the carbine, all of them short, though a heavily clad hunter seldom complains about that. The old double-curve carbine buttplate was flat enough to distribute recoil nicely. Deeply hollowed in the center and rounded at heel and toe, it got where it was going, fast, and it stayed there. Then there was the almost perfectly flat shotgun butt, with so little down-pitch that it was no more comfortable, and definitely less secure when you levered the gun at your shoulder. At about the time when a useless inch or so came off the front of the forestock the buttplate got the pitch it needed. All these plates were of steel, and Winchester carbine stocks, unless mighty special indeed, have had straight grips only. We'll except the M-1 Service .30 carbine.

The comparatively light Model 64 rifles have enough barrel weight and length to balance finely, for most of us. They come up responsively on or close to the mark, right away. Their pistol grips sit far enough back to still feel handy when we wear gloves, and you learn to shove gloved fingers through a lever loop quickly, after a bit of practice. To the average taste, the size of their semi-beavertail fore-stocks isn't overdone. Perhaps they lie a little more steadily in the hand than the slim forestocks of the 1894 rifles, and the later but not often seen 55s.

The apparently longer distance to lever-throw added by the curve that must follow the pistol grip is no never-mind. Inconsequential. With any 94 or 64 or their ancestors the shooter must remember to give a final forward hitch to the lever loop. If he fails to, the carrier doesn't lift a fresh round from the magazine. A spot of practice in dry firing blends this effort into the unregarded—or nearly so. On the shorter throw lever actions—'86, '92, 53, 65, and the current 71—this last little hitch is less noticeable. The Marlin carrier rises on the return trip of the lever.

The 64 Deer model has the extras of checkered grip and forearm, grip cap, and a one-inch gunsling on quick-detachable swivels. Such a light rifle with two-piece woodwork may show different striking points on the target, down or up, when the sling is or isn't used and the loads are of .30-30 or .32 Special power. For off-season varmint hunting the sling is worth while, and for carrying in open stretches of country it's a help, too. It is possible to put up varmint rounds for the 64 that give the accuracy needed at one hundred yards or so. Even *carrying* a deer rifle around in summertime is good practice. It makes the gun feel more familiar, come the turn and fall of the leaves. The stalking up to one-hundred-yard or shorter ranges is good preparation, too.

Winchester 71

Barrel: 24 inches.
Sights: open rear and hooded, ramped front. Receiver is ready for peep sights, with Lyman 66 A and a blank in the rear barrel slot being regular factory issue when chosen.
Magazine capacity: 4 .348 caliber cartridges.
Safety: half cock notch in exposed hammer.
Weight: about 8 pounds or slightly over.

There are slight differences in action design between the 71 and the 1886 rifle. Even with the modern rifle's sharply curved finger lever the throw is still short and easy. The big hammer and the trigger—which is more curved than those of early 71s—wait where they should. Thumb and forefinger find them promptly: you cock the rifle as it jumps to your shoulder.

The 71 carries well, for its big but not too big receiver is rounded at the bottom. Cold? Yes, steel receivers can get that way, but it seems natural to tote a rifle in the left hand, ready for action, if you're a right-handed shooter, and what hunter could object to wearing a glove or mitten on it?

The breechblock is locked shut by a pair of heavy

Winchester 88.

lugs that slide almost straight up into cuts in the block and the receiver sidewalls. Harold MacFarland has given the action strength of the 71 and of late '86s (over 26,000 serial number) as 45,000 pounds per square inch. It has plenty of backup for .348 factory rounds, but handloads of higher pressure aren't to be recommended. This holds good for practically any lever action repeater and with a bolt gun too it's common sense. The stretch of brass is often not serious to the owner who reloads his .348 empties, and the case is a strong, heavy one. It's been used for various wildcat cartridges of larger caliber and great power. Opening the neck of almost any case can give that extra foot-poundage. Case shoulders naturally build up pressures, though generally we need them to get what we want from a given length of brass, or to burn certain powders.

There is a good deal of body taper to .348 brass, and the inside diameter of the base is large. At the instant of discharge the case can't grip the chamber walls as well as a more straight-bodied one like the .308 or .358, and it drives back hard through the slight tolerance that practical headspacing gives it. The force of this thrust is augmented by the big inside head dimensions. As Colonel Whelen pointed out long ago, it's best to keep both the .348 chamber and the brass free from oil. Then the case has a chance to hold on as it is simultaneously expanded and driven back. A few cents buy a soft bristle brush with a wire handle, the kind we might use to grease barrel and chambers of a .45 sixgun. With that we can get into the chamber, clean it, and leave it dry.

For such a heavy, comparatively short rifle the 71 has good lines. The semi-beavertail forearm is wide, not deep; its lines blend well. Late stocks have the comb shoved much farther forward than before, the target rifle inheritance showing up again. This does no harm except that it might cramp a big or a heavily gloved hand, and the short upper tang would make the mounting of a peep sight there pretty difficult. However, this sort of sight seems to be going out of favor—none now made, that I know of, has any windage adjustment—and only a few shooters wanted or should have had one on a rifle like this, with approximately .30-06 recoil. There's more than danger of the sight's being driven back into the eye on an uphill shot or when the rifle is held loosely. It has happened. I have seen it once, and *that* time it was not tragic: only the lower lid of the eye was cut open. On a lever gun the receiver peep sits almost an inch

nearer the eye than the usual sort on a bolt action, mounted over the receiver bridge. This much extra closeness helps a little in catching the sights quickly, and at least on a hammer gun it's not too close.

Since the .348 sometimes is used against dangerous game, the easy side-loading of its magazine is important. Winchesters and Marlins of this tubular magazine type can be refilled while the action is closed and ready over a cartridge in the chamber. The detachable magazines of the modern Remington pumps and autos, the Savage 340, and the Winchester 88 are almost as good, and so is the side-door Krag or the cellar-door Schultz & Larsen. But it's easier to get at least *one* extra round into the tubular magazine, and fast.

The .348 has been called a universal rifle for American big-game shooting. If stalking can reduce ranges to 150 yards, or about two hundred at most, it can qualify. Lots of deer hunters like its anchoring power and its flat-nosed bullets' pretty high reliability in brush. The gun has been used on varmints to some extent—it naturally would be—and up to 100 yards and a bit there can be the accuracy for such small targets. Cast bullet reloads are interesting to work up, and they have their hunting purposes. A hollow point can be made of lead soft enough to break up and avoid ricochets if the shooter is careful. Although a 12-inch rifling twist isn't exactly designed for lead bullets, a gas check cup on the bullet base lets us go a little easy on the amount of hardening alloy we must put into the pot.

Winchester 88

Barrel: 22 inches.
Sights: the usual supplementary type for a scoped rifle, folding open rear and hooded, ramped front. Receiver ready for scope mounts or peep sight.
Magazine capacity: 5 in detachable box that when fully charged is inserted from below when the breech is open.
Safety: cross button at front of trigger guard.
Weight: about 6½ pounds.

If the Model 71 .348 is a universal American big-game rifle the 88 might with almost equal justice be called an all-round rifle—if you believe there is any. For such a stretch of usefulness most people would choose it in .308, the caliber in which it first stepped out, back in 1955. Some who never plan to hunt anything heavier than deer or antelope, and who do a lot of varmint shooting, might pick the .243. A hunter whose main interest lies in game considerably bigger than deer perhaps would take the .358. If he understood handloading with cast bullets, or with the light 9 mm. and .38 auto-pistol pills, he could use this .35 caliber for small-game shooting.

The 88 might be called a lever operated bolt action rifle. It's faster than the other high-power lever guns, and much faster than straight-pull bolts like the Mannlicher-Steyr, Lee, Ross, or the more or less experimental Newton variant of turn-bolt operated by a standard lever of generous size. It has the accuracy of a bolt action of similar build, weight and power, for its three locking lugs are about as far up front as lugs could be unless they were hitched to the muzzle. The one-piece stock, through-bolted to the receiver, stiffens the assembly, and the steel is bedded carefully into it.

Most people find the 88 attractive in lines. It has the smoothness of a streamy hammerless and of a rifle stocked to about average iron-sight dimensions: 13½ inches long; comb drop, 1⅝; heel drop, 2½. It looks still better with its magazine in your pocket. Carl Saddlemire, a muzzle-loader devotee who's at home with modern arms too, told me when the 88 first came out that he wished they'd made it with one round less capacity. Then that box magazine would have sat flush. Knowing muzzle-loaders so well, Carl knows what gun lines should be, and he's seldom a hard person to agree with. This time it was doubly easy because he'd just got there first with that comment. I let the wind out of my lungs and we went on from there.

This rifle's speed of action usually seems to be the first thing noticed. Lever stroke is listed at 60° and that of a 94 Win, for instance, is close to 90, starting from the lower line of the straight-gripped carbine's tang. So the action is about as fast as that of a pump gun giving similar recoil, and I think that no more words need be expended on this topic.

The safety is quicker and handier than that of the unaltered Savage 99, but not nearly as convenient or even as foolproof as an exposed hammer. A more commonly useful foolproof detail is the trigger. It goes down with the lever on the opening stroke instead of staying put, waiting to mash your forefinger on the return if you forget to hold it out to the side. If the shooter is rattled and hauls away on that trigger while he works the action the rifle doesn't fire as it goes shut. An interrupter blocks it. Ease off, and the trigger is ready again.

The 88 is deliberately lightened in the featherweight style now so popular. The pistol grip cap and the buttplate are of nylon, not steel; the buttstock is hollowed about as generously as that of the old '86 .45-70 Extra Light Weight; and the barrel, like that of the littlest 70, is turned down nearly as much as it can stand and still have enough stiffness for first-rate hunting accuracy.

The action has a great margin of strength for the high-intensity cartridges it handles. There's not only the support of three goodsized bolt lugs. There's also the snug enclosure of the case-head in barrel breech and bolt-face, much in the Remington fashion. Like those highly modern actions it has a built-in extractor and ejector: no channel through the receiver ring for the first; no slicing through the bolt-face or—worse —through a locking lug for the second. Today's designs have advanced far from the 1898 Mauser, to which they owe so much. For front lugs that rotate into their seats in the receiver ring reliably, as these do, are trustworthy in plan and in strength. It seems to make little difference whether they are solid lugs, as on this Winchester and on most bolt actions, or serrated, as on the Remington pump and autoloader, and some of the old Newton, Ross, and Niedner designs. The serious trouble with certain Ross actions was that they could be so reassembled that the lugs didn't turn when the straight-pull bolt handle was thrust forward.

Tom Florich mentioned one possible objection to the built-in ejector when the Remington 721 and 722 bolt actions came out in 1948 and recalled attention to this system. He stressed it as a theoretical objection. Pressing hard on one side of the chambered case, the ejector would push minimum-tolerance brass farther away from the bolt-face than it would force maximum-tolerance. With a possible difference of some .006 inch, ignition might vary. And in a loose chamber each cartridge would lie diagonally across the chamber. As a fired and expanded empty it could be a trifle eccentric, too. We know that both 721 and 722 actions have done well as the basis of bench rest rifles. For that matter, the built-in ejector has been common in Winchester lever action repeaters for many years.

Probably the 88's extractor could be said to weaken one lug—slightly. However, the two remaining lugs are solid enough.

If a primer is punctured or a case-head bursts, the escaping gas could hardly reach the shooter. This rifle is hammerless, closed at the rear like the Remington pumps and autos. Even its ejection port is so small that snow or rain could hardly pour in. This opening is about where your hand would cover it, too, unless you wanted a heavy scope on the receiver, and pretty far back. The .358, obviously, is a good bit more muzzle-light than the .243. There's a big hole bored through a barrel for bullets of that size.

This rifle is stocked for iron sights and the standard open rear notch is set too far forward on the short barrel to give even as much sight radius as a 94 carbine has. A peep sight at the end of the long receiver makes good iron-sight shooting possible, and on this hammerless side-ejector a hunting scope can be set as low as ingenuity permits. The usual mountings on the 88 are low enough for a rather full-faced shooter, and the accuracy of this arm deserves a scope for the rather long ranges at which it performs so well.

IN THE kind of story that occasionally stinks up the printed page, we may read, if our gullibility and our stomach are strong enough, of 400- and 500-yard shots at big game. They do happen, and—don't mistake me—sometimes they're made with complete success. There's a quick kill or at worst a disabling hit that lets the matter be settled promptly. Yet it's seldom *necessary* to take such a shot.

Estimating Distances

But even with no intent to deceive, many a hunter will tell of one when he knows little about judging distance. It looked like 400, or 500, and the guide said it was, and he ought to know, hadn't he? Agreed: he ought, but does he always?

It takes a lot of pacing of distances—over all sorts of terrain, up and down as well as straight-out, and under different light conditions—and then looking back, studying and trying to memorize the more or less indefinite, to become able to make any sort of reasonable estimate by eye. The tape is better, and it's been used. Next best is the pacing, all the way, or sharply estimating the places where we do well to put one shoe ahead of the other at all.

This is a nuisance—though how it does pay off in sight adjustment or overhold!—and it's easy to slur it along with other nuisances that make hunting and marksmanship skill. Lots of capable hunters have little judgment of distances over 100 yards, or over 50, if they stick to the timber. They can state with complete honesty that a shot was made at "close to 400" when in reality it was a bare 200 yards. Even so, it was creditable shooting.

Then there is the fellow who is, let's say, enthusiastic. *He* never shrinks a good story. We all have some of that tendency, I presume, and it keeps the world—yes, even the outdoorsman's world—from getting too dull. Haven't you noticed, as I have, a sort of drag in your leg muscles when you were pacing a shot? It takes moral and physical effort to stretch out to a full 36-inch pace. Some of us are short-legged, too, and I bring up that matter to excuse the fact that I have to deduct about 10 per cent from my paced figures to get the yardage. It's easy to determine your personal par on a measured 100 yard range. If you really want to learn to estimate you'll catch yourself earnestly gazing down every rifle range you come to in your travels, whether it's 50 feet or 1,000 yards.

For Your Stomach's Sake

In the first paragraph of this chapter we said something about stomach ease, inner contentment. In mind was "the ghastly type of shooting"—so Teddy Roosevelt, Jr., once described it—that often results when a hunter takes on a shot that's too much for his skill. Those results can be nauseating, to a civilized mind. No normal person "likes" to lose crippled game, or to wonder how and when death finally gave it the

CHAPTER 8

BIG GAME RIFLES FOR THE OPEN

ticket, whether the wound was physically mortal or whether it took the more roundabout route of depriving the animal of its ability to feed, or maybe to defend itself against predators.

Post-season wandering over hunting grounds can come up with stories that are best soon forgotten, if that's possible. At the moment of discovery they can be physically nauseating. Poorly placed bullet or inadequate bullet, there isn't much difference in the final accounting. The various ways and degrees of horror, though, through which the end came, have variety enough and too much.

Popularity of the Long-Range Rifle

A cheerful note, long overdue in this chapter, is the growing preference for the long-range hunting rifle.

It isn't only the need for economy that brought this about, though the mere resighting and restocking—or simply stock alteration—of a good, used military piece gives us a rifle that'll reach out and do the business. Nor is it due altogether to the unthinking acceptance of, say the .270 or the .30-06. "Everyone knows they're good," though in some kinds of woods hunting anything in that class *may* be a rather poor choice.

J. C. Higgins 51.

It's more, and it's wiser. Almost every long range rifle has varmint rounds waiting for it, in factory cartons or in components for handloading. Nearly every one is effective, too, in military-style competition, a fascinating sport where you "meet the right kind of people," the really right kind, I mean. Most of these rifles have the weight and balance, and the accuracy with peewee handloads, to be efficient in the small-game woods, and they're more fun to use than a meal-ticket shotgun. The majority of their calibers also can be accommodated with loads that serve well in deep forests.

Now we're getting to it: the all-round centerfire rifle. Maybe it doesn't exist. But the closest sneak we can make up to it is pretty likely to be classifiable as "a long range rifle."

The fewer we use, the better we shoot. You don't quite believe that? Neither do I. Always there are exceptions, and we could be profoundly thankful to have in our hands at the right moment a rifle that's highly specialized for the work. More thanks are due if we are completely familiar with it. So if time and opportunities are limited, too many special jobs might never pay off. Not any of them.

The factory demonstrator has to learn to use quite a variety of arms, but time and a fabulous ammunition supply are on his side. With most of us, it's different.

In this chapter we discuss only American factory production in the long range rifle class—bolt actions—although some rifles of almost any other breech system can qualify for this kind of use in the hunting field.

J. C. Higgins 51

Barrel: 22 inches, chrome plated bore.
Sights: open rear with square Patridge style notch, ramped Patridge gold bead front. Receiver ready for peep sight or top mounted scope.
Magazine capacity: 5 .270 or .30-06 cartridges.
Safety: thumb lever, wing type, at left rear of bolt.
Weight: about 7½ pounds.

The 51 replaces the Model 50, a somewhat plainer rifle. Both have the Belgian-made Fabrique Nationale Mauser action which has become so popular here. Barrel and stock are made and assembled to the action in the United States.

There's nothing newsworthy about this sort of international marriage: it gets no headlines. In the last century and in the early years of this one it was common form for some of our best makes of double shotguns to be fitted with barrels that had been made abroad, quite commonly in Belgium. This fact wasn't stressed in advertising. Instead, the copy writers got to work on the bolting, firing and ejecting mechanisms, and on the handling qualities of the complete guns. They could be eloquent, and they were, for they had some beautiful upland, marsh and trap guns to write up.

The 1898 and revised versions of Mauser actions are no strangers here. Thousands have been imported, and thousands "liberated," too. This one has the familiar bolt stop with pull-out thumbpiece at the left rear of the receiver. The trigger doesn't have to take on the extra duty of bolt release, as it did on the old 54 Winchesters and many other rifles, some still made. In time, some such double-duty triggers *can* develop a creepy pull that they never had before. Some have stood up finely. The 51 normally comes with a good pull, and it ought to keep it.

The safety is the simple Mauser wing at the rear of the bolt. Raised to the locked position, this one isn't quite upright; so a scope's eyepiece can be pretty large and far back without making the safe unhandy to shove down fast with your thumb.

To clear a low scope, the bolt handle is curved outward. For saddle scabbard riding, though hardly for any other travel or use, a closer-lying bolt handle would be preferable. A good gunsmith can bend one to almost any desired slant, and no harm done.

A shooter unfamiliar with the Mauser action needs to be cautioned about single-loading, it seems likely. On the target or testing range with most of our American bolt guns we can, if we like, simply slide a round into the chamber and close the bolt on it. With a standard sporting or military Mauser, however, it's best to press the cartridge into the magazine, so that the extractor can pick it up as the bolt goes forward. This is easy and natural, anyway. But a gunsmith can grind a gentler angle on the claw of the extractor to let us use direct barrel-loading. With the usual unaltered Mauser, like this one, it's considered good form to load only to full magazine capacity, not barreling an extra round.

The 51, like the Model 52 Higgins .222, is one of the growing number of high velocity rifles—custom or semi-custom, mostly—that regularly come with a chromed bore. This isn't for appearance, or even primarily to prevent rusting. It's to lengthen barrel life, and the case for that seems proven.

The pistol grip of this rifle's stock has a hunting,

Marlin 455.

The 455 Monte Carlo stock is meant for use with either receiver peep or scope sight.

not target-range curve, and it's capped for looks. Both the grip and the semi-beavertail forestock are checkered. This stock is described as being of telescope height and it could be just that, depending on the glass, the mount, and the face behind them. A gunsling and quick-detachable swivels are standard equipment.

The open sights on the 51 deserve a kind word. Sure, in practical hunting, open sights are at least 75 years out of date, but these are better than most. Patridge, a competitive pistol shot of the first years of this century, designed the type. Today it's as standard on good handguns as the large-apertured Lyman type of rear peep is on good rifles.

The square, flat-topped front sight fits into the square notch of the rear sight more surely, more uniformly, than a round bead fits into a semi-circular notch. It's quicker and more accurate than the bead and the U-notch or the picket and the V so common on European rifles. Why this system is still so rare on rifles I don't know. Cheaper to make the other kinds, or perhaps they're considered more bumpproof, or maybe open-sight rifle shooters aren't credited with any sense at all? Make your own guess.

Be sure that square rear notch is wide enough to show plenty of light on both sides of the front sight post. It's quicker that way, far better in poor light, and the eye naturally centers things. It's doing the best it can, but hardly what a peep sight or a scope would do if the brain behind the rig knew the right answers.

Marlin 455

Barrel: 22 inches, Micro-Groove rifling, stainless steel.
Sights: Lyman 48 receiver peep with micrometer adjustments, and ramped, hooded bead front. Receiver ready for top scope mounts.
Magazine capacity: 5.
Safety: Mauser wing type at left rear of receiver.
Weight: about 8½ pounds.

This new rifle is Marlin's first bolt-action high-power, and it's laid out on the long view, it seems to

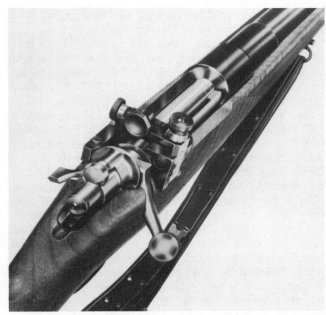

Breech of Marlin 455, showing F. N. Mauser style of wing safety for use under a scope tube.

me. Featherweights are attractive and they certainly have their uses. Most of us sometimes, and a few of us always, need them. But the typical American hunting rifle for long-range shooting is still fairly heavy.

In that respect and in others the Model 455 qualifies. With sling it goes to about nine pounds. The barrel is stiff, of good sporting rifle weight, and it has that amusing, abrupt little stepdown ahead of the chamber, typical of so many Mausers. It's American made, though, like the stock. It should be long-lived, as a hunter demands if he has the opportunity and the excellent good sense to do lots of practice shooting. Stainless steel and the shallow grooving of the Micro system—16 lands, usually—help it resist erosion. In any of its larger calibers—.270, .30-06, .358, and the .308, that bandwagon on which so many factory and custom makers are climbing—it should

Remington 721, 24-inch barrel.

Remington 722, 24-inch barrel.

give fine accuracy for well over 5,000 rounds unless a good many rapid-fire strings rip through it. The .243 and .244 should last for over 4,000.

Other calibers might follow. The same outside barrel contour, with a rifle built like this one, would simplify production of a confortable, potentially accurate bigbore such as a .333, .35 or .375 of standard .30-06 overall length.

The stock is heavy, a marksman's design, with a few ounces pared off by the use of a light, hard rubber buttplate instead of a steel one. Grip and forestock are sizable and a Monte Carlo comb gives the scope-height drop that would suit most shooters. Gunsling and quick-detachable swivels are standard equipment.

So is the Lyman 48 peep—no fooling around with open sights on this rifle. That sight isn't necessarily the very best of its type, and it's certainly one of the oldest. But more than any other it made durability and precision of adjustment the details that an exacting buyer demands as a matter of course. "48" is part of the rifleman's vocabulary, like those familiar symbols that identify rifle models without our having to name the make: 03, M-1, 52, 70, 71, 721, 722 and a few others. Add more that in time will be as familiar, and go back as far as 1886, lest good things be forgotten.

The action is the FN Belgian Mauser with Sako trigger that has a short, clean pull, adjustable for weight. The wing of the safety sticks out to the left in scoped-rifle style, but not far enough to annoy the average iron-sight shooter. Since it's quicker and handier, by a little, than the military Mauser safe, he'd probably like it.

About the only criticism of the rifle is one that would be registered immediately, if at all. White spacers under grip cap and buttplate violently offend some people. "Gingerbread, and iced at that!" The remedy, if it's prescribed, starts with a screwdriver.

Remington 721 and 722

Barrel: 24 inches, except 26 on .222, .244 and .300 Magnum.
Sights: open rear, ramped bead front. Receiver waits for peep sight or top scope mounts.

Magazine capacity: 4, except 3 in .300 Magnum and 5 in .222.
Safety: thumb-piece at right rear of receiver.
Weight: 721, 7¼ pounds; 722, 7; .222 and .244, 8; Magnum, 8¼. All are approximate.

Action. When these rifles came out in 1948 they were at once appraised as having great action strength. They have it, and so have many other sporting and military rifles. But I think that quite a number of prospective buyers, and users too, overlooked the other sort of strength, new in American bolt-action sporters, at least in my memory.

That is the almost completely gas-proof action. The face of the breechbolt is deeply counterbored, enclosing more than the mere rim of the case, and it fits into a snug, square-cut recess in the barrel breech. This is no coned breech barrel. The square-cut shoulder of the firing pin, up front, makes it difficult if not impossible for gas from a pierced primer or burst case to travel back along that pin. Getting that far, it would meet another hurdle, the square shoulder of the firing pin head. But the bolt lockup is exceptionally strong, too. Shortcuts in manufacture didn't weaken it—such as the bolt cylinder and receiver being made from round, not machined stock. No bolt lug is slotted for the passage of the ejector, and no highway is cut for the extractor at the right side of the receiver ring. Ejector and extractor are built into the face of the bolt.

The only objection to that sort of extractor is that you can't press hard against it to give it more grip on the rim of a sticking case. But really not so much can be done in this way to assist a bolt gun's extractor; the claw is too far under the receiver ring. On a lever gun like the Winchester with exposed hammer, you certainly can make that hook grip. I've done it time and again when reloadable brass was scarce and I had to get the full measure of service from what I had left.

An NRA-conducted test of this rifle and of a Mauser World War II, Springfield, and Enfield in the same .30-06 caliber was a horrible affair! The *proof* cartridge, giving about 70,000 p. s. i. pressure with 180-

A Remington 721 with receiver peep sight and gunsling.

Remington 722 BDL De Luxe
Special with 26-inch .244 barrel.

grain bullet, was overloaded to capacity, and all but the Remington suffered a little. But these people could still open and load them, and they began shoving 220-grain bullets into the rifling ahead of the proof pill. Eventually all the rifles were locked shut, the scoreboard of endurance reading: Springfield, 1; Mauser, 2; Enfield, 3; Remington, 5. But no rifle—but no rifle—is recommended for that sort of buckshot loading!

Dismounting the bolt to clean and lightly oil the mainspring and firing-pin tip is less handy than with the Winchester 70, for instance. Before you unscrew the bolt plug you must pull back the firing-pin head against the strong spring—the little notch on the bottom will help—and slip a coin or washer or suchlike between plug and pin head. On the 70 you simply push in a little button and turn the bolt-head to the left until it's clear, first having set the safety at intermediate.

The Remington bolt-stop button lies just ahead of the trigger, and a diagonal up-and-back press actuates it. When the gun is dismounted, the screw that adjusts trigger weight is easy to get at; it's just ahead of the trigger and pointing toward it. The pull is usually clean, with backlash, if any, just noticeable if you try to find it. That effort doesn't seem worth while.

Quality. Any new rifle model may give trouble to the buyer, although the factories go all out to exterminate the bugs before they turn it loose on the public. Some years ago, when the 721 was pretty new, a friend of mine was asked to sight in a couple of them. They were a .270 and a .30-06, as I recall. He was long familiar with his 70 Winchester, an action that still is one of his favorites, but he became disgusted with these Remingtons. Each one hung up several times. That was 'way back, and now I think, we'd have to go far and look sharp to find a dissatisfied user.

They are basically inexpensive high-power rifles, though they come in various grades of finish and ornamentation, the Premier fluttering a price tag that reads around a thousand dollars. The first step up is

the BDL or De Luxe, which has selected wood, checkering, and quick-detachable swivels and sling.

If the stamped-out trigger guard and floorplate are unbearable there are custom-made replacements to be had. The factory's policy is outlined in a letter from the Company.

"If the shooter wants a rifle for hunting, or if he wants to install a target-type stock and heavy barrel for bench rest or slow-fire target shooting, the Model 721 will give him good service over a long period of time. However, if he wants milled parts for looks and a standard rifle, the Model 721 will not give it to him because to get in the price range we are in, we had to prepare for strength where it was needed and use lighter materials where strength is not needed."

Variety. Probably most American shooters know that the Du Pont policy—they took over Remington Arms, Union Metallic Cartridge Company from Hartley & Graham in 1934—has been to streamline production. That means cutting down the variety of models, calibers and loads. Sometimes that seems remorseless, but the sales target is the average Joe.

Yet these rifles do offer a pretty wide choice. There's the special short action of the 722, the first American one of this type, for highpower stuff, since the good little Savage 1920 went out in 1928. At the present the 722 offers .222, .244, .257 Roberts, .300 Savage and .308 Winchester calibers. The shedding of an inch of action length means that much less weight to carry, or to hold between the hands in snap-shooting. With a short action a light barrel and a stock feel good, giving no suggestion of breech-heaviness.

The 721 takes the .270, .30-06 and .300 Magnum. All of these, too, are popular calibers. The gun still feels light and, more important, easy to carry because of its small mid-section. These Rems hold one less round in their magazines than we'd been taught to expect. For years we'd had .270, .30-06 and similar caliber sporters that took five in the mag for the scarcely logical reason that military prototypes did! The 721 and 722 snapped that tradition.

Standard-grade Winchester 70 with 24-inch barrel.

Standard 70 with Monte Carlo comb and folding rear sight as a spare when the rifle is scoped.

Winchester 70

Barrel: 22 inches on Featherweight; 24 on standard weight sporters, except 25 on .375 and .458, and 26 on .220 and .300.

Sights: open rear, a folding variety on Featherweight and on Monte Carlo scope-stocked rifles and the .375; adjustable and locking open rear on the .458. Standard front sights are white metal beads. Redfield full length gold bead on the Super; silver bead on the .458. Receivers are ready for peep sights or top scope mounts.

Magazine capacity: 5, except 4 in .300 and .375, and 3 in .458.

Safety: thumb lever at right rear of bolt.

Weight: Featherweight, 6½ to 7¼ pounds; standard, 8¼ to 8¾; .375, 9; .458, 9¼. Caliber, barrel length and outside dimensions, and density of wood produce these variations. A sling adds from about 6 to 8 ounces.

Action. Brought out early in 1937, the action isn't ultra-modern. It is a refinement of those excellent systems, Mauser 1898, Springfield 1903, and Winchester 54. It isn't radically different. The barrel has a coned breech and the case-head protrudes beyond its extracting cannelure, virtually unsupported. A soft-headed case *can* make trouble in this sort of action, but such a case is extremely rare. I've never encountered one and I hope I don't. When a .250 case split lengthwise in front of a 54 action only a moderate amount of gas came back. I was wearing glasses, and neither the rifle nor I took any harm.

The 70 bolt is vented for gas escape, and this common precaution would help if a primer were pierced. Like late 54s, it has a pin that runs through a slot in the striker. This would prevent that part from being blown out to the rear in any sort of ruction that even a nightmare would be liable to project on our mental screen.

Of course the lockup of the bolt is strong. The lugs are sturdy and not weakened by slotting. Some rifles have larger receiver rings, but good design and excellent materials make the 70 about as strong as any. The .458 round carries a lot of powder and lead and jacket, even though it's loaded to moderate pressure for use in hot countries. Griffin & Howe,

long-established and critical gunsmiths, use the 70 action for their custom .416 Rigby and .425 Westley Richards magnum rifles. (The latter is a big case, though its head is shrunk down to 8x57 rimless military size for use in standard Mauser actions.) The .300 and .375 Magnums are stiff loads, in factory and in blown-out shapes. For years the only American mass-production actions to take them were the 70s—and the earlier 54s made for the .300. No question about 70 action strength, within reason, and that's a pretty healthy place to stay within.

The striker fall is short enough, well under one-half inch, like that of late 54s, just before the Hornet cartridge came along. Trigger pull is adjustable for weight, with three nuts locking it, and I haven't happened to see a creepy one. In fact, this rifle set the pace for bolt-action sporter pulls. Trigger stops are gunsmithed, sometimes home-made, to cut the backlash. There's so little that you practically have to anticipate it to notice it even on a target range, but that is one way of passing the time pleasantly, some think. If the pull changes in ten years' pretty steady use, then I'm an insensitive brute. Could happen with 'most any rifle, either striker or hammer action.

A flange on the bolt cylinder rides along the runway to prevent cramping when the throw is long, as with the .300 and .375 calibers, though these are engineered pretty short in the 70. Magazines and bolt throws vary in length according to the rounds they feed. The Hornet—apparently on its way out because so many less expensive and still more numerous lighter arms of this caliber are made now—has a special short magazine and an opening yawn not much wider than that of a .22 rimfire.

Magazines for the .220, .243, .257, .308 and .358 are blocked off, and the throw is shortened by an extension of the extractor collar. For handloads longer overall than factory standard, especially desirable in .257, the block can be removed and a .30-06 magazine follower substituted. The extractor-collar extension can be cut off, or a new extractor fitted. Just being able to do this is a decided advantage, to a rifleman.

Changes. From time to time the 70 has been altered to keep up with changing tastes.

The early safety lock was almost as handy as an exposed hammer. It was at the top rear of the bolt, pivoted at the right, and you drew it back to release it. Under a low scope it was most unhandy; so we find the present type, a push lever over on the right side.

Also changed to adapt the rifle to glass sights was the bolt handle. Its top has been milled away so that it can't touch the scope tube. The slant to the rear always was handy, like the 54's. Much more recent is the hole drilled into the lower surface of the bolt knob, which might provide a little suction to the palm's grip in rapid fire. Can't think what else it's for unless to carry a brace of vitamin pills.

The upper rear tang has been shortened and it now has no reverse curve. If M70 stocks had split under recoil, the new shape might prevent recurrence of such a mess and mishap. Possibly the recoil shoulder up front might need closer bedding, in the heavy calibers.

Stock lines have changed just a little. Those made now in standard grade are less trim behind the pistol grip, and the Montes have come in, with the cheek-piece at the side carried farther forward than that of the old Super Grade without that raised comb—a type that seems to be headed for history, excellent though it was with iron sights. Just at present you must have a scope even for 35- and 40-yard shooting or be classed with the underprivileged, who used to be called "poor people."

No more 20-inch barrels are furnished. They came in most calibers except the Swift and the Maggies. The .375 barrels are now of reasonable weight, and beautifully tapered. The first ten or so were of standard weight, meaning medium light, or really light in that boring. They kicked the stuffing out of a few who agreed to try them, and they were succeeded by crowbars that made you think of .22 match rifles until you'd seen the hole at the muzzle.

The ramp for the front sight is shorter than before, and the Super's grip cap now is steel, not hard rubber. Perhaps we had best put away the miscroscope before we get eye-strain.

There's been a decided change in calibers available, though. Several newcomers are becoming familiar, and production dreams no doubt go on. Some of the long-gone are the .250 Savage, 7x57 mm. Mauser rimless, .300 Savage (just a few of those), and .35 Remington. All are good, but the little .35 belongs, perhaps, in a lighter, faster-operated rifle, and the .257, .270 and .308 replace the others in *general* popularity. Those three and the .220, .243, .30-06, .300 and .375 H&H Magnums, .358 and .458 make up the present lineup of 70 calibers.

Quality. Most people use the 70 as a basis of comparison when American factory-built bolt actions go under discussion. It isn't cheap, even in standard grade, and 20 years of use have proved its quality.

It was about the first of its class to have a clean, crisp, durable trigger pull that was adjustable for weight, and its accuracy in any caliber was at least good, and frequently outstanding. The milled trigger guard was artistically curved, the stock well shaped, useful and shootable with irons, not a bit clubby. The hinged floorplate couldn't be lost, and it was just easy enough—not too easy—to open when you wanted to

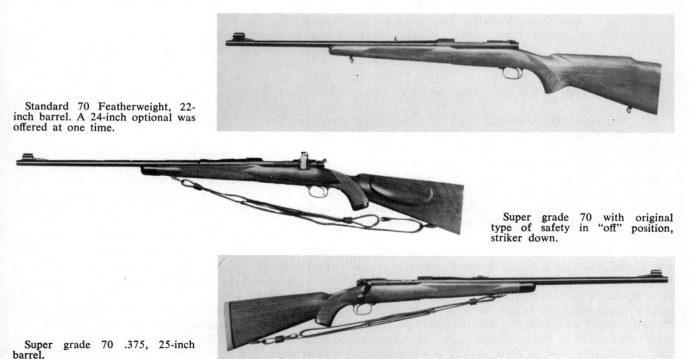

Standard 70 Featherweight, 22-inch barrel. A 24-inch optional was offered at one time.

Super grade 70 with original type of safety in "off" position, striker down.

Super grade 70 .375, 25-inch barrel.

A Super 70 with 26-inch barrel.

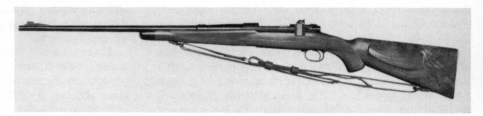

The Super 70 with 24-inch barrel and Lyman 48 rear sight. Rear sight slot in barrel is filled with a blank piece.

empty or clean the magazine. The release was where it belonged, in front of the guard and out of the way, not inside where you *might* kick it off by mistake, or out where your hand felt it when you carried the rifle at trail. In working up this model, Winchester brass consulted a lot of folks who toted rifles and used them a long way off from chimneys and guttered roofs.

Variety. Styling as well as caliber choice has changed through the years, but almost from the first there's been wide latitude. We needn't discuss the target or varmint 70s here.

Just at present the *Featherweight* comes in .243, .270, .308, .30-06 and .358. The barrels are really light, only 22 inches long, the 24-inch optional having gone where less popular items go—into memory and satisfied use here and there. The stock is hollowed to get rid of maybe three or four ounces, and the aluminum buttplate, guard and floorplate save weight, too. The gun doesn't seem muzzle-light, as one might expect.

No open sight is a blazing bargain, and the one on this rifle is much too far forward, especially for a short-barreled rifle. But it folds down to let us use a peep or a scope.

For iron sights the standard stock is right unless you mount your irons high. The Monte is primarily for scope use, and a jaw-cracker in the calibers above .243 when you scrooch down to see a peep or a crotch sight. That little 6 mm. kicks back fast, but not hard. Forward, the Monte is ⅜ inch higher than it is back aft. Even with a scope it's for the individual to decide whether or not to sand it down, up front. Many people use it and like it as it is.

This is a delightful little rifle to carry, so well balanced and light that it seems to weigh nearly a pound less than it does—or to gain not more than two pounds during a nice long day in the hills! At this writing it's the only American factory issue in its class, though custom and foreign featherweights are legion, with some of them much overdone in this matter of airiness. Or so lots of us think, before or after taking.

Not always after, though. Build can mean much; the stocking, that is. Yet light people often can take more recoil than the heavy-set: they ride it out because they learn so soon that there's nothing else for them to do.

The featherweight does have a good case in court. Shoulder recoil is less punishing than face recoil, and if the upper line of the stock suits the user he can do all right in spite of some extra kick. We get more from a light upland shotgun, though it doesn't seem to arrive as fast. However, a pet of that kind is often made to fit us. As a rule it's far from cheap, and the extra dollars do more good in stocking than they would in decoration.

The *Standard Grade* made the 70's reputation and, in the main, holds it. It gets around. In most calibers it's easy and pleasant to shoot, though comments on the Monte Carlo styling of the Featherweight can apply, for stock dimensions now are identical. The small calibers make up into fairly heavy rifles, but with the .30-06 and .300 we get into lightness and liveliness. The .375 seems a bit heavy, but certainly not logy. A thin, light man or woman *who is trained in marksmanship* can shoot it comfortably in the game fields but hardly would care to fire long strings with it on the target range. The old "any .30 caliber" ruling would seem pretty sensible there!

The *Super Grade* isn't custom, built to measure, and I doubt that the usual *Custom Grade* is, either. The money is more likely to go into magnificent wood, art work, and precious metals. But the Super is good-looking, and better finished than many so-called custom jobs, alack and welladay.

The wood has more checkering and is set off (now) with a steel grip cap and the familiar black plastic forestock tip. Monte Carlo at present is standard on this grade, and the cheekpiece on the left always was. The one-inch swivels are quick-detachable and a sling is included in the price. Engine-turning decorates the bolt, extractor, extractor ring or collar, and the follower or cartridge cradle in the magazine. Selected barrels are said to go on this grade, though 70 barrel excellence is pretty much a standard item, and the outside finish of steel seems to get extra attention.

For the M70 buyer who'd just as soon pay more to get an article with obvious but tasteful extra good looks the Super is the choice. The styling is conventional in every respect, as far as I can see, and it's not liable to be outdated soon.

Since the walnut used in this grade is no longer of "fancy" or "selected" quality—unless it's wanted, available, and paid for—a home gunsmith could come close to duplicating a Super, with a Standard 70 to work on. It would take time and skill and a few extras to buy, not many. I confess that my 70 stock has been refinished and slightly reshaped twice, but so was the wood of a single-shot match .22 that I used for quite a few years. Some of us who become fond of a certain rifle can't leave it exactly as is. A number of husbands, I've heard, have got into trouble by trying to remake the personality of their wives—in their own divine image, mebbe. Further thoughts on this attempted parallel are confusing; so I'll drop the lid on this chapter.

NOT encouraged in the usual methods, I tried a different way of pestering my friends. I'd ask them—singly when necessary, though groups were more fun—what *one* firearm they'd keep or buy if they could own no more. It was to cover the full line: fun, practice, small game, big game, home protection, and guerrilla fighting too, if that ever came up.

These fellows were experienced outdoorsmen and shooters, and by virtue of those interests, individualists. They understood the question and they were deliberate and, at the last, positive in answering it.

A veteran of many years in the Navy chose the .45 Colt automatic. (And how he can shoot it!) He figured that he could always have it with him, that it was reliable as he handled it, and that he could hit with it at almost any range that might be necessary. It has the power, and his own pet has the accuracy, because that's been gunsmithed into it. Being a woodsman, he knows how to use cover. Even though he's an Expert Rifleman many times over and a big- as well as a small-game hunter he chose the pistol. With both arms his target skill and all-round familiarity are about equally high.

Another's choice was about as different as it could be. He too picked a familiar weapon, a 12-gauge double shotgun with two different chokes, full and modified, or full and improved cylinder—I don't remember which. With buckshot he'd be deadly at about 50 yards, with rifled slug to 100 or more. He'd be using the gun of his lifelong choice, and he knows what it can and can't do.

A third fellow owns just two guns, a 67 Winchester .22 single shot and a 721 Remington .270. He likes them both and shoots them well, but the .270 would stay with him because he's a handloader and on that rifle he has his choice between iron sights and a bright, wide-field 2½-power scope. A varmint hunter and deer hunter, he knows his .270 well. He too would do all right.

So would another friend, who named the light little 69 Winchester .22 bolt action, clip repeater. It too would have to give the choice between iron and glass sights. He'd plan to be able to hit what he had to, as far off as he had to, and I think he could. The little gun is reasonably handy in a car, and he wouldn't need much time or gas to get to places where he could shoot it, often. So could all of his family, and the same goes for the .45 Colt mentioned three paragraphs back.

The fifth man, last to be impaled on this stick, makes a living as an expert, painstaking gunsmith. He built his own last-ditch firearm, restocking a 1903 Springfield to fit him. Barrel length of about 21 inches lets it travel in his car on the too-rare occasions when a gunsmith like him gets a little free time. He's a good hunting and target shot with rifle, pistol and shotgun, but this is his business gun. Accordingly, it's stripped to the rugged necessities: gunsling, receiver peep and

CHAPTER 9

COMBINATION GUNS AND ALL-ROUND RIFLES

square gold bead front, and no scope, for his eyesight is good. Oh yes, he did put on a special magazine floorplate release and a little pistol-grip cap. The sling swivels are quick-detachable for handiness, and the forestock goes up to the muzzle for balance. Weight complete, as I remember, is about 8 pounds, but it feels like less because of the balance. Something like this would be my choice, except perhaps in .257 Roberts. But you've heard the rebuttal to that: "You can always get 06 ammunition."

These men are the sort of gun-lovers who like all kinds—rifle, shotgun and pistol. We have our specialists in this country, target shots and/or hunters. To one kind, hunting appeals only through the challenge of woodcock and grouse; another will use only a rifle, and for nothing but deer or a possible bear; yet another is a woods-wanderer and packs a pistol. So it goes, through a great variety of happy people.

To some a gun is a tool, though it may give them much pleasure, too. There's the law officer with his handgun, the farmer with his shotgun, the woodsman, plainsman or mountaineer with his rifle or carbine. I've seen a guide hunt a mouse with his long-barreled .30-30, a little shamefacedly, but then, what else was there to use? (Oh, yes, the mouse got out of sight; he knew when he was licked, and he never came back to

The business Springfield.

Typical German *Drilling.* Sixteen-gauge barrels on top, an 8x57 rimmed-case rifle barrel below. Left-hand cheekpiece. *Courtesy Combat Forces Press.*

camp.) A man with one gun is likely to be handy with it and get quite a variety of service from it.

COMBINATION GUNS

The idea of multiple-purpose firearms is old. Rifle-and-shotgun muzzle-loaders were fairly common, the barrels over-and-under or in the lop-sided balance of side-by-side.

Some 50 or 75 years ago the full-length barrel inserts for double shotguns were much used in the deer woods. You loaded one barrel with buck, then dropped a .38-55, .32-40 or maybe a .30-30 into the tube you'd inserted in the other. Poor balance and not much sighting equipment? Yes, but it was economical and you didn't have an extra gun to care for and to store away after the season had closed.

Since that time, various short inserts have been marketed, mostly in light calibers such as rimfires or .22 Hornet. Typical is the .22 rimfire from the Armax Co., 3401 West Rosedale St., Fort Worth. It comes in 12-, 16-, or 20-gauge chamber size. There's still the problem of sighting. Irons can be fitted, such as a folding peep and a front sight that's high enough. Some shotguns already carry a scope, often without magnification, but the reticle or the dot sharpens the aim. In open shooting this sighting does well for many people, and for rifled slugs it's fine. It could be adjusted for .22 shooting.

Multi-Barrel Guns

In Europe, three-barrel Drillings and four-barrel Vierlings aren't considered freaks. There's a considerable variety of carefully preserved game; and sometimes the law, or rules of sportsmanlike conduct that are equally respected, require the hunter to use a bullet, or to use a charge of shot. Even the shot size for certain game may be specified.

Almost all possible combinations are made. The four-barrel may have paired shotgun barrels, a small rifle tube on top and a big bore below, or the little one may be snugged under the shot barrels, with the heavy caliber below it. Common smallbore tubes chamber the .22 rimfire, or the centerfire 5.5 mm. Vierling. That one was in use before our Hornet, and like it, a near match to the old .22 WCF single-shot black-powder cartridge.

Most three-barrels have two side-by-side shot tubes on top, the rifle barrel below. Sometimes this is reversed, two paired rifle barrels upstairs, the smoothbore down under. Or the shot barrel may be directly above the heavy rifle caliber, with a small rifle barrel stuck on off-side and about midway in height between the other two.

Doubles

The double barrels are almost always over-and-under, usually with the shot tube above. Down low, the high-power rifle load has less leverage to work against the hinge pin in the frame. When well made, these combination guns can give fine rifle accuracy. They lend themselves to handloading of the brass with light or standard charges.

Double rifles, side-by-side, don't. Although each good barrel may be accurate by itself, the trick is to make them print close together at a practical hunting range, such as 100 yards. A load definitely and correctly put up for them will do this. Change the loading components, and the points of impact spread. A highly skilled handloader like my friend Bert Shay can, usually, load them to line up. This isn't easy, and persistence can't always whistle up success. With only one rifle barrel to feed, our problems are more interesting than frustrating.

Double rifles give two quick shots, and if *one* firing pin ever breaks, that's as hard luck as a person can expect in a given emergency. Usually these arms have superb balance, though they rarely come as featherweights in medium-power calibers like the .303 British, which is practically a .30-40 Krag equivalent. The big .465s, .470s, and so forth commonly weigh from 10 to 12 pounds, and need to. Some delightful little varmint and small-game calibers have been made, too. It's quite normal to scope a double rifle in a deer-stalking caliber like .240 or .303.

One combination gun, used quite a lot in the past, was the Paradox for black powder shot-shells or shells holding a short, soft lead bullet. The last few inches of the barrels were rifled, and as a result the shot spread fast and rather wildly, but the bullets flew point-on to a considerable range. Some bullets were hollow-pointed for quick expansion, and some, as I remember, had iron points to give better penetration on heavy African or Indian game.

Over here, the double rifle often has been longed for, but not enough people have put through a call. Colt made a few 1886 model .45-70s of the type, and Winchester turned out one .405 on the Model 21 shotgun frame.

But an over-and-under combination double is useful, at least where ranges aren't too long. These guns, and three-barrel combinations, are imported right along. Stoeger has them, and in the Abercrombie & Fitch used-gun catalogues that come out once or twice a year there's always a tempting list of them. Many of these imports, like World War II loot, take foreign rifle cartridges, rimmed, and difficult or expensive to buy here. American brass can be formed to oblige most of them, and our bullet molds and custom-made jacketed bullets cover a wide range of calibers. Frequently the shotgun barrels are chambered for shells shorter than our modern standards, and then either special handloading or rechambering ought to be done. A few of the older barrels shouldn't be used with our heaviest factory loads.

Some of the more recent imports are made with American ammunition supplies in mind. New at this writing is the over-and-under "turkey gun" from Flaig's Lodge, Millvale, Pa. On top is a 12- or 16-gauge barrel, and the choice below includes .22 Hornet, .222, .257 Roberts, .270, 7x57 mm. and .30-06. Barrels are 24 inches long, making a very short gun, with the breakdown action, and weight is listed as 6½ pounds. The maker is the old Franz Sodia firm.

American Over-and-Unders

There have been three familiar makes of American over-and-under combinations. None of them was suitable for big-game hunting.

Marble Game-Getter. The first, the easiest to pack, and the hardest to shoot well was the Marble Game-Getter, .22 rimfire on top, .44 smoothbore below. The steel tubing stock wasn't meant to be detached, but it folded down along the barrels and made carrying in the issued leather holster pretty convenient even beside a trout stream. Barrel lengths were 12, 15 and 18 inches—only the last being now legal to own or sell without paying the $200 federal tax imposed on a "firearm."

The early model had a well-shaped revolver style grip with hard rubber sideplates, and the sights were gold bead front and a Marble folding peep behind the hammer, at just the right distance from the shooter's eye. The second model had a flat, slabby grip with plain-looking wooden sideplates, and the rear sight, just ahead of the breech, was a combination folding peep and open V notch. You filed the ears off the V and were ready to go and sight in.

A hinged hammer extension was easy and fairly quick to move up or down for barrel-firing selection. The thing to do, in hunting, was to remember whether it was set for shot or ball.

With shot, that gun was effective on most small game to perhaps 50 feet. Up in Canada's canoe country, or in jungle or bush that rarely screened another human hunter, or even along mountain pack-train trails, the Game-Getter lived up to its name. The .22 barrel was beautifully rifled, and the gun closed up tightly and wore well. But with no comb to rest your cheek on it wasn't easy to hold steadily for rifle shooting or to mount quickly and surely, always at the same place on your shoulder, for shotgun work.

Its shot charge was light, loaded with the black or smokeless powder and the wadding into a tapered brass shell only as long as the overall of the .44-40 Winchester and Marlin rifle cartridge, so that those repeaters could handle it, too. However, you could use in the Marble the .44 X-L shotshell, .44-40 brass with a long cardboard cylinder out front, to hold a heavier load.

The special ".44 G. G." round-ball cartridge carried a 115-grain soft lead pumpkin peeping out at the mouth of the short rifle case. The propellant was 30 or 34 grains of black powder, or a smokeless equivalent, and velocity must have been around 1500 f. s. This bullet fitted the smoothbore Marble barrel well enough to give fair accuracy at 25 or 30 yards, enough for the woods, and some deer were killed with it. This load could be used in rifled .44-40 barrels, but even with their lazy twist as slow as one turn in 36 inches there was sometimes unmerciful fouling. Certain makes of G. G. ammo definitely shot more cleanly than others, though none that I've seen had any bullet lubrication except perhaps a greased wad behind the lead.

Later Game-Getters took both the .44 and the two-inch .410 shell, and some were dangerously under-bored for the .44 ball, which is a museum piece now, fortunately. I asked the factory if they could put a choke in the .410 barrel for me, and they came across with a good one. I've yet to see any .410 do really well with rifled slugs, and a chunk of 80-odd grains of lead at about 1300 f. s. isn't much of a killer on large game.

Marlin Over-and-Under. A year or so before Pearl Harbor the Marlin people brought out a well balanced and rather businesslike combination gun, a special barreling of their Model 90 over-and-under shotgun. They used the .410 frame, with boring of that size underneath, but on top there was the choice of .22 Hornet or .218 Bee as well as the little .22 long-rifle.

This gun weighed about 6½ pounds and was nicely stocked. The little Game-Getter wasn't much heavier than a husky sixgun, such as a .38-40 New Service Colt with 7½-inch barrel, a pleasant-shooting gun in that much maligned caliber. The two Marlin barrels had the same outside dimensions giving plenty of muzzle-steadiness, and a person could do good work with either barrel. Since there were two triggers, the rear for the rifle barrel—in effect, to shorten the stock for that kind of shooting—it was safest to load only the .410 chamber when bird-hunting. Rifle accuracy was scopeworthy, and there was enough metal on top to permit careful mounting of a glass.

The price of nearly $40 in depression times kept this gun from becoming popular. In quality it was worth the price, gun-equivalent to a good three times that now, but it didn't handle deer-hunting rifle loads and therefore was more or less a "novelty," not practical for most shooters.

Savage Model 24. This .22-.410 first came out under the Stevens name, and at one time it was stocked with Tenite, not wood. At a distance this stuff had the color and grain of superb walnut, but closer up it looked like the plastic it was. Grip and forestock checkering were generous in amount and beautiful in

execution, but they weren't done by human hands! The stock was hollow—"Tonk, tonk" it would answer to finger-taps—and none too rugged. Tenite was used for a number of rifle and shotgun stocks soon after World War II, but now you seldom see one, and a good thing, too.

During that war, thousands of Stevens .22-.410s were bought by the Air Force as survival weapons. With proper stock material it always was a serviceable little gun, and now as the Savage 24 it's stocked with good quality walnut. The 14-inch pull, from trigger to middle of buttplate, is of about average shotgun length, but since the wood butt is obligingly flat it's easily shortened a half inch or so to rifle dimension.

One trigger and one hammer fire the barrels, as with the old Game-Getter. But the Savage selector is at the right side of the receiver, not on the hammer nose, and more convenient for most of us. A southpaw opens the gun without trouble, for the top lever is two-way, unlatching the breech lock with either a right or left push. The barrels are made short for woods work, 24 inches, and the weight of about 6¾ pounds is steady-holding without being burdensome.

A 1⅝-inch drop at comb and 2⅝ at heel are about average for either a hunting rifle or a field shotgun. Although this gun at first feels different from any other I know of, it needs nothing but the universal

Savage Model 24 .22-.410.

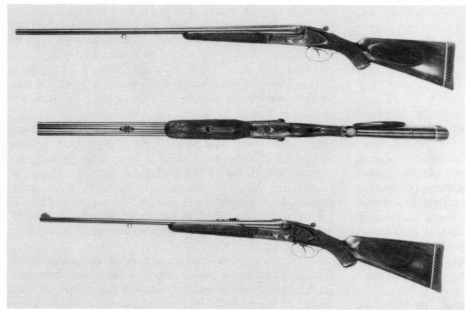

Custom-built double-barrel rifle *and* shotgun combination by Pachmayr Gun Works of Los Angeles.

Savage Model 219 single-shot rifle.

requisite, practice, to make it team up with you even in woodcock cover. Naturally, .410 killing power is minimum—some would say sub-marginal—and .22 rimfire deadliness has sharp limits even with the most expert shooting. This Savage is a gun for a leisurely, careful hunter, not for a beginner, and not for the character who feels that filling his license is a necessity and an inalienable right. Back in real wilderness where game is relatively unwary it could do well. For a 25-foot shot at a deer's neck, though, nothing we could safely stuff into it would equal the .44 round ball from the Game-Getter. For that gun we'd have to buy a mold and cast those Marble marbles now, unless we were lucky enough to find some ready-mades that ran closer than the common .01 or .02 inch variation.

Interchangeable Barrels

Some imported shotguns have two sets of barrels, shot-and-shot and shot-or-bullet. The latter are less often seen than interchangeable shot barrels with different borings, as frequently made here.

Long ago, Stevens put out their single shots with interchangeable rifle and scattergun barrels as a regular thing. About 25 years ago, Savage offered .410 tubes for Model 99 takedown rifles, but they chambered the weak and now long-discontinued two-inch shell. The idea has been used a good deal, with rather indifferent success, as measured by sales.

Single-shot enthusiasts have used single-barrel shotguns as foundations for rifles of moderate power. A rifled insert is fitted permanently into the smoothbore tube, the gun is supplied with iron or scope sights, and a serviceable heavy-barrel target or sporter results. An extra barrel from the factory makes a shotgun-and-rifle combination.

Savage 219-220. This deserved to stay around. The 220 hammerless shotgun is still made, a popular single in 12, 16, 20 and 28·gauges, and .410 bore. It *should* be made, for it's a clean-lined thing, its top tang safety is quick to reach, and it's the only hammerless single at a moderate price. The old Iver Johnsons, Harrington & Richardsons and so on are long gone.

Sold as a rifle, the model number was 219, but shot and rifle barrels were made interchangeable, each having its own forestock. Rifle calibers were .22 Hornet, .25-20, .30-30, .32-20 and, I think, a few .25-35s. All are good ones in their fields of operation.

The locking cam bears against the barrel lug, taking up wear and keeping the assembly snug. So the accuracy of this rifle with ammunition that suited it was

good, effective in varmint hunting within the various calibers' effective ranges. It compared well with the work of British and German singles with respected old names and priced at easily ten times the 219's figure. The original price of that gun was about $15. Cash was scarce then.

ALL-ROUND RIFLES

Hardly anyone except a hunter of woods game is interested in a rifle-shotgun hookup. But almost any rifleman is intrigued by the thought of an all-round rifle. Catch one fondling a bigbore rifle and, if he knows anything at all about the fun and the year-'round practice of shooting a smallbore, ask him, "How'd you like to have a .22 rimfire just like it?"

Almost always the reply will be prompt, decisive and affirmative. "I should say I would!"

That's one way of getting an all-round rifle—get two —but it's hardly the easier way. The other and more common effort to reach this perhaps unattainable is to choose a centerfire, carefully. You consider the highest and the lowest in power that fill your game and target needs. Then you forget the .22 rimfire understudy or just buy any .22 that hits your fancy.

Understudies

It will be hard to make a .22 the twin of your high-power. Superficial likeness in action is easy enough. But take an extreme example of this from the past, the Remington Model 16 .22, Model 8 high-power, and for good measure, the Model 11 shotgun.

All are autoloaders, with the bolt handle on the right of the flat-sided receiver. The 16's safety is a post inside the trigger guard, up front. You shove it to the left for off. The safe of the Model 11 12 gauge of that time, similarly located, must be shoved forward. Later 11s have a cross button, at the *rear* of the guard. The Model 8's safe is a big flat lever with a turned-up lip, and it's·on the right side of the receiver.

But there are many more details than the safety catch to consider. Equal weight and similar weight distribution or balance are important; the sights should be identical in design and location; the throw of the bolt, lever or slide handle should be the same. The two rifles must feel and operate exactly alike. That's perfection, the ideal.

Understudies were easy to find in single-shot rifle days. The offhand Schuetzen target shot bought or had made to his order a heavy-barreled .32-40 or .38-55 for the 200-yard range, then backed it up with a .22 with the same size of action and·barrel for indoor practice at 50 feet or 25 yards. The smallbore barrel was shorter, so that the weight and balance of the two rifles were for all good purposes identical. In between, for practice up to a full 200 yards on calm days, there may have been a .25 rimfire or a .25-20, -21 or -25. Similar teams of single-shot rifles stocked and sighted for hunting weren't hard to figure out. A heavy single shot for the .30-40 Krag cartridge was an accurate and fairly flat shooting rifle for the mountains or plains, and its handloading possibilities in a sturdy rifle like the Winchester high-wall ran from original .30-06 power to cellar-range popping.

Probably the best non-custom understudy .22s in bolt action were the M-1 and M-2 Springfields. Now and then a used one can be bought in good condition. In weight and balance they were close to the Armory's NRA sporter in .30-06, their barrels just a little heavier because of the smaller boring. Even so, they are light-barreled for close prone competition, or would be considered so today. The M-2 had a speed lock giving quick and uniform ignition, but its bolt throw was shortened to average smallbore length. This latter fact made the rifle slightly less useful as an understudy. Both .22 and .30 in this styling weighed about 9¼ pounds without sling, but the heavy stocks and extremely thick steel buttplates were open to alterations. For iron sight shooting they were well stocked. Custom work could fit them to an individual's taste—and often did. We refer to the NRA stocks, not the Type B commonly seen on the .22s sold to Association members in 1957.

Springfield no longer manufactures these rifles, and I know of no factory-made .22 actions that match up so closely with bigbore mechanisms. In general operation, though not in size, the Marlin 39-A is similar to the 36 and 336 deer rifle, and the Marlin 56 hammerless lever gun is a little like the Winchester 88.

There really isn't much popular demand for understudy .22s, and never has been. Winchester, for example, made fewer than 20,000 Model 1873 .22 rimfires, out of a model total of more than 720,000.

But there is a solution, short of fine custom work which can do almost anything. You build up a smallbore, or cut one down, and it *can* be a rumpus room or attic job, or staged on a floor in between. Some light, inexpensive .22 bolt guns have fairly long and heavy actions, not essential to the project, however. You hollow wood here and there, and weight it to bring the gun to the heft and balance of your centerfire sporter. The worst poser is the lightness of the .22's action and barrel breech. (Even the heavy barrel 52 is considerably smaller at the breech than the Model 70, to say nothing of the much lighter smallbores we'd choose to work on.)

Or you can buy a longer-barreled and more expensive .22 like the Mossberg 144 or Winchester 75 (the Remington 513 is practically a heavy-barrel), and with these target models still avoid the metal-work of

shortening or turning down a barrel, provided your bigbore weighs pretty close to nine pounds.

You can't do much about the bolt throw of the rimfires now made, and they're all short, compared to a high-power. But you can work on the trigger pull, refining it if it needs such attention, and putting in a stop to cut the backlash if there is any. With a trigger pull spring scale you can test the release weight of both rifles, and these smallbore target guns have adjustable pulls. The Winchester has a side-lever safety, just a little one, it's true, but you could build it up, and on the Mossberg a side lever could, I think, be engineered to work smoothly and to lie almost where the one on your big rifle is located.

The final result won't be a rock-steady match .22 for hot competition, but instead a practical, hunting-weight understudy, helpful to use all the year 'round. It could go to camp with you in the fall, if the travel is easy, though by that time the feel of your big game rifle will be familiar, thanks to its humble, homespun brother, the done-it-yourself .22. You'll have small game subloads for the centerfire.

Just One Rifle

The usual try at solving the all-round rifle riddle leaves the .22 out of calculations. There's still enough to figure out.

Naturally, regular four-position indoor shooting with a match .22—and outdoors whenever you can get it, even in pretty rough weather—are fine practice for a big-game hunter. The shooting should include rapid fire, undesirable though its *necessity* certainly is in the hunting field, because it keeps us from going poky in sight alignment and trigger squeeze. Smallbore is fun in itself, and it's infinitely better hunting-rifle training than half a box a year loosed off in pre-season "practice." Most of us can find or build a smallbore range.

Caliber. But year-'round shooting with the centerfire is the thing for the hunter, and it can take in small-game and varmint hunting as well as paper-punching. For these uses we need an all-round caliber.

Choosing it depends on where we live and where we plan to do our big-game hunting. We want flat trajectory and well sustained energy for long shooting, but in the woods less power, usually, and always less range make the best choice, even though the bullet may be of larger diameter, and heavier. These general rules apply to the lineups of both deer cartridges and of loads for much heavier American game. Incidentally, almost any caliber up to .358 *can* be handloaded down for small game and gallery practice shooting.

More depends upon the hunter's skill, patience and marksmanship than on the size and vitality of his game, which vary greatly in any species. To go rather to extremes, one deer hunter might be well gunned with a .30-30 for the woods, or with a .220 Swift for the open country, if his State laws permitted that caliber and if he took no shots at deer over 200 yards away. Another deer hunter might need a .348 or .358

for the woods, or a .30-06 or even a .300 Magnum for the long-look country. First he'd have to learn how to shoot them, and some useful ballistics are harder to master than others are.

Weight. The all-round rifle for the average man must be well balanced and fairly light. It shouldn't have to stay home when outdoor holidays come up! The purpose in getting an all-round rifle is to use it a lot, become completely familiar with it.

It can, however, be so easy to carry that it's unsteady to aim, either quickly as in the woods or immediately after strenuous climbing or sidehill gouging at high altitudes. If the barrel is extremely light there can be serious shifting of zero. Not always can even the first two or three shots be relied on to print exactly where they're held unless that barrel has been bedded properly. This may mean free-floating, semi-bedded, or full length contact, rifles being individuals in their likes and dislikes.

As a rule it's best to go to the heavy side, but only a little. Unfortunately, the place to determine proper weight is outdoors, and across plenty of it, not in a gun-store. If a rifle feels a trifle heavy at the end of a day it's probably just right.

Action. There's no ruling that the all-round rifle must be a bolt action. Most of them are, but most hunters expect to do some long-range shooting—dream about it, anyway. Lever actions like the Savage 99 and Winchester 88 can do good work at distances where almost all other repeaters of the type would fail. The latest pumps and automatics extend the range of precision well beyond that of earlier sporters in those classes. Not many hunt big game with a single shot today, but those who do generally appreciate, demand and can use fine accuracy.

But some big-game hunters stick to the timber and have absolutely no need of three- or four-inch group-ing at 200 yards. Their all-round rifle could be a lever gun in .30-30, .348 or .35 Remington caliber, to mention just a few.

For reloading with full charges the bolt actions—and a few single shots—are the favorites. The latest lever, pump and auto rifles also breech up tightly, giving comparatively little chance for brass to stretch and become temporarily unreloadable. Since the .30-30 shooter almost always gets by far his finest accuracy with light reloads, the old type actions in good condition serve him well.

Sights. These we'd choose for the primary purpose, fall hunting. It pays to have the familiar gold, red, ivory or black post or bead come into view each time we bring the stock comb to our face. Using a small-apertured, wide-rimmed disc in the peep sight for slow-fire target shooting or varmint hunting doesn't seem to do any harm. When we take it off we find it easy and natural to use the big, thin-rimmed aperture for quick work.

The principle of primary purpose holds for scope-sight reticles and scope-sight powers. A compromise between woods hunting and open-field varmint shooting could fall far short of perfection for either. Which is more important? Some varmint hunters use a power-building attachment like the Litschert or Edwards and take it off when the leaves start to turn. Then they get the larger, original field of view through the glass, and that's certainly welcome in most kinds of big game hunting! There are also the variable-power scopes.

* * * *

Some people will tell us that there's no such thing as an all-round rifle, and never can be. Others will let us know that they have one. To an extent, both are right. At any rate, the second group at least has had the fun of trying, unless their rifle shooting is purely oral.

B Y the nature of unknown lands our first American game guns were imported. They came to the edge of a virgin wilderness. Out from the Atlantic's rise and fall, her dip and roll and pitch, they made land-fall with the colonists. They were essential equipment to those folk who came here to live out their years, not to look and plunder and then pull anchor. But as the new world labored through its generations it grew less and less dependent on the industries of the motherlands.

It was a Swiss gunsmith, we're told, Martin Meylin, who set up the first American rifle-boring mill, near Lancaster, Pa. There were others of his former countrymen, and men from the German Rhineland too, in that community, and what they had forgotten or never known of the art they began to learn from him. So in time we had that specialized American weapon, the Pennsylvania or Kentucky rifle—made primarily for use on the Kentucky frontier, it seems.

It was and is an arm to arouse pride in the mere contemplation. Personal ownership isn't necessary. It helped to bestow on us two great gifts, the modern American rifle, and the right to possess and use one.

Yet all through the few centuries of our history the imported arms have been prized, not by all of us, but by a constant few. Some were cheap and shoddy; some were superb. From the latter—and of late years to some extent from the cheaply built weapons of war—our gunmakers have learned techniques of the trade. Finally some of them began to surpass their teachers.

But in the early years of this century it was a commonly accepted saying that the Germans made the best high-power sporting rifles and the English the finest double shotguns. There were two great favorites among the sporters, the Austrian Mannlicher-Schoenauer and the German Mauser. In New York City the firm of Abercrombie & Fitch featured the Mannlicher for years, later turning to the British Jeffery with Mauser action and chambered for the .256, .280, .333 and .404. Downtown, Schoverling, Daly & Gales specialized in Sauer-Mausers. Their calibers were our own .30-06 and the 7, 8 and 9 mm. Mauser rimless rounds with 57 mm. case length. This period was quite a while back—pre-1914, most of it—and today it's amusing to remember that the Sauer ordinarily was fitted with a half-octagon barrel. That was a sort of super-refinement on lots of our single shots and lever-guns of the time, and some inexpensive little rimfires like the Stevens Favorite had it, too.

Double- and single-shot rifles have been imported right along, but not in numbers to compare with the bolt-action repeater. The main exception to that sweeping statement would be the Flobert, a single shot .22 that came in various grades, some of them truly beautiful. In the late 1800s they were common enough, before our little rimfires had displaced them by their reasonable or good quality, low price, *and* the ready availability of spare parts. That last item almost always is a matter for some thought.

CHAPTER 10

IMPORTED SPORTERS

Most of the more or less contemporary imports are no problem in cartridge-case identification. Soon after World War I the ammunition companies began to find in their mail, fairly often, carefully packaged chamber casts made of sulphur. "What is it? Do you make these cartridges?" The cast was formed by plugging the barrel a little ahead of the chamber and pouring in melted sulphur. Usually the result was a bit wrinkled and undersize, having shrunk to less than normal case dimensions, as a rule. Now we have a material called Cerrosafe, with low melting point and minimum shrinkage. It's sold by Bob Brownell, Montezuma, Iowa, and Frank Mittemeier, 3577 E. Tremont Ave., Bronx, N. Y.

MAUSERS

Here we are looking at the 1898 Mauser and later issues of the type. These include all American bolt-action high-powers now made; advanced and improved, most of them, but essentially Mauser.

Plenty of earlier Mausers are carried in our game fields and they are doing all right, too. The 1888 in carbine form still helps to keep American-made "8 mm. Mauser" rounds on dealers' shelves, ready for us to buy. Its magazine is a Mannlicher pattern, open at the bottom so that the clip or charger which embraces the bodies of the quintuplet gunful can fall free as the last round is barreled. But its bolt is mainly Mauser, not much different from those of the 1871 single shot and 1880 tube repeater in the service 11 mm. or .43 caliber. The '89 Belgian 7.65 or .30 brought in the solid Mauser bolt cylinder, bored out from the rear, and the five-shot clip that held the rimless cartridges by their extracting grooves. Sporterized, a few got here. One of the party picked up an empty not many woods miles from our Adirondack camp in the fall of 1913. (I wasn't very big then, nor am I now.) The first thought was that this odd little brass bottle had been flung out from an automatic.

Other Mausers got here sooner and later. After the War of 1898 the 7x57 had become a well known cartridge. Spain had switched from the 1891 7.65 Mauser to the 7 mm. in late 1892, and in December 1893 she took up the new model with double-column magazine. This right-left-right-left-right apartment system eliminated the protruding single-column magazine.

The 1898 Mauser had the two front locking lugs of earlier rifles of this name, and it added a third lug at the rear for extra safety. That gave us the modern rifle. Some older specimens have been modernized, as we'd expect.

There have been various makes of Mauser sporters, those from the Oberndorf plant naturally being quite favored, for that was the home of Peter Paul Mauser. Right now, the factory of Wilhelm Heym, Munnerstadt, Bavaria, is perhaps the only one in West Germany that's making the original Mauser '98 action.

F. N. action with the new Sako Micro-motion adjustable trigger.

The F. N. Magnum action.

Outside of Germany several makers are turning out slightly modified '98s, and they are well hooked up with American importers. Many of these rifles are coming in and we'll look at some of the leading brands.

Fabrique Nationale

These Belgian rifles are a specialty of the Firearms International Corporation, Washington 22, D. C. Various grades are offered, with or without receiver sights of American make. Actions only, and actions with installed barrels, are available, a rather common choice in recent importations.

As this post-war FN became known it built a reputation for refinement, though it was not greatly changed from earlier Mauser sporters made in Germany. The safety was handy for a scoped rifle, and quiet in release, and the trigger had no slack to take up, and no creep. Barrels were finely finished for accuracy, and well bedded in the stocks. In general the rifle was noteworthy for its custom appearance and behavior. Double-set triggers are a regular item, at extra cost.

Calibers now offered are the .222 on non-cancellable order, and the .220, .243, .244, .250 and .300 Savage, .257 Roberts, .270, 7 mm, .308 and .30-06. At this writing a fine, heavy action is listed for the .300 and .375 Magnum cartridges. Its lower line is smooth, not protuberant as on some of the early German magnums, which of course were excellent arms, and available before anything of the sort was made by our American factories—except some of the Newtons, that is, and the Canadian Ross Model 10.

It's no wonder that FN actions are used widely by home and custom gunsmiths. They are good, standard items, easy to obtain. You don't have to look around for a factory or arsenal rifle, American or foreign, with shot-out barrel, and ready-barreled FNs come in the popular calibers. If you want to build a bench-rest rifle there's the special single-shot action in three styles. The standard takes rounds of .30-06 head size, and there are actions for the .222 and for the Magnums, .300 and .375, not that anyone would be likely to choose the latter for bench—yet. The trigger can be the standard non-adjustable, the Sako that is adjustable, or absent, so that you can fit your own choice.

Sporter actions have their magazines—the box is integral with the trigger guard—of definite lengths for the cartridges used. Magnum is 3⅝ inches; standard, 3-3/8; .244 and .308, 2⅞; .220 Swift, 2-13/16; .243 and .250 Savage, 2¾. Not all of them as prescribed would suit riflemen who like to set the bullets of their handloads well out to touch, or almost touch, the rifling lands. The receivers are drilled and tapped for peep sights and top-mounted hunting scopes. There is a button for detaching the magazine floor-plate, whereas the old military rifles demanded a bullet point or some other sharp instrument for this job. Some of us would prefer the old sporter release in the trigger guard,

Husqvarna light-weights, top one with Esquire four-power scope.

used on Japanese rifles, too, or maybe the old lever that lay along the floor plate.

Most of us would like the FN's smooth receiver contour, and be glad, too, that the thumb-slot on its left wall is gone. In a way it was handy, when we shoved in a clipful of cartridges, but it certainly didn't add to the receiver's stiffness and it became a nuisance to explain to people what the thing was *for*. The clip slots at the rear of the receiver opening also disappeared in the streamlining. Few would want them except on a target range, and even there we might prefer to exempt a rather expensive rifle like this one from the rigors of rapid fire. A hunter seldom gets himself into a jam where he has to cram in five more rounds in a hurry.

Husqvarna

Swedish Husqvarna actions, barreled actions, and complete rifles come from Tradewinds, Inc., Box 1191, Tacoma 1, Wash. (You don't follow "q" with "u" in pronouncing that name, and it's a respected name, Swedish steel and Swedish workmanship being of high grade.)

The full length rifle weighs about 7¾ pounds, has a 23¾-inch barrel, and at present is listed in .220, .270, .308 and .30-06 calibers. A lightweight model of some 6½ pounds has a barrel only 20½ inches long and the calibers are .243, .270, 7 mm., .308 and .30-06. Both straight-top and Monte Carlo stocks are offered, the wood being European walnut, as we'd expect.

This too is a refined Mauser-type action. It has a small-diameter receiver ring, hinged floor-plate with out-of-the-way release, single-stage trigger pull without slack or takeup, and in late models, a slide safety on the right, behind the bolt handle, instead of the

three-position wing at the rear of the bolt. Scope users like the new safety, and the stock can be had with a Monte, but iron-sight users accustomed to older Mausers might prefer the wing. Set in the middle position, it let them empty the chamber with the striker locked, and before taking a quick shot in the woods they found it easy to jab that wing over to the left when it had been sitting upright. True enough, the unlocked bolt handle could rise and cause a misfire— just a little brush against undergrowth was sometimes enough—and unless they'd diverted some of their time from woods-watching to rifle-watching they'd not know until it was too late. Fairly tight, often reloaded cartridges helped to prevent this, but they *could* be tight enough to stick in the chamber when a quick second shot was needed, bolted in with the gun at the shoulder.

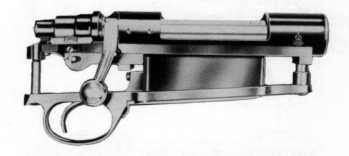

Husqvarna action, No. 1 length, for .308.

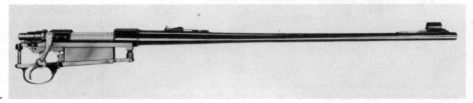

A barreled action.

Sako high-power Mauser rifle.

Like the Winchesters, this Mauser bolt has no cut through the left (or top) locking lug to clear a way for the ejector. This adds to at least the theoretical strength, though 1898s of the later years certainly were strong, and it seems that good Mausers never have had "hard," brittle receivers like those of the Russian Moisin and early Springfields. Some Mausers have been soft, and in time a few did perhaps develop excess headspace from constant battering, but they weren't at all liable to let go suddenly under the abuse of insanely hopped-up loads. Husqvarna receivers are of modern sporting type, and the drilling and tapping for peep or glass sights come as a matter of course.

The Brevex Magnum Mauser Action also is imported by Tradewinds. It's a splendidly planned job. Between front and rear guard screws it measures 8 11/16 inches as compared to the 7¾ of the standard Manser. It gives even more magazine length than we'd expect, 3 15/16 inches. This magazine is milled one-piece with the guard assembly.

Model 300 takes .300 and .375 Magnum cartridges, Model 400 the .404 Jeffery, .416 Rigby, .505 Gibbs and so on. Only the extractors and bolt-faces of these

models differ, and the actions are right for many big wildcat cartridges present and presumably to come. The floor-plate is hinged, with its small, unobtrusive release lever set in the front inner curve of the guard. Chrome vanadium steel is used for this action, but it can be had soft for engraving, to be hardened afterward. The barrel thread is listed as metric, 29 mm. diameter, with 12 turns to the inch.

Either the three-position Mauser safe or the scope safe can be had. The wing of the latter clears the left side of the scope when it's on, and it's curved and grooved to let a gloved finger get at it and press it down. The bolt handle is curved so that a glass can sit low, close to the receiver, which is drilled for the mounts and for a peep sight, in late models.

The Brevex is a heavy, strong action—it weighs about 3¼ pounds—and the recoil lug at the front of the receiver is big. For those who want a strictly modern magnum action, and prefer one made abroad, it should be a good choice.

Sako

Made in Finland, the Sako rifle earned respect in short-action, small-size style and .222 barreling. Firearms International imports a big-game Sako, too, with Belgian FN Mauser actions fitted with Sako adjustable trigger. The standard rifle is made in .270 and .30-06, the magnum in .300 and .375. Barrels are of Finnish steel and credited with long accuracy life, and they carry a good sort of emergency sights, to substitute when a scope is out of order, or useless in fog or heavy snow. The ramped and hooded front sight is a flat-topped Patridge, not a bead, and the open rear is fixed, with an extra folding leaf for more elevation.

The stock is only 13 inches long—just right for quite a lot of people with short reach—an inch shorter than that of the FN Mauser. It has more drop, 1 13/16 inches at comb, 2½ at heel, compared to 1⅝ and 2⅛. Many would say that its Monte Carlo is well shaped for looks, comfort and shootability, all three. Barreled actions are available for those who want them, and parenthetically, most of us do our best work with our own stock, one that's been correctly fitted to us. This isn't always practicable, and it takes a good deal of shooting even to know what we want.

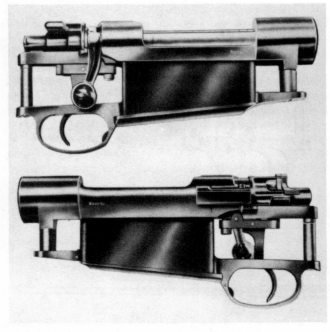

Brevex Magnum Mauser actions. Upper, with the familiar Mauser military-type safety. Lower, with the scope safe.

Brno

This Czech firm began in 1922 to make a reputation with its light machine guns. Mauser-action sporters came here after the war, some pocket auto-pistols, too, perhaps best known by the trademark ZB—Zbrojovka Brno.

The importers, Thalson Co., 682 Mission St., San Francisco 5, tell me that none of the sporters has come in since 1952. At this writing they still hope for deliveries, may get them.

Although these rifles are adapted in several ways to American tastes, they have an overseas look. They come with short or with full-length forestocks, are described as hefting just under seven pounds, and have 20½-inch barrels. The barrel has two distinct stepdowns at the breech end, and the sling swivel is attached directly to the barrel band, well out front, and not to the forestock wood. Triggers are double-set, the rear of the guard forks in a double shotgun style—old rifles, too—and the open rear sight with fixed and folding notches is set far back toward the breech.

The rear of the receiver is smoothed off, except for the usual Mauser bolt-stop box, and the safety is small and neat, but handy except possibly for a southpaw. To prevent objectionable sun-glare when we use iron sights, the top of the receiver is matted.

Calibers are distinctly foreign as catalogued now: 6.5, 7 and 8 mm. Mauser, all with 57 mm. case length. Yet all are well liked here and the 6.5 is, practically, just a neck-expanded .257 Roberts like those so popular in rechambered Japanese service rifles. Of course the Mauser cartridge came long before the wildcat. If the Brno is imported again it probably will blossom out in half a dozen or more American calibers. That would be almost necessary. The styling might be changed a good bit, too. There are small Brnos in Hornet and in .22 long-rifle calibers.

Birmingham Small Arms

This great old firm puts out a considerably modified sporting Mauser, a series of them, in fact. These are the short-action varmint rifle, previously discussed, the medium, and the standard. All are styled alike, and the importer is Al Freeland, 3737 14th Ave., Rock Island, Ill.

The short action is made for .22 Hornet and .222 Remington, the latter being usually the one wanted. It will take small cartridges up to 2.3 inches overall. The original medium action BSA caliber seems to have been the 7x57 Mauser, since early days so popular with British sportsmen and called the .275. The .257 Roberts, .300 Savage and .308 Winchester came later, and the .243 and .244 may follow. For bench-rest shooting this action is offered without a magazine. At this writing the long action is scheduled for .30-06 and perhaps .270 cartridges.

The medium and long actions are of average size and weight for their calibers, and the striker fall of 5/16 inch shouldn't give the trouble that some .222 users have met, Bert Shay tells me, in the short BSA and Sako actions. This is a serious trouble, the fre-quent hangfires of Winchester 116 primers, which in the Remington Model 722 fire reliably and give the even ignition that results in tight groups on the target. It often happens that some make of primer has tougher cups than most of the others and such primers are a natural choice for heavy loads if a rifle's striker is up to using them. All standard American rifle primers work well in American rifles, almost without exception.

The lines of the receiver are clean, even to the hunting scope bases mounted fore and aft like those on the small Sako. Although the flat, oblong striker head or cocking piece looks odd at first, this assembly does flow cleanly into the breech lines. The safety at the right is handy and its red indicator is more than just nice to look at. Not only is the trigger adjustable for weight of letoff; it's also stated that either a double- or single-stage pull can be had—same trigger. It serves as the bolt release.

The magazine is of standard Mauser type carrying four rounds, with a fifth in the chamber, and its floorplate is hinged. The release is in the front of the trigger guard.

English and American types of forestocks and of rear sights are or have been offered. Both style stocks have cheek-pieces and rather subdued Monte Carlos. The British forestock tip turns out in a medium-sized snobble; the American is fuller and rounded off. The British (or German) open rear sight is of the tangent style used so often on old Luger automatic pistols with seven-inch or longer barrels. Elevation goes on as you slide the adjusting sleeve forward. Much more popular here—and perhaps the only one to be imported in the future—is the two-leaf folding open sight now so common a stand-in on a scoped rifle. The bead front is ramped and hooded, and it seems that the late BSA imports have their receivers readied for peep sights. Kesselring, Parker-Hale and Stith ring mounts for a scope are among those available for the BSA.

Without scope and sling this rifle goes to about 7½ pounds and its barrel is 22 inches long. It's an attractive arm. British rifle workmanship was famous in the past, like that on their good grades of revolvers and automatic pistols, though hardly the equal of that on their shotguns in "Royal" or similar listings. We should get quality in this rifle, rather a newcomer at the moment, or demand it. Knowing "the reason why" wouldn't be satisfaction enough. A featherweight version has been added, and an 8½-pound 458. Lots of rifles have been or will be made for that instantly popular American caliber.

MANNLICHER-SCHOENAUER

The 1903 Greek service rifle and the sporter of the same year were among those rifles that are outstanding in workmanship, and through the long years they have kept up that reputation for quality, almost without a break. It's true that some sporters imported

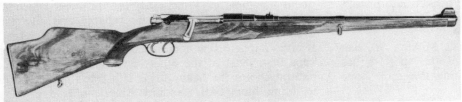

Mannlicher-Schoenauer carbine.

Left side of the carbine.

soon after World War I weren't up to standard. That plague didn't last long.

Both 1903 rifles handled the distinctive 6.5 mm. cartridge in a five-shot revolving magazine. The clip for the military piece is a beauty, no throw-away. Instead of having a fragile, narrow brass lip at each end it has flexible steel claws a good quarter-inch wide, and it can be picked up and re-used indefinitely after it has been ejected by the forward motion of the bolt. Or you can simply pull it out and pocket it after the rounds have gone home.

Similar, but rimmed, 6.5 rounds were used in Rumanian 1893 and Dutch '95 Mannlichers with single-column magazines loaded with long clips that gripped the case bodies. Sporterized, they made the early game-killing reputation of the caliber. Long, heavy smallbore bullets have advantages: light recoil, good accuracy and trajectory, deep penetration in game and frequently through brush screens, too. The 1903 Mannlicher-Schoenauer became popular at once. It still is.

Lately there's been difficulty in getting these 6.5x53 cases, sometimes called 6.5x54. They often measure close to 54 mm. but must not be confused with the Mauser 6.5x54, a much shorter-bodied case loaded with light bullets for the short or *kurz* Mauser action. Norma now makes the rimless 6.5x53 brass, and the rimmed cases have been formed from .303 British with good success, even to accuracy delivered by the handloads. The rimless 6.5x53 loaded in Canada by Dominion is commonly imported.

Other special, more or less proprietary calibers came, the 8x56 and 9x56, not to be confused with or substituted for 8x57 and 9x57 Mauser, and the 9.5x57, which in English fiction or fact accounts usually is a ".375." The factory of Johann Peterlongo, at Innsbruck in the Austrian Tyrol, turned out some fine early M-S sporters.

The bolt-head is detachable and its locking lugs lie a little farther back than those of the Mauser '98. It has been described as an action with 45,000 pounds

per square inch working pressure, like the Lee-Enfield, Mauser '88 and Norwegian Krag. This figure might apply to early M-S rifles and to regard it as their limit is sensible. It is some 5,000 p.s.i below late Springfields and 1917 Enfields, some 10,000 below the Winchester 54 and 70, Remington 30 and 720, and Mauser '98. Naturally these figures vary with vintages and individuals.

The M-S has been brought up to date. Later calibers included the 7x57, 7x64 (practically a .270), 8x60, 9.3x62 and 10.75x68, as well as our .30-06. Stoeger Arms Corporation dealt in most if not all of these calibers, and their Mannlichers now, from the plant at Steyr, Austria, take in most of the desirable big-game calibers below the magnum class. They are the old familiar 6.5 (sometimes called 6.7), the Mauser 7x57, and the American .243 Winchester, .257 Roberts, .270, .308, .30-06 and .358. The last practically duplicates in performance the much longer 9x56 M-S, though no 280-grain factory bullet is made for it at present. Modern emphasis usually bears down on velocity, not on slug-heavy bullet weight. But weight certainly has its uses.

The 1957 magnum rifle has a new and rugged action. The rear or "safety" lug, supplementing the two front locking lugs, is long, consisting of the entire bolt rib. Calibers are .458 Winchester Magnum, 6.5x68, and 8x68. The latter two are fast, the 6.5 sending a short 93-grain bullet at a listed 3937 f. s., the 8 a well balanced 186 grain at 3280. In shoulder angle the 6.5 resembles the .243, the 8 the .358.

The spool magazine is made to take a particular shape of cartridge, hold it so that the jar of recoil can't batter a soft lead point, and finally deliver it in line for the breech-bolt to pick up and chamber on the closing of the action. With and without cartridges —and there's a great difference in some rifles—the M-S is known as one of the most smoothly working bolt actions. It's in a class with the Krag, the Schultz & Larsen, the M-2 .22 Springfield and a few others. To empty its magazine of cartridges when the breech is open you press a stud on the right side of the receiver. Out they come.

Mannlichers have been made as takedowns, somewhat in the manner of takedown American Newtons. These Austrians gave fair accuracy when other things were working well, for really they, like the Newtons in this style, were only rifles with easily detachable stocks. So they'd group in about 3 or 4 inches at 100 yards. The British Jeffery with Mauser action, by contrast, was no arm of precision when made as a takedown, for its barrel, with the forearm attached, came right off the receiver. Since these Jeffs were made in potent calibers, most of them what we'd call magnums, they could scarcely combine that slice-in-two takedown with a useful grade of accuracy. Many .22 rimfires can and do, and even some .30-30s of this breed aren't entirely hopeless at woods ranges of 50 or possibly 75 yards.

The set triggers so common, once almost universal on Mannlichers, have had free and varied comment. Some riflemen just don't like hair triggers, and never will. Others, who've become familiar with them, find them helpful on long shots when there's time to aim, provided their trigger fingers are warm and sensitive enough to make such wishing-off of the shot possible. Unset, some of almost any make are too heavy, but usually a good gunsmith can cut the unset weight to three or four pounds. The pull may not be velvety, but we could use it, and these weights aren't too much when we shoot at moving game. So most of us think.

Iron-sighting the M-S always was a problem unless you were content with open sights. Almost invariably the standard rear has been a fixed notch with an extra fold-down for longer range—ranges to determine by test, not by reading print. The early-developed Lyman 36 suits this rifle that has a split receiver bridge through which the bolt handle commutes back and forth. With swinging, spring-returned arm, the 36 solved the problem, though the nicety and handiness of elevation and particularly of windage adjustments don't put it in the target class!

Then came the English Parker-Hale mounted on the cocking-piece nut—on the cocking piece itself, for Mausers. It is heavier and more expensive than the 36 and its weight could affect ignition. If the bolt has a loose fit in the receiver, the play could affect the grouping of shots on the target. This sight, and short-stemmed Lyman peeps mounted on a cocking piece, do have the advantage of bringing the sight aperture close to the eye, just as Lyman had planned when he started in business.

The 1950 M-S rifle's bolt handle permitted lower scope mounting, badly needed. A flat surface milled out on the left of the receiver had a dummy plate set in, ready to fill with a scope base. An extra safety catch on the right of the receiver, push type with quieting rubber buffer, was independent of the regular wing safe.

The variety of stocking and of barrel lengths and calibers has been great, as we'd expect in so old and popular a rifle. Barrels were usually light, to keep gun weight almost always under eight pounds, sometimes as light as 6½ in carbine form; and stocks were slim, too. The full-length carbine or old rifle forestock really didn't put much weight out front, and wasn't intended to. But it helped to protect the thin barrel in rough travel and usually was so beautifully seasoned that it was unlikely to warp and make the shooting go haywire.

There have been changes in styling, as in the 1923 model; then in 1950, '52 and '56 we had more. We now find the M-S up to date in Monte Carlo stock form, the pistol grip close up as on the '50, and with white spacers setting off the buttplate, grip cap, and the rifle's forestock tip. Rifle barrel length is now the popular 22 inches, but the carbine is still made in all current M-S calibers. Some of the old 6.5 carbines were under the legal 18 inches, it seems, but such barrels can be made acceptable by fitting an extension tube to the muzzle, permanently, as by welding.

We still have the choice between double set triggers and a plain single trigger. The pull-weight of the latter is standardized at 4½ pounds, which could be lightened with benefit to most shooters. Between the two types there's no difference in price.

The standard gun with open sights now retails at about $200, a rather high price, though many "extras" of finish are thrown in as a matter of course. "Why not? *This* is a Mannlicher," would be the reason given.

Its importers and most of its owners are proud of it, and one reason is its history. In 6.5 caliber this rifle has been a favorite of explorers like Charles Sheldon and Carl Akeley, and of closer-to-home but just as exacting woodsmen like Kenneth Fuller Lee and William Monypenny Newsom. It's given good service all over the wild parts of the world—has even squeaked by as an elephant rifle—for close-range, exactly placed shots with its full metal jacketed bullet of about 158 to 162 grains' weight.

In most styles and in larger calibers too the gun was light to carry, well balanced in firing, and reliable in action. At first it was used mostly by experienced hunters, men and women who rarely needed to rely on rapid fire. They did well with it, and they talked

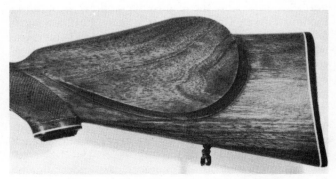

The new Mannlicher-Schoenauer stock.

Schultz & Larsen sporter. *Photo courtesy of GUNS magazine.*

or wrote about the way in which it had backed them up.

So its popularity persisted in spite of one or two serious faults. It's a slow action, almost impossible for most of us to work handily from the shoulder: the bolt handle is too far out, and too flat. "Butter-knife," it's been called. This flatness and its low-lying position make it an easy brush-threader, a fine companion until a second shot is needed, quickly. Modern handles are slanted back, and this helps but doesn't cure. It's no rifle for a lead-slinger.

The other "fault" may not be serious. If you demand a really low-mounted scope you'll say it is. But don't judge this matter by inspecting an old Mannlicher with a glass riding high enough to let you use the tube as a sort of handle—suitcase fashion—in carrying the rifle. Yes, some of us used to do that, with stiff, steel-tubed scopes riding high above a rather light rifle. I've done it myself, but with such fearful dread and trembling that I soon gave up the practice and went back to stretching my short fingers across the gun's floorplate. Incidentally, lots of the old European sporters wore high-mounted scopes a-purpose: the owners controlled or politicked access to private preserves where they fired at the driven game from a high perch, railed off to prevent hunter casualties induced by human excitement and plain old terrestrial gravity. Great sport if you liked it.

The rarely unbroken merit of the Mannlicher-Schoenauer, added to the romance of the name, ought to keep it on the market for years to come. It's seen its brief worst days and now is sailing along through the decades of its best. Not that the real oldtimers aren't splendid. They are.

Schultz & Larsen

Sharpe & Hart Associates, Emmitsburg 1, Md., import this rifle, and the California address is 4435-G Piedmont Ave., Oakland 11. It is made by the Schultz & Larsen firm of Otterup, Denmark, made to suit those who are exacting in workmanship. Although it's a comparatively new rifle in America, and rather expensive, enough have been sold and put into use to make it known and respected.

7x61 Cartridge. Its own special cartridge is the 7x61 mm. Sharpe & Hart, which started as a wildcat inspired by a chamber cast of an experimental French army autoloader identified as "M. A. S. 1907. No. 4." The wildcat based on the chamber cast ended, finally, as a medium length, big-bodied case, rather straight-sided, and very sharp-shouldered for a factory round. Norma makes it. The case was designed to burn Du Pont 4350 powder and to be a handloader's, even an experimenter's shape and size.

Although it looks somewhat like the belted .275 Holland & Holland Magnum it is nevertheless a distinct development, the result of years of trial of various forms. Here are some general measurements, fairly exact. Case lengths: 7x61, 61 mm.; .275 (or 7 mm.) H&H, 63 mm.; .300 H&H, 72 mm. Belts run about .531 inch diameter; the brass ahead of belt, about .512 to .513. H&H rims (for extraction) mike .527-.528, but the S&H rim is decidedly wider, .535-.536.

So we see that the 7x61 is a little like the .275, but only a little. We can't call it a derivative; it is a special, *modern* job. As ballistics engineer A. E. Ellinger explains clearly in P. O. Ackley's 1956 handbook, both body shape and shoulder angle have considerable effect on the burning of our modern progressive-combustion powders—of which 4350 is an advanced example. (At first we shooters thought it was only for big cases and heavy bullets, but later we learned that it is extremely flexible, considering its grain size.)

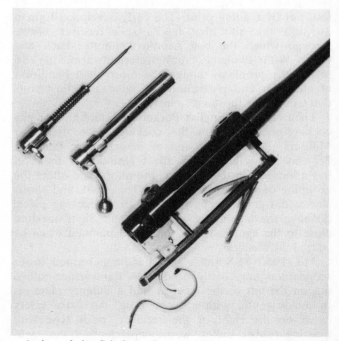

Action of the Schultz & Larsen. Note gas ports along bolt cylinder, square-shouldered striker, and heavy receiver with its small ejection port. *Photo courtesy of GUNS.*

A short case has its values, and the 7x61 gives us about standard .30-06 overall length even with pretty heavy bullets loaded with their bases inside the neck, not down among the powder grains—though fine target cartridges like the .300 H&H Magnum Match often are so assembled. In a short case the powder grains get clubby in a tight little meeting; so ignition is easier and more thorough, and more combustion takes place inside the case, relatively, than out in the barrel's throat and the first little length of rifling, that critical place for accuracy, where barrels start to burn out. A straight-bodied case, too, improves combustion, lowers rearward pressure, reduces possible forward flow and stretch of the brass neck, and lengthens barrel life because there's less funneling and breaking up of powder grains on their way to the lobby and the exit door.

This lobby, or shoulder below the neck, is useful under today's conditions if it is reasonably abrupt, like that of the 7x61. The well-known theory is that "It burns the powder in the case, not out in the bore." Mr. Ellinger goes on to explain a theory, which appears sound, that the powder blown into the bore from behind an abrupt shoulder enters as a sort of plug, giving more time for the rest of the charge to burn inside the brass. Quickly converging shoulder angles also blow the unburned powder grains against the sides of the neck instead of against the sides of the rifling throat, reducing the erosion of steel, and usually preventing the thickening of case necks from forward flow of brass.

We have had a few factory cases with abrupt shoulders, the .250 and .300 Savage, the 7.65 Belgian Mauser, and some others. The .275 H&H is one of that sort. When our powders lacked the kind of deterrent coating used now and therefore burned faster, this case was reformed to a more gentle neck slope to handle those powders. It was the .276 Dubiel, a still remembered and respected wildcat. But time has brought changes, and the shorter, straighter body and steeper shoulder of the 7x61 give advantages over the factory-made .275. For some years the Western Cartridge Company made that splendid cartridge, loading their (rather contradictorily) round-nosed and boat-tailed 175 grain 7 mm. bullet in it to give about 2760 f. s. velocity. Handloaders had and took a choice of other bullets, and now for the 7x61 there's a wide selection.

Bullets from 110 to 210 grains—almost .30-06 latitude—were tried in developing the new round, with rifling twists as slow as one turn in 20 inches for the short, varmint-hunting bullets, and as fast as one in six for the long ones. The Norma factory cartridge sends a 160 grain at 3100 f. s. Early H&H loads developed 100 f. s. less with the same weight of bullet, but later the powder charge was cut. The Schultz & Larsen is a strong rifle, and recommended handloads—with the bulky Du Pont No. 4350 powder only—fill the case to the compression stage. Pressures are rather

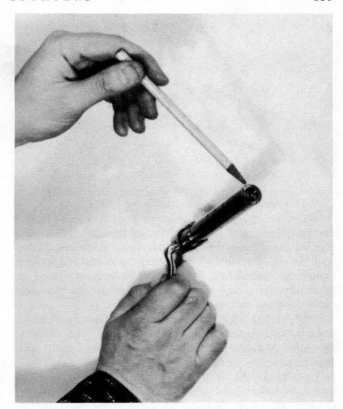

Bolt face of the Schultz & Larsen helps in the tight case enclosure. Pencil points out the built-in ejector. *Photo courtesy of GUNS.*

high. If the bullet won't seat properly you know you have an overload. However, maximum powder loading with this cartridge, or with any other smokeless round, is not for the beginner. The experienced rifleman and handloader realizes that he has rather rare need for such power, and he values the accuracy life of his barrel. With a big case like the 7x61 he has lots of practical leeway, up and down.

Already this caliber has done well on American big game, and it's a likely candidate to win the 1,000 yard Wimbledon Match. In a way it's an improved .280 Ross, which was a consistent winner overseas. Phil Sharpe's work in developing it is something for us shooters to appreciate.

Rifle Strength. The 7x61 was developed with scientific aids, not by guesswork. Sharpe explains that pressures were tested in the Modern-Bond Universal velocity and pressure gauge in his laboratory. With the receiver assembly costing about $1,250, and barrels—good for some 300 to 500 rounds—at around $200 apiece, the work wasn't inexpensive.

The case-head itself is strong, and it's well supported in the bolt-face, much in Remington 721-722 manner. There are plenty of gas ports in the bolt cylinder, and the lockup is strong. The big new .378 Weatherby Magnum was no trouble for this action to corral.

So the locking lugs are at the rear, not close up to

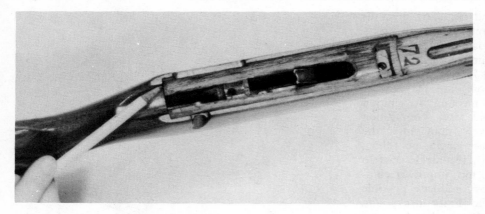

Pencil points to the rear recoil shoulder of the Schultz & Larsen stock. *Photo courtesy of GUNS.*

the cartridge head as in a Mauser design? There are four of them, and the extremely snug assembly of the bolt in the receiver—lap-fitted—prevents buckling under the backthrust of firing. The receiver, too, is unusually stiff; only a small opening is cut out for single-loading and ejecting.

This M-54J sporter action weighs just over three pounds, compared to the 3¼ or so of the Brevex *Magnum* Mauser. The Schultz & Larsen bench rest action goes to about 4½.

To add to the sporter's durability—for it can be had as a rather light and heavily charged rifle—there is an extra recoil shoulder at the rear of the receiver inlet in the stock. The recoil shoulder up at the front of the receiver is of good size, would in itself stand up to most stresses. But some barrels and actions, such as old, light-weight Newton .35s, have almost literally "shot themselves out of the stock," and in this advanced S&L design about every possible liability has been considered and guarded against.

Handiness. Even if this rifle were converted to top-loading there'd still be some who'd object to it because it's "different." Personally, I think its loading system would be handy in most situations except rapid fire on the target range, the shooter bound tightly with a sling. A top-loader with a low-mounted scope isn't always easy to charge, we should remember. With the S&L you simply open the hinged floorplate and drop the cartridges in. This you can do while the bolt is closed on a chambered round; pretty nice after one or two shots have been fired and you might need

another soon. At this writing the calibers offered are .244, .270, .30-06, 6.5x55 and 7x61.

In 1957 the M60 was announced. Its bottom- or top-loaded magazine carries cartridges in staggered position instead of in the straight, single-column line of the 54J.

There's some criticism of the bolt handle's being small. But it's curved out and slanted back, and you lift it only about half as high as one of Mauser type. The back-and-forth slide of the bolt is smooth, so easy in fact that a few early ejectors broke, I've heard, under the handling of shooters accustomed to stiffer actions. This weakness was corrected.

Bert Shay is enthusiastic in praising the trigger's location. It is well back, almost touching the guard, and it leaves plenty of room for a gloved finger, being in this respect much like those on many lever guns. Pull is adjustable from three to six pounds.

When made up with a light 22-inch barrel the S&L weighs about seven pounds without scope or sling. The receiver is ready for peep sights and the standard barrel is *not* sliced across for an open sight. Amidships, the rifle is deep rather than wide, because of its straight, single-column magazine, and many will like this carrying feel.

For a light rifle it shoots well: accuracy is built into its barrel and snug action. Inletting is carefully done, and that French walnut stock is shootable. The comb is a Monte Carlo, with a forward slope-down for comfort, not misery, when we shoot heavy loads.

RETIRED military rifles often are useful in civilian life. The best of them—and few reach that rating—can be made superior in some worthwhile ways to the factory sporters. Gunsmithing spent in converting them to the hunter's use may be an excellent investment.

There is another side to the cost sheet. Sometimes it's only sensible to discard stock and barrel, for there remains the action, a foundation on which to build a sporter. If it is sound and reliable, okery-doke. Not all of them are. Restocking and rebarreling (with exact adjustment of headspace) usually are expensive jobs today. Perhaps we might as well buy a factory rifle and refine the bedding for accuracy, if it needs it. In resale value—not always to be considered by those of us who are far-sighted and know what we'll like and continue to like—the factory article may be ahead of the sporterized military piece. Appreciation of military actions varies, actually, in different communities. German or Czech Mauser, British Lee-Enfield, Japanese Arisaka, and even our own Springfield—all are liked or disliked somewhat geographically. Personal experiences, related with or without a reverent eye on the goddess Truth, do sway local opinion. It's much less trouble to sell a rifle to a customer you see than to one you hear from in the morning mail.

Buying a big-game rifle economically when we have to, or as a cheap, knockabout spare or "lender," is quite different from building a dream sporter. Some of the ex-service rifles do well in the hunting field with no more refinement than a new set of sights, if that much. They make their owners happy and they do, often, kill game in as clean and sportsmanlike a fashion as the high-priced custom jobs do. Any American who goes to the trouble of arming himself and learning to use his weapon is an asset to our Country. There's no room for snobbishness among shooters. It's silly, and it stinks.

Springfield 1903

In this brief discussion, or in any discussion of military arms suitable for hunters' use, the Springfield deserves first place. We still use it as the basis of comparison when other bolt actions come up, new or old, military or sporting. Among the oldsters there's a tremendous amount of affection for the 03, and among youngsters too, who know the score. Used as it should be used, it isn't outdated.

Strength. The earlier receivers were single heat-treated or case-hardened, those up to 800,000 at Springfield Arsenal and 285,507 at Rock Island. Double heat treatment went from 800,000 to 1,275,-766 serial number at Springfield, from 285,507 to about 319,921, and a few later and higher numbered, at Rock Island. The higher Springfield numbers, most of the higher Rock Islands, and the World War II receivers made by Remington and Smith-Corona, are nickel steel. It pays to be choosy when we can.

Many authorities do agree that the "hard" or

CHAPTER 11

MILITARY RIFLES FOR HUNTING

"brittle" single heat-treated receivers have been maligned. They've proved safe with perfectly normal service or factory rounds in .30-06 caliber. One shooter I knew played safe by firing his low-numbered Springfield only with cast-bullet reloads. That may have been an extreme precaution, but he had several rifles and certainly did enjoy his old 03 in such use.

There is, too, the matter of being your brother's keeper, though we needn't always expect a like return. For example, I let a young chap fire some of his handloads in an old .32 Colt Police Positive Target I had, giving them only a casual look. Evidently his bullets were oversize, and too hard, for later that evening I saw that the thin barrel breech had been belled. Something new had been added, for I do know my pet guns. For once I had the sense to count to about 1,000 and keep still. Later the old six-inch barrel was shortened from the breech, down to 3¾, and now I just love to have that little shorty in a holster on a wintertime hike.

But suppose it had been an old, "brittle" 03 rifle and the kid had loaded super-maximum powder charges behind .311-inch bullets made for a Japanese rifle. The results might not have been so happy.

The single and the double heat-treated actions are known for their smoothness. A hard skin on steel, *with proper workmanship,* can turn up that sort of slickness. The double is considered even stronger than the final nickel steel type, but both have adequate strength for .30-06 and in fact for .270 rounds, in normal, sensible loadings. The 03 isn't considered a good choice for conversion to .300 Magnum, and with so many suitable actions available for that purpose there'd be little sense in using it.

The "old" Springfield and the Winchester 1895 rifles are the chief reasons for the underloading of factory .30-06 cartridges. Considering some of the other stuff that gets by under the name of ".30-06 rifles," it's just as well that the commercial ammunition is held down in pressure. Reference is made to casual conversions and rebarrelings that sometimes are foisted on the buying public.

"Faults." These are few. The two-piece firing pin probably seemed a good idea when the rifle was designed, but it isn't liked today, and more rugged one-piece strikers have been made by gunsmiths.

A warning by R. A. Thompson (p. 72, *American Rifleman,* March, 1956) was timely. We know that protruding firing pins, rusted tight in the breech face, have caused premature explosions when breech-bolts were slammed forward, and not fully locked. As he says, this *could* happen with the 03 if the little collar of the striker, or the doll's head of the firing-pin rod, were broken. It may seem improbable; so do many other causes of serious accidents, before they happen.

Some object to the cocking piece at the rear of the firing-pin rod. It is just what the name implies, put there to let us cock the rifle with thumb and finger if we get a misfire. It isn't, of course, to let us carry the 03 with the striker down on the primer of a chambered round. We can cock the rifle by raising the bolt handle, but who wants to do this if the misfire might prove to be a hangfire and let go when the action was unlocked?

No doubt the weight of the cocking piece slows ignition. Yet it may by its weight make ignition a little more sure and even, and it does give less chance for primer metal to flow back into the firing-pin hole in the breech face. Anyway, the headless striker put on the fine National Match grade of 03 before 1931 didn't fire the 1930 National Match ammunition properly. That stuff had been made with Berdan primers, it's true, but Ordnance went back to the striker with a cocking piece, and that was that.

Another advantage of a cocking piece is that it acts as a sort of shield if a primer is pierced. True, the one on the Springfield .30 would divert gas more effectively if it were more square-shouldered up front, like that of the M-2 .22 training rifle, but it's better than nothing.

Some don't like the magazine cut-off. Turned down to "OFF," it prevents the bolt from going back far enough to pick a cartridge out of the magazine. The early twentieth century idea of a battle may have been that of an engagement where rank and file sniped deliberately at each other with the deadly new long-range rifles. Keeping a magazineful in reserve, to stop a charge, seemed like a fine idea, though the German Mauser didn't employ a cut-off, and our rifle was patterned after that 1898 model. Turning the cut-off

to "ON" lets us clip-feed the Springfield, if we wish, and the magazine feed is extremely reliable with .30-06 rounds or those of similar dimensions.

But—and this we've been saving—the cut-off also acts as a bolt release when it's set in the middle position. Springfield trigger pulls are usually good, or else agreeable to great refinement. No trigger should be asked to perform an extra, part-time job like serving as the bolt release. That's the general impression. There is, however, the embarrassing fact that thousands of .22 rimfires, some of them light little fellows and far from expensive, have dual-purpose trigs and still somehow retain the clean, crisp pulls that they had at birth or were endowed with later.

Some don't like the 03's double-stage military pull with long, soft takeup and a final clean release? Well, it stands up to a lot of use, without changing the weight, and you learn to use it. Shooting at running game, even, is only an advanced refinement of military rapid fire. A professional infantryman or marine is apt to learn it quite fast. At Perry, up to 1940 or so, when 03s were still issued, we learned to "take up the slack" before starting the final pressure, in rapid as well as slow fire. For a purely snapshooting rifle a single-stage trigger is better—less liability of over-shooting if we snatch rather than squeeze! But I think that learning to favor any sort of rifle—provided it's at all accommodating and really good—has its advantages. We are more deliberate and more serious, more mindful of the gun. There are few forms of sleight-of-hand performance, quick, smooth, mastered through long practice, that suffer from an alloy of common sense and self-restraint. I'd prefer to spend money on having a Springfield pull smooth and lightened, if it needed either or both refinements, than to have it converted to single-stage. However, that's a personal opinion, and probably you've noticed that most people who like the 03 get personal about it. The old rifle is a somebody, not just a thing.

General Desirability. For use with the .270, .30-06, .35 and .400 Whelen and simliar cartridges the 03 action is a good choice. The pressures of the factory-loaded .270 are close to 55,000 p. s. i. and the later Springfields handle them. For high-intensity wildcat rounds, the 03 isn't so good, the main reason being the tendency to overload them and get the velocity the designer (one kind of designer) promised, or a bit more! The barrel has the coned breech common to the Enfield, Winchester 54 and 70, and Remington 30, 30-S and 720, and the bolt-face isn't deeply countersunk for the case-head. Generally we can get the power we need, and better accuracy along with longer barrel life, by loading to some 50,000 p. s. i., or below.

The 03 is a bit conservative and some of its users are, too. Yet between them they continue to get good results. Quality of Springfields made in peacetime, at least, is outstanding, obvious. You notice the finish and the fit of action parts, the smoothness of cartridge

The Springfield NRA or DCM Sporter. Standard except for scope blocks, Redfield square gold bead front sight (not the present Sourdough), and the sling keeper attached just about midway of the strap. The M-2 .22 Springfield is closely similar in appearance to this NRA rifle. *Courtesy, Combat Forces Press.*

handling and firing mechanisms, the careful assembly of wood to steel. (That gap behind the upper tang of the receiver is there for a purpose. A service rifle stock mustn't split, in any climate, with any normal loads.) As a military rifle the Springfield always has been outstanding in performance, and in looks, too. It's been probably the greatest of all favorites of those who have had custom rifles built precisely to their order, like a custom suit or overcoat or pair of shoes. At least until recent years about its only rival has been the Mauser, the sporting action as a rule. A good issue of the 03 is up to sporter standards, or above them.

Types. The most desirable types were the National Match, with standard weight, star-gauged, close-tolerance barrel, and pistol-grip stock of good length and plenty high at the comb for iron-sight use, and the slightly heavier barreled N. R. A. Sporter. The latter had a hunting type stock with short forearm, not the long military sort that reaches to only a few inches below the muzzle. It was an oversize stock, like those on some of our match rifles, so that the owner could shave it to suit him. The bedding for accuracy was splendid, and most of the peacetime service rifles were excellent in that respect, too. The Type T was a heavy-barrel, for target work, and it's been used in International competition.

The old Type S service rifle had a short stock, about 12¾ inches from trigger to buttplate. With it, people of average ranginess of build learned fast, in the hard way, to hold their thumbs straight out, not crossed over the comb. Trustfully placed so, the thumb came back hard on recoil, and the nail tasted human flesh. A recoil pad would have stopped that, but the hole under the trap in the buttplate is a useful cache for the string (thong) cleaner and oil-can, or for matches paraffined into a bundle, or for two or three extra cartridges done up in an oiled rag with matches thrown in! Those last-ditch rounds would be dried before we chambered them.

World War II Springfields usually have a stamped-out guard instead of a finely machined one, and some of their barrels are cut with two grooves instead of the usual four. Yet they are strong, serviceable rifles, and as a rule they shoot well. Some have a woods-useful peep sight on the receiver, quicker and more accurate to aim with than the old ladder sight out on the barrel breech. We'd have to juggle handloads to zero in for the woods, of course.

Springfield 1873

This rifle belongs in good company, and commonly mingles there. The .45-70 ammunition is still made for it and for other rifles, and it had better be! The only reason why the Springfield 1866 is an unsocial recluse is that it's so hard to get the .50-70-450 ammo for it. However, .50-70 cases *are* made from .43 Egyptian brass by the Shell Shop, 8709 Sunset Blvd., Los Angeles 26, and they should do nicely for the black-powder loadings we'd use in that caliber. Tools and molds still ought to be available from Lyman-Ideal.

About ten varieties of the original 1873 .45-70 were made. Like the 1866 it has the flop-up, "trap-door" breechblock, hinged up front. Quarter- and half-cock hammer notches let it be locked shut, or flipped open when the hammer is in a safe position. The automatic ejector speeds reloading, though it wouldn't be called a strong extractor by modern standards. However, we reload that rifle with black or low-pressure smokeless powder, keeping pressures down to 25,000 p.s.i., and good brass will give many firings before it's swollen enough to make extraction hard. Chambers are beautifully cut, like the rest of the metal work.

The rifle is heavy and long, easy to shoot off-hand but maybe a bit unwieldy in the woods. In carbine form, or shortened to 22-inch rifle, it's a handy gun, still heavy enough out front for good holding, and a killer as far as we can count on placing its big, slow bullets.

The .45-70 Springfield and Winchester caliber was the .30-06 of several 1800 decades. As late as 1914 the Winchester Company catalogued 20 different loads for it, with bullets ranging from the 140-grain round-ball gallery marble to the long, deep-penetrating 500 grain. Oddly enough, soft-point and full-patch jacketed bullets were loaded in front of black as well as smokeless in this and other calibers, probably on special order. More than those 20 standard .45-70 rounds could be used in the Springfield, Winchester and others of that size. There were the .45-85 Marlin, .45-85 Bullard, .45-70 and .45-75 Sharps paper patched, and the short .45-60 Winchester 1876—unless its rim was too wide to seat in certain chambers. The .45-85 (or .45-83) Colt had a case just a trifle too long.

Today the .45-70 is loaded in the nearly all-round big-game weight of 405 grains, and this soft point, smokeless powder charge is safe in good, sound Springfields. About the only criticism of this rifle as a hunting arm is that left-handers might find its side-mounted hammer and breechblock latch unhandy.

Of course it is a single shot. We can dispose of that matter briefly and, I hope, clearly enough, by saying that a single shot *makes* you learn to shoot carefully and if you're already a good, careful shot you get a little extra kick from killing your game with that kind of rifle. Some hunters have no business with such a gun, and in certain kinds of hunting it might be dangerous to rely on it. I suppose that latter consideration depends on how adventurous the hunter is. There's no need to moralize on this matter or even expatiate on the days of Lewis and Clark, when grizzlies actually came running out of the hills, ready for a showdown.

Krag-Jorgensen 1892

Several revised editions came out, and lots of these rifles are in use. Krags are slow to wear out! The action is a sturdy one for cartridges in the 40,000 p.s.i. pressure group—a limit it's wise to observe considering the age of any Krag—and it stands up to several rebarrelings. Its .30-40 case has been necked down to form the .25 Niedner-Krag, and this round and the .25-35 (with necessary magazine alterations) have been used in the Krag. When the Hornet was new and less powerfully loaded than now, single shots for it on this action were rather popular.

But most that we see now have the original .30-40 barrel, and that caliber is still one of our most useful. Properly loaded, it does well on all but our largest big game, at moderate ranges. It is hard to give the 110-grain varmint bullet as much velocity as most of us want for this kind of hunting. For the long-throated Krag barrel it seldom makes up into an accurate load, and then too, the rifling has a 10-inch pitch for the 220 and the special 230-grain bullets, which was passed on through inheritance to the Springfield. One of my friends has a fine old 30-inch Krag rifle, beautifully balanced for offhand, and he loves it. For woodchuck shooting he handloaded the Western 150-grain .30-30 open-point bullet, which is rather lightly jacketed. He found that it shot well, killed reliably, and gave no ricochets. But then, he's a careful hunter.

The eight-pound 22-inch carbine is a good pound lighter than the rifle and handles so well in the woods that it's scarce and hard to buy. But most Krag rifles that we see now have had their barrels cut to 24 inches or shorter.

Although the action has only one front locking lug, which turns into a solid seat in the receiver, the lug formed by the bolt handle is reassuring. Very few Krags indeed have blown their bolts, and when this happens, under abuse, the rear lug tends to throw the long bolt to the side, away from the shooter. It pays to inspect any bolt lugs pretty regularly for signs of weakening.

The Krag is still considered a safe rifle with the right ammunition, and it's one of our few bolt actions above Hornet and Bee power that use rimmed cartridges. These get their headspace right on the face of the chamber. If the case shoulder is set back

in neck-sizing, the rim, like the belt of Holland & Holland Magnums, still does its job of positioning the brass in the chamber. Rimless rounds, and semirimless like the .220, usually are positioned by their shoulder angle, and *that* area the handloader has to watch.

Some, not all, rimmed cases give trouble in Mauser type double-column magazines. But a Krag, properly loaded, is reliable. And it can be charged when the bolt is closed. Pry open its side door and roll the rounds in, being careful to see that the rim of each following cartridge lies behind that of the one ahead. Snap or ease the cover shut and it's done, a slower business than clip-loading for full recharging, easier and faster than partly refilling a Mauser type top-loader.

To get rid of the side door and the porch, Krags have been altered to top-loading. This reduces magazine capacity from five to three or possibly four rounds but makes them handier for the trail carry. The standard Krag is one of the slickest of all bolt actions: the top cartridge, as it comes around to the left to wait for the bolt to pick it up, isn't in any tearing hurry. It presses only lightly against the bolt cylinder.

The issue stock fits most shooters rather well, being a little under 13½ inches in pull length and reasonably high combed for iron sight shooting. Probably most restocked Krags—and there are many of them—carry a pistol grip. The majority of us think we must have one because it's customary.

The magazine cut-off holds the top cartridge in the magazine back out of reach of the bolt, but the safety operates in Springfield fashion. Since not many Krags are scoped, the safety is completely satisfactory to most owners. As with the Springfield, the striker and firing pin rod are separate units. Under reasonable care, without spare parts in the kit, and weeks' or months' travel from gunsmiths, both rifles have done all that could be asked. Many have done it under abuse, too. Before any such trip with any rifle—and this sort of escape from today's world is much too rare—it's wise to ask a gunsmith what replacements, if any, to roll up in cloth and pack, and how to fit them, too.

Enfield 1917

When the British were planning to put in service a high velocity .276 cartridge,* practically a magnum, they built a special Pattern '13 rifle for it. Next year, the terrible August of 1914 shattered the complacency of the thoughtless and the conviction of the civilized and intelligent. It really had happened, an all-out war with most of the European nations savagely engaged in it.

As Pattern '14 the revised new rifle handled the

*Philip B. Sharpe once said that its 165-grain steel-jacketed, cupronickel plated bullet started at 2800 f. s. velocity. Case body was larger than the rim.

.303 British ammunition, *fairly* large stocks of which were on hand. In two world wars the 1914 rifle served alongside the old Lee-Enfield. Our entry into World War I in 1917 made necessary the conversion of the rifle to .30-06 caliber. It proved to be more than a makeshift. As a service arm and as a sporter it's done so well that it is highly respected.

The barrel has the coned breech, doesn't enclose the case-head as well as the square-breeched Mauser, which itself gives nothing like the complete enclosure of the new Remingtons, Winchester 88, the Schultz & Larsen, our M-1 Garand and M-1 carbine, the Russian Tokarev and German Gewehr semi-automatics, and the Japanese Arisaka bolt action. But its heavy nickel-steel action is strong, quite a favorite for modification to handle magnum factory or wildcat rounds. Remington and Winchester Enfields have a reputation for strength, but Eddystone receivers have been "too hard." If they won't take a file or if they show little lengthwise cracks, look out.

Just as issued, the Enfield does right well as a hunting rifle. Its fixed battle sight is set for some 400 yards with the old service load, a 150-grain spitzer bullet at 2700 f.s., but handloads can be worked out to zero at 100 yards. A 170-grain .30-30 or 190-grain .303 Savage soft point at about 2500 f.s., or less, does the trick and is deadly on white-tail deer. For reduced loads with cast bullets the sliding peep on the folding leaf comes in handy. Both apertures are good-sized, well back on the receiver, quick to aim through. There's no windage adjustment in the rear sight, but the front sight can be driven from side to side for zeroing, if this proves to be necessary.

The issue stock has no comb at all, and its small pistol grip is too far back to be of much use except in bayonet fighting. Most of us want a comb buildup or a restocking job, and more streamlined sights or a scope. The side lever safety is handy under a glass and was used without much change on Remington rifles for almost 30 years.

There have been some minor action troubles, and some rare ones. Among the latter would be the breaking of the firing pin, its spring, the extractor, or the ejector. To play absolutely safe, the owner might lay in spares. Having them, he'd probably never need any of them! This 1917 rifle does remarkably well for an adaptation, one not originally designed for the .30-06 cartridge we use in it.

Blunt, soft-point bullets often get their noses shaved in being fed from double-column magazines, and the Enfield is frequently hard-hearted in this respect. Various remedies have been applied, one of the best being a reshaping of the loading ramp in the receiver. This must be done carefully so as not to weaken the hold of the metal behind the lower locking lug. W. B. Thomas, Alderwood Manor, Washington, worked out a magazine insert for this rifle and the Springfield that makes the top round in the magazine go straight in. This reduces magazine capacity, which means little, and after all, that's the way in which loads *should* feed in any repeater, isn't it? Sometimes metal strips attached to left or right of the front of the magazine will do the work; they're an approach to central or straight-line feeding.

Special triggers can be had for the Enfield, as for most military rifles popular as American sporters. They come in the chapter on accessories, for really they aren't essential to a good many of us. The standard pull is usually rather clean, and it's not difficult for a reasonably skilled tinkerer to adjust. There was a great buying of Enfield parts for the Remington 30 when that model was new and carried a single-stage trigger that so often was multiple, traveling back in a series of creeps.

There's plenty of criticism of the cock-on-closing feature that the issue Enfield shares with many old rifles, the Lee-Enfield, the Japanese, and some early .22 repeaters. Raising the bolt handle cams the empty case loose in good Mauser fashion but it doesn't cock the striker—which, by the way, is a two-piece job much like the Springfield's. The mainspring is only coiled back by the bolt handle's upturn; the real resistance comes in the last inch or so of the forward, closing shove.

Which is easier, to wrench a bolt handle up against a strong spring, or to send it forward against that resistance at almost the end of the trip? The answer tells whether or not you'd want the action altered. It might depend on the length of the stock. Is it short enough to let you throw the bolt easily, offhand, with the rifle at your shoulder?

The Enfield's bolt release is like that of the Mauser, no thing of beauty, but serviceable. The trigger is left to do its own special job, same as with the Krag and Springfield.

The waistline of the '17 rifle is bulgy, and we don't need that full capacity of a six-shot magazine, do we with a seventh cartridge in the chamber? Cut to five magazine rounds and with the floorplate flattened out, the Enfield carries much more easily, for as issued it's a lot of rifle to tote at trail with your fingertips straining their utmost not to loose hold on the huge receiver section. Restocking can lighten the weight, too, and chopping off two to four inches of the stiff 26-inch barrel makes a trifling difference. Personally I like a .30 caliber barrel of good length, except in tough country. What it adds to velocity is little, if anything, but it does reduce muzzle blast, and still better, it makes a rifle hold more steadily. That's for me. You may prefer an 18- or 20-incher, and I've used them too and liked some of them. But for the less strenuous sort of hunting I prefer barrel length.

Garand M-1

Easy and comfortable to shoot, almost completely reliable, and accurate enough for most big-game hunting, the Garand has been around in the wilderness.

Now that individual ownership is available to NRA members we can expect to see it a little more often away from the target ranges. There it affords much fun—and develops skill in practical marksmanship.

But it's unlikely to become a popular hunting rifle. It weighs some 9½ pounds, it's so large in mid-section that carrying it long miles at trail becomes no pleasure at all, and it's not particularly well adapted to scope mounting. The issue sights are about the best that ever went on a standard military rifle, and the rear peep click adjustments for windage and elevation are exact and close enough for almost any hunting purpose.

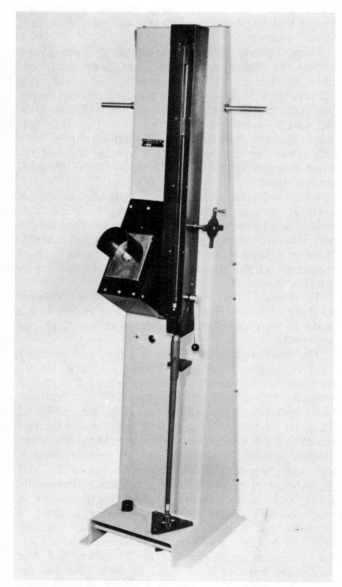

Kollmorgen Optical Company's barrel-straightness tester has been used by the Government in a program of studying the effects of barrel differences on accuracy. By changing the dimensions of the polished steel mirror it is possible to adapt this device to testing barrels of different external sizes and contours. Since this Kollmorgen device costs some $2,000 or more, it's beyond the practical reach of the average gunsmith.

For bigbore target competition many of us find the sight good enough, and that's saying a lot.

Yet only a few experienced hunters seem to want a semi-automatic rifle. Most of them don't need one. In some states the self-loader's capacity is set by law at no more than six or even five rounds, and the M-1 uses that eight-shot clip, though an adapter can be had.

The trigger pull isn't as brittle as an icicle; neither is it mid-March slushy. It's perfectly usable and consistent: you learn it and it stays with you. There are no temperamental shifts in weight or length of draw—at least in my own M-1 experience—and the safety is one of the handiest ever put on a hammerless rifle. It lies in the front of the trigger guard, and a forward push releases it. If there's time, you move it with thumb and forefinger, noiselessly.

At first the insides of the Garand seem complicated; later they seem beautifully planned for long wear and for reliability. It isn't a cheap or quick rifle to manufacture, but it was *the best* our Ordnance Department could design. Our servicemen's lives aren't considered cheap. When throw-away weapons are subject to stoppages or breakdowns they're for slave subjects.

Some tutoring or else some careful study of the manual is necessary to make us familiar with the care and even with the operation of the M-1. The effort is worth while, and the gun deserves the care.

Garands have been sporterized and reduced slightly in weight. Here I think the effort wasn't worth while, for there was little if any improvement in woods-handiness, and the general appearance was something of a nightmare—or so it seemed to me. Most civilian riflemen would choose the M-1 sooner than the M-14 of 1957, if only for its appearance. It looks like a rifle.

Lee-Enfields

These British service rifles have gone through several modifications. The Rifle No. 1, Mark III, and the No. 1, Mark III*, a 1918 revision, have rather light barrels, heavy enough, though, for most sporting purposes. World War I taught the British the necessity for simplified manufacture of small-arms, and the Rifle No. 4, Mark I* came out. This has a heavier barrel and is preferred by some shooters for that reason.

Ten-shot, removable, staggered box magazines are standard, and so are two-piece stocks, joined just ahead of the grip, except on the light No. 4, Mark I* carbine that weighs only about 6¾ pounds. To most of us American riflemen these weapons, even the little No. 5, Mark I* jungle version, would seem clumsy. The 10-shot magazine is reliable enough, and quickly charged with five-round clips, but it hangs 'way down below the trigger guard, unsightly and awkward, and we seldom use a .303 for casual plinking! Very careful fitting of the stock is necessary for good accuracy, and one needs considerable familiarity with these particular arms to do the inletting well. And at least the earlier rifles demanded precise, even

Ackley sporter on a Mauser action. See thumb-slot in receiver for clip-loading, and the magazine floorplate release in the front bow of the trigger guard.

bearing of their locking lugs if they were to shoot at all well. But the No. 4 and No. 5 are, even today, unusual military rifles in having a peep sight on the rear of the receiver.

Despite its faults the Lee-Enfield is a considerable favorite for remodeling into sporter style. Many gunsmiths admire its quality, its capable action, and the short and easy bolt-throw that results from the rear location of the locking lugs. This lockup is strong enough for the mild pressures of its .303 loads, and the cartridge is useful. Our factories regularly load it with a 215-grain soft point at 2180 f. s., and there are custom bullets and plenty of molds for the handloader. Since the case is rimmed, the enclosure of the brass is snug, no problem even for these old bolt actions.

The British Rifle No. 3, Mark 1* is the Pattern '14. Since our 1917 Enfield was adapted from it with almost no changes except in magazine, bolt-face and barreling, it looks familiar. The magazine holds five of the rimmed .303s, plenty for a hunting rifle. A good many have come over here in recent months.

Mausers

A major on World War II stateside assignment told me that one of his hobby ambitions was to collect specimens of all military Mausers. He was one of the most efficient and determined young men I ever knew, and a thoroughly right guy too. I've wondered how he made out.

W. H. B. Smith's books on *Mauser Rifles and Pistols* and *Small Arms of the World* cover the field, even the variations in styling, and it's a big field. Here we look at it only from the viewpoint of the hunter who may think of buying a Mauser war rifle for conversion.

Probably he won't be interested in the 1888, also called Mannlicher from its magazine and some of its bolt details, even if he sees it as a Schilling or Haenel sporter. The need for a special clip to charge the magazine, the unsightly and awkward protuberance of that magazine, and the bolt handle 'way up front are serious drawbacks. Even more serious could be the fact that it must be used with the 7.7 mm. ammunition, not the 7.92 S (spitzer or pointed) military issue that came along in 1905. Groove diameter of the old rifles averaged .319 to .321 inch; in the modern service rifles it runs between, say .323 and .3256. Ammunition was made accordingly, although our own modern factory stuff, the 170-grain soft point at 2570

f.s., is loaded down to be safe in the '88s, and the bullets are thin-jacketed, practically .32 Special or .32 Remington slugs. They are good deer loads.

The Belgian '89 in 7.65 caliber is uncommon here—though Winchester did chamber the Model 54 rifle for that round—and so are Turkish 1890 and 1895 and Argentine 1891 7.65s, and the Portuguese 1904 and Swedish 1906 6.5s. Mexico was rather early and ingenious in developing semi-automatics—witness the Mondragon of 1908—but her main reliance has been placed on the turn-bolt Mauser-type repeater. The latest, in .30-06 caliber, has more Springfield than Mauser characteristics, and her early 7 mms. have been on sale recently up here. They aren't to be compared in strength to a later German Mauser sporter in that caliber, but our own conservatively loaded factory cartridges should be safe in the Mexican rifles that are in good shape.

The Czech VZ 1924 in 7.92 is one of the best military Mausers in workmanship and in the steels used. The shortened Model 33 form became the 33-40 under German control of Czecho-Slovakia, and the bolt handle is turned down instead of left standing straight out as from the 1924 rifle. This piece has a fairly small receiver ring and makes up into a nice, light sporter, still having strength enough for cartridges in the 7.92 (or 8x57) and .30-06 class.

Poland's 1929 7.92 was a good model, with turned-down bolt handle and general German Mauser characteristics. Her 91-98-25 rifle was a Russian Moisin 1891 action converted to 7.92 in 1925, not at all desirable. It could be a hazard. The Yugo-Slav 1924 is uncommon, but it might be worth more as an 8 mm. sporter than as a curio. If we get one of the carbines with barrel less than 18 inches long it's a "firearm," in Federal parlance, and must be registered at a high fee or given a permanently attached muzzle extension. The *action* is a good '98 Mauser type with a little more complete case-head enclosure.

Mauser '98

Various forms of this model are what we mean when we speak of German Mauser military rifles. Some, not all, of those made before 1905 were rebored to take safely the larger-diameter pointed bullets. Miking a tight-fitting lead slug that has been driven through the barrel is sound practice to follow with any military rifles, sporters too. Firing a high-velocity jacketed bullet even .001 inch over groove diameter is an introduction to peril. Though most of these military Mausers are strong, no rifle is completely foolproof.

There were various forms of service cartridges that we'd never care to fire in a sporter, and some we'd not dare to fire in any *rifle*. The Germans were about as fiendish as any other people, if not more so, in the stuff they sometimes loaded. Salvaged battlefield rounds seldom are a bargain, anyway. Some of the worst 7.92s are the following: armor piercing or tracer, red lacquer around primer; a. p. or a. p. tracer, copper colored bullet with one-half inch of tip blackened; incendiary or explosive, black lacquer around primer; super high pressure aircraft machine gun load, green band about one-quarter inch wide, halfway between bullet tip and the case mouth, when the round is loaded, ready for firing; contact-explosive bullet, dangerous within 50-yard radius of its point of strike, identified by its having no crimping cannelure and by a black lacquer coating from its boat-tailed base (which I for one have no wish to see) to within one-half inch of its copper-colored tip. There may be others. Unless the salvage comes from a sealed carton (15 rounds) labeled for rifle use, why take the chance of firing it? And why fire it when we know our own American 170-grain sporting stuff is safe, and our sensibly put up handloads, too? Sporting ammunition imported by a reliable firm is OK—though even then we'd check bullet and rifling groove diameters—and we just might want it for heavy-bullet 7.92 loadings.

The condition of any captured military Mauser ought to be checked, I think, by a competent gunsmith. There's small liability of its not passing inspection, but it pays to play safe. If the bore is ruined the action may be splendid for rebarreling to an American caliber. There are many such ex-military jobs in our hunting fields and on our target ranges.

The hunter who uses a low-mounted scope won't like the standard Mauser wing safety; it's hard for him to get at in a hurry. Here are some that lie conveniently at the right side of the bolt sleeve. The Doc Line Company's safety is a do-it-yourself installation, and the address is 18440 John R. St., Detroit 3. The Fischer designs come from Modern Gun Shop, 2522-R Chicago Drive, S. W., Grand Rapids. The standard model locks only the striker, but positively, and the Auto-Selection model has as an extra a manually operated button to lock the bolt shut. This bolt lock goes off, as we'd insist, when the firing safe is pushed ahead for ready.

Sub-Caliber Practice. The Germans made .22 caliber insert barrels for some of their military rifles, the same idea that fathered the sub-caliber inserts for Luger pistols, those little tubes that took a bottle-necked copper cartridge loaded with a round ball of about .15-inch diameter. The idea was good, the application usually satisfactory.

More military practice came from air rifles made to resemble the service musket, and from .22s built on similar lines. A few have got here. Perhaps we have more of the sporter type Mauser .22s, single-shot and "clip" magazine bolt-actions with shortened forestocks. These smallbores look good, they perform rather well on target paper, and they're something different. The elaborate machining of the bolt cylinder calls forth admiration. It's an intricate, beautiful job, but the gasproof qualities of at least some of these Mauser .22s are not to be relied on. In firing almost any open-breech rifle it's wise to wear shooting glasses or at least the 16-hours-a-day specs, and actions like these make such protection mandatory. Case-heads of our modern rimfire ammunition rarely burst, and indeed some of the old, weak, strictly black powder design actions still in use demonstrate graphically how much our cartridge brass can bulge without bursting! But insurance is for the unusual.

Loose chambers are rather common in these little Mausers, and trigger pulls are liable to be neither this nor that—neither double-stage nor single-stage with clean release. Perhaps a spongy trigger pull helps in training recruits: never knowing when it's going to give, they can't flinch, and people do sometimes flinch when firing even a .22. But our American riflemen are trained to appreciate and use a clean, crisp trigger, and all in all I can't see a Mauser .22 trainer as a bargain if the same chunk of money will buy a Remington 513 or Winchester 75 in equally good condition. The weights of all three are closely similar, and in a rifle I'll gladly trade unquestioned accuracy, shootability, and the ready availability of spare parts for a rakish, sporty appearance and neat workmanship where it doesn't greatly matter.

Japanese Service Rifles

"Transformation?" That could be the word. You find a long, clumsy, distinctly odd-looking 6.5 mm. musket, inspect the bore and action, find them good, and give the gun the works. Off comes the two-piece stock, snugly though the halves are joined along a line running back from the lower part of the pistol grip. Away go the service sights, European style V rear and inverted V or barleycorn front. If our gun has one of the dust- and snow-proof sliding bolt covers we don't want that, either: unnecessary in ordinary hunting and inclined to be noisy. The straight-out bolt handle gets turned down, and unless we have one of the 19-inch carbines, which is short enough, anyway, the 30 (plus)-inch barrel comes back to 24 or so, and it'll handle nicely.

A restocking job, plain or fancy, built either for the iron sights or the scope we choose, is somewhat more than just a luxury, though the orginal wood can be altered and built up, too, if necessary. The result is a fine little deer and varmint rifle at pretty much the cost we've named, ourselves.

Brass? Norma now makes the semi-rimless 6.5 with American-style primer pocket, and loads it, too, if so

A Williams peep sight on the receiver of an Arisaka.

ordered, with 77- or 156-grain bullets. The same brand of cases, with 180-grain hunting bullets if wanted, comes in the other common Japanese caliber, the 7.7 or .303 or .31 with case length of about 57 mm.

Until this special brass became available it was customary to rechamber these issue barrels. The 6.5x50 became a 6.5x57 taking neck-expanded .257 Roberts cases and other forms, blown out or longer. The 7.7s have been used with reformed .30-06 brass, or chambered for that size. Either 7.7 method is dangerous.

Bert Shay gives a good, clear explanation. "The main worry about the 7.7s is strictly the *ammunition*, where cases are made of .30-06 brass, which is .012 to .015 inch too small at web [bottom of case], and particularly with WW2 fired brass (or new, for that matter) is dangerous with around full power loads. Instead of the case bulging, it *may* give out at the web, and here is the danger of the Model 99 action, the 7.7, because—and this is the *only* dangerous part— when the bolt is closed the slot through the locking lug for the ejector is *up*, and slanted toward the shooter's head. So if a case lets go, the particles of brass are directed at the shooter's head. This has caused one death that I know of."

The safe way out, and it was known years ago but isn't always followed, is to cut off the 7.7 barrel at the breech and rechamber for .300 Savage or .308 Winchester. Then we have a serviceable .30 caliber rifle, which usually does better with custom .311-inch bullets than with those of the standard .30-caliber .308-inch size.

Model 38 6.5 Arisakas are usually of better quality than the Model 99 7.7s. Some 6.5s were made for Japan by Italy, with Mannlicher-type bolts and Mauser-type magazines, and there have been Austrian made 6.5s, or Japanese copies, with hook safety on the cocking piece. These are uncommon, and they rate more thorough examination and test firing than the Arisakas, which, now they are rather well known, are considered among the best of bolt action designs. I think that it was gunmaker P. O. Ackley who first

proved their strength, over here, with exhaustive test firings. Practically everyone was surprised at the results he turned up. They can be regarded as definitive of the general class, though test of any possibly doubtful specimen—of any rifle—is certainly in order.

The enclosure of the case-head is practically complete. The steel may not equal the best modern types, but it's unlikely to be inadequate to the job. After all, proof-firing of any firearm is mandatory, isn't it? The best factories and arsenals do it.

In quality of finish the Model 99 is inferior to the 38, more stampings are used, and in general the rifle is less attractive to most of us. But when used with proper ammunition it is considered a safe arm. Slotting a locking lug to make passage for the ejector's blade to ride through isn't good modern practice. On the Winchester 70, for instance, the bolt face at the left of the top lug is slotted, and on the Remington 721-722 and the Schultz & Larsen there's no slot at all, the ejector being built into the bolt-face. The main thing is to use sensible loads in brass that fits the chamber correctly, and to have glass in front of your eyes when you fire any open-breech rifle, whether it's bolt, lever, slide, or single shot.

These Japanese actions have the cock-on-closing bolt and a rather unusual safety; otherwise they're practically '98 Mauser. The safety is a large button at the rear of the bolt—push in and turn right to lock—and it has the merit of affording some protection from gas if a primer is pierced. It isn't woods-handy, but it could be altered or replaced. A somewhat similar safety on the Italian Carcano 6.5 made for Japan turns left to lock, then goes back an inch or so to ease tension on the mainspring. These rifles aren't common, and neither are the 7.7 Japanese copies of our Garand. Only collectors who need a specimen would regret their scarcity.

French Rifles

France has used a great variety of military rifles, the 1886 8 mm. being about the first of all smokeless-powder smallbores. The one we are most likely to find in this country is the 1907-16 Lebel, carbine or rifle. After World War I a great many went into the woods after game, and our factories loaded the 8x50 rounds with a 170-grain soft point at 2640 f.s. velocity. It was a good killer of deer and black bear. Three-shot clips were used, and five-shot for the 1916 model.

The French service bullet, Balle D, was finely pointed and boat-tailed, too. It was truly a "solid" bullet, being made of copper alloy, with no lead core, and the weight ran from about 197 to 203 grains. Such a bullet might dive and cartwheel in heavy game, as the old 150-grain full jacketed .30-06 often did, and either might fail to do anything but needle straight through.

In its day the Lebel served well as a cheap but sound hunting rifle. Deer shooters were much better equipped with it than with some of the little .25-20s and .32-20s we still see carried in the woods by hunters who don't know better. Those who understand the game usually demand a reasonably powerful cartridge, no pipsqueak, even though their skill *could* let them use a pistol-type load and kill cleanly with it when everything worked just right.

If 8 mm. Lebel rounds go off the market it is possible to form cases from .348 Winchester brass. Loading tools, molds and jacketed bullets ought to be available indefinitely.

The succeeding French rifles—though all sorts of arms had to go into service in both world wars—are even less desirable than the Lebel, to the average American hunter. These are the MAS or MAC in two versions. The Model 1934 uses a Mannlicher type of action, but with a staggered or double-column box magazine, and the 1936 resembles a Mauser. By some curious psychological quirk the designers slanted the bolt handle *forward*. Like the Lebel, these rifles have no safety lock. Bolt lugs lie at the rear, and this action is not recommended for conversion to an American caliber. Neither should .30-06 brass be reformed to fit the chamber of this .30 caliber, a 7.5x54. The head of the case, just above the extracting groove, is of about .015-inch greater diameter than the 06, and that's too much. On the credit side we can say that the bolt cylinder is generous diameter, and that up front it makes a good enclosure for the case-head. Yet these rifles are for the collector, not the hunter. That would be well to remember if, as seems unlikely, a number of them was to be dumped in our import warehouses.

But the old 8 mm. Lebel has earned a place among our big-game rifles of the past. Few would care to buy it now, except perhaps as a spare.

Candidates for Go-By

There are a few other foreign military rifles on which the best advice might be to "give 'em the go-by." Most of them have at least a few admirers who are grateful for the good service they've had from them. Yet none of them seems to offer any particular advantages except economy. Usually a few more dollars will buy a satisfactory old American sporter— bolt, lever or slide—in equally good condition and taking a cartridge that's still made here.

The ill name of the *Moisin-Nagant 7.62x53 Russian* came from conversions. Rechambered for .30-06, some of them blew up, and there were tragic results. The hard, "brittle" receiver is considered safe with good 7.62 mm. ammunition, which for some 20 years was made here in sporting style but now has been dropped. It isn't a case to try to duplicate, as I see it. Efficient, of course, but in shape it is about as oriental as a pagoda. For some reason its base is round, not flat. Perhaps that is to ease feeding, though a special interrupter prevents more than one cartridge at a time from climbing out of the magazine. Some of the cases for the straight-falling-block Remington Hepburn single shot were rounded at the bottom, but not like this one.

Good shooting on the range and in the hunting field has been done with the Russian rifle, and more yet will be done. For it has its following, and some specimens have been sporterized to nice appearance and lively handling. Bullets for it should mike about .310 inch, generally, though it has done all right with the usual .308-inch jacketed. In handloads it's taken the standard .30-caliber line from 110 to 220 grains' weight.

But there remains the matter of case supply, and few would want them made to order. Just wouldn't be worth it. There also remains the thought of where that rifle saw service—unless it was one of the many that never got out of this country—and of the kind of service it rendered.

The *Russian Tokarev 1940* semi-automatic is an interesting military arm, and no more. Case-head enclosure is practically complete, not difficult when a rimmed round is used, and the gun is a little less clumsy than the *Simonov 1936*. Its shorter box magazine holds 10 instead of 15 cartridges. Full automatic models also were made, but those we couldn't use for hunting if we wanted to. We can let them all go by.

The *Rumanian '93 and Dutch '95 Mannlichers* in 6.5 rimmed occasionally get here, quite a number of the latter, in fact, a few years ago. The cartridge is excellent in design and performance and has been a favorite for single-shot and double rifles, too, as well as for combination guns. It's as useful to the hunter as the closely similar rimless 6.5 Mannlicher-Schoenauer, but the difficulty of finding or making brass (as from .303 British) keeps it out of general use here.

These Dutch and Rumanian rifles require a special five-shot clip when used as repeaters. So does the *Austrian Mannlicher-Steyr*. This is a straight-pull bolt action that locks up front, not at the rear by means of a swinging wedge on the under surface of the breechblock, in the manner of some earlier and more clumsy-looking Austrian rifles. The cartridge is the rimmed 8x50, short and stubby, but capable of being handloaded to woods usefulness. It might be possible to form this brass from .33 Winchester cases, which themselves are becoming a little difficult to buy. The 8x50 is only about .004 or .005 inch smaller, just above the rim. This suggestion isn't meant to be downright *practical* or to apply to full-power loadings. It's only for the advanced experimenter. Any radical re-working of cartridge brass down near the head can be dangerous, and the 1895 action hasn't a great margin of strength. With its own arsenal loads it has built up a long record of fair service.

The *Italian Mannlicher-Carcano,* originally an 1891 design, also has the open-bottom magazine, with the clip falling out as the last cartridge is picked off by the forward moving bolt. Calibers are 6.5 and 7.35 mm., not easy to obtain here. The 6.5 case is about one millimeter shorter than that of the Mannlicher-Schoenauer sporter, and some of these Carcanos have been so sloppily chambered that perhaps the M-S rounds could be forced into them. This isn't advisable; in fact, the Italian rifle is a good one to steer clear of. At least one man was killed when one of these arms failed. Escaping gas from a pierced primer drove the firing pin straight back out. It isn't secured in the bolt like that of the Winchester 70, for instance.

Danish and Norwegian Krag-Jorgensens are well made, but their single front locking lug holds them down to ammunition of about 40,000 p. s. i. pressure. So conversions to American calibers hardly seem worth while. We have our own Krag and the fine .30-40 cartridge to shoot in it. The Danish rifle dates back to 1889 and uses a rather large-bodied, rimmed 8-mm. case. Its loading gate swings forward instead of out to the right as on our Krag and the Norwegian. The latter takes a special rimless 6.5-mm. cartridge, and some of the later rifles were made in sporting style with short forestocks, for snipers, and for sale to hunters.

The *Swiss Schmidt-Rubin* in 7.5 mm. is practically a .30 caliber, and an exceedingly well made arm, as we'd expect. Like most other military models, our own included, it has gone through a good many variations. The action is a straight-pull bolt, and the odd-looking ring at the breech is the safety. Some of these rifles have been imported lately and offered for sale at low prices. However, the unusual features of the action, its rear locking system, and the lack of American-made ammunition keep it from becoming popular as a hunting arm. Although it's a far better arm than the French 8 mm. Lebel, which saw much use here for 20 years or so after World War I, there are so many other rifles available now—and plenty of loose change to spend on them—that this good Swiss job hasn't much chance. It doesn't seem likely that our ammunition factories will tool up for this size. All but one of them have their own rifles to sell, anyway.

You don't see as many of the *Canadian Ross* straight-pull .303s as you used to. Many have worn out, for it became customary to chamber the military arms loosely in order to ease case extraction under the rough conditions of trench warfare, which sometimes included prolonged rapid fire, and extraction was almost impossible after it got hot. The Ross couldn't pry a battered or dirty case loose with the comparative ease of a good turnbolt. Surplus military rounds loaded with cordite powder were cheap to buy after the war, but not cheap to use, for they burned out barrels pretty fast.

Then there is the bad safety record of the Ross, still debated, but there it is. Almost any Ross centerfire—perhaps not the straight-pull single shot .22s—can be assembled improperly, so that the locking lugs won't grip when the bolt is shoved forward. It seems that Mark III and Model 10 rifles with serrated lugs were the worst, though the 1905 Mark II or Mark II** bolts, with solid lugs, also have been assembled wrongly, and have blown out. Correction has been made, as described in Chapter 21, but too late to save the *general* reputation of the Ross.

We find a few riflemen who know and like this rifle, but they understand it and take due precautions. Sporters came in desirable calibers, the Ross .280, an early magnum, and the familiar .303. A few were made in .30-06 and .35 Winchester. Too many rifles of Ross make have been chambered so loosely and overbored so much that accuracy was practically non-existent. Yet one of the few sophisticated riflemen I've met who admitted ever having found a brand new factory rifle satisfying in every respect was a Ross owner. His particular pet was a Model 10 .280. This man was the author of perhaps the first full-size book ever published on handloading ammunition, and of course he was particular. If such a rifleman is to give full approval, every detail must be right, and this rifle had them: trigger pull, action smoothness, ballance, sighting equipment, and that ultimate, the record punched out on target paper.

Ammunition Supply

Before we buy an odd-sized foreigner the question of feeding it had better come up. A double-barrel elephant rifle is going to fire imported rounds, and for the purpose that's all right. We buy enough for practice, too, not wanting any mere nodding acquaintance with the gun before we emplane for the tropics. For extensive use in this country, ammo supply is to be considered.

At present this problem, when it exists at all, is simpler than at any former time, barring the fact that some good old rounds have gone out of production in overseas factories. Many of these were long popular for use on the thick-skinned or "great" game. But here are a few sources that may help when we can't form American brass and be sure that the product is safe to use.

Norma rounds include the 6.5 and 7.7 Japanese, 6.5x54 (or 53) Mannlicher-Schoenauer, 6.5x55 Swedish, sporting 8x60, which isn't too hard to make from .30-06 brass.

The Shell Shop, 3705 Sunset Blvd., Los Angeles 26, has 6.5 brass for the Japanese Arisaka, Italian Mannlicher-Carcano, and Austrian Mannlicher-Schoenauer.

Philip J. Medicus, 18 Fletcher St., New York 38, is a well-known ammunition specialist. He handles modern, obsolete and foreign cartridges.

Any of these three, and others like them, can be expected to extend the range of their offerings as demand and opportunity warrant it.

Frank H. Miles, Box 324-R, Bedford, Va., turns cases from brass. They go from black-powder obsoletes to odd but often desirable foreigners like the 7x73 Vom Hofe magnum. He duplicates the size and shape of your sample.

CHAPTER 12

SOME of the most pleasuring shootin'-irons I ever had were second-hand when they came my way. A few may have been third-, fourth- or fifth-hand. No matter: they gave good service and were no end of fun to use. At least three or four were the best I ever saw or heard of in their class, and I'm not trying to kid myself or anyone else.

There was a dark fringe to the picture. Time and again I was cheated when buying sight-unseen, and who hasn't been? More about those perils, later.

ADVANTAGES

There are good reasons for buying a second-hand rifle, even a rather old one. Outstanding, in a certain mood, is the thought that rifles made over 15 years ago, let's say, have a quality of workmanship and finish, though hardly of any raw materials except the walnut, that we meet today only with amazement! That's laying it on a bit thick, but notice, next time, and compare.

Notice the joining of wood and steel; run your fingernail over it. Are there abrupt stepdowns? Well, maybe some, and wood does swell with heat or dampness, and contract with the opposites, but on a high-grade rifle or even an inexpensive little .22 pump, maybe, the junction is likely to be pretty smooth. Note the quality of the walnut. A standard-grade rifle that cost perhaps $25 some 50 or 75 years ago—if we look that far back—may have stock wood that today would be of super-de luxe quality. This is natural: military and sporting requirements have made good walnut scarce. The quality of steel finish seen so often now can't be helped, I suppose, with the costs of labor, material and overhead as high as they are. We get our values in other matters, equally and in fact more important.

There's the unquestioned strength of modern actions, the generally superior bedding of steel in wood for accurate shooting, and the still fluid detail of stock design that's planned to make marksmanship a less difficult art to master. Different methods of rifling, such as broaching, the use of many more grooves than were commonly seen in the past, and new protection of rifling, like chrome or moly-kote covering, are fluid too, no longer experimental though probably not yet fully exploited for good.

There were famous barrels in the past—usually too exceptional—though it's common to find run-of-mill oldtimers without the faintest sign of tool-marks running down their grooves and lands. Notice also their sleek outside finish. As a rule we have to pay a pretty high price not to get a modern factory barrel that isn't triple-purpose—just a barrel, not a nail-file and a match-scratcher in overtime.

Special Purposes

Some of us buy a used rifle for a special purpose. There are, for instance, no light, long-barreled lever actions made now. In that class, about 22 inches is

USED RIFLES

the longest; the 24-inch styles are heavier. But Winchester and Savage both made them in the past, the former up to 26 inches in .25-35, .30-30, .32-40 and .38-55—and later in .219 Zipper—and the Savage up to 24 inches in .300. Their weights went little if any over seven pounds, and for a bigbore brush gun there was the 22-inch 1886 Winchester .45-70 that was still lighter. Sure they're hard to find, for people still like them for certain kinds of hunting, but they haven't passed out of existence. Then there are the old heavy-barreled lever guns, standard weight in their time. With plenty of muzzle-steadiness they're often worth buying, worth restocking, too.

Some of us like an old model better than a current one because of its lines, because it carries more easily, because the hang of its trigger and the location of its safety or hammer spur seem handier—any number of reasons. It could be caliber, too, and your real crank sometimes buys a rifle for which the ammo is no longer made. He has or can get or can form a supply of brass, and though he's a crank he's practical, too. He knows just what he wants in the ballistic line, for some kind of shooting he loves to do.

Interest

Lots of us buy old rifles because some romance of the past makes them interest us. Or our interest may be more practical: we want to know what a certain rifle and its cartridge will do. Therein lies challenge, and the results of our loading and firing may turn up something that's entirely "practical." That'll put the hard-headed guys at the club in their place, won't it?

How I wish I'd bought that low-wall Winchester single-shot .32 Ideal back in the mid-'thirties! Perfect

173

in and out, tools, mold, and a fair supply of still re-loadable brass with it. When those cases had worn out and if I couldn't get any more I could have had the barrel cut off at the breech, shortening the chamber about 7/16 inch for .32 Winchester Self-loading brass. Then I'd have had a "new" black powder case to develop loads for! Yes, those .32s also were discontinued two or three years ago, but you bet I'd have had laid in a stock of them. All I'd have needed was their brass: the bullets would have been nearly .003 inch too small for the Ideal barrel, most likely.

That is the sort of figuring a fellow's apt to do when he buys an old rifle for the interest it holds for him. Yet there's any number of less pleasant ways of going insane, and something like the one just hinted at would be my choice.

Economy

There is also the matter of economy, and we needn't have ancestors from north of the Clyde to be able to figure that buying a used rifle in perfect or as near as never-mind perfect shape for about 75 percent of retail shows sense, if the gun's going to suit us. If it's a discontinued model—though thoroughly satisfactory—we might get it for still less. Some of these do command a high price because so many shooters regret their ever having been dropped. Examples are the Remington 81 auto and 141 pump, and the Winchester lever gun when barreled for that still popular .218 Bee. The Remingtons went out because new and radically different models succeeded them, and the 65 Bee was replaced by bolt actions, several of them, not all, made until recently.

Then too, we can get a perfectly serviceable used rifle at a much lower price than a new one costs, unless we're concerned about the outside appearance. Refinishing the wood is an interesting home workshop job, and reblueing isn't expensive when you think of the cost of a new rifle.

OBJECTIONS

There can be drawbacks to this business of buying a used rifle. Perhaps the most serious is the matter of ammunition. Even the handloader can be stumped. At the close of the chapter preceding this one we listed, just as a hint, a few sources of supply.

There's also the want ad. *American Rifleman* columns are helpful in tracking down hard-to-get ammunition—or guns, for that matter. So is *The Shotgun News*, Columbus, Nebraska, which is almost 100 percent ads, many of them asking for or offering real oldtime metallic-cartridge stuff.

Three of the many ways to keep an oldtimer in service. *Top:* Like it enough to never quite let it go. It began as a 1903 or 03 for its .22 Winchester Automatic cartridge, later was restocked in modern style by Thomas Shelhamer. After the Model 63 came out, for .22 long-rifle ammunition, the old 03 was sent to the factory and its stock and sights transferred to a 63 action and barrel. Rear sight is a Marble Flexible, front a Redfield gold bead, flat-topped Patridge style.
Middle: Like it enough to have it converted. A rusted-out .22 short Low Wall Winchester single shot was rebarreled by Charles Canoll with a .25-20 WCF Model 43 Winchester bolt gun tube, then fitted with one of his gas-proof firing pins. Sights are Lyman 1-A rear and ivory bead front. The original wood was used, only the top of the forestock touching the barrel, and excellent accuracy resulted.
Bottom: Like it so much that someone takes pity on you and makes up brass for handloading. Ammunition for this single-shot, rolling-block Remington, .40-50 bottle-necked, was rarely available after the 1920's. Tom Florich formed cases by necking down and shortening .45-70, and this 70-odd-year-old rifle is still active. Sights were installed by William Lyman himself. They are the old woods favorite tang peep and ivory bead front. *Courtesy Gun Digest.*

All this sort of thing is for the specialist, the rifle-crank who's rather well informed, and willing to go to some trouble to get or to work up what he wants. The average shooter is generally better satisfied with buying a rifle that takes currently made ammunition. If arms are still being made for the caliber of his choice, that's better yet. When none has been manufactured for 20 years or so he'd best be a bit dubious. A fellow hates to say it out loud, for fear of giving ideas to the streamlining school of thought at Bridgeport, New Haven and East Alton, but here are some examples: .25 Stevens, .25-35 Winchester, .303 Savage, .32 Remington. All are excellent cartridges still, and we have absolutely nothing ready-made to fill the place of the first one. It's a bitter admission to make, but a business handling an excess of detail must slim down or shut down. We still ask for new types of factory cartridges, don't we? Who hasn't thought of certain gaps that ought to be filled? Some of us even write in and make a suggestion.

Action Strength

Practically any old centerfire American rifle is safe with the ammunition made for it today—and usually made for later models too, some of them still in production. This is distinctly not true of rimfire rifles. There are cheap ones like the old Hamilton single shot and pump repeater, and ancient, light, black-powder designs such as the Stevens Crack Shot, Marksman and Favorite, and the Remington No. 6. A few of the more expensive old repeaters, and one old automatic, are hardly to be recommended for use with .22 long-rifle high-velocity cartridges, even though the power of these loads is limited and their cases are made strong to protect those who just will take the chance of firing them in arms designed when today's rimfire ballistics were only a dream.

The centerfire rifle in sound condition and originally made for a cartridge still being manufactured can almost without exception be considered safe. Just one "high velocity" type of oldtime cartridge that needs comment is still loaded, the .32-20 with 80-grain hollow-point bullet. It is *not* for 1873 Winchester repeaters or Colt or Smith & Wesson revolvers, and probably not for light single-shot rifles like some of the Remington rolling blocks. The Colt slide action rifle has used it, but I doubt that it was really wise to try it. The .25-20 repeater cartridge came out for a new, strong series of rifles, Winchester '92 and Marlin '94, and both the 60-grain hollow point and the old 86-grain soft-point High-Velocity loads were safe in all standard arms of this caliber.

But there are conversions—rechamberings and rebarrelings—to give shooters more power. An old .38-55 Savage, for instance, made over into .300 might not have the necessary action strength. This sort of thing is a bit uncommon, though when we buy a used rifle we do well to dig back into its history, if we can.

Parts

Long-obsolete models in sound condition may suffer a broken part and be hard to repair except at a high price. Most of the good ones go through two or three human generations without breakages, provided they get decent treatment.

Modern guns too can break down, but the parts are available. Even in fall time, two or three weeks at the most ought to bring in the spares, and we may not even have to ask a harried gunsmith to fit them. But many oldtimers have no stock of parts laid by for them at the home factory. Making them by hand takes time and skill, both marketable items that bring a good price today. Even so, this liability needn't scare us off from buying an old rifle that we really want.

Stocks

The usual Kentucky rifle stock had excessive drop at comb and heel and its buttplate was curved for off-the-arm firing. This design was popular, without much change, right up into the 1920s. Today's stock is straighter, its comb is likely to be a high, forward-sloping Monte, and its buttplate is by comparison to the Kentucky as flat as some parts of that fascinating empire called Texas. Probably half the rifle shooters of today—more, when you think of the thousands of kids who are learning the game on NRA-sponsored ranges—never saw the rounded steel crescent of a "rifle buttplate."

These old stocks are more usable than some of our best shots seem to think, but they are distinctly not for scope sights. Except for Schuetzen target rifles, which had fairly high combs and usually cheek-pieces too, hardly any had a scope in front of them. Before World War II, practically all American sporters that were stocked for glass were custom built. By that I mean, here, they were specially stocked either at home or in a shop. Even the full-faced individual wasn't really well fitted for scope shooting with the usual factory stock, though some cheek-pieces helped. There were a few exceptions, the Remington 30-S and 720, some Mossberg .22s—not many others.

So the scope shooter who buys a used rifle may have to figure on a stock buildup, wood or pad, whichever suits him. But suit him it must, if he's to develop every bit of the skill that's latent in him.

Sometimes a lower front sight will do a good deal for an old, crooked-stocked rifle. Or there can be a buildup, if it's needed for irons. Or the shooter may find—some do—that a little more drop than is modern will do all right when he's wearing heavy clothes. They put his face farther back on the stock, where it's thicker, and not always much lower. For snapshooting in timbered country the additional drop may be just right. I shouldn't call this a common experience.

Resale Value

A discontinued model is usually hard to sell. So is a rifle with a pitted barrel, when so many good ones are around, most of them made since non-corrosive ammunition came in. Resale may never come up, if we become fond of that old rifle.

On the other hand, an oldtimer may bring as high a price as was paid for it, or higher. It pays to keep it in good shape, not to use loads that will burn out its barrel—loads it never was meant to take—and to treat it with the respect and care it deserves. Refinishing the wood helps; reblueing, unless it's well done, is worse than leaving it alone. Lots of us admire the signs of honest wear, for they're different from the signs of abuse!

There must be no hurry in selling it. Somewhere, almost surely, there are potential buyers who'd love to have it. Usually you find them by advertising in the sort of print that guncranks read. These folks are of three kinds: collectors, shooters, and both.

HOW TO BUY

The bargaining is your own business. In fact, it may never come in. Someone has exactly what you want and you're willing to pay a fair price for it. He asks just that, and there you are. To try to go further is fun to some people; to others it's pointless, and the sale or the swap is made.

There are responsible dealers and individuals who offer used guns for sale, and there's the other kind. From the latter a description of the gun's condition may be as meaningless as any lie—just a noise made with the mouth or a foul-up of written words that carry no message of reality.

In its "Arms Chest" department *The American Rifleman,* the NRA's monthly magazine, has set up a code of description that dealers all over the country follow, or pretend to follow.

"New" means just that, and "New—Discontinued" means that the gun has never been sold at retail, although it's one of a model that's gone out of production. A "perfect" gun—or its bore condition, outside finish and so forth—is like new in every respect. "Excellent" implies little use, no marring, no blue wear except at the muzzle or on sharp corners. A "very good" gun is in perfect operating condition, shows no appreciable wear on working surfaces, no rust or pitting, and only minor dents or scratches. The term "good" is more elastic, less definite: it implies safe working condition, no broken parts, only minor wear on working surfaces, and no rust or pitting that will interfere with proper functioning. Here we'd want to know exactly the condition of the bore and the woodwork, and the snugness of the breechup. "Fair" is safe but not much more. A "poor" gun is badly worn. It may need rather extensive repairs to put it into working condition.

In a way, a would-be seller's failure to regard these terms as having any meaning may not be too serious to a careful buyer. Those who ship guns for inspection should agree to accept a return and to make refund if the piece is unsatisfactory. If we ask for

inspection privileges in the delivery office before we accept the gun, we should get them. As a rule we have to pay the return charges as well as the incoming. Credit offered instead of a refund isn't good enough, it seems to me. Our money is our own, to spend where we like.

Unless the dealer has a hard mover, a gun he hasn't been able to get rid of in a reasonable time, he may not be willing to take it off his rack long enough for it to go out on approval. There are noteworthy exceptions, however, and these fellows are likely to believe that their stuff is up to claim and worth the price they ask. Shipping on approval is part of their service to the public.

INSPECTION

Time for inspection may be limited, as in an express office, or it may include test firing, if you've asked for it and are known to be the sort of person who gives proper care to a gun. Usually the look-over takes place in a store, in the seller's home, or in our own home.

Barrel

In a rifle, bore condition is of first importance to most of us. For woods hunting of deer and bigger game, or of rabbits, a barrel *can* be in rather bad shape and still do satisfactory work. If the rifling lands at the muzzle and for a foot or so below it still stand up sharply and aren't badly pitted we might get about half the accuracy, with jacketed bullets, that the barrel used to deliver. We might get more, but a rough barrel seldom shoots worth a hoot with lead bullets, even when they're full- or slightly oversized, and hardened. A high-intensity varmint rifle, eroded above the chamber, isn't likely to give more than, say, a quarter of its original accuracy. All these degrees vary with the condition of the individual barrel, and with the general assembly of barrel, action, and stock.

Many barrels in calibers that haven't been made for a long time, or even for a few years, are not replaceable at the factory. They could let us in for reboring and rechambering, or for complete rebarreling. Such corrections could be worth while. The action, the woodwork, the engraving, or just the rareness or unfamiliarity of the model may tempt us. Why not?

But usually we look at the barrel first, and it must be clean and free of oil if we're to see its condition. For examining the breech end of solid frame lever guns, and some others, a barrel reflector like the old Winchester or the current Borescope is essential. Use a good light. It does no harm to wipe out the barrel, yourself, with two or three really tight patches. I've known of a bigbore tube that had been doped up with beeswax!

A super-accurate bench or varmint rifle that's lost half its accuracy may be offered at a surprisingly low price, with no pleasant surprise awaiting the buyer.

Newton cartridges were respected so highly that many special rifles were made for them in later years. This Griffin & Howe .256 has a 26-inch Poldi Anticorro barrel, Zeiss four-power scope in Griffin & Howe double-lever side mount, and Model 1898 Oberndorf military Mauser action. With correct loading and holding, 1¼-inch 100-yard groups are common. *Photo courtesy Combat Forces Press.*

Often it's hard to see the throat erosion with the naked eye.

Action

Most modern and fairly modern actions will wear out several barrels. Some lever and pump guns may not. Headspace gauges check the breech-up of bolt actions and some others, such as single-shot falling blocks of good quality. Any obvious, abnormal gap at the breech of a pump or lever gun is bad. An extremely slick action may be off-color, too: someone may have polished essential steel off the locking lugs or the locking bolt. This can increase headspace dangerously.

A broken firing pin or extractor may escape a casual look-over. So may the *general* suitability of an old action for modern loads. An unusually light trigger pull may have been adjusted so, or it may have worn because the engaging parts are soft. If the pull is really ragged, full of creep, that fact may mean little to a skilled home workman, though the pull of some hammerless rifles is difficult to smooth into a clean release. Check the hold of the half-cock notch on a hammer rifle.

Stock

A beat-up appearance of the stock and the outside of metal parts may be a sign of less obvious damages caused by abuse. Such a stock seldom accompanies a perfect barrel and it may go along with broken or rusted action parts. Or it may mean that only a refinishing job is needed.

Cracks running down from the receiver tangs may have come from serious abuse or poor inletting, often from both, and a stock that's badly cracked can't be expected to contribute to good shooting with loads of even moderate intensity. Poor bedding around the receiver of a bolt gun usually, not always, indicates indifferent accuracy. If a forestock bears hard against one side of the barrel and not against the other we can expect that barrel to "walk" its shots across the target as it warms up. Skilled amateur bedding, as with glass, can correct most if not all faults.

Sights

The particular and we might say the skilled rifleman seldom finds any "as is" sights to suit him. But good iron sights for hunting aren't expensive, and anyone who plans to buy a first-class hunting or target scope expects to spend quite a piece of money on it.

It is true, of course, that the light plinking scopes are worth several times their price in actual seeability, compared to irons, unless the shooter has remarkably fine eyesight.

Sometimes we get an entirely satisfactory set of sights on a used rifle. If the rear sight—a tang peep, particularly—has worn loose, it can be tightened at the factory or at a gunsmith's.

Most old model hunting rifles except the bolt guns and the Winchester '95 lever action had holes ready drilled, and plugged, for tang sights. Now attention has gone, in most cases, to the receiver; it's the popular type of peep sight today. Lots of rifles aren't ready for either peep or scope, but having them drilled usually costs little. It pays to see that you get competence and care in this little job.

Now we can go on to examine the main types and a few examples of the rifles that are most commonly offered in desirable used condition. Contemporary models and military arms needn't be discussed here, only a few of the "obsolete" but still useful rifles of American make.

BOLT ACTION

Early models like the black-powder Hotchkiss and Remington-Keene, or the .30-40 Blake high-power with its big seven-shot spool magazine, are collectors' items. Some do go hunting, but we'd hardly buy one for that purpose alone. For less money we could, almost always, get a more modern arm that would do as well or better in the field.

Newtons

Occasionally one of these sporters goes on sale, though it seems that most Newton curators like to keep their own for the good that they have done and still do. The cartridges were famous as being among our first really high-velocity rounds. Only four have been used at all commonly, and perhaps most of those rifles never fired a Newton bullet.

Charles Newton's thoughts on almost any shooting subject deserve a digression from any carefully planned-out discussion of rifles any old time; so here goes! When most high velocity bullets were jacketed with cupro-nickel he had the sense to use plain copper instead. It cut down barrel fouling, and how! He also tried paper insulation around the soft lead cores of jacketed bullets in the hot class, for some, like the

.22 Savage High Power, actually had melted in flight, and once in a great while we see that today, or at least a little swirl of lead around a bullethole in target paper, when a soft nose melts. In the latter case we do sometimes get fine accuracy, still and all.

He knew, and so did others, that a plain soft point can be badly blunted when it shucks forward in a box magazine, under recoil. So he designed one that couldn't—not ordinarily, at least. There was a two-diameter wire in the nose of his bullet. The small end, up front, was a protection against magazine battering, and the square shoulder below it helped to prevent setback of the lead when the bullet took off in a hurry.

His bullets in 123-grain .256, 172-grain .30, and 250-grain .35 are collectors' gold now. In their day they were bought, when available, for handloading almost any cartridges of those calibers.

The smallest Newton caliber was the .22 with that long 90-grain bullet of about .228 inch diameter. Its case was a neckdown of the 7x57 mm. Mauser. Shortened .30-06 brass formed the .256, which Western Cartridge loaded with a 129 grain open point bullet. The other Newton cartridges, except the standard .30-06, were built on a special big-bodied, rather straight-sided rimless case of magnum size. The popular .30 and .35 were Western loaded with their 180- and 250-grain open points. The .276 (or 7 mm.), .280 and .333 are rare, but at least the barrels were made and used to some extent. Most Newton velocities were around 3,000 f. s. And all these calibers are strictly for handloaders now, with original brass scarce, though it can be duplicated.

Many varieties of "Newton" rifles were made, and the story is well told in Harry O. Dean's "America's First Wildcatter," in the April, '56 number of *Guns*. Mauser and early, single heat-treated Springfield actions were used, as well as Newton's own Mauser-type designs. Some of the early pattern Newtons with the small bolt handle—not the later type with a backward curve like the Enfield's bolt handle—were made improperly during the 1918 receivership of the company, and these wouldn't be considered safe. The Mausers are good, and the early and late Newtons. Proof-firing of any doubtful specimen is certainly advisable.

Newton actions in their various forms used one or more interesting features. The bolt sleeve safety lever lay at the right, about where we'd reach for a modern safe. Drawn to the rear, not shoved forward, it was ready for firing.

Some of these rifles had the serrated or multiple locking lugs like those of some Ross rifles, and coil instead of leaf magazine springs were used on a number of them, also in Ross fashion, Mr. Dean points out. A floorplate release button in the front of the trigger guard was similar to the one on the Model 70 Winchester, and takedown Newtons used the floor-

plate as a lever to turn the big stock dismounting screw. Not a good idea at all, in theory, though some of these takedowns shot rather well. On the other hand, many Newtons showed what we'd call mighty poor accuracy, not even good enough for big-game shooting at medium ranges. The chief reason seemed to be the oversize boring. This reduced pressures, and Newton wanted his rifles to deliver the advertised velocity. Some did, and in those days it was really fast, especially with bullets of reasonable weight for their caliber, like his.

There were also Newton set triggers, maybe the first on American bolt-action rifles, and some had the setting, not the firing trigger, reversed and up at the front of the guard instead of at the rear. A sort of Metford form of rifling was tried, too, with the grooves rounded and cut on an arc with shorter radius than that of the bore. Grooveless oval boring was advertised, but whether or not Newton used this old and seldom satisfactory form I don't know.

The outstanding contributions of Newton were his high-velocity cartridges and the stocking of his rifles. When he designed the .22 and .250 Savage loads he was held down in overall length by the size of the Model 99 lever gun's magazine. So bullet weights had to be low to develop the velocity figures needed for advertising. His stocks were not quite in the modern hunting-rifle style—their pistol grips were a little far back and their combs were a bit low—but they weren't far off from what we like today.

Winchesters

The Model 54 Winchester is still a long way from being outdated. You see quite a few of them. At first they weren't stocked even as well as the Newtons, but the NRA stock that came along about 1930 is highly satisfactory for iron-sight shooting. It has the full, close pistol grip, high comb, and buttplate slanted to give plenty of downpitch. The snobble came off the forestock tip and the forestock was made wider, though it's narrower than the one on the 70. Toward the last, the firing pin was locked securely in the bolt in 70 fashion. A transverse screw in the bolt sleeve does it.

There's no question of the strength of 54 actions for the cartridges they were made for, which in the later years included the .300 Magnum. If you find one in good condition and like its caliber, its build and its wing-type safety, that rifle is worth your thoughtful consideration.

There have been various changes in Winchester .22 rimfire bolt guns, mentioned before. Almost always we'd prefer the latest versions, though one discontinued rifle, *the Model 57*, is still called for in an occasional want ad. It's been described as "a little Model 52." This junior target rifle, made for .22 short- or long-rifle, with appropriate box magazines that will fit in other Winchesters of the type, has a 22-inch barrel and weighs only about five pounds. There's a great deal of drop to the stock and the pistol grip is rather bashful, but these details trouble a really small kid less than they do a grownup. Within limits, they help, if the stock is short enough.

The Model 56 is less often seen. It's similar to the 57 except for the sporter type forestock and lack of a barrel band to take the front swivel. The 57 is a solid frame gun, steel and wood anchored fore and aft, and it earned a great reputation for accuracy. We don't seem to have anything quite in its weight and style class now.

Remingtons

The Model 30 Remingtons that came out soon after World War I used the heavy 1917 Enfield action with few changes, and they were popular for only a few years. Not enough hunters had been converted to the bolt action, and it wasn't a good enough bolt gun. Basically it was sound, without question, but the trigger left much to be desired and the spindly stock was a transitional model from old to new. The steel butt-plate was narrow and curved, uncomfortable with heavy loads, the pistol grip small and too far back, and the forestock excessively tapered. In between lay the big receiver. Barrels were light and only 22 inches long. The .25, .30 and .32 Remington Auto-loading calibers gave no great punishment, but with the .35 Rem you began to feel recoil, and in .30-06 this rifle was something of a bruiser.

With well-fitting stocks, such as Belding & Mull supplied for a while as a varminting specialty for the accurate .25 caliber, the basic design of the 30 began to show its possibilities. In fact this custom job was excellent in almost all the details we look for now.

The improved Model 30-S Remington was modern, and we're more likely to see it than the old 30. Added calibers were the .257 Roberts and 7 mm. Mauser. The Roberts displaced the .25, the only Auto caliber regularly supplied in this model. Even the standard stock was satisfactory for a low mounted hunting scope, and the heavier barrel and woodwork brought the weight up to eight and one-half pounds or more. The *Model 720* followed it, with more refined lines that made for somewhat easier handling. To the standard 24-inch barrel length of the 30-S were added the 720's optional 20 and 22. We were getting closer to some modern preferences. The 720 added the .270 Winchester cartridge to the line.

Long before this, Remington had got away from the creepy "single-stage" trigger pull of early 30s, and the Enfield cock-on-closing striker. Although the .25 Remington was a pleasant-shooting little varmint cartridge up to about 200 yards, under average field conditions, it didn't survive the rest of the Auto line as bolt-gun ammunition for many years. After Remington had developed the .257 from Major Roberts' experiments with his super-accurate .25 wildcats, a few shooters did stick with their old .25 Rems. But some others had rechambering and bolt-face alteration jobs done. Rifle and ammunition tastes were changing.

We might still find one of the early Remington bolt-action single-shot .22s offered for sale. Essentially they're modern little guns, about as safe as the usual bolt action rimfire is from gas blowbacks, and well planned for accuracy. Remington didn't get into this field in the early days, as the other big companies did. The short-lived but popular *Model 34* tubular magazine repeater is still a good design, and all that I've seen showed the results of careful workmanship.

It will be a long time before the heavy-barreled *Model 37* target rifle becomes scarce on our smallbore ranges. Various minor improvements in lockwork appeared in its lifetime, and stocks grew heavier and more close-up at the comb. A 37 in good condition is still a sensible buy, at least for the beginner in target competition. As his shooting habits and technique develop, he may alter the stock to suit him. Plastic wood buildups may not look pretty, but we see them on target rifles because they help some people to shoot better. However, the latest 37 stocks are more likely to need sandpaper than wood putty, if they require any workover at all.

Savages

The Model 1920 Savage was, almost certainly, the first short-action high power bolt gun built by an American factory. It cost a lot less than the imported short Mausers and in most of the practical ways it was just as good. Bolt lockup—and the waggle-tail looseness of the bolt when it was drawn back—resembled those of the Mauser, and the Savage had the rare handiness of a shotgun type safety on its tang.

The light barrels measured 22 inches in .250 and 24 in .300 Savage, and gun weight was only about seven pounds or less. Yet accuracy was generally good, for these little rifles were well made. To get it you really needed a restocking job or a buildup, for this was an *early* American high-intensity bolt gun. The snobble-tipped forearm was small, the pistol grip too far back, though sharply curved, and the aluminum buttplate (or sometimes steel) was set on without enough down-pitch. Like contemporary lever actions, this rifle had a low stock comb.

These 20s, still often seen, would be worth rebuilding except for one fact, the far more gas-proof case-head enclosure of the 722 Remington short-action. If the shooter is conservative and safety-minded in his ideas of breech pressure, and if he's careful to use good cartridge brass, the old action might suit him to perfection. If he does much woods hunting with iron sights, that handy little sliding safe would tempt him. A later, longer Savage action of this type took the .30-06 as well as shorter rounds, but it's seldom seen. In barrel and stock lines this rifle resembled the early 54 Winchester.

Savage 40 and 45 rifles—the 45 had the extras of checkered wood and a peep sight—were rear-, not front-locked, but they were safe in .30-06 and in the lighter calibers offered—.250, .30-30 and .300. Detachable box magazines helped to keep the price down, but the familiar lever guns outsold them by a huge margin. Those rear-locking lugs shortened the bolt throw but couldn't put the gun into the lever-action speed class. The early model magazines protruded enough to make trail carrying slightly unhandy, and all in all, the public wasn't ready for a bolt action that sold at or a bit below the price of a lever gun. These Savages aren't bad at all, and in some ways they're more refined than the present Model 340. They cost more, too, considering the dollar's buying power at the time.

The Savage 1919 match rifle and 1922 sporter started a long line of truly revolutionary models: highly accurate but inexpensive bolt-action target smallbores and much better than average .22 hunting rifles. The first thing you noticed about that 1922, when you picked it up in the store, was its solid, substantial weight, six pounds or more, and the steadiness with which you could hold it. In a way, it instantly made the old favorite .22 pump actions and automatics obsolete. You still loved the little guns that had given you so much pleasure, but this new one was more businesslike.

The match .22s became heavier and better-stocked, with the *Model 1933 NRA* being still a desirable trainer. There were heavy-barrel .22s also, and some later action refinements such as fast locks. Most of these Savages are light enough for hunting, and within the limits of .22 rimfire power they do well. Some of them are light enough for some of us to use for snapshooting.

The 1923 and 23-A sporters really branched out. There were stock improvements, and in time the speed lock. What's more, this model number went into centerfire calibers. A longer and stronger action took the .25-20 and .32-20—23-B and 23-C. The 23-D was apparently the earliest factory Hornet, for Winchester developed the cartridge before adapting the big 54 action to it. These centerfires weighed around 6½ to 7 pounds, though there was a much heavier Hornet in semi-target styling. The 23-AA was the final and most improved .22 rimfire in this line.

Cash value depends on the lateness of the model, though not as much as on gun condition. The popularity and respect that these medium-priced bolt actions earned through the years—including the long stretch of a decade when most of us had few easy-spending dollars—warrant their quality. A well-kept specimen is certainly worth consideration, and only the early ones were poorly stocked for modern marksmanship technique. All of them—and many current rifles too—were designed without much thought of gas-proof security. With good ammunition there's no trouble, but a defective case can come along any time. As far as maintaining headspace under Hornet back-thrust is concerned, I think I'd prefer a modern 340 Savage. It takes the .222 Rem as well as the Hornet,

and there have been some complaints about the 23-D's durability. Naturally, handloads put up by a certain kind of rifleman would void any such criticism. If they could only breech up a battleship to a barrel they'd be all right.

In quality and comparative cost—bringing the dollar down to date—there doesn't seem to be any rim- or center-fire like the 23s made now. Perhaps a place between the Savage 340 and Winchester 43 would be the bracket. But streamlining economy killed the 43 in 1957.

Others

Light, inexpensive old single-shot .22s of Savage, Remington and Winchester make still show up, though the *Stevens Little Krag* is a rare one. Those with breech-bolts tapered up front, barely covering the case-head, are poor selections. Various odd repeaters turn up, including perhaps the scarce *Hopkins & Allen,* which is a real museum piece. When we get to the 1920s and '30s there are the *Mossbergs.* Those people were about the first to give us good stocking jobs on light .22s, and to feature inexpensive scope sights too.

The 44 Mossberg isn't greatly different from the present 144, and the *44-US* was a World War II training job. The only serious objection to the 44s is their forestock shape—deep, not wide. It seems to be no great handicap to some junior shooters I've coached, and they do well with the regular issue of iron sights.

LEVER ACTION

Our earliest form of popular repeater is still the biggest seller in the centerfire line, for big game, at least. The three familiar names hang on: Marlin, Savage and Winchester. There was nothing wrong with the *Stevens Model 425* that took the Remington Auto Rimless quartet, from .25 to .35, but time has nearly washed out even the memory of it. Once in a while one shows up in a merchant's stock. It can be a specimen or a shooting-iron, depending on its condition and on our need and interest.

Marlins

So many 1893 Marlins for the .30-30 class of cartridge were made that a few still turn up. The *1894 Model,* from .25-20 to .44-40, seems to be scarcer, and the *1895 Marlin* was like the 1886 Winchester, comparatively few made, for they were heavier, more powerful rifles. Its calibers ran from .33 Winchester smokeless to .45-90. Only the .45-70 rounds are still made for the '86 and '95 rifles. Earlier Marlin centerfires, most of them top-ejecting, are rare pieces. Few indeed still go hunting.

These '93 to '95 rifles in good shape are all right to fire with factory cartridges now made for them. The case-hardened receiver used on them continued down to the early years of the *late Model 36* .30-30 and .32 Special of almost identical design. A good '93 or 36 is a sensible buy, except one of the former made for Marlin's only proprietary smokeless cartridge, the .25-36. This case hasn't been manufactured for many years. It's a little larger at the base than the .25-35 Winchester, and its body is longer. Shoulder and neck aren't much different. If a case resizing die can be had, it isn't difficult to form its brass from .32-40, which is of about the right length.

Only Marlin has made lever action rimfire repeaters in great quantity and variety. The early solid frame .22 of 1891 is practically never found in good shooting condition. Small action parts and the barrels usually have worn or rusted out. However, a friend of mine has an 1892 in .32 rim—or centerfire—interchangeable firing pin—that's mirror-bright inside. He's done fine shooting with it, including short-range stuff with a cast round ball. Finally he decided to have it rechambered to take the .32 S. & W. Long case with its heavier, inside lubricated bullet, and the results were splendid. Charlie Canoll, in Waverly, N. Y., did the work. He's capable, and what's much more, careful.

The 1897 Marlin .22 (later the less age-revealing "97") is a little scarce. Like the 39 and 39-A that followed it, it's a takedown. With the 39-A came the modern high-comb stock and semi-beavertail forearm. The 97 seems to have been the last one made with octagon barrel, and the beautiful half-octagons went out long ago.

The Savage

The 1899 or 99 Savage has had its changes, few of them basic except in the strength of steel used in the action. Early models with the loaded-chamber indicator at the front of the breech-block were made for the .25-35, .30-30, .303, .32-40 and .38-55. If they're sound they should handle modern factory loadings with ample safety. They are rather doubtful actions to convert to .250 or .300, perhaps, not to mention the newly adopted .243, .308 and .358.

So far, the only discontinued Savage round is the .22 High Power. You still see its rifles offered for sale, and in solid frame they're tempting if the bore is good. That .22 is a fine little medium-range varmint caliber using .228-inch custom bullets, and .25-35 brass is a natural for case-forming. Hardly any factory loaded .22 HPs can be found now.

Winchesters

Most Winchester lever guns from the '86 on down stand around in used-gun racks—until someone snaps them up. Already there's a beginning of an old-Winchester-collecting hobby; so some that deserve to may never hunt again. Since most of the black-powder and a few of the strictly smokeless cartridges have been discontinued, the matter of ammunition supply crops up when we look over these guns. The only 1886 caliber left is the .45-70, and the 1895 box magazine rifle isn't much better off. All the 1892 Calibers—.25-20 to .44-40—and the 1894—.25-35 to .38-55—are still manufactured.

Later versions of these last two models are also OK on the nutrition problem, even with two added mouths to feed: .218 Bee in Model 65 and .219 Zipper in Model 64.

The Model 53 was a light-weight '92 for all the calibers except .38-40, and the *Model 55* was a standardized edition of the special 1894 Extra Light Weight. It took the straight smokeless rounds only: .25-35, .30-30 and .32 Special. These guns came in both solid frame and takedown styles. The former are still good hunting rifles if you don't mind a rather low comb, straight grip, and small forestock. To change the angle of the buttplate and give more down-pitch is easy when you fit a flat-surfaced recoil pad, not so simple when you use the slightly curved steel buttplate that came on the rifle.

The Model 65—a varmint or biggish small-game gun in .218 Bee, .25-20 and .32-20—seems not to have been made since World War II. It had a high-comb stock, pistol gripped, and most of the forestocks were rounded out and wide along the midsection. Quick-detachable sling swivels could be fitted to it at the factory, as to the recent Model 64. Few bolt actions in these three light calibers outshoot a good 65.

SLIDE ACTION

The black-powder Colts with exposed hammer are seldom seen afield in any of their calibers, from .22 short to .50-95. Still rarer is the Burgess .30-30, not a pump gun in the usual sense, for its pistol grip slid back and forth to operate the action. The forestock was fixed. There was also a Burgess-Colt .44-40, but this one was a lever action repeater.

Remingtons

The Remington slide actions date pretty well back, the *Model 12 .22* being a 1909er. In 1936 it became the Model 121.

These rifles, and the centerfire *Models 14, 14½ and 141,* were hammerless repeaters, Nothing new. The Savage 1899 deer rifle and 1903 .22 had won respect long before 1909.

Any of these Remingtons in good condition is desirable for practical use at moderate ranges. They are well-made arms in the high-price brackets. In planning them no attempt seems to have been made to undersell competitors. Model 12s we see now are usually the worse for wear, very much the worse for neglect and abuse. For most of these rifles, and the later 121s, spare parts should be available. These .22s had few and rugged parts, but before buying any discontinued rifle that needs replacements it's well to make sure.

The 14 took the rimless .25 to .35 Autoloading cartridges, but the 141 seems never to have been made in .25. The 14½ cost a little less than the 14 and its ammunition was inexpensive, .38-40 and .44-40. These two were fairly common as 18½-inch carbines.

Not many *Model 25* rifles or carbines seem to be left. Calibers were .25-20 and .32-20, of little use except in an accurate rifle, and the M25, like the rest of these early Remington pumps, was a takedown. Some shot better than others, the caliber being important, and the tightness of the lower tang that fitted into the open bottom of the good, solid receiver.

The Model 25 had the smooth breech lines of the .22s—some of the most beautiful little rifles ever made, really—and it was not much larger. The 14 and its followers of this type that preceded the 760 were less streamlined at the breech, more humped than flowing. Compared to a good many big-game rifles, though, they're glamorous.

The Standard Arms people made a hammerless pump action and a gas-operated autoloader for the Remington Rimless series. Now they are seldom seen afield, in a shop, or in a collection. Their lines were far from beautiful. More seriously, their reputation for smooth, reliable handling of their ammunition was exceedingly low.

It was too bad that the company hadn't the necessary big financial reserves to go on and perfect the actions before sending the guns out to market to bring in a cash refill. We *should* have had a gas-operated sporting autoloader of good repute long before we did.

A Bunch of .22s

Around the time of World War I a ".22 repeater" always was a slide action. The big companies made them—Savage, Winchester, Marlin and Remington—and never cut corners on variety. Sure, there were Marlin lever guns in almost any conceivable styling, and *Savage's Model 1911* bolt action .22 short was made for about four years. The parallel magazine tubes held a supply of 20 cartridges, and the one I bought and used for a while was a reliable little trick.

But when the kids in school talked .22 repeater they meant a pump gun. That was what perhaps 25 percent of them had set their hearts on, with an easy 25 percent more stringing along just to be normal and masculine and assertive.

You will actually find *Winchester 1890 and 1906 .22s*—stamped 90 or 06 after 1919—in used-gun racks. Almost always their barrels are as smooth and bright as a brick chimney that's listened to generations of human foolishness and sense. But some might be worth rebarreling, and the Model 62 is still made, isn't it? with scarcely any action changes except the coil mainspring instead of the flat one.

Marlins are less often seen—always were—though nearly all of them were good rifles, too. *Savages* got around, but the oldtimers have become scarce, even the *Model 1914,* with shotgun type safety. The *Model 25* with trigger-guard safety button never was as handy for the first shot. It had only four years of production life as compared to the ten of the '14.

The box magazine hammerless 1903 and the *lighter 1909* always fascinated some of us—still do. They were easy to load *and* unload, and we never minded missing the sight of a long mag tube out under the barrel. According to a recent Savage parts catalogue, all these rifles are now without parts or repair service, including the Model 25. The Savage 29, sometimes called Stevens 75, succeeded the 25 and is made in modern form as 29-G.

Let's not think that gun guts have eggshell durability. Few are that bad! A Savage 1914 still comes down to our junior range once in a while and functions perfectly, by ruling, as a single shot down there. Probably it'd handle a magazineful of mixed shorts, longs and long-rifles without any fuss, and many older rifles would do as well. It does seem that when using a split-receiver rifle, old Savage or Marlin, it's not a silly precaution to wear glasses. The receiver of the Remington 16 automatic, the one that uses special .22 cartridges, appears to be as gas-tight as almost any. Its two-piece assembly comes in handy only when we clean the action; it has nothing to do with the barrel-and-stock takedown business.

One comparative bigbore, the *Marlin Model 27 slide action* take-down with exposed hammer, got into this section with miscellaneous .22s. The round-barrel model took the .25 rimfire Stevens cartridge, and so, it seems, did some Stevens pump guns of much earlier vintage. The .25-20 and .32-20 Model 27 rifles had octagon barrels. Perhaps no one knows why, today.

One of these 27s with a good barrel and all its action parts in healthy condition could be a real find. The .25 rimfire—and the other two in light, small-game-hunting handloads—ought to shoot well in spite of the takedown feature. The gun was nicely styled, though a bit old-fashioned, and smooth operating in good Marlin manner. It weighed about six pounds and was meant for snapshooting. Barrels were 24 inches long and we wouldn't, today, call them featherweight.

Semi-Automatic

Among the oldtimers not much choice is left. The Winchester 1905 .32 and .35 and 1910 .401, like the Remington .25, are among the late and really quite often lamented factory cartridges. Each one did have its little domain of usefulness, and the .25 could almost have been an all-rounder, out east, anyway.

Winchesters

The .351 caliber Model 07 depended on the law-enforcement trade for its survival, I suspect. It used to be a pretty popular deer rifle in the woods, and some even went out west. A great many Model 1907s were sold, and their square little boxes of cartridges wait for the sweep of your eye along the shelves of most dealers. In 1957 the 07, along with the Models 43, 64, and even the .348 caliber 71, was discontinued. Some kinds of streamlining don't seem brilliant, at least to a few of us!

The original 1907s, and *the 07s as made for many years after 1919,* are alike to the thirty-second of an inch, we might say, but they're quite different from later-made 07s. They weigh about a half-pound less, and have hard rubber instead of steel buttplates. Their stocks are long—14 inches from trigger to buttplate, slimmer and trimmer, too, with a small pistol grip farther back; and their forestocks are a good deal thinner.

Corrosive-primed ammunition with Sharpshooter powder pitted most early .351s at the breech, and forestocks split under careless handling. The action was and is outstandingly durable among *all* types of repeating rifles. A semi-automatic is a self-operated repeater, while it works. These Winchester center-fires were famous for keeping on the job without quitting.

Our first semi-automatic rifle in general use was the *1903 Winchester* that took its own .22 cartridge. The round is still made and should hold out for a few years' production if those who own one of these top-quality beanshooters will occasionally buy some beans for it.

I couldn't calculate the hundreds or thousands of happy miles the old 03 rifles—both of mine were stamped so when I bought them new—have given me. Just to remember the places they were carried or canoed to, fits well into a pipeful of tobacco smoked on a hillside with the breeze in my face. But in view of the ammunition status I couldn't recommend the 03 to any buyer. Conversion to .22 long-rifle has been done, but it might cost more than buying a current Model 63, which has the shotgun-butt, high-comb stock that makes good shooting easier.

The Winchester 74 came first in .22 short, then in long-rifle. A later version cut the 24-inch barrel to 22 inches and slightly modified the stock. They were smooth rifles to handle and easy to shoot well.

Since the Model 77 succeeded the 74 only recently, the latter is a safe buy. Parts ought to be stocked for some time.

Remingtons

The Remington Model 8 high power is an old one—a 1906 model—and in 1937 gave way to the *modern styled 81,* which lasted until 1951. There were practically no changes except in the woodwork, although in its later years the 81 was adapted to the .300 Savage, with a head quite a bit larger than that of the old .35 Rem, and a good deal more backthrust.

In any caliber except the discontinued .25 either of these models is satisfactory for deer shooting up to about 150 yards, accuracy considered. Drawbacks to this action are so minor that the gun has made friends by the thousand, and it is not at all surprising to find a used one that's priced a little higher than a currently made 740 in equal condition. For some years, until people have forgotten the 8 and 81 record of satisfaction, this comparative valuation ought to

stand. Some dislike the protruding box magazine and bolt handle; yet these rifles have gone to far places in the hand. Guides soon learned to like them, and woodsmen of that profession are particular.

The Remington Model 16 .22 is most attractive, but its special cartridge is expensive, like the Winchester 03's, and not easy to find. High speed .22 longs, not .22 long-rifles, have been substituted, but the 16-inch rifling twist is much too fast for their short bullets, and not many riflemen like to be caught using this ammuntion, anyway.

The Model 24 for .22 short or long-rifle, not both, was a high grade arm. The only cheap thing about it was the ammunition, and for that dispensation everyone was thankful. The original barrel was only 19 inches long. Then came a 21, as I recall, and the re-stocked, modernized *Model 241* had the old favorite length of 24 inches.

Any 24 or 241 should handle either high or low velocity cartridges without trouble if the action is clean and oiled. Dismounting it to give it care is easy. To avoid shift of sighting zero, be careful not to change the adjustment of the ring at the barrel breech. It's to be used only when and if a tighter assembly becomes necessary.

One of the best shots at our old club in Lynchburg had a 241 he'd fitted with sling and good iron sights. He liked to use his own rifle instead of the club's M-2 Springfields, and in spite of the 241 handicaps of light weight and the takedown joint between barrel and receiver he was one of our most dependable, consistent scorers. It seemed to me that his practice was unusually sensible—for he was a small-game hunter, too—and no one in the crowd had more fun than he did.

After the 241 went out of production, only one old-line, high-grade, expensive .22 auto-rifle was left, the Winchester 63. The newer crop of smallbore automatics, usually designed with the simple, easily made tubular type of receiver, has its various faults. But there are the virtues, too: pretty fair reliability when they're given a little care now and then, a reasonable degree of ruggedness, and quite often superior accuracy, thanks mainly to their one-piece stocks.

A Savage

A Savage Model 1912 just might show up at a dealer's. It was our first inexpensive automatic for the economical .22 long-rifle cartridge, and it should be safe with the low-velocity standard or target rounds made today. High-velocity stuff comes back with a much harder jolt than the action was balanced to handle, and parts for the M12 would have to be made by hand. They're discontinued at the factory.

This rifle had the smooth, flowing breech lines of the 1903 and 1909 slide action "clip" repeaters. The magazines were similar if not identical, though the auto was made to take the long-rifle cartridge only.

These three, and the 1914 slide action, had the handy sliding safety on the top tang, right where your thumb would reach for it. If the M12 could have hung on just a few years longer it would be easier to find one in perfect shape today. The old smokeless ammunition was viciously corrosive, in .22 rimfire, and the semi-smokeless, Lesmok and black-powder loads fouled up an autoloading action so fast that some of the boys decided to use smokeless, anyway.

SINGLE SHOT

Here's where we have little choice if our used-gun buy is to handle factory-made ammunition and equal a modern rifle in the kinds of performance most hunters want. Single-shot bolt actions of high grade are popular for target and bench-rest shooting. The hunter who uses a single shot from choice has his reasons and his satisfaction, but he's a bit uncommon, and in big-game country most people would call him a crank. His ratio of cartridges to kills might change their ideas.

Collecting old single shots can easily become so fascinating a hobby that they overflow the gunroom. Fear not: there are some beautiful specimens that could easily be tolerated on the walls of other rooms. Nearly all the "britch-loaders," as some woodsmen used to call the single shots even in quite recent years, have most graceful lines. Stock refinishing almost always brings out pretty walnut, and sometimes the shading and figure are breath-taking.

Most of these oldtimers are in poor or even hopeless shooting condition, but now and then a good one comes along, and for the others there are the remedies of reboring, relining or rebarreling. Occasionally a good barrel for an obsolete, hard-to-find cartridge like the long, slim .25-20 Single Shot is cut off at the breech and rechambered for a currently made, not too high pressure size—in this event the .25-20 WCF or Repeater. Modern brass often can be reformed to fit old chambers. In fact, almost any rimmed case from .22 Hornet to .45-70 could be or has been used in this way.

James J. Grant's book on *Single-Shot Rifles* is full of suggestions on how to make the old ones live again. His listing of American rifles of this type is as complete as could be wished, within reason, and you needn't read far in it before you find how involved and fascinating the study is. Some of the facts may never be known, as he implies—though with the undimmed hope of the enthusiast. Always there remains the possibility of full discovery, or of proof of what we suspect.

Stevens

The Stevens is one of the oldest makes, and one of the latest, too. In variety, this line compares favorably with any other.

For use with the more nearly modern cartridges most of us would want the *Model 44½*. It is prac-

tically a falling-block. When you throw the lever down, the breech-block does fall sraight, for a short distance; then it rocks backward to make loading easier.

The earlier 44 action has the rocking block, and its receiver is cut straight down, for a little way, just behind the barrel breech. The 44½ receiver walls come up higher, in a graceful curve, and they offer more support to the breech-block. Some have been made to handle cartridges as powerful as the .30-30, at least, but for pressures of this class there are more suitable makes of single shots.

For a few years preceding World War II Stevens manufactured a most satisfactory line of single-shot rimfires in the moderate price range, junior and senior models. Any of them in good shape could be a real prize today, and now and then one turns up, too often impossible to pry loose from its owner. They were stocked in modern style with pistol grip, high comb and fairly large forestock. And they were equipped, ready for use: they came with sling and peep sight, and either with target scope blocks attached or with holes already drilled for them. The *heavy Model 417* and the *light little 418* were target arms in .22 long-rifle caliber. The corresponding senior and junior sporters, *417½* and *418½,* offered a choice of .22 long-rifle, .22 WRF and .25 Stevens. No more suitable modern small-game rifle than the 417½ in .25 has been made by any of our factories.

A few heavy Hornets similar to the 417 smallbore match .22 were made. There has been some complaint—how well founded I don't know—about the durability of that action when used to back up Hornet pressures. The report was that in time the hammering of those rather hot little rounds set back the breech-block slightly, increasing the headspace. We do know that genuine old 44½ actions have given satisfaction with more powerful smokeless cartridges. Excessive handloads can account for quite a number of gun troubles of various kinds.

In general, Stevens single-shot rifles have served more on the target range and in meadow and woodlot than in remote wilderness. These kinds of shooting are more readily available to the great majority of us. Stevens barrel accuracy in low, medium and high priced rifles has been famous and well sustained. It played a real part, through the generations, in working toward that still unattained goal, Nation of Riflemen.

Winchesters

It seems to have been durability, not the numbers manufactured, that made the Winchester single-shot action the most common still found in first-class condition. The heavy high-wall action with blued receiver has backed up the pressures of rounds as powerful as the .300 and .375 Magnum. In general, a rimmed case like the .30-40 Krag, .303 British, .35 or .405 Winchester, or wildcats or foreigners' rations based on them, is as high as most of us want to go in our use of a single shot.

Blued low walls, not the really old case-hardened actions, are considered safe for the Hornet, but not for cartridges of higher pressure. They aren't recommended, either, for loads of similar pressure, such as the .218 Bee, in cases with larger inside head diameter. That would give the backthrust of gas more area to work on. The standard factory Hornet load is a heavy one, and no attempt to "improve" it should be made in front of low wall breech-up. It's better to load the 45-grain bullet, which balances the Hornet case capacity so well, to not over 2400 f. s. Let the factory rounds be the magnums for this caliber and action.

The variety of Winchester single shots still puzzles the collector. And this is true of other makes, for the single shot was a specialist's arm, even in its day, and many were made to order. Yet the collector, and the shooter who's followed this line, and the experienced gunsmith, all know pretty well the suitability of one of these action types for a modern cartridge. Those who know and love this action—and there are quite a few of us—are likely to be a bit conservative in stating just what sort of present-day calibers a certain specimen is suitable for, in conversion. We don't want an old friend to take on a job for which he's unfitted.

As with other single shots, an occasional Winchester is ready to use when you get it. Bore is good, action and woodwork sound; even the sights may be acceptable. And there are cartridges for it. A rare run of luck.

Usually some gunsmithing is called for, and if we can find a smith who is himself a devotee of the britch-loader, we and the rifle are in good hands. Charlie Canoll, referred to before, is one of these. That must be why he has done better work for me in this line than a couple of nationally prominent firms. The jobs came to a fellow who was interested. There's apt to be a gleam in the eye of an enthusiast when your perhaps casual talk hits home. In fairness to Charlie I can say that his other work is done carefully, too. And I ought to know.

At the opposite extreme are the tinkerers who think that almost any makeshift will do for an old rifle that shoots low-pressure loads, anyway. But how would you like to use a .22 Hornet that has a piece of nail for a firing pin? This conversion of the modified low wall—originally a .22 long-rifle musket—had a good ordnance steel barrel from a .22 M-1 or M-2 Springfield, and a new, tight firing pin could have been fitted and bushed in, but I'd had enough. So back it went, prepaid of course, but to get rid of it was worth the fee.

The Winchester has its faults, even its weaknesses, but perhaps it has fewer than other single shots of its time. Almost any of them needs a smaller, snugger firing pin for modern non-corrosive centerfire primers.

Various designs have been made, and I've seen one high-wall Win in .277 Elliott Express—a 7 mm. neckdown of .405 brass, practically a magnum—that had a hammer that rebounded into the half-cock notch. Since the standard action eases the firing pin back before the breech-block starts to fall, I can't see the necessity for that alteration. Seems better to have the firing pin support the primer cup during the instant of discharge. A spring-retracted firing pin is good if the hammer stays down on it after the trigger has been pulled, and a strong spring makes us feel sure that the pin *will* be drawn back, not broken off as the breech-block falls. This is the sort of behavior that Canoll builds into his gas-proof firing pin for the Winchester. It has to have the spring because his firing pin is snugly housed in the breech-block. It has no lower arm, like the factory model, to act as a lever for retraction. That is how he closes an open place where gas might slip through if a primer were pierced.

Even the small parts of the standard mechanism wear well, though the extractor shouldn't be asked to do the heavy work of that hook on a good bolt action of Mauser type. Firing pins stand up well and in general are satisfactory with low pressure loads, including the .30-40 Krag cartridge. But even the .22 rimfire firing pin isn't gas-proof, by any means, unless there's a hole in the breech-block drilled down from above into the firing pin's chamber. Some were made that way at the factory, and not only in .22 calibers. Usually they carry out .22 rimfire gas from a burst case.

Sad experience taught me that the hammer pin may not stand up to the constant use of long-loaded bullets, set so far out that considerable force is needed to seat the cast lead in the start of the rifling as in the Winchester Model 52 .22 rimfire. First one, then another of those brittle, slotted pins broke, and at last the message filtered through. This rifle is one of the old models with flat mainspring, and the hammer comes to full cock when the lever is drawn back on closing. I rather doubt that the hammer pin in the later coil-spring action would be broken in this way, at least if the hammer were one of those that come only to half cock on the closing of the breech. Then P. O. Ackley devised and installed a pin that I think will last. Period.

Other Single Shots

An enormous number of *Remington-Rider rolling block rifles* was made for the world's armies, and thousands of sporters too, in almost all the good American calibers of the time. Yet these rifles in even fair condition are uncommon, and few are chosen for rebarreling.

Many were made in smokeless military calibers like the 7 mm. Mauser and 8 mm. Lebel, and a few in sporting sizes of similar power. Some 7 mms. were imported lately. Even though the 7x57 American factory load is kept down to moderate pressure, the

Remington-Riders in this size definitely should be checked for headspace before they are fired.

The Remington-Hepburn was a sporting action, a straight-falling block operated by a thumb-piece, and in some specimens by an under lever. These arms have been converted into medium-power varmint rifles like .22 Hornet, or the wildcat .22-3000 Lovell or the larger-capacity 2-R Lovell, both formed from the old and now scarce .25-20 Single-Shot cases. Better, stronger cases, however, were factory-made for Griffin & Howe. It took an entirely new factory cartridge, the .222 Remington, to make the good 2-R "obsolete." Plenty of those who know and use the caliber would object to that adjective. Well, they're right. My own 2-R was chambered so snugly I didn't have to neck-size the brass. That called for moderate charges, but how they would shoot! It was a high-wall Win, but the Rem-Hep seems to breech up as tightly. Of course the steel in it is older than that in the later Winchester.

The Ballard still does excellent work on smallbore ranges. Converted to .22 long-rifle, this old lever action falling-block became one of the best custom-made match rifles. Its hammer fall is reasonably fast, the breech-up snug, and the long receiver tangs help to make stock assembly tight. Its currrently made ammunition is familiar: .22 and .32 rimfire, .32 center-fire Colt, .32-40, .38-55, .45-70. The cases of its .40-70-330 and .40-90-370 were shorter and more tapered than the Sharps Straight rounds using similar charges. They are among the hard-to-find, like the .44-100-530 and .45-100-550.

Uncommon because it's hammerless, the *Sharps-Borchardt* always attracted attention, and it stood up well under inspection and use. Ignition is fast, and the strongest actions nearly equal the Winchester in ruggedness, though this rifle wasn't made in the years of high-pressure smokeless ammunition. For .22 rimfire and moderate varmint-hunting calibers, and for its own big black-powder rounds, the Borchardt has been highly satisfactory. Although it has backed up some powerful modern cartridges it doesn't seem to be a first choice for such conversion. Few but the large and reasonably late Winchesters are.

The old side-hammer Sharps, like the Borchardt, came in a good variety of styles and big calibers. In .45-70, or altered by chamber shortening to take those cartridges, it would be a more generally desirable rifle than the Government Springfield in that size. Its lever action is handier and its breech-block lock-up apparently much stronger. Nearly all that we see now are collection pieces, but some are entirely suitable for big-game hunting in the woods, and a few of them get there. Sharps rifles in the old, odd calibers are in use when brass can be had for them.

Probably the most famous today, and the most respected for its killing power, is that old grandfather .50 Sharps Straight with 3¼-inch case. Its black powder charges ran from 140 to 170 grains, and its standard paper-patched bullet weighed 700. This was the lord of all buffalo calibers, but the 2½-inch brass for the .50-90-473 should be easier to find, by far. The .50-70-450 (or 425 grains in paper-patched target and hunting style) was a Government round, bottle-necked and only 1¾ inches long. Even after the .50-70 Springfield was superseded by the .45-70 of 1873, a lot of these half-inch rifles stayed in the service of National Guard outfits for many years more. Until lately, .50-70 brass hasn't been scarce, and Sharps and Remington rifles used it too.

The Savage 219 hammerless was the last centerfire single shot made by our factories. In design and materials it's modern, with ample strength for the cartridges it chambers. Only a few of us, perhaps, would appreciate and have use for the .25-20 and .32-20. The M219 Hornet could be rechambered for a slightly larger case—and used with bullets of the correct diameter. That detail we could find out by slugging the bore and miking the slug. The .30-30 cartridge always is useful, somewhere and for some sensible purpose.

CUSTOM-BUILT rifle is a glib phrase. It slides so smoothly off the tongue that it's used perhaps too freely. We all have our idea of what it means.

My notion is that it's built for a certain person, like a custom suit or pair of shoes. Outstanding appearance isn't essential. Indeed, a certain class of men who have their clothes made to order hate anything that's in the least conspicuous, and the same goes for custom rifles that they'd be likely to buy.

But the "custom rifle," to use the most exacting definition of the phrase, must be so tailored to the shooter that it lets him do his best work. It develops rather than limits his ability.

Who makes it? Why, probably a gunsmith, though one or two of our big factories are still in the business. But it can be made by the shooter himself, a true amateur gunsmith. Tom Florich stocked his .30-40 Winchester single shot to suit himself, in target style and for a target scope only, no iron sights, and the results on the range justified the free hours he'd given to the job. It's superbly accurate.

No, he didn't make the complete rifle. He didn't bore, rifle and chamber the barrel, or assemble it to the receiver. He took an oldtimer in good condition and did what was necessary to make it shoot and to fit him so well that he and the rifle, as a team, were able to deliver the accuracy of which they were capable.

I have no such skill, and I've owned but a few custom rifles. The first I had, about 30 years ago, was an early model, standard grade 54 Winchester .270 that I'd never laid eyes on till it came back from Dowagiac, Michigan, where the now dissolved Niedner Rifle Corporation was located. The Niedner stock— made by Tom Shelhamer, I presume—was built to order. I'd written to Colonel Whelen, telling him my build and stating that I planned to use the iron sight equipment the factory offered on the 54, a Lyman 48 receiver peep and 1/16-inch gold bead front hunting sights. So the stock was built to fit me, and it did. It was the first strictly modern-marksmanship stock I'd ever owned or even seen. They weren't too common then. In fact, *at that time* the Colonel advised me to have the stock custom built because none of the factories would fully understand the terms used in describing it.

Was this a custom rifle, with its standard factory barrel and unaltered action, only its stock specially built? Was it custom, without any embellishment whatever except the neat, sharp checkering and the pistol-grip cap? Why, I guess it was. It fitted me, as I said before, and it gave me new concepts of hunting-rifle accuracy, for it shot much better than I could aim and hold. It gave me lots of room for improvement, in using it.

The next was also a Niedner, and maybe anyone would call that custom, for stock, barrel, and scope mounts were made by that company. It was a 52

CHAPTER 13

CUSTOM-BUILT RIFLES

sporter, before the factory made any 52 sporters. Its scope was a 2¾-power Hensoldt, with the magnification and brightness I needed for small-game hunting, and the auxiliary sights were Lyman, a 48 in back and a special tall-stemmed gold bead up front. The stock didn't have a Monte Carlo comb or even a cheekpiece. Durn little gun balanced alive-like, came up fast, and held pretty steadily in spite of that extremely light 22-inch barrel. The whole rig, with sling and scope, didn't go eight pounds.

It looked good, too: smooth lines, dark, nicely figured walnut, blueing a bit glossier than a factory job. The stock fitted correctly for scope use, for it was high at the heel as well as at the full, rounded, under-cut comb. To get down to the irons I really had to force my face against the wood, but there wasn't any recoil, and I made out all right. Unless there was fog or rain or snow, or unless I felt exceptionally lazy, the scope was usually in place, with the irons going along in reserve.

Another one certainly wasn't a custom job. It wasn't made for me. It was a high-wall Winchester single shot with a heavy Model 52 barrel, .22 long-rifle caliber, and it had been stocked for the fellow who sold it to me, unless he too had got it as a used gun. This smallbore was beautifully accurate, the best I ever used, maybe. As time went on, things happened to its woodwork. The stock was shortened, by degrees, a full inch or more, thinned down, hollowed, oil-finished at least twice as the outside surface was shaved away. The forestock got the reducing treatment, too. Finally it fitted me, and I'd done 95 per cent of

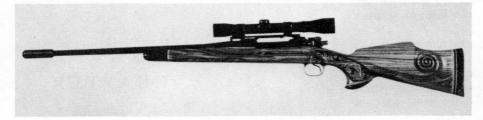

One of Anthony Guymon's standard-production Streamliner light-weight rifles. Muzzle brake to reduce recoil. Stocked in mesquite, with high, forward-sloping Monte Carlo comb. Springfield action with Dayton-Traister trigger.

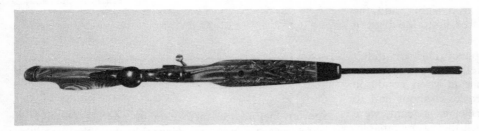

Right side view of the Guymon rifle.

Bottom view shows beavertail forestock, rolled-over Monte Carlo, and *no* magazine floorplate, for this rifle has a 4-shot "blind" magazine; the mid-section of the stock is not inletted clear through for the magazine box. This feature adds something to the stiffness of assembly and leaves wood, not steel, to grasp on a cold day's carry.

the work. So it couldn't be custom, could it, an amateur job like that? But I thought it was, because it taught me so much about marksmanship.

PRO AND CON OF A CUSTOM RIFLE

One advantage in buying, or making, a custom rifle is that you get what you ask for. Or you should! You write the specifications. If you order, let's say, a 7½-pound gun, you ought to get it, not an 8- or 8¼-pounder. It is no consolation to be told, about 4 p. m. on a long, full day, that "Walnut varies greatly in density." So do customers' skulls, and it's time that they registered a demand that they get what they pay for, whether it's custom or run-of-mill.

One terrible disadvantage is that not all firms are dependable. The following story is almost unbelievable. But it's true; the thing did happen. Like this:

A friend of mine sent his pet .30-06 Enfield to one of the scope-sight makers, an old and prominent company. When it came back with the new glass mounted, the bore was rusted. It looked as if some knothead had spilled bluing solution into it. My friend reported this matter, and did he get satisfaction? He didn't think so; they sent him a polite letter of apology, and that was all. So the affair ended, though the memory lingers on.

It pays to know whom you're dealing with and how far his responsibility extends. Most custom makers will turn out what you ask for if your specifications are explicit enough. A few of the best will use their own ideas, developed by long experience and the sort of originality that pays off in rifle appearance and efficiency. In these rare cases you get something better than what you'd asked for.

Of late years, since the term "custom rifle" became so well known, so commonly used, it has been maltreated. Almost anything that isn't a straight factory rifle has been glamorized by that title, and in many cases we'd be far better off with a factory rifle. And really a lot of these jobs look as though they'd slid off an assembly line. They lack individuality. Much worse, some of them lack the proper assembly that makes accuracy possible.

When a rifle is classified, say, as "semi-custom," we know about where we stand. Many of our good gunsmiths produce such a line, usually with the custom job, the individualized rifle that fits a certain person, available at extra cost. That is honest dealing. In that way we may get a caliber, an action, or a form of stock that can't be had from a factory. If material, workmanship, inspections, and proof equal those of the factory rifle we get just as good an article, and it's what we want. The time is past when gunsmiths couldn't get the best of barrel steel. A custom .250-3000 barrel that came to my order and was badly throat-eroded after not more than 2,000 shots wouldn't be duplicated today, in all likelihood. It was an accurate barrel, with one of the two or three best names of the time on it, and it shot no excessive charges and almost no rapid-fire strings. The maker simply hadn't been able to procure the material that I know he'd wanted.

But when you do get a good custom rifle that fits you—as that .250 certainly did fit me—you've bought yourself a definite satisfaction. The pride of owning something that was made specially for you may or may not mean much, though most of us feel at least a glow of quiet pleasure in it.

Using an arm that really fits, that almost at once becomes responsive and familiar, does things for your shooting—good things. Your hand curls naturally around the grip—a nicely rounded shape, no slab-sides—and your face settles instantly into place on the stock comb, your eye in line with the sights or the scope. In any of the shooting positions, unless it's a

specialized rifle, the piece fits more adaptably than any other sort of rifle has done. It carries well, too, and—again, unless it's specialized, as for varmint or target shooting—it seems lighter than it is. The weight has been distributed to make it ride and handle well.

That is the custom rifle at its best, and it's still available. Probably more are being made than ever before. Not quite every one comes from a gunsmith, though in a sense too many do.

Or too many are made too soon. No rifleman can profit as he should from a custom gun until he's had considerable shooting experience. He may have the best of instructors and coaching, but nearly all of us, as we go along, develop our own techniques. Only in slight ways do they differ from the standard system of

This angle gives a better view of the Guymon rolled-over comb.

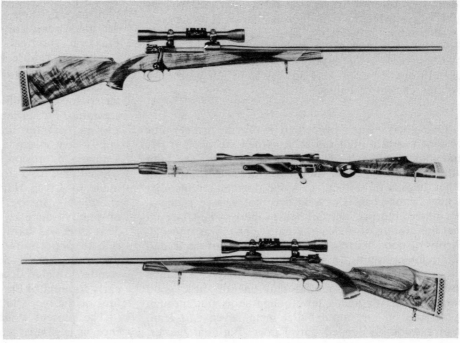

Three views of the Weatherby De Luxe Magnum rifle. This standard product is marketed in gun stores throughout the country.

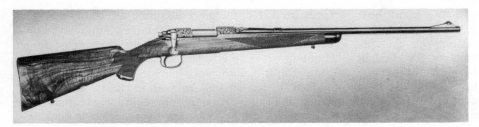

Remington 722-F Premier. A fine example of custom work done at one of our big factories.

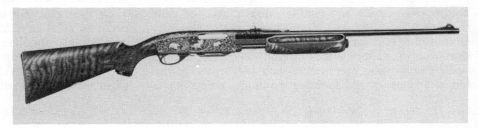

Remington 760-F Premier with gold inlays.

American marksmanship, and you'll notice that that system, properly taught, does allow some leeway. It has to, for we're not all built alike.

The best way that I know to find out what we need is to peel and patch away on a pretty standardized stock. This might be and really should be an operation that extends over more than one year of fairly regular shooting, an average of at least one trip a week. Meanwhile, the built-up and sanded-down stock is no beauty—except maybe from a rarefied intellectual point of view—but it's the vehicle that takes us along the road faster and more surely than trying this and that at random, whatever comes up in borrowing or buying.

When we know what we want in balance, weight, and carefully taken measurements it's time to order or make the custom rifle. It must be a replica of the "try gun." For instance, if the outside barrel contour is to be the same, it wouldn't do to decide that a .257 Roberts—now that we've learned to shoot so well—had best replace the .30-06 we'd been using. The .257 barrel would be noticeably heavier to us, for we'd have become critical of balance.

BARRELS

One great source of delight in having a very fine custom barrel is that it's slick. When we wipe it dry and look through it toward a light we don't see faint little tool-marks running down grooves and lands. Most other barrels have them to some degree. I remember a new factory barrel of long ago that was so rough—not pitted, but just not finished properly—that I could feel the grating of a cleaning patch. That was unusual. Plenty of good barrels that make minute-of-angle and still tighter groups do show the marks of the rifling cutter plainly, though the lands may be much smoother. It seems doubtful that one of these good barrels, after it's had a few fouling shots put through it, scrapes off any more bullet metal, even cast lead, than a smoothly lapped barrel does. For that matter,

old fouling left in the bore *can* do it. Such ill-treatment of bullets in any average, good barrel is trivial. Think of the many fine match shots who never give their .22 rimfires a cleaning until after the season is over, if then.

It certainly seems true, however, that a smooth boring and rifling job is less prone to rust, and less open to erosion, than the average barrel. But again, the difference is slight. For the most exacting service it's natural to want the best. Bench-rest shooters, for example, are particular about barrel workmanship, and they should be.

Barrel Steels

Soft steels are more easily machined than hard ones, and with black-powder temperatures and pressures they can give barrel life that runs into the tens of thousands of shots. Some of these tubes on old standard-grade arms are beautifully rifled, and still show it, thanks to good care ever since they were made.

The .22 rimfire barrels of soft steel last and last, and we have records of 250,000-round accuracy life—and better. In general, rather soft steels are still preferred for .22 rimfires. The "Winchester Proof Steel" stamping, for instance, means the kind of steel that's proved best for the particular purpose. That could imply easy machinability, not great hardness and resistance to erosion where those two qualities aren't needed. Yet hard steel can do well, the stainless barrels made by Clyde Hart, for instance.

Stainless Steels. Winchester Staynless steel barrels on some of the early Model 52s never became popular. This steel was hard; it was more difficult to bore and rifle to perfection—or near to that ideal state—than the softer steels. So in general the less expensive, standard material turned in better scores, and the early formula of Staynless went off the market. Centerfires of the type did, too.

The present Winchester Stainless (note the difference in spelling) is of a different formula. It's meant to be heat-resistant. That is the problem now, for with modern ammunition the danger of corrosion scarcely exists, except under downright neglect. A recent letter from Winchester states: "No figures are available but we estimate about triple the barrel life in these high intensity calibers." The reference is to the two hottest numbers from New Haven, .220 and .243.

Winchester is by no means the only company to use steels of this sort. Equally well known is the fact that experiment and development are moving fast. It is perfectly possible that a new and improved steel, far ahead of what we have now, will be bored and rifled before the first Stainless has had, let's say, 15,000 rounds put through it. And one barrel for that test wouldn't be enough, anyway.

Now we do get good long service from standard high-velocity barrels, manganese and molybdenum alloyed, and so on, that haven't changed a great deal for some years. A .22 Hornet might last for over 30,000 rounds—some have, at least with lighter than modern factory loading levels. A .30-30 should go 10,000 with full power cartridges, a .30-06 4,000, a .257 Roberts 3,500, a .220 Swift 3,000. Any of those figures means a considerable outlay for jacketed-bullet ammunition, even if we handload, and the opportunity to know our rifle and become expert with it.

That's about all that those figures do mean! They represent a groping sort of estimate, a witches' brew of records, a grab through a maze of variables. Steels,

chambering, boring and rifling all vary. Still more does the way in which we use the rifle. I don't mean the care we give it, for except in damp climates only a little bore-swabbing is necessary or desirable—usually. We do know that oversize bullets, unnecessarily hot primers, hot powders and heavy charges of any powder are members of that robber band that steals the gilt edge of accuracy from our barrels. We know that rapid fire in the military courses is hard on barrels, and some of us use cast bullets, with their light, cool powder charges, for these events.

But rapid fire, such as 10 shots in 70 seconds, isn't necessary! Slow fire, one minute per shot, can heat a barrel fast enough. This is notably true of small, high-intensity calibers like the .220, which becomes a stove after just a few shots under a hot sun. If we want long barrel life in a pet sporter with standard steel barrel, we get to our range early and stay late, and we don't let our barrel get too hot to grip, not just to touch, with our hand. In fact, we don't let it become anywhere nearly that hot. It cost me a new barrel, a couple of weeks of wait and repent, and a complete new sighting-in and recording of adjustments to find that out. But no doubt it was good experience, and if anyone wants it he can have it for himself sooner than he thinks. It doesn't take long.

Chromed Barrels. So our hunt for longer barrel life goes on. Marlin used the 16-groove or Multi-Groove system first on their .22 rimfires, then on the center-

Winchester 70 Custom Grade, engraved, inlaid, and carved.

Closeup of some of the work on the same Custom 70.

fires, which include some hot numbers. It seems reasonable to suppose that those 16 lands might hang on to accuracy longer because there are so many of them. Then too, they develop less friction because they don't need to stand up as high as the usual 7, 6, 5, 4 or 2 lands. We'll probably see further and more wide-spread development along this line, in high-intensity calibers. Barreling is in a state of flux, with new and hotter loads coming up, and almost anything could happen, even a re-trial of grooveless oval boring, which never did seem to give great satisfaction.

Chrome plating is the popular thing now. It's had a lot of publicity, which it deserved, and a number of standard rifles come out with chromed barrels.

P. O. Ackley uses, at this writing, a different method. His ball-lapped barrels are impregnated, under pressure, with Molykote or molysulphide. This should reduce friction and add to barrel life. The steel itself is of a new formula, with tensile strength of 145,000 pounds per square inch and Rockwell testing at C-30 or more. Molykote lubricant can be bought in small tubes at low cost, and its effectiveness is shown when you put a little drop of it on the contacting surfaces of a revolver's trigger pull. It will reduce the weight of let-off up to a pound or more, and this result lasts for a long time.

Chrome plating was described concisely and clearly in John P. Young's article, "Chromium for Gun Bores," in the February '56 *American Rifleman*. Its chief advantage is that when properly applied it can give as much as four or five times the normal barrel life. Since we already have high-velocity rifles and are tortured with the thought that we could have much higher *if* the bores didn't wear out so doggoned fast, we're really desperate to increase barrel life in any practical way. There's not much sense in having a supremely flat-shooting, accurate, and perhaps amazingly deadly rifle if its throat is burned out well before the 500-round mark. By that time acquaintance has barely ripened.

This smooth, slippery chromium coating gives higher velocity in many instances, it shortens the cleaning job and reduces the wear from the rod, and it helps to eliminate the sticking of cases in the chamber. Even a somewhat worn barrel, with the rifling in reasonably good condition, can be chrome plated. First it is electro-polished to a smooth inner contour, then plated to original diameters. But plating with chromium doesn't fill in pits and furrows, and if the throat of the rifling has been eroded badly this restorative may not be worth while, at least at the present time. Electro-polishing isn't necessary if the plating is to be only about .001 inch thick, and at the time of Young's writing no one was doing it commercially. The .001-inch thickness is minimum, he states, and high velocity barrels need from .002- to .003-inch thickness of plate. In no case should the thickness exceed two-thirds the height of the rifling lands, for beyond that we'd be liable to get into trouble with the chrome breaking away from those lands.

Chromium is about three times harder than hard rifle-barrel steel, and its melting point is some 3,000 to 3,600 degrees Fahrenheit as compared to about 2,250° F. for the steel. It won't melt at gun temperatures, and it won't rust, but it *can* crack when it's hot enough, and then the steel under the cracks is no longer protected.

However, it is one of the present-day good and popular remedies for that headache of high velocity barrels' wearing out so fast. Many new rifles, both custom and factory, are coming out with the chromium plated barrels. Some shotgun barrels have them, too, and the smooth finish should let them throw evener shot patterns.

"New" Rifling Method

Cutting the grooves in a rifle barrel takes time. During wartime pressure and under the towering labor costs of post-war manufacture, time is valuable. We now have a method of cold swedging the rifling into a bore that has reached high toward perfection. Some factory and custom barrel-makers use it freely and

Floorplate and guard work on the Winchester Custom 70.

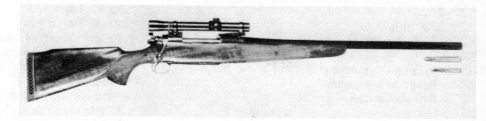

A Gibbs .505 caliber rifle built
by Al Weber.

successfully. Multi-groove barrels are an example.

The button or ball or whatever this swedge is called —various names are used—is drawn or pushed through the smoothly finished bore. Grooves ground into this tool produce the lands of rifling. Or we can say that the raised portions produce the grooves.

Once the work has been set up correctly it goes fast, and the results are excellent. Even under close inspection, few barrels indeed have to be scrapped.

The method is a logical development in our modern world and there seems to be no reason to regard it with suspicion. It isn't that new!

Special Calibers

From the custom maker we can get, if we wish, barrels that are chambered and rifled for cartridges not at present produced by our American factories. These may be obsolete but still desirable black or smokeless powder rounds, foreign calibers that fill in gaps between our current ready-mades—or go beyond them in size and power—or wildcats that serve all sorts of special purposes, sometimes including the satisfaction of curiosity or even of self-esteem. I'd be one of the last, though, to belittle wildcats, because of the direct and indirect good they've done us.

Here we'll look at just a few examples of special-caliber jobs. They are purely representative. Others could have been chosen, and this story is impartial. I'm trying to illustrate, not to catalogue.

The .505 Gibbs rimless is a famous African caliber. Like some other big British cartridges it's been used elsewhere than in Africa. Since one or two of my friends regularly hunt white-tailed deer with a .375 Magnum, and by good shooting get their game—dead right there, with few if any trail-ups—and find the destruction of well-placed shots not excessive, I see nothing wrong with using an "elephant rifle" in Alaska or the Yukon or our own Rockies, wherever game as tough as big bear, elk, or moose is to be killed.

Al Weber, R. 1, Box 154, Lodi, Calif., makes up a .505 in American, not British or European sporting style. It's a big gun—has to be—but it's nice-looking. Forestock and pistol grip are large, to help a fellow take up recoil, and since the stock is rather high at heel as well as at comb, there shouldn't be unpleasant whip-up of the comb to belt the shooter's chops.

The 10-inch cylindrical receiver is 1⅝ inches in diameter and its recoil lug is up between the receiver ring and the barrel shoulder, to allow more wood

between it and the magazine. The large locking lugs are ½ x 3/16 inch in size, and ⅝ inch long. A three-shot magazine is integral with the trigger guard, and the smooth, adjustable Dayton-Traister trigger is standard.

Weber has also made actions for the .50 caliber machine gun cartridge, with rearward bolt thrust quoted as 21,113 pounds. His figures for the .505 Gibbs, .416 Rigby (for which this sporter of his is also available), and .30-06 are 12,620, 10,715 and 7,189 pounds. English Cordite loadings for the .505 and .416 are a 525-grain bullet at 2,350 f. s. and a 400 grain at 2,300. Since most big-caliber Cordite loads are held down to be safe in tropical heat, power can usually be increased with the more stable American powders. The .416 and .505 seem to have considerable life expectancy. About ten years after World War II the British manufacturers were obliged to streamline ammunition production, as our people here had to. Abercrombie & Fitch, Madison Ave. at 45th St., New York 17, stock those two foreigners and many others.

Ackley Wildcats. The list recently received from P. O. Ackley reminds me of Adolph Niedner's repertoire of long ago, except that it's even more extensive. Both men made standard caliber rifles too, as most of our gun-makers do.

Here are the wildcat calibers which Ackley has made or could make. Of course not all are of his own design. Those starred (*) are his special recommendations. The word "Improved" he calls "an unfortunate selection." It is, because it means primarily that the chamber will take factory cases, which are blown out to greater capacity when they're fired. A shooter might be satisfied with .30-06 power, for instance, and see no advantage in his buddy's 06 Improved. When we burn more powder of the same type we shorten barrel life, other things being about equal, and the steep-necked, straight-bodied, improved cases sometimes are hard to develop accurate cast-bullet handloads for. Not always, though.

*.17 Hornet
*.17 Bee
.17 Lovell (Woodsman)
.17-.222 Standard
.17-.222 Improved
.22 K-Hornet
.218 Mashburn Bee
.219 Improved Zipper

*.22-.250
.22-.250 Improved
.220 Swift Improved
*.22-.30-30
.228 Magnum (recommended for some purposes)
.228 Krag, two versions
.228 Belted Express
*.240 Cobra
6 mm-.250-3000 Standard
6 mm-.250-3000 Improved
6 mm Magnum on .300 H&H case
*.25-35 Improved
.255 Dean (a .25-20 WCF Improved)
*.250-3000 Improved
*.257 Roberts Improved
.25 Niedner (standard .25-06)
.25-06 Improved
.250 Magnum
6.5x54
*6.5x57 (Spence Special)
*6.5x57 Improved
6.5-06
6.5-06 Improved
6.5 Magnum
.270 WCF Improved
.270 Magnum
*7x57 Improved
.285 OKH
7 mm-06 Improved
7 mm Magnum
*.30-30 Improved

*.30-40 Improved
*.30-06 Improved
*.30 #1 Short Magnum
.30 #2 Short Magnum
.300 Magnum Improved
8 mm-06
8 mm-06 Improved
.333 OKH
.333-06 Improved
.333 Magnum
*.35 Whelen
*.35 Whelen Improved
.35 Brown-Whelen
*.35 Magnum
.375 Magnum Improved
.404 Magnum, short
.404 Magnum, full length
.450-.348
.450 Magnum
.475 Magnum

Some of the Ackley wildcat cartridges, including quite a few that he especially likes, are shown in the accompanying photographs. I quote his caution to handloaders, and his remarks on the separate cartridges. Note the word "approach." He means it, for he's an experienced rifleman. These top loads are listed in his book.

* * * *

A few loads are given for each of the following illustrated cartridges. These loads are in no way guar-

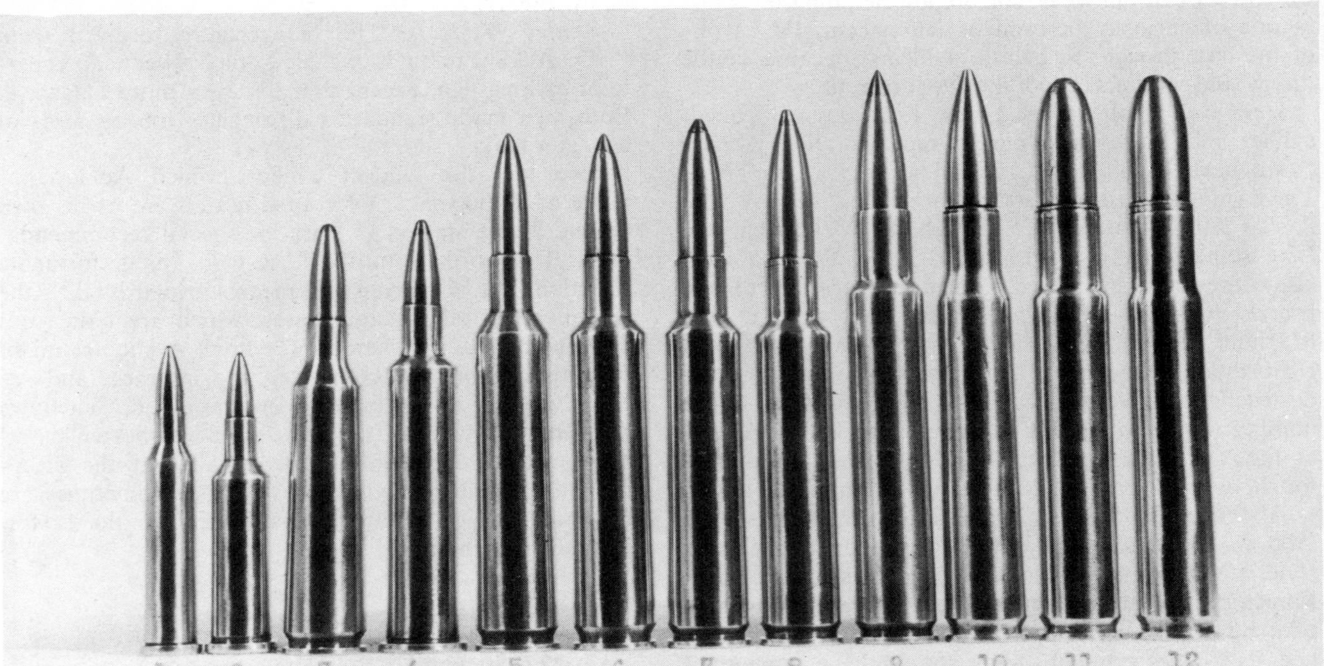

Ackley cartridges. 1. .17 Hornet. 2. 17 Bee. 3. .22-.250. 4. .22-.30-30. 5. .228 Ackley Magnum. 6. "Improved" .257. 7. The same necked up to .270. 8. "Improved" 7x57. 9. Ackley "Improved" .30-06. 10. Standard .30-06. 11. "Improved" .35 Whelen. 12. Standard .35 Whelen.

13. Original short .30 Ackley Magnum. 14. No. 2 Ackley short .30 Magnum. 15. .333 Ackley Magnum. 16. .35 Ackley Magnum.

anteed and the customers are cautioned to approach the top loads with care.

Neither Mr. Ackley, the author nor the publisher takes any responsibility for damage that might occur in loading rifles with the loads shown in this book.

1. .17 Hornet. This is probably the best of the various .17 calibers and is recommended for small-game and varmint shooting. It has proved to be highly satisfactory for shooting woodchucks and jack rabbits. Bullets are available in 20, 25 and 30 grains.

2. .17 Bee. This is also a very satisfactory cartridge for this small caliber, and uses the same line of bullets as the .17 Hornet. It is slightly more powerful and appeals to many shooters because of its shorter case and slightly higher velocity.

3. .22-.250. Cases for this cartridge are made by necking down the .250-3000 brass, and it has proved to be one of the best and most popular super .22 cartridges. It is becoming very popular for bench-rest shooting as well as varmint shooting and is well adapted to use in all bolt-action rifles.

4. .22-.30-30. This is a new cartridge presented here because of ease in forming brass from .30-30 or .32 Special cases, as compared to similar cartridges such as the Improved Zipper, .219 Wasp and others. It produces somewhat higher velocities than these versions and is highly recommended for use in single-shot rifles.

5. .228 Ackley Magnum. This cartridge has proved to be an exceptional killer of big game and has been quite popular for use on such big game as antelope, deer, etc., and for varmint shooting such as long range rabbit, woodchuck and coyote shooting. Bullets

are available in 60, 70, 75 and 80 gr., but the 70- and 75-gr. have proved to be the best. Bullets are available only in heavy-jacketed type; therefore, this cartridge is not particularly recommended for use in thickly settled areas for varmint shooting because of the tendency to ricochet.

The .228 bullets as made by Barnes are Spitzer type with soft points with 6-caliber ogive. The Sisk has about 8-caliber ogive and a very small hollow point. Both have tubing jackets and will not blow up under any normal conditions. [Note: These are big-game bullets, primarily, and also made to stand very high velocities.]

The reason why the .22 high-power [.22 Savage, now discontinued by our factories] bullets give trouble in the .228 is the quick twist used to stabilize these long-pointed bullets. Many .228 barrels are made with nine- and ten-inch twists and the centrifugal force or RPM's imparted to the thin jackets cause the bullet to blow up on the way to the target.

We have conducted quite a few interesting experiments on such things. I doubt very much if the trouble is due to the lead melting. If you spin a small lead wheel fast enough it will fly apart because the tensile strength of lead is insufficient to hold it together after a certain number of RPM's are reached.

The Remington Korelokt are somewhat better than some of the Winchester, Western or others, but do have a tendency to blow up on impact, which is

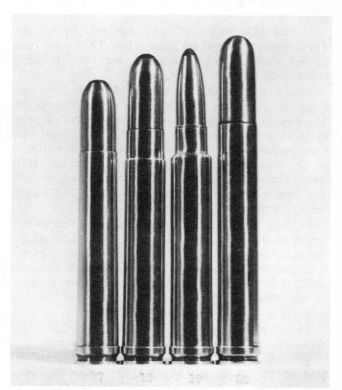

17. .458 Winchester Magnum. 18. .450 Ackley Magnum. 19. "Improved" .375 Ackley Magnum. 20. .475 Ackley Magnum.

exactly the thing which gives high-velocity rifles in general a black eye.

6. Improved .257. This is one of the most popular of the Ackley series of "improved" cartridges. It has been widely chambered for by gunsmiths all over the world. Cases are made by simply firing factory ammunition in the "improved" chamber. Factory loads fired in the "improved" chamber show a reduction in velocity of approximately 100 f. s. but the fire-formed cases can be reloaded to considerably higher velocities, and this cartridge has definitely proved itself on all types of large game in the United States.

7. .257 "improved" case necked up to .270. This is a new cartridge, but preliminary tests have shown it to be highly efficient and it produces ballistics comparing very favorably to the larger .270 cartridges, including the various .270 Magnums.

8. "Improved" 7x57. This is basically the same cartridge as the "improved" .257 and cartridge #7. It is one of the best of all the "improved" cartridges, and like the "improved" .257, cases are formed by firing factory cases in the "improved" chamber.

9. Ackley "improved" .30-06. This is another "improved" cartridge which has been widely chambered for by gunsmiths all over the world, and when properly handloaded it equals the ballistics of the factory .300 H&H Magnum loads. It has been proved on big game through North America, including the large Alaskan brown bear.

10. Standard .30-06. Shown for comparison purposes only.

11 and 12. "Improved" and standard .35 Whelen. These cartridges need no description. They have been proved over a long period of years to be highly efficient on all types of big game.

13. Original short .30 Ackley Magnum. This cartridge is sometimes referred to as the #1 short .30 Magnum and has proved over a long period of years to be about the best of any of the .30 Magnums ever experimented with. It easily duplicates the ballistics of the standard .300 H&H factory cartridge. It is short enough to work through all standard actions, and its design makes for high efficiency. The overall length of the case is 2.450 inches.

14. No. 2 Ackley short .30 Magnum. The overall length of this case is 2.532 inches. This cartridge has the same design as the #1 short .30 Magnum except it is slightly longer to make it possible to clean up old .30-06 chambers when such barrels are rechambered. Ballistics are very similar to those for the original #1 Ackley short .30 Magnum.

15. .333 Ackley Magnum. This is basically the same case as the #2 Ackley short .30 Magnum.

16. .35 Ackley Magnum. This cartridge is also basically the same as the #2 Ackley short .30 Magnum and is one of the best Magnums available for the largest North American big game and even African game. Bullets are available in 180-, 220-, 250-, and 300-gr. weights, and in both soft-point and full metal patch, round nose and spitzer points.

17. New .458 Winchester. This is Winchester's answer to the demand for a cartridge for large, dangerous game. Although not as powerful as the .450 Ackley Magnum, it will work through standard-length actions.

18. .450 Ackley Magnum. This is one of the most powerful Wildcat cartridges available. It is especially designed for use on heavy, dangerous game for the sportsman who wishes to have a surplus of power. Cases are made from un-necked Norma Magnum brass, or necked-up .375 Magnum brass. Bullets are available in 300-, 400-, 500-, and 600-gr. weights, in thin and thick jacketed type, also in full patch. The 500-gr. bullet is especially recommended for the largest game.

19. "Improved" Ackley .375 Magnum. Like other "improved" Magnums, its cartridges are formed by firing factory ammunition in the "improved" chamber. It is suitable for large game.

20. .475 Ackley Magnum. This is the largest cartridge of the Ackley line and only 600-gr. bullets are available for it. This is a cartridge recommended only for use on the very heaviest and most dangerous game.

Further Notes by Mr. Ackley. The best .17s are the .17 Hornet and the .17 Bee, but we make some using the .222 case, and have even made them on the .250-3000 and the Swift case, but the case capacity of the .17 should not be over 14 to 15 grains. As soon as we go over that we are going down hill.

The .228 as I originally made it was nothing more nor less than the .22 Niedner. At the time I had never seen the .22 Niedner and simply necked down the .257 case, but I later found out that the .22 Niedner was a 7 mm. case necked to .22, which made the two cartridges identical except for the bullets. I used the 90 gr. and he used the 70 gr.

Subsequent experimentation has shown that the bullet over 75 grs. is not too practical, and it is better to increase the bore diameter after that. The .228 probably offers more difficulties than any other Wildcat because when I developed it I had both Barnes and Sisk make bullets, all of which were heavy jacketed and with long streamlined points, made expressly for big game.

These six- and eight-ogive bullets required a twist of nine and eleven inches, but as soon as many customers get one of these rifles they immediately start using ordinary .22 high-power bullets or 63 gr. Sisk designed for the .22 high-power, and none of these bullets will stand the RPM's imparted to them by the short twist. Trouble results immediately, and is always laid to the gun. Now I refuse to make a .228 unless it is clear in the customer's mind that he must use the right bullets.

The .250 Magnum case can be made from the

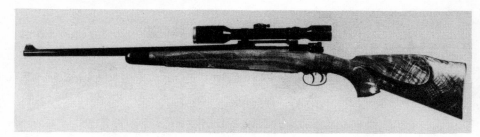

Ackley 7 mm. Magnum rifle on F. N. Mauser action, French walnut stock. Weight, 8½ pounds.

The same 7 mm. Ackley. Note bolt-handle alteration for saddle use.

.275 or .300 Magnum brass, but the .300 is usually used because very few .275 Magnum cases remain in circulation. My own .250 Magnum has an overall case length of 2.450 and it is entirely too large for the .250 bore. The same case is a whiz in .30 caliber, but even in .270 or 7 mm. it is not too hot.

The #1 short .30 Magnum is simply the .250 Magnum necked up to .30; that is, the cases are identical except the neck diameter, and the same is true of my own .270 and 7 mm.

The .404 Magnum can be furnished on either the #1 or the #2 short .30 case.

Weatherby Cartridges

Weatherby's, Inc., goes on, we might say, from where the Ross and Newton rifle companies left off. Roy Weatherby believes in velocity. He's gone out and killed big, heavy game with it. So have some of his customers. We shall discuss bullet weight, bullet construction, and explosive effect in the latter part of this section. These fellows did what they did.

At present Weatherby furnishes seven special calibers. His barrels are throated out ¾ inch, he states, to give plenty of seating room for long, heavy bullets, and to relieve initial pressures. That is not the European system of free-boring, in which the smooth, unrifled section extends considerably farther. His testing equipment includes a chronograph, and pressures are taken for him by the H. P. White Ballistical Laboratory at Bel Air, Md., where so much of the NRA testing is carried on, and by the Norma ammunition makers in Sweden.

The .220 Rocket is an improved Swift, its cases fire-formed from the factory ammunition, just as the .300 and .375 Weatherby Magnums are blown-out factory cases. The .257, .270 and 7 mm. are belted, rimless brass, too, of magnum size, and the .378 is a special, much larger case. Weatherby has Waterbury-Farrell loading machines such as big ammo factories use, and he does lots of handloading for tests, as any wildcatter should. However, his cartridges aren't wildcats, but commercially available

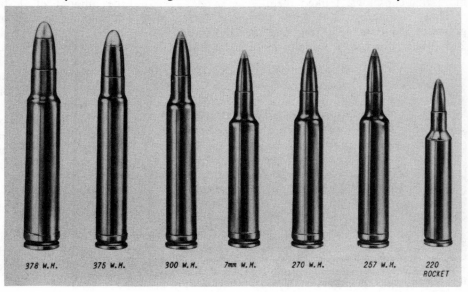

Weatherby Magnums—.378, .375, .300, 7 mm., .270, .257—and the Weatherby .220 Rocket.

378 W.M. 375 W.M. 300 W.M. 7mm W.M. 270 W.M. 257 W.M. 220 ROCKET

Weatherby Custom Grade .300 rifle with French walnut stock has monogram plate, laurel leaf carving, pearl inlays. Scope is Weatherby four-power Imperial on Buehler mount.

rounds. Norma makes the special brass for him.

There's no question about an ultra-high-velocity rifle's capability of accuracy, if it and its ammunition are made correctly and matched to each other. For those who need such sustained long range power and flat trajectory the type is most useful, provided they are seasoned to recoil and muzzle blast, know how to estimate distance, and what to do about it after it's estimated. As for accuracy, Tom Florich says, "Some of his .300 jobs have grouped like a National Match or a DCM sporter, and of a hunting rifle you could hardly say more."

For examples of Weatherby velocities the .270 and .300 should serve, both with what are practically standard-weight bullets, and both loaded to pressures comfortably below the very high 55,000 pounds per square inch, as taken and reported. However, Mr. Weatherby, like any sophisticated rifleman, would be quick to point out that pressures vary greatly in different barrels and with different cartridge components. His book, *Tomorrow's Rifles Today,* and P. O. Ackley's book are both worth reading. The latter, I understand, plans annual editions to answer questions that are sent him.

Both books list a good many handloads and also carry a number of articles on subjects that interest us riflemen. I doubt that these books are money-makers, or intended to be, but they help to make us all more rifle-conscious. I liked them.

That Weatherby .270 with 130-grain bullet, 67 grains of Du Pont 4350, and the special Federal No. 215 primer turns up a velocity reported as 3364 f. s.

P. O. Ackley used these ten-quart cans filled with water for demonstrating the explosive effects of bullets.

from a 26-inch barrel. That would be 224 f. s. higher than the factory .270 Winchester cartridge, a 24-inch barrel being used.

More gain is apparent in the .300 Weatherby caliber. With 180-grain bullet and 79 grains of 4350 the velocity is 3225 f. s., 305 f. s. above that of the .300 factory Magnum, both with 26-inch barrels.

The ".378," a trade name, for it takes .375 Magnum bullets, gives us a series of three American .375s somewhat like the old, familiar .30-40, .30-06, and .300 Mag series of .30 calibers. Muzzle velocity of the Winchester 300-grain factory .375 is 2550 f. s., of the Weatherby .375 some 2700 or more, and of the .378 at close to 3000, perhaps all of that, or higher. At this writing, the tests aren't finished. It would be our fastest large-caliber bullet of good weight, probably, and the Norma case that holds it is a strong one. Evidently Schultz & Larsen actions have been used for at least some of these .378s.

Bullet Strength and Explosive Effect. If high velocity is combined with enough accuracy and the bullet weight that can fight cross-winds with fair success, it lets us make hits—and better, *place* the hits—at long ranges. First we must have mastered that advanced form of rifle shooting. Some of us deserve long-range rifles; some don't, yet.

But even a well-placed bullet must have the killing power needed for the game we hunt. That depends on the amount of destruction of tissue, more or less, depending upon how vital it is. A heavy *and* long bullet penetrates well. Lighten it and send it faster and it may not. Penetration in game seems to require two factors, bullet weight (with reasonable length to steer and drive it), and the right bullet construction. We must have one of them; sometimes we might need both, within reason.

So with this advanced Ross-and-Newton type of ammunition, the Weatherby rounds, we must choose our bullets for strength of construction if we're to shoot heavy game at short ranges. If we're to use these cartridges as super-long-range loads, we can choose the most nearly equivalent factory bullets, such as .30-06 or .300 Magnum for the Weatherby .300, for it will add some 100 yards to our killing range, and out near the limit its velocity will be similar to that of the standard .300 H&H Magnum, at *its* corresponding practical limit.

These Weatherby cartridges have killed well with

A 150-grain .30 at 3300 f. s. muzzle velocity smacks in. Range was 50 feet.

Similar loading, but bullet was tough enough to hold together and penetrate one-inch oak backstop.

A .30-caliber 150-grain Ackley controlled-expansion bullet at only 1800 f. s. raises some ruction. Passing out, it made a ⅝-inch hole in the can.

Another hit from an 1800 f. s. 150.

regular factory bullets. But when any doubt of their stiffness comes in, we'd do well to test and finally choose a custom bullet, or maybe a steel-, not copper-jacketed foreign bullet, such as the full metal-cased or hardpoint .375 for the biggest African game. Of course a copper jacket *can* be made heavy and tough enough for almost any purpose.

But most of us would need an expanding bullet, and this might be one of the Barnes variety, for an example, with specially thick and tough jacket. Or it might be one of unusual construction. This could be the Ackley controlled expansion, which carries on further the idea of the old German DWM Strong Jacket, in which the last third or so of the jacket was about as thick as the lead core inside it. The Ackley jacket is thinned at the front, for expansion, and its lead core goes only a little more than halfway down, the rear section being solid copper. Ackley has made, and may make again, a solid copper bullet with hollow point. It gave, he says, even better expansion than the cored bullet, and less loss of weight in its path through game. "Another thing," he says, "is that the bullet is made of dead soft copper which is much tougher and less prone to metal fouling than gilding metal. Gilding metal used in this kind of bullet has a tendency to break off so that it is only a square slug left, thus losing considerably more weight than a solid copper bullet."

The old French 8 mm. Lebel military bullet, Balle D, was of solid copper, or copper alloy. Naturally a lead-filled bullet of the same weight as a copper one is shorter and requires less rapid twist to stabilize it, but the difference is not so great. The specific gravity figures of lead and copper respectively are 11.34 and 8.92. Barrel wear of copper bullets is hardly worth considering in a sporting rifle because just about any of us would use these bullets mostly for special purposes. For that matter, tough, hard jackets of gilding metal sometimes wear barrels faster than mild

Some of the recovered bullets. The two at left were Ackley controlled expansion at 1800 f. s. Third from left was a controlled at 3300, and the remains at right are from a 150-grain factory expanding bullet at 3300.

Junk.

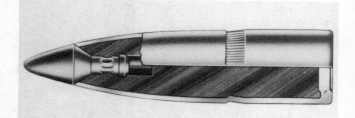

Some 180-grain Remington .30-caliber bullets, sectioned. This one is the Bronze Point with cavity below the bronze tip to increase breakup.

steel jackets. Most of the latter, in the standard expanding types, aren't really thick jackets.

Then there is the Nosler partition jacket, something like the old German H-Jacket. Its core is in two parts, the lower section encased in jacket so that it will hold together and plow on through.

Another good bullet was factory-made, the Peters belted—outside belted, to distinguish it from the later inner belted, which is the same as the Remington Core-Lokt. A heavy belt between the soft tip and the bore-bearing section limited the expansion so effectively that in 225-grain .30 it was quite a favorite for hunting African lions. Other weights and calibers were made: 180-grain .30-30, .303 Savage and .32 Special, 180-grain .30-06 semi-pointed, 210-grain .35 Remington, and so on. The slightly heavier than normal weights for the smaller cartridges made some mighty effective deer and black bear loads in these sizes. Gone. Not made any more.

Bullet makers have the opportunity to know their product. People write in, sometimes drop in. So the makers aren't going to recommend an elk or a grizzly bullet for eastern white-tails, and we do well to consult them, stating our problems clearly. You bet they'll be glad to help.

As to the shock of so-called "explosive effect," we must remember that some of the largest game seems to be not very susceptible to it. What still higher velocities would do isn't too well known as yet. A surface wound from a lightly constructed bullet can't be expected to be lethal—not with confidence—though such things have happened, mostly when the game wasn't what we'd call really big.

It seems to me that Weatherby's chief contribution has been to make super-velocity rifles and ammunition available to more people, which results in more extensive testing in the game fields. That's what we must have to learn about them, to carry on the further developments about which he—with plenty of thousands of others—is so keen. His standard rifle, without embellishments and not stocked to your order, is expensive, but not as steep as you might think. And you can buy the ammunition ready-made. If you don't want to go into reloading—poor soul, for that I'd pity you!—you can have it done at his place. He's sort of domesticated the wildcat, I reckon.

ACTIONS

We have a few custom-made actions such as the Dunlap and Morgan-Johnson for smallbore match shooting, the Weber, Taylor & Robbins, and Auston for bench-rest, and the Weber magnum. We could expect many to be developed in the future. Like wildcat cartridges, they put ideas into the world of the real and existing, and their contribution to firearms development may be equally valuable.

But most custom makers use a standard action, refining it if such work is needed or wanted. Most

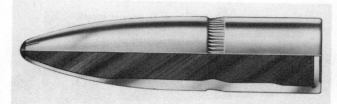

Pointed soft-point Corelokt is made sharp, too, for long-range efficiency. Jacket is thick at midsection to prevent lead core from shedding its jacket along the path through game. Slits at tip of jacket are to help get even, sure expansion.

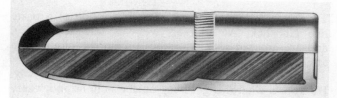

Round-nosed soft-point Corelokt for woods use.

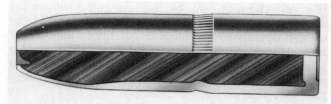

Hollow-point Corelokt is made for those who prefer this pattern to a soft point. But notice the dimple of lead at the nose, which makes this bullet a modified or limited hollow point.

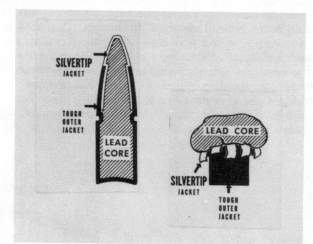

Diagram of Winchester 180-grain .30-caliber Silvertip, another type of factory-made controlled-expansion bullet.

gunsmiths who turn out complete custom rifles, even as their main activity, do have a little time to work over customers' actions as a special job. And such work can be mighty satisfying to the customers.

It's true that some pretty stiff factory actions do mellow considerably after the first box of cartridges has been fired ahead of them. There's also the home working of the action—open and shut, open and shut, hours of it, really, being no chore to the rifle-crank.

A left-hand bolt-action job by Pachmayr.

This we can do dry, or with the lubrication of a paste like Gunslick. At intervals we wipe the action dry, and are amazed at what comes off on the cloth, even after dry working.

But a gunsmith can do it better, more completely. He knows where to get busy on the action, and where to leave hands off, such as not removing any metal from the engaging surfaces of locking lugs. The jewel-like perfection of fine English shotguns, with every action part polished whether it needs it or not for smooth operation, is seldom called for in any of our rifles. It costs plenty at today's prices for the time of a really skilled man. Perhaps some of us would prefer such an investment to outlay on the exterior surfaces that everyone sees.

Engine-turning or damascening of the bolt and its raceway looks nice, to most of us. In the raceway, particularly, it is more attractive than the rather black, rather rough finish of so many factory jobs. The same applies to careful polishing and rebluing of all outside metal parts. Not all standard production rifles need it.

Converting a bolt action to left hand operation can be a ticklish job. Removing steel from the receiver ring may result in serious weakening of lockup strength. Except on the Remington 721 and 722 actions the work isn't easy to do correctly. Dale M. Guise, Rt. 1, Gardner's, Pa., does it, chamfering the edges of lug recesses for smooth operation. This, of course, is con-

sidered harmless. Erven P. Barber, 3326 N. E. 57th, Portland 13, Ore., also reverses these two actions.

The Mathieu is a special job, featured by Weatherby. P. O. Ackley is prepared to make left-hand conversions, and so is Bob West, 3520 Christine St., Salt Lake City 6, Utah. These are named only as examples.

It's only fair to repeat that some of the handiest men with a bolt gun are southpaws. You see them competing in military rapid-fire courses—where bolt actions are still used, that is—as well as carrying rifles in game country. The way in which they reach over and wrench up the bolt handle, slide it back and forth and then slap it down—this last, mostly with the trigger finger alone—makes you admire their adaptability. Actually, they don't seem to be handicapped at all, except with a scoped rifle. Any of us needs plenty of dry practice in bolt throwing, to master a rifle of this type. How much, if any, more they require I don't know. An IBM calculator might tell, and in a robot world it'd be no trouble at all to work out the percentages.

Hauck Single Shot

Wilbur Hauck, RFD 1, West Arlington, Vt., has made up single-shot rifles on the Winchester and the German Stiegele actions, maybe on others. For some years he has been making his own, a hammerless falling-block lever action with flowing lines that rather suggest the Savage 99 receiver. It has a speed lock, with only three-eighths-inch hammer fall, and both hammer and firing pin are retracted before the breech-block starts to go down. This prevents liability of the firing pin's sticking in a primer that has flowed back, under high pressure, and breaking off as the breech-block falls.

In other ways this entirely modern action is built to handle modern ammunition, practically everything from .222 Remington to .375 Magnum. The firing pin is lined up with the bore axis, not slanted, as in the

Hauck varmint rifle with cheek-piece for a left-handed shooter.

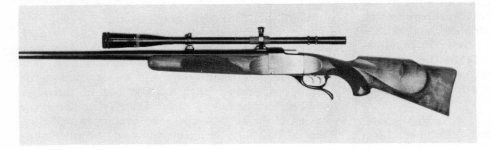

Hauck single shot with cheek-piece and target scope.

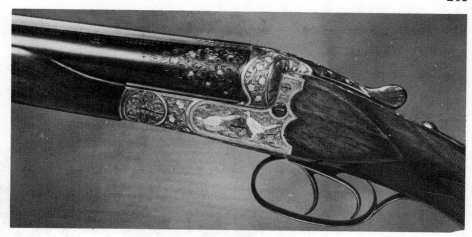

Pachmayr engraving on frame, breech and top lever of a double shotgun.

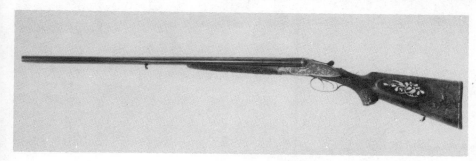

A Jules La Bantchni custom 12-bore, engraved, inlaid, and carved. French walnut stock.

Gold-embossed ducks by Griffin & Howe decorate thi s Model 21 Winchester double shotgun.

Side view of the same G&H job.

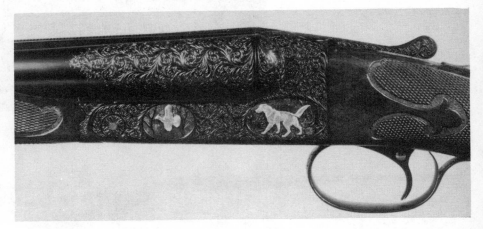

Full-length view of a Winchester Model 21 Custom Grade shotgun. Recoil pad is leather covered, muzzles are engraved, and in between there is plenty more handwork.

Here is some of the work between muzzles and butt-pad. Engraving, inlay, stock carving.

On this side, a pheasant instead of a grouse.

old Stevens, which in the largest, strongest models had a safe limit of about .30-30 or .30-40 pressures, it seems probable. When the action is in firing position the breech-block is locked firmly in place, and the cartridge head is completely covered. There is an internal gas port for added security.

This rifle shoots high-intensity cartridges with accuracy. The barrel shank that enters the receiver is long, and thus adds to the stiffness of assembly. So does the bolt that binds the stock to the receiver. Finally, the forestock is floating: it's attached to a metal hanger that is screwed into the receiver.

A Mauser type of double-set trigger is available. Those who are familiar with a "hair trigger" find a good deal of use for it in varmint hunting, and a really skilled still-hunter of woods deer sometimes has the chance to profit by it. I've known of one or two instances. Close-up, the faint click of setting the trigger

could alarm a deer, and it would take a mighty cool snapshot to use a hair trigger on running game! That sort of trick isn't commonly turned. Quite likely it was in muzzle-loading days, though it seems more than doubtful that even in the most lonely and primitive wilderness many folks went around carrying a set trigger set.

The Hauck single shot is well adapted for use with rimless cases, when so ordered. Few others pull much-reloaded and unresized brass of this type reliably, but this rifle has to be modern, and it is. For those who love the single shot and need the power-and-accuracy combination that modernized oldtimers may not be able to give them, it's perhaps the best choice, at least among rifles made in our own country. Some bench-resters use the Hauck, but it seems to be more popular with varmint and big-game shooters.

ENGRAVING

"Gun engraver from Europe, recently arrived to this country. 30 years' experience. All kinds of styles. Standard or top works. Reasonable prices. J. Michelena, 2551 S. W. 11th St., Miami, Florida."

You know as much as I do about him, and maybe more, for by the time that this gets into print Mr. Michelena should have had a start in making his reputation, good or not, in our Country. I came on the ad last night, going through "The Arms Chest" columns in the *Rifleman*.

I like good engraving on a gun and have been privileged in hunting a lot in both rough and easy country with a few that were tastefully decorated in this manner. There have been dozens of others, however, perfectly plain, that I remember with equal affection.

Remington and Winchester still have this work done on their shotguns and rifles, and on these and others we get, it seems, about what we pay for. Quality and quantity both cost money. Let the purse choose, or the taste!

Most of the prominent custom makers do engraving, or have it done, to individual order. Ackley, Griffin & Howe, La Bantchni, Pachmayr—the list could go into the dozens.

The magazine floorplate of a bolt-action high-power takes engraving nicely. Well executed, it looks good— and it actually feels good as you carry the gun! The work of A. Griebel, illustrated here, is a splendid example. His address is 4724 N. Keystone Ave., Chicago 30.

Alvin A. White, 72 Verndale Ave., Attleboro, Mass., does fine work for various gun-makers and some directly for his own customers. "This sort of thing," he says, "was in style in the old target rifle days. . . . I did a Ballard with a bullfrog shooting scene, somewhat the same as was used on old Peabody rifles."

(The Peabody, which later evolved into the hammerless Peabody-Martini, was a single-shot action, its breech-block hinged at the rear.)

The life and the vigor of White's pictorial work are obvious, it seems to me. He has caught the friendliness and fun, the give-and-take that prevail on the target range. Who hasn't had a similar experience? All shots in the bull except that sour one that was pulled clean out into the lake at one o'clock. The embarrassed bear's friend is doubly delighted—at the riddled bull and at the off-shot, too. (See cut on page 207.)

Or see the receiver ring and side wall of La

Bantchni's sporter, or the receiver of the Remington 722 Premier, or the Winchester 70 custom grade, or the De Luxe Fabrique Nationale Mauser. You choose the amount and the type of engraving you want. Of equal quality, the work can be conventional, reserved, subdued, or the reverse, like the custom tailoring of clothes.

You ask for what you like and can afford, and for what you think you'll enjoy living with for years and years, if you're a real rifle-lover. Who is to say that your taste is either timid or flashy? And why should you care? In a custom rifle you please yourself; you are the individual who judges. This goes for any custom job, even if it lacks any decoration at all and is "purely functional," built up or whittled down or altered in any way to let you be a more efficient and therefore happier rifleman.

Gun Digest directories list a good many engravers. Only a few are named here, as examples. To some of us, some of these names ring a bell more clearly than others do. It is safe to assume that all are craftsmen. At any rate, having a rifle engraved isn't like buying a rifle, even a custom rifle. We may know

A magazine floorplate engraved by Griebel.

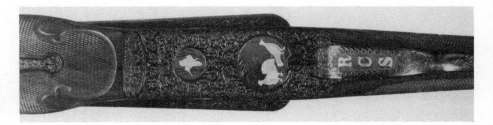

Woodcock and grouse. Note that last little touch of the custom job, screwhead slots pointing north and south.

pretty much what we want, but if we're sensible we listen to the artist's suggestions.

I do remember a seasoned still-hunter who, in placing an order for a factory job on his custom-built '94 Winchester, put in one sentence of caution, "Do not make neck too thin." So that buck's head looked natural, and the work was really beautiful. I'd never forget that rifle, and I was permitted to do all the

Griffin & Howe floorplate engraving and inlay.

hunting with it that I wished. Father may never have heard the term "Custom-built rifle," and I'm sure I hadn't then. But that .30-30 fitted him, was stocked differently from any other rifle I've seen, and good reason why: he'd sent a full-length, professional-type drawing along with his order. Flat-sided receivers take engraving well.

Here are some engravers listed by the *Digest,* not mentioned so far in these pages:

Cole Agee, 2300 Christine, Fort Worth, Texas.
E. D. Averill, Rt. 3, Miller Creek Rd., Missoula, Mont.
Max E. Bruehl, 4956 Elston Ave., Chicago 30, Ill.
Dan Clark, 427 Crawford, Norman, Okla.
Adam David, 1401 Ridgeway Pl., N. W., Canton 9, Ohio.
Jos. Fugger, c/o Griffin & Howe, 202 E. 44th St., New York 17, N. Y.
Charles H. Jerred, 853 West 1st St., Fulton, N. Y.
E. C. Prudhomme, 305 Ward Bldg., Shreveport, La.
Woodie Ward, Rt. 1, Box 927-R, Silsbee, Texas.

CARVING AND INLAYS

Carving and inlays on stock wood have one thing in common: some like them, some hate them. We hear of "the Western school"; yet a liking for such embellishment is by no means confined to that part of the country.

Sometimes carving is a part of the checkering pattern, uncheckered designs standing out separately from the diamonds, as in the work of Hal Hartley, custom Winchester, Anthony Guymon, Roy Weatherby, Jules La Bantchni, and many, many others.

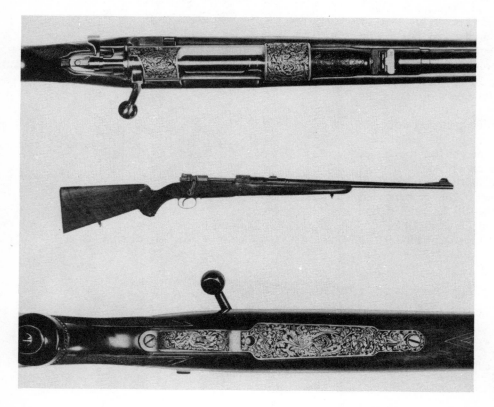

A Presentation Grade F. N. Mauser from Firearms International.

To answer the demand for carved stocks at moderate prices, Guymon had designed for him a machine that reproduces the carving from the original master stock. He continues to carve to order, too.

There may be inlaying of wood or precious metal in wood, or of precious metal in the steel. Those who do this work are carrying on a tradition, one that the Kentucky rifle, a while back, carried on, too. In this work and in engraving it would be interesting to study and compare the English and German influences on the native American—where the latter is influenced at all, for since it's American it's pretty independent, and salty, too, at times.

Whether we like embellishment or not, whether we even think it "belongs" on a rifle, much of it is done with artistry. That we have to admire. It goes 'way back in firearms history, back to ancient ordnance as well as sporting arms. It is something more, something that a few people always have craved, and that thing is beauty. There's a beauty in simplicity, and a different kind in intricate elaboration. Each has its followers. We can choose either sort of rifle embellishment, or none at all, being most satisfied with the beauty of line alone, and with no coloring effects but those of steel and wood.

STOCKS

Here we consider the woodwork chiefly as it helps us toward marksmanship. Most of our custom stockers develop a distinctive style and stick to it, changing their design only slightly as time goes on and brings with it different tastes and different theories as to what is most helpful in certain types of shooting. A stock and forestock can be specialized for target work—four-position, prone, bench-rest, International, or Schuetzen offhand—or for hunting. And in hunting our needs could vary, too—varmint, big game in the woods (snapshooting, usually, except for the most expert and patient hunters), big game in mountains or on the plains, or all-round prospecting.

It is natural that a stocker should standardize his work to some extent, for he has his convictions as to what is right for certain purposes. Yet most of them will make a stock to fit the customer, if that individual needs—and knows that he needs—something quite different from the usual length, drop and

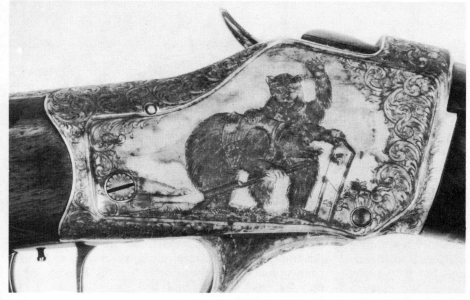

Delicate engraving decorates receiver ring and sidewall of this seven-pound La Bantchni rifle. The wood is French walnut.

A study in chagrin by Alvin A. White. Bruin has four in the bull, and one clear out at one o'clock. Forgot to wipe the oil out of the old High Wall Winchester, maybe.

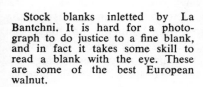

Stock blanks inletted by La Bantchni. It is hard for a photograph to do justice to a fine blank, and in fact it takes some skill to read a blank with the eye. These are some of the best European walnut.

A seven-pound .30-06 sporter stocked by La Bantchni. Unfinished.

Rigby .416 caliber stocked in French walnut by La Bantchni.

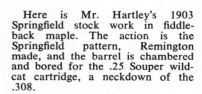

A Hal Hartley stocking job on a Winchester Model 63 .22 automatic with Lyman Alaskan scope. "The Winchester 63 wood," says Mr. Hartley, "is 'quilted' maple showing a wide, deep, wavy effect. The 1903 is maple showing a fine, close fiddle-back figure. These two are almost the extremes in maple.

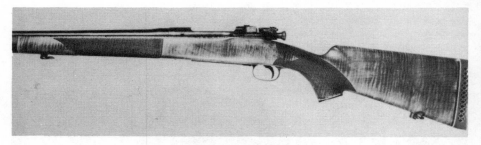

Here is Mr. Hartley's 1903 Springfield stock work in fiddle-back maple. The action is the Springfield pattern, Remington made, and the barrel is chambered and bored for the .25 Souper wildcat cartridge, a neckdown of the .308.

pitch specifications. This fitted stock may or may not cost the buyer more than the rather standardized form made by the gunsmith of his choice. An extreme example of the fitted stock is the goose-neck. It lets a person who has lost the sight of his aiming eye fire from the same familiar shoulder. Such a rifle is hardly well balanced for carrying, but it can pay off when there's shooting to be done. We carry a hunting rifle much more than we fire it, but which is the more important activity?

Stock Woods

Walnut is the great favorite of stock woods, used most widely when it's available and will fit into the cost accounting. Factories have used gumwood and birch as substitutes for plain American walnut.

The weight of the wood to be used may figure as more important than its price or its appearance. It would be foolish to have a custom rifle built with extreme lightness in mind—short, thin barrel, aluminum buttplate, floorplate and guard, even the receiver lightened where it's safe to do so—and then have it stocked in beautiful but heavy burl walnut that's excessively hollowed out.

Plain American walnut, Honduras mahogany, mesquite, and western maple are somewhat similar in weight. Big variations exist, as we'd expect. Burl American walnut, eastern maple, rosewood, and European walnut are likely to be noticeably heavier. Birch may be, too. Cherry and koa generally are lighter than "standard" American walnut, if there is such a thing, for wood is organic; even when it's dead you can read some of its life history.

In walnut alone there's a tremendous range of choice as to weight, color, figure, and of course the cost. There's been a tendency to disparage American walnut, of which so many of our stocks are made, both factory and custom. Some of the standard-grade stocks made of it long ago have a color range and a figure that make our hands itch to hold and caress them, to take them out into bright sunlight and study the depth and the solid goodness they have. World wars cut seriously into our walnut supply and range of choice. Yet it is still fairly common to find a factory-made rifle with a stock that repays oil-finishing with genuine beauty, even though that American walnut may be too soft to take clean, sharply cut checkering finer than, say 20 lines to the inch—and keep it under reasonable hunting use. The less expensive factory stocks come without checkering, though this feature was a regular "extra" on almost any inexpensive stock in the past, and some took and held it to our utter admiration. For that matter, some of the same grades still do.

Most imported walnut now goes under the name of "French," and usually it is strong and heavy. Even so, we want it to run pretty straight at the grip, a weak point in almost any stock except some of those that are made for bench-rest, and we want the grain of the fore-end (on a bolt action) to be pretty straight too, and running diagonally forward up toward the barrel. That's for accuracy in a light or a fairly light rifle.

The French walnut usually has fine, not coarse grain, and if it's been seasoned slowly and properly it isn't liable to warp, although an oil finish, at least in the barrel channel, gives less protection against warpage than a lacquer, varnish, shellac, plastic or other finish that keeps out dampness. A coating of oil or gun grease in the barrel channel, and in the magazine and action well too, seems to do no harm to the shooting and is mighty reassuring when the canoe upsets and there's no screwdriver in the kit.

French walnut is durable, rarely develops "checks," a name for slight cracks that may never grow larger or deeper for years and years, and it rarely becomes porous, even at the end-grain, where wood fibers have been cut across, as at the forestock tip. This wood—and much American walnut, too— often is a feast in colors, from light tan through browns to "black as your hat." In contrast, California "Claro" walnut has a bright figure, not a bit subdued, and it's become popular chiefly for that reason. Like any stock wood it needs and generally gets close inspection—which, let us hope in every case, comes not too late!—and so does mesquite. The latter has been called gaudy, but some people frankly like gaudiness, whether or not they've read the dictionary's definition. Why shouldn't they? I'd hate to see riflemen regimented in thought or feeling, wouldn't you?

Now maple: there's a great old favorite. It was a standby for the Kentuckies, and you know what we owe to those rifles. Most of this finely figured wood, so rich in curls or waves or tiger-stripes, comes from the northeast or from Oregon.

Hal Hartley, Lenoir, N. C., has been a specialist in maple for years, and he's an artist with the blowtorch. As he uses it, this treatment makes the grain distinctive.

"I do specialize in maple," he writes, "and I believe the rifle stocks will run eight to one over walnut. I also make about 50% of the shotgun stocks

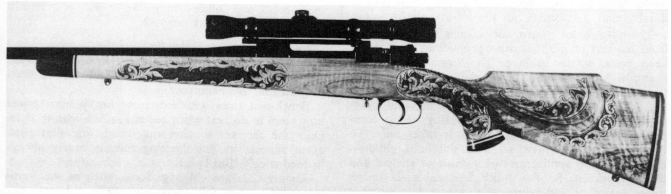

An Anthony Guymon stock of Oregon myrtle built to the customer's specifications.

Another view of the Guymon myrtlewood stock.

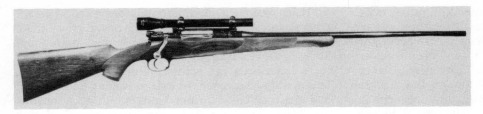

Mauser action .270 stocked in rosewood by P. O. Ackley.

of maple. People are getting more conscious of the beauty of maple woods, and as figured maple is getting scarce they will have to get it while it can be had. The northern border States have most of the hard, figured maple. Canada has a fair supply. Here, in the Blue Ridge and Appalachian mountains, the supply is about exhausted."

We seldom see cherry or apple stocks now, but myrtle, properly air-seasoned, has a good following, and its grain is often prominent and beautiful. Mahogany, however, is seldom well figured and it may be porous, though it'll take a good finish. Rosewood is used to an extent, and it can be made up into a fine-looking stock, a little heavy, perhaps.

Stock Finishes

Any custom sporter deserving the name has a well-finished stock. Usually this work takes time, though special, fairly new preparations like George Brothers' Linspeed Oil can shorten the job and still produce nice work. Most custom stocks have an oil finish that is durable and that brings out the beauty of the wood.

There's also the varnish or lacquer finish, different from the sort of job that mass production must do to keep costs within balance. The French finish, for example, looks at first glance like an especially fine varnish job. It isn't just that! It gives some depth to the appearance of the wood, and it brings out practically all of the grain's inherent beauty, being comparable in this to a fine oil finish. It takes time. To bring out the polish—which need not be a glitter—there are many applications of varnish or shellac and elbow lubricant. So this finish is durable. It resists minor scratches and bumps that nature lets fly at it in the field, and after 20 years of steady though careful use it looks about as good as it did at first. There is, of course, no darkening or enriching of the grain, as with an oil finish. Weatherby, I think, uses a plastic finish on some stocks, durable, and rather glossy. It isn't like the French finishes I know, but a lot of people like it. The main thing is for each of us to have his pick.

This brings in the do-it-yourself, so popular now, sometimes matter for cartoon comedy. But it is encouraging as a return to what was (with a big *maybe,* when you think of it carefully) a more self-reliant America. It's fun, and it isn't liable to ruin a stock, for at first try the beauty or the opposite isn't likely to be more than skin deep. Just one sheet of sandpaper now costs a scandalous price downtown at the store, but it can be worth buying.

Most of us choose an oil finish if we put it on ourselves, and there are new and good formulas to use if time is of the essence. (It shouldn't be, but we all live differently.) Only a little while before this writing the Wood Craft Laboratories, Box 52-R, Northfield, Ill., brought out their kit for the home workshop, kitchen, or off-duty card table. It's complete, with sandpaper, steel wool, filler, sealer, drying oil, and wax, and the cost is considerably below that of a box of .30-30 hulls. Not a mere surface job, it penetrates the wood.

Linseed oil is a favorite, usually the raw kind, for the drier in the "boiled" variety can hide the grain of the wood. So it's said, though I've seldom known it to do so and I rub 40 coats of the stuff into my stocks—raw or boiled, whichever's handy. Old linseed oil can gum on a stock, though I've had some that had been kept around for several years, tightly capped, and it did all right. Some mix varnish with it to fill the pores, and others may use coats of varnish, sanded down, for that purpose.

Bedding

As for bedding barrel and action in the stock, "the situation is fluid." There is no standardized method that is unequivocally *it.*

Bench-rest rifles with extremely heavy barrels just now seem to do best when bedded in full-floating style. Only the receiver touches the wood, and that part, as in almost any fine-shooting rifle, is nearly always bedded snugly. But bench-rest is a laboratory.

Rimfire .22s are obliging. Some, such as the Remington 513 target job, shoot beautifully with only one stock screw for assembly, and lots of smaller ones that do creditable shooting are bedded pretty casually. Few of these float, intentionally. Just at present the Winchester 52 target barrel is next door but three to free-floating, having only an adjustable band up front, and three narrow rubber pads, one ahead of the receiver, one at the rear, and the third behind the barrel band.

Except perhaps for the ultra-accurate, custom-stocked .22 match gun—which may not *always* outshoot a good factory job—the real problem is the high-power sporter. This one can be temperamental. Full-floating often works, even for rather heavy barrels. So does the system of contact that extends a few inches up from the receiver. Some stockers like a slight upward pressure at the forestock tip, or near it, to dampen barrel vibrations. There's also glass bedding, as with Herter's preparation, for instance, and full-length bedding in wood, a long, exacting job that so far certainly hasn't proved worthless.

Some 30 years ago, factory bedding left much to be desired. Custom competition—why buy a high-grade factory stock if the rifle wouldn't shoot well?—and the natural desire to improve have changed the picture. The standard grade but more expensive sporters—52, 70, 721, 722 and so forth—now are bedded rather well, almost always. Most of them show a slight, or a considerable, improvement in accuracy if worked over by a first-class stock man. Naturally some rifles that are called custom don't shoot to factory standards. We always have that kind of work, less of it now, perhaps, than about ten years ago.

Stock Design

Custom stocks vary in shape, size and purpose. They vary in styling, too. All this is healthy, just as a running stream is more attractive than stagnant, green-scummed water!

Light Rifles. Light-weights are fashionable now, though it would be truer to say that their purposes are more generally recognized than they were a few years ago, when most of us felt that a big-game rifle should weigh some eight or nine pounds, less scope and sling. We'd been conditioned to such weights, in the better factory jobs, for some time. But taste is a pendulum and we no longer have to look for an old-timer in good shape if we want a seven-pounder or a still lighter woods or mountain rifle.

It is custom gunsmiths who are still out in front, leading this return to the featherweights. Many of them hunt, when they can get time to, and they tell us the old story: you do a lot more walking than shooting.

Usually these custom featherweights have short, light barrels. Muzzle brakes—nozzles to reduce recoil —are in favor, naturally enough when gun weight is so low, and at least one, the Sha-Cul, doesn't fling an unearthly blast back into our ears. But stocks get lightened, too.

First of all, we'd choose the wood. A burly piece may be beautiful, but it's heavy compared to a straight-grain. Then we'd plan the design: light forearm, just big enough to afford a good grip *if* we use cannon-fodder in the pinweight and have to hold tight; small mid-section, stiff enough for the accuracy we really need in the hunting we're to do, and a four- or three-shot magazine capacity would be plenty; stock fairly thin, just long enough and high enough to fit us in our hunting clothes, and with buttplate or pad sufficiently big to ease recoil, no more; and pistol grip small—or even no pistol grip, though it helps when recoil is heavy, and custom bolt guns without one scarcely exist. Still, this is *our* rifle, built to our ideas, and who else is going to carry it? And you know we

hunt rough country, being he-men and rugged as all get-out.

Hollow the stock? Why, certainly. It helps to give steadiness to that light barrel. Hollow the forestock, too? It's been done, square sections taken out up along the line, subtracting maybe two or three ounces. That otherwise full-length-bedded job shot like a match (not a bench) rifle. It was a .250-3000 weighing a sure eight pounds, and it could have been 10 percent lighter and still a good, accurate sporter.

Let's consider a rifle that L. H. Brown, Kalispell, Montana, built for himself. It's described in the September, 1955 *Rifleman,* his article on "Light Hunting Rifles." Brown took over much of Niedner's equipment when he went into custom work on his own. He's a big-game hunter, finding time for it even though he's a gunsmith.

The action of this 6½-pound rifle, .35 Whelen caliber, is a G 33-40 Mauser, seven ounces lighter than the German military. Barrel measures 20 inches, two inches longer than those of some featherweights of the same power, more or less. The gun has a shotgun safe, quick to get at, no scope, for it's a woods rifle. The irons are a light receiver peep, folding notch sight on the barrel for emergency use, and the front on a slim ramp.

As we'd expect, the stock has a recoil pad, well worth its weight on this sort of rifle, a Monte Carlo comb sloped forward to go easy on teeth and jaw, hollowed butt, and short forestock. The latter feature puts the front sling swivel out on the barrel; ahead of the little snobble: not right for long strings at target but OK for the two or three carefully pulled shots a hunter might have to use. If bullet impact varies when we fire with and without the sling—even when sling tension is very light—a careful rifleman will know the allowance to make.

A cross-bolt runs through the stock, behind the recoil lug in the receiver. This strengthening, so common on Mauser rifles, is to prevent the receiver from setting back in the wood, or even splitting it at the rear.

Combs, Grips and Forestocks. These give us the revolutionary, the conservative, and the in-between. We are all, stockers and shooters both, working for the same two things, shootability and beauty. About all that we—or most of us—agree on is that the butt-plate should be flat! And some do like a little more shoulder-gripping curve in it than others do.

A conservative stocker isn't necessarily unprogressive—far from it! Some of the most comfortable, most shootable stocks are made by craftsmen of this sort. They dislike abrupt lines, even if they're curved, as of course those of the most "extreme" stocks still are.

Makers of the latter type of stock aren't trying to be funny, or even sensational in the meaning that the sensational is only temporary. They're working hard toward the same two goals, but taking longer steps, that's all. And they plan their stocks to give the best possible results in performance and looks "not for just

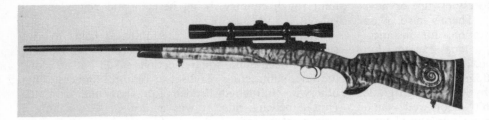

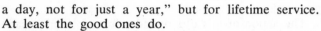

A standard production Streamliner by Anthony Guymon. Tor-
toise-shell hard-maple stock.

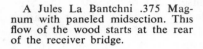

A Jules La Bantchni .375 Magnum with paneled midsection. This
flow of the wood starts at the rear
of the receiver bridge.

a day, not for just a year," but for lifetime service.
At least the good ones do.

As an example let's take Anthony Guymon. His
address is 203 Shore Drive, Bremerton, Wash., a location that naturally has something to do with that
phrase, "the western school."

He believes in his work. "Our streamliner design,"
he writes, "will not kick you under the cheek-bone.
It's designed to swing the rifle away from the face when
recoil brings the rifle back, 20 degree rolled over comb
away from barrel line."

The sloped-down Monte is accepted now and has
been for years. Elmer Keith was one of the first to
publicize its value. Shoot a heavy load in a light rifle
with *sloped-up* Monte and the lesson comes smack on
the jaw. Hurts.

Guymon's wide forestock is meant to lie comfortably
in the hand, to afford a grip if you must hold hard up
there, either under heavy recoil or when shooting in
a strong cross-wind. The pistol grip of "coolie hat"
design is "extreme," sure enough, but it could have
its purpose. Most of us hold farther back on the grip
when we fire from that most accurate unaided field
position, prone with sling. Change of grip on a moderately light rifle, not necessarily a featherweight, can
easily produce change of zero. So a shooter with a big
hand, or one for whom the stock, in prone, is a bit
long, could use that sharp curve for consistent positioning of his hand. In the Adirondack witch-hopples
or in the thick, almost jungle growth of some rarely
hunted parts of the West Indies I shouldn't care for
that coolie. But in caliber and build most of Guymon's
rifles are for mountains and plains, and he has a
special varminter style, too. I doubt that he stocks
many lever actions, and few gunsmiths do many of
them now. It is possible to produce an extremely
beautiful rifle on this action, with or without pistol
grip. The long "under-belly" of a full or even three-
quarter-length tubular magazine wouldn't help, but
those who would restock such a rifle, or have it re-
stocked, usually aren't of the type that wants any
such warehouse of firepower.

La Bantchni and Ackley stocks have an unusual

panel effect in mid-section. It goes around the sides
of the receiver and flows back into the grip. Scarcely
anyone would be likely to call it an "extreme" touch,
and in fact these two men are representatives of the
conservative school. The additional wood does give
strength and rigidity where a marksman would want it.

Some Custom Stockers

A few custom stockers advertise rather extensively,
but probably the majority do little of it. Some depend
entirely on word-of-mouth reputation, which can be
extensive if it's duly earned. Most lists of men in this
profession are noteworthy for their omissions, and perhaps this one is outstandingly so! A printed recommendation seldom means as much as a personal visit
to the shop—don't hang around too long!—or even a
careful examination of just one of the stocks recently
made by a craftsman whom we're considering.

Some of the men, or their work, mentioned here are
known to me, some are not, and I realize that others,
forgotten or overlooked, will come to mind too late.
I believe that all of them are "good," but anyone's
work can depreciate or improve as time goes on. The
same can be said of almost any model of factory rifle
that's being produced.

P. O. ACKLEY, Box 185, Murray, Utah.
AMRINE & OVERLY, Marysville, Ohio.
APEX RIFLE CO. Sun Valley 3, Calif.
ERVEN P. BARBER, 3326 NE 57th, Portland, Ore.
E. C. BISHOP & SON, Warsaw, Mo. (Finished and unfinished
   stocks.)
L. H. BROWN, Kalispell, Mont.
CHARLES H. CANOLL, Broad St., Waverly, N. Y.
REINHART FAJEN, Box 115, Warsaw, Mo.
AL FREELAND, 3734 14th Ave., Rock Island, Ill.
GARTMAN CUSTOM GUNS, 12 Richfield, Cranston 10, R. I.
DALE GOENS, Box 224, Cedar Crest, N. M.
GRIFFIN & HOWE, 202 E. 44th, New York 17, N. Y.
GUNREBLU, Biltmore 3, N. C.
ANTHONY GUYMON, 203 Shore Drive, Bremerton, Wash.
HAL HARTLEY, R 5, Box 708, Lenoir, N. C. (Maple.)
WILBUR J. HAUCK, RFD 1, West Arlington, Vt.
R. HICKS, 9013 Cordova NE, Albuquerque, N. M. (Modern
   Kentucky rifles.)
HOLTZ GUN SHOP, RD 1, U. S. 22, Ebensburg, Penna.
   (Maple.)

Griffin & Howe bigbore. Open sights, for different ranges, on short rib; heavy, high comb; G&H double-lever side scope mount; Winchester 70 action. Calibers include .350 Magnum, .404 Jeffery, .416 Rigby, .425 Westley Richards, and .458 Winchester Magnum. Strengthening bolt through stock, much in .458 Winchester 70 fashion, eases the strain on the recoil shoulder.

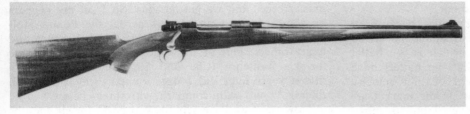

Ackley sporter with Mannlicher type of forestock.

Merton L. Hueber, Springer, N. M.

Paul Jaeger, Jenkintown, Penna.

Kess Arms Co., 3283 N. Green Bay Ave., Milwaukee 12, Wis.

Jules La Bantchni, Olympic Custom Guns, 2202 Pico Blvd., Santa Monica, Calif.

Harold E. McFarland, 741 Copper Basin Rd., Prescott, Ariz.

Mashburn Arms Co., 112 W. Grand, Oklahoma City, Okla.

Leonard Mews, 932 W. Summer, Appleton, Wis.

Morton Gun Works, 2115 Santa Fe St., Wichita Falls, Texas.

Pachmayr Gun Works, 1220 S. Grand Ave., Los Angeles 15, Calif.

M. S. Risley, RFD, Earlville, N. Y.

Thomas Shelhamer, Dowagiac, Mich.

Shenandoah Guns, Berryville, Va.

Smokey's Gun Shop, Wyanet, Ill.

Keith Stegall, Box 696, Gunnison, Colo.

D. W. Thomas, Vineland, N. J. (Stock blanks.)

Roy Vail, Warwick, N. Y. (Supplies French walnut.)

L. R. Wallack, Northville, N. Y.

Weatherby's, Inc., 2781 E. Firestone Blvd., South Gate, Calif.

Al Weber, R 1, Box 154, Lodi, Calif.

* * *

We've saved the dessert till the last of this chapter, comment from a few custom makers who took time to write it—this profession is no forty-hours-a-week one—and perhaps whistled up a bit of courage, too. I can't help liking them all, for they obviously believe in their work and their words.

Then too, "I can but think," as an English professor might say, that they· up and made the effort not only for any publicity value that might accrue, but also for the good of the game. Their ideas and styling vary a-plenty, but they're all working for that same goal, combined utility and beauty in the stocks we put to our faces. The stock of the American sporting rifle is far from being perfected, but we're getting there. When and if it's finally evolved, I believe, it will improve our field marksmanship vastly, and it won't look like a burp gun's stock, either. I think we'll aim pretty close to the barrel, not through some points up in space.

Comment by P. O. Ackley

We try to be flexible enough to furnish something the customer wants so that when he gets it, it will look like something he had in mind instead of something that the stockmaker thinks it should. This is a very common fault with many inflexible stockmakers because all of their stocks look as if they have been cast in a mold, regardless of whether some are light or some large and heavy.

You will notice from the pictures of the rifles that I prefer the conservative type.

I usually try to talk people out of ornate things like the ridiculous inlays that we have seen in some of the stocks, the very radical humpback Monte Carlos which are so badly out of place in a hunting rifle, and work on the theory that a stock can be beautiful and useful at the same time.

I hate to take a very beautiful piece of wood with a great deal of character and then throw a ridiculous inlay in the middle of it, or to carve it up in the ornate manner that we see in so many. To me, this indicates a lack of taste.

The stocks shown in the pictures are very well made with a #1 checkering. Most have 24 lines to the inch, and it is surprising how universal the fit of these stocks is. In other words, for hunting purposes or out in the field, they fit almost everyone with either a scope or iron sights, where it is ordinarily impossible to get a stock to work with both types of sights.

We try to make the pull to fit the individual customer and the standard pull is approximately 14 inches, which would be entirely too much for women or smaller men. The rest of the universal stock can remain the same and still fit a large percentage of the people.

I still am at a loss to understand why the American stockmakers get the "club" accent. They seem to think it necessary to have a pistol grip close enough to the trigger so that you have to turn yourself inside out to get a hold on it. This might be all right for the Bench Rest profession, but on a sporting rifle it is completely out of place.

We also have this Monte Carlo complex, or sort of a monstrous creation with the comb slanting down or up or crosswise or what have you.

I think that if some of these guys would try it out they would find that a straight stock without a Monte Carlo would not whip as much as these radical ones, thus making it more pleasant to shoot.

It is entirely wrong to criticize rifles because of their velocities because the criticism should be aimed at the real source of the trouble, which is the bullet itself. All that it amounts to is that the bullets have not kept up with the development of high-velocity cartridges. Most of the bullets now on the market are very little better than the first jacketed bullets introduced in 1909; by that I mean that if you were able to find some jacketed bullets made fifty years ago, you would probably find them just about as good as anything you had now.

CUSTOM RIFLES IN AMERICA
By Jules La Bantchni

Writing words is out of my line, but I will try to make my viewpoint interesting to the reader on custom guns, as well as to the real gun enthusiast. Also to the artists and men who appreciate and know quality of craftmanship in a really fine gun—and there are many of these men.

In my twenty-five years of making guns I have not yet found the Ideal Gun (and I've seen them all). The gun that came closest to this ideal was a Griffin & Howe. Their guns were a little heavy at times—stock a little heavy, too, but the workmanship was superb.

Naturally, as do all creators, we look at the other masterpieces and we get an idea. So I set my peepers on some Master Gun Makers across the Pond—Holland & Holland, Westley Richards, Merkel, Sauer and many others. Out of this study and comparing came the La Bantchni Rifle and Shotgun. But not until fifteen years later did I dare compare my work with theirs. *Now* I will compare with their best.

Nowadays we have schools you go to for six months or a year. Or, better, yet, you tear down an old Springfield, get a semi-inletted blank, some glass bedding and wood putty. Put an ad in a well-known magazine and tell the public that the "canoe paddle" they see advertised *had* to look like that. It was made for a shooter who wants to use a scope sight. The proud owner who buys this highly publicized product puts it up to his face for the first time. Now he wonders why he can't see through the scope without moving his head around in five or six different positions to

Light La Bantchni sporter.

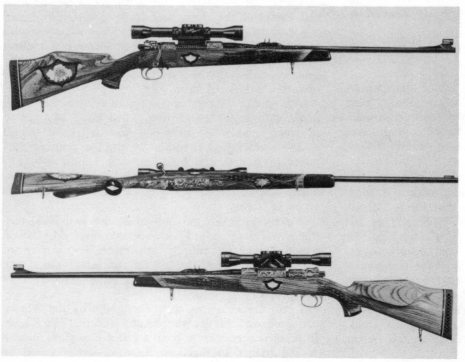

Weatherby custom-made .300 for the Shah of Iran. California mesquite stock with ivory inlaid map of Iran. The royal crest is engraved inside the map.

get in the right place. But to the parlor hunter it's okay. He will probably never use it, anyway. He will keep it in a gun cabinet or show it to his friends, explaining to them that the stock had to have a Monte Carlo with three-inch drop at comb. Oh, yes! Cast-off* half an inch, so when you cheek your gun you can see what the gun looks like along the right side of the barrel.

Then there is another class of Gun Maker. The *art* of making guns doesn't mean a thing to them, because they know they cannot possibly compete with the few fine artists we do have. To begin with, they start blowing out cartridge cases from .22 Hornets into .375 Magnums. When the case is stretched to the limit and resembles a milk bottle with a nipple on it, and has great appeal to the individual . . . then comes the problem. What name can they give this dream shell, that the public will go for? By all means, this gun *must* have a flashy stock—anything *but* walnut! Another *must* is elaborate inlays all over in red, yellow, purple and white. Instead of a gun, it looks as if the hunter is carrying a Navajo blanket. And he must never forget that this gun will kill the largest game on the Continent, with only one shot.

As in everything else, some things are made for

*Cast-off, for a right-handed shooter, sets the toe, the heel, or even all of the butt a short distance to the right, usually a small fraction of an inch, a quarter being common. A cast-off toe can reduce or eliminate the jab presented to a high-chested shooter. A cast-off heel, fairly popular on side-by-side double-barrel shotguns, can make it easier for a heavy-chested person to see instantly down the rib between the barrels when he snaps the gun to his face. Cast-on of the butt, to the left, is the reverse. It can partly reduce the cheek-bump delivered by a comb that's too high, or that rises too abruptly, by in effect moving the comb to the right. Stock design often can eliminate the need for cast-off or cast-on, though it's true that many fine shotguns made in England for discriminating customers have one or the other, and perhaps the idea started there. —H. S.

purely commercial purposes. Other items are made for a more discerning public who want, and appreciate, the finer commodities of life. There is lots of room for improvement on both kinds.

The man who *knows* guns always prefers European walnut. The cost is a little more, but you have the finest in stock wood that grows. As a critic would express it, "Wood fit for a king!" Here's hoping that our new gun-makers will try a little harder to turn out a finer gun. As for myself, I hope I never lose that thrill that comes when I see a real masterpiece in wood and steel, called a Gun.

COMMENT BY ROY E. WEATHERBY

My greatest ambition in life was to some day build for the discriminating sportsman and hunter the finest, most accurate and beautiful rifle in the world, coupled with a service just as outstanding.

It was in 1945 that I started this great undertaking in a very meager way, with no employees. Finally, one by one, they were added. Each year that passed, the number of skilled, select men grew and grew. The popularity of and the demand for my products grew likewise, until today I find myself well established, building what I honestly and conscientiously feel to be what I set out to accomplish some eleven years ago —the finest rifle the world has ever known.

Power—killing power—was my first achievement. I felt that if I could get any bullet traveling fast enough, one could kill any animal on the face of the earth with but one shot—even if rather poorly placed. I have proved this theory time and time again on the North American continent, Africa, India and other parts of the world.

At first my customers consisted of only the real high-velocity enthusiasts and those who could afford and demanded the finest in a firearm. At one time 90 percent of all our rifles built were strictly custom

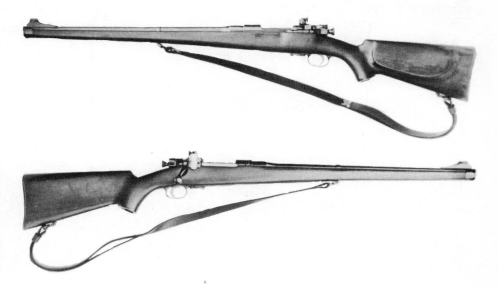

Please remember that a custom rifle is built to increase *one* person's efficiency, and to suit his tastes. Charles Canoll made this Springfield sporter for himself. About the only non-essentials are the quick-detachable version of sling swivels, the pistol grip cap, and the Mauser type of magazine floorplate release. As for full-length forestocks, or cheekpieces, you like 'em or you don't.

made, with beautiful, exotic woods; inlays of ivory, ebony and other rare materials; checkering by the finest craftsmen; and finish of sheer beauty and durability.

However, I found it somewhat difficult to find a sufficient number of those people demanding such ornate work, and started building the Weatherby Deluxe rifle. Even though 90 percent of our production today is of this Deluxe model, the remaining 10 percent of custom-built rifles number into the thousands.

Some people ask why any man would want a rifle built with such a beautiful stock, inlaid with rare woods, fancy checkering, engraved action and barrel. That can be answered in this way. Why is it that people like chrome strips on their automobiles? Why do they not all buy black cars? Why do people build homes decorated with expensive flagstone and equipped with gadgets and modern conveniences? It is because there is always a certain number of people who want something different. They know just what they want and are willing to pay the price.

Naturally, the finest, most elaborate stock does not make a rifle shoot any better. But it is the pride of ownership—and that goes a long way in this world in which we live. The remark has often been made, "Why, I would be afraid to take that rifle on a hunting trip!" But one need be no more concerned about taking an elaborately stocked or engraved rifle on a hunting trip than about taking his nice shiny new automobile on a vacation trip. The rocks and pebbles from the cars ahead batter and mar the hood and windshield. The parking lots seem to get their fair share of paint chipped off the sides of automobiles. But these automobiles are still in use, and when one becomes a bit shabby it is taken to a body shop and a repaint job makes it look new again. Thus, after people have used one of our custom rifles a few seasons and perhaps have it marred to some extent, a refinish job will put that rifle right back in its original form at but a fraction of the cost.

Another reason for these custom rifles is that many people want and are willing to pay for a rifle specific-ally fitted to them. It is not uncommon to have people fly completely across the country just for a personal fitting so that when that rifle comes up to their shoulder, their eye is in the middle of the scope field.

We have literally hundreds of people throughout the world with these beautifully engraved and inlaid creations who hunt with them every year. Mr. H. W. Klein of Dallas, Texas, has at least twenty of the most elaborately built rifles we have ever produced, and he has used all of them on various hunting trips throughout the world. As this is being written he is using one for polar bear hunting in the Arctic.

We just finished one for the Shah of Iran, with the map of Iran inlaid in ivory and the gold crest of Iran inlaid within the ivory. Five of our Custom rifles were built for Ex-President Miguel Aleman of Mexico. Also Dr. Heinz Nordhoff, the president of the Volkswagen Company in Germany; General Nate Twining; General Curt LeMay; General Robert L. Scott, Jr.; Ed Quinn, president of the Chrysler Corporation; John Wayne; Robert Taylor, and hundreds of other well-known businessmen and celebrities, as well as royalty.

However, we build hundreds of the ordinary Weatherby Deluxe rifles, stocked in a nice grade of walnut with the same type of special finish as on the most expensive custom model, but naturally without the ornaments.

Our main cartridges are the .257, .270, 7 mm., .300 and .375 Weatherby Magnums, and finally the new .378 Weatherby Magnum—the world's most powerful cartridge as far as killing power is concerned.

We take great care in selecting our skilled craftsmen. We have men from Germany, Finland, Iceland, England and other foreign countries where men have spent their lifetime working on the finest quality firearms. It is gratifying to receive the many letters from people of all walks of life—from royalty to the laborer—praising the accuracy, killing power, beauty and workmanship of the Weatherby rifle. We will always strive to continue manufacturing this sort of product and to give the finest possible service to our customers.

SINCE the time when the muzzle-loading caplock rifles went out of general use, most of us have owed the thrill of our first shooting to rimfire ammunition. It's true that there was a time in the last century, and reaching pretty well into this one, when a certain kind of hunter rather looked down on the .22 and even larger rimfires. They didn't seem worthy of any serious beginner's attention.

Sometimes the oldtimers advised the wasteful and unwittingly cruel method of "learning on the game." Target shooting, they thought, didn't amount to much as training. If the youngster was to hunt deer, let him start with a deer rifle. A few shots at a hatchet-blaze on a tree ought to be enough, hadn't they? Thing to do was to learn to *hunt*. Then your shots at deer would be close-up, and the shoulder's a big mark, isn't it? After the kid had been blooded a bit he could go fancy if he liked, and learn to break the neck. Nice shot, and your deer dropped right there.

We know better now. Whether we're young or mature when we start to learn we generally have sense enough to begin with the .22 rimfire, and our affection for that caliber is likely to stay with us. If we go on and really learn rifle marksmanship our respect for it grows. We may call it a pipsqueak, but if we know the score, that's a pet name, no insult. In its field the .22 is as satisfying as any other caliber.

Modern Rimfires

At the outbreak of World War I, more than 30 different rimfire cartridges were being made, about a dozen of them for currently manufactured arms. Many of the small ones came in various loadings, too. The most popular .22s gave a powder choice of black, smokeless and semi-smokeless. Peters used the King's Powder Mills brand of semi-; the others generally loaded Du Pont's Lesmok. About that time, Western loaded its Nublend semi-smokeless, at least in some of the small centerfires.

All the .22s except the BB and CB caps came with either solid or hollow-point bullets, and so did the two Stevens .25 calibers. Most of the smokeless .22s could be had with hardened, greaseless bullets. They didn't pick up grit in your pocket and carry it into the rifle chamber and throat.

Now we have nine calibers left, some of them perhaps living on borrowed time.

They are well made. At least the .22s, possibly not all the larger calibers, are more accurate than the stuff made a half-century ago. Some calibers and types are vastly better, for better sights, improved stocks, and usually snugger actions and superior barrels have kept up with the tremendous increase in popular demand—demand for more rifles and demand for better performance. The ammunition had to improve, too, and it did. The refinement of accuracy is held down more by retail cost limitations than anything else. Otherwise the sky would be the top floor.

CHAPTER 14

RIMFIRE CARTRIDGES

Case Material

But the increase of power is limited by the strength of the brass cartridge case. A rimfire holds its priming mixture in a hollow in the rim—what we might call its extraction flange. Ignition comes when that rim is pinched, suddenly and violently compressed, by the blow of the striker.

In the .22s we could have noticeably higher velocity and power if it weren't for two liabilities. Many old rifles and pistols that get lots of use wouldn't have the striker blow to ignite priming compound in much tougher cases—some have a hard time as it is—and a certain percentage of them lacks the breech-up strength to be safe even with the present high-speed loads. As for gas-proof qualities, some of our modern actions are inferior to a few of the best oldtimers, though at least when they're made by a reliable, recognized company they almost surely breech up snugly. Thus there's little chance for brass to burst in them. Look at the base of an empty. Unless it's been fired in an autoloader it should be as flat as it was before it went into the gun. The best autos leave them so, too.

It's a high compliment to the strength of modern cases that so few of them let go in old, badly set-back actions, or in chambers rusted or worn into practically bottle-necked form. Such guns are with us and will be for a long time. They set up a barrier against much increase in rimfire power with the case materials we have now.

The modern high-velocity .22 long-rifle develops about 22,000 pounds per square inch pressure, and for convenience and extra safety nearly all of our rim-

BB and CB caps (both obsolete), .22 short, .22 long, .22 long-rifle, .22 Remington Autoloading, .22 Winchester Automatic, .22 Winchester Rimfire, .25 Stevens (long), .32 short, .32 long. *Henry Way-Silvers Photo.*

fire cases are now made of brass. Copper has practically gone into the discard. Government pressure figures for the .45-70-500 Springfield service-rifle load went up to some 25,000 p. s. i. That cartridge or its smokeless equivalent—both handloads, of course—is still suitable for our biggest American game at moderate ranges. The lighter .45-70-405 Government load occasionally was put up in copper cases, 'way back when. These cartridges looked like rimfires, but the indentations above the head gave them away: they held the inside primer in place. The cases were fairly strong, though not meant for reloading. A few of these rounds are still unfired, but they're hardly suitable for accurate range work. Long-loaded black powder cakes or crumbles under the compression. In the latter event, up go the pressures.

Bullets

Most of the bullets loaded into our rimfire cartridges are of close to pure lead, so soft that the stepped-down heel of the .22 long-rifle, for instance, is upset to full or practically full rifling .groove diameter by the blow of the powder. Slightly harder lead is sometimes used, as in Remington Match long-rifles. The purpose may have been to reduce lead fouling in spite of those bullets' lack of grease grooves, as in the earlier lots. Neither idea is new, though both are well used in this target round. The old "greaseless" bullets in early .22 Winchester Automatic loadings, for example, were hard, like chilled shot. They didn't foul a good barrel. At least ten years ago Federal Cartridge introduced their Air-Line bullets: no grease grooves except a tiny ring, like that on the Remington Match. The single milled groove up front was decorative: that part of the bullet's ogive didn't touch the rifling lands. The type was successful and it's still made.

Well over 20 years ago, Western brought out their Lubaloy coated .22 long-rifle bullet, the soft lead carrying a thin wash of copper alloy. This round was loaded with Lesmok powder and it became a fair favorite on target ranges. Similar coating is now used on most Western lead bullets except the low speed .22 short-long-and-long-rifle trio and target rounds for bigbore handguns and .22s. The Winchester high

velocity or Superspeed .22s have it too, and the .22 Automatic.

In a general-purpose bullet, not for the finest target work, there's no serious objection to this plating. Bore wear may be a wee bit greater and the expansion in game slightly reduced. We must remember, though, that this coating is really thin. There's also the remote possibility—not quite as remote as the planets we read of in space stories—of electrolytic action rusting a barrel left uncleaned after using this ammo. I've heard only of the possibility, never have seen or heard of an instance.

The advantages too are slight. Since the coated bullet is harder because of that thin skin, it needs less lubrication. Dry wax serves well, and it's less liable to pick up grit than soft grease is. But this fact itself is a hazard: it *can* pick up some foreign matter; it isn't foolproof. It's still best to carry those cartridges in a clean belt, pouch or carton. Few of our .22 rimfire bullets except those made primarily for targets now carry a soft or at all sticky lubricant.

Copper alloy coating does shorten the unnecessary, even harmful bore cleaning that never stops while a single faint, gray smear shows on the patches. You can "clean out" a good barrel with this type of bullet, if you want to. It seems to whisk out all the old but harmless lead fouling.

With the improvements in automatic machinery we're probably getting more nearly perfect bullets than we did a comparatively few years ago, and better complete cartridges, too. In the popular target sizes, competition is keen. It may not be as sharp in the hunting and plinking types. One thing that most of us who are a bit particular would like to see in the stuff we use for hunting or even for casual field practice—which needn't be as casual as most plinking—is more careful bullet-seating. When a third of the bullets in a box of cartridges practically rattle when we shake them, a third turn 'round and 'round under light thumb-and-finger torque, and the rest are crimped in solidly, we sigh for a greater degree of uniformity. That's an exaggeration—few are quite so bad—but possibly the irritation is justified. Uncrimped .22 bullets have shot well—once were the great favorite—

and hard-crimped bullets have shot well, but mixtures aren't for us. We prefer the stale monotony of having them all alike.

Storage Qualities

Rimfire ammunition carried over a hot summer needs reasonable coolness and dryness. Our present non-corrosive priming compounds are much more stable than the first lots of that breed, when mercury was a member of the firm, and probably they are superior to nearly all the corrosive, potassium-chlorate types of the past.

But they have to do a hard job, igniting smokeless, not black or semi-smokeless powders. The latter were mostly black, anyway, with a shot of guncotton or similar vitamin that gave them greater strength, weight for weight, and almost invariably more accurate results on target. They fouled less than the black.

Loosely crimped rimfires are practically in the primer class, storage problems considered. We could, if we liked, keep them over summer in sealed glass jars. Yet in most climates it's enough to give them reasonable protection from dampness and heat. So taken care of, they almost surely stay reliable, surefire, for ten years or longer. Accuracy, in rimfires, seldom holds out that patiently, but five years' successful storage isn't at all amazing, at least for ammunition that's good enough for serious practice. When we get a fine shooting lot of .22s we take the best care of it that we can, for possibly we'll never find another that will do as nicely in a certain rifle.

Modern lubricant holds up well. Sometimes it can run off in hot sunshine, but we don't expose it to that, even on the firing line, if we can help it. When bullet grease is dry, caked and brittle it has small value as a lubricant. If we have some old, discontinued, and therefore mighty important size in that condition it pays to remove the flaky stuff—carefully, not letting any solvent get inside the case—and relubricate it. Ammunition of current manufacture isn't liable to get into that shape before it's used up.

Ballistic Tables

Factory ballistics, quoted in this and following chapters, are rather well standardized by the Sporting Arms and Ammunition Manufacturers' Institute. Sometimes, in fact, we find slightly different bullet weights given the same velocity *and* energy figures. Sounds screwy, but variations in bullet weight and velocity naturally exist even in ammo from the same factory box. Private laboratory tests often come up with different figures, and not every figure used is the result of actual tests. Here's a quote from a fairly recent Winchester ammunition handbook: "By plotting velocities over a series of ranges, a curve can be established from which muzzle velocity may be closely estimated." That is perfectly all right, it seems to me.

We can take the factory figures with confidence for all practical purposes, almost without exception. Factory mid-range trajectories are useful for comparisons, but they are taken from a line between the rifle muzzle and the bullet-hole in the target. But iron sights are above the bore, and scope sights usually higher still; so our actual firing trajectories work out quite a bit flatter.

Grains, feet per second velocity, foot pounds energy, mid-range trajectory and so forth are abbreviated. Here, then, are our rim-fire cartridges as made at present. Few have changed in any important respect for the last decade or more.

.22 SHORT

	Bullet in grs.	FS vel. at muzzle	100 yds.	FP energy at muzzle	100 yds.	MR traj. at 100 yds.
Standard velocity	29	1045	810	70		
High velocity	29	1125	920	81	54	4.3"
HV hollow point ...	27	1155	920	80	51	4.2"

The .22 short is our most accommodating cartridge, and our least accommodated. More people have fun with it than with any other, and in doing so they gain at least some familiarity with firearms. Maybe, if the coaching is right, they acquire a lifelong tolerance for firearms, safely used.

Some of them learn a *lot* of basic marksmanship with the short, our most economical cartridge—unless you handload a centerfire with primers bought from the Director of Civilian Marksmanship and cast your own lead bullets. At this writing, though I tremble at mentioning our rocket-powered living costs, shorts sell at a penny apiece.

They make little noise and, with due permission, can be fired in out-of-town places where a louder report and apparently far more dangerous charge might not get the green light. The short is dangerous enough, deadly up to many more hundreds of yards than we can see ahead in lots of country, and its full and serious range must be well over one-half mile, wind and weather permitting, for dampness does accelerate bullets—some. But a backstop for it is much easier to build than one for any centerfire rifle cartridge, and we learn safety best when the odds at first are somewhat on our side. Sure, the short is an accommodating little round.

But not one rifle out of 100,000, I'd reckon, does justice to it. Only two models are made for it, and furnished on special order, the Winchester 62 hammer gun, a pump repeater, and the Remington 550-2G Gallery Special, an autoloader. This cartridge requires a short chamber and .22 short rifling, with one full turn in from 20 to 24 inches of barrel. In the usual twist of 16 inches, correct for long-rifles, the bullet is badly over-stabilized. It spins too fast, madly, in fact. This is the great handicap. True, the much too long l-r chamber makes the bullet take a running jump into the rifling instead of being eased in. But target revolvers do the same thing to their bullets, now that the .38-44 S&W case of full cylinder length is a collector's treasure, and the .22 long, which at least fills .22 l-r *chambers,* shoots comparatively little better from them than the short, as a rule.

In spite of its great handicap the .22 short does pretty well on 50-foot ranges. Time and again a junior shooter whose spending allowance isn't on an on-call basis will prove that five of those maltreated bullets will stay inside the 8-ring (.817 inch), with most and sometimes all of them in the 9 (.483), and a few, not purely by luck, in the 10 (.150). That is good accuracy with a whirling dervish of a short fired from a barrel made for its college-bred brother who had most of the advantages in life. Sometimes it does better, sometimes worse.

In the best of target rifles that were specially made for it, this cartridge should come close to making 50-foot possibles, and probably it could do that, frequently. There is no selected, target grade ammunition made for it at a premium price, and never has been, as far as I know.

It's a good old cartridge, Smith & Wesson designed in 1855 or '56.

Standard Velocity

Now that first the CB and then the BB caps have fallen out of load lists, the "low power" short is our lightest cartridge. Yes, "Standard Velocity" is the correct term; it sounds more impressive.

The BB (bulleted breech) seems to have been the first rimfire cartridge, dated about 1840, practically a percussion cap then, with a rim bumped on it and a round ball set in its mouth. Though it is doubtful that it was loaded with a "round ball" after 1900 or so, the description continued long after the cylindrical bullet with rounded nose was adopted. The description distinguished it from the CB (conical bullet), which carried a bullet shaped much like that of the .22 short, and sometimes it was identical.

Most "smokeless" BBs had no powder at all, and you can imagine what the undiluted old-time priming did to barrels, if you enjoy nightmares. The black-powder charge for both these caps was about one and one-half grains: not much dilution of primer salts there, either.

Late ballistic figures credited the 18- or 20-grain BB bullet with 780 f. s. velocity, and the 29-grain CB with 720. Special NRA Junior rifle qualification courses at 25 feet were set up for these cartridges, for even that close they were considered safe from splash-back because of their low power. The bluff, square-shouldered BB cut rather clean holes in target paper, easy to score in a casual fashion, but the better balanced CB usually was a lot more accurate. Some factory lots of it did really well. After all, the low velocity meant fewer RPMs; so it wasn't as badly over-stabilized as the .22· short.

The low-power short is the best we have left to fire, at our own risk, in those little old pistols and rifles that probably shouldn't be used at all, the collectors'

items. But it has its practical uses, too, close-range practice when economy and the need of keeping noise to the minimum are important. With a muzzle velocity comfortably under the speed of sound it doesn't "crack." The report is too light to be heard at any great distance.

High Velocity

The high-velocity loads are only a bit faster than the standard, but their snappier report and the labels on the cartons give them sales appeal. Comparatively few stores bother to stock the low speeds, short or even long-rifle.

The high-velocity short is of course a hotter load than the slower one; yet bore wear hardly enters the picture. Most of us who value our .22 rifles use few .22 shorts, though we may have a modern auto-pistol that's made specially for them. Before World War II, High-Standard put out a field or plinking grade of .22 short autoloading pistol, and now there are top-notchers in this and other makes.

Actually, shorts aren't's really vicious. Once I ran 2,000 of them, including a few caps, through a K-.22 S&W target revolver and at the end of the shooting there was no visible erosion at all. We'd have to divide that figure by six—or at least by five, for the usual target string with a sixgun—to get a true report of chamber erosion. Even so, this 2,000 was by no means an unusual record. Most of the fear of using shorts in a long-rifle chamber stems from what used to happen when priming was corrosive and a few of the terribly destructive oldtime smokeless rounds got in by chance. However, I'll go along with those who fire few shorts, if any, in a match gun chambered for long-rifles.

No .22 short is a game cartridge, and we should remember that rats are as hard to kill as gray squirrels. Large game has been bumped off with .22 shorts, when the shooting was a push-over.

Even the hollow-point short is ineffective. It does sell *because* it's a hollow point, and lately you seem to see more of them in the showcases or on the shelves. But to expand properly, a bullet needs velocity, and it doesn't hurt to have a good, weighty cylindrical section behind the point, shoving it along. The hollow point short has neither.

Gallery Loads

These are not refined for accuracy. Both types, in a way, are novelties. One sends a 29-grain bullet of compressed lead dust at standard velocity, 1045 f. s., though earlier lots were as slow as 970—nice and quiet in a small indoor gallery. The other, fairly new, uses a 15-grain bullet of sintered iron, powdered iron with binders. Velocity quoted by Winchester is 1710 f. s., the highest of all rimfires.

"Spatterpruf." This is one of the trade names of the lead dust bullet. The thing was designed originally to be safe from splash-backs from steel target back-stops, and it is. Later it was found that gallery air could carry enough of the invisible dust to endanger

a fellow's lungs, and this hazard is now pretty well recognized.

For outdoor galleries, as at concession stands—"punkin fairs," for instance (and may they hold on for a generation to come, now that circuses are going underground), this load is just right. Often the shooting is done at less than 15 feet, and with perfect safety.

This cartridge has another use, and that is in field shooting, not hunting, but firing at safe, inanimate marks. That's a lot of fun, and even with this puny load it teaches us something, through that useful teaser called "relativity," about range and wind estimation. It's possible to make these bullets glance from slanting stones, but they're safer than the solid lead ones, or even the hollow points.

"Rocket." It was early in 1955, I think, that Remington brought out this fast load under the name of *"Rocket."* The thin little boxes sold fast; still do, pretty much.

For field shooting this type has its place. It is about as free from ricochets as any bullet, even the special high-velocity varmint-shooting slugs in the most advanced centerfire calibers.

But for hunting it's out. Pat Lashe, a young friend of mine and an Expert Rifleman many times over, told me of shooting a woodchuck with a Rocket. The bullet went to pieces in the shoulder, giving some degree of shock, of course, but almost no penetration. Pat quickly threw in a long-rifle that finished the short-range job. Perhaps the Q-99 ingredient now used stiffens them. I don't know.

Down at our junior gallery this type of short has a certain popularity. The sharp report and long, bright muzzle flash have their appeal, and if lights are dimmed you see a flash on the backstop. Bullet-holes in target paper are clean-cut, drilled right out. I doubt that this load is the most accurate .22 short at 50 feet, and a certain percentage of the Rocketeers is appalled when you tell them they're firing iron bullets through their pet rifles. Maybe I would be, too! The stuff jumps at a magnet, a graphic illustration of what it's made of.

For the first stages of junior qualification the Rocket type loads do all right. You don't see many of the Sharpshooters and Sharpshooter bar workers using them. Most of those who shoot shorts, and many do, prefer lead or copper-coated bullets. Still, I doubt that a few hundred rounds of the stuff would chew up a barrel so that you could notice it. But some of us want maximum bore life when we have a good rifle and have learned to use it. The load is a special-purpose job, not for general use.

The .22 long hasn't had a chance since black powder days. Some 1873 and 1890 Winchester and 1887 Colt repeaters were made especially for it. For reasons of economy most buyers chose the .22 short guns, it seems by the evidence of what's left. A few Winchester lever-action single shots were made for the long, and the 1900, 1902, 1904, and Thumb Trigger bolt guns, junior-size single shots. After a while the latter three were made with chambers reamed out for the .22 extra long, considered a fair game cartridge in its day. These were about the latest of a great many .22s, Floberts and others, that were intended to use longs. In our time one or two pocket-size foreign auto-pistol models were designed for this orphan.

For years our factories have loaded it in only one style, at velocity as high as 1375 f.s. Cutting it to 1240 no doubt increased its accuracy, and certainly made it somewhat safer in old, weak arms—which shoot far too many high-speed long-rifles, anyway. It is no size to choose for precision shooting, as anyone knows who knows much about .22 ammunition. The other kind of people usually buy it, and a lot of it. You see it in most gun stores.

But it is worth indenting this page for a new paragraph in which to state that at least in some rifles made with 16-inch long-rifle twist, some lots of it do shoot with accuracy that would amaze most of us who haven't given it a recent trial. Five-shot 50-foot possibles *are* possible, or at least mighty close to being so. Long use of it in a match rifle could bring the grief of an eroded bullet seat for the long-rifle load.

For .22 short rifles that have been rechambered to take the long-rifle it's probably the best load. Their slow twist can't spin the l-r bullet fast enough to keep it point-on at ranges much over 25 yards, usually. And if the ream-out job has been done a bit roughly, why, the long case covers up some of the defects. If the chamber's really rough, any cases longer than the shorts will swell and stick. Many fine old .22 short rifles have been ruined by this operation. Another way to spoil such a barrel is to rechamber it for .22 Hornet. This was quite a popular operation on Winchester .22 short single-shot muskets when that good little varmint cartridge was new. The result often shot well with 35-grain jacketed bullets like those of Sisk make, but the soft steel was burned out rather soon, as we'd expect.

Still, the .22 long keeps on selling; so it stays in production and probably will for years to come. People buy it until they hear about the .22 long-rifle or find that the shorts give nearly equal accuracy to that of the longs, in guns made for the long-rifle.

For some reason, perhaps because quite a few repeaters handling no other size were in circulation, the long was chosen as the size to load with the tiny No. 12 shot. Its old-style copper case was lengthened to overall .22 long dimension and its mouth crimped over a thin cardboard top shot wad. The BB cap also came in this style, though its overall was more like that of

.22 LONG

	Bullet in grs.	FS vel. at muzzle	100 yds.	FP energy at muzzle	100 yds.	MR traj. at 100 yds.
High Velocity	29	1240	965	99	60	3.8"

the CB, the one with conical .22 short bullet. Our present .22 shot cartridge is the long-rifle, its mouth crimped hard to hold the No. 12s without a top wad. For busting the miniature clay birds it's just right. Other practical uses don't exist. Somehow—perhaps the shot are harder than those that went into long and BB rounds—it doesn't lead a good rifled barrel as seriously as we might expect. Patterns are ragged, for rifling whirls and scatters a shot charge, and some Spanish-made brush guns have been rifled at the muzzle for just this purpose. The special smoothbore .22s show what this practice load can do.

.22 LONG-RIFLE

	Bullet in grs.	FS vel. at muzzle	100 yds.	FP energy at muzzle	100 yds.	MR traj. at 100 yds.
Standard velocity ...	40	1145	975	116	84	4.0″
Modern match	40	1105	970	108	84	4.1″
High velocity	40	1335	1045	158	97	3.3″
HV hollow point	36 or 37	1365	1040	149	86	3.3″

A keen rifle-crank could easily "stay young" as long as this cartridge has succeeded in doing. Many do, and all of us, if we've had any luck in living, know other men and women with completely different absorbing interests who have the secret that Ponce de Leon missed finding.

The birth date of the long-rifle has been named as 1887, though Walter Roper, who certainly knew his stuff, said that it was 1886. Peters and Stevens went into a huddle and brought it out.

It used the .22 long's five-grain charge of black powder in the long's case, but five grains or more of lead went on to the front end of the bullet. The heaviest long bullet had been only about 35 grains. Thus the long-rifle had from the first the benefit of a well-balanced bullet, and what was then a rather fast rifling twist, a turn in 16 inches, was worked out and standardized for it. The cartridge was less powerful than the .22 extra long rimfire, some nine or ten years older, but it had an overwhelming advantage.

It was accurate, just as had been planned. For one thing, its heavy bullet with long bearing burned black powder well. Contrary perhaps to the usual opinion, it wasn't necessary to swab out the barrel after every 10-shot target string. Except in dry, hot weather the cartridge shot cleanly for 50 rounds or so, giving what was fine smallbore accuracy in the old days.

And its bullet had enough weight to buck the wind much better than the lighter .22s had done. So the long-rifle's value for outdoor practice was recognized early; yet its light report, even in pistols, made it a gallery favorite. Smoke? Yes, but we stood it. My earliest gallery shooting was in black and Lesmok powder days. A fellow just expected to cough a bit, down on the range. Actually the fog was no more annoying than the rank and sharper odor of some smokeless shotgun powders under fancy and not too

familiar names. If there was time, when you extracted the red or yellow case, you turned down-wind to do it!

Standard Velocity

In the average small store this load is almost as uncommon as the low speed short. But on the thousands of indoor and outdoor ranges it's general issue. Nearly all rifles shoot it more accurately than the high-speed stuff, which *can* take a slower twist of 17 or 18 inches and like it. Sometimes the superiority of low- over high-speed ammo in the regulation 16-inch twist isn't as great as we'd expect, but always in the gallery its lighter report is appreciated. On most indoor ranges, if we use the high-vel, we're liable to get what cross-word puzzle writers call "a sidelong look." Four letters: "leer."

Outdoors, though it takes longer than the high-speed bullet to get to the target, there's less "delay" and a lower percentage loss of velocity, and wind affects it less. Remington quotes flight time over 50, 100 and 200 yards as .138, .287 and .616 second for standard velocity, and .121, .259, and .565 for the Hi-Speed. The latter type buys this fast travel at the price of more rapid loss of speed and energy; its bullet is bucking the air too fast for its own good.

Someone once remarked that the .22 long-rifle certainly could use a boat-tailed or taper-heeled bullet, provided that one could be manufactured and loaded with the necessary precision, and at a reasonable price. He was right. A boat-tail does little good on a jacketed, soft-point bullet for big game, for it hasn't much effect in retaining velocity until the rate has dropped below the 1100 .f s.* or so of sound. But at that time a boat-tail really goes to work, as in long range machine-gun fire, for instance.

To load a .22 long-rifle bullet of this form would offer problems. The tail, seated inside the case, would decrease powder space, increase loading density, though powders could be had or devised to take care of that. However, the bullet is about as completely standardized in weight and composition as any that we have, despite minor variations in its bearing surface and in its shape up front. It's a 40-grain pill of nearly pure lead.

So it's soft. It never really was hard, even in the old "smokeless, greaseless" type, the early semi-pointed Winchester Lesmok Precision, the present copper-coated or the old cadmium-coated, or the new Remington and Peters Match. It seems quite too liable that a boat-tail of soft lead, if one were applied, might be upset unevenly by the blow of the powder, just as the present stepped down "heel" is upset to almost if not quite full diameter when the cartridge is fired. If the upset of a soft-lead boat-tail were trivial, or if it were uniform, the project would seem more promis-

---

*1089 at 32° F. Add 1-plus foot for each degree of rise in temperature. Humidity and barometric pressure also have some effect.

ing. But who wants to bet that we'll never have such a .22 bullet?

Since the low-speed long-rifle is accurate and not at all noisy, it's used to some extent by squirrel hunters who know just what they're doing. With brain shots it is of course deadly, but it's only for the expert to use. The rest of us, who aren't so sure of placing our bullet properly, would do better with the high speed hollow point, and better still with a cartridge that fires a larger diameter bullet at a little lower velocity.

Most factory lots of standard long-rifle are accurate if they and the individual rifle are compatible. Without any special effort at selection we should get one and one-half-inch grouping at 50-yards from nearly any well-sighted, well-aimed and held rifle if we squeeze off the shots carefully. Better and worse can be done, as most of us well know. Except by target standards we can hardly call any lot sour, and that speaks well for mass production, doesn't it?

Clubs affiliated with the NRA, and NRA members too, generally have the privilege of buying .22 long-rifle standard velocity ammunition from the DCM at prices that compare pretty evenly with that of the .22 short at regular retail. Naturally transportation charges vary with distance and weight. Some of this ammunition comes in standard packaging; some is put up more impersonally! No matter: it's almost invariably good. Nearly always it does well in any one of the different rifles and pistols found on a healthy club's range, and in some of them it shoots possibles. Poor lots are at least as rare as they are in the regular trade production.

Match Loads

About the first of the higher-priced special target cartridges were Winchester Precision 75 and 200. The former carried a lighter dose of the Lesmok powder and it was meant for 75-foot shooting. The other stuff was for 200-yard work.

Other early target loads were Remington Palma, Peters Tack-Hole and the United States Cartridge Company's USNRA. For a time at least the latter sold at standard prices, though it was a match cartridge of a little higher velocity than the usual 970 f. s. or so. Toward the end, it was furnished in hollow point, too, and it was our best long-rifle hunting cartridge until the high speeds came along.

There were a couple of interesting bullet variations made by Remington, the "flat end bullet" of about World War I time, and the Hi-Speed wadcutter of the late 1920s or early 1930s. The first one I've never seen, though I presume it was a target load and I'm almost certain that it had Lesmok powder behind it. The Hi-Speed punched clean holes in target paper, just as today's .38 Special sixgun bullet of almost identical shape does, but it got little use on rifle ranges. At that time the accuracy of high-velocity .22 rimfires was not good, though as usual, some lots did a little better than others. So this interesting cartridge wasn't with us for long, though it was really about as effective on game as the hollow point hunting load. Most rifle magazines handled it all right, though some autoloading pistols, as I recall, didn't care for it.

Match bullets generally have been shaped a little differently from the standard-price variety, with a good many minor variations through the years. A couple of years ago there was a radical change— or nearly that—when Remington brought out the new "Match" cartridge.

There was a change in nomenclature, too. Before this time, factory personnel at our various plants had racked their brains, thinking up new and catchy names for the product: Precision, Tack-Hole, Dewar Match, Wimbledon Match, All-X Match, Palma Match, Police Match, Police Targetmaster, and so on. Then, with a tired and happy sigh of relief, they settled on the plain Anglo-Saxon "Match." The earlier names won't be forgotten for some time. Too many of us have shot some of our best scores under one or more of those banners.

This new cartridge, and the Peters like it, featured a gentle slope from the bullet's bearing section down to a long, rather slender point, evidently something of a breeze-splitter, as the ballistic figures at the head of this section suggest. The match loads made for some years before this new type had had identical ballistics—so at least we were told—to those of standard velocity ammo. The advantage claimed was that you could practice with cheap ammunition, then switch to match stuff when competition came up and was important. You often could, too, with little if any more than the usual sighting-in changes of your scope or receiver sight settings. Winchester and Western production still includes the standard velocity match rounds, at this writing.

These two companies didn't fool around long. They soon came out with their Improved Low Velocity EZXS and Super-Match Mark III. (That S-M name has been around for a generation and is worth something in publicity value.) These loads have similar bullet shapes and velocities to those of the Rem-Pete Match, though all that I've seen carry grease grooves, as the late R-P do.

The 1100 f. s. velocity match cartridges had been wanted for a long time, to replace the last of the Lesmok powder target loads that had developed that easy, result-getting speed. But Lesmok and other semi-smokeless powder rounds had to go: they were dangerous to load, compared to the smokeless. For a long while the last remaining batches of them in private ownership were treasured by the knowing. Their almost invariably good accuracy was due in part to the ease with which the old powders were ignited. For rifles with rather light hammer or striker blow they were considered best of all, and there was target-paper proof of the theory. Almost any that's left now is too stale to be accurate, but our current stuff is nearly always excellent indeed, and new main-springs *can* be bought or made for practically any rifles.

National competition—and l e s s "important" matches, too—prove that not all makes and lots of match fodder have equal average accuracy. Every good rifle deserves a tryout with all of the current makes and lots we can get hold of, including stand-ard-priced and standard-velocity rounds. Just as it's always been, down through smallbore target history since 1919, one year a certain brand is tops, one year another. But the news reports shouldn't be taken as definitive proof of what's best for us individually to use.

Almost always it pays to shoot match ammo in outdoor competition, and a lot of the fellows and girls stick to it indoors, too, though some fine lots of standard will stay in the 10-ring with nearly if not quite perfect consistency. Still, a few of us remember having bought rare lots of standard that copied the distinctive shapes of the older match bullets. Obviously these hadn't quite made the grade; so they were sold at the lower price. It is highly probable that in some rifles they'd have cleaned up handily on match stuff of some different make that wasn't one of the rifle's own pets.

Under the best conditions, match bullets should stay in the 10-ring, with most if not all of them in the X-ring, at 50 and 100 yards. On a calm day or on an indoor range they should come close to it at 200 yards. There are such enclosed ranges; in fact, Remington has one up to 600, I'm told. At those three smallbore ranges, 50 to 200, the 10-rings go .89, two and four inches, with X-rings .39, one and two. Smallbore shooting is about as good training as we can get in judging the *force* of winds, and their angle to the line of fire. When we go to bigbore we use far smaller allowances, but we're wind-wise from our tribulations with the .22.

Just as an example of what close, hard holding in smallbore is—and what a fine-shooting rifle the pipsqueak is, too—here's "A Letter from Al Wood," which appeared in the June, 1956, *Precision Shooting.* He was firing prone with sling, his friends from bench, at 100 yards, and his groups were the smallest. He gives his explanation *purely as supposition.*

"I suspect it may be the result of what happens during the comparatively long-barrel time of the small-bore ammunition. Most of the more successful small-bore shooters shoot in a low (legal of course) posi-tion with a tight sling and considerable cheek and shoulder pressure. This may hold the rifle in line a little better during the long barrel time than when shot from the bench. I suspect this does not happen in the high-speed benchrest guns because of the extremely short barrel time and the energy required to move the greater mass in so short an interval."

High Velocity

These are the popular, easily found .22 long-rifle loads, although from a practical viewpoint there seems to be little use for these cartridges loaded with solid bullets. On game as small as squirrels the expansion of their lead is none too sure, and the bigger small game, like turkeys and varying hares or snowshoe rabbits, just aren't in the .22 rimfire's bracket. These weak loads don't kill them with the sureness and all-round reliability we ought to demand.

But the high-speed long-rifle is snappy, it shoots flat, for a mere .22, and in plinking it delivers a sensa-tional smack; so folks buy it. I remember one little store, the anteroom to a firstclass gunsmith's shop, where this solid-bullet load was *not* stocked. You could get the standard, the match, and the hollow point, but not this one. The omission was intentional.

Then too, this cartridge has had a pretty smelly reputation for accuracy, at least until lately. Early lots gave a velocity of some 1200-plus f. s., just a little over the speed of sound, and a curious *zing-g-g* as they went down the 100-yard range, cracking through the sound barrier. Later velocity figures went to 1375 f. .s for the solid, 1400 for the hollow point. Now we have the conservative 1335 and 1365, and the non-mercuric feature that early non-corrosive priming needed so badly.

One day at the bench rest last fall I decided to try a short string of hi-vels at 100 yards, and to my amazement the five shots made a one-inch vertical and a one and one-quarter-inch horizontal. At bench I'm still deep in the tyro stage, seldom doing a whole lot better than I could prone with sling, but how I wish I'd fired a few more groups, including some 10-shotters! Still, that lone target leads to pretty much the same conclusion that Larry Moore's more ex-tensive firing did, as reported in the August, '56, *Guns,* from 1.80 to 2.52 inch 10-shot group *averages* of four strings each with different makes of rifles and high-velocity ammunition. So most of our 100-yard shooting could stay in the 10-ring *when* everything worked just right, though we take more care in choosing a stand-ard velocity load for our target rifles because on the whole it's more accurate, and also a lot less sensitive to wind drift. But match shooters need X-ring accuracy.

But it is encouraging to see the improvement the factories have made in their fast loads, and to the average shooter this means a good deal. A hunter can sacrifice a small degree of accuracy—not much—if he gets a decidedly flatter trajectory. He has to esti-mate ranges, not just take a careful surveyor's or tape-toter's word for them; so unless he's an excep-tionally good judge of distance—and too restrained and sportsmanlike to take silly chances, we might add —the flat trajectory is for him. For these reasons the old .45-90 outsold the .45-70 in some hunting areas, even though it was considerably less accurate. This kind of choice is a makeshift, there's really nothing good about it, but it's fairly common.

In sound rifles, including a few of the old ones, the high-speed long-rifle is an interesting and rather useful cartridge for some purposes. It shoots about the same as the hollow point we'd choose for the hunting we'd do with a .22. But neither style should ever be asked to do the work of a competent little centerfire like the Hornet or Bee, or like the .25-20 or .32-20 in brush country. Used rifles of efficient caliber are so cheap that there's little excuse for wobbling along as a hunter with a .22. For a few kinds of game the little one does OK.

For the fast long-rifle does have a few limited uses in the field. Even the solid bullet, high or low speed, obviously has the power needed for brain shots on any sort of small game, if we can be sure of making them. The fact that deer and larger animals have been killed with .22s cuts no ice. Such shots were setups or bull luck.

On small game the hollow point is sometimes too destructive, too "deadly." Rake a squirrel lengthwise and he's badly smashed up. None of us wants to do that. The ideal shot is in the brain, the forward part of the spine, or in or close to the heart. Using a hollow point instead of a solid gives us more leeway, but sometimes not much. There's so little resistance, broadside, in a squirrel's body that the hollow point may fail to mushroom. Again it may mushroom too much. On cottontail rabbits this load is rather effective; they're easily stopped. The soft body of a grouse may be badly smashed by the cave-nosed bullet, though it is much more than possible that he may get away in spite of what *looks* like a well-placed shot. Almost any .22 cartridge will kill frogs, but the big old fellows sometimes are so hard to kill outright and pick up that a minimum load for them could be the hollow-point short or the faster bullet of the .22 long. The low speed long-rifle is about right.

After all, the .22 is a target size. Its purpose is to make us efficient with more powerful arms of military or sporting type.

It pays to inspect hollow point ammunition. Some lots are much better than others, not only in evenness of crimp and the absence of lead fins drooping down over the case mouth, but also in the precision with which the hollow is made. Off-center stuff occasionally shows up, and in my experience, at least, it hasn't proved out on target. When well made, it seems to shoot as well as the solid. We must remember that some extremely accurate big-game hunting ammunition has been made, comparing favorably with military rounds with sharp, full jacketed bullets. Western 220 grain "tip-o'-lead" and 180 grain hollow point, both boat-tailed at the time, I think, come to mind as the earliest outstanding examples. Benchers today favor the hollow point in their precision bullets; at least, a lot of them do.

Expansion of a hollow point can be more or less cut down by filling the cave with hard grease, an old trick in lead-bullet days and sometimes used on modern bullets that are jacketed. Since most of us shoot comparatively few hollow point rimfires at game, it's no great effort to take a pin of the right size and go into the cavity to make sure it's free of grease—and to find how deep and wide it is, too.

Some hollows are deeper than others, and some lead tempers softer than others. The best way to discover any real differences in performance is to try various brands in pine board. This is less sensational than shooting up soap, but I believe that it gives a truer picture. Almost anything is better than finding a deficiency in the hunting field.

As for barrel wear no doubt the fast loads are quicker, more accomplished thieves of prime precision than the slow ones are. They develop higher temperatures. But .22 rimfire bullets as now made seal the bore promptly, allow little if any gas to cut past into the rifling, and that is one of the big causes of throat wear. If the loads fill the chamber and the start of the rifling is close up to the bullet, maybe cutting into it as in most match rifles, not much gas gets past. Those who use .22 high speeds a lot seldom do half the shooting per year that the targeteer does with his lighter charges. A truly worn-out smallbore barrel is a rarity.

.22 AUTOMATICS

	Bullet in grs.	FS vel. at muzzle	100 yds.	FP energy at muzzle	100 yds.	MR traj. at 100 yds.
.22 Remington Autoloading	45	920	...	84	..	5.5″
.22 Winchester Automatic	45	1055	930	111	86	4.6″

Each of these cartridges was made for a special rifle, the Remington 16 and the Winchester 1903 or O3. The former stayed in production from 1914 to 1928, the latter from the late 1903 or early 1904 to 1936, when slight alterations to the action and a thorough modernizing of the stock made it the Model 63 in .22 long-rifle caliber.

These auto rounds were special-purpose jobs when self-loading .22s were a new venture. Greasless or inside lubricated bullets kept the actions clean, except for some sifting-through of half-burned powder grains and the usual scattering of oil. Standard bullet weight was seldom if ever below 45 grains, even in the hollow-point styles that hung on till about the time of World War II. The slugs were heavy enough to boost recoil, and their usually rounded noses slipped into the blink-open chambers with nary a hitch, as I recall, and I used both models a lot. About the only cause of jamming was a weak round in a dry, unoiled action. Then the empty case might fail to pop out, and it would block the chamber.

These cartridges—non-interchangeable—and their rifles really did well in their day, and that day won't end as long as the ammo is available. It is over-priced, out of line with the .22 WRF or Special, for instance, and that may be a warning sign. The same thing happened to BB and CB caps shortly before they were discontinued. So perhaps before this book is in print they will have been lopped off, at least the Remington, for though the M16 was a good little rifle and had one or two advantages perculiarly its own, it never became as popular as the older and better-known Winchester model.

When and if these loads become purely collectors' items, not shooting ammunition, more people than you might think will be unhappy. These folks are scattered all over the world, and some of them live in fine game country. Those early auto-rifles took down in the middle and went into small packing space; they became travelers. Sure, their owners in the islands, jungles and wilderness outposts of places with queer-sounding names had to "order the ammunition special," and six months could be a short wait for the ship that brought it. But people became fond of those rifles, and depended on them. They could hang one on pegs over the door or fireplace, chamber empty and the magazine partly filled, to ease the spring tension. When the clock ticked on the instant of danger it was quick and sure to bounce a load into the chamber, then snap off a couple of warning shots in one second. If that message didn't get through to the brain, the third bullet sure could.

.22 WINCHESTER RIM FIRE

Bullet in grs.	FS vel. at muzzle	100 yds.	FP energy at muzzle	100 yds.	MR traj. at 100 yds.
45	1450	1110	210	123	2.7"

Only a few new rifles chambered and bored for this excellent cartridge were available after World War II, and none is made now. The last repeaters were the Winchester 61 and Remington 121, pump guns. Little bolt-action single shots in .22 WRF or the identical .22 Remington Special went out at about the same time. They were good hunting rifles for boys, for the hollow-point bullet still was available in some stores, and the old solid bullet always was a pretty fair killer.

It is of slightly larger diameter than the .22 long-rifle, and Winchesters for it were rifled at a standard .226 inch across the grooves, though some other makes were as tight as the .223 to .224 that is about maximum for the long-rifle. Most barrels used a 14-inch twist for the WRF, except the Remingtons, which were 16, same as those for the long-rifle, long, and short combination, really meant to please the first of the trio. Chambers were oversize for ordinary .22 cartridges, for the WRF carries the lubricated and bore-bearing section of its bullet inside the case. Clean to handle and pack, and water-tight.

Even in the days of black and semi-smokeless powders, when the velocity of the 45-grain bullet was only about 1110 f.s., the WRF was a killer, compared to all other .22 rimfires. Its bullet was heavier and faster than the standard types, and its flat point delivered

more smash on small game and usually mushroomed better than the round-points. Still, it paid to buy hollow points—39, 40, and a full 45 grains—for the good velocity expanded them pretty well at close range.

Now only the solid bullet is loaded, and it gives us, within 100 f.s. or so, the speed of the heaviest old .22 Winchester *Center* Fire loads that the factories put up for single-shot rifles. That cartridge had a great reputation in squirrel country, at least for its killing power. Some rifles shot it with the necessary accuracy up to about the limit of actual ranges usually fired at, some 50 yards.

It was noteworthy that when the velocity of the WRF was raised over 300 f.s. above the earlier loadings the accuracy increased. The .22 long-rifle's precision went down-hill at the change. However, the extra speed put the WRF bullet well above the sound barrier, and it didn't drop to that level until it had gone 100 yards or so. Probably improved manufacturing methods helped, too. In good rifles the modern ammunition has grouped within an inch at 50 yards. We need something better than that grouping for squirrel shooting, but few of our shots in the woods stretch out much over 35 yards.

Larger small game, definitely not including woodchucks, is killed with fair reliability by the WRF, even with its solid bullets, though for light stuff, with small resistance to lead, the hollow point .22 long-rifle almost surely would be better. None of the rimfire cartridges deserves consideration for turkey hunting. Most of them have been used on these big, hardy birds, but they simply haven't the sure killing power under all conditions that we need.

.25 STEVENS

Bullet in grs.	FS vel. at muzzle	100 yds.	FP energy at muzzle	100 yds.	MR traj. at 100 yds.
65 or 67	1130	985	184	140	3.8"

Only the standard or "long" .25 is still made. Until about ten years ago the short was more or less available, though officially it had been discontinued. Usually it carried the standard bullet, though some were listed as a couple of grains heavier. Hollow points in both lengths went out long ago. They really weren't needed.

For this is no varmint cartridge, either in flatness of trajectory or destructive power. It is simply a small-game cartridge, and quite likely the best ever made for short-range work. On squirrel, rabbits, grouse and so forth its reputation was high—clean, sure killing with a minimum of mess and destruction.

Some 10 or 15 years ago an attempt was made to speed it up. Results were excellent: good accuracy, flatter shooting, more smash. It was still not a varmint cartridge, and its power was more than was wanted for most small game hunting. No doubt the speed alone would have sold it, and perhaps new rifle models for it would have come out. But the manufacturers were wise not to market it. A lot of old, weak little rifles in this caliber were in use—still are, though it's getting hard to find a .25 rimfire in gun-crank shape. The risk was too great. A bottle-necked .25 would have led to rechambering of some unsuitable rifles and a necked-down .25 wouldn't have been greatly superior to the high-speed .22 WRF. And volume sales would have been essential.

Accuracy of the old black and semi-smokeless loads and of the modern non-corrosive smokeless rounds has varied a good deal. It is also true that rifles' potential accuracy varied, for poor lots of .25s seem to be awfully rare, at least in our time. Yet old rimfire priming mixtures were in some formulas less stable than the best we have now. Almost any weak flash could ignite black, Lesmok, or King's Semi-smokeless powders, though not always with uniformity. So such ammunition, deteriorated under poor storage conditions, could be most disappointing.

Then too, some otherwise fine .25 rimfire rifles were not adjusted to give perfect, even ignition. For this, the rimfire's copper or brass case must be struck hard and briskly, clear across the hollow rim that contains the priming. If a .22 match rifle doesn't shoot well, one of the first details to check is its ignition. This is equally important with the .25. Its case is a long one and the density of loading is low. The powder has plenty of room to shuck back and forth inside this one. Black powder filled it to the base of the bullet, in customary fashion for that propellant. We have stronger and really better priming compounds now, and we need them.

.32 SHORT AND LONG

	Bullet in grs.	FS vel. at muzzle	100 yds.	FP energy at muzzle	100 yds.	MR traj. at 100 yds.
.32 short	80	945	840	158	125	5.3"
.32 long	89 or 90	945	850	178	144	5.3"

Like the .25 Stevens, which always has been a little more expensive, these .32s are good cartridges in the woods. Their killing power on most small game is just right, and the report is low, not sharp enough to broadcast a general alarm. Drop the muzzle velocity of any rifle bullet below the speed of sound and the difference stands out. Well out beyond their reliable range of 50 yards or less they hold their velocity and power with a miserly grip, compared to the fast .22 rimfires. There's little lag. Any, but any, rifle must be used with great care in settled country, or anywhere else, for that matter.

These so-called .32s are really .30 calibers, over-bored a bit, but still .30s. Barrel-groove diameter runs from about .309 to .315 inch. They are little if any more destructive than the faster .25 rimfire with its flat-nosed bullet.

Rifling twists vary from 20- to 26-inch complete

turns, and these leisurely rates and the larger bores made the .32s slightly easier to clean and keep in good order than the .25 rimfires with a standard 17-inch spin. This meant something in black-powder days. On a day's hunt, when perhaps half a dozen careful shots were fired, your barrel was less liable to foul and become inaccurate if the twist was slow and the bullets were heavy in proportion to the powder charge.

Now we'd·hesitate before buying *any* rimfire arm that isn't made for either the .22 short or .22 long-rifle, or both. All the other cartridges except perhaps the .22 WRF have a too uncertain life expectancy, and we can't form, prime and handload rimfires in a home workshop. Priming mixture is much too dangerous to tinker with.

But a lot of these now "odd-size" rimfires are in use. Until recent years I generally had one or more of them hanging around, and going out on trips. Maybe the ammunition factories will be more obliging than some of us expect. In a practical way, acquaintance with .25 and .32 rimfire ballistics is important. Handloading .25 and .30 caliber high power cartridges of quite respectable case capacity can include duplication of these old loads. In the small-game woods such prescriptions are right up top.

Most rifles that took the .32 short were chambered out enough to accept the long also, though towards the last of the Winchester single shot's life it was made in this size for the .32 short exclusively. For small game it's a good little round, especially when its bullet point is rounded off more bluffly than that of the more powerful long. Since these bullets are of heel type, the front section practically of cartridge case diameter, the slow little .32 short bullet slips up through the long chamber and into the rifling without great dismay or suffering. Old rifles chambered for the .32 extra long are rare. That load was almost the equivalent of a .32-20; it packed 20 grains of black powder under the standard .32 long bullet.

Our present .32 rimfires parallel the still current .32 short and long Colt centerfires. Actually, though, the modern long Colt is the old .32 long-rifle, which was made in both rim- and centerfire with an 82-grain inside-lubricated bullet, to keep your clothes clean. Its base was hollow, and the quick blow of black or semi-smokeless powder upset the soft lead to seal the bore. This is hard to do with a smokeless rifle powder.

It's never good form to sneer at the accuracy of the .32 long rimfire. Some excellent rifles were made for this once extremely popular cartridge, and certain factory runs of current ammunition have been splendid. No reason why the load shouldn't shoot: it's practically an oversized .22 long-rifle.

There seems to be little chance of the .25 and .32 rimfires' being revived. Small-game seasons are short—they have to be—and most hunters carry a shotgun. They want game, and if there's a fair chance at a fine bird like a quail, grouse or pheasant they want to be able to take it.

The .41 short rimfire pistol cartridge actually was restored. Though long gone from factory-load lists, it still crops up fresh and reliable. So it's being made, all right. Collectors probably were mostly responsible. They had a natural hankering to fire the old Reming-ton, Colt, National and other derringers, and the rather few revolvers, such as the Colt Cloverleaf four-shooter and the five-shot House Model, that were made for this stubby cartridge or for the far less popular .41 long, with its bluff, man-stopper bullet and the equivalent of a .22 short powder charge added for more bump.

TIME was, you didn't see many rifles carried in or out of town except in the fall. Kids, though, would tote their .22s around in any old weather, but they were just kids, and a smallbore rifle wasn't considered of much account. A grown man or woman who used a rifle off-season and legitimately was an odd one.

Now we have more hunters, plenty of cars to stow the guns in, shorter game seasons, and as sharp an itch as ever to use a rifle on any full- or half-holiday that we want to. So there are more target shooters and more varmint hunters than ever before.

Each of these sports now exists completely in its own right. Though they give valuable training to the big-game hunter, they aren't necessarily so considered. A person can be happy in either one, and never plan to "go farther."

In black-powder days there were comparatively few varmint cartridges. Those up to .32 caliber, at least, could be handloaded nicely for squirrel, grouse, ducks (then legal rifle game), rabbits and so on. The .32-35-165 Stevens and Maynard and the .32-40 trio— Bullard, Remington, and the still current Ballard, Marlin, Savage and Winchester—were the lightest of a long series of deer cartridges. Practically all calibers from .22 to .50, and of course the .58 Musket and any amount of muzzle-loaders, were used on varmints. But few cartridges got much if any publicity as being particularly suitable for woodchucks or coyotes, and almost no one made a hobby of hunting crows with a rifle.

The varmint rifle and ammunition industry is a big one now. Generally, speaking, it started with both custom rifles and wildcat cartridges, and both these kinds of production are still in full swing, though not many *new* wildcat case forms are coming out. But before the revival of bench-rest the varminting trade was quite possibly the chief incentive to the wildcatter, plus his own natural curiosity, the desire to find out and to improve. Then too, custom-made .22 bullets had reached a high degree of precision. If you wanted to design a wildcat that would shoot, the .224-inch rifling groove diameter was inviting. Given good components and a good rifle to use them, almost any caliber or case form can produce accuracy.

The factories now make special varmint-hunting cartridges, each of which to *some* degree stems from a wildcat. With the powders and bullets we now have, the field is pretty well covered by ready-made loads, packaged in the familiar colors and under the well-known brand names. They stand on the hardware or sport store shelves, waiting.

Close neighbors to these cliff-dwellers, perhaps touching them, are those we could call adapted varmint loads, the 87 grain .250 Savage and .257 Roberts, the 100 grain .270, and the 110 grain .308 and .30-06. These too have lightly jacketed bullets, designed to break up fast on impact, thus killing small animals promptly and being almost completely sure not to

CHAPTER 15

VARMINT CARTRIDGES

ricochet off rocks or shale. They are *not* intended to be used on any big game. But the standard loadings are, and for that reason these calibers are to be discussed in later chapters. As a matter of fact, almost any big-rifle cartridge can be handloaded for safe use in varmint hunting.

Here we consider special varmint rounds—.22 Hornet, .218 Bee, .219 Zipper and .222 Remington, along with one midway caliber, the .220 Swift, and two deer, antelope, *and* varmint sizes, .243 Winchester and .244 Remington. A pair of oldtimers, the .25-20 and .32-20, close this chapter. They, like the .270 and .30-06 (don't laugh, please), have been modernized for the varmint hunter by way of short, light, over-stabilized bullets.

.22 HORNET

	Yards	Velocity	Energy	MR trajectory, inches
45 gr.	0	2690	720	...
s. p. or h. p.	100	2030	410	.8
	200	1510	230	4.3
	300	1150	130	13.0
46 gr. h. p. ..	0	2690	740	...
	100	2030	420	.8
	200	1510	235	4.3
	300	1150	135	13.0

The Hornet has been around for well over 20 years and the .22 WCF case it came from goes back to 1885 or so. Some Hornet chambers, tight enough to contribute to minute-of-angle accuracy, will accept that black powder design, but we don't use it. The fouling from just one shot would make it a bit risky to fire a jacketed Hornet bullet through the dirty barrel, and the .22 WCF cartridge is a valuable item for collectors.

229

The .22 Hornet isn't falling off in popularity because of its age; it's the .222 that's responsible. When high-velocity .22 rimfire ammunition was new and startling, some dealers charged a little extra for it, but the stuff sold just the same. There's a bigger disparity between Hornet and .222 costs, but not enough to curb the overtake by the latter round. People buy the .222 for its speed and range and smack.

Yet for some purposes the Hornet is a better cartridge.

Its report is mild. When we hunt in a country of small farms, with houses less than a half mile apart, and roughly parallel roads not much over a mile away, it's possible to get back into night pastures, unused in the daytime, where the sound of our occasional shots won't annoy anyone. Naturally we should ask permission before barging in on a person's land, but the slim little Hornet looks a lot less formidable than a .30-06 or even a .220 Swift cartridge. Of course it has a long danger range—so do all our cartridges— and any hunter must be careful of the background even if he's carrying a shotgun after woodcock and the load is three-quarters of an ounce of Number 9s.

With soft-point bullets the Hornet is pretty safe from ricochets if we limit our shots to 200 yards, about the extreme sure-killing range on varmints, and 150 is a whole lot better if there's even a light breeze, up to 10 miles an hour. Hollow point Hornets don't do as well. It's a common experience to dig them out of an earth backstop and find them scarcely distorted at all. The jacket usually fails to split open, the hollow fills with dirt, and that's all. Yet in some 12 to 15 years of fairly steady use of the Hornet and Bee I had, as far as memory serves, no ricochets whatever. Most of the shooting was with soft points, but not all, by any means. Some of the hollow-point Hornet jackets are entirely too thick up front, and our fac-

tories ought to remedy this matter.

The original 2350 and 2400 f. s. Hornet loads were deadly on small game and on varmints up to woodchucks. Turkey hunters found them effective, except sometimes on the largest of those birds, and the destruction seldom was excessive. For the big gobblers they preferred something more powerful, such as the original .22-3000 Lovell wildcat based on the .25-20 Single Shot case and not blown out to 2-R form. Heavily loaded, the Lovell sent the 45-grain Hornet bullet at about 3000 f. s. The modern Hornet has proved to be a good turkey load, even though privately chronographed velocities seldom stack up with its catalogued figures.

It kills woodchucks reliably if the hits land in vital areas, and usually without an excess of ripping or blasting. Some of us prefer to have our varmint kills like that; some don't. Small game handloads with soft-point, full-jacketed or cast lead bullets are easy to put up. The usual 16-inch Hornet rifling twist is just right for 45-grain bullets, with a latitude of some 20% in either direction, unless the speed of the heavier bullets is low, or their points long and slender.

Standard and reduced loads give the Hornet one of the longest barrel lives of all our high-velocity calibers. Cases fired in a well breeched and reasonably tight chamber last indefinitely. And being rimmed, they offer no headspace problems in a properly made rifle, compared to those of rimless or semi-rimmed brass, like the .222 and the .220. The Hornet is positioned by its rim, not by its shoulder. This means that squib loads don't shorten the case bodies under the kick of the primer itself. With pressures held down to the common lever-action high-power brackets, 40- to 45,000 p. s. i., there's little if any stretching or forward flow of the brass.

The Hornet is an economical cartridge to buy, and

.22 Hornet; .218 Bee; .219 Zipper, handloaded hollow point; .222 Remington; .220 Swift; .243 Winchester; .244 Remington; .25-20 WCF or "Repeater"; .32-20. *Henry Way-Silvers Photo.*

to reload. It's one of the few modern calibers that can give us almost full power with our home-cast lead bullets. A velocity of 2400 f. s. is practicable in its slow twist, and I know of one shooter who used little or no hardening alloy in the Hornets he cast. A gas check on the bullet base helped keep lead fouling down, and he got accuracy and killing power. Even a rather hard cast bullet, given a deep, wide hollow point, and shot from a properly handloaded Krag or Springfield, for instance, is deadly on deer, sometimes *too* destructive. A solid, almost pure lead bullet at similar or more likely greater speed than the .30 expands on varmints, all right, not having the stiffening of a copper or gilding metal jacket.

At longish ranges the factory Hornet or its equivalent in a handload would shoot flatter and be more deadly. But most people who thoughtfully choose the Hornet, plan to get some stalking as well as shooting experience. It's good to be able to make our own bullets with simple, inexpensive equipment if for any reason the supply of custom or factory jacketed slugs should dry up.

The Hornet has obvious limitations in velocity, even when we use sub-standard bullet weights, so much more sensitive to wind. Blown out into wildcat shape, it gives us more speed if we need it. That's one way to do it. "Just get a bigger case to start with" is good advice to those who want more power. Overloading is never the solution.

Next to the .22 Hi-Power Savage, which in its time was promoted and used as a deer cartridge, the Hornet is our oldest factory-loaded special varmint round. It still is good, and has its place. Next came the .220 Swift, the in-betweens in .22 caliber easing in later.

.218 BEE

	Yards	Velocity	Energy	MR trajectory, inches
46 gr. h. p. . .	0	2860	835	. . .
	100	2160	475	.7
	200	1610	265	3.8
	300	1200	145	11.5

In 1938 the Model 65 lever gun was given two inches more barrel (full 24-inch length), a semi-beavertail forestock, a factory peep sight like those still seen on old Model 64 .219 Zippers and 71 .348s —and this new cartridge. The .218 case is a neckdown of the .32-20, not of the shorter-bodied .25-20, and it holds just a little less powder than the pioneer .22 Niedner Baby Magnum, wildcatted .32-20 brass.

Its reception by experienced riflemen was hesitant and dubious at first. Then it was found that accuracy from the light lever-action repeater was really good. The .22-caliber barrel naturally had a rather thick wall, and the breech lock-up of the 65 was not very springy with its moderately powered cartridges. Full-length case resizing almost never was needed. Handloaders found the .218 good to work with, for it burned powder well, even in squib loads, thanks to its short body and its reasonably steep shoulder.

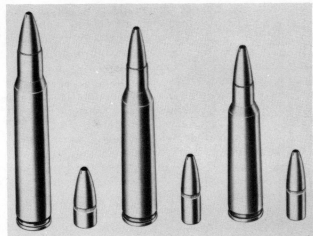

Adapted varmint loads. Remington .30-06 110 grain, .257 Roberts 100 grain, and .250 Savage 100 grain. All are pointed soft point, with slits at jacket nose to help make expansion sure and even. The Western-Winchester .250 and .257 varmint bullets weigh 87 grains and are short pointed to give long bearing on the rifling.

Historically it's interesting. The Bee is a lever-action-rifle variation of the Hornet like the .25-20 WCF or Repeater variation of the old Single Shot .25-20 which resembles the Hornet in its proportions. But unlike the .25-20 WCF the .218 has greater powder capacity than the case that sparked its development.

It is just noticeably more powerful than the Hornet, and at present the retail prices of these two rounds are the same. Pressures are much alike, though the larger inside head diameter of the .218 gives a greater area for backthrust to work on. Generally speaking, the same action strengths are adequate for both, and neither should be loaded beyond factory power for use in a light, rear-locking bolt action like the Winchester 43, for instance, or in a light lever action like the Winchester 65 or the low wall single shot of that make. In fact, the latter isn't advised for standard Bee rounds.

Heavy .218 handloads have been recommended. No doubt most of them are safe in front of a big, strong action, but after all there are larger .22 caliber cases if we want extra power. Old "maximum" recommendations can be downright dangerous to follow with cases made since World War II, for Bee brass, like some other sizes, has been thickened and made heavier. This adds to strength, but not in proportion to the increase in loading densities. We must cut such charges.

Although the Bee is less popular than the Hornet, which had a much earlier start and was a unique factory load at that time, it isn't hard to find or liable to be discontinued. Model 65s are scarce, but new bolt guns have been made in .218 and they're a good choice for those who don't want .222 power, noise and ammunition expense.

As for accuracy, there is no good reason why the

Bee should be inferior to the Hornet, all the important qualities of load and rifle being equalized. It should satisfy those who prefer a Hornet to be in blown-out shape because it seems to burn powder better than the gently shouldered factory case. The various "improved" Bees and Hornets can use the moderately coarse-grained 4198 Du Pont that burns well in fairly heavy charges in their cases, and poorly in the unaltered Hornet with 45-grain bullets. It isn't necessary to seek the highest velocity when loading this powder in these cases. In fact, it's sensible to load it as lightly as it'll burn cleanly, and the gain comes in lower temperatures and just a little longer barrel life.

.219 ZIPPER

	Yards	Velocity	Energy	MR trajectory, inches
56 gr. h. p. ..	0	3110	1200	...
	100	2440	740	.6
	200	1940	465	2.9
	300	1550	300	8.3

When the Zipper came out in the spring of 1937 it reminded some of us of the old .22 Niedner Magnum, a wildcat that had given good service in single shots and remodeled Krags. The Zipper too is of .25-35 shape, with reduced and shortened neck, and there's nothing wrong with it.

However, the Model 64 Winchester lever action, like the old 94, seldom gives remarkable accuracy with anything like heavy or high-intensity loads. The spring-back of the breech is considerable, for the locking block doesn't cover the end of the breech-bolt fully, and it slants to the rear. Some 64 Zippers shot better than others, depending partly on the tightness of stock attachment and breech assembly. For one or two consecutive shots, the usual limit for a varmint hunter of some experience and ability, the 64 .219 did fairly well. It certainly was no 10-shot grouper unless the string was fired in a mighty leisurely fashion. Custom bolt action and more or less custom single-shot Zippers have brought out the good accuracy the cartridge really has. The locking design of the Marlin 336 lever gun appears to be a bit less elastic than that of the 64, and though this Zipper is made at present only in carbine form it should kill woodchucks realiably up to 100 yards and a little bit more. It isn't meant to be a long-range rifle.

One improvement in factory .219 Zipper ammunition was the dropping of the 46-grain hollow point at 3390 f. s. The 16-inch twist was not much too fast for this short, speedy bullet, but the surviving 56 grain spins well enough, thanks to reasonable velocity and moderate length, and it's less affected by wind. Cutting bullet weight *and* speed to Hornet levels can improve the accuracy of a lever-action .219 repeater, but most people buy a Zipper because they want Zipper power!

The factory cartridges always were considered safe in tubular magazine repeaters, for they are blunt-pointed. In this they have the form of the .218 Bee, though Winchester did load a few Bees with round-nosed 45-grain soft points—and accurate cartridges they were, too, fully up to standard. Most of my hand-loading for the 65 Bee was with bullets of this type, uncannelured Hornet soft points, for I used no crimp and didn't need one. All the Bee and Zipper factory bullets I've seen have had the crimping groove.

The soft points shot well in the Bee and seemed no more dangerous to stuff into the magazine than the hollow points with their hard copper lips. Bee recoil didn't batter their noses too freely, though the setback of a Zipper might do so.

For long-range work the owner of a Zipper or Bee should seriously consider using pointed bullets. Accuracy should be fine unless their overall length is too great for the twist and velocity to stabilize them. They shoot flatter than the blunt bullets, and they hold their energy longer. The overall of the complete handloaded cartridge, in .219 Zipper, shouldn't be too great for the lever action repeaters to handle, for the case neck is short, remember? But for safety's sake, only *one load* should be placed in the tubular magazine. It would be just a reserve, one we'd hope never to have to use, but the time might come when it would stop a cripple, even though we'd be using that rifle with the care and restraint that go into the handling of a true single shot. Yes, the point would be battered by recoil. Even so, the reserve load should shoot closer to sighting than the blunt-nosed factory round, though they were of identical weight.

The .219 is a good cartridge, and the recent barreling for it by Marlin, under the Micro-Groove system, has extended its life expectancy. It is about the handiest brass, too, from which to form the .219 Donaldson Wasp, a great favorite with bench-resters. And don't forget that it's a rimmed case. Bolt actions can be adapted to handle it, and if they were as well made as we'd reasonably expect, away would go our headspace worries.

It can be handloaded to give more power than the smaller (and less expensive) rimless .222, and in blown-out versions it bridges the gap between .222 and .220. In fact, it can come fairly close to .220 Swift power, but in those brackets the "improved" .219 is for the shooter who gets his pressures tested scientifically, not by guess.

.222 REMINGTON

	Yards	Velocity	Energy	MR trajectory, inches
50 gr. s. p. ..	0	3200	1140	...
or m. c.	100	2650	780	.5
	200	2170	520	2.5
	300	1750	340	7.0

That metal-cased or full-patched bullet is loaded by Remington and perhaps some others. It isn't meant to convert this popular varminter into a squirrel or bunny rifle: the explosive effect of anything like 3000 f. s. velocity is much too much for that. But this load could kill medium-sized fur-bearers without terrible destruction, and where it's legal to use a rifle on carp it'd be just the thing. We'd have to be careful not to fire at low angles to the water, for fear of ricochets, and quite likely a round-point bullet of equal or better weight would punch a straighter path to these destroyers of game fish.

So much for a perhaps uncalled-for introduction to this 1950 cartridge that's had phenomenal growth in popularity. Now we can go on and save space by not elaborating on its great bench-rest reputation. Its excellence is well known. At standard loading density it gives desirable velocities with good, uniform combustion of its powder.

The .222 case was no close copy or reforming of any earlier shape. It was an entirely new design, though I don't know that there's any particular virtue in that fact alone. In general proportions it somewhat resembles the 7x57 Mauser or the long-necked .30-1903 Springfield.

A comparison with the 2-R Lovell wildcat was natural to a good many riflemen when the .222 first came out. Both were more or less midway loads between Hornet and Swift, and the 2-R was a proved, good cartridge. It was the blow-out of Hervey Lovell's .22-3000, which was a simple neckdown of the long, slim .25-20 Single Shot case. In good bolt actions and single shots the 2-R gave fine accuracy. It earned the reputation of being an unusually well balanced round that would burn almost any American rifle powder of fine enough grain, and do well with it. In trajectory and wind-bucking it ranked well ahead of the Hornet and Bee; yet its report was still comparatively mild. For practice and for small-game shooting it shot nicely with cast bullets, too.

But it wasn't an over-the-counter factory job and most good rifles for it were fairly expensive, custom made at least in chambering and usually in some other details. Since the factory .25-20 S. S. cases were never very rugged there was a demand for special brass, which Griffin & Howe and, I think, the late J. Bushnell Smith answered by having factory cases made for them. This excellent brass was thicker, and gave less powder capacity, at least in some lots. Others were rather weak.

The only serious fault of the 2-R wasn't its own! For some years the caliber was so attractive and such remarkable results were attributed to it that handloaders of a certain kind raced each other in seeing how much powder they could stuff in for still higher velocities—and many of these loads were published. So the 2-R was probably the most overloaded of all cartridges. I used to wonder how they could pack in as much propellant as they did, but perhaps my rifle had a tighter than usual chamber! At that, it was the only one I ever had that never required neck-sizing of its cases, either .25-20 or G&H, to hold jacketed bullets of the right diameter for its barrel. That barrel was a relined job, a No. 1 soft steel octagon bored

out to receive the tough steel tube for the 2-R. Admirers of relining cherish a theory that such barrels outshoot solid ones, other things being equal (a rare thing, such equality, in the rifle world!), and maybe they're right. That 7½-pound sporter shot much better than I could hold it, and I wonder what it would have done from a bench rest. Too late to find out.

The .222 is in no sense a derivation from the 2-R in shape, though it certainly is in purpose. For almost any purpose it fills the place of the old wildcat, for even a single shot *can* be adapted to handle a rimless case and pull 'most any brass when you throw the lever down. There are fewer good single shots available, now, for a much greater number of folks who want varmint rifles, and the .222 parent rifle, the Remington 722, is a good, accurate, reasonably priced arm. Less and more expensive bolt guns followed in .222 chambering, and the ball is no more than started. In fact, it hasn't had a chance to pause for punch and smokes and "Have you got *every* dance taken?"

Maybe a part of .222 popularity is due to the packaging of those small but businesslike rounds. They're 20 in a box, just like the big-game stuff, and probably the slimmest ever to be so put up except the long, straight .22-15, .25-21 and .25-25 Stevens blackpowder cartridges. Convenient for the handloader, too: no up-and-down stacking of his product, for each one has its little stall.

Head-size made necessary the use of the small rifle primers. There was no question of their ability to ignite the powder in the short-bodied case, for primers in this class are quite hot today, but some of us wondered if the primer cups had the strength to hold the rather high pressures. It seems that we needn't have worried. Some of the foreign rifles, Bert Shay discovered, actually haven't the striker blow to give full or even sure ignition when the Winchester No. 116 is used. They do all right with the Remington 6½, and the Winchester primers do all right, too, in the Remington .222 rifle—and of course in lots of others.

Any comment like this necessarily has only temporary meaning. Investigation, and change when advisable, go right along in our gun and ammunition factories. The strikers of the Savage 340 .222, and of the Winchester 43 for Bee and Hornet cartridges, seem to have plenty of slap for our rifle primers.

Pistol primers have thinner cups—though there's been some talk of making just one single, combination small primer—and they shouldn't be used for anything like full charges in the rifle cases that accept this size. The only exception in factory loading seems to be the standard velocity .32-20. So many revolvers use it that at least one company, Winchester, primes it with the pistol stuff, so easy to indent with a light hammer blow. The mild pistol primers do well for extremely light handloads in most rifles.

There have been warnings against the use of Du Pont 4227 in handloading the .222 to full power. The advice was good, for 4227 replaces No. 1204, which was tailored to Hornet, .25-20 and .32-20, a rival to the more concentrated Hercules 2400, which is still made and useful in lots of loadings. However, use of 4227 in *moderate* .222 charges is OK, and this fine-grained stuff runs easily through a mechanical powder measure. It's economical, too, though hardly for use in attempting to duplicate factory .222 ballistics! That attempt could end with a blown-up rifle and most serious personal injuries.

Giving an easy, comfortable 100 to nearly 300 f. s. velocity increase over the 2-R, and still without ear-cracking muzzle blast, this Remington cartridge has won great popularity. In fact, few of our newer shooters have heard of the Lovell cartridges, the first widely used wildcats to "show what the Hornet could do, *if* . . ." They have missed some interesting shooting and experimenting, but plenty of both lies ahead for them in the standard .222, which of course has been wildcatted and blown out, too. The most rewarding research would center on its accuracy, for it is well shaped and balanced to get the most out of the .22 components we have now or are likely to have soon.

Almost the only possible objection to choosing the .222 as a one-and-only varmint rifle is the small size of its cartridge. With a bigger case we can have power in our pocket, ready if we want it for a longer shot or for some serious, even grim need that might come up. Larger cases *can* be handloaded down to .222 power and still give the hunting accuracy we'd require. On the other hand, the real enthusiast with a one-and-only rifle of any class is apt to shoot it awfully well, and the .222 is no peewee.

There's one caution about this caliber that should be sounded. It's just so popular that a good many Hornets have been chambered out for it, and with adequate breech strength that's fine. But some Hornets, early ones at least, were only about .223 or even .222 in rifling groove diameter, and most Bee, Hornet, and .222 bullets we buy are a full .224 or close to it. Oversize bullets do increase pressures, though often they shoot beautifully—undersize ones, too, sometimes—if they're uniform. But since .2225-, .223-, and .2235-inch bullets are custom made and cost less than factory bullets, for instance, it seems wise to push a tight lead slug through the barrel of a conversion and measure it with a micrometer.

.220 SWIFT

	Yards	Velocity	Energy	MR trajectory, inches
48 gr. s. p. . .	0	4110	1800	. . .
	100	3490	1300	.3
	200	2930	915	1.4
	300	2440	635	3.8

Here is the first of our tabulations in which 300 yard velocity and energy figures have much practical meaning.

The Swift came out in 1935, and up to 300 yards it still has the highest velocity and the lowest trajectory of all our American factory cartridges. But that 300 yards is a long shot at any varmint, too long for most of us to be justified in taking with any rifle, and the bullet weights to which the Swift is limited get pushed around plenty by a good, fresh breeze, that far out. It's a fine 200-yard cartridge, and a bit more, for the hunter who's at least fairly skilled in reading wind.

Several factory loads have been put out, even a full-patched 48-grain. The blunt 46- and 56-grain hollow points at 4140 (old 48-grain speed) and 3760 f. s. never were popular for varminting. They lost their speed too fast and were less glance-proof than the sharp soft point. For a while Winchester loaded a 55-grain spitzer soft-nose at 3720. This was a fine cartridge, but it hadn't the sensational appeal of the 48-grain racer and by 1946 or so was unavailable. For years before that the more streamlined 55-grain Sisk Express had found favor with handloaders, of which there have been plenty for this caliber since it first came out of the warehouses. Now we have a lot of such bullets in various weights and makes.

It was generally believed that the high intensity of Swift loadings led the powder manufacturers to quit recommending changes, for any caliber. This happened in the late summer of 1935. Du Pont had issued a most helpful little book, in which the .220 was included, but it was withdrawn almost immediately.

Certainly this cartridge requires careful loading, for factory charges run up to or near the high 55,000 p. s. i. level and too often there's the temptation to "better" just any factory product. Swift case necks do thicken with the forward flow of brass, even in 10% or slightly more reduced loadings; necks lengthen too, and both these changes increase pressures. But the real reason for stopping press on load recommendations seems to have been the experiments going on in primer compositions. Different lots varied considerably, and some were right hot.

The .220 is still a somewhat critical cartridge for handloaders who insist on "full power." Though the case is thick and strong—even the extracting groove cut is shallow—it does have a fairly steep body taper, can't grip chamber walls as firmly, at the instant of discharge, as a straighter-bodied case like the .308 or even the .30-06. But it does burn any American rifle powder well, with the right weight and composition of bullet ahead, and up to the limit of its deadliness it's one of our most versatile cartridges.

Its lowest usefully accurate limit is about that of the .22 long-rifle rimfire, and some cast bullets with the pistol powers are even quieter. What is its highest limit of deadliness?

Answers vary as big-game country experiences with it have varied, or almost as much. The .220, like the .22 Savage Hi-Power before it, has been accepted as effective in Scottish forests, and the big stags there take killing. But the hunting is quite different from much—altogether too much — of ours. I don't mean that it's restricted to the rich, the noble, or their friends. That may be generally true. But it's the way of hunting that's restricted. Often the rifle is empty until game has been seen and appraised. And then it's up to the hunter. Landowners don't tolerate sloppy shooting. The kills must be sure, with no game wounded, lost and wasted. The hunter knows he has to do right by the game.

Equally careful hunters on this continent have done well with the .220. In some states it's legal to use a high-powered .22 on big game. Not all of them let it in, and since game laws cover the personnel from A to Z, Mr. Admirable to Mr. Zero, such ruling has its points. To bar .22s and admit the .25-20 and even the .25 rimfire isn't funny. It happens, and it's tragically silly.

Where the Swift has been used in open country, at ranges not over 200 yards, it's been a killer on broadside and front-on shots, hardly reliable and certainly not justified on rear-end or raking shots. The fast bullet, when it still is fast, destroys a good bit of tissue; it seldom has a whole lot of penetration. Some hunters who have used this type of cartridge on deer have found that at times a hit that looks final and sure, just isn't. The game, though mortally wounded, gets up and moves on. So these fellows wait a bit, ready to fire once more, before they walk up closer.

The above is an over-simplification of the Swift as a deer load. Few would choose it deliberately for this purpose. Those who own a Swift and no more suitable high-power rifle could take it anywhere, even into the woods, on a deer hunt. They should do all right *if* they have the guts to resist temptation and never ask for the improbable. It's not likely that the .220 bullet will cut one husky twig without blowing itself up, or that it will reach out till its speed scarcely exceeds Hornet muzzle velocity and kill like a Magnum. You have to place your shots on deer or bigger game when you use this cartridge.

But some have the patience to wait till the time is right, and the shooting skill to use that moment. They are hunters and riflemen of the highest order. Many others, equally high, would feel much more comfortable in any deer country with a considerably bigger caliber. Their minimum might be a 7 mm., or possibly a 6.5, both good in brush when their heaviest standard bullets are used. Up or down, take your choice, but .22 is pretty small unless the bullet is longer and heavier than a Swift's 14-inch twist can handle. Knowing your gun and your game are the big things, and how few of us do know them.

The .220 is a good target cartridge, even pretty fair at benchrest, and its trajectory, short time of flight, and light recoil can improve our marksmanship if we've never before used a rifle of this type. In full or nearly full loads it's noisy, and even cast-bullet charges heat the standard-weight barrel so fast that it's no gun for military-style rapid fire. But almost any good handload shoots well in it—really well—and costs can be held down to .22 long-rifle retail after we've bought our tools *and* mold.

Primarily it's for varmints, with jacketed soft points at good speed. For long range work and for decisive, sure killing at any practicable or sportsmanlike distance, long or short, it's by far the best of the factory .22s. An equally good barrel for the wildcat .22-.250 might outlast a .220, since powder charges are generally a bit lighter for about the same velocities, and the steep shoulder angle does help to "burn the charge in the case." But the Swift ammunition is ready in nearly all gun stores, and its brass is heavier at the base than that of most lots of .250. The new Winchester Stainless barrels should last well.

In windy country the 6 mms. are more reliable varmint cartridges, but they're noisy, too, seemingly as high-pitched and with fully as much volume. Some shooters don't mind muzzle blast. They do as well in spite of it as they would with a rimfire, but some people who own our hunting lands do mind it.

It is certainly convenient to drop the power and fury of the Swift to Hornet levels and practically Hornet accuracy, too, though perhaps oddly, in full to say three-quarter full loadings a Swift usually beats an equally fine Hornet in precision. We can't do quite that well with the 6 mms., I think. Their twist (10 inch for the .243 and 12 for the .244) is fast for short bullets, and their slugs would need almost one-third more weight to balance up like the 45-grain Hornets. Weight of bullet or of powder adds to noise. If a good deal of our shooting, but by no means all of it, must be pitched in a minor key, the Swift is a cartridge to think about.

.243 WINCHESTER

	Yards	Velocity	Energy	MR trajectory, inches
80 gr s. p. ..	0	3500	2180	. . .
	100	3080	1690	.4
	200	2720	1320	1.8
	300	2410	1030	4.7
	400	2140	810	9.4
	500	1910	645	16.5
100 gr. s. p. ..	0	3070	2090	. . .
	100	2790	1730	.5
	200	2540	1430	2.2
	300	2320	1190	5.5
	400	2120	995	11.0
	500	1940	835	18.5

This one and the .244 Remington were announced in the same month, July, 1955, and almost at the same time. Wildcats in 6 mm. had been legion, and a few hunters never had ceased to regret the disappearance, about 20 years before, of factory feed for the 1894 or '95 Lee 6 mm. Navy caliber. That was a fascinating little cartridge, and one of the first to use plain, uncoated, copper-jacketed bullets, though some of its later issues had tin-plated copper in the common .30-30-and-all-the-boys style.

Ballistic figures quoted above are from the factory. Results obtained with the 80-grain at the H. P. White Lab showed up less impressively, though the 22-inch barrel was used there instead of a 26-incher, and no ballistic data is to be taken as absolute, since barrels and bullets, powders and primers, all vary to an extent. Unfortunate, but so far unpreventable.

At any rate, the .243 has what its buyers want, long-sustained accuracy, velocity, and power for varmint hunting under the most challenging conditions, and reasonable to startling deadliness on mountain and plains big game up to deer and antelope. It is a big game caliber for the smallbore enthusiast. At 300 yards, that is, it is listed as having the same velocity as the 130-grain .270, which itself would be called a smallbore by some .30-caliber users.

The .243 and the .244 Remington, too, do have their advantages for game as well as varmint shooting. With the heavier factory bullets they carry up well and hold a respectable punch at 300 yards, and even in light rifles their recoil isn't heavy, though it comes in a hurry; it's no slow push like that of some of the bigbore loads. These two 6 mms. have accuracy, and more than fair wind-bucking ability out to 300. Longer shots can be made, with luck, skill, or a wedding of both, but the sixes are a far way from being our best long-range big-game loads. Many of their publicized "advantages" over pretty competent .25s, even, to say nothing of larger calibers, can be put down to natural enthusiasm over a new product.

To most of us the 6-mm. caliber *is* new, and therefore interesting. The .240 Holland & Holland Apex is an old, good English cartridge. It sends a 100-grain bullet at from 2900 to 2950 f. s. With bullets of that weight the .246 Purdey develops 2950, the .242 Vickers, 3000. Energies are from 1940 to 2000 foot pounds. Since these are British loads, they were designed more for game than for varmint shooting. They are not over-size cartridges.

The .244 H&H Magnum is. Announced in 1956, this one is a neckdown of .375 Magnum brass. It carries a 100-grain copper-tipped bullet, expanding, but stiffened a bit to stand the stresses of magazine handling under recoil and the setback of inertia when it leaves at high velocity. Such stresses are rough on sharp, soft lead points.

Muzzle velocity is given as 3500 f. s., with 2275 left at 500 yards, a pretty much academic range, that one, too far out to decently try in hunting any big game with so light a caliber, if with *any* caliber. Energies at muzzle and at 500 are listed as 2725 and 1150 foot pounds. Some of us would say that this cartridge is grossly over bore capacity, burning a lot of powder to gain its added velocity at the cost of short barrel life. Some would like it. Sour grapers, those first, since the rifle comes to nearly $400 exclusive of duty and delivery charges? Not entirely, I think!

We can be happy with our own 6 mms. in varmint hunting. Both .243 and .244 are much less wind-sensitive than the .22s with their lighter bullets, and accuracy is good. Most if not all of our custom makes offer a variety of 6-mm. bullets, for varmints or for deer and antelope. The Winchester 100-grain, incidentally, is considered by some to be a little too stiff even for game, the Remington 90-grain possibly too frail for shots that take the long way to vital spots. We can expect changes in these and other bullets if they're proved to be advisable. And as long as there's game to hunt we can expect changing conditions.

Another kind of accuracy, an obliging sort, often shows up in these rifles as it does at times in some .220s, .25s, .256s, and .270s. Bullets of widely different weight frequently print close together at 100 yards and a bit farther, inside two or three inches or even less. To the keen varmint hunter this means little: he works up one good load and sticks to it. But it's an interesting phenomenon and could on occasion be helpful, though few of us deliberately hunt varmints and big game at the same time.

It seems to come from a combination of small caliber, fairly thick barrel walls, quick barrel time, and high velocity. In a .30 or larger caliber it's more unusual, though the Remington Model 30-S and 720 .30-06 barrels did well at planting light and heavy bullets close together at moderate ranges. This was more noticeable in small calibers, .25 Remington and .257 Roberts, than in the 06. These were quite heavy barrels, a good deal like the longer one on the 1917 Enfield, and they had that thick breech and steep taper to smaller size ahead of the chamber. Ross .280s were a little like them, though there the effort was to equalize the strike of bullets sent by powder charges that varied in weight, as all do.

The rifling twist of the .243 is 10 inches, same as that of the new Holland & Holland .244 Maggie, as compared to 12 inches in the .244 Remington, which is fast enough for its 95-grain factory bullets, and for some of 100 grains. At woods ranges it's possible to use a longer and heavier bullet than a twist is meant for, and still keep it point-on. The 117 grain .25-35 in the .250 Savage is an example. It did OK up to 50 yards or more, and I think, though I'm not sure, that my rifle had the 14-inch twist that was then the .250 standard. Nothing unusual about that experience. For years there was a special custom bullet for the .250, 115 grains and pointed. That was a fairly long one, and it was primarily meant for deer.

.244 REMINGTON

	Yards	Velocity	Energy	MR trajectory, inches
75 gr. s. p. . . .	0	3500	2040	. . .
	100	3070	1570	.4
	200	2660	1180	1.9
	300	2290	875	4.9
	400	1960	640	10.0
	500	1670	465	18.5
90 gr. s. p. . .	0	3200	2050	. . .
	100	2850	1630	.5
	200	2530	1280	2.1
	300	2230	995	5.5
	400	1960	765	11.0
	500	1710	584	20.0

There's little choice between the .243 Winchester and .244 Remington as cartridges. The .244 has a loading capacity of about one grain more weight of powder, and its sharper shoulder angle, some 26° as compared to 20° of the .243, .308 and .358 Winchester trio, "burns more powder in the case and less out in the bore." These differences, like the others, are trivial. Both cases can be loaded with the same weights and styles of custom bullets, though the faster Winchester twist favors long bullets, and with equal charges the velocities will be pretty similar.

The short neck of the .243 permits "long loading" of the bullets in factory rounds. They seat a little farther out in the rifling throat than those of the Remington do. For cast bullet loading, with grease grooves covered by the brass and therefore unable to pick up dirt or grit, the long-necked Remington is a better case. Some of us who shoot our high-intensity rifles a lot use a good many lead bullets to get the practice we need before the barrel's worn out!

Full power loads with jacketed bullets give more trouble when we handload a case like the .243, with its long, sloping shoulder. Brass flows forward, thickening and lengthening the neck. Although we can ream and trim those necks, the operation does shorten case life. Then too, the body slope of the Remington case makes it fairly easy to form its brass from .30-06, a size that hardly ever is in short supply. The straighter-bodied .243 would call for some blowing out if we used 06 brass to build up our case inventory.

These differences don't mean much. Both cases are of thick and strong brass. They should stand a good deal of full-length resizing, when that becomes necessary, before they are seriously weakened.

Except for its smaller neck and more abrupt shoulder the .244 case is quite similar to the .257 Roberts and 7x57 Mauser. Their shoulder slope is only a tiny bit steeper than that of the .243 Winchester. Head-size of all these cartridges is the same, except for the tolerances allowed in manufacture. They are direct descendants of the .30-06, from the grand-daddy 8x57 Mauser rimless.

A good many rifle models are being adapted to the .243 and .244, and more can be expected. At first the .243 got more attention, for it seems that Remington was a bit slower than Winchester in putting its 6 mm. rifles and ammo on the market in good supply. The greater weight of Winchester bullets in factory rounds may have had something to do with it, too. Yet the Remington .244 bullets stand sharp (and theorizing) inspection a little better. They are of the fairly new "pointed soft point" design, with only a pinhead of lead exposed, and they get quick expansion at high velocity from the lengthwise slits at the front of the jacket. So they take magazine stresses better than the long-exposed points of the .244s. For accuracy, the base of a bullet is the important end, though a seriously battered nose doesn't help in the most exacting long-range shooting, or in squirming up from the magazine. The 80-grain Winchester is quite famous for factory-bullet accuracy.

Both cartridges are attractive in appearance, the Winchester a bit unusual in shoulder and neck proportions, but that sort of thing seldom hurt a cartridge's sales. The belted H&H Magnums when first introduced here aroused plenty of interest even among those who didn't at first glance take in the purpose of those belts. The belts on the old, heavy Peters biggame bullets helped sell that excellent but now long-discontinued ammunition by their odd and businesslike appearance. The Hornet had its appeal because it was such a lean and hungry-looking little thing, and what a tiny cartridge it was to have a jacketed bullet! Same thing goes for the .17 caliber wildcats. Some of the Bullard black-powder specials, their cases shaped like ink bottles, caught a second look, all right, and occasionally their first local sale right afterwards, no doubt. Within limits, the system works. If the goods do as well as these new cartridges are doing, "a bright future is assured."

Why aren't more cartridges made with really abrupt shoulders like the .275 H&H Magnum, .300 Savage, and 7.65 Belgian Mauser? Not so easy to massproduce as more leisurely angled ones are, but that gives the wildcatter a chance.

.25-20 WINCHESTER

	Yards	Velocity	Energy	MR trajectory, inches
86 gr. lead ..	0	1460	405	. . .
or s. p.	100	1180	265	2.6
	200	1030	200	12.5
	300	940	170	32.0
60 gr. h. p. ..	0	2250	675	. . .
	100	1660	365	1.2
	200	1240	205	6.3
	300	1030	140	21.0

The long, gently bottle-necked .25-20 Single Shot, an 1889 development for the Maynard and a lot of other single shots, was so good for target work and for hunting in the little wildernesses near home that almost everyone except Grandad and fussy old Uncle Jim wanted a .25-20 repeater. They stuck to the .32-20, mostly, not having much use for smallbores.

But a repeater for the .25-20 S. S. "couldn't be made." The round was too long for 1892 Winchesters and 1894 Marlins, too short for the '93s and '94s that had been built around .32-40 and .38-55 cartridges. So the old favorite .32-20 case of 1882 was reduced to .25 caliber for the short '92 and '94 actions. Various rifles were made for this .30-30-shaped round, off and on, until the 43 Winchester dropped it from its line, along with the .32-20, in the early 1950s, while that rifle model was still new.

Consequently there are a good many used .25-20s on the market, and others that you couldn't pry loose. Those made since non-corrosive ammunition came in the late 1920s are likely to have good barrels. Most of the others vary from complete ruination to an insistence on jacketed bullets if they're to give useful accuracy.

Classing the .25-20 with varmint cartridges could amuse some people, including a few who've never used it. Yet its presence on this page isn't entirely the result of wondering, "What other chapter could it fit into, for gosh sake?" It is a varmint load for those who can hunt close-up, where its 60-grain bullet still has some blow-up effect. In general this isn't much beyond 50 yards, and even then it must be well placed. For coyotes, foxes and jack-rabbits it's pretty light. In most parts of the West a high-trajectory cartridge isn't of much use, anyway. Sure, there are exceptions.

The .25-20 is also a small-game cartridge, and except for the .32-20, it's the last centerfire of that type made for us. On grouse or squirrels the low-velocity 86-grain load is entirely too rough, except for head shots. Even the lately discontinued full-patched bullet was too destructive, for it had the usual wide, flat point. For turkey and big hares the soft-point or lead bullet is quite good, at woods ranges. Some would pick the fast, rough 60-grain to be more sure.

But the .25-20 can be handloaded nicely for grouse and squirrels, doing the work of the .25 rimfire, or more if it's asked to. And in general it's one of our best small cartridges for the woods loafer, since it gets through brush, not wonderfully well even as an 86-grain, but decidedly better than the Hornet tribe. None of its bullets has the length and weight we need for such shooting, chancy at best, but the heavier ones at least are slow. The rate of the discontinued "High Velocity" 86-grain was only 1710 f. s. Such handloads shoot well in the .25-20.

No .25-20 load fired from the usual 24-inch barrel makes a great deal of noise, and the 18- or 20-inch Remington, Winchester and Marlin carbines aren't much worse. The pitch of the report is so low that at a few hundred yards a .25-20 sounds like a .22 rimfire nearer by. This fact can mean a good deal in some kinds of hunting and target work.

But is it an accurate caliber? The bullets are seated so deeply that usually all the bearing surface lies within the case, and to make this worse, most .25-20 barrels are fairly long-throated, like the average .30-30 tube.

It depends on what sort of accuracy we need. With factory ammunition, good solid-frame rifles run about two- to three-inch groups at 100 yards. But the .25-20 is scarcely a 100-yard rifle; it's for the woods. The best 50-yard group I ever saw one make was three of the 60-grain hollow points, not very fresh factory cartridges, in just under one-half inch. It was fired from bench with a 1/16-inch ivory bead front, unshaded, and a Lyman tang peep sight with its small fold-down aperture removed and stowed away. Bert Armstrong, who shot it, and I always felt sorry that we hadn't more of that ammunition to plunk into that group. We think it indicates that a good .25-20 will stay in an inch at 50 yards, and as a rule the heavier, slower bullets do just slightly better than the 60-grain. The rifling twist is 14 inches in most .25-20s except the Stevens single shot, which uses 13.

The rifle Bert fired was a low-wall Winchester, single shot that Charlie Canoll had fitted with a light Model 43 barrel. A stiff assembly, and the single shot breeches up closer and tighter to the case-head than most repeaters except those of the Mauser type do.

The 86-grain bullets seem to have overcome their common failing of long ago, when the speed of 1380 f. s. from muzzle couldn't always stabilize them, and you got a few keyholes. A 77-grain bullet is still good, and once it was factory loaded. For single-loading use it pays to seat almost any .25-20 bullet far enough out to touch the rifling lands. This isn't for added powder space, but for better accuracy.

The other day Bert Shay sent me a five-shot 100-yard group he'd made with his '92 Winchester .25-20, from bench. I mention it to show what custom bullets and loading, plus good holding, can do with a hopelessly outdated old caliber! The first shot went high; the next four went into less than 9/32 inch, center-to-center of bulletholes farthest apart. A 13/16-inch measurement took in all five centers.

Load was nine grains Du Pont 4759, don't know what primer, and round-nosed 75-grain soft point made by Bert, its jacket a fired and formed copper .22 long-rifle case. It was not the first load tried with that bullet in that rifle: it had been worked up for that particular gun. The scope was a little 329-S Weaver, old but good, and taken care of.

The .25-20 cartridge is nice to handload. Its brass is light and not difficult to work with precision in almost any good tool, and it's quiet and pleasant to shoot. Messing around with it, a person can learn a good deal about ballistics and what makes them, almost in his back yard. None of us expects new rifles to be made for it, but the caliber is still popular enough to hang on, it would seem, for a long time to come. Its brass is easy to form from .32-20, and even the Bee cases could be reshouldered and then neck-expanded, if we absolutely had to.

The .25-20 Single Shot held a bit more powder, two to three grains extra in bulk black measure, and burned any suitable powder well. In heavy single shots with nickel steel barrels (made to order) its case held enough progressive burning powder to send jacketed bullets right along, and such loads when properly put up were accurate and rather deadly in varmint hunting. Few can shoot the old cartridge today because its cases are scarce and no other size, it seems, can be reformed to replace them, except the Lovall or 2R, which came from .25-20SS.

.32-20 WINCHESTER

	Yards	Velocity	Energy	MR trajectory, inches
100 gr. lead .. or s. p.	0	1290	370	. . .
	100	1060	250	3.3
	200	940	195	15.5
	300	840	155	38.0
80 gr h. p. . .	0	2100	780	. . .
	100	1430	365	1.5
	200	1090	210	8.5
	300	950	160	24.5

With full-weight lead bullets—the good 115-grain has been dropped from manufacture—we get better accuracy from the .32-20, or certainly should, than from the .25-20. The long lead bullet of the .25 extends clear through the case neck into the powder chamber, and as Bert Shay has proved time and again, a lead base fuses when it's surrounded by hot powder gases.

These two cartridges are rather similar in their design, and general accuracy runs about the same. In William Lyman's day the .32-20 was considered useful and accurate, and it still is a good one in the same sort of country as that where the .25-20 shines. Its report is a little louder, but not much. It isn't sharp in any loading.

One great advantage of the .32-20 is that its bore is large enough to make the use of a round-ball load entirely practical. Fascinating to use in indoor galleries, too. Sent at about 900 f. s. by a pinch of pistol powder, it is an excellent short-range charge for squirrel shooting. It's deadly but not excessive. This means using the rifle as a single-loader, for the ball is pressed gently into the case mouth and greased outside, or with a wad of Ipco or similar lube behind it. Some good barrels might deliver quite a long string of accurate shots with no grease at all on the round bullets, which should be cast to fit, not bought as buckshot.

When black powder had to be used for all charges a straight-sided case like the Stevens .32 Ideal was better for such pea-bullet loads. You could seat the ball right on top of the shiny kernels, for better combustion and less fouling. With smokeless we get the advantage of having the lead up front, closer to the rifling throat, and powder burns well in this .32-20 case. Modern primers are hot, and not much gain could be expected from the old trick of upending the cartridge, or the gun muzzle, to drop the powder down against the primer. Another way, at target, was to roll the case to settle the powder evenly along the line from base to neck.

The full charge .32-20's killing power on varmints is generally enough better than that of the .25-20 to notice. A wider, heavier bullet, even though definitely slower, is what does it. At close range the 80-grain load sometimes tears woodchucks quite badly, but even so it absolutely requires good placement for sure work.

On small game the 100-grain bullet, shot from revolvers and starting at a little over 1000 f. s. when a long barrel is used, has made a great reputation. Some of the old sixguns with fixed sights were zeroed at the factories for 115-grain bullets, and they throw the present 100-grain a little low. Filing down a front sight to add elevation is easy, but it shouldn't be even started until long sessions at the range have answered the question "How much?" A .32-20 revolver in good shape brings a rather high price today, and sixguns were much easier to keep free from rust, using the old corrosive smallbore ammunition, than the rifles were. Apparently more of the primer salt was blown outdoors, where it belonged. This cartridge is noisy in a handgun but it's not in the class of the .357 and .44 Magnums! The fast 80-grain .32-20 is not for pistols.

Just like the .25-20 the standard velocity .32-20 is a good useful load in the woods. It's conservative, excessively so if you like, far from startling in speed, smash, or even accuracy. But with the best iron sights it'll shoot where you hold as far as you can see in close timber, and it's far and away ahead of a Bee or Hornet if it has to clip a twig or two on its way. Of the three essentials in hedge-trimming—low velocity, wide, flat point, and good length and weight—it has the first two in generous allotment. It is quite a decent turkey cartridge, as most experienced hunters of those birds would tell you. For the handloader who buys more molds than half the price of a big bench-loading press would come to it's a daytime dream that keeps him awake at night. Pressures and burning temperatures with the right powders are low, and the standard 20-inch .32-20 rifle twist lets him get almost full, high velocities with 100-to 115-grain cast bullets without gas checks. Not that a gas check hasn't its uses in any rifle or pistol caliber, but it's one more thing, one more variable, and there are quite enough of them, anyway, when we load for uniformity.

Rusted-out .25-20 barrels can be rebored handily to .32-20, P. O. Ackley being one of the few who do it. With the wide difference between .257- and .310-inch grooves there's plenty of leeway when rust has chewed in deep, compared to that between the .308 and .321 of the .30-30 and .32 Special; yet he and probably many others have done that, too.

I've heard of worn-out .30-30 barrels being merely rechambered for the Special, and fired with that ammunition. But in a certain black mood a person can think that we live in a world rather well stocked with horrors.

AMONG riflemen, "deer cartridge" is as indefinite a phrase as "grouse load" is among shotgunners. Some of the smallbore experts kill their birds cleanly with a .410 bore and No. 9 shot, close-up and in early season. At the other extreme are hunters who use "4s for everything," and their gun is the 12 or possibly the 16 gauge. In between, loads of No. 8, 7½, or even 6 shot, in bores big enough to pattern them well, are chosen carefully. All these fellows, except quite likely the chap with the 4s, do OK with what they know and believe in.

So, too, a good deer cartridge is what you know and believe in. But first we must know. The right answer depends on where and how we hunt. For long range and for big deer, like the western muleys for instance, we need a decidedly different load from the one that is good, and perhaps much better, on the Columbian blacktail of the Pacific slope, or the white-tail, who lives almost anywhere. Incidentally, he varies more than most other big game does in his habits, size, vitality and that imponderable will-to-survive.

Deer are big game. They can and sometimes do take as much killing as almost any American animal, and this element of the uncertain should be remembered when we choose a caliber for hunting them. The long array of "deer cartridges" is bewildering because it contains so many that are suitable only under certain conditions, and still more, only for certain people. Some of us use the obsolete or the almost if not quite sub-marginal because we know these cartridges *and* the rifles we fire them in. A number of the calibers covered in this chapter should never be chosen by an inexperienced hunter or a poor shot.

.25-35 WINCHESTER

	Yards	Velocity	Energy	MR trajectory, inches
117 gr. flat nosed	0	2300	1370	...
s. p. or	100	1910	945	1.0
m. c.	200	1600	665	4.6
	300	1340	465	12.5
117 gr. rounded	0	2300	1370	...
s. p.	100	1950	985	1.0
	200	1680	730	4.6
	300	1460	555	12.0

The round-nosed soft point wouldn't stay round very long in the tubular magazine of a Winchester repeater, but it'd do all right in a single shot or in one of the old Savage 99s made in this charming caliber.

For it is charming, no less, not noisy even in a 20-inch carbine, and its recoil is just a little tap, about half that of the .30-30. It's accurate, too, though like other smokeless sporting loads of the 1890s—and some later arrivals—its bullet is so deeply seated in the long neck that all or most of the bore-bearing section is hidden under the brass. The 220-grain Krag, now, or even the more tapered .30-1903 Springfield of that weight, had some part of their long bullets far enough out to reach into the rifling seat.

The last arm to be chambered for the .25-35 was the 94 Winchester carbine, available in this size until

CHAPTER 16

DEER CARTRIDGES

the early 1950s. Along about 1914 one of our best authorities, a man for whose memory I have the greatest respect, for he was a rifleman and a sportsman, predicted that the .25 Remington would outlast the .25-35. The Rem was of the modern rimless shape, and it was slightly more powerful, having additional powder room. The prediction was logical, but .25 Remington rifles dropped out before World War II and now the cartridge itself is obsolete. Winchester price ranges reached further down, and a lot of people like lever guns, at any rate.

Both these cartridges, and the .25-36 Marlin, are fun to play with, and they were just about the only sizes that may have been pointed at the varmint hunter of fifty years ago, though they were considered acceptable for deer and even far-out antelope. In .30-30 days they actually were fairly long-range loads. In spite of their quick rifling twists, eight-inch for the Winchester, nine for the Marlin, and a conservative 10 for the Remington, a lot of cast bullet designs were worked up for them. Some interesting and satisfying shooting was done, too. Yet as a rule, as good reduced loads were put up with the short 86-grain .25-20 jacketed bullets, which before World War II cost less than a cent apiece. Yes, jacketed stuff: soft point or metal cased.

At one time the .25-35 and .25 Remington were recommended as calibers for sportswomen and teenagers, and the thought was sensible. These loads are easy to master, and in almost all rifles, including the takedowns, they have woods accuracy. Precision comes in good part from not being afraid of your gun. Solid frame arms, bolt- and even lever-action repeaters, developed excellent varmint-hunting accuracy, and trajectory and wind didn't bother much up to about 150 yards. Heavy-barreled single-shot .25-35s could whip a good many bolt-action sporters on the rifle range, or tie them at least.

But these calibers aren't for the huntress of today. A little more practice, a gradual working up of handloads to the necessary power, and she does better work with a heavier caliber than her mother or grandmother could do with the little .25s. And as for the teeners, though they can't walk 200 yards unless they have to—or want to, from some prehistoric urge that wells up in them—they're tough. They can lug and shoot a man-size rifle, or darn near it, if they're given time to soak up the right kind of training.

The .25-35 has practically the same penetration as the .30-30—often hard to tell the difference in game country—though of course it hasn't the smash. If the bullet is placed right it kills deer neatly, sometimes without any need for a trail-up. But with this cartridge many opportunities ought to be passed up. It has to be favored. You and I know that lots of experienced hunters swear by it.

Its rim and body are smaller than those of the .30-30, but I've seen first-rate cases made for it from the latter. This was done only for convenience. My friend had lots of .30-30 brass on hand, and a new .25-35 he'd made up. rebarreling a carbine with a slightly turned-down rifle tube. This good caliber is still made, and we hope it hangs on.

.25 REMINGTON

	Yards	Velocity	Energy	MR trajectory, inches
117 gr s. p. . .	0	2320	1400	. . .
	100	1980	1020	1.0
	200	1700	750	4.5
	300	1470	560	11.5

Almost always this now discontinued cartridge has been loaded more heavily than the .25-35, though its extra powder space never was fully utilized by the factories because of limitations of the rifle it was made for back in 1906. The autoloading Rem was a strong rifle, but its action was nicely balanced to handle a more or less standardized load. Modern .25 factory ammunition added about 300 f. s. velocity, whereas a strong bolt action could take an extra 100 f. s., or even 200, using the old Du Pont No. 16 powder and the milder potassium chlorate primers. Corrosive, yes, but this caliber and the .25-35 could be kept in perfect shape throughout a normal barrel life of 8,000 rounds or so—normal for this type. It seemed that the higher burning pressures sucked enough of the corrosive salts out the muzzle, or else that the heavy powder charge diluted them. Anyway, it was so, and you could use reduced handloads too, within reason, and still keep the bore uncorroded. There was simply no comparison between the barrel life of these calibers and the .25-20 and .32-20 when smokeless powders were used with the old primers.

Cases can be formed from the .30 Remington rimless, still made, and the .25 Rem deserves handloading. Like the .25-35, it's a well balanced cartridge.

.250-3000 SAVAGE

	Yards	Velocity	Energy	MR trajectory, inches
87 gr. s. p. . .	0	3030	1770	. . .
	100	2660	1370	0.6
	200	2330	1050	2.5
	300	2060	820	6.4
100 gr.	0	2820	1760	. . .
rounded s. p.	100	2350	1220	0.6
	200	1970	860	3.1
	300	1670	620	8.4
100 gr.	0	2820	1760	. . .
pointed s. p.	100	2500	1390	0.6
	200	2210	1080	2.8
	300	1940	835	7.1

The original claim of 3000 f. s. velocity was startling. The .256 Newton and .280 Canadian Ross were the only American factory loads that beat it in muzzle velocity, though out at 300 yards their remaining speeds were a bit over 2400. They used long bullets.

Experience has classed the 87-grain .250 as a varmint cartridge. The 100-grain or a slightly heavier custom bullet is the one for deer. For the woods we'd choose the round-nosed bullet, for the open, the sharp one. The semi-pointed Winchester-Western Silvertip falls between them in trajectory and remaining velocity, and it is well liked. Within 200 yards, about the extreme effective limit of the .250 on deer, the actual difference between the 100-grain bullet designs isn't much. Thing to pick is the one that shoots most accurately in a given rifle. This is worth finding out, for the length, body taper and shoulder of the .250 resulted in an accurate cartridge that did well with the old powders and with the new ones, too, in spite of their deterrent coating.

Most rifles for it use a 14-inch twist, but some have been made as steep as 10. Yet it's a good cast-bullet size, obliging with almost any weight between about 65 and 100 grains—latitude enough. Case necks are usually thick, requiring careful resizing and expanding to fit the cast lead.

If a light cartridge is wanted for a woman, girl or boy, this is a sensible one to think about. Recoil is light, muzzle blast from 22-inch or longer barrels not extreme, at least with the 100-grain load. The explosive effect of high velocity counts; 2700 f. s. was about as high as we could comfortably go with the .25-35, handloaded or factory, and that was with a lightly jacketed 87-grain varmint bullet.

For the beginner it is not a good brush cartridge, or even a long-range load. It's done well in both kinds of country in the hands of experienced hunters. In killing power on deer it is generally a little ahead of the .30-30, though it's vastly different in its effects, and for all-round use, including plenty of target practice and maybe some serious, careful hunting of varmints, there's no comparison between the two.

.257 ROBERTS

	Yards	Velocity	Energy	MR trajectory, inches
87 gr s. p. ..	0	3200	1980	...
	100	2840	1560	0.5
	200	2500	1210	2.2
	300	2190	925	5.7
100 gr.	0	2900	1870	...
pointed s. p.	100	2580	1480	0.6
	200	2280	1150	2.7
	300	2000	885	6.7
117 gr.	0	2650	1820	...
rounded s. p.	100	2280	1350	0.7
	200	1950	985	3.4
	300	1690	740	8.8

The .25-06 Niedner was considered over bore capacity—though it's still used successfully—and the smaller .25 Niedner Krag was thought to be just about right. In Krags and single shots it was a fine wildcat cartridge.

The 7x57 mm. Mauser having about the same powder capacity as the .30-40 Krag, it was a natural for Major Roberts to choose in his experiments with long-range varmint rifles. He eased the shoulder of the 7 mm. into a more gradual slope, and the result was excellent combustion of the powders then available, and splendid accuracy with bullets of about 87 to 100 grains' weight—and at least very fine shooting with the blunt-nosed 117-grain .25-35 and .25 Remington bullets. He tried a lot of forms.

Remington, adapting this wildcat to the 30-S rifle, restored the 7-mm. shoulder angle for manufacturing convenience, and loaded it with 87, 100- and 117-grain round-nosed, hollow-point bullets. They were ballistically poor, but at the time the Roberts seemed to be giving its best accuracy with that general shape.

It was odd that for years hardly anyone believed that the .257 would shoot as well or better with sharp-pointed bullets. Some handloaders found out, of course, and now they've had their way, or half of it! For .257 magazines were blocked off—and in the case of the Remington 722, built—to accept the short overall rounds. The 100- and 117-grain bullets therefore are seated deeply, their bases going clear through the neck and chumming up with the powder kernels. This minor ballistic crime, or so at least it seems to be, does no great harm when jacketed bullets are used. At the instant of discharge the case neck expands, and out they go into the short rifling throat of the .257. Thousand-yard Wimbledon Match accuracy has resulted from similar loading of a good many .300 Magnums. The bench-rester wouldn't admire this style of bullet seating.

Now the Roberts is an accurate cartridge, and rather mildly loaded by the factories. Perfectly sane handloading can increase the velocities of its 100- and 117-grain bullets, and improve accuracy too. With a long, sharp 125-grain custom bullet it can be decidedly improved for hunting, and greater weights can be used, for the 10-inch twist has a lot of stabilizing ability. The .257 is no elk or moose cartridge, though it has killed such game, and so have the .25-35 and lighter rounds.

But it is a good deer cartridge, of the lighter sort, and for open shooting a long, rather heavy spitzer is the natural prescription.

Factory barrels, unless they're considerably eroded, normally must be throated out to receive long bullets seated far out to give almost 7-mm. Mauser overall length. Winchester magazines are no problem: they can be fitted with .30-06 springs and followers, and the extension of the extractor collar shortened to give full rearward travel to the bolt. Lengthening the Remington 722 magazine in a practical, safe manner is limited. A Roberts barrel on a 721 action would be one solution. When we use true rimless cartridges like the .257 in a slightly over-length magazine there's little if any trouble. A semi-rimmed case like the .220 Swift can be a nuisance, sometimes serious, if the lower rims ride ahead of the upper ones when we load or empty the magazine.

For those who like a comparatively smallbore rifle for deer hunting the .257 is one of the best. Honesty compels us to classify it as "a small deer cartridge" compared to the more powerful .30 calibers of similar powder capacity, or a bit less. Yet it has made a good record, rarely blemished by failures due to anything but carelessness or lack of skill. It is a pleasant shooting cartridge to master and it remains one of the best all-round calibers on the rather light side. In trajectory it is much inferior to the 6 mms., but it does handle heavier bullets, less sensitive to wind as velocity falls, and decidedly more reliable if brush screens the target.

In factory loads the 117-grain is for the woods, the 100 for the open, and the little, lightly jacketed 87 strictly for varmint hunting. The Silvertip 100-grain in its present form doesn't shoot quite as flat as the pointed soft point, the midrange height at 300 yards being seven inches and the velocity only 1920 f. s. In actual use the difference means a level teaspoonful more than nothing. For most of us the Roberts is barely a 300-yard cartridge on any game.

.30-30 WINCHESTER AND .30 REMINGTON

	Yards	Velocity	Energy	MR trajectory, inches
150 gr. h. p. or	0	2410	1930	...
ST °	100	2020	1360	0.9
	200	1700	960	4.2
	300	1430	680	11.0
170 gr. s. p., .	0	2220	1860	...
h. p. or ST	100	1890	1350	1.2
	200	1630	1000	4.6
	300	1410	750	12.5

° ST: Silvertip, Western or Winchester.

Perhaps in some ways the 1895 Winchester cartridge deserves to be the most popular deer load, which it is, by the token of sales. It's made in great and in fact unnecessary variety. Remington still loads the original 160-grain weight in full-metal-cased style, and apparently always has since the beginning. The Winchester-Western design is 170 grains, and there is some call for these bullets from people as different in their occupations as trappers and security guards.

The 150-grain varmint bullet isn't offered in the

Remington rimless case, which so closely resembles the original rimmed Winchester. Both cases were loaded with a 110-grain hollow-point varmint bullet for years. Velocity ran as high as 2750 f. s., but accuracy up to a full 100 yards was a bit uncommon, to say the least. A Peters 125-grain hollow point was much better balanced, but never popular.

As a deer load the 150-grain can be dismissed, I think. It was an attempt to make the .30-30 a long-range rifle. However, it's still furnished in pretty rugged build, the Corelokt reinforced-wall soft point by Remington and Peters, slower at long distances than the Silvertip, which is a delayed expansion type. So the attempt goes on. For varmint shooting the hollow point 150-grain is probably safer from ricochets than the 170-grain soft point at lower velocity.

With the heavier bullet there's no great need to choose the type carefully. All of the expanders mushroom when they hit a deer solidly at reasonable range, up to 150 yards, say, considering the accuracy and power of .30-30 rifles. For the rimless cartridge, you know, at first was headstamped ".30-30 REM."

Often the modern .30-30 bullet goes clear through, letting out some sort of blood trail. A hit too far back is unfortunate, to say the least; no 150- or 170-grain .30-30 has the velocity to give much rupturing effect. This cartridge will serve the careful, experienced deer hunter well, and it's killed almost all sorts of game, but it's a poor choice for the beginner unless he hunts and shoots like a really skilled oldtimer. With a considerably more powerful caliber he'd kill his deer more quickly, and he'd get some that he might lose with the modernized 1895 cartridge.

Since the .30-30 was our first popular smokeless load for big game, there's some affection for it, which I share with millions. It does fine shooting with cast bullets and only in a short-barreled carbine are its full charged cartridges noisy. Recoil is light in arms of good and properly distributed weight. With a 170-grain long-pointed bullet at full speed, burning its powder with open throttle, it just might be a winning International Match caliber. A heavy bolt-action or single-shot .30-30 can convince anyone that this cartridge is not inaccurate. But then, few are.

.300 SAVAGE

	Yards	Velocity	Energy	MR trajectory, inches
150 gr bronze point	0	2670	2370	...
	100	2410	1930	0.7
	200	2170	1570	3.0
	300	1950	1270	7.5
150 gr. Corelokt s. p.	0	2670	2370	...
	100	2270	1710	0.7
	200	1930	1240	3.3
	300	1660	915	9.3
180 gr ST or pointed s. p.	0	2370	2240	...
	100	2160	1860	0.9
	200	1960	1530	3.7
	300	1770	1250	9.2
180 gr. rounded s. p.	0	2370	2240	...
	100	2040	1660	0.9
	200	1760	1240	4.1
	300	1520	920	10.5

Most careful choosers pick a 180-grain for the woods, or for game larger than deer. For 'way-out deer the 150-grain Remington Bronze Point is a flat-shooting load, with the Silvertip not far behind it. Winchester-Western furnish a special long-exposed soft-point 150 for varmint hunting, only. It shoots flatter than the second load detailed above. Notice the difference in 180-grain types: the blunt one is for the woods, the sharp one for open country.

The .300 Savage is well over 40 years old and may be superseded by that efficient upstart, the .308. That would be too bad. In well selected factory loadings it has just the right power for deer—though some competent hunters call it a bit excessive—and it's not hard to learn to shoot if the beginner is eased in with moderate handloads. Even without them—and most of us shooters are—it's not too much for an experienced .22 rimfire and shotgun user to assimilate.

Although its case neck is short for cast-bullet loading, such formulas have been put up in it and have shot well. Overall cartridge length is short because of the 99 Savage magazine it was designed to fit. Long, heavy lead bullets that we might choose for the .30-06 wouldn't do for this case, but a blunt hollow point of about 150 grains could have its uses. So can shorter and lighter bullets, for the 12-inch twist is the same as that of the .30-30.

Rifles and cartridges in this caliber are in good supply, and likely to stay so for many years. Since the .300 has the same case-head size as the .30-06 and its body taper—as far as it goes—is almost identical, we have that brass to fall back on for case forming. As always, the capacity of the product should be checked with that of the rifle's own brass, and lower capacity means lower loading levels, for safety.

.30-40 KRAG

	Yards	Velocity	Energy	MR trajectory, inches
180 gr. pointed s. p. or ST	0	2470	2440	...
	100	2250	2020	0.8
	200	2040	1660	3.5
	300	1850	1370	8.5
180 gr. rounded s. p.	0	2470	2440	...
	100	2120	1790	0.8
	200	1830	1340	3.8
	300	1590	1010	9.9
220 gr. ST	0	2200	2360	...
	100	1990	1930	1.4
	200	1800	1580	4.4
	300	1630	1300	11.0

In power this cartridge slides between the .300 Savage and the .308 Winchester. Like the .257 Roberts in comparison to the .250 Savage, it takes much heavier bullets than the shorter American cases of the same caliber.

Most .30-40 rifles and carbines are heavy, eight pounds and up, though I remember a carbine that belonged to an old, experienced hunter who was one of the soundest writers we've had on the subject of sporting rifles and their ammunition. He used it in the far north, and I doubt that it went much over seven pounds.

The average Krag or '95 Winchester .30-40 owner

Deer Cartridges, Plate I: .25-35 Winchester, .25 Remington, .250 Savage, .257 Roberts, .30-30, .30 Remington, .300 Savage, .30-40 Krag, .303 Savage. *Henry Way-Silvers Photo.*

Deer Cartridges, Plate II: .303 British, service load; .32-40; .32 Special; .32 Remington (point filed off, possibly for brush shooting); .35 Remington; .351 Winchester selfloading (point has been flattened as by magazine stress under recoil); .401 Winchester self-loading; .38-55 with black powder and lead bullet; .38-40; .44-40 with black powder and lead bullet. *Henry Way-Silvers Photo.*

may not realize how fine a weapon he has. Even in factory loads the choice is wide, and practical. The old 150-grain cartridges have been discontinued, but the sharp 180-grains are good varmint loads if a person is careful about the background, glasses it so he'll run no risk of hitting a rock. The round-nosed 180 is the choice for deer hunting except at long ranges, and the 220 is for big stuff, has been used a lot on moose.

The 220-grain Silvertip listed above has the new semi-pointed profile and shoots a bit flatter than the blunter soft or hollow points. At original velocity of about 2000 f.s. the plain soft point had about the highest reputation of all our relatively smallbore, smokeless cartridges for use in brush. Some deer hunters actually choose this weight still, in spite of its increased velocity, though it's a rather poor killer of white-tails unless it's placed right. Our modern

220-grain bullets, and for that matter the old ones, are designed for deep penetration in heavy game.

The Krag case is the handloader's delight. Powder and lead combinations have been home-laboratoried for it by the dozen, and proved on target paper. Rifling twist is 10-inch. Still, I've seen a Krag put buckshot—one at a time—into the 9 and 10 rings right along at 50 feet. Versatility, utility, killability— the .30-40 has 'em all.

Bert Shay has loaded two round bullets in its long neck, just for a gag, but the results weren't hopelessly bad, at that. With a short lead bullet like the old Marine Corps' 87 grain (Ideal 308245) and a little snifter of pistol powder the 25-yard results are excellent.

Regardless of "paper energy," the 190-grain is the choice for woods hunting. True, the original bullet weighed only 180, but its low speed of 1840 f. s. let it get through brush better than the early 160-grain

.30-30 at about 120 f. s. higher speed. With the advent of the 190 and the discontinued 195-grain soft points the .303 fell into its rightful place, a little Krag, close to midway between .30-30 and .30-40 for those who wanted a timber cartridge.

.303 SAVAGE

	Yards	Velocity	Energy	MR trajectory, inches
180 gr. s. p. . . .	0	2140	1830	. . .
or h. p.	100	1810	1310	1.1
	200	1550	960	5.4
	300	1340	715	14.0
190 gr. s. p. . . .	0	1980	1650	. . .
or ST	100	1680	1190	1.3
	200	1440	875	6.2
	300	1250	660	15.5

Only for hunters who know it like the back of their hand is it a 200-yard load, though its heavy bullet bucks wind and holds its punch rather well, by actual field proofs, and in good solid frame 99 lever guns the .303 is accurate. The long bullet actually makes it a little different from the rest of the .30-30 family, and large game has been killed cleanly with it. For caribou, black bear and on up we now have so much better cartridges that it should be kept for deer hunting only. At ranges over 100 yards the modern 180-grain loads have obvious advantages, but this caliber shines in the timber. It does all right if shots are placed correctly, and the penetration of its bullets is plenty.

The case is a good one for the handloader. At the base it's larger than the .30-30, and the brass is strong. The short powder chamber burns light charges well and the neck covers the grease grooves of any cast bullet we'd be likely to choose for it. We can use sharp points, for the 99 magazine holds the hulls side by side, not bullet to primer.

.303 BRITISH

	Yards	.	Velocity	Energy	MR trajectory, inches
215 gr s. p. . . .	0		2180	2270	. . .
	100		1900	1720	1.1
	200		1660	1310	4.9
	300		1460	1020	12.5

Only the plain soft point without inner or outer stiffening is loaded in this cartridge by our U. S. factories. Dominion, up in Montreal, furnishes a soft point and a sharp, capped point in 180-grain, also a 215-grain in full jacketed, and Western used to make an open point boat-tail of about 174 grains. Velocities run within less than 300 f. s. below that of the .30-06 180 but hardly convert the .303 into a long-range rifle.

In various forms the .303 British caliber rifles have served hunters all over the word. Single-shot, double-barrel, and repeating sporters have been chambered for this size. The 215 grain cartridge is much like the Krag 220-grain, perhaps a little surer to expand on deer, since the bullets made here aren't so stiff, maybe not quite as suitable for the heavy stuff. Practical differences are mighty small.

Custom bullets of about .311 inch fit most .303 British barrels, and they come in various weights. Cast bullets might need to be larger, .313 or over, to fill the grooves, and military rifles made under wartime stress have their natural variations. The .303 case neck is short, but not excessively so.

In Canadian, Australian and African game countries the .303 user wouldn't need to worry about ammunition availability where such stuff is sold. Most people who have given it a fair trial in the United States like it. Far more rifles have been made for it than for the .30-40, for it was the standard British caliber long before and for some time after the two world wars.

.32-40 WINCHESTER, MARLIN AND SAVAGE

	Yards	Velocity	Energy	MR trajectory, inches
165 gr. s. p. . . .	0	1440	760	. . .
	100	1250	570	2.4
	200	1100	445	11.0
	300	1030	390	28.0

Notice how this old coot hangs on to the velocity that's given it? Not much lag. It was a famous 200-yard offhand target cartridge, with bullets up to 210 grains cast for it, and a two-diameter 185 with bearing bands of .316 and .323 inch, slightly over the average land and groove diameters, respectively. Barrels were throated out for this big bullet, on order.

Most target bullets were pre-loaded, pushed down from the muzzle with a short starter and a measured rod, or forced into the breech by a starter like the one Ideal used to make. But even with fixed ammunition some loads shot well. A few years ago an old fellow walked off with the honors from a shoot against a slew of modern rifles. His was a heavy single shot in which he'd been using the 165-grain soft point .32-40, factory loaded. In any loading this caliber is pleasant to shoot, win or lose.

Old factory High Power rounds went up to 2065 f. s. velocity, but the thinly jacketed soft points opened fast and gave little if any more penetration than the low-speed stuff. Of course they were more deadly. Penetration could be had with modern or oldtime .32 Special jacketed bullets in handloads of necessarily lower velocity than that 2065 figure. Such .32-40 modernization would be only for strong rifles like sound '93 Marlins, '94 Winchesters, '99 Savages and Winchester high-wall single shots (the low wall *has* been barreled .32-40), and nickel steel or "special smokeless steel" had best be the barrel composition if it's to last long.

Favoring less sturdy arms of the great variety once made in this caliber, the modern factory load is kept low in pressure. It always was about the most accurate variety we could buy, though practically anything that was useful could be had. For squirrels there were the Short Range and Miniature cartridges with 98- and 100-grain lead and metal cased bullets. The black-powder full charges were cheap to buy, and the High Velocity at about 1750 f. s. was a deer load for well breeched rifles with soft "black-powder steel" barrels.

Almost anyone would say that the present factory cartridge is too light for deer and be right. Good shots and good hunters who know and like the caliber wouldn't agree, but they're a minority group, I hope there are enough of them to keep the .32-40 in circulation for a long time to come.

.32 WINCHESTER SPECIAL

	Yards	Velocity	Energy	MR trajectory, inches
170 gr.	0	2280	1960	. . .
rounded s. p. or	100	1920	1390	1.0
h. p.	200	1630	1000	4.8
	300	1410	750	12.5
170 gr. flat-	0	2280	1960	. . .
nosed s. p. or	100	1870	1320	1.0
ST	200	1560	920	4.8
	300	1330	665	13.0

In late years the .32 Special sometimes has been embarrassingly absent from the roll-call of some rifle and carbine models, but at the moment it seems to be fully reinstated and likely to stay. And why not? Since the beginning the mere word "Special" has helped to sell this caliber.

It is sort of special, too. The 16-inch twist lets us shoot black powder in it if we have to or want to use it behind cast lead. With smokeless the plain-based lead, without gas-checks, goes at pretty fair speed before it fouls up the rifling grooves. 'Way back, .32 Special factory velocity was some 100 f. s. ahead of the .30-30s, and perhaps a difference in killing power could be noted in 100 or more carefully autopsied deer. Now there's little to choose between, even in factory .32 Special variants, as is obvious in the tables back there.

One advantage claimed for the .30-30 is that a badly rusted barrel will still spin bullets out with fair accuracy. Few of us *have* to hunt with such barrels, and the slow .32 twist makes for a little longer life.

So it's a toss-up. Unless we take as light a rifle as a .30-30 to the far north, where ammo for it is practically currency, or unless we want factory-loaded full-jacketed or varmint rounds, the .32 is as good a choice as the .30. The lower sectional density of its bullets means little.

.32 REMINGTON

	Yards	Velocity	Energy	MR trajectory, inches
170 gr s. p. . . .	0	2220	1860	. . .
or h. p.	100	1890	1350	1.0
	200	1610	975	4.9
	300	1400	740	13.0

Different case shape and powder capacity keep the .32 Remington's velocity below that of the .32 Special, and we must remember this fact in handloading it. Rifling twist is 14 inches, as standard, not 16, and this tends to increase pressures, but not much.

This cartridge is a perfectly acceptable .30-30, a recognized and in fact honored member of the family. But it was never much of a mixer, never well known.

Until rather lately it was priced, like the .32 Special and .303 Savage, the same as the .30-30, and it looked

A sectioned .35 Remington Corelokt soft-point cartridge. From base of case to nose of bullet: primer cup, priming compound, paper seal, primer anvil, flash-hole in case's primer pocket, powder, bullet jacket, bullet core.

as though we were getting more for our money in buying the less popular sizes. Perhaps we were, even if it was something intangible, like confidence.

.35 REMINGTON

	Yards	Velocity	Energy	MR trajectory, inches
200 gr. s. p.,	0	2210	2170	. . .
h. p., ST, or	100	1830	1490	1.1
m. c.	200	1540	1050	5.2
	300	1310	760	14.0
150 gr. pointed	0	2400	1920	. . .
s. p. Corelokt	100	1960	1280	0.9
	200	1580	835	4.6
	300	1280	545	13.0

As a deer and black bear cartridge the .35 Remington has had a long and successful time of it, with growing rather than fading popularity. It came out with the Model 8 autoloading rifle in 1906 and almost always there have been plenty of new, current rifles available for it—Remington, Standard, Stevens, Winchester 70 and Marlin 336. There were custom jobs on the short Mauser action. Second-hand rifles for it received careful consideration, and still do. It's a fine load, with just the right amount of power, good accuracy, and not too rough recoil or report from well-built rifles of reasonable barrel length. Reasonable, that is, to suit the average.

For moose, elk, grizzly or Alaskan brown bear it's light. The 200-grain bullet is stubby, shorter than that of the .32 Special, which is a squatted-down .30-30. Long, heavy bullets get through the hard flesh and bone of our biggest American game, straight through as aimed, pretty much, but short ones may be deflected or even stopped before they reach the vital organs inside. Though this .35 has killed such game, and some African game too, its sure capability ends with deer and black bear. So it is, really, just the sort of cartridge that most of us need, our opportunities being limited by our travel.

With the advent of the .358 Winchester, so quickly adopted by many rifle makers, the question of the .35's survival pops up. A lot of hunters go for power, too often more than they need. A more easily mastered, entirely adequate lighter cartridge lacks the appeal of the buster. Any answer to the question of the .35's life expectancy must be temporary. All we can say is that two popular rifles, the Remington 760 pump and the Marlin 336 lever, are being sold for it right along, not to mention the used guns.

There are at least three other cartridges in its deer-and-black-bear class, all recently dropped from U. S. manufacture. More rifle models, and probably more rifles, have been made for the .35 than for the other three combined. All of them fire a 200-grain bullet at about 2200 f.s. muzzle velocity.

The vanishing trio, still in use as ammunition supply permits, consists of the 8x56 Mannlicher-Schoenauer, .33 Winchester and Marlin, and .401 Winchester self-loading. The smaller the bullet diameter, the greater the ranging power. All except the 8 mm. are essentially woods cartridges. That one is a .32 that *can* be handloaded for fairly long shooting.

Recently Remington has attempted to extend the range of the .35 with a poorly balanced 150-grain sharp soft point, a revamped form of the long discontinued 150-grain hollow point at 2360 f.s. The newer 150 needs a word of caution: it should *never* be used in a straight-tube magazine like the Stevens or Marlin, in point-to-primer loading.* The old Remington 14 and 141 slide actions have spiral magazine tubes, and these guns were safe even with the old pointed, full-patched bullets once loaded in all of the rimless Rem quartet except the .32. When it was legal to shoot ducks with a rifle there was some use for them, though not many seem to have been sold.

Handloaders of .35 Remington cases take care not to set shoulders back in neck-sizing. In heavy loads they gain little if any velocity, but this big caliber comes close to becoming an all-rounder with cast-lead .38 revolver bullets sized to fit the particular barrel, .358-inch being about standard. There are special molds for gas-check bullets heavier than most plain-based revolver slugs we'd use for "small shooting." The Norma make of 9-mm. Luger bullet, soft point, might suit some .35 barrels, now that the .38 Auto Colt no longer comes in anything but full-jacketed style. Such a short bullet gives no well-sustained accuracy or speed even in the slow 16-inch .35 Rem twist, but it can make a safe blow-up load for varmints that aren't too far off. Handloaders should remember that some .35 Rem. rifling groove diameters run only .356 inch, not the usual .357 to .358.

This old .35 case looks like a shortened and neck-expanded .30-06 but actually it's a good bit smaller.

*Yes, modern rifle primers normally have thick, tough cups, and this practice has been sanctioned by manufacturers. But on this question I'll stay obstinate.

Rim sizes for them are .454 and .468 inch, and the heads just above the extracting groove go .451 and .4665—all approximate. Head and rim differences are about average for cases that we call "true rimless," to distinguish them from semi-rimmed sizes like the .220 Swift or 6.5 mm. Japanese.

.351 WINCHESTER SELF-LOADING

	Yards	Velocity	Energy	MR trajectory, inches
180 gr. s. p. or	0	1850	1370	. . .
m. c.	100	1560	975	1.5
	200	1310	685	7.8
	300	1140	520	21.5

Right from the 1907 beginning most people looked doubtful when they saw the small size of the .351. But it burned the dense Hercules Sharpshooter smokeless at contemporary .30-30 pressure, about 39,000 pounds maximum. The stubby little bullet spun out pretty fast, for those days, beating any standard black powder loading and most of the smokeless revisions called "High Velocity" or "High Power."

Its effect on deer always has been marginal; some would say it's submarginal. Though penetration is good, the bullet has neither weight, width or velocity. At maximum it's about a 100-yard load, and hits beyond that distance have demonstrated failures of the soft point to mushroom well. Up close, its killing power is like that of the .25-35, if we can compare the effects of a moderately heavy and slow bullet with those of a moderately light and fast one.

On the credit side, most of us agree that it will kill deer cleanly when it's pointed right—it's done so time and again—and that the .351 rifle and cartridge combination is easy to shoot in the country it's meant for. Recoil from the heavy rifle is trifling, the bark of its report mild though rather distinctively abrupt, and the accuracy good enough for short-range work.

For a snap-shooting rifle the trigger pull is heavy, liable to disturb the close coordination we need, but that's a less serious fault than a too-light release. Of all the centerfire self-loading sporters except the old .25 Remington it's the easiest to shoot fast *and* well. Muzzle upchuck is slight; the gun settles back fast into alignment.

That is as careful an estimate as I can make of the .351. It shouldn't be taken too enthusiastically, except by those who know it well. It absolutely isn't the gun for an over-eager hunter. Those who like it appreciate its steady, muzzle-heavy feel, its great reliability and ruggedness. As for its being an automatic, they know that its first shot must be made to count, because of its low power. They also know that sometimes, in spite of a hunter's best efforts, one or more follow-up shots may have to be sent in, fast and accurately.

Comparatively few now buy this rifle for deer hunting. There are lighter-weight and more powerful self-loaders available, and perhaps more of the same in the works. But to a considerable extent it's a standby of law enforcement agencies. It has plenty of power, but not the range to make it liable to carry into the next county, where someone else is sheriff. So the full-patched or metal-cased bullet survives in this caliber and it's likely that the soft point will, too. Though the rifle went out in 1957, a lot of them still get used.

.38-40 WINCHESTER

	Yards	Velocity	Energy	MR trajectory, inches
180 gr. s. p. . . .	0	1330	705	. . .
	100	1070	455	3.2
	200	966	370	15.0
	300	850	290	36.5

A gunsmith friend of mine called this one "probably the most useless cartridge ever developed." Of course he knows what it will and won't do.

As late as 1920 or so there were heated arguments between .38-40 and .44-40 fans. The small one, actually a .40 caliber, had more velocity in all standard loadings, and in High Velocity an impressive 1776 f.s. compared to the .44's 1569. (Velocities sometimes were listed to the tenth part of a foot, which meant if possible less than nothing, bein' as how things are.) The .38 was a little more accurate, on a hair-splitting average, having not quite as stubby a bullet. It kicked less.

And that, it seems, was the reason for its production. This early factory wildcat, a neckdown of the .44, seemed like a good caliber for ladies and juniors. Back in the 1870s, everyone knew, didn't he, that the .44-40 was *a big game cartridge?* Mild it down a bit and see if it'll catch on. It did. From 1879 to 1915 or so it sold pretty well. It never became the world-wide caliber that the .44-40 did, though it's hard to tell the difference in their actual effectiveness.

For revolvers to be used in real wilderness the .38-40 has been a longtime favorite. It shot plenty fast and flat, and the blunt nose of its bullet helped make up for its lack of weight.

.38-55 WINCHESTER, MARLIN AND SAVAGE

	Yards	Velocity	Energy	MR trajectory, inches
255 gr. s. p. . . .	0	1320	985	. . .
	100	1160	760	2.9
	200	1050	625	13.0
	300	1000	565	32.0

Like the .32-40, this nearly true .38 diameter bullet is a miser of the velocity it starts with. This was the heavier Schuetzen offhand favorite, and as with the .32, sometimes its rifles were recut to larger bore and groove diameters to extend barrel usefulness. To distinguish them, shooters called them .33 and .39.

The standard .38-55 load, still made, has a long and well-built reputation for deer killing. Its big, slow bullet gets through brush well, gives good penetration, and at short ranges usually splits its jacket and mushrooms as it's supposed to. With almost any slow load, hits on deer must be placed carefully, and we'd do well to remember that in black-powder, lead-bullet days the .38-55 wasn't one of the big cartridges. But it was factory loaded up to 1700 f.s. for use in the strongest rifles, and most guns for it were lighter and slightly less expensive than those for larger cartridges. It survived.

Handloading safely for a particular rifle can add to .38-55 killing power on deer, and a hollow-point cast bullet of the old 235-grain Ideal standard is worth considering. Through brush, though, deep-cavitied lead makes poor progress; it's easily persuaded to turn off on a side trip.

The .38-55's full handloading variety is tremendous, even in fixed ammunition, assembled snugly in the brass. Possibly this caliber will be revived for matches that are restricted to black-powder rifles, or those using lead bullets. At least for the first sort of competition it's one of the best. Over-the-counter hunting ammunition has its uses for those who understand what it can and can't do.

.401 WINCHESTER SELF-LOADING

	Yards	Velocity	Energy	MR trajectory, inches
200 gr. s. p. . . .	0	2190	2130	. . .
	100	1650	1210	1.2
	200	1220	660	6.3
	300	1010	455	19.0

Already this discontinued cartridge is hard to find, though hoarded stocks should last for years. Its report and recoil seemed excessive to the average deer hunter, when it came out in 1910, and the heavy rifle didn't sell in volume to compare with that of the .351.

At close range, as the figures indicate—and those up there are the highest ever claimed for it—the .401 is a killer. The long-gone 250-grain bullet at 1875 f.s. was for game like moose, but the lighter, faster 200 stayed on the market much longer. Both did kill game as heavy as grizzly and Alaskan bear in spite of their short, poorly balanced build and the fact that they were too light for the job, anyway.

Sometimes the .401 was tried at too long a range for even the 200-grain soft point to expand well on deer, and after the first five years or so Winchester designed a special copper-tubed hollow point for both weights. The short lead exposure at the tip was kept, but the air in the thin tube at least appeared to improve the bust-up, and the copper stiffened the bullet nose against battering in the magazine. A thoroughly experienced European hunter called the .401 just about the most deadly of its type—bigbore, medium-game brush load. The tubed design was a revival of the soft-lead express bullet, but jacketed with copper to take the higher velocities. An Ideal cast bullet can be given good deer-killing power.

.44-40 WINCHESTER

	Yards	Velocity	Energy	MR trajectory, inches
200 gr. s. p. . . .	0	1310	760	. . .
	100	1050	490	3.3
	200	940	390	15.0
	300	830	305	36.5

This 1873 cartridge was a carefully worked-out design. It used practically a duplicate of the famous .44 Henry rimfire's bullet—not heeled down to enter the case mouth, of course—and a slight bottle-necking* of the case let the manufacturers pack in 12 extra grains' weight of black powder, a full 40, without greatly increasing the overall length. What was then considered a rather compact repeating action could handle it.

So the .44-40 gained world popularity, and in out-of-the-way, fascinatingly wild parts of this world it's still active. Sometimes it's used as money. All this started because of the speed of lever-action operation; the cartridge never was or could be a wonderful killer of big game. In revolvers—mostly Colts, though Smith & Wesson made a few for both .38-40 and .44-40—the load is a practical one: lots of smash from its flat-nosed bullet, and noticeably less recoil than a 255-grain .45 gives.

This deer I think of now was less than 30 feet away and the standard velocity .44 soft point took him in the shoulder. Meat was needed. He stumbled forward his own length and piled up. A clean *and* quick kill.

For a setup the .44 is an all-right deer cartridge. It's improved by handloading to safe, higher velocities without cutting bullet weight, for it needs what it has to steer its way through resistance. Some hunters still use it, their success depending upon their ability to get an easy shot and to make good on it.

In woodchuck country, sport can be had with a .44-40, or a .38-40. It is not too simple. Fifty yards is about the longest sure range, accuracy and trajectory being considered, and the bullet must hit an instantly vital spot, *not* the paunch. The background must be watched, for slow bullets ricochet easily from rock or shale, sometimes even from hard, baked earth. So a hill backstop is best, and some chucks live along hillsides and are, I think, more alert than the others. The fox is one of their few natural enemies, and he loves to hunt that kind of terrain. This sort of chuck hunting, by man or fox, must be careful in every way. This sort of hunting is no punishment.

SHOTGUN SLUGS

Some of us have to use these lead cylinders for our deer hunting. Their accuracy is far inferior to that of almost any rifle bullet, but more than twice as good as that of the round "punkin balls" that the factories used to load.

They were sub-caliber, to go easy on choked muzzles, and the general impression was that they bumbled up the bore, bouncing back and forth from side to side. Probably, though, the thick, perforated felt wads at bow and stern held them fairly well in line, and a straight-cylinder barrel wasn't bad at all

———
*Look at a rifle or sixgun chamber and you see that bottle-neck.

with handloaded shells. You wrapped the ball in a cloth patch small enough to make it fit.

The best slug shooting I ever happened to get from many trials came from a full-choke 20-gauge single barrel, four- to six-inch five-shot groups at 50 yards. For aiming there were the usual round bead front sight and a notch in the breech face.

So far I've never seen slugs do well at cutting brush. The nose is blunt enough, the velocity of about 1410 to 1470 f.s. low enough, but the weight is up front. That location is fine for accuracy, but the slug's very deep hollow base hasn't the steadying effect that's needed at the stern of a brush bullet. The deep cavity in the base of 265- and 275-grain .455 Webley Mark II revolver bullets certainly didn't stabilize them. That and the long, tapered nose resulted in a chunk of service lead that could and sometimes did tip on impact.

Compared to a .45-70-405 the slug is poor against brush interference; compared to a .250 Savage or even a heavy .257 Roberts it's good. Much of this is generalization about a subject that never seems to have been investigated fully, and that would be difficult to run definitive tests on. In the natural course of events a good many deer have been killed by shotgun slugs that have clipped twigs and somewhat heavier wood.

Weights in 12, 16, 20, 28 and .410 bore run 1, ⅞, ⅝, ½, and ⅕ ounce, closely paralleling old round-ball standards. An ounce is 437.5 grains; so the 12- and 16-gauge slugs resemble .45-70 rifle loadings. With the 20 gauge we're getting into the light stuff, and it's a shame that the 28 and .410 ever were put out in ball or slug. Yes, the Hudson's Bay Company's trade gun was a 28-gauge muzzle-loader—shot, ball or sometimes both went into it—and it killed game. The game was close-up, and a tragic lot of it was lost, too.

Do slugs spin in the air? It's been denied on good authority, and the weight up front would seem to be enough to stabilize them to a useful extent. The long, straight sides also must help to give them good head-on delivery from the gun muzzle, better than a loose round ball gets unless it expands to fit the bore—and is sized down again by the choke. The spiral grooves swaged into the slug's sides may be for looks; some carry clear down, some are blocked off at the base, and the fired lead does appear to have been shortened by inertia and by the boot the powder gas gives it.

Some early experimental slugs had a hole right through the center, with fins designed to spin them. They weren't successful. The imported Brenneke slug had a wad permanently attached to its base, and it shot well. That ammunition was expensive, and after our factories had brought out their slug loads there wasn't much demand for the Brenneke any more.

LONG range is relative. For lots of us a 200-yard shot at a standing deer or even a larger animal is too much to try with just a reasonable expectation of a sure and quick kill. Losing wounded game is bad in every way, for all concerned. A few hunters are so skilled as riflemen that they can judge distance, allow for it and for wind, and with a clear conscience take a shot twice that long, or a bit more.

But conditions vary a great deal, and they have to be somewhere near "right" for any 'way-out shot. The hunter must be in good form, not winded or trembling from exertion or altitude, and he must be able to fire from a decently steady shooting position. This may be with or without a rest such as a jacket folded over a boulder or his extended arm leaned against a log, the rifle not touching the rest, of course. And parts of our finest hunting country, so beautiful and wild that they remain forever in the memory, are the lands where the winds are made. Some days just aren't fit for long shooting. Though we may be able to fire from a sheltered lee we may find it impossible to judge the wind's force if no vegetation, dust or snow flurry takes the place of a rifle range's wind flags.

Long range opportunities don't come up only in the West. The East has them too, across a beaver meadow or a burning, over farmed or not-long-ago-farmed land, from rugged mountainsides that you find fairly often in Pennsylvania, for instance. Some who know these places and their productiveness of shots that the average hunter would pass up or fail miserably in trying, arm themselves with the best long-range rifles and ammunition they can get.

There are not many factory-loaded American cartridges to choose from, though we have some good ones. Among them there is variety enough to satisfy most of us, right now, and possibly some new ones may come up, a 6.5 mm. or .256, a 7 mm. or .275, and a caliber above .30, like .33 or .35. They'd be rather large cartridges, some of them of belted magnum type, almost certainly. The .256 Newton on shortened .30-06 brass probably won't be revived— even with the minor changes usual when such a thing happens—for advertising reasons, and for a quite different one. Nobody wants to produce a new, strong centerfire rifle, and its ammunition, of a size that's identical to an oldtimer made by a less-well-established and, frankly, less responsible outfit. For though there have been good Newtons—just as an example —there have been substandard ones, too.

Most of our factory-made long-range cartridges are derived at least indirectly from military rounds that date back to the early 1900s, or earlier. At that time, military thinking visualized fighting at extreme distances, with armies taking full advantage of high-pressure smokeless powder and long, lean, jacketed bullets.

In the nature of things the .22s, 24s, and 25s will be the long-range big-game cartridges of the future.

CHAPTER 17

LONG-RANGE HUNTING CALIBERS

Still smaller sizes in time may prove worthy. But since we have only begun to develop high velocities, the minimum now—for game such as moose and elk, let's say—would be about .270 caliber. Bullets kill by weight and/or velocity, roughly speaking. They must also have strength or stiffness for good penetration, though as velocity falls away over the long distances they need less sturdy construction to penetrate well before they expand or, possibly, blow themselves to pieces.

Wildcat cartridges can give higher velocities to standard, accepted bullet calibers, and they can add new calibers not in factory production here in the long-range class, such as .33 and .35. For that matter, though, the 270-grain .375 factory magnum travels like a 180-grain .30-06 and therefore is a long-range load for a good many people and purposes. Recoil? Yes, but more hunters could handle it than think they can.

In 1925 the first modern Winchester bolt-action high-power, the Model 54, came out in this caliber and the .30-06. Experimental work on the .270 began at least as early as 1920, and cupro-nickel jacketed spitzers, full metal patched in military style, were part of the material of research and development.

The commercial cartridge fired a sharp 130-grain protected or capped soft point at 3160 f. s. and people began to find that they could make long-range hits with it a little more surely than with the .30-06. The first of these .270 bullets were lightly jacketed with tin-washed gilding metal—or possibly copper—and at times they broke up too quickly on impact at high velocity. Later this design of bullet was more thickly jacketed near the base and often, not invariably, gave good penetration on game a lot heavier than deer.

The 130-grain is the factory weight for big-game shooting at long range; the 100-grain is for varmints. The latter is thin-jacketed and can be had with long, parallel sides and a quick, conical nose taper, something like the old "U.M.C. Thomas" .30 calibers Remington made in the good weights of 160 and 172 grains. So these little .270s have reasonable bearing surface and shoot fairly well from the quick 10-inch twist that's standard. Handloads for varmints can use heavier bullets, 110-grains being quite a favorite.

.270 WINCHESTER

	Yards	Velocity	Energy	MR trajectory, inches
100 gr. s. p. . . .	0	3580	2840	. . .
	100	3160	2210	0.4
	200	2770	1700	1.7
	300	2400	1280	4.5
130 gr. Bronze	0	3140	2840	. . .
Point	100	2880	2390	0.5
	200	2630	1990	2.1
	300	2400	1660	5.1
130 gr. pointed	0	3140	2840	. . .
s. p. or ST	100	2850	2340	0.5
	200	2580	1920	2.1
	300	2320	1550	5.3
150 gr.	0	2800	2610	. . .
rounded s. p.	100	2400	1920	0.7
Winchester	200	2040	1380	3.0
	300	1750	1020	7.8

Ballistically there's probably less choice among the 130-grain bullets than there is in their accuracy in an individual rifle, and much the same could be said of custom bullets in this weight. We don't need minute of angle accuracy for long-range big-game shooting, but if our load and rifle come pretty close to it, that's a help.

The 130-grains have killed big bear, also elk and moose. For these species they're light, many experienced hunters would agree. The .270 is deadly on deer, caribou and black bear and it *has* been used with complete success on much heavier game. Lately it has become somewhat favored as an African caliber for meat in the pot, not for large or dangerous game.

Originally the 150-grain bullet was for deer, its velocity being some 2700 f. s. or less, to avoid excessive destruction. Western pioneered it, along with the round-nosed .30-06 180-grain soft point. Now it's being pushed as a heavy-game load and at least in some makes its construction has been stiffened. The heaviest factory bullet is the 160-grain Dominion, and custom bullets seldom weigh more, though some makers, such as Barnes, do jacket certain bullets to order, plenty stiff for deep penetration. It seems that a 170-grain round-nose could be stabilized up to 200 yards, at least, and it wouldn't be for long-range shooting, anyway, except in a .270 Magnum. Speer now makes a 170-grain round-nose, and Barnes furnishes heavy bullets up to 180-grains.

The .270 has been popularized partly by men like Townsend Whelen and Jack O'Connor, who've used it a lot and know what it will do. It is of course a long-range cartridge, but an odd thing is that its popularity is universal: we're as likely to see it in close timber as on the plains. When it gets through brush it's a most quick and certain killer of deer, the shot being placed reasonably well, but many who choose it seem never to think that a larger, heavier, slower bullet might be much better for their kind of hunting. To use it in country where we can't see more than 75 yards in any direction is a little like firing up a hot-rod to travel a similar distance from the house to the mail-box.

However, it's a fine, accurate cartridge, and its rifles commonly outshoot .30-06s of the same models. This is largely due to the greater weight and stiffness of their barrels, but so many buy it for its accuracy that the loading factories don't let them down—or they'd better not. Small caliber though it is, and with a 10-inch rifling twist, the .270 is a good cast-bullet size. I've never tried it except with really hard alloy, but I believe that it's like most cartridges and could be loaded down to squirrel hunting or 50 foot target practice with short, plain-based bullets of soft lead and a little bit of fast-burning powder. It is certainly one of our best sporting sizes, and as Americans we can be proud of it, for it is really quite different from the foreign .275s or 7-mms.

It does kick less than the .30-06 hunting loads—about the same as the M-2 service round—though perhaps a bit more suddenly, and its bark is sharper. In that respect it's pleasanter to fire than the .220 and the modern 6-mms. A lot of women and kids use the .270 and like it.

.280 REMINGTON

	Yards	Velocity	Energy	MR trajectory, inches
125 gr. pointed	0	3140	2740	. . .
s. p.	100	2840	2240	0.5
	200	2550	1800	2.2
	300	2280	1440	5.5
	400	2040	1160	11.0
150 gr. pointed	0	2810	2630	. . .
s. p.	100	2580	2220	0.6
	200	2360	1850	2.6
	300	2130	1510	6.5
	400	1920	1230	13.0
165 gr. round-nosed	0	2770	2810	. . .
s. p.	100	2460	2220	0.7
	200	2180	1740	2.9
	300	1930	1360	7.4
	400	1700	1060	14.5

Naturally there were varied reactions when this cartridge came out in the summer of 1957. Some jobbers and dealers groaned audibly at having another caliber to stock, and the old wartime thought, "Is this trip necessary?" came to a number of sophisticated riflemen. Just about everyone realized that anything new is good for business, giving at least a short impetus, and good for the sport, too.

Some of us felt bad because the .280 Rem wasn't in the magnum class. A new 7-mm. had long been wanted, its birth announcement expected almost any day. Sure, there was the 7x61 Sharpe & Hart, a fine load, a magnum somewhat like the .275 Holland & Holland belted that Western had made, briefly, but never pushed for use in a popularly priced rifle.

Others wondered at the choice of boring and bullet diameters. Why not bring out a true 7-mm. since so many bullets of .284 inch diameter are made? The Rem .280 bullets run .283 to .2835, the rifle's bore diameter .277 to .278, groove diameter .283 to .284. Discrepancies are small, but a combination of minimum .280 Rem barrel and possibly oversize 7-mm. bullets would call for some caution in loading top charges. American 7-mm. rifles go as large as .2845 and even .2855 in the grooves. The fact that German arms run as "over-bored" as .2854 to .2874 means little, since the European system employs, or did employ, high-riding rifling lands. Remington's four-groove .280 rifling and the by no means deep grooving tend to lower pressures. Still, the .280 Rem handloader should measure both barrel and bullets when he works for top velocities—if he does.

That seems to be the chief objection to the new caliber, and it needn't be serious. The cartridge is almost certain to become popular. As General Hatcher pointed out in his fine, careful coverage in the August, 1957 *Rifleman,* working pressures of factory loads are low, well under those of the .270, so that the .280 will function nicely in the Model 740 autoloader's gas-operated action. As he explains, such an action can be adjusted to any reasonable pressure. But by using a slightly larger caliber than the .270, with some 4½ percent more bullet base area, pressures can be held down and high velocities still obtained. It's the dental surgeon's "Open wider, please" technique that makes the .35 Whelen so much more potent than the .30-06.

Introducing the .280 in the autoloader was business-like. Since World War II a lot of hunters have gone for speed of fire; so lever, pump and auto rifles, both centerfire and .22 rimfire, have come out in new forms. They sell fast. Trading on the great popularity of the .270 and going it better in the sustained velocity of the 150-grain, and in the blunt-bullet weight of 165 available in factory stuff, was smart, too. That bullet, stiffened like the others in Remington Corelokt and the identical Peters Inner Belted fashion, should be deadly on the biggest American game, given a fair chance. With 10-inch rifling twist the .280 can handle heavier custom bullets, which should come especially for it. Most .270s are 10-inch, and the blunt Speer 170 and Barnes 180-grain bullets give it penetration, and added stability in brush. It's doubtful that the .280 will displace the .270, or that it was seriously meant to.

Cases of .270 and .280 are almost identical in length, some 2.535 to 2.54 inches, but the .280 body is longer, its neck short to prevent its being fired in a .270. That could be disastrous! And the .280 can't be inserted in a normal, well tapered 7x64 mm. Brenneke chamber. Wall thickness, General Hatcher reports, gives the .280 slightly less powder capacity than the .270s.

In overall, the heavy-bullet factory .280s may run longer than .270 rounds now made, but that's immaterial. Most American .30-06 type magazines are meant to handle longer hulls than the sporting 270s and 06s as now loaded. The original .270 bullet, the 130 grain pointed expanding, was of almost identical length to the current 130-grain Silvertip, but it was loaded farther out. Modern 220-grain .30s with thicker jackets and consequently lighter lead cores are longer than most old 220s with rather long-exposed soft points; so most of them go clear down through case necks. This overall shortening of some modern rounds, including a few .30-30s and others, helps to reduce nose-battering in box magazines. It helps in some Mauser conversions, too! As for accuracy, well, the .300 Magnum match bullets often are seated clear through case necks. We hunters needn't worry about the system.

The .280 Rem is pretty sure to be wildcatted, blown out to greater capacity and altered up and down in calibers. The heavy brass and well-forward shoulder invite all that. And as factory-loaded it's a good all-rounder for the hunter, better than the .270 for a few of us who really need heavy bullets, but by no means the equal of the .30-06.

Brass for it could be made from 06, a little short, or from .270, just about right. Bert Shay describes a commonsense method. By loading bullets out so the rifling bites them one creates some excess pressure; so one reduces the load quite a bit. The bullet holds the case back against the bolt-face so the primer will be smacked by the firing pin. In a couple of firings the brass will flow forward. Sizing necks up or down to take the .280 bullets isn't much of a chore.

7x57 mm. MAUSER

	Yards	Velocity	Energy	MR trajectory, inches
175 gr. s. p. . .	0	2490	2410	. . .
	100	2170	1830	0.8
	200	1900	1400	3.7
	300	1680	1100	9.5

Handloads or imported ammunition make this durable old cartridge almost equal the .270 for long-range shooting. Greater effectiveness has been claimed for some loadings, but the pressures at times were questionable, and the velocity figures usually are based on the 29.1-inch barrel of the old Spanish military rifle. A reliable listing, no doubt with that rifle, was that of the American 139-grain at 2900 f. s.

This bullet weight has been discontinued here, along with the later 150-grain Winchester and the 160-grain U. S. Cartridge Company boat-tail. The latter was a splendid design, with the old Ross-type capped hollow point, very sharp but pretty rugged in magazine handling, compared to a plain soft point. Actually that long, streamlined bullet was better for the 7-mm. magnums, though the standard American 10-inch rifling twist could spin it, and it was easy for the old German pitch, a fast 8.66-inch.

Our surviving load, the 175-grain, is similar to the 220-grain .30-06 in speed and trajectory up to 300 yards—really too long a game shot for either of these heavy-bullet rounds—and it's similar in deadliness, too. They don't kill by explosive effect, but by proper bullet placement and their good weight and penetration. They are woods loads, and our present commercial 7-mm. is just a little .30-06-220.

But since there's a wide choice of sharp-point, expanding custom bullets, the 7-mm. is a fine long-range caliber for the handloader. He can also use heavier bullets, if he wants to, than he could in a .270, both having a 10-inch rifling twist. The old Remington 30-S and Winchester 54 and 70 rifles for the 7x57 have considerably stronger actions than the Spanish military pieces with no safety or reserve locking lug at the rear of the bolt. Then there are the Mauser sporters, old and new, on the essentially modern, sometimes rechristened, 1898 actions.

Most loads, including our present factory output, give noticeably light recoil in a well built rifle of about eight pounds' weight. So the 7x57 has been a long-time favorite of the huntress, and a small, lightly built man needn't be ashamed to carry it. Better to kill cleanly than to flinch and louse up a good, fair chance, and this old favorite is about the smallest we have for all-round American shooting. With the right bullets it can take anything that walks this hemisphere, and do a good job. About a dozen different countries chose this caliber because it seemed like a sensible minimum when ballistic qualities, rifle weight, and moderate recoil were stirred together in the thinking. The hunter can carry a lighter-weight rifle than the soldier does because he fires so few shots in a day.

7 MM MAGNUMS

The excellent ranging and killing qualities of the caliber, with moderate gun weight combined with comfortable shooting, are so inviting that many magnum 7-mms. or .275s have been brought out by factories and custom shops. Some of them are the 7x64, the 7x65 rimmed, the .275 Holland & Holland Magnum, and we could include the slightly larger diameter .280 Ross and .333-.280 Jeffery.

Right now we have two good magnums of American design, the 7x61 Sharpe & Hart and the 7-mm. Weatherby. Imported Norma ammunition is available for each. Both are handloaded a good deal, with bullets from 120 to 175 grains, and somewhat heavier weights could be used for short-range smacking power. The 160-grain spitzer can be given good velocity and trusted to hold it well out at long hunting ranges. But the shooter who doesn't handload needn't worry. These rounds are commercial and therefore beyond the wildcat stage—though that is an ungrateful way to speak of a class of ammunition that time and again has proved worth the trouble that sometimes comes up in getting the loadable brass.

The big .276 and .280 Newtons were barely if ever on a real production basis, and now they're almost forgotten. So is that single-shot rifle special, the rimmed .405 case necked down to .277 Elliott Express. How I did admire the Winchester I saw for that caliber, a finely balanced, scope-stocked rifle of about 8½ pounds! Its hammer had been altered to rebound into half cock, and a retractor spring pulled the firing pin back out of the primer indent. But its owner loaded that rifle sensibly and had no trouble with brass flowing back into the firing pin hole. Even so, the rifle was a powerful one and you knew when you'd shot it. The .303 Elliott on the same brass was practically a .30-06.

The Dubiel Magnums were among our earliest wildcats of this .275 to .280 caliber. John Dubiel's .275 or 7-mm. used the .275 H&H case with a decidedly eased-back shoulder slope, and his .280 was a .300 H&H neckdown. The Charles O'Neil, Elmer Keith and Donald Hopkins OKH wildcats include an excellent .285, necked-down .30-06 brass, which gives high velocity in a standard-length, standard-sized case, yet still is a 7-mm. magnum in power.

7.62x53 MM. RUSSIAN

So many of these rifles were made here during World War I, and undelivered after the Russians went Bolshevik, that thousands were offered to NRA members at low prices. At the time that was a real favor to Association people, and some useful sporters were gunsmithed out of these arms. The Russian is considered safe with its own 7.62 ammunition but is *not* for conversion to .30-06.

The short cartridge was efficient. American loadings gave about 2800 f. s. velocity from the 31.5-inch Moisin barrel. Winchester's bullet was a 145-grain Ross-type copper tube, Remington's the 150-grain bronze point. Sometimes more powerful handloads were used, and the case took the full line of standard .30-06 bullets from 110 to 220 grains.

Our factories quit manufacturing this cartridge during the early 1950s, and the odd-shaped brass, rounded at the base, isn't one to try to duplicate from currently made sizes. So this caliber of rifle and cartridge isn't to be considered for purchase, and our .30-06 is decidedly superior from any practical viewpoint.

.308 WINCHESTER

	Yards	Velocity	Energy	MR trajectory, inches
110 gr. s. p. ..	0	3340	2730	. . .
	100	2810	1930	0.5
	200	2340	1340	2.2
	300	1920	900	6.6
150 gr. pointed	0	2860	2730	. . .
s. p. or ST	100	2570	2200	0.6
	200	2300	1760	2.6
	300	2050	1400	6.5
180 gr. pointed	0	2610	2720	. . .
s. p. or ST	100	2390	2280	0.8
	200	2170	1870	3.1
	300	1970	1540	7.4
200 gr. ST ..	0	2450	2670	. . .
	100	2210	2170	0.8
	200	1980	1750	3.6
	300	1770	1400	9.0

Some long-range hunting cartridges: .270 Winchester, soft-point hand-load; 7x57 Mauser rimless; 7x61 Sharpe & Hart; 7.62 Russian, service load; .308 Winchester; .30-06; .300 Holland & Holland Magnum; 8x6 Mannlicher-Schoenauer; 8x-57 Mauser, the 7.92 service load; 8 m/m Lebel, service load. *Henry Way-Silvers Photo.*

If this 7.62 NATO is adopted as our service cartridge—and now there is no "if" about it—a lot of our sportsmen are going to approve heartily. It is short and compact, just noticeably lighter in recoil and blast, I think, than the .30-06 when the two are used in rifles of the same weight and build. Ballistics are only slightly below those of the 06, and already the .308 is extremely popular—and deserves to be.

Alongside the 06 it is not quite a two-inch case as compared to a two and one-half. Its neck is shorter and its sides are straighter, adding to the powder capacity of that two-inch brass. More or less theoretical objections are that it is therefore less well adapted to holding cast bullets with their grease grooves covered, and more liable to give extraction trouble when the rifle is hot from firing. These "drawbacks" are trivial, especially the latter, for the shortness of the case eases extraction of empties when the rifle gets hot under firing that's more rapid and continuous than any hunter would give it. The .308 is a carefully designed military round, and you can't say much more than that for any cartridge.

The 110-grain bullet is for varmints. Fired at a stated velocity 80 f. s. lower than that of the .30-06 110, and from a 12- instead of a 10-inch standard twist, it might average a little more accurate, other things being as equal as they could be made.

A long-range big-game shooter has his choice between 150- and 180-grain weights, and for game heavier than deer or antelope he'd probably settle on the latter. Long bullets hold their punch and their penetrating ability better than short ones. The recoil of the 180 is definitely more noticeable than that of the 110, but between 180 and 150 there's little apparent difference.

The 200-grain Silvertip cartridge came out in late 1955 and at this writing doesn't seem to be well known.

It was an attempt to make the .308 a more all-round caliber. In recent years the 180-grain .30-06 has been fully as popular a moose load as the old reliable 220 grain, and it's been used on Alaskan bear, too. Its velocity of 2700 f. s. puts it right up there, when it fires a correctly built bullet. The 200-grain .308 is only a negligible 40 f. s. faster than the 220 06; so the inference is easy. For the heaviest American game it certainly would require better shooting, more careful placement. This loading is well ahead of the discontinued Peters 200-grain belted .300 Savage in velocity, 2450 vs. 2220 f. s. What about its bullet's ability to penetrate, compared to the belted? If that is wanted, custom bullets can supply it.

.30 SPRINGFIELD 1906

	Yards	Velocity	Energy	MR trajectory, inches
110 gr.	0	3420	2850	. . .
pointed s. p.	100	2940	2110	0.4
Remington	200	2490	1510	2.1
	300	2090	1070	5.6
150 gr.	0	2970	2930	. . .
pointed s. p. or	100	2670	2370	0.6
ST	200	2400	1920	2.4
	300	2130	1510	6.1
180 gr.	0	2700	2910	. . .
rounded s. p.	100	2330	2170	0.7
	200	2010	1610	3.1
	300	1740	1210	8.3
180 gr. pointed	0	2700	2910	. . .
s. p. or ST	100	2470	2440	0.7
	200	2250	2020	2.9
	300	2040	1660	7.0
220 gr. ST . .	0	2410	2830	. . .
	100	2180	2320	0.8
	200	1980	1910	3.7
	300	1790	1560	9.2
220 gr. s. p. or	0	2410	2830	. . .
h. p.	100	2120	2190	0.8
	200	1870	1710	3.9
	300	1670	1360	9.8

These are the common commercial loads in .30-06. The 150-grain Winchester-Western semi-pointed, with long lead exposure for varmint hunting, shoots a little less flat than the 150-grain bullets described in the

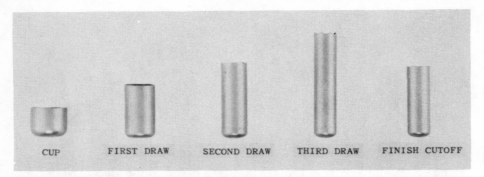

CUP   FIRST DRAW   SECOND DRAW   THIRD DRAW   FINISH CUTOFF

The start of a .30-06 180-grain Silvertip cartridge. Drawing of the jacket.

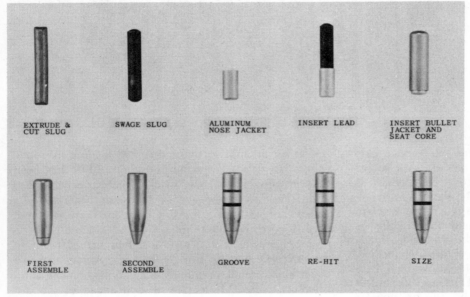

EXTRUDE & CUT SLUG   SWAGE SLUG   ALUMINUM NOSE JACKET   INSERT LEAD   INSERT BULLET JACKET AND SEAT CORE

FIRST ASSEMBLE   SECOND ASSEMBLE   GROOVE   RE-HIT   SIZE

The core or slug, the nose jacket or "Silvertip" (it seems that German silver was used at first), and the jacket take on assembly and final shape.

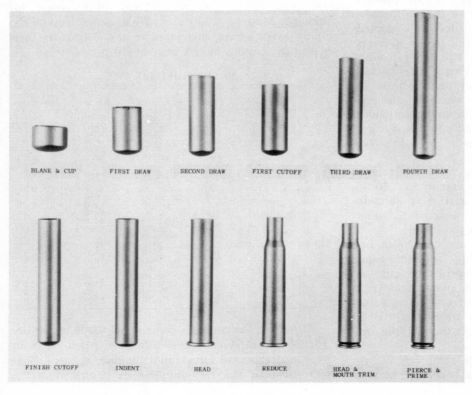

BLANK & CUP   FIRST DRAW   SECOND DRAW   FIRST CUTOFF   THIRD DRAW   FOURTH DRAW

FINISH CUTOFF   INDENT   HEAD   REDUCE   HEAD & MOUTH TRIM   PIERCE & PRIME

Manufacturing the case or shell for this cartridge is no one-two job.

table, and the 150-grain Remington bronze point shoots slightly flatter, as this design normally does. The 180-grain boat-tail or taper-heel match is a long-range target load, and out beyond the short military-target range of 300 yards it fast outdistances our factory-loaded hunting bullets. Full metal cased, it is not for hunting, though such bullets have been used in 150, 160 and 172 grains' weight with varying degrees of success. They tend to dive and cartwheel through heavy game, but in almost any direction. They're unpredictable, and few people hunt with them now.

The 110-grain Remington bullet shoots a bit flatter than the Winchester-Western design, but this means little. Most .30-06 rifles are so long-throated and so fast in rifling twist that varmint-hunting accuracy with these short pellets seldom extends much beyond 150 yards. Their great advantage is that they usually break up on contact with the ground, but the 125-grain custom bullets are nearly as good in that respect—possibly better at times—and they're more stable. This custom weight has become quite a favorite for deer shooting in open country.

For that, most hunters prefer the 150-grain or even the 180, though some of this preference certainly is due to long-accepted usage. The 150- to 154-grain pointed, full jacketed was and is a famous military bullet, and in Government loading was easier for the average shooter to handle than the boat-tailed 173 grain M-1. The 150-grain expanding of almost any type is a pretty fair varmint bullet, and in the good bit of varmint shooting I've seen done with it, and occasionally done, myself, I don't remember having once heard the shriek of a ricochet. Naturally we were careful.

The great all-rounder for the .30-06 is the 180-grain, at modern velocity comparable to, though different from, the 220-grain in its effects on American big game. The round-nosed soft point is for the woods. Years ago it was designed by Western as a not too destructive deer bullet, though it can hash up plenty of meat, at that. But deer fairly hit with it almost never are lost. Why this company and Winchester discontinued the semi-pointed 180-grain Open Point Expanding I don't know. It was deadly on game from deer to large bear, and accurate, too. Its trajectory figures were less impressive than those of the pointed 180s. Could they have been considered so important?

The 200-grain hollow point and the 225-grain belted Peters bullets are gone, too, along with some other weights, 145-grain Ross type, 160-grain full jacketed, 172-grain hard and expanding, and the old Remington subload, a long-exposed soft-point 190 at about 2200 f.s. Nice loading for deer in the woods, that one was.

The favorite heavy bullet stays on, for that 220-grain is famous for big game at moderate ranges. A few use it for deer, despite its uncertain expansion on such light game. The Barnes custom 250-grain

Now they've got it made.

soft point has been found excellent by one or two of my friends who have tried it in the woods. They handloaded it to full, safe speed, and the soft copper jacket, less brittle than gilding metal, split open and made it a bang-up good deer bullet at moderate ranges.

Custom-bullet styles and weights are almost unlimited. There are so many that a person has quite a time in trying to find the two or three different and wanted types that shoot best in his rifle. Then there are the molds, dozens of them. Name the use, and *some* 06 load almost surely can be bought or made up for it.

Up to the limit of its killing power, which is considerable, the .30-06 is still our best all-round cartridge. Few smaller sizes handle round bullets so accurately, and at the other extreme, 250 grains is a respectable weight—in a long bullet like a .30—for any American big game. Naturally one's shooting opportunities might be such that a .257 Roberts or an even lighter cartridge would be as good and in fact a better all-round choice. But if he ever has to shoot for keeps, at long range and in a brisk breeze that's flapping the uniforms of an invading force, a .30 caliber beats most of the smaller ones except maybe a magnum .270 or 7-mm. There's also the matter of ammunition supply on an emergency basis.

Magnum cases seldom are as obliging as the 06 in

reduced-load accuracy that builds marksmanship at low cost and without much racket.

.300 HOLLAND & HOLLAND MAGNUM

	Yards	Velocity	Energy	MR trajectory, inches
150 gr. ST ..	0	3190	3390	...
	100	2870	2740	0.5
	200	2580	2220	2.1
	300	2300	1760	5.2
180 gr. pointed	0	2920	3400	...
s. p. or ST	100	2670	2850	0.6
	200	2440	2380	2.4
	300	2220	1970	5.8
220 gr. h. p.	0	2620	3350	...
	100	2320	2630	0.7
	200	2050	2050	3.2
	300	1830	1630	8.2
220 gr. ST ..	0	2620	3350	...
	100	2370	2740	0.7
	200	2150	2260	3.1
	300	1940	1840	7.7

This is a super-military, special sporting cartridge, not an adapted or revised service type. Military designers, as they would, have used and advanced the magnum idea—a lot of powder to give high velocity to a relatively small caliber projectile. There was the Germans' long-range "Paris gun" of World War I that arched its shells high and far to drop them into that city, and in World War II there were a couple of rifle-caliber anti-tank guns, 8 mms. The German Pz. B. 7.9/13 was a huge, slope-shouldered brass bottle that sent a 225-grain bullet, tungsten carbide-cored and packing tear gas and tracer, at 3968 f. s. Its case was 3.71 inches long, would make the old 3¼-inch Sharps or Winchester Express brasses look stubby, or at least the Polish Pz. B. 35 would, for it measured 4.21 inches. This one fired a bullet similar to that of the German horror, except that the tear gas capsule was absent, at 4000 f.s. Its long case is tapered and abruptly bottle-necked. These and other 8-mm. rounds are described in M. D. Waite's article, "Some 8-mm. Cartridges," in the January 1956 *American Rifleman,* an excellent, definitive story.

In it are tabulated, too, the various 8-mm. sporting magnums, from 60 to 75 mm. in case length, that bracket the .300 H&H in power, most of them being below it. The .30 or .300 is our caliber, just as the 8-mm. is the Germans', and we have an enormous variety of bullets in this size. That helps to account for the popularity, and the usefulness, of the .300 H&H and of other .300s based on it. It's a good ballistic middle-of-the road between .275 and .33.

Standard factory rifles for the .300 weigh about 8¼ pounds, minus sling and scope. Most custom rifles made for it before the late Winchester 54s, the 70s, and the Remington 722s came out were a pound or two heavier. They were easier to shoot, better adapted to bringing out the fine long-range accuracy of the cartridge. But recoil is relative, hunters seldom agreeing on what it is or does, and much lighter .300s have been built, with short barrels, too.

It is a long-range cartridge, and meant for such use, but at close range it has lots of stopping power when the right bullets are chosen. Although the case

was designed for British powders and has a scandalously long, tapered neck and considerable body taper, it's still accurate with modern American components. The 180-grain boat-tailed match bullet, originally at 3030 f.s. but later cut to 2920, has a good 160 f.s. edge on the sporting 180 at 300 yards, and it still is a fine 1000-yard load, not to be proved but to be beaten in wind-resistant accuracy. It *can* be beaten by heavier .30 caliber loadings and no doubt by some 7-mm. magnums. But the match .300 is a standard factory load, with much data available on it.

So too the sporting 180-grain is a familiar hunting cartridge, about as heavy as most of us can use with our full accuracy potential. It's hardly an exaggeration to say that it adds 100 yards to .30-06 deadliness, for those who can shoot it that much better.

The 150-grain factory load may seem to be an experiment, though it's not new; it's been furnished in one or two other bullet designs, long ago in this country. It shoots slightly flatter and faster at game ranges and gives a bit less recoil than the 180. Most people would be satisfied with a 150-grain .30's killing power on deer and antelope. The 180 should fight a cross-wind better, 'way out.

Choice between the 220-grain bullets depends on accuracy from a particular rifle most of all, not so much on remaining velocity and energy. The Silvertip 220 could be called semi-pointed, whereas the hollow point or "mushroom" is blunt. Both have done well on big game, and so have the 180-grain bullets. For such shooting, sturdier and sometimes heavier bullets than these weights at times are chosen. But when ranges are well beyond 200 yards the stiffer construction is less often necessary to prevent too quick expansion or breakup.

The .300 is less easy than the .30-06 to handload for accuracy with cast bullets and light powder charges. This might be said of the custom magnums, in spite of their much more abrupt shoulders that improve combustion.

AMERICAN 8-mm. CARTRIDGES

	Yards	Velocity	Energy	MR trajectory, inches
8x50 Lebel, ..	0	2640	2630	...
170 gr. s. p.	100	2260	1930	0.7
	200	1960	1450	3.4
	300	1700	1090	8.9
8x56 Mann-	0	2190	2130	...
licher-	100	1880	1570	1.1
Schoenauer,	200	1630	1180	4.9
200 gr. s. p.	300	1430	905	12.7
8x57 Mauser,	0	2570	2490	...
170 gr. s. p.	100	2140	1730	0.8
	200	1790	1210	3.9
	300	1520	870	10.5

Wildcat .300 Magnums are fairly numerous. One of the earliest was the Hoffman, with the shoulder made more abrupt, the body of the case not blown out much. The Weatherby is an example of extreme blow-out. Since its ammunition is factory-loaded by the Norma people, it isn't a wildcat any more.

A perhaps elderly but certainly tireless rumor has it

that Winchester will answer the call for .275 (7-mm.) and .333 magnums. Will they be based on long .300 or .375 brass, or on short .458 Mag? A .333-.300 shouldn't be over bore capacity, wasteful of powder, and maybe not a .275, either. But short cases are handy, modern, and obliging to a slew of existing .30-06 action openings.

As far as I know, these cartridges never were factory-loaded in this country in any long-range hunting style. They could have been, and the handloader could do it, for only the Model 1908 Mannlicher-Schoenauer is a sporting design; the others are military. Yet it has nearly the case capacity of the Mauser, for which it never should be substituted in firing, as it's too short to give safe headspace. Its shoulder is farther back.

This round was discontinued by its American makers, Peters and Western; so it must be imported for the Mannlichers here that need it. Brass for handloading it can be formed from 8x57, .30-06 and some other sizes. Most Mannlichers now brought in take modern American calibers, from .243 to .30-06 and .458, though the 6.5x53 (or 6.7 or 54, as sometimes listed) and 7x57 have hung on and are in good demand.

The Lebel 8-mm., and particularly the Mauser, are underloaded here. The Lebel, which goes back to 1886 and was the earliest smokeless powder, military bolt-action round, finally was given a 198-grain spitzer bullet of solid bronze (plenty of bore resistance there!) at a little under 2400 f. s. That is a rather formidable load at about lever-action pressure, a bit under 40,000 pounds per square inch. A lighter, sharp soft point of about .323 inch diameter could replace the 170-grain factory soft point, which is better shaped than our Mauser bullet of that weight—practically a .32 Special or .32 Remington, that Mauser is.

It is possible to form Lebel cases from .348 Winchester brass, which is slightly smaller at the rim but a very little larger at the head than the French cartridge. The base of the Lebel is rounded, though not in the extreme 7.62 Russian fashion. In spite of the well-known strength of the .348 case it seems advisable not to use such worked-over brass for heavy charges. In fact, the Lebel rifle and round make a hard combination to "modernize" except in pretty conservative ways.

Such work would require careful, knowledgeable loading. The Lebel action is well bolted shut but it wasn't meant for modern pressures. About the same can be said for really old Mannlichers for the 8x56. The 1886 Lebel had an 8-shot tubular magazine and the case carried a 232-grain flat-nosed bullet, Balle M. The 1907 and 1916 rifles were of box-magazine type, clip-loaded, three- and five-round capacity respectively, with the pointed Balle D ammunition.

Barrels of any of the three 8-mm. calibers mentioned in this section should be calibrated with a lead slug, and the use of oversize jacketed bullets scrupu-

.348 Winchester; .358 Winchester; .375 Holland & Holland Magnum, 300-grain soft-point bullet; .405 Winchester; .45-70, black-powder, 500-grain lead bullet; .458 Winchester Magnum. *Henry Way-Silvers Photo.*

lously avoided. This slugging is most important with the general run of Mausers; they vary so much. The 1888 model, sometimes called 7.7 mm., has *approximately* .312-inch bore diameter, .321 groove, and the latter dimension is fairly easy for most of us to measure, at least when grooves are of even, not odd number. The 1898 or typical Mauser rifle with double-column magazine and rear safety locking lug was modernized in 1905 to 7.92 mm. Groove diameter goes to about .325 and its bullets are around .323. Case lengths are the same, 57 mm., and it is possible to insert World War II 7.92 ammunition into at least some if not all of the old rifles. It would be extremely dangerous to fire it in those weapons.

To roil up this slough of despond, or at least of frustration, we simply must remember that German manufacturing standards in 8x57 have wobbled about considerably. Before 1914, when this caliber was common in fine sporting Mausers like those featured by Schoverling, Daly & Gales in New York, you could know about what you were getting. The 236-grain soft point at a bit over 2100 f. s. was standard ammo, and not of great pressure, either. The rifles were well made. But after 1918 almost anything turned up, even rebored military jobs, slicked up because they'd rusted out just a mite.

These perils are exorcised by our factory-loaded 8x57 Mauser rounds. The 170-grain bullet is so thinly jacketed and comparatively light in weight that it can be upset to fill large barrels or "squoze" down in tight ones. Rifles in good condition take these cartridges safely, but 8-mm. hulls *can* be loaded into some .30-06 chambers, and to fire them there would be disastrous. This method of instantaneous bullet sizing accounted for practically all Winchester '95 rifle blow-ups that ever occurred, and for some wrecked .30-06 bolt guns, too.

If we make our 8-mm. brass from 06 stuff we need to keep the handloads strictly personal in our pocket, not leave them where a friend can pick them up and fire them in his .30. Such a mistake comes easy when a person's none too familiar with ammunition and the stuff is head-stamped by one of our factories or arsenals that load .30-06. Some 06 cases formed to 8x57 have lower capacity than the latter's own brass, and powder charges must be cut to avoid trouble.

The wildcat 8-mm. 06 uses neck-expanded .30 brass and is a good one for those who handload it correctly.

For deer shooting up to 200 yards our factory 8-mm. rounds are really effective. In power they are glorified .32 Specials, and some of the old military rifles shoot them with pleasing accuracy. In this department, however, there's considerable variation. Few have what we'd call varmint-hunting accuracy! But with carefully chosen custom bullets that fit the barrel the limit of the attainable is pretty high, provided the gun's a good one.

THE ELK, the moose, and the big bears—grizzly, Alaskan brown, and Kodiak Island—are our heaviest game, usually the hardest to kill. In vitality they vary by species and as individuals, but all of them deserve consideration. No game should be hunted with a popgun.

So the choice of a cartridge especially for game of this class is more than justified. It can be used on smaller animals too, with bullets that expand well against the light resistance. You may remember the saying, "If you want a good deer rifle, get a moose rifle."

Cartridges described in this chapter range from at least medium to big bore, though smaller calibers could just as well have been included in the listing. Time and again the .30-06 and .300 Magnum have proved their ability to kill our heaviest American game cleanly. Magnums of .275 and .280 caliber compare well with the .300 in bullet weight and the velocities required for the job, there is a host of suitable wildcats of .30 caliber, and below and above, and most of us know that the little .256 Mannlicher has performed well on the largest game on this continent—when used by the right people. Its long, heavy bullet has one of the essential factors, penetration, though its "shocking" and "knockdown" powers—to use debatable expressions—are comparatively small.

A hunter does his best work with a rifle that suits him. It's absolutely true that a man or woman who could qualify physically and temperamentally to hunt our largest game might be armed best with a lighter caliber than any of these, starting with the .348, that have fallen into this chapter. Overgunned, a hunter has two strikes against him. One is the rifle's recoil; the other is its weight, which for him must be considerable if that recoil is to be even halfway bearable—permit him to group his shots in a bucket at 75 feet, let's say. But there's nothing funny about a hunter's being overgunned. It's tragic for him, the guide, and the game.

.348 WINCHESTER

	Yards	Velocity	Energy	MR trajectory, inches
150 gr.	0	2890	2780	. . .
s. p.°	100	2360	1850	0.6
	200	1860	1150	3.2
	300	1420	670	9.0
200 gr. ST, s.	0	2530	2840	. . .
p. or h. p.	100	2140	2030	0.8
	200	1820	1470	3.8
	300	1570	1090	10.0
250 gr. ST ..	0	2350	3060	. . .
	100	1970	2150	0.9
	200	1660	1530	4.4
	300	1410	1100	11.5

° Slightly flatter trajectory is given for the Silvertip 150-grain.

The heavy Model 1886 Winchester cartridges came close to equaling the most powerful Sharps, Remington and Ballard single-shot rounds, and the '86 lever action was one of the handiest and most reliable repeaters ever made. Right down the decades it was sold to experienced hunters who wanted plenty of

CHAPTER 18

CARTRIDGES FOR OUR HEAVIEST GAME

power for big American game, and in 1903 the "high power smokeless" .33 modernized the old rifle. That cartridge was practically a reformed .45-70, just as the .348 of 1936 is a worked-down and shortened .50-110, decidedly bigger than the .33. The newer cartridges have slightly smaller rim and head sizes, respectively, by one to three thousandths of an inch or so, when they're miked alongside the big ones.

For the .348 the Model 71 rifle was designed, a modernized '86. At this writing no other 71 caliber has been offered, but the strong .348 case has been wildcatted for a number of rifles, including its own. An example is the .450 Alaskan by Johnson's Kenai Rifles, Cooper Landing, Alaska. It shoots a 400-grain .45 bullet at 2100 f. s. That is about 100 f. s. faster than the old, lightly jacketed .45-90 High Velocity 300-grain, and the modern custom bullet gives deep penetration in heavy game. With the old primers and Du Pont No. 16 the .45-90 300-grain could be speeded up to more than 2300 f. s., and with modern primers and No. 4198 to 2200 and a bit, but the bullets break up fast at such velocities.

The .348 itself is no baby, though it isn't a cartridge that lends itself to much "improvement" in velocity by handloading. There's a good deal of body

261

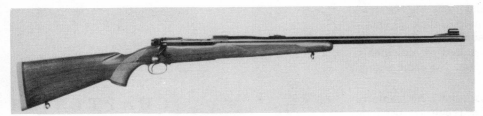

Standard grade 70 .375 Magnum rifle.

taper to the case, and the rifle chamber should be free of oil when it's fired, for even when dry there's considerable backthrust. The sloped brass can't grip the chamber walls, and the big inside head diameter gives plenty of room for rearward pressure to get to work. Although the 71 action has adequate strength for factory ammunition it is, after all, locked at the rear and meant for some 45,000 pounds normal pressure. In case shape the little .218 Bee resembles the .348, except for its proportionally longer shoulder.

On our big game both the 200- and 250-grain bullets have been used successfully. The 250 came out late, in answer to appeals for a heavier slug, and in the meantime the now discontinued Peters 210-grain belted at 2510 f. s. bridged the gap. Handloaders who need tougher bullets than the Silvertip 250 can get them in various weights from custom makers, and a good many do get them, up north and out west.

This heavy Silvertip is much like the old 250-grain .35 Winchester '95, though a bit slimmer and longer. Safe .35 handloads almost reached the Silvertip's velocity, and the rounded bullet point helped in ranging out. But now the .35 rifle is obsolete and hard to find or feed.

The .348, however, is extremely popular. A lot of people have bought it for deer hunting and been glad that they did. For the brush the 200-grain is their bullet choice; the short, fast 150-grain has its admirers for more open shooting, though no .348 load is to be considered for shots much if any over 200 yards long. Up to 100 yards and a bit more the light bullet gives considerable blow-up or rupturing effect. The 200-grain is more reliable; in fact, it's one of our few good brush bullets for the deer hunter. All .348 bullet noses must be flat, for safety in the tube magazine, and this improves their short-range killing power.

The 250-grain bullet's velocity, weight, length, and extra wide flat nose fit it for use in close cover, but it may not expand reliably on deer unless it hits a fairly solid part. The 71 was called a "universal big-game rifle," and up to a rather impressive point it is.

It's been suggested that its heavy cast-lead bullets are suitable for deer shooting, and so they are when hits are well placed. Many shooters using this sort of handload in any caliber under .375 or .38-55 like a good, deep hollow in the point so that there'll be at least some wreckage if the hit lands too far back on the deer. At good velocity rather hard lead alloy can be used when there's a cavity up front.

Will it make the .348 cartridge and rifle obsolete in a few years?*

The 200-grain .358—both weights are semi-pointed —is a souped-up .35 Remington. Based on .308 brass, it's a smashing deer, caribou, sheep and black-bear load. The 250 grain is similar to the long-proved .35 Winchester, and both of these .358s shoot a bit flatter than the .348 counterparts. They hold their energy considerably better.

.358 WINCHESTER

	Yards	Velocity	Energy	MR trajectory, inches
200 gr. ST ..	0	2530	2840	. . .
	100	2210	2160	0.8
	200	1910	1610	3.6
	300	1640	1190	9.4
250 gr. ST ..	0	2250	2810	. . .
	100	2010	2230	1.0
	200	1780	1760	4.4
	300	1570	1370	11.0

In its first year or two this 1955 cartridge was introduced in three good, accurate hunting rifles, the Winchester 70 bolt and 88 lever actions, both featherweights in .358, and the Savage 99. All breech up snugly and only the latter has a two-piece stock. These guns are light to carry, about 6½ to 7½ pounds in this caliber.

The Model 71 .348 goes to 8 pounds, frequently several ounces more, and in spite of its good balance and its slim, flat-sided receiver it can feel like all of that and then some, carried in rough country. It doesn't suit the hunter who likes a light rifle, though 8 pounds is not really heavy. Average accuracy makes it about a 200-yard gun, a fact which means nothing in the sort of hunting it was meant for.

Along toward sundown it can feel burdensome, might slow up some of us on a quick shot. Well stocked though it is for iron sights, with no upgraded Monte Carlo to loosen our bicuspids and molars, it can kick if it isn't held right, and if it is too, times have been. It's a man-sized rifle with man-sized smack, and we have to pay for that smack. Payment can be reduced by a recoil pad, and quite a few 71s have one, like some .30-06s of similar weight.

Recoil? What goes forward from a rifle's chamber must come back, too, and a featherweight rifle comes back harder and faster than a heavy one. The three models of .358 just mentioned do have good, flat buttplates, though the ones on the Savage Feather-

---

*It obsoleted the M-71 rifle in 1957, as far as production is concerned. And so many of us had dreamed of a 71 in still larger calibers!

weight and standard EG 99s are smaller than those on the 99-R and the Winchesters. Perhaps some of us could feel the difference, though there's more in the way a particular rifle fits a person. Most of us would benefit from having a fat, soft recoil pad on any of these light .358s. Heavier models may come along, and the cartridge deserves them. The 8½- to 8¾-pound .35 Winchester '95 didn't seem too heavy when you were shooting it, though it's true that few of those rifles ever were stocked at all well.

There's another advantage to the 71 .348 lever gun which may help to extend its life span. It is heavy enough for good offhand shooting, slow or snap, and the weight is well distributed. The gun is neither butt-, breech-, nor barrel-heavy.

It's fast in reloading, too. The lever goes forward and comes back while we're recovering from recoil, even though those motions are longer than the 88's cycle. Recharging the magazine is quick and easy when the rifle is ready to fire, though the box clip of the 88 is like that, too. But best of all, perhaps, is its handy hammer. This *pays* when opportunity is brief. The side safety of the 70 and the top tang safety that can be gunsmithed into a Savage are quick, too; it would be hard to tell the difference. But most of us began our shooting with a cap pistol, and not quite all of them are double action! One can be serious and not appear a fool when he brings up the fact that the lever-action hammer gun is peculiarly American, ingrained into our breed. It's quick, safe, and noiseless when we know it. Holding back the trigger until the mule-ear has passed full cock becomes completely instinctive.

It seems that the .348 and some other hammer guns will be around for years to come. So its cartridges are bulky and they cost three cents more than .358s do? Some of us have seen the time when three cents was money to think about, but let us hope we never get a reissue of that.

The .358 should be popular for years. It's a little cartridge, but as powerful as most of us would need for any hunting in this half of the world. In fact, some will be overgunned with rifles of this caliber, unnecessarily, when one for the .35 Remington or the .308 would give all they actually need, and be easier to master. The .358's shortness makes it compact to carry, and it is of just about the right length to handle and stuff easily into a magazine.

Being a .35 caliber, with about .358-inch bullet and rifling groove diameters, it's a natural for the handloader. He has a big variety of jacketed bullets to choose from, since .35 Remingtons in any weight, and cast lead from about 250-grains down to .38 revolver slugs and round balls, all should fit. The rifling twist of 12 inches, same as that of the old .35 WCF, isn't really steep; so a slew of varmint, practice, small game and gallery loads can be worked up.

Definitely a bigbore, it is still a fairly all-round caliber. The small powder space puts it below the class of the 9x56, 9x57, .35 Whelen and similar big .35 rounds, but it helps in assembling accurate subloads. Whether or not a longer factory .358—though the name would have to be changed to avoid confusion—will supplement it is worth guessing about, and at the moment worth not much more.

.375 HOLLAND & HOLLAND MAGNUM

	Yards	Velocity	Energy	MR trajectory, inches
270 gr. s. p. . .	0	2740	4500	. . .
	100	2460	3620	0.7
	200	2210	2920	2.9
	300	1990	2370	7.1
300 gr. ST . .	0	2550	4330	. . .
	100	2280	3460	0.7
	200	2040	2770	3.3
	300	1830	2230	8.3
300 gr. m. c.	0	2550	4330	. . .
	100	2180	3160	0.7
	200	1860	2300	3.6
	300	1590	1680	9.3

The British designed this super 9.5 m/m as an all-round African load, and with India too in mind, no doubt. At short range the little 9.5x57 Mannlicher-Schoenauer firing a 270-grain bullet at 2250 f. s. had proved effective against lion, though its penetration on heavy game was not too good. In Britain it was known as the .375, just as the 7x57 Mauser was the .275 in common discussion.

First reactions to the .375 Mag as an African cartridge—and they still hold good, to a considerable extent—were that it was too light for elephant and rhino, and rather rough in its recoil for routine meat-in-the-pot shooting of the various antelope species, though its lighter bullets held up well at pretty long ranges. Now we have perhaps, and let us hope so, more riflemen who are thoroughly trained by range practice and game shooting with cartridges like the .30-06, and heavier ones. Teamed up with .375 Maggie, they do all right, and a lot of .375s go to Africa, for residents' use or with visiting hunters. Many professional "white hunters" still rely on a heavy double, or at least a husky bolt-action caliber like the .505 Gibbs, just as our Alaskan guides often favor the .375 when they're out with a client who carries an 06. It isn't a case of the customer's always being right, but of his always being alive at the end of the trip.

The .375's recoil with 300-grain bullet has been listed from about 33 to 41 foot pounds—and rifle weight means much—as compared to 19 for the .30-06-220 and 28 for the 300-grain .405. Standard weight for the latter two would be around 8½ pounds.

The .375 sounds formidable, and it is. So is a 12-gauge shotgun weighing some 7½ pounds and loaded with the regulation old high velocity shell, 3¾ drams powder, 1¼ ounces shot. The two aren't much different in actual recoil, although a rifle's kick usually does seem to arrive faster! But the jolt of the .375 has been discussed so much that too many people are afraid of it, and *without* good reason. Light men and ladies have used it comfortably, maybe not for several successive 10-shot target strings, but as a hunter fires it. If a little 120-pound guy like me can take it and not feel abused—and I've done it with relish—probably you can, too. With any rifle it's easier to concentrate on hitting, and hit, for a few shots, than for a boxful of hulls. It's the one or two or three bullets that count, out hunting, and the first chance is the best. The .375 gives a big push, but no jab, and it has no unearthly sharp report, like so many of the little calibers.

Rifle weight and build, as always, mean a lot. Winchester has put out at least three barrel weights: first the standard, a pinweight when bored out to .375; then a heavy like the tube of a .22 long-rifle match gun (unless you glanced at the muzzle); and finally a prettily tapered barrel that resulted in a nine-pound rifle.

That weight is as light as most folks want in a .375, and a husky man could carry it all day in Africa, never have to look back for his gunbearer and possibly find him AWOL when opportunity or emergency broke. Much lighter custom .375s have been built and liked, though the first ones commonly went to 10 pounds or so, before the Model 70 appeared. One of about that weight, which Charlie Canoll built for Paul Matthews, is actually a target rifle. We all agreed that it was sweeter to shoot than the average .30-06.

The 270-grain soft point has, in a sense, superseded two other factory weights, an unusual accomplishment. Some years ago the 235-grain hollow point went off the market. It started at 2870 f. s. and at 100 yards had dropped to 2564. At all ranges it fell below the 270-grain in power, and its poor sectional density disqualified it for all-round, shots-as-they-come use on heavy game. Only a few people liked it, and it's no longer loaded in America.

Although the original 300-grain soft point did well on big game, the succeeding Silvertip sometimes expanded too soon, and a good many Alaskan hunters choose the semi-pointed 270-grain instead. The heavy, slower bullet is used quite a bit for deer shooting, even in our eastern states. It's less destructive than most people think it would be.

The flat-nosed metal-cased or full-jacketed 300 grain was meant for African and Indian heavy game. Its ballistics beyond 100 yards, or at least beyond 200, are inconsequential, and the 270-grain is really the only factory weight for long shooting. Up to 300 yards it carries like a 180-grain .30-06. The metal cased 300 is jacketed with thick Lubaloy. Like the British Nobeloy, that composition is 90% copper, 8% zinc, and 2% tin. Gilding metal is 90% copper and 10% zinc.

This bullet sold well, much better than the Western-Winchester .30-06-220 full jacketed, also made with a blunt nose to prevent deflection by heavy bone. That stiff .30 is a special-order job, whereas the metal-cased .375 is standard. These bullets are the exact opposite of the "delayed mushroom" 220-grain .30

that Remington made about 30 years ago, with the full jacket drawn thin at the point so that it *could* expand. That was a moose and bear bullet.

But copper alloy jackets often fail on the heaviest African game, and the steel jacketed foreign .375s now have preference.

A good variety of .375 custom bullets is made, for the caliber is popular. Foreign bullets for it and for the 9.5x57 widen the hand-loader's choice. Some riflemen, like Paul Matthews, have made their own.

The Gould 330-grain hollow point .45.

Then there are the molds, and we can use .38-55 bullets, too, home cast or factory jacketed in thin gilding. Most of them go a split hair over the standard .375 inch but could be resized. That would be more for accuracy, if it were needed at all, than for lower pressures, for we wouldn't send them fast. Quite a mild deer load can be put up in .375 brass if it's wanted! To avoid fouling trouble we should remember that .38-55 standard rifling twist is 18 inches,* as compared to the .375's 12. But in emergency shortage even black powder could be used in the .375 for one or two accurate shots before fouling choked up the bore. We'd want cast bullets, too, and possibly the gas check on the 278 (or 280) grain Ideal would swipe out some of the sludge. At any rate, it's a well balanced bullet for the .375.

.405 WINCHESTER

	Yards	Velocity	Energy	MR trajectory, inches
300 gr. s. p. or m. c.	0	2204	3236	. . .
	100	1897	2399	1.04
	200	1623	1740	4.85
	300	1384	1290	12.82

Those figures, averaged down to a hair in the old-time fashion, apply to the intermediate type of .405 bullet, a blunt one. The original 1904 loading—only 2150 f. s. claimed then—carried a finer lined slug, and so did the last issues, up to the early 1950s. On

---

*With increased black-powder velocity the .38-56-255 and .38-70-255 were cut with 20- and 24-inch twists, the .38-72-275 with 22 inch.

the late ones an unusual amount of lead was exposed at the point, and this unbaring didn't help the .405's reputation as a killer of the biggest American game. However, that reputation was built in a busy half-century, and it holds good.

In penetration, its sister cartridge, the .35, born a year earlier, always exceeded it. The case is shorter and its 250-grain bullet is longer, with much better sectional density. Up to 300 yards both calibers shot about as flat as the modern .30-40-220 soft-point Krag, but they were 200-yard cartridges for the hunter. Out at 300 their expansion was not reliable.

But they were good. Their passing has been mourned by those who know them—more people than you might think.

The .35 ammo was discontinued in the late 1940s, and long before that both the full-jacketed bullets had gone. There was little real use for that style. The .405 was tried on heavy African game, with less than middling success.

The .405 brass can be formed to .35, but it's already scarce. Rim and head dimensions of the .30-40 Krag are similar to the .35's but the case is about 3/32 inch too short. Still, it could be used, and probably has been. Neck-expanded, then carefully blown out to fit, it would appear to be safe for standard 2200 f. s. velocity, though perhaps not with thick-jacket custom bullets of 250-grain weight, meant for use in magnums. It would be safer to use .35 Remington or even .358 Winchester bullets of 200 grains, at velocities not over 2400 f. s. With its own bullets and cases the .35 could be handloaded to a bit over 2300.

.45-70 SPRINGFIELD

	Yards	Velocity	Energy	MR trajectory, inches
405 gr. s. p.	0	1320	1570	. . .
	100	1160	1210	2.9
	200	1050	990	13.0
	300	990	880	32.5

In studying this cartridge we don't "start by reading the menu from the right." Its energy and trajectory figures mean little, for it has a smashing effect that foot pounds do not describe, and it's a 100-yard load. It's killed game at longer ranges, even with the none-too-accurate 300-grain High Velocity at 1888 f. s. starting velocity, a popular load in its time. But when we recall that the .22 Winchester Rim Fire is an almost perfect 100-yard understudy for the .45-70-405 we realize rather vividly that the latter is no mountain and plains caliber.

Back in 1914 there were 23 Winchester ball cartridge loadings for the .45-70, one or more different weights in other makes, also shot cartridges, blanks, military specials, and Bullard, Marlin and Sharps rounds in the standard 2.1-inch case. Some rifles were fed the 1⅞-inch .45-60 WCF 1876 as a subload, in spite of its slightly wider rim. The .45-70 we have left in production is the most all-round useful.

Although its bullet is thin-jacketed it gives reliable penetration at standard velocity, and much faster handloads can be put up for late, strong 1886 Winchesters, all with blued, not case-hardened receivers that have serial numbers at least as high as 126,000. At this point the change was made to blued steel of essentially modern type, stronger than oldtimers of that color. Winchester single shots with blued, WP monogrammed proof-marked receivers are rated as even stronger. The factory loading is for all .45-70s that are in good condition.

Speeding up a lightly built soft point can decrease its penetration after a critical point has been passed. The remedy doesn't lie, I think, in using tough .45 custom bullets meant for wildcat magnums. Even though most .45-70 rifling grooves are shallow, pressures could go high. There have been few complaints about the standard .45-70's penetration on any American big game; yet it is a deadly deer load too, with good placement of hits.

Using a cast lead 330-grain Ideal hollow point, the Gould design, we get a surer deer cartridge, though this bullet is poor in heavy brush. A great variety of cast bullet weights and shapes has been on hand for years, and as Paul Matthews once remarked, this cartridge is one of the few left that will give full power when you can't find jacketed bullets.

Not all its rifles were heavy, or needed to be, though 8¼ to 9 pounds was standard. The Extra Light Weight '86 was listed at 6¾ and felt like it. In takedown form this featherweight with 22-inch barrel was only a quarter or half pound heavier. Jerry Fuller and I used his solid-frame Extra Light a lot, with factory and home loads. Sure it kicked, but the broad, flat shotgun buttplate eased the shove and we shot it as well as we could hold. If we'd gone in for much target work it quite probably would have been bad for our holding! But factory rounds were fairly expensive, and it took a good deal of time to dig enough .45 molding lead out of backstops; so we didn't expend too many rounds too often. The little rifle was absolutely a delight to carry over the hills and through the woods, and it was in fine shape, well sighted, and accurate. Up to about 100 yards it was a woodchuck gun, but you had to know your overholds. One or two longer shots were made, but they didn't prove anything.

My father used a similar rifle in the British Columbia mountains at ranges that seemed long after his many annual hunts in the Adirondacks of New York. When he had learned the curve of the 300-grain High Velocity bullet he did his usual excellent shooting. If there is "no such thing as knockdown effect" it would have been hard to get him to sign approval to any statement to that import. He'd seen the thing happen.

The .458 Model 70 African Rifle and its cartridge went on the market in 1956, after more than a year's testing by game wardens and professional hunters on that bright continent. It had made good. One of the wardens told of having shot an elephant between the eyes—a placement ordinarily to avoid because of the mass of honeycombed bones that protects the brain—and the full-jacketed bullet penetrated more than two feet of that structure and stopped at last under the skin of the shoulder.

.458 WINCHESTER MAGNUM

	Yards	Velocity	Energy	MR trajectory, inches
510 gr. s. p.	0	2125	5110	...
	100	1840	3830	1.1
	200	1600	2900	5.1
	300	1400	2220	13.2
500 gr. m. c.	0	2125	5010	...
	100	1910	4050	1.1
	200	1710	3210	4.18
	300	1520	2520	12.0

This type of Winchester bullet was designed to be the stiffest lead-cored slug available, and reports seem to rate it so. The jacket is of steel, coated with gilding metal, and it's about .10-inch thick at the nose and .067 along the sides. This casing alone weighs some 222 grains and the total weight of the bullet is 500 grains, its length about 1⅜ inches.

The 510-grain soft point is shorter, being more dense. It's a shade longer than the old .45-70-500 factory lead bullet, which had three wide grease grooves and a hollowed or "dished" base. The 510 grain has good lead exposure to assure expansion; yet its gilding metal jacket, thinned a little up front in modern style, is made tough for adequate penetration on the largest of the cat and bear species. It could become a favorite with Alaskan hunters—and guides, too, perhaps—who want lots of close-range power. Muzzle velocity of 2125 f. s. is listed for both bullets, and their great mass makes them hold their speed rather well at ranges beyond those that most hunters would consider practical for a hard-kicking rifle, one in the elephant class.

The factory muzzle-energy rating is over 5000 foot pounds. We must figure on the caliber, and the weight that gives the bullet its good sectional density, the length and mass behind its hard or soft nose that make for reliable and straight penetration in the kinds of game these bullets are designed for. We must remember at the start that it's not a heavy African cartridge, though it certainly isn't a light one.

The .600 Nitro Express, three-inch case, is the big one. Unlike some other old favorites, such as the .500 and the .577 Nitro Express, it probably will be available for a long time. The 900-grain bullet has 1950 f. s. velocity and 7510 foot pounds energy, though a lighter 1850 f. s. load also was made. Its "solid" or full metal-cased bullet, when jacketed in steel, penetrates well, and obviously its shocking power is enormous.

The .500 Nitro Express—570-grain giving 2150 f. s. and 5850 f. p.—was a more powerful load than the new Winchester. The .470 Nitro Express—500-grain at 2125 and a listed 5050—is an old favorite. Its bullet is efficient, as years of exacting service have proved. though it lacks the sectional density of the .458. These British cartridges are for double rifles.

The .505 Gibbs is for bolt-action repeaters. It's a proprietary size, though custom rifles are made up for it over here. The figures are 525 grains, 2300 f. s., and 6180 f. p. Sectional density isn't great, though this bullet is far from stubby and its deadliness has been proved, thoroughly. The .404 Jeffery rimless has figures of 400, 2125, and 4110, or 300, 2600, and 4500 for its light bullet.

Choice between double barrel and bolt action fires up an old feud. The double is quick for its two shots, well balanced, short for a given barrel length, and quiet to reload if it's made without automatic ejectors. If a firing pin breaks, there's another. The bolt action can use smaller, high-intensity cartridges of equivalent power in many instances, it holds more cartridges, and it can be built lighter, of reasonable weight to carry all day and have ready in your hands at any moment. In close-up jungle shooting the noise of operating its action for follow-up shots sometimes might be a terrible hazard. The click of an action is more easily placed than the blast of a shot.

The Holland & Holland-style belted .458 case is about 2½ inches long, not much even as compared to the 2.1-inch .45-70 and 2.4-inch .45-90, favorite old moose loads but never very useful in Africa. As an African cartridge the .458 is short, even with its long bullets, seated well out as they are. Although it's compact and easy to handle, the pressures are kept low so that tropical heat can't raise them to excess, although our modern powders are less sensitive to temperature changes than the British Cordite.

There is little taper to the case body, and .45-70 type subloads naturally occur to a handloader. The belt assures headspace as reliably as a rim does, and we could use anything from a round ball to the 535-grain Postell cast bullet, an old Ideal favorite for long-range target work with the .45-70 single shot. Rifling twist is 14 inches as compared to 20 in Winchester .45-70's and 22 in Springfields. We still have plenty of easily ignited powders to choose from, for straight cases.

The Rifle

At present the .458 comes in the Super Grade 70, with bolt cylinder and neighboring parts engine turned for looks. Rifle weight of 8¾ to 9¼ pounds is low for the power, and the recoil is about 70 foot pounds. But like other elephant rifles, this one shoves rather than stabs in recoil. The stock is less straight than those of other 70s with Monte Carlo: at comb and heel they go 1 5/16 and 2 5/16, whereas the .458's figures are 1¾ and 2¾. The stock is shorter, too, 13¼ vs. 13½. A lower hand-hold results from the upper part of the small of the stock being not quite so high, and with this sort of grip—not overdone, of course—it's easier to take heavy recoil. A thick rubber butt pad is standard equipment and it's set on with good down-pitch.

To prevent the barrel and action from being "shot out of the stock," a Mauser-type cross-bolt is run through from side to side. It bears on the rear of the receiver's steel recoil lug. The forearm screw is reinforced, too.

The sling and its forward attachment are of European style. It's a carrying strap, not a loop sling for marksmanship, though it could be let out and used as a hasty sling, by most shooters. The swivels are quick-detachable, in Super 70 fashion, but the front one is attached to a barrel lug (not a band, another method, and also OK for this style of rifle) ahead of the fore-stock tip. This strap weighs only five ounces; the Army style of 1¼ inch leather generally goes to a full half pound.

Magazine capacity is three rounds as compared to four in the .300 and .375 70 Magnums. This change was made to assure easy feeding, and the total of four shots, with a cartridge preloaded into the chamber, gives us twice the capacity of the double barrel rifle. Recharging speed—for just two cartridges, let's say— would be about the same. In repeat fire the bolt action is the slowest of all except the single shot, and the double and the autoloader are the fastest; yet a handy rifleman with a bolt gun that fits him is pretty fast. His reloading can be done in the time he needs to recover from heavy recoil and get his sights realigned.

This rifle has its own standard sighting equipment, a 3/32-inch silver bead front with detachable hood, and a set-screw adjusted and locked open rear. Silver is no material for a front sight that's to be lined up for a long, difficult shot, but it shows up in poor light for an equally difficult and much more critical close shot! And it can be blackened or hooded.

The rear sight is slid forward to add elevation and it is described as adjustable to 400 yards. That is beyond an elephant rifle's practical range, naturally, but the extra up could come in handy for subload practice. A peep sight can go on the receiver, but unless the aperture is a good bit larger than the biggest standard choice on Lyman, Redfield, Vaver, or Williams models the open sight should be about as fast as a receiver peep, so far from the eye. A receiver peep with rearward extension like those used in .22 rimfire match shooting is nice on a light-recoiling varmint and deer rifle such as an 8- or 8½-pound .257 Roberts, provided the shooter knows this type of sight and is careful about what he's doing. With the standard large aperture it improves our shooting in dark woods, and our snapshooting, too.

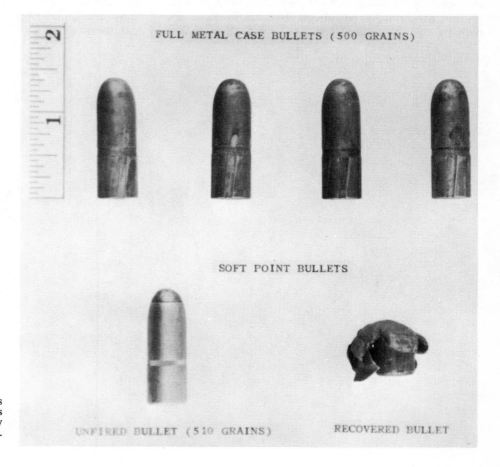

FULL METAL CASE BULLETS (500 GRAINS)

SOFT POINT BULLETS

UNFIRED BULLET (510 GRAINS)

RECOVERED BULLET

Some .458 Winchester bullets from African game. Two elephants and two buffalo were dropped by the four full-patch bullets shown. The soft point killed a rhino.

The African Winchester and a gunful of its compact cartridges.

Make one entirely of soft rubber and it would be harmless on a .458!

Just as it happened with the .375, it can be expected to occur with the new Magnum: a lot of riflemen buy our heaviest American caliber because it interests them, and use it, if at all, on game much smaller than it was meant for. There's certainly no harm in that, and both .375 and .458 can be handloaded for white-tail deer and even for woodchucks. Meanwhile, there is the power if you ever need it.

About the only serious fault found with the new rifle and cartridge by the NRA technical staff— Major Hatcher gave a characteristically sound and interesting report on them in the August, 1956, *Rifleman*—was the battering of soft points in the magazine, under recoil. This was expected, and it would be hard to correct with straight-cased cartridges in a double-column magazine, or in almost any magazine except perhaps one of rotary type like the Savage or the Mannlicher-Schoenauer. The only remedy, at this writing, seems to be to use up the battered rounds first. They'd have to be in really bad shape to interfere with functioning, or to affect short-range accuracy.

The "African Winchester"—a title that used to apply to the 1895 in .30-06 and .405 calibers—is a special Super Grade and costs $295 this particular afternoon. Full-jacketed loads retail at $11.00 per box of 20, the soft points at $7.20. Per hundred, the 600 Nitro Express rounds are listed at $90.00, .425 Westley Richards 410 grain at $56.50, and .404 400-grain Jeffery at $52.50. Most of the big double rifles cost twice or more as much as the 70 .458, and a fine bolt action like the Holland & Holland in .404 is around $500. It seems likely that many of the Winchesters will be exported, for the gun and cartridge are already proved, out where the game is, and they are standardized in production, supply and maintenance.

A COMMONLY accepted definition of a wildcat among riflemen is: any cartridge not available from the regular production of our factories. The manufacture of ammunition on a military or commercial scale, like any other mass-production problem, involves large financial outlays for the plant, toolroom and laboratories. Many people are required and they must be gathered from fields requiring highly specialized knowledge.

Our factories in the United States comprise our Government arsenals and the commercial plants of Peters-Remington and Winchester-Western combines, with Du Pont and Hercules in the powder field. There is also Federal, maker of .22 rimfire cartridges, shotgun shells, and centerfire primers, and north of the United States-Canadian border is the Dominion establishment, manufacturing a wide variety of ammunition for the sportsman. There are also our new and good Cascade Primers.

Those of us who have been privileged to spend time in one of those huge, sprawling areas leave it thoughtfully, awed by the large portion of plant space devoted to laboratories—physical, chemical and ballistic. In those laboratories no effort is spared to check raw materials and components as well as the finished product that you use in your rifle.

If it were not for the uneconomic aspects that face the factories there would be no wildcats. Sadly enough for us riflemen, they just cannot afford to make up 500 or 1000 special cartridges, cases, bullets and primers—or special powders, for that matter. Hence the enterprising, enthusiastic riflemen who have ideas that they wish to follow must either make their own or farm out the work to individuals or small shops that cater to the wildcatting segment of rifle users.

No small shop or individual has the lab facilities or equipment the big plants have. In fact, though chronographs are fairly common in the hands of small shops or individuals, pressure guns are distinct rarities except in the large establishment. So much so, that in spite of the great number of wildcats developed in the last twenty years, we have seen pressure data on exactly four! Luckily, the information from factory tests and empirical results has spread to the shooters over the years. A wildcatter has this data for a guide, even though he lacks a pressure gun for a final check-up of his results. Many excellent factory cartridges exist today because of intelligent wildcat development by shooters who followed an idea through in a sane fashion.

For the rifleman and handloader who approach the field of wildcats with critical logic, some knowledge, and reasonable expectations, the observations that follow—being the results of tests and experiments of three avid wildcatters—may result in avoidance of wasted efforts and perhaps even a nasty accident. Wildcatting adds enjoyment to rifle shooting, fits rifle and cartridge to your own particular needs, and teaches much in a fascinating field.

CHAPTER 19

WILDCAT CARTRIDGES

BY THOMAS C. FLORICH,
THOMAS C. FLORICH, JR.,
AND ALBERT J. E. SHAY

Speed Limit XX Miles Per Hour

To the enthusiast who thinks he can get speed or power by virtue of magic formulas denied to the hard-boiled technicians in plants and arsenals, who spend their lives in this field, all we can say is "You'll be sorry." The craze for speed and power from the automobile has given us more than we need. The fact that each year more people are maimed or killed in automobile accidents than were lost in the entire Korean Campaign bears grim testimony to the deadliness of greater speed and power than are needed. Now we know that drivers do not try to have accidents, but the availability of excess power tempts the enthusiast to "make it go faster," and the tragic record builds up, day by day. The automobile is just a means of transportation, but rifles are deadly weapons, designed to bag game or kill an enemy. Used as designed, they do either job efficiently.

Start wildcatting and abuse that design, and it may become deadly at both ends. Strangely enough, one rifle accident occasions more adverse radio and newspaper publicity than do fifty routine—but perhaps fatal—automobile accidents. *If you are not prepared to be ultra-conservative in your wildcat work, stay out of it.* One ill-advised move on your part can cause an accident that will splatter all over the front pages of newspapers and give the finest sport in the world a bad name. Frankly speaking, the rest of the riflemen, handloaders and wildcatters will resent it. In addition you will have a wrecked rifle, probably have personal injuries, and suffer a complete loss of confidence in yourself. Do your work conservatively and you will avoid accidents. In many respects wildcatting is an unknown field that, over the years, has produced innumerable "wonders" that were complete flops and died a-borning.

But there are also some cartridges that are not wildcats today because cautious experimenters saw an approach that promised some improvement and then carefully developed it at the cost of much hard work—without secrets, magic or repealing the laws of physics. The results now are listed among standard factory rounds.

Cartridge Brass

Experience backed by laboratory tests shows that cartridge cases do the work the plants or arsenals designed them for. There is a popular conception that when a case is wildcatted "You build up your load until the bolt-lift becomes hard, then back down two grains, and you've got a safe load." That is nonsense. Pressure tests indicate that "when the bolt-lift becomes hard" the pressures are close to the 60,000- to 70,000-pounds-per-square-inch class. Those are proof pressures, never fired from the shoulder. Forget the "two grains" magic formula; it just is not so.

By actual tests, here is one crumb of knowledge. A magnum case using around 60 grains of 4350 or 4831 powder and a 160-grain bullet showed right around 50,000-pounds-per-square-inch. An increase of 1½ grains of powder added 5000 P. S. I., and the original load reduced by 1½ grains dropped 5000 P. S. I. None of the three loads showed any difference in the bolt-lift!

When you consider that the best brass made is designed to operate at 55,000 P. S. I. or less, the business of "adding to the charge till the bolt-lift is hard" is idiotic. When it's hard you're in serious trouble already, and cutting the charge two grains will not give you a safe load, for over 60,000 pounds is *not* safe, as even the free-wheeling wildcat enthusiast will admit.

Load Development

Starting with a new wildcat and lacking a pressure gun, but with chronographs available for nominal fees at commercial laboratories, a shooter can only follow a technique of load development which conservative developers have used in the past. All details of the rifle being ascertained correct, all components having been proved normal in loading normal loads in a comparative case for a rifle of similar caliber, the unknown wildcat is compared to the known cartridge in powder capacity. (Bear in mind that these techniques are crude, not definitive, and at best an intelligent guess for the unknown cartridge.) Start with the

known cartridge's top load in the unknown, increasing the charge 2 percent at a time toward the prognosticated charge. Stop immediately when the primer flattens to the same extent as is observed in the known cartridge load.* If the case web (the solid base or head) shows any increased diameter on the micrometer, cut back to the best grouping, most accurate load on the target that is below the primer flattening charge. Beyond this point you are in the unknown and only a pressure gun can give you definitive information. Some case webs are heavier than others, even in the same factory calibers, and in actions that do not enclose the casehead completely (or nearly so) pressures above the critical point can make this unsupported web flow—enlarging primer pockets and actually spreading the brass. Miking the web—just above the rim of a rimmed case, or just above the extracting cannelure of a rimless case—before and after firing will show any spread of this web, the heaviest part of a case.

In Phil Sharpe's *Complete Guide to Handloading* the high and low pressure figures are available, in his tabulation of loads, in every combination that Du Pont or Hercules had ascertained and published. Later both companies stopped issuing such information for several good reasons, variables both human and mechanical that are not hard to guess.

There is also the method of plotting curves, on squared paper, of the low and high safe charges for a known cartridge with a given bullet and propellant. Let the horizontal scale be the charges in grains, the vertical scale the velocities. If you have one velocity reading for the larger case with the same bullet and powder, which obviously and safely should be the heaviest safe charge from the known cartridge, plot that point and draw a parallel to the known curve only as high as the top load point of the known cartridge, which is the top safe-pressure level of the powder. You will have a charge beyond which it is unsafe to go on the parallel curve. Work up 2 percent at a time toward the charge indicated. In one cartridge this method was within one-half grain of what one

---

*Primer flattening. During the time that the non-corrosive, non-mercuric primers were being developed, the many mixes used gave such variable flattening effects to primers—sometimes just a primer fired without a powder charge would scare you to look at it!—that one could place little implication of pressure signs on the primer. During the past several years, Ordnance in placing ammo orders made tests and liked the mix that Federal used. They specified it on all contract stuff, and our large rifle primers use that mix, which gives flattening effect on the primer similar to the effect of the No. 70 mix used in the No. 26 Frankford Arsenal primer. This flattening and cratering (firing pin indent with built-up walls) of current primers is not of itself foolproof or definitive evidence of specific pressures, but in conjunction with other pressure signs it is a big and fairly reliable help. Remarks to the contrary, made during the development days, were well founded, but they apply to a much lesser extent today. Though modified, the flattening is still a comparative help.

rifle—and within two grains of what another rifle—seemed to handle without pressure signs, and the velocity was within 40 f. s. of what the parallel curve indicated as likely for the unknown case.

An example of the time-honored method of case comparison is the 7x57 and the 7-mm. wildcat based on the larger .30-06 case. The known safe 7x57 load of a 175-grain ball ahead of 47 grains of 4350 was the starting point for the 7-mm. 06, and the charge was increased 2 percent at a time. The 7x57 holds about 55 grains of 4350, and the 7-mm. 06 holds 63 grains—struck measure case full, but check your own cases, as different makes vary slightly in capacity. The difference in capacity of eight grains could not be utilized in the larger case, as it was found that 52 grains of 4350 in the 7-mm. 06 was the mean top safe load in several 7-mm. 06 rifles. The reason? Propellants have a burning range and a balance point, and the 7x57 mm. load mentioned happens to be one very close to the balance point of 4350 as it gives 2590 f. s. with 48,000 P. S. I. pressure. In this instance a larger charge of a slower burning powder in the 7-mm. 06 does better with the 175-grain ball. But during the working up of the 7-mm. 06 load from 47 grains to 52 grains all indications of pressure were carefully watched, as these details are gone into hereafter—primer flatness and cratering, case expansion, flash, blast, groups—and over 52 grains of 4350 in the 7-mm. 06 seemed too much, from these visual signs.

The brass case will not stand abuse. To add to the problem, though some cases are drawn as they always were, shortly after 1940 in the .30-06 the extrusion process was highly developed because it is faster and cheaper. The extrusion process today is being used on more and more cases adapted to the method. The sad fact emerges that although a drawn case has a head better adapted to wildcatting (the extra cold-working in the drawing process gives the brass a better crystalline structure), even it handles anything above 55,000 P. S. I. none too well. The extruded case-head is not as strong as that of the drawn case and somewhere between 50,000 and 55,-000 P. S. I. the extruded case starts to give. If you fire Armor Piercer M-2 ammunition with extruded heads you will find that three to five or more primer pockets per hundred are loose when you decap the cases. The AP M-2 load has a maximum pressure permissible of 55,000 P. S. I. If you fire M-2 ball loads in similar extruded cases where pressures are kept under 50,000 P. S. I. you will not run across any enlarged primer pockets.

In addition to the various books on handloading, all of which are good, there is for the advanced handloader-experimenter with rifles the fine, exhaustive treatment by Earl Naramore, *Handloading Ammunition*. A lieutenant-colonel of Ordnance, he gives a wealth of detail on the technical analysis of all components used to assemble ammunition for rifles, from the standpoint of the proof of Ordnance. The wildcatter owes it to himself to read it.

Case Shape and Case Capacity

In wildcatting much store is set on "case shape." The long, slender one is sneered at today as being inefficient in burning the charge, and the short, squat case of the same capacity is stylish. "It is more efficient." There is no question that in the field of high explosive the shape of the charge is a most important factor in its efficiency for particular purposes, but we use a propellant in our rifle cases, not high explosives. The propellant burns, the high explosive detonates, and we are not concerned with detonation in a rifle. If it ever occurs—God forbid!—it happens only once in a rifle's useful existence, and the shooter is a casualty. We will not go so far as to state that case shape cannot contribute to cartridge efficiency, but we state flatly that with existing components available to us, case shape is one of the minor factors of efficency, among a host of others yet to be mentioned.

What price case shape? The cartridge on the left is the 6.5 or .256 Clipper, the .257 Roberts with neck opened up to take .264-inch bullets and the case fire-fitted to enlarge it to the same capacity as the old reliable .256 Newton case, which appears on the right. Read the table of their velocities and see what the chronograph recorded for identical loads fired in each. *Thomas C. Florich Photo.*

Back in April 1946 *The American Rifleman* began publishing an article by C. C. Meredith, entitled "Common Sense Applied to Internal Ballistics." It carried on through the June issue and related in detail the experiments conducted with three .22 wildcats. One was a .35 WCF with gentle shoulder slope, one a .303 British with abrupt shoulder, and one a .303 British with reverse curve shoulder, an extreme but not unknown shape. Capacity and loading density of the three were equal. Velocities and pressures were nearly equal. No case was obviously more "efficient" than the other two.

With existing components, *case capacity* still determines a cartridge's efficiency.

We took the .256 Newton case, chambered a 6.5 mm Japanese rifle for it. Then we took a .257 Roberts case (named of course for rifling groove diameter, not bore diameter), opened the neck to hold the same .256 bullets, and blew the case out till both held the same weight of powder when filled to the top of the neck. Then we chambered another rifle for it. This second Japanese rifle chambered for the .256 Clipper (the .257 Improved opened to use .264-inch bullets) had the same barrel length, twist and bore diameter.

Two loads that had proved good ones in several .256 Newtons were put into both cartridges. The .256 Newton case is 61 mm. long and has the slender tapering body and shoulder that are passé today. Bullets were seated to the same depth in both; so having started with the same capacity in both, the loading densities were the same. Ten rounds each were fired to get an average, as this was a specific test. In a routine test, five rounds tell us what we need to know.

Here is what the Potter Counter recorded, the charge in each instance being 50.5 grains of Du Pont 4350:

Bullet		Rifle	Foot seconds velocity (mean instrumental at 60 feet)
Rem. 150 gr. SP	6.5 Jap Clipper		2750
Rem. 150 gr. SP	.256 Jap Newton		2746
Speer 140 gr. SP	6.5 Jap Clipper		2706
Speer 140 gr. SP	.256 Jap Newton		2701°

°Evidence that No. 4350 is a heavy-bullet powder. Although it gave decent velocity and good accuracy with the 140-grain, it was more efficient with the 150-grain bullet.

Instrumental velocities are the recorded readings over one-half the bullet's travel. The British use the term "observed velocity," which is really more descriptive. Arsenals and plants use various distances for placing their screens that the bullet cuts, such as:

(a) First screen at three feet from muzzle, second 100 feet beyond the first. Instrumental velocity is given as at 53 feet—half the distance between screens, 50 feet, plus the 3 feet to the first.

(b) First screen at 3 feet, second 150 feet from first gives them an "instrumental at 78 feet."

(c) At Phil Sharpe's the first screen is 10 feet from the muzzle, second 100 feet beyond the first. "In-

strumental velocity over 60 feet" is the expression we use.

(d) The H. P. White Laboratory at Cleveland, Ohio, often uses short-spaced screens and reports instrumental velocity at 20 feet or whatever other distance it works out to.

Any of these methods is okay, as from the *recorded velocities* they work out the muzzle velocities, and the actual tables of fire show that these muzzle velocities are just about correct.

Now, a little arithmetic discloses the fact that in our .256 tests case shape possibly accounted for a velocity increase of less than fifteen one-hundredths of one percent with the upper loads, and under one hundred eighty-five one thousandths of one percent with the lower loads. If that is what the case-shape school of thought calls "efficiency of burning," they can have it!

At that point in our lives we three wildcatters stopped worrying about case shape and turned our attention to capacity, which field offers more fertile ground for the wildcatter—but not without its problems, as the following notes reveal.

Cost Accounting of Velocity

Much work, and some of it highly successful, has been done by taking existing cases and increasing their capacity, thus sending the bullets at higher velocity. Miller, Ackley, Weatherby, Mashburn, Kilbourn and others have taken everything from the little Hornet up to and including the .375 Holland & Holland Magnum case, blown it out changed the shoulders to "modern" slopes, and increased the capacities to get greater velocity. Propellants available today make such "improvements" possible. With the group of riflemen who hold that velocity is the answer to ballistic progress, or with the school which holds that heavy bullets at moderate velocity are the sound answer, we take no sides. We have seen game killed with rifles of both classes and they were dead elk—all one-shot kills.

Number one with 175-gr. 7-mm. ball at 2300 f. s.; number two with 250-gr. .35-caliber ball at 2700 f. s.; number three with 180-gr. .30-caliber ball at 2700 f. s.; number four with 130-gr. .270 ball at 3140 f. s.—and as we stated, they were all dead. In each instance the ball was properly placed, and we lean toward the school that holds that a properly placed ball is most important.

We know of one Montana hunter who takes his elk with one shot each year with a .32-20, 115-gr. ball! But he is a neck-shot artist who refuses to spoil good meat; so he stalks up close and follows his lights in this ballistic argument. All of this proves that a well placed shot bags game neatly; no more, no less. There is no question that velocity is a most desirable ballistic quality.

Yet reflections based on experience disclose that for big-game use a bullet's velocity can be detrimental, unnecessary and even undesirable. Most American big-game shooting takes place in wooded or brushy terrain at short ranges where a long, heavy, blunt-nosed bullet will be deflected much less than a lighter spitzer bullet from the same rifle. In cases of extreme high velocity bullets, contacts with brush or twigs have so disrupted the bullets that no part of them reached the beast.

Students enrolled in the high-velocity school cite the thickness and hardness of the steel their creations penetrate. They are correct: the higher a bullet's velocity, the greater amount of steel that can be penetrated. But since long range game targets are not protected by boiler plate, the virtue of steel penetration applies in no way to the hunter, or to the target shooter.

For the hunter, the long, heavy, blunt-nosed bullet helps to insure not only the arrival of the bullet through twigs and brush, but also the penetration on impact to the vitals of the game, through the heavy bones and muscles that protect these vital areas. These facts are borne out by the published experiences of famous hunters, and they cover game of all sizes, all over the world.

For the long-range hunter requiring a bullet to be used at upwards of 250 or 300 yards, the high-velocity type is most desirable. Over canyons, valleys or plains the spitzer at high velocity delivers the most energy, with the flattest trajectory. For such work every slight addition of velocity is of great help in avoiding errors of range estimation and in delivering the greatest possible blow to the animal.

But the question, for most of us, is: "What do I have to pay to exceed factory velocity in my wildcat?" The facts are that enlarging the case makes possible the use of larger charges, which increase velocity. The price? First, a disproportionately high increase in the powder charge used. Let us make an odious but possibly revealing comparison. The National Rifle Association published loading data on the .30-06 and .300 H. & H. A wildcat developer published loading data on a blown-out .300 H. & H. case of much enlarged capacity. We have the same weight bullets and same propellant in all three.

.30-06 factory case—180-gr. Silvertip—57 grs. 4350—Winchester 120 primer—2761 f. s. at 20'—51,460 P. S. I.

.300 H. & H. factory case—180-gr. Norma boat-tail—67 grs. 4350—Win. 120—2938 f. s. at 20'—49,100 P. S. I.

.300 H. & H. blown-out—180-gr. Silvertip—77 grs. 4350—primer not stated—3205 f. s. muzzle velocity—50,000 P. S. I.

All three are excellent game loads. All three have recoil that does not encourage the firing of 100 rounds per session; they are heavy loads. The second has more recoil than the first, and the third more recoil than the second. All three loads are so close to the top safe pressure levels that a cautious handloader would not go farther, for variations in individual rifles

of the same caliber with the same ammunition could produce greater variation in pressure, necessitating some reduction in the load in another rifle, for safety. For 6.4 percent velocity increase over the .30-06 the .300 H. & H. factory case requires a 17.5 percent increase of charge, with increased recoil and the erosion which shortens the barrel's accuracy life. For a 9 percent velocity increase from the .300 H. & H. to the blown out .300 a charge increase of 14.9 percent is required. But from the .30-06 to the wildcat .300 H. & H. a 16 percent increase in velocity requires a 35 percent increase of the charge. The law of diminishing returns is in operation, and erosion is getting in its dirty work of shortening barrel-accuracy life.

For the specialist hunter a 500-round barrel life may be worth while. For the man who gets a gilt-edged barrel and wishes to preserve that accuracy life for a possible 5000 rounds it isn't worth while. Further, we know that the pressure levels of factory and arsenal cartridges are kept within safe limits. The wildcat case cited is one of the extremely rare ones where pressure data are available. Another instance was the N. R. A. data on the .30-06 compared to the .30-06 Ackley Improved. The results showed no significant velocity gain, on test, but some higher pressures for the Improved. There are only two other wildcats of recent years on which pressure data have been published, that we know of.

This being the fact, the reasonable rifleman is naturally cautious when only velocities are given, sometimes based on chronographed data, sometimes estimated. Sometimes the velocity data result from comparison of bullet-drop figures. Here just a change of the forward shape of a bullet alters the same weight-of-bullet's drop. The shape and weight of a bullet are important factors in its remaining velocity out where the game is hit. Taking bullets of the same weight and muzzle velocity and differing only in shape, look at firing data from a factory ballistic table. It gives us the picture. The following data are based on 180-grain .30-06 bullets only, loaded by one factory to 2700 f. s. m. v.

Bullet type	Velocity remaining at			Loss f.s.	Front Shape
	100 yards	200 yards	300 yards		
Metal cased taper heel	2520	2350	2190	510	Pointed
Bronze point flat base	2480	2280	2080	620	Pointed
Core-Lokt flat base	2470	2250	2040	660	Pointed
Core-Lokt flat base	2330	2010	1740	960	Round-nosed

The full-jacketed 180-grain boat-tail is used for 600- and 1000-yard target shooting and it does that job superbly. As a long-range big-game bullet the 180-grain bronze point delivers the most energy at hunting ranges, and a 300-yard shot at big game is longer than 95 percent of it is shot at. The pointed soft-point Core-Lokt was more recently designed for game than the bronze point, and its velocity is only

A COMPARISON OF CENTERFIRE CARTRIDGES

Cartridge	Bullet in grs.	Muzzle velocity	Remaining velocity at 100 yds.	200 yds.	300 yds.	Loss at 300 yds. foot seconds	Per cent
.22 Hornet	45 Mush.	2690	2030	1510	1150	1540	57
.218 Bee	46 Mush.	2860	2160	1610	1200	1660	58
.222 Rem.	50 S. P.	3200	2650	2170	1750	1450	45
.220 Swift	48 S. P.	4110	3490	2930	2440	1670	41
.270 Win.	130 Br. Pt.	3140	2880	2630	2400	740	23
.30-40 Krag	180 S. P.	2470	2250	2040	1850	620	25
.30-06 Spfld.	180 S. P.	2700	2470	2250	2040	660	24
.300 H&H Magnum	180 S. P.	2920	2670	2440	2220	700	24
.300 H&H Improved	180 S. P.	3205	Data not available				

40 f. s. less at 300 yards; so pay your money and take your choice. The 180-grain round-nose, soft-point Core-Lokt is good in brush and has desirable penetration-expansion characteristics for short shots in brush on heavy game. Each load does the job it was designed to do. The importance of bullet shape is self-evident from the comparison quoted above.

Although muzzle velocities as high as can be obtained safely in any cartridge are unquestionably to be desired, the velocity delivered to the game at the ranges you must take your shots at is the velocity that pays off. Air resistance slows down the bullet's velocity. Sir Isaac Newton stated that law simply as "Air resistance varies as the square of the velocity." His experiments on which he based his conclusion were made with falling objects, none of which had a velocity equal to the speed at which sound travels. Later experiments by ballisticians disclosed the fact that as velocity goes above the sound barrier, Newton's "square of the velocity" does not apply. Other, and higher, powers of the velocity are used rather than the square, as velocity increases. Simply put for practical purposes, as velocity is increased, the air resistance increases at a disproportionately high rate.

Your weighing of the advantages velocity offers as compared to disadvantages of shorter barrel life at the higher velocities, increased recoil and muzzle blast, disproportionately larger powder charges, specially built rifles and more expensive ammunition for the wildcat, will enable you to make a decision. Certainly the long-range (600 to 1000 yard) target shot will make almost any sacrifices necessary to attain the greatest remaining velocities at long range. Experience over the years has shown the value of higher remaining velocity at long ranges. At hunting ranges your choice is guided by one question: does the cartridge have sufficient velocity at the ranges at which shots will be taken for the particular species? A comparison of firing data will tell you all you need to know. Data following are based on the 180-grain pointed soft-point Core-Lokt bullet of .30 caliber.

Cartridge	Muzzle velocity	Velocity remaining at 100 yds.	200 yds.	300 yds.	Loss at 300 yds. foot seconds	Per cent
.30-40 Krag	2470	2250	2040	1850	620	25.
.30-06 Spfld.	2700	2470	2250	2040	660	24.4
.300 H&H Magnum	2920	2670	2440	2220	700	24
.300 H&H Improved	3205	Data not available				

If we assume that such details as the toughness of the bullet's jacket and of its lead core are the same, we are safe in saying:

1) The .30-06 will do at 200 yards what the .30-40 does at 100 yards.

2) The .300 H & H will do at 300 yards what the .30-06 does at 200 yards.

3) The .300 H & H Improved will do at 400 yards (or more) what the .300 H & H does at 300 yards.

Your decision is now based on what velocity you need at the ranges at which your shots are taken.

Before we leave this consideration of velocity, a comparison of several centerfire cartridges, each of which is good, will give you a broad look at the cumulative effects of bullet weight, bullet shape, case capacity and the loss of muzzle velocities at game ranges. Half of these were wildcats before being adopted by our factories, and the rest were strictly factory designed.

The above table is based on actual firings and shows the importance of bullet weight x its diameter squared, which the ballisticians call "sectional density." This factor of sectional density coupled with the shape of the bullet (such as a good long radius forward and possibly a boat-tail base) will determine the missile's ability to retain velocity at long ranges.

Other Factors of Velocity

The foregoing paragraphs must be considered with these following to fairly judge the improved high velocity cartridges of increased powder capacity. There are factors like free-boring, bullet weight and diameter, and using boat-tailed bullets rather than flat-based ones of the same weight. Even case shape may help a trifle. Certainly seating bullets out a bit does help by reducing the loading density, and the chrome lining of bores may help. So the sober-minded developer uses all these factors, which are legitimate ones, in getting added velocity. Do not forget that barrel length-velocity tests seem to prove that a 26-inch barrel gives the best length-velocity relationship with modern, slow burning propellants, currently used in large capacity cartridge cases .

Boat-tailed bullets have less barrel bearing surface than do flat-based bullets of the same weight, and by offering less friction in the bore they increase the acceleration. Back in the mid-'30s, when we bought Government powders through the Director of Civilian

Marksmanship, Frankford Arsenal sent a mimeographed slip with the powders, and one of these is one of the few definite velocity-pressure clews on boat-tailed bullets we have ever seen. Here is the data from Frankford Arsenal, dated April 8, 1924, on Pyro DG,* Lot 540, Powder, CP (Carney's Point) as checked by PA (Picatinny Arsenal) for the Model 1903 rifle:

Bullet	Charge	Instrumental velocity at 78 ft.	Mean pressure
150 gr. service	49 gr.	2656	44,220
172 gr. cal. .30 M1 (uncannelured)	47 gr.	2550	49,770

Pyro was a *regular burning powder*. Today's Improved Military Rifle powders are *progressive burning propellants*, with a much more favorable time-pressure curve, which means greater acceleration for the bullet. If one attempted to reason arithmetically from the arsenal's sheet that a 22-grains-heavier bullet required a 12.8 percent reduction of the charge and gave a 12.8 percent reduction of velocity, a big discrepancy is apparent. All we can say is that the boat-tail helps somewhat. British data on the .303 Mark VII and Mark VIII cartridges—both of which are 174-grain in bullet weight, the VII flat-based, the VIII boat-tailed ("streamlined," they call it), using similar powder charges—these data state 2450 f. s. velocity for the flat-based and 2500 for the boat-tail. Although 2 percent velocity increase is of itself trifling it could, with the cumulative increase due to other factors here discussed, add up to a significant enough total velocity increase in a wildcat.

The factor of free-boring is even more favorable than the boat-tailing of bullets. Tests show that free-boring a barrel one-half to three-quarters of an inch ahead of the neck of the chamber, before the throat or lands is cut into the lands of the rifling, reduces the pressures by 5000 P. S. I. or more. If the pressure level was 50,000 P. S. I. without free-boring, a compensating increase of charge in the free-bored barrel will still operate at 50,000 P. S. I. with an increase in velocity from the greater volume of gas generated by the increased charge.

Aside from free-boring, just the variation in the leade or rifling throat makes a huge difference in pressure. A rifle throated for a long, heavy bullet when using a lighter, shorter bullet—with the jump or free travel it has to make to reach the rifling—has shown nearly 10,000 P. S. I. less pressure than the same load in a throat in which the lighter bullet fits closely, allowing no jump into the rifling. The importance of the throat cannot be exaggerated. In a .25-06 round with a 140-grain bullet giving an 85 mm. overall length, used in a barrel throated for it, the pressure runs 55,000 P. S. I. Such a round fired in a barrel throated 5 mm. shorter (for the 117-grain bullet) gave 68,000 P. S. I.! Taking that 140-grain bullet and seating it

to 80 mm. overall length lowered the pressure to 60,000 P. S. I. in the short throated barrel!

The now obsolete .275 H&H Magnum and the .276 Dubiel (they are alike except for a more gentle slope to the .276 shoulder) were originally throated for a round as long as the .30-06 magazine would feed. In a Magnum Mauser action the length of the round could be increased, and the throat was cut for the long round. That made possible an increased charge and gave better velocity.

There is evidence that chrome lining a bore reduces barrel friction. It is worth looking into, and chrome-lined barrels are available.

A word about tight chambers. They were quite popular with exacting riflemen 20 or 30 years ago, and when cases were die formed and the necks reamed while the case was in the die, the ammunition gave uniformly good groups and neck resizing was not needed for reloading. It was considerable and exacting work. Fortunately, the improvement of bullet uniformity since that time has been much advanced. The bench-rest riflemen of today can, with his excellent bullets, make groups we oldsters never hoped for with our hand-drawn and reamed cases for our tight-chambered rifles. But the tight chamber was not practical, for feeding and extraction problems were possible, particularly under wide temperature variations. The practice passed into the same place where the moistening of Lesmok powder driven .22 rimfire bullets reposes.

If a bullet .308 inch in diameter is used in a rifle of .30 caliber with lands of .300 and grooves of .308, experience shows that the relationship promotes good groups. It is also true that .309 bullets shoot tight groups out of a .308-inch barrel, but they increase pressures. Beyond that .001-inch oversize bullet in a .300 bore, .308 grooved barrel, groups spread out and pressures rise to an alarming degree. The canny wildcatter will make his pets take advantage of this fact by using .309- or even .310-inch grooves to handle .308-inch bullets. As this eases pressure, he can increase his powder charge somewhat. We mention this only because we have seen it. Rarely, to be sure, but in the interest of sound practice remember the closer the bullet diameter is to the full groove diameter of the barrel, the more likely you are to have a good grouper and fewer problems in reloading. American practice is to have bullet and groove diameters the same.

Pressures

Judging pressures by staring a fired case earnestly in the face of its primer end is of but little help in arriving at pressure figures. If a primer is quite flat, all you are justified in saying is that the load is "hot," and a flat, cratered primer is "too hot." But how many pounds per square inch are "hot," or "too hot"? Although there is no substitute for a pressure gun, as previously mentioned, when the bolt-lift becomes hard one is definitely justified in saying the load is "much

---

*Diphenylamine as stabilizer; graphite for coating.

too hot." In this instance, "much too hot" is in the proof pressure class. A load that enlarges primer pockets so that a new primer slides in with no help from a loading tool is certainly "much too hot." A further check is to mike the case webs of new brass before and after firing. If anything more than a .001-inch increase is noted it may be from a slightly loose chamber, but it may as well be an overload or a near maximum load that is spreading the brass, just as it occurs with a small percentage of AP M-2 loads in extruded brass. Stop and ascertain the cause, in the interest of safety.

When you finally have your load worked up and want to be certain of its safety, a pressure gun check of five rounds will definitely establish the sanity of the load. With wildcats, this is expensive, but to an individual wildcatter it is insurance. A commercial wildcatter's failure to use a pressure gun may be an attempt to kid the public, but an accident with one of his creatures may be held to be negligence on the wildcatter's part, if the case gets to court!

Lest the uninitiated, prospective wildcatter decide from the foregoing that it's a risky, uncertain and possibly dangerous field, be it stated that our experiments cover many years, many types of actions, and cartridges so numerous that we could not recall them all from memory. We are for wildcats and will be while we have enough strength left to squeeze off a shot—out of a wheel-chair, if necessary. Take the advice of level-headed shooters and technicians and you will be safe, and some day the ".30 — —" will be listed with your name where the dashes appear. Beware the extreme enthusiast and consider only groups on the target, the readings of the chronograph, and the figures of pressure tests of any new wildcat. All else is dross. Take it from cynics who still enjoy wildcatting in spite of all we have learned thus far—and we have not scratched the surface.

Stalking the Wildcat

There are many approaches to any wildcat cartridge. Just a large stock of usable brass sitting around often tempts the nimble-minded developer, including ourselves. So the .22 Orphan was developed by necking down the .276 Pedersen, an Army experimental form, to .22 caliber. With reasonable charges a pretty good varmint cartridge resulted—with no major problems.

Then there is the desire to get greater velocity from a given case. Usually its shape is changed to hold more powder to nudge the same bullets, but faster. Within reasonable limits you can pick up velocity, but in blowing out brass there is a greater or lesser loss from the splitting of the case bodies at neck or shoulder. At current prices of cases this loss may or may not bother you, but psychologically it is frustrating even to dyed-in-the-wool cranks like us. And it is not particularly good for your rifle chamber if it occurs pretty regularly. Some lots of World War I .30-40 (for training) and .30-06 ammunition split almost regularly after a

few years' storage, and the good Ordnance steel and nickel steel chambers of those times weren't pleased.

A more extreme approach is to blow out your case radically and increase capacities by as much as 20% or more. Sure, you get increased velocities. You also get these things: (1) increased recoil and muzzle blast; (2) much shorter barrel life from increased erosion, and if you think 1½ inches of erosion with fewer than 200 rounds with a very hot .25 caliber Magnum is humorous, you are wrong. The thing was not even sighted in with all loads when a new barrel was needed. Then (3) a large percentage of case bodies split in the blowing-out process. We know by bitter and shameful personal experience. We necked down a .375 H&H Magnum case to use .280 bullets, blew the bodies out to hold a charge of 84 grains of .50 caliber machine gun powder—getting about 25 percent splits in process—and we secured exactly 100 f. s. more velocity with 180-grain bullets than the .280 Dubiel gave without any trouble. To make the lesson stick, we found that in the ".280 Milkbottle" 71 grains of 4350 gave the same velocity as the 84-grain charge of .50 caliber M. G. powder gave. We know better now.

A variation on the preceding is to take a .375 H&H case (and this one we actually did, too), cut it from 72-mm. length to 66-mm., put it through four different dies to form the shoulder and neck for holding .257-inch bullets. There were various trimmings between stages, together with annealings, too. Then we blew it out to give powder room, and when we got through it eroded the barrel so quickly that to this day all we know about the thing is that it was stupid to have started.

There is also a legitimate experimenter's approach. A popular factory case is necked down, or the neck opened out, for different diameter bullets. Even the factories do this and the results are often good. The first rimless high-powered case was the 8x57J (Infantry) Mauser for the model 1888 rifle. From that case various developments have resulted in the .22 Newton, .244 Remington, .257 Roberts, 6.5x57, 7x57, 7.9x57 Js (or 1905 Mauser with spitzer bullet), 9x57 Mauser, 9.3x57 Mauser, and the 9.5x57 Mannlicher-Schoenauer. The .30-06 has been worked over quite as extensively, for we have the 6-mm. 06 by Gipson, .25-06, 6.5-mm. 06, .270 Winchester (with a little longer neck, much like that of the .30-1903), 7-mm. 06, .280-06, 8-mm. 06, .333 OKH, .35 Whelen, .375-06, and a .400 Whelen. Or take the .300 and .375 H&H Magnum cases. They've been necked up or down so much we have had .22, 6-mm., .25, .270, 7-mm., .280, 8-mm., .333, .35, .400, and .450 calibers—all Magnums.

Of these some were nothing to brag about; many were quite satisfactory and pleased the wildcat fans and factories. All were made with a minimum of work. One lift of the loading tool lever and the case is opened or reduced at the neck. The body is rarely changed and the shoulder is seldom altered from the original. But now the developer has the options of having his barrels rifled with fast twists for long, heavy bullets or slower twists for short, light, varmint bullets, for combinations or purposes that the factories could not, because of the limited demand, add to their line of cartridges.

It is a fertile field for the wildcat rifleman, and some worthwhile ballistics are developed, well suited to particular types of hunting, or to certain species of game. This field is far from being exhausted in spite of the imposing lists above.

There remains the field of truly advanced ballistic reesarch, involving the designing of cartridges to take advantage of newly developed components or actions. The arsenals and factories are continually striving to obtain improved ballistics. For the individual such work involves much knowledge, much mechanical skill, as well as the availability of a machine shop, chronograph, and pressure gun as a minimum. In this field today's wildcat cartridge becomes tomorrow's issue ammunition for an Army, or the popular over-the-counter round for target shooter or hunter. Is it any wonder that so many riflemen are loyal members of the Wildcat Lodge?

Any attempt to append a list of currently used wildcat cartridges would be futile, as whole volumes are available on the subject for the interested shooter. Particularly helpful are Phil Sharpe's *Complete Guide to Handloading* and Dick Simmons' *Wildcat Cartridges*. Then, if you can find it, there is J. R. Mattern's *Hand-loading Ammunition*. It was written when a different series of Du Pont powders was in use, different primers too, and before wildcatting had been done by any but a few specialists, such as Adolph Niedner, who worked with the famous Dr. Franklin Mann. But it is based on deep experience and on principles that always made sound practice, with the components then available.

Wildcats Using .22 Caliber (.224") Bullets

R-2. Hervey Lovell's original .22-3000 was the .25-20 Single Shot case necked to use. 224-inch bullets. On the R-2, the shoulder angle was changed to slightly increase the capacity. It offers about 20 to 25 percent more velocity than a .22 Hornet, making it a practical varmint rifle for up to 200-yard shots under favorable weather conditions. Brass may be unavailable, and since the .222 Remington is available and gives slightly better ballistics, be certain of the brass supply for an R-2. The .25-20 WCF or Repeater case is entirely different from the Single Shot.

.22 or .219 Wasp. This is widely used by bench-rest shooters. It is the .219 Zipper case cut down and blown out slightly. Any rifleman interested in bench should give this one consideration, as it seems so well suited to such work.

22. Gebby Varminter. This is the .250-3000 case necked down for .224-inch bullets. It has produced fine groups with loads from the Hornet class right through velocities of the Swift type. It is used in bench-rest shooting and is a fine varmint cartridge as well.

Some wildcat cartridges for big-game hunting. From left: .25 Whelen, .35 Whelen, .400 Magnum on Newton brass, .400 Whelen Magnum on .375 H&H brass, .400 Whelen, .265 O'Neil-Keith-Hopkins on 7x57, .285 OKH on 06, .333 OKH on 06, .334 OKH on .300 H&H, .280 Dubiel, .300 Hoffman Magnum, .300 Weatherby Magnum. The last has become domesticated in Norma factory production. *Photo courtesy Combat Forces Press.*

.220 Swift modifications. A number is made, with slight modifications of case shoulder, body, and neck. The Wilson Arrow and Weatherby Rocket are well known examples of many that have been used in bench-rest and on varmints. The Arrow is a bit unusual in that it will fit in most if not all factory Swift chambers: its sharper shoulder was given it to improve powder combustion, not to increase powder capacity. Not all handloaders have confined themselves to this intended purpose in using it.

Wildcats Using 6-mm. (.244″) Bullets

There are several, of which the *Rockchucker* is an example. They use bullets from about 75 to 105 grains in weight, for bench-rest, and the heavy bullets for game the size of deer. The .244 Remington and .243 Winchester resulted from 6 mm wildcat developments over the past years.

Wildcats Using .25 Caliber (.257″) Bullets

In this group a wildcat fan can find just about anything he may desire. Everything from the Hornet and .25-20 WCF up through the big Holland & Holland Magnums has been wildcatted into a special .25.

Herbert Longo wanted a low pressure, reloadable .25 to about equal the .25 rimfire, and by expanding the Hornet neck he got what he desired. Designers of the velocity-effect school worked on H&H Magnum brass and got what they were after. Bullets as light as 60 grains and as heavy as 150 have been used in .25 wildcats, by selecting the case, powders and pitch of rifling for the weight of bullet. For some 70 years, if we go back to Rabbeth's work with the long .32-caliber Wesson rifle case, experimenters have been busy with special .25s. Names like Mann, Niedner, Newton, Howe, Roberts, Keith, Whelen, Miller, Weatherby, Gipson, Cottrell, Ackley, Hopkins and O'Neill come to mind. Their developments were used widely as wildcats and sometimes taken up and put into factory production. Though so much has been done, there is still fertile ground for the earnest experimenter. We are guilty, ourselves, with a .25-06 case using 140- and 150-grain bullets in a barrel with one turn of twist in eight inches. It is easily made, and a 140-grain bullet at nearly 2900 f. s. in .25 caliber makes a good long-range target load as well as a big-game round for magazine actions. Similar ballistics come from necking down and blowing out the .30-40, as exemplified by the *.25 Gipson-Ellinger Krag.* Magnum cases of larger capacity than the .25-06 give greatly increased velocities to 100- and 117-grain bullets, but thus far erosion is a bad problem.

Wildcats Using 6.5 mm or .256 (.264″) Bullets

What holds for the .25 is to a lesser extent true of 6.5 mm. Everything from the 6.5 Mannlicher Schoenauer through Magnum brass has been adopted. In this sized bullet a good selection of heavy types gives the sectional density school their opportunity to experiment, as shown by *Fred Barnes' 6.5 Magnum* using a 200-grain bullet with .50 caliber machine gun powder for propellant. At the other extreme was the *6.5x68 R. W. S.* 1939 development. Here a six-gram (93-grain) bullet was given 3900 f. s.! And just about everything between is there for the asking, by choosing case, bullet weight, powder and proper barrel twist. The *.256 Newton,* being no longer available from the factories, falls into this group. It is still a good cartridge for open country, big game hunting.

Wildcats Using 7 mm (.284″) and .280 (.289″) Bullets

This group parallels the 6.5s, in that long, heavy bullets give the sectional-density experimenter free rein. Although rifles of .280 caliber are no longer made, most advanced wildcat gunsmiths have made cases like the .280 Dubiel (for rifles which had .289″ grooves) or other rifles with .284″ grooves to use the 7 mm bullets of .284″ diameter.

A recent development by Phil Sharpe of the *7x61 Sharpe & Hart* cartridge probably belongs under factory classification. Schultz & Larsen of Denmark make the rifles, and Norma of Norway the brass. Having seen the years of development that went into it, we can state that it was tried out with twists of one turn in six inches through one turn in 20 inches, and with bullets weighing from 75 through 210 grains. With the slow twists the lighter bullets, and with the fast twists the heavy bullets, gave excellent velocities and groups. Loads were chronographed, pressures taken, and when announced to the public this wildcat was practically a factory job.

There are other 7-mm. wildcats of less and greater capacity. Ballisticians lean toward 7-mm. as the ideal caliber for a shoulder arm—great velocities with moderate recoil—and we'll be disappointed if the factories don't soon announce a 7-mm. Magnum. They have been experimenting in this caliber for years; so it is about time that they put out a standard cartridge using this potential which wildcatters have worked on so long. With well-shaped heavy bullets, the 7-mm. group offers excellent 600- and 1000-yard target possibilities, as was proved by Sir Charles Ross with his .280 Ross match rifles, before World War I. The usual Ross match bullet weighed 180 grains and was finely streamlined.

Wildcats Using .30 Caliber (.308″) Bullets

In this group everybody and his brother have been active—factories, arsenals, ordinary riflemen and ballistic engineers, as individuals and in professional laboratories. Bullets as light as 90 grains and as heavy as 250 are available, making any approach possible, from high velocity to great sectional density. Cases have been designed for very short and very long actions, the "carbine, cal. .30 M 1" cartridge being at one end of the scale, and the huge, blown-out Magnums like Weatherby's, Miller's, Ackley's, Hoffman's and many others at the other.

Since it is our own Army caliber, it is a safe wager

A Griffin & Howe .35 Whelen. Cocking piece rear sight, ramp front. Notice how near the iron-sight line is to that of the Lyman Alaskan scope. *Courtesy Combat Forces Press.*

Mauser-action .35 Newton with 26-inch Griffin & Howe barrel, curly maple stock by Hal Hartley, magazine lengthened and bolt handle turned down by Vernor Gipson. *Courtesy Combat Forces Press.*

that the future promises plenty of room for further development. In .30 caliber we can say, "You name it. Someone's got it for you, right now." Currently, the best long-range target results are obtained from .30 caliber, in the .300 H&H case and modifications of it.

Wildcats Using .33 Caliber (.333") Bullets

For the sectional-density experimenter this is nearly the ideal size, as the bullets are long and heavy. The lightest standard was 200 grains in the old .33 Winchester cartridge, now obsolete, not made. The heavier bullets of 250 grains (pointed) and 300 grains (round nosed) have been used by *Griffin & Howe* in the .333 Magnum, which is the .375 H&H Magnum necked down. *O'Neill, Keith & Hopkins* made a series of .333 cases, using the 7.9x57 mm, .30-06 and .375 H&H. Existing propellants give good velocities, and penetration on heavier game. The factories have been working, and likely we shall soon have a standard American .333. For heavy game it is just too good a caliber to overlook, as the old British .333 Jeffery proved.

The .333 wildcats are built to use .333 Jeffery bullets, which run about .333-inch in diameter. The old .33 Winchester and .33 Newton bullets go about .338-inch.

Wildcats Using .35 Caliber (.358") Bullets

Like the .333, this group offers much for shooting heavy game. The two standbys are the well-known *.35 Whelen,* made by necking up an 06 case, for American game, and the *.350 Griffin & Howe Magnum,* a neckdown of the .375 H&H, to fulfill Leslie Simpson's specifications for a cartridge for large, non-dangerous game in Africa. Using 250- to 300-grain bullets at velocities giving practical trajectories for the game hunted, and good penetration on impact, the .35 Whelen is still widely used even though both the arm and its ammunition are strictly custom jobs.

Wildcats Using .40 Caliber (.410") Bullets

For some years this field lay fallow. The *.400 Whelen* was a .30-06 necked up, and the *.400 Whelen-Magnum* was a .375 H&H opened up. They suffered at the very first from a lack of choice in bullets: only the 300-grain round-nosed for the .405 Winchester was to be had. In more recent years several bullet makers turned to .40 caliber, and 300, 350-and 400-grain weights gave the experimenter the chance to develop cartridges that work through long magnum actions and give ballistics equal to or a bit faster than those of old, reliable Cordite powder loads the British provided for their double rifles for African and East Indian game. There are already several good .40-caliber wildcats, and they are acceptable relatives of the .400 Whelen, .400 Whelen-Magnum and *.400 Niedner* (.35 Newton opened up), which heavy-bullet fans liked so well in the past.

Wildcats Using .45 Caliber (.458") Bullets

Since the end of World War II, particularly in Alaska, hunters have wanted and designers have provided large-capacity .45 cases using 300-, 400-, and 500-grain bullets. The .458 Watts is a prime example, and it has ballistics equal to the old reliable British .450, .470, .475, and .476 Cordite cartridges for large, dangerous African game. We've seen and shot an experimental factory rifle with 500- and 510-grain bullets, and the fired case goes neatly into the chamber of Todd Craig's *.458 as made by Ackley!* This tends to prove that regardless of whether a wildcatter or the factories approach a specific problem, existing components often make the final result so close for either as to be virtually interchangeable.

Put another way, the advanced wildcat developer follows the same conservative, safe reasoning that the arsenal or factory labs pursue. The laws of physics apply to the lab technician and individual alike, and when they come up with the same shape and capacity of case it is more than a coincidence—it is something inevitable. In this instance it is once again proof that the wildcat developer who obeys his reason and the laws of physics knows exactly what he is doing.

THESE calibers always are interesting to the rifle-crank—people like you, perhaps, and I'm certainly one of that bemused fellowship—and many of them are of first-rate usefulness. They fill the gaps between American factory loadings and sometimes supply the specialized kind of service that our manufacturers seem to have forgotten or—just possibly—never to have heard of.

The obvious objection to buying a rifle for an oddy is the problem of feeding it. That can be serious in out-of-the-way places, where game tends to live. But lots of us already own such rifles, and keep 'em going. When a cartridge is both obsolete and foreign we may have a problem. Yet an old rifle, or a bargain rifle, or any good rifle deserves to go afield now and then and have the dust blown out of its barrel.

This activation may call for handloading, even for bullet-casting too, but so what? It's fun. If we can't buy or form the brass we *can* have it made to order. This effort can be worth while.

In this chapter, tempting though the bypaths are that stretch out to the backwoods of crankdom, we'll try to focus discussion on rounds whose value resides in the hard fact that no American cartridges similar to them in performance are being turned out. "Obsolete" refers to calibers that are no longer factory-made here, and "foreign" denotes the European and British sizes that ordinarily have to be imported, including a few that once were loaded by American plants.

OBSOLETES

Some were discontinued only recently, in the early 1950s; yet they may be harder to find than much older sizes, such as one or two that you can't use! Although a good many rich old mines of obsolete ammunition were gutted during World War II by customers anxious to get anything that would shoot, even for the powder, lead, and primers it contained if the brass was useless to them, you still do run across some great finds. The powder may be weakened by age, or if black, crumbled into dust that would burn at dangerous pressures; the primers may be corrosive or, far worse, early non-corrosive stuff with a mercuric content that ruins the brass when the cartridge is fired*; but the cases may still be strong and springy enough for safe first firing and considerable reloading. And bullets last indefinitely, though the grease in the grooves of lead pills may have to be removed and replaced—not always after 50 years or longer storage, however.

At least the old cartridge forms a model from which dies can be made for reforming adaptable brass from a current size, if any such luck turns up. "Single specimens" for collectors are handled by a lot of

*Some corrosive (potassium chlorate) primers were mercuric, too. In fact, this double-trouble type goes into Western-Winchester .30-06 and .300 Magnum Match cartridges because of its contribution to accuracy in those particular loads.

CHAPTER 20

SOME OBSOLETE AND FOREIGN CALIBERS

dealers. Here is a list from editor John Amber's 1957 *Gun Digest*, always a useful annual to buy.

C. G. BATTLES, 215 Magyar, Wellington, Ohio.
JACK A. BRICKELL, 8531 S. E. Taylor St., Portland 16, Ore.
FRANK DAVIS, 47 Robinson St., West Englewood, N. J.
THE GUN SHOP, 1070 N. Henderson, Galesburg, Ill.
HOWE FUR CO., Coopers Mills, Maine.
MCDANELD & WHEELER, Osborne, Kans.
PHILIP J. MEDICUS, 18 Fletcher St., New York 38, N. Y.
MILLER BROS., Rapid City, Mich.
PLATT B. MONFORT, 14 Bouton Pl., Huntington, L. I., N. Y.
MARTIN B. RETTING, 5851 Washington Blvd., Culver City, Calif.
THE SHELL SHOP, 3795 Sunset Blvd., Los Angeles, Calif.
PERRY SPANGLER, 3510 Fenton Rd., Flint, Mich.
ERNEST TICHY, 632 Galapago, Denver 4, Colo.

At times such dealers can supply box quantities or more, in some sizes, and they may stock foreign cartridges, too.

Black-Powder Cartridges

Practically all of the black powder centerfires can be handloaded with smokeless, and except for some special, and rare, old single-shot sizes, most of them were. Hercules Sharpshooter smokeless could dupli-

Some of the popular old black-powder designs in the "medium" calibers, .38 and .40. From left: .38-56-255 WCF, .38-70-255 WCF, .38-72-275 WCF, .38-90-217 Express (solid bullet), .40-45-265 (.40-50 Sharps Straight) with paper-patched bullet, .40-50-265 bottle-necked and paper patched, .40-60-210 WCF, .40-65-260 WCF, .40-70-330 WCF, .40-72-330 WCF, .40-82-260 WCF, .40-90-370 Sharps Straight paper patched, .40-110-260 Express (hollow point, tubed). *Courtesy Combat Forces Press.*

cate nearly all black-powder rifle cartridge ballistics, with extremely low pressures at those levels. In the small calibers it was considered highly erosive, but I doubt that it was ever tested fully with modern non-corrosive primers. When they came in we had plenty of other powders to use, and most of us did use them, being scared stiff by Sharpshooter's 40 percent nitroglycerine content. That meant hot burning even when pressures were low.

For soft-steel barrels like those of old single shots and early repeaters a straight black-powder charge, ignited with a pistol primer if its thin cup is safe in the magazine handling, undoubtedly lengthens bore life. I know too well that modern large rifle primers, even with black powder, are hard on very old, soft steel.

Usually we've chosen the cartridge for its original black-powder power, haven't we? Priming with a pinch of smokeless, as described in the handloading chapter, doesn't seem to be hard on the steel if we go easy. Some printed recommendations have been pretty steep. After all, we want only to reduce the bore fouling enough to maintain accuracy during a day's hunting. It isn't necessary to sweep the barrel clean with hot and high pressure charges.

Now, any black-powder cartridge is fascinating to play with, and generally it's useful, too. But here we want to bear down on the sizes that aren't readily duplicated by hand- or factory-loaded modern stuff.

So for small-game or possibly short-range varmint shooting it isn't necessary to revive a .22-13-45 Winchester, .22-15-60 Stevens, .25-21-86 Stevens, .28-30-120 Stevens, .32-30-125 (.313 inch) Remington, .32-25-150 Ideal or any of the dozen or so others in this once highly specialized class. We can duplicate them with lead-bullet handloads in small or good-sized modern .22, .25, 7-mm., .30- and .32-caliber cases. But it *is* most interesting to work with them and develop accurate charges, and the little cartridges, big enough for their job, are light to carry, seldom go tinkle-tonkle in your pocket, and, frankly, are fascinating durn things to handle! They're also unusual, too unusual.

Many of the larger sizes, if not the best, can come close to being that when we hunt American big game from deer on up. Their killing power depends on thick, long, heavy bullets—which must be well placed, it's true—and this kind of slug is one of the most dependable in brush. For long shooting they are out. Their effective range, everything considered, is from 75 to 100 yards.

The service they rendered in the woods gave their generations of users the chance to classify them as to deadliness. The long .38s, from the .38-55-255 to the .38-72-275, were deer loads. Going up to .40 caliber generally made a deer hunter feel more secure. From the .40-50-265 or 285 bottle-necked Sharps, Remington and so forth, and the .40-65-260 Winchester and Marlin to the .40-82-260 and various .40-70-330s there was a good spread of choice.

The heaviest .40s, with long bullets like the .40-72-330, .40-70-370 bottle-necked, and 40-90-370 bottle or straight case, could be used on the largest American game. But the big .44s, .45s and .50s were better, for hunters who could handle them. And we must remember that recoil, though sometimes heavy, never was quick, or even a jab, if your rifle had a flat, shotgun style buttplate.

It would be foolish to doubt the killing power of such once common, popular rounds as the .44-105-520, .45-120-550 and .50-100-450. They could still be quite enough for the biggest game on this continent, and close-up they'd be among the best.

There were popular deer sizes in those bigbores, too, such as the .44-40-200 and the .45-60-300. The first was marginal and today is considered submarginal; the second had plenty.

Folks had just as much fun then as now. Case shape, for instance, was a fine football. Some said that a bottle-neck slung a bullet out harder; others held to it that black powder always burned better from a straight case. So factories supplied both kinds in hunting and target sizes, and you took your pick. Some of the Bullard bottles looked as though they'd been fashioned to hold leprechaun wine.

The rifles, large and small, had relatively slow-twist rifling. Though modern quick twists, from .257 Roberts to .458, would do better, no doubt, with cast bullets a bit harder than the old alloys, it is worth noticing what proved out in both accuracy and killing power when these cartridges were made.

In 1904 some of the Winchester formulas ran like these: .22 Extra Long and WCF, .32-20, .32 Ideal, .38-40, 44-40: no alloy, pure lead.

.25-20 to .25-25 (fast twists): 1 part tin, 60 parts lead.

.32-40 and .38-55 full power: 1 to 40.

The same in "Short Range," with light bullets: 1 to 20.

Most long .38s and .40s: 1 to 20.

Long, heavy .44s, .45s and .50s: 1 to 15 or 1 to 16.

Paper-patched lead bullets: usually 1 to 20.

Smokeless Powder Rounds

Obsolete cartridges like the .25-36 Marlin and .25 Remington were delightful to shoot, but we can load bigger .25s down to their level. The same goes for the 6-mm. Lee.

Early high-intensity American calibers such as the .280 Ross and the Newtons are still useful as is, in good rifles, even though we have modern wildcats and standardized Weatherby rounds that give similar results, or more. The .256 Newton could be called a magnum 6.5 mm., though it's lighter than the .270 Winchester. With equal bullet weights we get greater sectional density than with the .270, and the .256 Newt is a fine long range caliber. Special rifles, not Newtons, have been made for it, and cases are formed by shortening the .30-06 after setting its shoulder back, and neck-sizing. (Reduce the 06 neck to hold .257-inch bullets and we have the once super-varmint case, .25-06 Niedner.)

The .30 Newton has no advantages over the .300 Magnum that I can see except that it's shorter overall

A few of the black-powder bigbores. From left: .44-60-395 Remington and Sharps, .45-60-300 WCF, .45-75-350 WCF, .45-85-295 Bullard, .45-90-300 WCF, .45-100-550 Sharps Straight paper patched in 2⅞-inch case (they were made up to 3¼ for heavier loadings), .50-70-425 Sporting with paper-patched bullet, .50-95-300 Express with copper-tubed hollow point, .50-90-473 Sharps paper patched, .50-110-300 Express in smokeless loading with jacketed bullet, soft *and* open hollow point. *Courtesy Combat Forces Press.*

Obsolete high-power rounds. All but the Army's experimental Pedersen were made in hunting style by one or more American factories. From left: 6 mm. Lee, 6.5x53 Mannlicher-Schoenauer, .276 Pedersen, .280 Ross, 7.65 Belgian Mauser (military bullet), 9x57 Mauser, .256 Newton with its designer's wire-reinforced soft-point bullet, .30 Newton with same type of bullet, .35 Newton with Western open-point expanding bullet. *Courtesy Combat Forces Press.*

and better shaped for modern powder. But the .276, .280, .33 and .35 Newtons would give us useful calibers below and above the .30 size—if we could get the brass and the rifles. These big fellows, including the .30, are as truly rimless as almost any cartridges. They mike about .526 inch at rim and head. They're pretty straight-sided and abruptly necked. Well shaped.

By comparison the .333 British Jeffery is .541 and .541, the .280 Canadian Ross .532 and .524, the H&H Magnums .528, .528, and only .511 above the belt, all approximate. Reworking one to duplicate another obviously isn't too practicable. Rechambering and reboring a turnbolt rifle—not the Ross straight-pull, many gunsmiths would say—might be worked out to great satisfaction.

FOREIGNERS

In the early 1900s a certain class of hunter used foreign rifles with imported ammunition, to be or to have something different. That was all right. A different class used them because we had almost no long-range bolt-action sporters, made here, and that was what they needed for the hunting they did. A few bought the .333 and .404 Jeffery type for great power, and they got it.

Now we have our own rifles and cartridges for long shooting or for plenty of short-range deadliness. The foreigners do little more than fill gaps, which may or may not be wide, depending a good deal on personal viewpoints.

High Velocity Smallbores

The comparatively new .244 Holland & Holland on Magnum brass is a high velocity varmint, deer, sheep or antelope round, and it will be used here to some extent. The 1903 6.5 mm. Mannlicher Schoenauer is no longer a fast load, but it's as useful as ever in the kind of country where it earned its reputation, virgin wilderness, with shots rarely over 200 yards. Yes, it has done longer shooting, all over the

world, but it wouldn't be chosen for that today. In brush it's one of the few good light calibers. Heavy-bullet weights vary, but 160 grains is about standard, and this makes a long bullet in 6.5, though much heavier ones have been used in wildcats. With velocity around 2200 f. s. it isn't too fast for deep penetration or for some stability among twigs and even saplings, and usually it's of a simple, reliable soft-point construction.

The 6.5x61 Mauser rimless starts a 155-grain at 2611, and the Schuler-designed 6.5x68—big-bodied, and necked and shouldered like the .243 Winchester—rips out a 93-grain at 3937. There's also a 123.5-grain bullet that goes at 3313 f. s. Now that the Newton .256 is obsolete we have no American factory-loaded 6.5, and there is a natural demand for one. Even in magnums there's a wide difference between .25 and .27 calibers.

There are plenty of good German 6.5s, and some of them can be taken care of by reformed .30-06 brass. The Mannlicher is a little fellow, but Dominion loads for it are imported for it right along from the north side of the St. Lawrence. Like many rimless European calibers it has its rimmed counterpart. This 6.5x53R is the old Rumanian '93 and Dutch '95 service round, and it's long been popular for single-shot and double rifles, and combination guns. Brass has been formed for it from the .303 British, and Tom Florich got excellent accuracy from 40 grains of 4320 and a 150-grain bullet. He used a single-shot Westley Richards with Farquharson-type falling block action. This load is a competent one, and he worked up to it carefully for use in that particular rifle, which is strong.

In 7 mm. or .275 the 7x61 Sharpe & Hart could replace the H&H Magnum and no doubt will, over here. But the 7x64 rimless has become reasonably popular and is accommodated with reformed .270 or .30-06 brass. German RWS tables credit it with driving a 172.8-grain bullet at 2776 f. s., and indeed its only advantage over the .270 is that its larger caliber lets it handle slightly heavier standard bullets. The rimmed version, 7x65R, gives 160 feet less velocity to the same weight of bullet. The old Spanish Mauser 7x57, made here for over half a century, has an RWS speed figure of 2526 for that bullet; so there's quite a difference unless we stalk close to our game, and sometimes we can't do that. The .280 Remington, though not of magnum size, now gives us a useful American 7-mm. It may need special-diameter bullets.

Weatherby's rating for his own 7-mm. is about 3000 f. s., 175-grain bullet. In comparing this with the ballyhooed .280 Halger of some 20 years ago— 180-grain at 3000—remember that Halger used the .280 Ross case, which is a lot smaller than the Weatherby. It was crammed with powder and the high pressure normally made extraction stiff. This abnormal condition wasn't enough to reach the 3000 f. s., it seems. Some creative imagination was called for, too. That's the consensus today, but boy, what a dream it was while it lasted!

There is excellent choice range in 6.5- and 7-mm. custom bullets, and it's fair in 8-mm.

Medium and Large Bores

But with 8-mm., about .32, we get into medium and large foreign calibers. The 8x68S drives a 186-gr. bullet at the RWS rated figure of 3280 f. s. and has no special advantage over 180-grain slugs in .300 H&H blown-out magnums except that it is a shorter cartridge.

The 8x60 rimless Mauser and Mannlicher Schoenauer gives enough power over that of the 8x57 military and sporting to be useful in its bracket. Its 200-grain bullet leaves at a stated 2600 f. s., and reworked 06 brass serves this caliber. Then there's the .318 Westley Richards, an oversize 8-mm. Bullets for this British cartridge mike about .328 or .329 inch, and the blunt or semi-pointed slugs of 250 grains developed 2400 f. s., the 180-grain 2700. The "Accelerated Express, L. T. Pointed" bullet has been famous for about a half-century. Leslie Taylor designed, it is something like the modern Silvertip, this semi-pointed affair; but steel jackets, tinned or nickeled, answer to the magnet—most specimens I have. Case head and rim measure about .003 inch under those of the .30-06, and the case is shorter in neck and shoulder. The 8-mm. 06 wild cat, fairly popular, would do the job of the .318, but for those who like a fine British rifle the Westley Richards is a good choice.

The .33 or .333 is a useful size to add. So the .333 Jeffery has been given a good deal of careful thought, trial and use by some of our big-game hunters. This cartridge, and wildcats of similar power, fill the space between .30 and .35 better than most .32s can, if you want good, husky bullets. The 300-grain Jeffrey is credited with 2200 f. s. speed—weight and starting velocity like those of the .405 Winchester, and far superior sectional density. The sharp 250 grain develops about 2500 f. s. Penetration of the full-jacketed heavy bullet is something to marvel at, and this caliber has been proved all over the world.

Nine millimeter or .35 caliber cartridges are rather well taken care of by our .35 Remington, .358 Winchester, .35 Whelen wildcat and bigger wildcats. The

Some British and European rounds, most of which have been reasonably popular in the United States. Bolt actions and/-or combination guns handled them. From left: 6.5x53 rimmed Mannlicher-Steyr, .275 Holland & Holland Magnum, 7x57 rimmed, 8x57 rimmed, 8x60 rimmed, 9x57 rimmed (cast bullet), 7x64, .333-.280 Jeffery, .333 Jeffery, .318 Westley Richards with round, capped point, 9x57 Mauser, 9.3x62, 10.75x68, 11.2x60. *Courtesy Combat Forces Press.*

9x56 Mannlicher and 9x57 Mauser were great short-range cartridges in their day, and still are, though more powerful loads are supplanting them. About 245 grains is the standard bullet weight, at a velocity of 2150 f. s. Handloads have given similar speed to the old 280-grain Mauser slug, though its regular rate was 1850, as loaded long ago, over in New England.

Following the usual practice, these 9-mm. Mauser and Mannlicher Schoenauer cases are different. The former is a little longer, and its shoulder may or may not be located at the same distance from the head as on the Mannlicher. I suspect that combination, interchangeable cases have been made, but it certainly would seem risky to fire special Mannlicher rounds in a Mauser. The headspace might be excessive, much in the manner of an 8x56 Mannlicher in an 8x57 Mauser chamber. The Winchester 54 in 9x57 was discontinued long ago, and now not one of our factories makes any foreign 9-mm. ammunition. The old cartridges were short and handy, effective on our big game in the woods, but the competition of large-caliber lever-action rounds was more than they could buck.

A step up, .365 or 9.3, is the rather familiar Mauser 9.3x62. About 285 grains is its standard bullet weight, with velocities from 2175 to 2329 f. s., depending on how you load, the temperature, bullet and bore dimensions, and what print you read. It's a well-justified caliber if we need something between .35 and .375, and many hunters think we do. The case is so much like the .30-06 that mutation isn't difficult, and Norma bullets of 201, 231 and 285 grains are imported for it. The cartridge is of the right length for 06 magazines. You can clip-load it if you want to and if your rifle's receiver is slotted for clip feeding. Don't laugh: one of our greatest American hunters, Stewart Edward White, carried clipped ammunition for his Springfield, and once among a pride of lions the instantaneous snickerty-snick reloading by his gunbearer came in handy as well as being for a moment a trifle awe-inspiring.

The 9.3 Brenneke seems to be less well known here than the Mauser development. It has relatively high velocity, as Brenneke cartridges usually do. Speed of the 275-grain bullet is listed at 2600 f. s. or a bit more.

Mannlicher Schoenauer's 9.5x57 is a little .375, in case length about midway between the .358 Winchester and .35 Whelen. It is slightly more powerful than the .358, for it starts a 270-grain bullet at 2250 f. s. Plenty of .375 bullets are available here, but jackets must be thin enough to permit expansion at velocities so far below those of the .375 Magnum. With British and European hunters the 9.5 has been popular. The little 20-inch Mannlicher for it can go as light as an actual 6½ pounds, and most of us over here would call it a plenty potent elk or moose gun. A variety of bullets was made for it overseas. Among them was a short, sharp spitzer with copper-tubed hollow point. This could break up quickly on game as light as deer, but it couldn't make the 9.5 a long-range rifle, by any means!

Between these calibers and the .458 Winchester a number of foreign rounds could fit in, if any seemed to be necessary. The 10.75x68 Mauser fires a .422 or .423-inch 347-grain bullet at 2200. In 73 mm. case length it's the .404 Jeffery Nitro Express, 400 grain at 2125, 300 grain at 2600. The .425 Westley Richards starts a 410-grain at 2250. Its fat, long-necked case has a rim much smaller than the head above the extracting groove and therefore doesn't need a magnum-sized bolt-face inlet.

The 11.2x60 is a real oldtimer. Its case is a modernized, rimless form of the Model 1871 black-powder design for "the first successful military bolt action, the Infanteriegewehr M. 71."* The big curved rim of the single-shot (later a repeater) cartridge was cut to standard Mauser 1888 8-mm. (or .30-06) size of about .469 inch, and an extracting cannelure turned in ahead of it. (This of course is the .425 Westley Richards system, too.) The head above the rim measures .511 inch.

The 11.2 jacketed bullet is of almost true .44 caliber, but its moderate weight and length and its rather low velocity disqualify it for use on Africa's heavy game. For hunting in America it is outmoded, but it was one of the early bigbores to be used in a good, reliable bolt action. It won some fame, and deserved it.

---

*Small Arms of the World, W. H. B. Smith, p. 63. Military Service Publishing Company, Harrisburg, Pa.

IN HIS work as a firearms and ammunition consultant Phil Sharpe built up The Philip B. Sharpe Research Laboratories at Emmitsburg, Maryland. The Sharpe & Hart Associates, Inc., is a different company, with which these writers have no connection. It features the Schultz & Larsen rifles and the 7x61 mm S&H brass.

Sharpe's friends of many years, Tom Florich and Bert Shay, are Associates, along with himself and Dick Hart. Tom Florich, Jr., has participated from time to time in their annual Schuetzenfests. Although Phil will use his lab facilities to help riflemen and handloaders, for a nominal fee, in research in rifles and ammunition, the bulk of the work that this crew has done has been largely pure research along lines that they agreed needed investigation.

Such opportunities as are offered in the way of a fine collection of all sorts of rifles, complete loading facilities and the shooting bench, Potter Counter (chronograph), Universal Receiver (pressure gun), as well their critical viewpoints as experienced riflemen and hunters make the opinions of Tom, Bert and Tom, Jr., of some worth to any reader of this book. Although each one of them will admit personal preferences in rifles and cartridges, they have proceeded always on the basis that the pay-off is the group on the target, the recorded velocity, and the pressure gun results.—H. M. S.

* * * *

This topic is probably the most controversial and misunderstood subject heatedly argued by riflemen. Fortunately the basic facts have been set forth plainly as the result of research, experiment and routine testing by Ordnance establishments and private plants concerned with the development and use of military or sporting rifles.

If personal preference, prejudices and particularized considerations are set aside, this short summary will help the guncrank in selecting the action type strong enough for the ballistic job he expects from his rifle. Time and extensive use have shown that any one of the bolt actions is strong enough for target, hunting or military purposes when it's used with the Arsenal or factory ammunition made for it and for the purpose in view. Therefore this question of strength has meaning primarily to the developer of new or wildcat cartridges, or to the experimenter with handloads.

The term *bolt action* in its broadest use includes the turn-bolts of the Mauser and Mannlicher types, the straight-pulls of the Mannlicher and Ross designs, and strictly speaking, some of the fairly modern gas-operated actions of the M 1 Garand, Tokarev, Gew '43 and similar autoloading rifles.

What Makes Strength?

The rifle parts connected with strength are the receiver, bolt, barrel, CARTRIDGE CASE, and the design of these parts.

CHAPTER 21

BOLT ACTION AND CARTRIDGE CASE STRENGTH

BY THOMAS C. FLORICH,
THOMAS C. FLORICH, JR.,
AND ALBERT J. E. SHAY

The materials used, the technique of manufacture, the exhaustive inspection and proof of the finished rifle, together virtually guarantee that normal usage, with normal ammunition, leaves a very definite assurance of great margins of safety. In fact, a "once over lightly" of the results of experience, experiment and tests of these parts discloses the fact that the strength built into them provides a margin of safety that only ill-considered judgment, flagrant mistakes, or plain carelessness can exceed.

Receivers. General Julian S. Hatcher, in his *Notebook,* cites tests on Springfield Arsenal production rifles in 1917, and these were the rifles we now speak of as "the old, unsafe, low numbered Springfields." Among these were some few that later studies indicated were "too hard" as a result of the heat treatment of that era used on them, but even these with proof rounds giving from 80,000 to 90,000 pounds per square inch did not fail. At 100,000 P. S. I. some of the "too hard" receivers did shatter. To the rifleman these figures indicate that even these single heat-treated, low-numbered receivers had about twice the strength that any normal load imposed on the receiver.

The General covers so many points of a basic nature of interest and value to the serious experimenter, and in such complete detail, that the latter is urged to familiarize himself with these highly ingenious tests. They are definitive, and so clearly commented on, that the non-technical-minded rifleman, too, will be enthralled by their completeness.

Bolts. The turn-bolt type actions were, with the advent of the 1898 Mauser and its descendants, made with a safety lug of one form or another. In his *Notebook* the General mentions the reduction of the front locking lugs on Springfield bolts to one-half, then one-quarter of their normal sizes and service rounds fired being held by the reduced lugs. Even more startling was the fact that complete removal of both front-locking lugs brought no failure with service ammunition, for the safety lug held. In the bolt the safety factor is much greater than in the old receivers, and much more than ample.

Barrels. Referring again to 1917 and 1918 production, General Hatcher's test established the fact that production line barrels withstood pressures of 130,000 P. S. I. In a special test, the barrel over the chamber was turned down to one-fifth of its normal thickness. Service rounds fired produced no apparent ill effects. These tests did show that the forging of the barrel blanks under wartime urgency was such that two or three per thousand had had the breech ends heated too high in forging, and these were weakened. By increasing the pressure of the proof cartridge to 75,000 P. S. I. the Arsenal men caught and eliminated these barrels in proof tests. The normal barrel's factor of safety is more than ample.

Cartridge Cases. Good cartridge brass withstands the pressures of normal rounds for which designed. Broadly considered, the older smokeless powder cases designed before the turn of the century handle about 40,000 P. S. I. The .30-30 and .30-40 fall into this class. More modern smokeless cases like the .30-06, .257, .220 and the Holland & Holland belted series handle 50,000 to 55,000 P. S. I. Above these pressures the brass starts to upset. In extreme instances of very high pressures this upsetting could be called *flowing*. If the upset or flow is, by the action's design, such that the gas gets into the action, the rifle may or may not fail.

The brass case is the weak link in the barrel-receiver-bolt-case chain of strength. Theoretically considered stronger, modern steel cases sometimes fail with normal pressures. Experience shows that the splits take place along the fine longitudinal scratches apparently incidental to the drawing operations. These scratches vary from those obvious to the naked eye, which of course are scrapped during inspections, to those so fine that they cannot be discovered by inspection although they result in case failure.

Design

At this point it becomes plain that the strength of actions is ample for pressures above those generated by the heaviest loads of normal types—armor piercing in military use, and high speed, heavy-bullet loadings of long-range target or hunting types. Tests and long usage have shown that variations of breeching design inherently offer varying degrees of gas-proof qualities. Simply stated, the more the case approaches complete enclosure—by the steel of the barrel, bolt and receiver—the less liable is gas to get into an action if a case fails, the more nearly gas-proof such an action type is. Parker O. Ackley's tests shortly after the end of World War II turned up the fact that a case completely enclosed, as in the M 38 or M 44* Japanese types, was virtually gas-proof. Conversely, when a lesser portion (Mauser or Mannlicher·), or greater portion (Springfield or Enfield), of the cartridge case · protruded or was unsupported by the barrel, bolt, and receiver, this gas-proof quality was, relatively speaking, lacking, when the rare, defective case was encountered.

These facts let the rifleman, with the help of the gunsmith, determine whether an action is suited to conversion from the original caliber to another cartridge

---

6.5 Japanese Rifles. The Model 1897 is also called "Thirty year" rifle, and a carbine in this model exists. Rather rare. It has separate bolt head as seen in Mannlicher rifles; magazine is of Mauser type. This rifle was quickly discarded by Japan as it was not foolproof. It could be fired without the bolt head being assembled to the bolt body, with disastrous effects. Hang it on the wall. Easily identified, as in addition to the two-piece bolt there is a large hook on the back of the bolt, the safety.

Model 1905, also called "Thirty-eighth year" rifle, has one-piece bolt resembling the Mauser's. This is the rifle commonly seen, and it has good ability to handle gas from a defective primer or case. Rifle has 31-inch barrel, carbine 18¼. There is a rarely seen rifle, made by Italy for the Japanese, which superficially resembles the Model 1905 but has the Carcano action (Mannlicher type two-piece bolt). Do not use it, as the bolt assembly of the Carcano is of questionable safety. This rare item is referred to as the "I type Japanese rifle."

Model 1911, also called the "Forty-fourth year" carbine, is of the Model 1905 action type and is identified by the 18.5-inch barrel and permanently attached bayonet which folds back under the barrel into the forearm. Model 1937, the "Ninety-seventh year" rifle, is the sniper's model: 1905 action with bolt handle turned down and a short scope fitted.

7.7 Japanese Rifles. Model 1939, the "Ninety-ninth year," has an action of the 1905 design. It is found in various barrel lengths. A good one has the excellent gas-proof quality of the 6.5 1905. Many, however, were made crudely. Some had cast receivers. The crude ones are not worth wasting time on. Those with cast receivers are death-traps and should not be fired under any circumstances.

This is as complete a summary as I can make, but as obscure as the subject of Japanese rifles is, it may be incomplete. T. C. F.

with higher operating pressure levels. The gunsmith's judgment can be verified by a Rockwell test of the receiver and bolt at the critical points, and this test, with the study of the gas-proof quality of the action in question, can resolve the final doubts of the action's suitability if the new cartridge is to be loaded above the conventionally accepted maximum of 55,000 P. S. I. This is at best an unwise liberty on the part of the handloader, but it can occur in experimental load development.

Mausers. The 1898 and later models are a good choice for any normal loadings, in any case the action will handle, if you are sure of the quality of the brass. If you unfortunately run into a soft-headed case (and it is rarely encountered) in a Mauser action, the gas that gets loose will raise the mischief. The bolt and receiver will hold, but what the loose gas does as a result of that unsupported portion of the case-head is a scandal. Although a case in the model 1924 Jugo-Slav-type Mauser action is more nearly enclosed than in the model 1898, it took three of us to open the bolt of one after firing a soft-headed case. In the 1898 we have personally seen: broken extractors, followers, and follower springs, floor-plates blown out, and the stock split around the magazine. The Mauser is strong, but far from gas-proof.

Mannlichers. The 1892 turn-bolts or later, which include the 1892 French, 1893 Roumanian and 1895 Dutch, all of which use a clip for *en bloc* insertion of the ammunition, as well as the 1903 Greek and 1905, 1908, 1923 and 1950 with the Schoenauer revolving-type magazine, all have separate bolt-heads bearing the locking lugs. These seem to be on a par with Mauser actions. The 1923 Mannlicher is like the 1903 or 1905 except that it takes longer cartridges, the 8x60 Magnum and 7x64 being examples, and both of these are loaded as heavily as our .30-06 and .270.

The amount of the case protruding is about the same as with the '98 Mauser. So the gas-proof qualities are similar to the Mauser's, and normal loadings are best in these Mannlichers.

The 1895 Austrian straight-pull Mannlicher is as strong as the Mannlicher types just described. However, its lack of camming, compared to that of turn-bolts, leaves something to be desired in seating and extracting cases. It is best left as is.

The model 1891 Italian Mannlicher-Carcano is in this group, but its weakness lies in a small lug that retains the firing pin and safety assemblies in the bolt. It seems wise to use this one as is—for 6.5 Italian ammunition only, for the breaking of this small lug would let the firing-pin assembly fly straight back into the shooter's face. This has happened.

The Russians' 1891 Nagant rifle and its later modifications are enough Mannlicher in bolt design to be considered here. Used with its own 7.62 Russian rimmed case the Russian has given no trouble, and the ballistics are in the .30-06 class. Some were con-

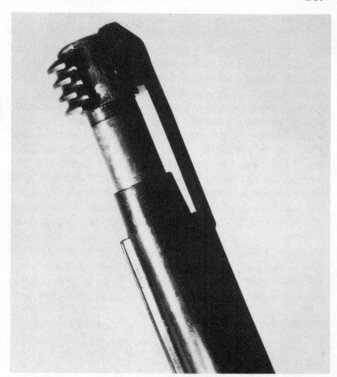

Note the white dot toward the back of the bolt. This is the pin inserted by Canadian gunsmiths after World War II, to preclude the improper or dangerous assembly of this model of Ross bolt. A simple modification, but effective. *Thomas C. Florich Photo.*

verted to 06 after World War I, and they were death-traps. Steer clear of such. During World War II some Russians were converted to handle 7.9x57 German ammunition. Never having seen one, we can't be sure of them. Leave them alone, for they may be and probably are as dangerous as the .30-06 Russians.

The breech end of the standard 7.62 Russian chamber is large enough to accommodate a cartridge whose diameter just above the rim is .483 to .484 inch. Add to that some .003- to .005-inch clearance, as is usual to avoid feeding problems with dirty or oversized rounds in a military rifle. If such a chamber is recut to take a 7.9x57 or .30-06 cartridge, both of which cartridge cases run not over .468 in diameter at the web (or head), there is some .020-inch excess room in the rear of the chamber, leaving the 7.9 or 06 case unsupported. Under such conditions the case expands and sometimes splits, allowing gas to get loose and wreck the rifle for sure, and possibly the shooter too. Incidentally, if the breech end of a 7.7 Japanese barrel is not shortened before rechambering to .30-06, a similar loose chamber results.

Short Model Lee-Enfield. These and the modernized type called the Number 4 rifle are normally classed as 40,000 P. S. I. actions. There is evidence that they will stand greater pressures. Use them as .303 only and you'll avoid the complications due to their somewhat thin barrels, complicated two-piece stocking systems, and rather lightly constructed actions.

Krag. The Danish 8-mm., Norwegian 6.5-mm., and our .30-40 Krags are considered to be in the 40,000 P. S. I. class. Strangely enough, the gas-proof quality —the case-head being almost entirely enclosed by the recessed bolt-face and barrel—is such that converted to low pressure (40,000 P. S. I.) smokeless cartridges they give excellent service. Some Springfield Arsenal Krags have turned up with "too hard" bolts, and hot loads have cracked the front lug, since they were heat treated by Springfield under the same technique used on low-numbered model 1903 rifles. A Rockwell test is indicated before any conversion. Used with normal .30-40 pressures and proper chambering, they give no trouble.

Ross. These in model 1905, 1910 and 1912 are amply strong, but the model 1910 and 1912 bolts can be assembled so that they don't lock in the receiver even though they appear to. In this condition they have

Closeup of a Model 1903 Springfield National Match receiver ring. The Arsenal's stamping is self-explanatory. Note the prick-punch mark on the ledge or shelf of the receiver ring, nearly in line with the "O" of the serial number. It indicates that Ordnance has rebarreled that receiver once. Note also the large aperture in the rear sight slide, at the top of the picture, that we oldsters favored to enable us to use the as-issued National Match rifles. The late and highly revered Al Woodworth, proof-master at Springfield Arsenal for years, worked it out; and this large No. 8 peep is "legal" under National Match rules. It's a lifesaver for "Grandpaw" on dull, misty or overcast days. The young chap of military age used to turn in his normally issued No. 6 peep for an even smaller No. 5, as it suited his vision better. *Thomas C. Florich Photo.*

killed shooters when the bolt blew straight back on firing. The Ross 1912 rifles sold since World War II show a hole in the top center of the bolt, with a pin inserted, and the end of the pin peened over. This was done to avoid the possibility of incorrect assembly, and these rifles are safe to use. As in all straight-pulls, the camming action is limited in insertion and extraction of cartridges, and in action during World War I they were troublesome in this respect when used by the Canadians in France.

Springfield. The model 1903, Springfield and Rock Island makes; the Enfield, Pattern 1914 in .303, and our own 1917 in .30-06; the Winchester models 54 and 70; the Newtons; and the Remington models 30, 30S and 720 are all lumped together, as the coned breech of the barrel (which contributes to their smooth feeding) allows ⅛ inch of the case to protrude when the action is closed. This protrusion, with a defective cartridge case, permits gas to get into the action. With receivers or bolts of the low numbered, too hard, Springfield or Rock Island type, gas might shatter a receiver or crack the locking lugs, though the safety lug will prevent the bolt from being blown out.

Not all low-numbered Springfield or Rock Island actions are "too hard." Seymour Griffin, who saw thousands pass through Griffin & Howe's plant over the years, developed a common-sense check before Rockwell tests were commonly used on rifle actions. In his experience, a much-used, low-numbered receiver that is too hard cracks off bits of the thin seat of the front guard screw on the under, forward portion of this slender seat, ahead of the recoil shoulder of the

Birdseye view (bird slightly tight) of the underside of the forward portion of a Model 1903 Springfield receiver ring. The big round hole with square threads is where the barrel is screwed in. The small hole at right angles to it is the seat for the front guard screw, drilled into the recoil lug. In the older low-numbered, "too-hard" receivers the thin guard-screw seat would sometimes show a chipping-away of this metal. In extremely hard low-numbered receivers, normal use has even cracked off the entire guard-screw seat and the whole recoil lug itself! In Remington and Smith-Corona Springfield receivers of World War II manufacture the recoil lug is square at the front, about twice as wide as this one, which is low numbered but shows the guard-screw hole intact. It was not too hard, and in fact it has worn out two Springfield barrels and is working on its third. This old action is sound, and it's as smooth as glass. *Thomas C. Florich Photo.*

receiver. In extremely hard low-numbered receivers, the whole seat of the front guard screw broke off. Some Springfields have had more than one replacement barrel shot out. If Ordnance replaced the original barrel, the receiver bears a prick-punch mark on the upper edge of the shelf on the upper portion of the right side of the receiver ring. If the original bolt was used, it was prick punched on the flat underside of the handle. Experience has shown that low-numbered receivers with no metal chipped off the front guard screw seat, bearing one or more prick-punch marks on the receiver, are safe to use with normal .30-06 loads. If there is any question, have it Rockwell tested, or better still, exchange it through the DCM for one that Ordnance knows is safe.

Enfield model 1917 rifles are usually strong. Some stamped *Eddystone* on the recevier have turned up, too hard, similar to some low numbered Springfields. A Rockwell test is indicated when any question exists. With normal ammunition the 54 and 70 Winchesters, the 30 and 30S Remingtons, and the Newtons (some of these last were too soft) have given no indication of trouble.

But for hot or experimental use the coned-end-type barrel can be safety breeched so the case-head is almost entirely enclosed, to improve its gas-proof qualities. The thoughtful gunsmiths like Sweeney, Gipson, MacFarland, and Dunlap, to name a few, have all worked to the minimizing of this case protrusion, not only on Springfields and Enfields, but Mausers as well, where experimental wildcats and high-pressure cartridges were involved. Such breeching when rebarreling an action seems wise if high working pressures are anticipated.

There remains a group of actions, the material and manufacture of which happen to be as strong as those mentioned before. In addition, the breeching is accomplished so as to completely enclose the case-head of the cartridge when the action is closed. The Remington models 721 and 722, the Schultz & Larsen M 54 J and 54 SS, the M-1 Garand, M-1 carbine, Tokarev, Gew 43, and the Japanese 6.5 mm. models 38 and 44 are such. In these, if a case fails, the gases are so confined that aside from the breaking of an extractor or ejector the gases cannot get out to damage the rest of the piece. These types are the experimenter's best choice, for cases do fail, and in these actions such instances are annoying but not particularly dangerous.

Precautions

Never forget that a breech-bolt, recoiling faster from a rifle grenade cartridge than it does from a ball cartridge, has cracked the upper rear surface of the Garand M-1 receiver. Although M-1 action and design are stronger than most others, no improvement in these factors is a guarantee against use showing up problems quite as serious as those that have trou-

bled us in the past, but of unanticipated types. Common sense demands that even in experimental work present limitations be departed from with GREAT CAUTION.

Considering the foregoing observations, common sense makes plain the few following points, which if followed will avoid the possible pitfalls in rebarrelling or remodeling a rifle for target, hunting, or experimental development.

1. Use any action only for cartridges that give pressures for which that action was designed with normal ammunition.

2. If the faintest question of an action's strength exists, consult a metallurgist or first-class gunsmith. A Rockwell test will give either gentleman concrete evidence for the advice you get from him. Be guided by his advice, regardless of the fact that an enthusiastic shooter of your acquaintance has got away with a

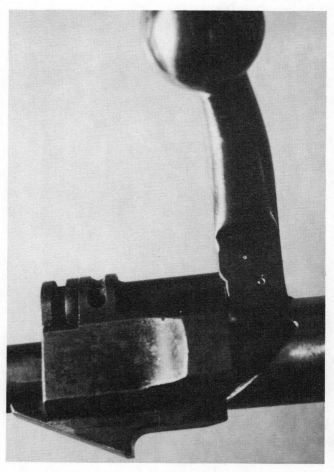

Upside-down view of the Springfield Model 1903 bolt handle. Note the figure 3, the manufacturing mark of interest only to Ordnance. The prick-punch crater above the 3 is the Ordnance mark indicating that this bolt is now assembled to an action rebarreled for the first time. Some bolt handles bear two or more prick-punch marks, indicating a second or still further rebarreling with that bolt. As any worn-out or questionable bolt is scrapped by Ordnance, the little crater says, in effect, "Ordnance found me okay for further use." *Thomas C. Florich Photo.*

practice that horrifies the metallurgist or capable gunsmith.

3. In handloading, stay within pressure limits of the brass. Only four cartridges were ever loaded by our plants or Arsenals to pressures approaching 55,000 P. S. I. This practice may be unavoidable for reasons of military requirements, but by a constant search for improved propellants, in three of these cartridges, powders giving the required velocities with pressures under 50,000 P. S. I. were developed and the ballisticians concerned were able to get a normal, nightmare-free night's sleep without sleeping pills.

In the fourth cartridge the results were not forthcoming; so the velocity was cut 100 f. s. to enable the pressures to be reduced from 55,000 P. S. I. to under 50,000. For that decision, made in our publicity-minded and highly competitive United States, we owe the plants sincere thanks. Stay under 50,000, as they do.

4. The safety breeching of actions to improve their gas-proof quality involves no removal of metal from the action parts concerned with action strength. But to lengthen an action for cartridges longer than it was designed for has in some conversions involved the removal of metal from the rear underside of the receiver ring, where it holds one of the locking lugs. Do not permit that. Buy a magnum action.

MOST born guncranks *unload* ammunition before they *re*load it. By unloading I mean dissection, breaking down the cartridge or shot-shell to see what makes it go boom and heave out the lead. That's instructive, and it can be done safely.

Paper shells are easy. Brass cartridges at first seem a hermetically sealed mystery. Then the kid finds that a steady, patient squeezing of the junction of brass and bullet breaks the crimp or the friction fit. By the time that his hands are sore from gripping the pliers the case starts to loosen and the bullet to work out. Later he may discover that a gentle tapping with a hammer around the junction performs the job faster.

Let's hope he doesn't, for some risk is involved. Various loading tools have collet bullet-puller attachments, and for quantity breakdown jobs—on old military ammo, for instance—they're fine. For single specimens in practically any caliber the hollow mallet of transparent plastic, sold by Guns, 4114 Fannis, Houston, Texas, does the work. It takes perhaps a minute to fit the case rim or the cannelure into the holder, secure assembly in the mallet, tap out the bullet, and put brass, bullet and powder into separate containers. Allow 10 seconds for looking over the products and admiring them. The bullet won't be marred, and the case will be perfectly usable, though now and then a rim is chewed by the holder if you haven't assembled the setup perfectly. This tool is *not* for rimfires; not safe, for the priming mixture is in the rim, which takes the force of the mallet blow.

So much for unloading. Now why do we handload, reload fired brass and sometimes charge brand-new cases with components of our own choosing?

Fitted Ammunition

We do it to fit the ammunition to the gun, the use, and the person, and who can say which tailoring job is most important?

Rifles are individuals, despite all the preciseness of modern manufacture. They do their best when treated as individuals. Often one that shoots indifferently with factory loads or with ill-fitted handloads steps into the minute of angle or better class when it's properly fed. More about this "in just one minute," as one of our often-listened-to commentators says.

Caliber use broadens when we handload for special purposes. From 25- to 50-foot gallery shooting to the longest range or the heaviest smack that rifle can deliver safely, this is the handloader's stretch. Also he can convert a rifle into an entirely different class. The .270, for instance, came out with a 130-grain bullet at 3160 f. s. original velocity, the .30-40 with a 220-grain at about 2000. Well-balanced 170- and 150-grain loads, respectively, *almost* put each caliber into the other's class, though there were some 32 years of active arms and ammo development between their birth dates.

We fit the person, ourselves, by choosing com-

CHAPTER 22

REWARDS
OF
HANDLOADING

ponents and balancing them to our needs. If we worship some certain make, we can use it! The product is distinctly our own—though for a long time we had best stick closely to recommended loads from a reliable source, starting low, always, and looking for pressure signs as we work up. Again, rifles are individuals: a heavy load safe in one might be disastrous in another of the same make and caliber, but with tighter bore and chamber. And how often do we need top loads and have to "work up"?

Now about that fitting of loads to the rifle. Some of us do it ourselves; some pay to have it done. I'll quote from one of Bert Shay's letters received last spring. Yes, he custom loads, also makes jacketed as well as cast bullets, and for me, they shoot. So they do for others I know.

"To my mind, custom loading means either of two things: If the customer orders 200 rounds of a given caliber, with specified bullet weight and powder charge and/or velocity, bullet type included, and the handloader produces them to specs, *that* might be called custom loading. However, I define custom loading as when the customer sends me the *gun* and asks me to tailor the *best* load that can be found for *that* gun, marking it specifically for that piece. You, being a prof of English, should be in a better position than I to vouch for the accuracy or inaccuracy of such a statement. [It's OK. Bert.]

"Most of the scribes, and Pharisees too, admit that each gun is an individual, a law unto itself. They also

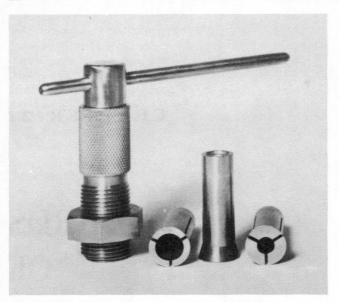

The RCBS collet-type bullet puller attachment for the bench tool.

admit (sometimes) that by handloading for it one gets the most out of its possibilities. But, do they go to the end of the line by saying that to do this *properly* the gun and the handloader must get acquainted real personal, be together a while and iron out their differences and idiosyncrasies? Naw, just have someone handload your ammo; *then* it will perform better. Bosh, folderol and—[Bert's an old Navy man]! Such small items as .010-inch seating *out* of the bullet farther than standard, 1.0 grain *more* or *less* powder, a change of primer or a different *make* of bullet of the same weight will make the difference between a run-of-the-mill load and *top* performance.

"There is no doubt that 'run-of-the-mill' handloads will about equal factory ammo in performance, sometimes by the very peculiarity of the change in components will do better, but this is accident. [Of course he knows that fired brass fits the chamber it comes from, isn't as undersize as new brass and therefore holds the bullet up more in line with the bore, but who can remember *everything* when he writes?] A different class of powder, or even a variation of the lot number, more often than not sets up different barrel vibrations which can either improve or disgust the gun, to say nothing of a change in velocity, which in many cases, a little bit *under* top permissible levels, produces surprising results. These are the things the handloader has to *find,* and he cannot do it with the gun 500 miles away. Neither is it within the bounds of reason that the prospective customer would care to pay for 20 rounds each of seven various makes of bullets and, let us say, three load variations of each, to find out for himself in shooting them. Such an assumption is preposterous.

"Occasionally an experienced handloader can diagnose a case without the gun, such as happened to me

six or seven years ago, when a budding handloader came to me about his Win. SS Hornet, I believe low-wall action. He said after he first got it from the gunsmith the first 500 rounds with a rather top load produced remarkable results, but after that his groups opened out to more than two inches, and what was the matter?

"I told him to reduce his load *one full grain* of Hercules 2400 and see. He came back two weeks later—and this is one case in a thousand, where the fellow *admits* it—and told me that it *worked,* that the gun went back to its original X-ring propensities."

COMPONENTS

From here on to the end of the chapter this will be brief. Sharpe's and Naramore's books, others too, including Mattern's out-of-print *Handloading Ammunition,* give the details and should be read, Belding & Mull, Ideal and Speer handbooks are small, inexpensive, but helpful, and the NRA *Rifleman* reprints on individual cartridges are excellent. But maybe in a chapter's span we can take in most of the cheerful points of the scenery and slow down for the dangerous curves and crossings, too.

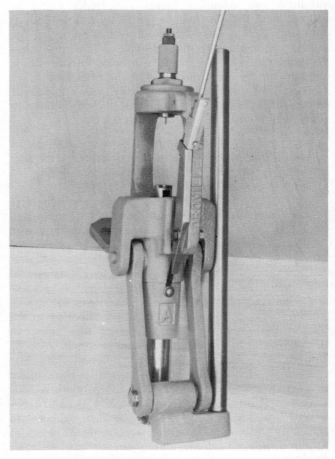

The RCBS Model A loading press is one of those that have the strength for making jacketed bullets.

Bullets

The primer has been called the heart of the cartridge, and it is, in reliability and to an almost incalculable extent in accuracy. But we have excellent primers—and all kinds of bullets.

Jacketed. Bench-resters will tell you that the bullet is the critical component, right now. They are correct. They like only a few makes because no more (except for their own manufacture in dies such as the RCBS) have given them the accuracy they need.

But there is constant competition, and who can say that X and Y makes will be at the top of the pile even next year? Minute of angle is good, useful hunting accuracy, even for varmints unless we try shots too long to be justified—justified for most of us, at least. Here is a list, not complete, of custom-jacketed bullets made by the comparatively small firms (or individuals in the business) that supply the hunter and sometimes the bencher: Sierra, Jordan, Shay, Hornady, Herter, Barnes, Nosler, Ackley, Speer, Pearson, Sisk, Baldwin—the last in .22 precision only. Add the imported Norma and our big-four commercials.

Most of their bullets come in soft- or hollow-point hunting style, and there are a few full jacketed. Sisk has made them in .22 for 20-odd years, I reckon, and a new one is a 100-grain .25 for turkey shooting, from E. L. Gardner, Box 1682, Rockford, Ill. There are others.

For varmint hunting don't overlook the Norma Lugers—93-grain .30 and 116-grain 9-mm. soft points—if they fit your rifle and you're willing to sacrifice some accuracy and ranging power by using a short, fragile bullet that's almost certain not to ricochet at distances up to 200 yards, let's say. That is beyond its accuracy range, I'm afraid, unless your rifle has a special slow twist and short throat.

A quite different example is the Sierra 130-grain hollow point .30, a target bullet too, with long bearing that helps in 10-inch twists, and a *steep* sharp point to pay for the bearing. Factories make some varmint bullets of both super-light and standard weights, but most handloaders buy custom stuff, often less expensive, often but *not always* better.

About big game bullets you can hear anything. Factories continually experiment, make little changes that they hope are for the better, and I suspect that some custom makers do, too. A certain brand and type at first was condemned as being too fragile; now it's called too tough. Perfectly natural from all viewpoints!

Well, no one could count *all* the variables, I suppose. Animals are individuals, some of the same species larger, healthier than others, or more gritty, and like us they have their moods. Caught unaware, they are more easily killed than when fleeing or fighting for their lives. Point and angle of bullet strike vary; so do ranges. A bullet may be expanded, or broken apart, or tipped by brush before it strikes the game.

Lead bullets, restricted to short ranges, were and are pretty consistent in penetration and expansion. Wrap one up in copper, gilding metal or steel and you have a variable. The old soft points aren't the big favorites just because they're old. Cap or hollow or drill the point and you have another variable. This doesn't mean that such bullets can't be reliable. The discontinued Western 180-grain .30, Open Point Expanding, for instance, was one of the best we ever had, but no type has won universal endorsement. Probably the capped or the hollow points are the high-velocity bullets of the future because there's no exposed lead to upset from inertia, or even flow away, when the start is super-fast. Ever notice those little whirls of lead-smear on paper targets? It doesn't always require a full velocity .22-.250 or .220 Swift to produce them at 100 yards and more. If they aren't lead, what are they? They don't invariably mean that good hunting accuracy is gone, either. And all that bullets have to do to shoot into or close to each other's prints is to be uniform in the way they act.

For deep penetration in our heaviest American game there are several designs. Barnes uses jacket thickness meant for specific jobs. The Nosler bullet is double-cored, with lead ahead of and behind the partition of gilding metal, integral with the outside jacket. It extends the idea of the German RWS H-jacket, still made, which has a rolled V or fold in the middle, *not* dividing the lead core. In a sense the Remington Corelokt and Peters *Inner* Belted, with thick gilding mid-section, use this method.

Double jackets (German D-mantle) have been tried, with success. An extra jacket can cover the point, or reinforce the main jacket. A varied form was the discontinued Peters *Outer* Belted. It had a tough, rather long ring of reinforcement ahead of the bore-bearing part, but the point was exposed.

The DWM Strong-Jacket is extremely thick at the base and along the lower sides, and the Ackley bullet carries on this system, to a higher degree. It has a long, solid base of pure copper, less brittle than gilding and, some of us are convinced, less fouling. At any rate, copper is a splendid jacket material, as was known in the early days of the 6-mm. Lee, when that bullet, sensationally fast at the time, was about the only commercial job in pure copper. The old tin wash—"white bullets"—did resist verdigris corruption in storage better than plain copper or gilding do now. It didn't make as pretty a bullet, however!

Bert Shay has built heavy bullets for deep penetration, including a 200-grain 7 mm. He is typical of too few, those who have the time and the sense for patient experiment.

Lead and Alloy. Don't overlook the factory offerings, the few that are left. Sixgun slugs may fit your rifle barrel and make buying a mold unnecessary unless you plan to do a good deal of small shooting. The .32 S&W short and long and Colt New Police

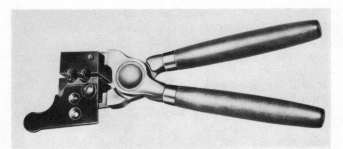

Lyman-Ideal double-cavity-bullet mould.

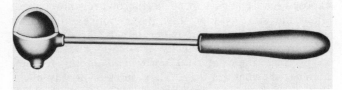

Lyman-Ideal lead dipper

A simple but precise cast-bullet sizer by Belding & Mull.

suit some .30-caliber barrels for gallery and small-game shooting, and almost any .35 can use .38 S&W or New Police, .38 Special and .357 Magnum lead. Also for short-range use there are the .25-20-86 and .32-20-100. The sixgun .45s are about .005 inch too small for most .45 caliber rifles.

Custom and cast bullets can be had, and Helmer Romness, Wanamingo, Minn., has had a mold rental service for many years, at least to NRA members. Target revolver shooters have found that swaging their bullets helps to reduce lead fouling at the throat of the rifling, but rifles (and auto-pistols) usually set the bullet so close to the rifling that a good barrel seldom is smitten by this terrible plague.

Many of us cast our own. The three most common makes of molds just now are the Ideal, Cramer or Saeco, and Hensley & Gibbs. I like a single-cavity mold for uniformity, but when the metal is at the right heat, well fluxed, and comes out of the bottom of an electric melting pot with plenty of weight up top, then the double, triple and gang molds do save time. However, I have plenty of time when I cast or handload. If not, I wait until I have. These things are

part of the hobby and I'm sorry when I get done.

Potter, Saeco, and others make melting pots, and Potter has an old, proved lead tester that tells the hardness of the alloy. That is one way; another is to buy the pure metals, lead and tin—or antimony for hardening, if you like. A third way is to use your thumb-nail. It works, for one batch of bullets, but hardly for exact duplication! Some barrels, especially of black-powder original type, were choosy when smokeless was used. And some target shots used to load and fire bullets in the order in which they'd cast them.

Knockout Mold Glaze comes from Price-Driscoll Corp., 520-R Fifth Avenue, New York 36. It makes bullets drop easily from molds, should eliminate tapping. It also gives anti-rust protection, but so does an oiled bullet in the cavity. And such protection has to be cleaned out thoroughly before we cast smooth, full bullets. Lighter fuel helps to get the oil out.

Pacific, Star, Ideal, Saeco, Wadman and others make lubricator-sizers, very handy. They size the cast bullet almost perfectly round, or should, and of a diameter to fill the rifling grooves. Some loaders prefer a *cast* bullet as much as .003 inch oversize for a .30 or .32, say, so it'll squeeze more lubricant out of the grooves when it's fired. Now a good many of us like them of exact rifling diameter, or a shade over. Tom Florich has found that a *jacketed* bullet only .0015 inch oversize can boost pressure about 5000 pounds per square inch, and that's too much. Worse, if it's extremely tough-jacketed.

Cast bullets can be lubricated by dipping them into melted grease, or better by standing them in a flat pan and pouring the grease round them. Simply peeling a bit of lube off an Ideal, Ipco or other stick and pressing it into the grooves with your forefinger *can* produce five-shot-string minute-of-angle accuracy, or contribute to it, for you learn to do this uniformly. You have to wash your hands after most bullet-greasing jobs, anyway, and I guess that feminine readers—if any—will scent the reluctant tone in that remark.

Bert Shay suggests stiff water-pump grease for extreme economy, Mobilubricant No. 6 or Texaco No. 5, and he's used them as ingredients in his own lubes, one third each of beeswax, paraffin, and water pump. The latter is not to be melted when it's used straight.

He says he's failed to notice any erosion from carbon particles in graphite grease wads at high velocity with jacketed bullets. I've used them only at moderate speeds, and generally with cast bullets. Sometimes these wads, which seem to stick pretty reliably to a bullet's base, make greasing the grooves of a cast bullet entirely unnecessary. They are a great help, supplementing greased grooves, when a slightly undersize cast bullet has to be used, with smokeless powder, in a barrel that isn't as smoothly throated as it should be. (Many black-powder rifles used undersize bullets as a matter of routine, and the quick blow of that powder expanded the soft lead to fill the rifling grooves.) A lot of people think that grease wads lengthen bore life with jacketed bullets. Bert is one of them, and he also recommends them as an aid in getting the best gas-check accuracy.

Gas checks seem to have been originated by Ideal, at least in this country. These shallow cups, usually of copper, protect the bullet base from fusion at reasonably high velocities, *if* the base is contained in the case neck. Black-powder express rifles reached about the limit for plain-base lead bullets. The .45-125-300 Winchester had a velocity figure of 1633 f. s. and was probably the highest, in standard loadings. Its bullet was soft, we'd say now, 1 part tin to 16 of lead, *and* the rifling twist was one turn in 36 inches. With faster spins and smaller calibers we can't go much over 1600 or 1700 f. s., using plain-base cast bullets, unless we use zinc or other metals that produce light, extremely hard bullets.

With gas checks we can go higher. About as fast as I've sent 'em is 2450 f. s., accuracy still good. Deeper gas checks, practically semi-jackets, and some other methods let us speed them up. Hensley & Gibbs molds machined for a coiled-wire stiffening of the lead are one way, and good. A *Rifleman* story (November, '55, p. 71) by James C. McCarrier told of using copper tubing instead. Sounds good. Wire-wound bullets aren't new, but they nearly dropped out of sight for 30 years or so. They're OK.

Gas checks in many calibers still come from Ideal, and Warner's, 2510 Pleasant Valley, Altoona, Pa., has been in business at least since depression times. Sierra and others also make them, and the Hornady type is unusual. Its cup is thickest at the top of the sidewall; so when the bullet and check are run through the sizer—hand- or machine-operated—that top is forced into the lead, crimped on. I've often found them, always still attached, on bullets that had pancaked in a backstop. The usual check is meant to drop off 15 feet or so from the muzzle—fire over fresh snow, to find it—and generally it does fall away. If some hang on and some don't, you haven't uniformity. But this trouble is rare. Gas checks have been used upside down behind plain-based bullets, and they worked. If it weren't for the extra variable that a gas check introduces, any accuracy hunter would be for it, no matter how theoretically his mind worked. It permits good velocities, and a wide range in velocity *choice* when we're looking for accuracy. If we had bench-rest competitions for centerfires with cast bullets only, probably the gas-check variety would win. Plain-base bullets demand the most careful casting and handling. Bases mustn't be dented or nicked. Horrible thought! Yes, I know that benchers are careful about everything that goes on, into or out of a rifle. The rest of us can learn from them, and should.

Gas-check bullets can be sent at far lower speeds than jacketed stuff; they have less bore resistance. Use the latter for whisper loads and they may not even burble out the end of the barrel. No fooling. And squib loads are fun.

So much fun that a lot of us go to considerable effort to work them up—or down, rather. In most .22s it's possible to keep the report well below that of the .22 long-rifle high-speed and still get pretty fair accuracy. Above .25, unless we use a round ball, we get more racket, and curiously, perhaps, more than equivalent loads give in cartridges designed to handle such charges. I asked Bert about this.

"I *think* I can logically answer the question," he replied, "about the noise of light loads in the large cases. I've found it all my life in '06, .30-40 and .30-30, plus a host of others, including my .25 Roberts. The whole thing sums up to the fact that there is *too much space* for the small amount of powder, and it all burns in the case, with not enough *resistance* from the bullet for good combustion. This is noticeable with 2.5 grs. of Bull [Hercules Bullseye, a pistol powder] in the .25, 3.0 in the 06 and Krag, and 2.5 in the .30-30 with 100- to 120-gr. lead. It is easily demonstrated by loading the *same load* in a .32-20 case, and in a barrel of the *same* length. There is not near the report, the small case causing the powder to burn or be consumed as the bullet progresses."

There's a saying that cast bullets "put a fine polish on a bore," and so they do. At least we get our shooting with a tiny fraction of the wear that jacketed bullets produce. This is not, really, because the lead alloy is softer and less abrasive, but because it upsets more readily, and more completely, to seal the bore against the hot powder gases trying to cut past it, and our powder charges are lighter. But the "polish" must be somewhat in the manner of wear, for even .22 rimfire and shotgun barrels wear out from firing, or would if they got enough of it, even with the right kind of care. And I'll readily admit that cleaning rods wear bores, too. Sometimes too much a-plenty. But cast bullets extend the rifle's usefulness, even to nearly if not quite all-round service.

A "no-sight-adjustment" reduced load, not a squib, can be put up, sometimes, with a cast bullet. A jacketed one may shorten the time of trial and error. This load, for small game or target, hits at 50 yards where the full-charge, big-game selection prints at 100, 150, 200, or some other chosen zeroing range. The old factory Short Range loads in .25-35, .25-36, .30-30, .30-40, .30-03, .303 Savage, .32-40, .38-55 and .45-70 had light bullets, usually of lead, though some were metal cased. If you held on the head of a sitting grouse you were liable to clip his toenails. We use light bullets, too, for most reduced loads, and often they're of lead, but by juggling weight and velocity, barrel time and barrel vibration (up and down), we sometimes can make up that no sight adjustment charge. Heavy barrels and fairly small calibers help. But after all, flat shooting up to 50 yards isn't for a squib load, and we don't want much midrange rise with this practical low-power charge.

The first cast bullet fired through a bore that's been fouled by jacketed stuff (and not cleaned) usually goes wild, as wild as almost any first bullet goes from an oiled bore. (In the latter respect some rifles are better than others, even apparently perfect, and thin oil, lightly applied, helps.) Small-game shooting with a bullet usually is precision work. Although the second and succeeding bullets generally get down to business, a squirrel or grouse seldom waits for us to fire fouling shots. So perhaps we'd better choose between hunting just one kind of game at a time and using a jacketed bullet. It can be sent pretty slowly, and one mild report sometimes doesn't disturb some kinds of big game a bit. At low enough speed an expanding bullet doesn't expand. Only a few rifle sizes come in full-jacketed, and the auto-pistol bullets of that type are so short and light that they don't offer much chance of success in this special handloading effort. But barrels vary so much that almost anything is worth trying.

Primers

We have just two standard sizes left, and a good thing, too! The .210-inch is large, the .175 small. The tiny No. 0 for .22 Extra Long Maynard* is gone; so is Frankford Arsenal's .205-inch .45 Automatic, also the .225-inch Winchester No. 225 for early non-mercuric, non-corrosive .30-06, .33 and other big sizes.

The corrosive and mercuric primers are about gone, too, except in Winchester-Western .30-06 and .300 Magnum match loads, and some black powder blanks, which are likely to be non-mercuric, at least.

Mercury makes brass brittle and unsafe, on the very first discharge, unless black powder lies ahead of it to coat the brass with fouling before the mercury can get in. Or at least I've been able to use this type of primers with much-reloaded, but cleaned, black-powder cases. Otherwise, we put mercuric primers into a pond or into a coal furnace, shutting the door right away. It was the potassium chlorate ingredient that made the old corrosive primers cause rust. The salt left on the steel attracted moisture, and with ease after the sun had gone under the hill.

Our American primers are at a high state of quality; they've got over the hump of conversion to non-mercuric and non-corrosive blessedness. In fact, they seem to have kept up with improvements in bullet manufacture, and that's to say a lot.

There are two strengths in each size, pistol and rifle, and some makes are stronger than others, or reputed so to be not long ago. At times we can inter-

*This came in two case lengths, the .22-8-45 in 1 5/32 inches, the .22-10-45 in 1¼.

change types, and at times we ought to, though not for handgun use. Over-strong primers *can* damage a sixgun's recoil plate, and possibly an automatic pistol's breech face, and their heavy cups often cause misfires, hangfires, or at least ragged ignition. For *light* loads in modern rifles, even some loads with jacketed bullets, pistol primers increase accuracy. They don't over-ignite fast burning powders and make shots string up and down. (Old, deteriorated rifle primers can cause this dispersion, too.) But their thin cups can be pierced by even a properly shaped centerfire firing pin, hemispherical at the point, if pressures go too high. They could be dangerous in tubular magazines, except in low-power cartridges like the .38-40 and .44-40, whose wide bullet flats scarcely contact them. I'd hesitate to use them in a black-powder rifle with poorly shaped or fitted firing pin, unless the load was mighty light. But their coolness is easy on old, soft steel.

Small pistol and rifle primers *may* not vary much in strength or thickness. Until the two types are officially made one—and there's been talk of that— I prefer to believe that they do vary, and to use them accordingly. Pressures change a good bit between .32 Short Colt and .222 Remington!

NRA members can buy large primers, either strength, at much reduced prices from the DCM, at least when supplies are available to that office. This is done to encourage marksmanship practice, and you bet it does. Generally they are made by a commercial outfit, though you might get some Frankford Arsenal. All are good.

Powders

First of all, read the loading book or booklet critically. Mistakes get into print with fiendish frequency, as any editor, copyreader or writer knows. If a load doesn't sound logical, reduce it plenty if it's heavy. We began to get progressive-burning powders about 1914. Their steadier push adds to velocity, but they aren't foolproof.

The books tell you what powders to use with almost any cartridge, and you may be amazed, as I am, at the versatility of some case designs, new and old. Mostly, the tables refer to commercial or "canister" powders, though the Government .30 caliber, 4895, almost always is listed, too. In strength it's *about* like Du Pont 3031, but different lots vary; they aren't held as strictly to standard as commercial lots are. Its accuracy can be and often is superb, but you stand a better chance of getting exact duplication if you stick to commercial numbers or names. It's a bit like buying .22 rimfire match ammunition: the lot number is important.

B. E. Hodgdon, Merriam, Kans., makes a specialty of supplying salvaged Government powders, including Western Ball, the sort that looks and feels like tiny, slightly lubricated birdshot, an advanced type of propellant. The 4831 service powder is much like

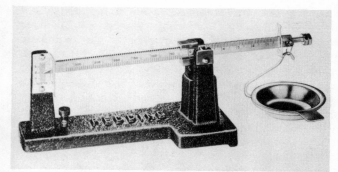

Powder scale by Redding-Hunter, Inc.

Du Pont 4350 canister. Paul Von Rosenburg, in P. O. Ackley's good little handbook, tells of No. 4814 machine gun powder being used in Barnes' .288 Supreme blown-out magnum. Ninety grains drove a 200-grain bullet at 3025 f. s. A special cartridge and load, but it has its uses. Barnes makes both custom bullets and custom rifles, and he's done a lot of experimenting and hunting.

Some of us use black-powder rifles with straight or duplex charges. "Duplex" ordinarily means the loading of two granulations of smokeless powder, a system that Elmer Keith used for high velocities with permissible pressure: one powder sparks the other.

RCBS powder measure.

He also employed flash tubes, joined to the primer pocket's flash hole, to burn charges from front to back. This was and is for the expert only, a person with machine tools, optical instruments, and judgment. His results were good.

But there's also the duplex loading of black powder, priming with smokeless in the bottom of the case, held there by the snug black charge above it. Little cartridges like the .25-20 and .32-20 can use as much as 25 percent by bulk (black powder) measure of Du Pont *bulk* smokeless shotgun powder, the only make of the kind still left. Larger cartridges must use less, say 10 or perhaps 15 percent, always starting low. Remember that storage under the usual black-powder compression can pulverize this soft powder, as well as black, and then pressures go up. It's better to use less compression.

Du Pont 4759 and the pistol powders are hard-grained, and the latter are vastly more powerful, weight for weight. An excellent charge for my .40-50 bottleneck Remington is four grains' bulk measure, about 2½ grains' weight, of 4759 over a large pistol primer and under 40 grains of FFG black. More 4759 upsets case heads, in time, and in this rifle they're practically everlasting (as the special, thick old Ideal "Everlasting" were) with standard black-powder loads. The load shoots cleanly enough for all-day

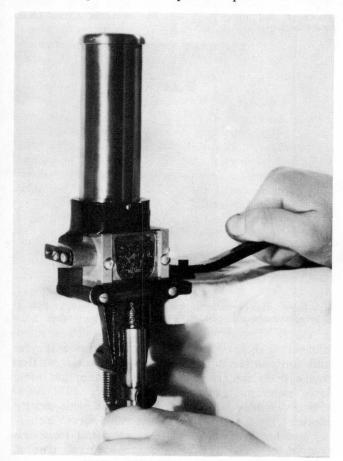

Belding & Mull powder measure.

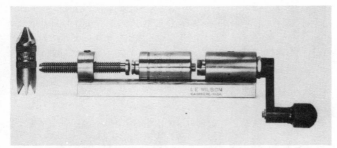

Wilson's Universal trimmer serves different cases with only the shell-holder used varying from size to size. Included is the hand-operated little tool at left, to remove burrs on inside or outside of case mouths.

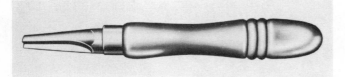

Lyman-Ideal case-mouth chamfering reamer.

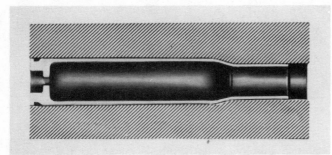

Cross section of case and Lyman-Ideal full-length resizing die.

Die and drift by Wilson for full-length case resizing. A knock-out rod comes with sets like this, the Lyman-Ideal, and others.

Wilson case-length gauge to detect any shoulder-to-base shortness that would produce excess headspace of brass in the rifle's chamber. It spots over-long case bodies, too.

hunting, and I was glad to arrive at it. Moderately sharp report is *one* indication of its moderate pressure.

Yes, FFG granulation is for pistol cartridges and rifle loads up to about .44-40. The very fine FFFFG is for .22 WCF and .32 S&W Short, the coarse FG for big cartridges, above about 40 grains' charge. But FFG seems to burn best in that rifle, and its faster rate of burning isn't serious, in this instance, for a lighter than standard bullet helps to keep pressure down—260 grains instead of the old 265, 285 and 296 for the regulation dose of 50 grains FG, black powder only.

Pretty stiff priming loads of pistol powder have been recommended, and they shoot cleanly, perhaps even making it unnecessary to wash cases with soap or detergent if they're to be stored for some time and not ruined by corrosion when we look at them again. For me, in large and small cases, a less condensed powder has worked better, keeping pressures low and maintaining accuracy during the day's shooting. After my Du Pont No. 80 was gone, 4759 did well. And there's still Du Pont bulk shotgun, which, by the way, must *not* be used in caseful charges for rifle or pistol. It's considerably more compact than

the very old Du Pont No. 1, which was made for bulk-for-bulk loading of black-powder cartridges. That was easy to use, and not easy to misuse, but some early single shots and the big-capacity 1876 Winchester series of calibers were better off with straight black.

Some handloaders weigh every charge of smokeless powder for any cartridge, and some, equally careful, never own a set of scales. They check their measures

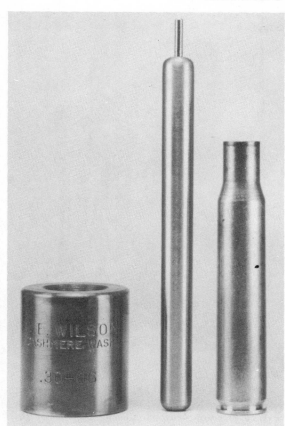

This Wilson punch-and-base set removes crimped-in fired primers common in Government cases—and in some old commercial lots, too. The point is made extra strong to do this job.

by another fellow's scales—the druggist's, maybe and they don't use top loads. So they do all right, and they often get bench-rest accuracy, too. Herter, Webster, Redding, and Pacific are some of the scales' names, and I think it was Bellows who introduced the scale damper. A paddle in a bucket of oil or other thick liquid cuts down the teetering time.

Among measures are the Belding & Mull, Ideal, P & O by Aurand's, RCBS, Redding, Herter, Hollywood, and Martin. Check any of them by scales: the maker would want you to. For speeding the measure-and-scale partnership the Little Dripper dribbles kernels of powder into the scale pan. You set the measure low, put in what it gives you, and fill the pan to balance, holding your breath and staring glassily until you get used to the job. The Big Dripper is motor-driven. For fast powder-charging the Mez-U-Rite tray holds a slew of loads, and capacity runs from 10 to 70 grains. It's accurate enough for safety, except for top loads, which always should be weighed, and you can check the charges by eye.

This pays, even when the cases are fairly well filled. A flashlight helps. Du Pont 4759 is a fine mid-range and small-cartridge powder. I like it a lot, no longer sigh for the No. 80 it replaced, but in the .22-caliber drop-tube of my measure it sometimes hangs up if

charges go over 10 grains—weight, not black-powder or bulk measure. In handloading you learn the little ways of the tools that help you, but always you're careful. What's the rush?

Brass

We get good stuff from the factories and arsenals, though in reloading we do well to stick to name brands unless the cases are specially made for us, and then the maker usually tells us their limits and how to use them, or can if we ask. We inspect all cases for neck-splits and signs of incipient rupture, crosswise marks near the base, and blackened when the situation is highly serious.

Slope-shouldered brass lengthens in use, even in

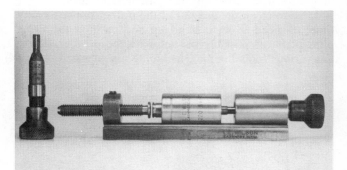

Wilson's inside neck reamer, shown by itself at the left, is used on cases that have had their neck walls thickened by the forward flow of brass in some high-velocity combinations. It is used with the case-neck *trimmer* setup.

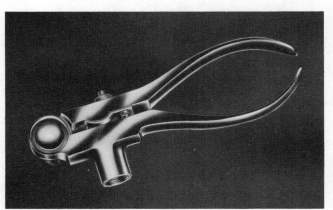

Lyman-Ideal No. 310 tong tool, without the dies.

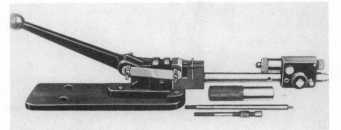

Belding & Mull 28 tool can be bolted down—or laid on a table or even held in the lap except when seating bullets in primed and powder-charged cases. Then it should be fastened or held upright.

tight bolt actions and single shots. Neck trimming for correct length, and full-length resizing, may come in; the former often does. Personally, I avoid full-length when brass is plentiful, though for no good reason, as I never put up more than maximum loads, and durn few of max. Wilson, Smiley, Grigsby, and Forster make some of the fine case trimmers on the market. A file, carefully used, can substitute up to minute-of-angle accuracy, at times. Then you chamfer the mouth inside and out to save your clothes and to make bullet seating easy and free from lead-picking. Over-long cases make extraction hard, sometimes, and always they boost pressures. Gauges like Wilson's and others show up cases that are too long or too short. I think that Wilson was first to provide a reamer for case-necks that were thick from the forward flow of brass.

I like to clean the ash out of the primer pockets every time; no need to let it build up and cushion the firing pin's blow, or possibly contaminate the powder. There are various tools for that, including a sharpened nail or

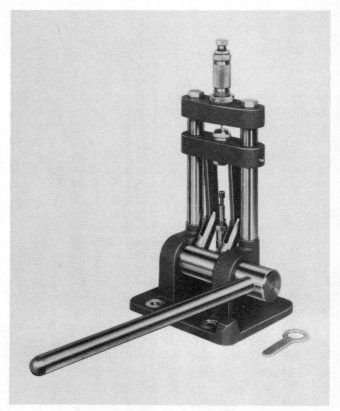

The C-H Precision Magnum loading press is of the "H" type.

Vickerman straightline bullet-seating die for bench tools using ⅞-inch, 14-thread dies, such as the Pacific, Universal, Hollywood, and Easton. Picture shows .220 Swift in seated position, and at right a shell-holder extension, in this instance for the .22 Hornet. Each size die—.22, 6 mm., etc.—will seat bullets for all cartridges in that caliber, and extensions are inexpensive.

a wood sliver, and an inexpensive one comes from Kuharsky Bros., 2425-R W. 12th St., Erie, Pa. It's a steel brush in a tube; use it by hand if you wish. Wilson's primer pocket reamer is one of the standards for a different job, taking the burr off pockets that were originally crimped over the primer. That system is OK for military use, but it never should have been applied to any sporting ammunition unless it was to go to the tropics.

Graphite eases neck-sizing, though light oil, lightly applied, is an old standby. Thin cases, like some of the little rifle sizes, take no great effort to neck-size, but a lubricant prolongs the life of dies. Graphite has the advantage of getting inside the necks, and of doing no harm there.

Case forming for wildcats is an art in itself and in the arguments that sprout up around it. Hydraulic pressure has been used but it's more fun to shoot a rifle. The light charges don't give much bore wear. A few grains of pistol powder and a cast bullet usually will do it, but true rimless cases must be swelled to a complete fit, so that they'll headspace correctly. Oiling them helps, but this is NOT for anything like full charges. Finally you get the right load and are happy. One way of forming, described in the *Rifleman*, is to use Bullseye under corn meal and a card wad. Always go easy with pistol powders, in pistols or in rifles. Bert

Shay sometimes seats a bullet out far enough to need force in chambering the cartridge, and a lighter than normal powder charge fire-forms the brass.

EQUIPMENT

Handloading popularity has revived so much in the last 10 years that to list and describe the available tools takes time and space in respectable amounts. When you're done, another new make or type almost surely will be on the market. That's one way of keeping young and alert, or of going nuts.

It's a good thing for our Country that handloading *is* popular. She needs marksmen.

Tong Tools

Only one seems to be left in manufacture, the Lyman-Ideal 310. It's a survival of many that appeared through the long development of handiness and precision: Ideal, Winchester, Smith & Wesson, Marlin, Modern-Bond and others, some made by the companies named, some probably made for them. The Bond was popular during the revival of shooting that followed World War I, though at least in my experience it didn't hold the cases as snugly and truly as the Ideal No. 3 and No. 10 (for rimless brass, that one) of that time.

The 310 is revolutionized, takes various-sized dies about as obligingly as any heavy bench tool, and it

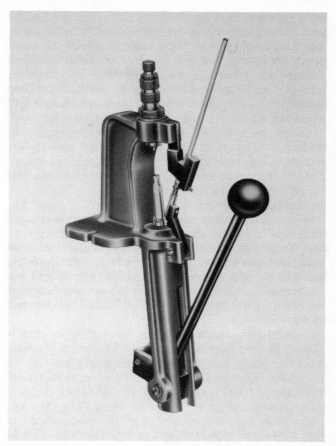

Lyman-Ideal Comet press is also of "C" type. Note the long, thin tube of the primer feed.

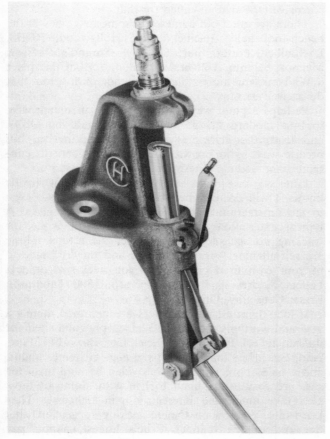

The C-H Precision Super is of the "C" type.

will put up minute of-angle-ammunition. The push and pull do not seem to quite as straight as with big, heavy tools, and there may be some uneven, lopsided case mouths as a result. I haven't noticed it with this tool as I have with some early models of this general type, the "nut-cracker."

But many old tong tools still do precision work, and these comparatively light ones get around. I've never seen a heavy bench tool in camp—maybe didn't go to the right places—but I've seen the nut-cracker there. We also see ancient molds dropping fine bullets in spite of the fact that their halves aren't hinged and floating for easy, sure lineup in the modern manner. They are aligned with a pin and the workmanship that went into them.

Bench Tools

This type must be at least a 100-to-1 favorite now, times being good, pocket money plentiful. So many old, new, and future ones are in the sky that choice is a bewildering chore to the beginner. Let him remember, if he pleases, that care, common sense, and the rather easily developed skill of operation have more to do with precision production than the brand name or price tag on the tool. Lot's more!

One of the least expensive and lightest to handle is

the Belding & Mull No. 28, faster than the old 26, but you'll notice that some loaders buy the 26 bullet seater for *that* particular job. These tools are called "straight-line," and so they are, considering their relatively small size and short leverage. The 26 seater is as straight as a fly-line with a trout at the end of the leader. You drop the bullet in, press it down with the hand plunger—or use a mallet for the tight resistance of jacketed stuff. Since the die is a close fit for both bullet and case, the bullet has to go in straight. This is an old idea for the perfectionists. It stems from Sharps, Remington, Niedner and other oldtimers. Other modern varieties include the Wilson and the Vickerman.

But the heavy bench tools seat bullets truly, too. Their enormous leverage helps to reduce the human variation in almost all operations except primer seating. There the sensitiveness that a light, lap- or table-held tool permits is a help. Perhaps. Bench-resters use the big machinery, and their product is and has to be the best. If they mashed a primer and broke up its pellet charge they'd go to bed with a temperature and an ice-pack.

Some heavy bench tools are of "H" type, double armed, like the Dunbar, and the C & H, some of which load shot-shells, too, that skeet and trap gobble up so fast. The Echo and Herter M. 3 Super have typical "C"-shaped frames, and the big Herter M. 81 Super is of double-barrel type, with two rams. The M. 243 Super is of turret type, with five rifle-case stations to speed production. A sixth one is for shot-shells. (These tools are being named pretty much at random; a book

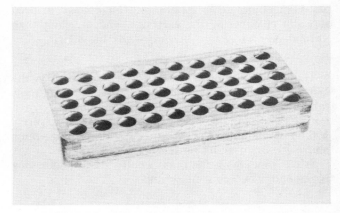

Loading blocks, one for empty, one for powder-charged cases, help the handloader to make sure that each case gets its ration of propellant, and no more. (Naturally, handloading is not for dreamy moments.) This block came from Belding & Mull.

could be written on loading equipment alone.)

Along the line of fast production, primer feeds were devised long ago for many bench tools. They're automatic and they save time, which is important to a person loading for a club or any large shooting outfit. But it pays to inspect *each* primer and see if its anvil and pellet are present and properly located. Defective ones are rare; so are opportunities at game, for lots of us. And again, primer pockets need cleaning, though the corrosive type seldom called for that.

There are great old names and some new ones in the bench-tool field: Pacific, Ideal, Hollywood, RCBS, Lachmiller, Potter, Star, Grigsby, Aurand's P & O, Meepos, Schmitt, Universal, Easton, Jordan, Harpster & Williams, and more still. Home-made outfits, too, that do as well as any.

Perhaps a good way is to start with an inexpensive tool—a modern or old nut-cracker would be OK—and learn the principles in the most primitive, but precise way. Who knows, you might not care to continue handloading. There have been such creatures.

Later one can go on and spend the money where he knows it will do him, personally, the most good, even to the satisfaction that a certain brand name gives! A typical extra that seems decidedly worth while for tracking up accuracy is the Bohler die setups. These are self-aligning, spring actuated, and they're made to fit your own fired cases when you neck-size or seat bullets. Address is Bohler Die Shop, 1500 Thompson Road, Coos Bay, Ore.

If loading and living quarters are cramped there's a new and worthy extra, a 12x32 inch plywood shelf for the bench tool. Huntington Bench Co., Box 4144, Portland, Ore. Handloading keeps a man at home, nights, and a wife appreciates that, provided he, and provided she, are easy and human to live with. Some of those girls take unaffected interest in gun tinkering. They learn fast. Pretty soon they're making suggestions that the lord of the manor, if he's honest, admits are sensible.

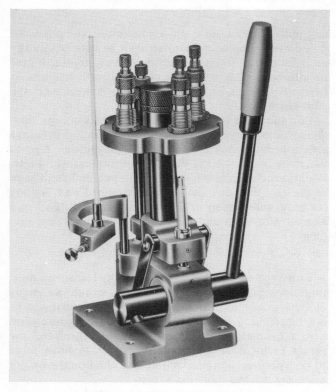

Lyman-Ideal turret-type loading press.

SIGHTS are the most critical equipment that goes on a rifle, for they so largely determine our accuracy of firing. And sight choice can be as persnickerty as rifle choice itself, for good reasons or for no reasons except to satisfy prejudice or eliminate the exercise of thought. Any personal opinions in this chapter are here for illustration.

We all vary in our perfection of vision. Some of us can't shoot a decent score with any iron sights, and people like that are helped more than others in actually *seeing* woods game, if they use a proper scope. Even if Fortune, that jade, is kind and they sight down the guide's arm and hand at a standing deer they may not see him unless they know what to look for. With a woods glass to help, the eye becomes an eye, the ear an ear, and that weathered old barkless branch an antler, by gosh!

Iron Sights

These are the least expensive, they are usually rugged—though not foolproof—and for some close-up work they can be the quickest because they "fit" almost any modern-stocked rifle. A scope fits a rifle that's made for it, but not too many standard models are, except some target rifles and some bolt action sporters.

Target Sights

Some of them are excellent for hunting, especially varmint or any long range shooting, when the light is good. But most of them live up to their name and are strictly for the black-and-white.

Rear Sights. In this class, unfortunately, lie most of the factory-made, inexpensive peeps issued on boys' rifles, light .22 rimfires. Their apertures are too small, and the steel circumference too large, for hunting when light is poor or shots must be taken fast. But they are more shootable than the best open rear sights, two-to-one better on target group size and proportionately in hunting, we could say, and most bolt guns have them as an extra. The average kid would far prefer to spend much more—or have it spent on him—and get a magazine reservoir of extra rounds, and the reason is obvious. Someone failed to train that kid, and to explain what is and isn't, about good shooting.

Special iron-sight matches in bigbore and smallbore have brought our target peeps to a high state of near-perfection. The as-issued Garand, for instance, has a dandy, the best rear peep ever standardized on a military rifle, and yet it's for the most serious business, too. Most bigbore match shooters use a type that led up to the M1 peep, a receiver sight just ahead of the bolt handle—if they shoot a hand-operated instead of the semi-automatic rifle. The Lyman 48 and Redfield 70 are typical. They stand about nine inches from the eye in offhand, and plenty far ahead for eye safety in prone.

Smallbore shooters generally pay more, though the 48 type does well on target paper and certainly makes for smooth handling if the match .22 ever goes to the

woods. The .22's extension peep can practically bung the eyebrow in prone, but no harm's done, because of the light tap of recoil. Usually there's back-and-forth adjustable mounting, anyway. Examples are the old Redfield Olympic, Lyman 524 High-Low, and the newer Redfield International. With the 524 you can get either iron or glass height mounting because of the two apertures, one above and one below the transverse cross-bar that carries windage adjustment. "Scope height" irons often aren't that: sometimes you can leave the tall iron front sight in place and never see it in the field of the scope!

At this writing the International is the most advanced, modern target peep regularly made in this country. The adjustment knobs are big, and spring-loaded for even tension between them and the adjusting screws and the slide. The Sure-X disc costs extra, clicks off each .004-inch change of aperture size to meet different light conditions. No new idea. The Merit iris shutter disc has been around for maybe a generation, and the Clark De luxe gives choice of rose, yellow, green, blue, and clear light filters. Williams makes a "Twilight" disc with a white reflector ring; could help in some lights. Usually it is large-apertured, meant for the hunter to use in dim light when, possibly, he couldn't see the thin rim of the Lyman type.

"The Tube Sight," by George D. Stidworthy, Jr., in the October '55 *Rifleman* covers this type of rear peep in clear, full fashion. Briefly, there are four main modern makes, Unertl, Fecker, Lyman, and Freeland, all precise, necessarily rather expensive. They stand as high as most target scopes and their exactness of adjustment is comparable, or superior.

Some receiver sights fail to give precisely what we ask for in windage or elevation, time and again, for years of steady use. Ordinarily such defects would be noticed only by a rather skilled shooter who has at least normal vision.

But the tube sight is for supreme accuracy, with irons, and it can give it when the front sight is located properly, centered in the view through the tube. The Unertl and Fecker have built-in diaphragms to eliminate reflections. The Lyman uses Polaroid material at the rear, adjustable to control light, and the front sight should have a Polaroid insert. These are long-tubed sights—17 inches or so, like a rather short target scope —and they give a tunnel effect in aiming. The Freeland has a short, large-diameter tube, stands a bit higher than the usual target scope, and its field is wide, without the tunnel effect. For this reason it's safer for the shooter who at times cross-fires on another competitor's target and loses points and possibly a pound of good-will in doing so. But the tube sight lets us know, by target blur, when we aren't lining up our sights properly, and some would call that its big advantage.

It is certainly big enough to matter in competition!

Front Sights. The new Redfield International front is an alloy rig for lightness in spite of the great size and 3½-inch length of its shading hood. In military style it's much shorter, with no enlarged rear on its hood. Even in rapid fire and poor (target shooting)

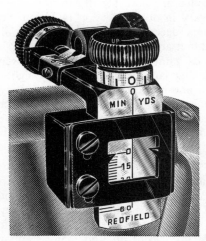

Redfield 70, similar style. Rounded, coin-slot knobs are for a hunting sight, and most models have them available on choice.

light it should be easy and fast to pick up. Green, amber and clear inserts come with these sights, and cross-hairs if they're wanted.

Redfield Olympic is smaller, less expensive, and the 63 to 68 series cost still less, though they're fine, precise jobs. Lyman's 77 and the 17-A are old standbys, with the Griffin & Howe Clear Vision and C V Junior, Freeland's Supreme and Junior, and probably others making up the list. They have to be good or they aren't around long.

Various-sized apertures and flat-topped post inserts come with the sights—even the very economically priced Mossberg match .22 has a fair selection—and a more or less useless round bead generally tags along.

Lyman 48 with target knobs for windage and elevation.

Redfield International receiver sight.

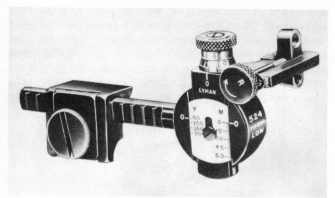

Lyman 524 receiver sight.

Merit iris shutter disc.

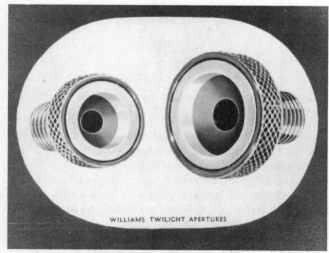

WILLIAMS TWILIGHT APERTURES

Williams twilight apertures are for hunting in dim light, and some eyes could use them a little earlier or later in the day than the thin-rimmed aperture of equal size. The last target shooter to fire, some winter afternoon on the range, might welcome either, especially in the rapid-fire stages.

An aperture rings the bullseye, more or less white showing, to suit the eye and the available light. Some of us overdo the use of small apertures, as trials may prove. Posts serve in training for service rifle shooting and in the too few rapid-fire courses we fire. Some prefer them for slow-fire scoring. Plastic inserts improve definition for some of us.

Hunting Sights

"Iron" hunting sights still go on the majority of rifles, and occasionally from thoughtful choice. Most of them are strong, and most rifles are stocked for their low plane. In some close cover they are the best, or at least so considered by a lot of us. They seldom are quite useless in fog or in heavy rain or snow, and they

Redfield International front sight.

Redfield Olympic front.

Lyman detachable 77, with scope-block type of base, and the screws to anchor the base to the barrel.

Lyman 17-A for Springfield .22 or .30.

Redfield 63, detachable, showing dovetail and scope-block type bases.

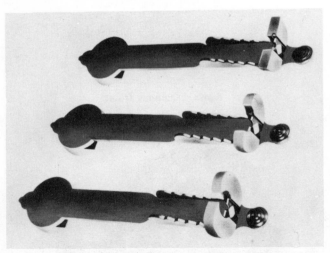

Well-made open rear sights, from flat-top to full buckhorn, by Christy Gun Works.

needn't cost much. In saddle or canoe travel they're handy.

Rear Sights. It is not for lack of good advice and convincing proof that open sights still ride on the majority of rifles! Maybe the average human bulls along in accustomed ways without much thought—though I'm not by nature a pessimist.

The V or U notch open sight is close to the barrel, rugged, and out of the way. Usually it's there when it's wanted, and it's seldom plugged with snow, rain or weed-seed. You aim better with it than with no rear sight at all! Changing light strikes it unevenly and your shots go wide, but close-up you aren't liable to miss from this cause. In a hurry, you fail to pull the front sight down into the notch, or even with the bar if it's a flat-top, and your shots go high. For quick work some like a notchless bar, with maybe a vertical white line

Marble folding open sight, an old favorite like the Lyman.

Marble Flexible tang peep sight is held in battery by a spring. Two sizes of aperture come with it.

Lyman 1-A is locked upright by a small lever on the left side.

pointing up the center. In deliberate fire it's impossible always to see the same amount of front beyond any open rear; so elevation varies.

It *can* do good shooting under the best conditions. I've seen one or two juniors (who hadn't the price of a peep) lay their five 50-foot shots into an area equivalent to 9-ring cutting. The groups weren't centered over the 10 because of the hammer-and-drift windage "adjustment" of these sights and their almost equally crude elevation. In older, much more experienced hands the open rear sight does some fair shooting—sometimes excellent snapshooting at close ranges—but it wins no matches of importance and most seasoned hunters have no use for it except as a folding spare if the peep or scope takes a vacation. The majority of open spares for the scoped rifle are set far out on the barrel, nice for a person plagued with far-sightedness but giving too short a radius between sights. This magnifies aiming error, which is plenty, anyway.

The best iron rear sights are peeps, and there are

two worthwhile kinds. One goes on the tang or small of the stock, the other on the receiver. The Redfield 70 LH on the Savage 99 is a cross—good sight, though.

Marble and Lyman make tang peeps for most rifles except the bolt guns, and I remember a Lyman 103 with special mounting that was just swell on the tang of my first Model 52. Like the later 144 it had sharp wind and el adjustments, but about all the tang peeps available now have only the latter, and not micrometer, minute-of-angle metering, either.* You get windage by driving the front sight to and fro or by shimming up one side of the rear sight's base. Work it out carefully, on an overcast day—for even good irons are affected somewhat by sunlight unless they're shaded or perfectly blacked. When it's found, leave this windage alone.

Tang peeps put the aperture closer to the eye than hunting type receiver sights do. Offhand, the figures average about six vs. nine inches, much less in prone or sitting, or when firing uphill. People who were thoroughly used to them employed these sights safely on rifles of rather heavy recoil, the .45 and .50 black powder arms, and they'd not hesitate to mount one on a .348 that fitted them. But a shooter unaccustomed to this type has no business with one on a rifle much above the .35 Rem in power. People have been seriously injured by recoiling tang peeps. I saw just one minor injury, and regretted it. Yes, I'd warned that fellow who wanted to try my .33, but he knew better. Only his eyelid was laid open.

The receiver sight puts the aperture up in the safety zone, though some experienced riflemen like an extension, .22 target-type receiver peep on a light-recoiling bolt gun such as an 8½-pound Swift or Roberts. It gives the quickness of the close-up but not too close tang sight, and the long-sight radius, too.

The standard hunting receiver sight is a dandy and I love it, except when I can use a tang peep or a scope. Adjustments are usually precise and durable. In general that sight wears longer than the tang type, which sooner or later develops play—exceptions are few—and must be held in battery, subconsciously, unfailingly, with the thumb. Since my thumb always crosses the stock I have no trouble in the uses a tang sight is meant for.

Some people object to seeing light under the receiver sight's crossbar. One of many simple gun-factory designs eliminated that. Those issue peeps on .218, .219 and .348 Winchester lever guns were rather good. Inletted into the breech-block, they certainly lay low. After a time they developed a shimmy, but that could be peened out. The Rice peep (Marcelona, Mich.) lies pretty low at the rear of Krag and Enfield

*The Lyman 52-A, described on page 185 of 1958 *Gun Digest,* does have windage adjustment, but it is at the top of the stem, not in the base as on 103 and 144, a location that might be awkward in woods use. Yet some of us would gladly put up with that drawback.

Redfield 80 with target knobs.

Redfield 80 with coin-slot "Hunter" knobs.

Williams 5D sight on Marlin 56 Levermatic.

receivers, has a big, woods-useful aperture, and is
moderate in weight, size and cost. (Some hunting
peeps weigh ¼ pound.) Adjustments are for zeroing
and letting-alone, not for the Wimbledon Match. A
simple, rugged hunting sight.

We want more latitude of elevation and even of
wind, and easily read and recorded settings, if we're
to use our rifle year-'round, with handloads of widely
varying power for a multitude of purposes. Lyman,
Redfield and Williams make most of the hunting type
receiver peeps. The Williams "Fool-Proof" does its
durnedest to keep all meddlers except those equipped
with a screwdriver from changing our wind and el to
see if the sight'll *really* move, and it's flat on top.
So are some Redfield and Lyman models. The sight
of a huge elevation knob sticking up neighborly to
the aperture disturbs some hunters, or it must, for
you see it mentioned in print. Coin-slotted knobs are
small and rounded, OK if you have the change.

Though I was lucky in having a peep on my first
rifle, and most of the others, no such bonanza is necessary. It takes an attentive person maybe three or four
short sessions to learn to look through (not for or at)
the peephole. Centering the front sight in the circle
comes naturally, and the bigger the circle, within reason, the better.

In target work (why do we fool writers call it
"work"?) with small-apertured peeps you do align the
sights consciously, with one final, farewell look just
before you give the trigger the ease-off that may fire
the shot. Or may not: that's the system for the beginner; never know when the rifle will fire. But in
hunting we usually employ a scope for long range,
deliberate shooting. The peep is mostly for fast
"work." Its thin rim is a ghostly blur, and meant to
be. Makes the front sight more prominent by contrast.

Form the habit of centering the front sight the
same way every time. The flat-topped post comes just
to the imaginary diameter line of the peep; its very
tip is centered in that line. In the same way a round
bead can be centered, though for me it's simpler to
center the whole bead, disregarding and scarcely seeing the thin stem on which it's mounted.

Front Sights. Hunting front sights come in many
makes and in two generally useful shapes, flat-top
and round bead. Others have been tried, even a
gilded aperture, the old Marble Vickers-Maxim. The
barleycorn or inverted V is used overseas, even yet.
If the point is blunt enough it needn't fade out.

In parts of our West a plain black front is good,
maybe undercut in Marine Corps style to sharpen
definition. On the typically overcast late fall days in
the East there's a hassle over three main colors of
bead or tip—red, ivory, and the "gold" of copper or
its alloy.

Ivory *will* show up almost anywhere in iron-sight
shooting light, though it can't equal a bright, low-
power scope. Even across snow it's no terrific handi-

Lyman ivory bead front sights

Redfield Sourdough with narrow base to give freeway to a
front sight hood.

Marble Sheard gold bead front sight.

cap, though there the red or gold is better. In some
lights red plastic looks black, but you generally see
the whole of the bead or tip, not only the lightward
side, and can aim as straight as with any other color.
Age may darken it, but it seems well to keep oil away
from it, just as from ivory, which goes yellow or tan
from the contact. Gold is more rugged, though sometimes invisible in dim light where ivory or red would
show. With reasonable care you don't break off an
ivory or plastic bead, and the soft gold isn't at all
vulnerable, *by comparison.* You can black the gold
for target, or for hunting in bright light, and you can
put the flame to the others too, just once, and no
return!

The Redfield Sourdough flat-topped, gold-tipped
front is a favorite with many of the well informed. It
uses an old trick, the slanting forward of the eyeward
face to catch the last glow of light. Saves the trouble
of putting a file on it. Another light-grabber is the
King, with chromium mirror throwing the illumination, if there is any at all, up where it helps.

Any bead or post should offer a flat surface to the
eye, and most of them do, except some factory-issue
stuff, soft and easy to file. This reduces the error of
aim, for light that hits the sunward side of a tapered
bead makes us shoot away from that light, usually.

One sight still made is all wrong, in theory. That
Marble Sheard bead is pointed, toward the eye. This
was the kind that went on Stewart Edward White's
.405 for his first African trip. It did the work: quick
aim, close-up, and in dim thickets and jungle. But
White always taught, and practiced, going light, and
next time the Springfield and the big double relieved

The Mossberg 4-power scope rides nice and low. Peep sight is shown swung out to the side.

Weaver B-4 with Tip-Off mount on Savage Model 6 .22 autoloader. This too is a handy combination, easy on or off.

the .405 from travel. This man had remarkably fine vision—may never have used a scope for any shooting —and he was one of the best short- and long-range shots that ever visited Africa. From what's been told, he used a sling only as a carry-strap!

For some kinds of open shooting the hooded target front—post, preferably, though maybe here that orphan bead insert could be worth its weight!—will do fairly well. Whitening the post (or bead) might help. The short hood or cover of some hunting front sights is really a protector, useful for travel. But occasionally it can help in game shooting. It darkens a red, ivory or gold bead and therefore adds something to precision, under a bright light, just as the detachable pinhole peep disc of a tang or receiver sight helps. In most hunting we want neither one. Remember that shading the bead calls for less elevation, usually. The old rifle range rule says, "When lights go up, sights go [must go] up; when lights go down, sights go down."

There used to be combination fronts: bead and post, large and small bead, ivory and gold, pinhead and post, maybe others. Few if any are still made, and to get them exactly of the correct heights, requiring no sight readjustment, would take some doing. Through the occasional perverseness of chance you'd have the wrong one up, at any rate.

Remember, please, that some of these comments

are, and frequently have to be, entirely personal. A shooter with better vision (maybe 95 percent of us) might get different reactions and results from a choice that has suited me. It pays to find out what we need, and a rifle range, hunting camp, or gun store is a good place to do it, looking over and through the sights. But it's best to find out months before you visit camp as a hunter!

SCOPE SIGHTS

These sharpen our vision, somewhat equalizing us, and have other obvious advantages. Included are those that mean so much to the hunter, knowing that his target is game, not a human, and sizing up its legal or merely desirable standing.

We have three general types, target, varmint, and big-game scopes. They are more or less interchangeable, and some riflemen would say that any scope is always better than an iron set. To a considerable extent they're right, except when heavy fog, rain or snow dims the picture.

Target Scopes

Their field of view is limited; so they're unsuited to most kinds of hunting except for varmints that aren't on a fast move. Most of them are heavy, and their mounts are a bit bunglesome in carrying. They have a reputation for being delicate, but then, any

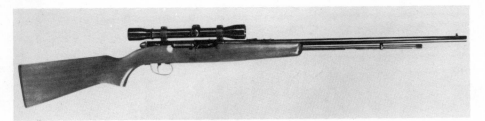

Stith dovetail scope bands fit on Tip-Off grooved receivers and come in ¾-, ⅞-, and 1-inch scope-tube diameters.

Lyman Junior Targetspot.

set of rifle sights must be handled carefully if it's to do the work it was made for.

The Scopes. A good target scope is one of the most satisfying of all rifle accessories. It brings out the accuracy of the piece, is invaluable for testing loads, and helps us improve our marksmanship. Few if any of us can shoot as well with the best of iron sights.

It is relatively cumbersome—long, heavy and high-mounted. Unless the rifle is stocked for it, a comb-raiser like the Stam or Jostam cheek pad is necessary for the best work. But the scope is easy to remove, and then we have our familiar old iron-sight rifle, changed only by the two unobtrusive little bases or blocks for the scope's elaborate mounts. Bases cost little, though they must be installed correctly—no simple job—and one good scope can go by turns on practically any rifle we own.

The kid can start with the least expensive glass, such as a Mossberg, Weaver, or Pan-Technics (Pan-Technics, Ltd., Encinatas, Calif.). Mounts are simple, and the base commonly no more than an already grooved receiver top. As soon as the youngster learns his scope he'll shoot better. Cost at present will be

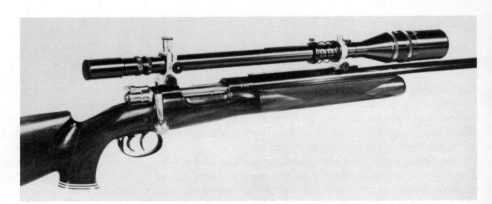

Unertl 2-inch targetscope has great light-gathering power in 10x, and adequate in higher magnifications. This one is mounted on a varmint rifle.

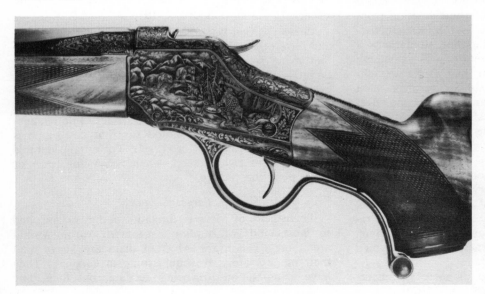

Sometimes a custom rifle barrel is half-ribbed to provide bases for target or hunting scope-mount blocks. This Griffin & Howe remodeled Winchester single shot has the half-rib for mounting an open sight that the customer wanted. I don't think that the rib destroyed the beautiful lines of the rifle, do you?

about $10. The beginner in serious target shooting will want to pay more for superior optical qualities, finer adjustments, and, probably, more power.

But power can be overdone. Though a scope "brings the target closer" according to its actual magnification, six times closer, or ten, or what-have-you, it also multiplies our tremor of holding by the same amount. On well-lighted 50-foot indoor ranges a good 10X glass lets us spot every shothole, easily. And 10X wobble is disconcerting enough to the beginner when he goes into offhand for the first time—and for the first few weeks of that effort. Many seasoned indoor shooters prefer a 15X scope, or thereabout, and I've wondered why, when so few of them—so pathetically few—get or take much chance to shoot outdoors at 50 to 200 yard ranges.

Scope weight counts in offhand work, usually on the wrong side of the ledger until we've become accustomed to it—and want it. At the same time the tyro is learning to be calm about that magnified weave and tremor, and how to dampen it. And, dog-gone it, we're trying to make the game *attractive* to beginners, aren't we? so that we'll have more U. S. riflemen. There's much to be said for a 10X target scope if it's to serve almost all-round, on the centerfire varmint rifle, too.

But the greater powers help—to some extent and at almost any range—when we've learned to use them. At present they go up to 30X in some if not all of the popular makes: Fecker, Lyman, Litschert, and Unertl. Thirty is mostly a bench-rester's power (with the 20s and 20-odds still doing well), but lots of prone shooters can use it with advantage under good conditions. Sometimes, oddly enough, it does as well or better against mirage as a lower magnification. The main thing, I believe, is not to jump to great powers too soon. Scopes can be raised in power by substituting a different eye-piece. But sometimes

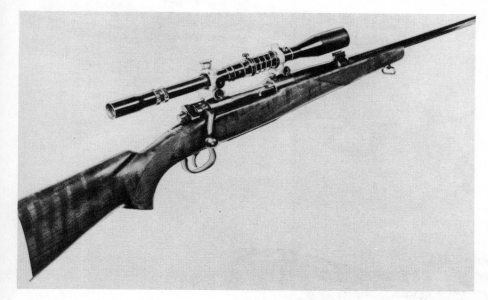

This Fecker Woodchucker scope (it comes in 4½, 5½, or 7 power) is using a short inter-base mounting to give the shooter the full field of the glass in offhand firing.

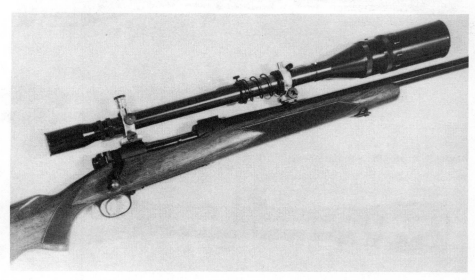

Unertl Ultra Varmint scope gives choice between 8, 10, and 12x, and like the Fecker outfit shown, it has a recoil spring to bring the glass back into battery after it has slid forward under recoil to prevent injury to the reticle. Objective cell is graduated for easy focusing.

Short-coupled mounting, plus the dehorned adjustment knobs, makes this Unertl-Winchester outfit pretty smooth to carry in the meadows.

Weaver K-10 on an engraved 52B Winchester sporter. Bolt handle is slightly altered to permit low mounting of the glass.

Weatherby 2¾ to 10x variable power.

Bushnell 8 or 10x varmint scope.

Leupold & Stevens 8x Westerner.

Unertl's Condor 6x is typical of scopes used for both varmint and long-range big-game shooting.

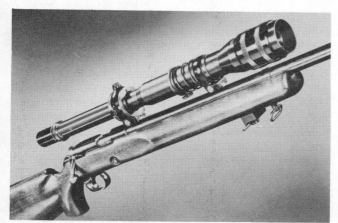

Bausch & Lomb Balvar, 6 to 24x, in B&L mounts designed for it.

a sadder, wiser purchaser goes down the scale, instead. If his home range is windswept, there's one reason.

No scope—or any rifle and its equipment of any sort—should be bought in a hurry. One of the great advantages of belonging to a rifle club is that members let you look over their various sorts of shooting stuff, and sometimes let you try it. This doesn't mean that the chronic borrower is necessarily the best-loved of all members.

Their Mounts. Mounts are of micrometer type, and the rear one clicks for quarter-minute wind and elevation, as a rule. Focusing for different ranges is done on the scope itself, of course, and it's necessary to get clarity and avoid eye-strain, exactly as with a binocular. A printed guide tells the settings, which usually are approximate; must be. Getting out parallax, apparent movement of cross-hairs as the eye moves

back and forth over the scope's *lateral* eye relief, must be worked out for the glass as an individual. That is what it is, just like a rifle.

Varmint Scopes

Almost any good scope will serve, though the target glass may be too heavy, too long, and of too great power at the cost of wide field and good light-gathering qualities. Its crosshairs, ideal for prone or bench, may be so fine that they become invisible under some field conditions.

The hunting scope may lack the needed power, and its cross-hairs—if it uses them instead of a post or some other reticle—may be too coarse. Adjustments for wind and el may not be exact enough for the precision work that long-range varmint shooting is.

So we have a *comparatively* new classification of glass sight, the varmint scope.

The Scopes. Objective-end attachments for low-power hunting scopes are one way out, and generally satisfactory, too. The Litschert is typical, 6, 8 and 10 powers. Fortunately they do not shorten eye relief: you still cheek the stock at the same familiar place. Neither do they magnify the reticle, but they do narrow the field, which means little unless we take running shots.

The old Belding & Mull scopes—they had their own special B&M mounts—carried big lenses. They gave lots of field, light, and resolving power. Literally they were eye-openers in their time.

Modern varmint scopes advance the idea. They are of two general types: "target" and "hunting," we could call them.

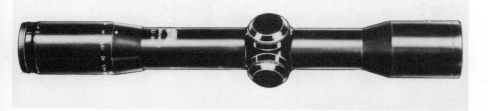

36 m/m objective Hensoldt Diavari D, 1½ to 6x by ½-power stages. Eyepiece is marked for each graduation and has click stops.

Esquire variable, 2½ to 8x.

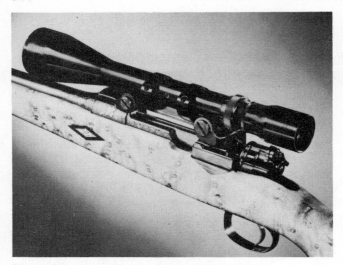

Bausch & Lomb variable, 2½ to 8x.

A typical slim, light but efficient 2½x scope, the Weaver J-25.

The first rides in target-style mounts, with similar precise adjustments. Fecker, Unertl, and the big Bausch & Lomb Balvar, 6- to 24-power adjustable, are examples. However, the typical varmint scope often is rather short, though big lenses call for high mounting.

The second type has internal adjustments, usually, and is less snaggy on the tote. (Not all varmint hunters travel exclusively by car, though this *is* one sort of hunting that the man who simply must take it

easy can follow and enjoy.) Weaver K8 and K10 scopes are of this sort, moderate in price. One of my friends, experienced, critical, and possessing, I should think, a full ton of shooting equipment, swears by his K10. Bushnell 8 and 10 Scopechief, Hensoldt Ziel-Dialyt 8, Pecar 8, V-IIS Vari-Power 4 to 10, Weatherby 2¾ to 10, and so on: to try to list them all now and hope to be complete in a few months' time would be impossible. Six-powers (and below) are liked, too, such as Unertl's Condor, Norman-Ford's Texan Sniper and Kollmorgen's Bear Cub. (Don't they choose these names well? Make your mouth water.)

Power can be low but effective because the resolving ability is so good, thanks to the brightness given by big lenses. So many combinations of light-gathering power and magnification are available that you wonder how a chuck or fox or coyote has a chance to survive, hidden in grass or brush. But resolving power has prevented tragic accidents. A brown-haired kid's head does *not* look like a chuck when you use a good scope.

Variable Powers. Maybe a note on vari-powers would fit in here. Perhaps they're the universal scope of the future, though a friend of mine never used the 2¾ X setting on his Weaver KV for years after he'd got accustomed to the 5X magnification and its smaller field. Even when deer-hunting he stuck to the 5, and did perfectly all right.

The Bausch & Lomb 6 to 24 is the big example just now, and plenty big, 36 ounces. Windage and elevation are in its rear mount, target style, and ring-shaped. The reticle stays the same apparent size, doesn't coarsen as power goes up, for the cross-hairs etched on the glass are wedge-shaped. Same with the B&L 2½ to 8 and some other scopes. Pecar has a 3 to 7 and a 4 to 10; Esquire 2½ to 8 (Tradewinds, Box 1191, Tacoma 1, Wash.); Kahles' Helia 2.3 to 7.7 and 3 to 10—and so on. Most of the good ones have a constant eye-relief distance, but width of field is normally a little bit less than with fixed-power scopes that are similar in other respects. Moss-

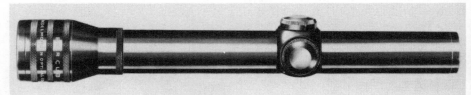

Kollmorgen 2¾x Bear Cub.

Tilden ring mounts. Front base and ring of the Tilden are a lapped, matched set for individual rifle and scope. When bore sighting and center of scope field coincide, rifle can generally be zeroed, at this given range, with the aiming point of the reticle close to the exact center of the scope.

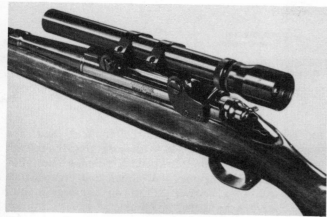

Bausch & Lomb 2½ to 4x variable.

Weaver K-2.5 is one of those that give good field and light at the cost of but little additional weight and bulk. It is still liked, despite or sometimes because of its low magnification.

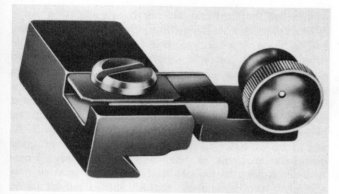

The Chilford Boone supplementary receiver peep sight.

berg's new 1A25 gives choice of 2½ or 5 power and goes on .22s with the now almost universal grooved receivers.

It is a rather uncanny experience to look through a vari for the first time, cranking the power up or down. For increase of light and field, with opposite effects on power, the thing in a way takes the place of several scopes, and that's canny Scotch enough.

Their Mounts. Target scope mounts often are "dehorned" for use on a varmint glass. That helps. Another improvement is to set the rear base on the receiver bridge instead of up front on the receiver ring. Then we can use a short scope—and some of

them are—and still get the full view of the field even in offhand.

The other type uses hunting mounts, in great variety. Some are more reliable than others, for we've still a way to go in that matter. Both internal adjustments, in the scope itself, and external are used. Either way, we want adjustments that can be read accurately, for the record or dope book, and for memorizing a few. Some adjustment dials that lack a scale can have one engraved on it. Some can't. Varmint shooting is precision work, and the usual rifle-crank doesn't settle down soon enough to one good load for varmint hunting. For experiment and development, the more the better, but not afield.

Big-Game Scopes

Some look as though they were meant to be played in a band, or at least for reveille. Shame to clap such a monstrosity on a beautifully built rifle! But the call is for more power, with equal or better field and light, and that means bigger objective and ocular lenses.

When hunting scopes, mostly imported, were just coming into fair use in this country a 2½ or 2¾X glass with 30-foot field at our standard 100-yard testing distance was considered splendid. So it was, too. Now we get 40 feet and more in those powers, and well over 30 in 4X. Even in the woods some use

Chilford Boone 2¼x scope.

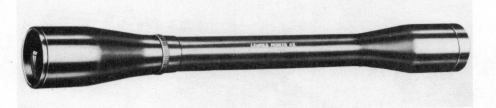

Leupold & Stevens Pioneer is one of the many hunting scopes in the popular 4x magnification.

Kollmorgen 4x Bear Cub.

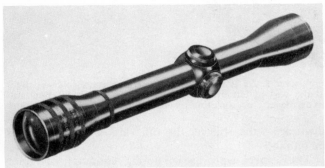

CHALLENGER

STREAMLITE
CHALLENGER
Lyman Scope.

Chilford Boone 4x.

6X scopes with 20-foot and better field, and like them. But extra power does magnify tremor, though we'd hardly notice the shake on a running shot. For a long while the beginner will notice that crazy dance of tree-trunks as he swings fast on a crossing shot, and it just can be a trifle baffling!

About 8X may be the maximum power popular for open, long-range shooting at big game, but if it is, wanna bet that it'll stay so? High magnification helps in searching and sizing up mountain and plains game, but a binoc is easier to use and with a rifle-range spotting scope you can *almost* see the spider-legged little Martians on a clear night. Man in the Moon winks right back at it.

The Scopes. If a fellow were heartbroken when a new model of his favorite make came out and he hadn't the cash to buy it, the climate of the U. S. A. would be as dewy as that of England. Lots of good oldtimers are still in use, and doing finely. From A to Z, Ackley to the old Zeiss, there's a host of new and used hunting scopes to study, and it's well to do just that.

Recent annual issues of *Gun Digest* have carried the listing in compact form: power, field, brightness, eye relief, eyepiece and tube diameters, internal or external (in the mount) adjustments, weight, and cost. There's the synopsis, a good one: for the complete story we just write the makers. Colonel Whelen's book on scopes naturally is fine. If it came out a few years ago, so what? The principles are there.

In the woods we want brightness, often to see what the unaided eye can't, and field, so the game will be in it as soon as we cheek the rifle—something like using an improved cylinder or quarter-choke for grouse. Power helps at long range, especially when the shot can be taken from a position steadier than offhand. It helps in searching for game, too, and the swing of the rifle muzzle needn't spook an animal if the distance is great enough. Of course a binocular or spotting scope makes it easier, and in some places some of us must go light.

A big objective gathers light, and as a rule, the larger the ocular the better it can preserve field and light as the power goes up. But huge scopes require high mounting to clear the rifle, and they demand unusually high-combed stocks. The rifle *must* fit, for steady hold or for quick, sure aim. An extremely heavy glass makes a rifle top-heavy, and a bulky glass makes it awkward to carry. These are costs to be considered, and they may or may not be worth paying. For

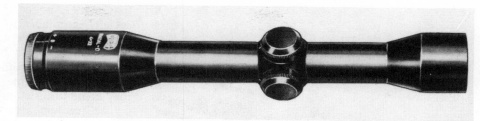

Hensoldt 4x Diatal-D made by M. Hensoldt, member of the Zeiss organization in West Germany. Imported by Carl Zeiss, New York City.

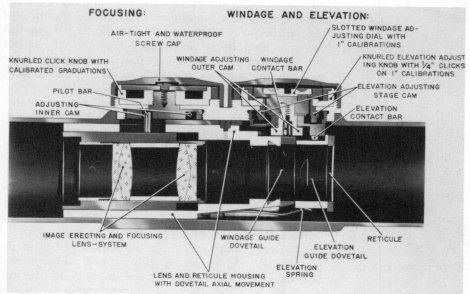

FOCUSING:

WINDAGE AND ELEVATION:

AIR-TIGHT AND WATERPROOF SCREW CAP

SLOTTED WINDAGE ADJUSTING DIAL WITH 1" CALIBRATIONS

KNURLED CLICK KNOB WITH CALIBRATED GRADUATIONS

WINDAGE ADJUSTING OUTER CAM

WINDAGE CONTACT BAR

KNURLED ELEVATION ADJUSTING KNOB WITH 1/4" CLICKS ON 1" CALIBRATIONS

PILOT BAR

ELEVATION ADJUSTING STAGE CAM

ADJUSTING INNER CAM

ELEVATION CONTACT BAR

IMAGE ERECTING AND FOCUSING LENS-SYSTEM

WINDAGE GUIDE DOVETAIL

RETICULE

LENS AND RETICULE HOUSING WITH DOVETAIL AXIAL MOVEMENT

ELEVATION GUIDE DOVETAIL

ELEVATION SPRING

Cutaway view of Weatherby Imperial.

Bushnell scope system.

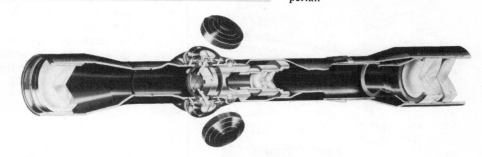

Bushnell 4x scope.

Esquire 4x and top mounts for Husqvarna rifle.

A graduated dial, like this one on a Kollmorgen Bear Cub hunting scope, lets the shooter read his adjustments and make a record of them. Screw caps keep out dust and moisture.

Williams Quick-Convertible side mount. Low iron sights can be used under this type.

that matter, no good rifle need have a scope to be socially acceptable, to impress the brotherhood! Yet all the costs, liabilities and inconveniences of a hunting scope can be worth bearing in—well, maybe 95 per-cent of hunting with a rifle. If the glass saves a human life its value is incalculable. Legislators just may come to insist on it.

The medium cross-hair reticle is becoming more popular for the big-game rifle. For hunting in poor light, most woods hunting in the fall, the flat-topped post probably will have its adherents for years to come; it used to be about the only sensible choice, but we do have better optics now. A sharp post can fade out unless the power is 6X or above, and a stack of posts is a nuisance: a reticle should be simple. Double cross-hairs do act as range-finders—the space between subtends a definite amount per hundreds of yards—and the lower one can be used for overhold. Some like a single cross-hair with a post, to show up canting of the rifle. And some like the Lee-type floating-dot reticle very much. For me, it does show up well even in shade, though we don't all see alike in matters pertaining to the rifle! It too can be used as a range-finder.

Internal adjustments for windage and elevation—and some external ones in the mounts—vary a lot in performance. Some makes have a bad name, some a good one, and individual specimens vary. If we don't get what we click for, no movement at all or maybe with a rush after three or four shots have jarred them awake, it seems that that outfit should be fired back fast to its maker for correction. We're doing a favor to other riflemen, too, when we insist on the stuff being right.

A rather old but very fine long-range stalking rifle by Griffin & Howe. Caliber, .280 Dubiel; scope, Zeiss Zielsechs (6 power); mount, quick-detachable side pattern. *Courtesy Combat Forces Press.*

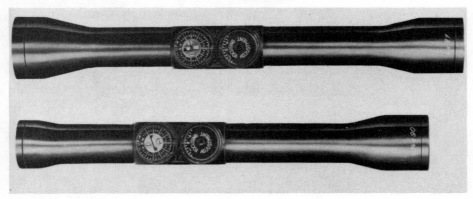

Adjustment dials on Weatherby scopes—focusing, windage, and elevation—are graduated, too, like those of some other scopes. Screw caps aren't shown in this photograph.

Their Mounts. Mounts and their fitting to the rifle *may* cost about as much as the hunting scope itself. They're nearly if not quite as important. Scopes add weight to a rifle, and mounts aren't balloons, either. For hard service we need strength in a mount, with its holding points on the scope not too close together. For easy, deliberate (and, I'll bet, productive) woods hunting no such strength or durability is needed as for horseback carrying. Then the quick-detachable mount with a scope holster often pays off, if the rifle has good irons for a short range opportunity.

"To state which is best for saddle use?" asked Tom Florich. "Until they make rifles with an integral hole to slip the scope in they will all be vulnerable to hard field use . . . All existing mounts are vulnerable

Redfield Junior scope mount, bridge type.

This Redfield Junior has split rings for a scope with large objective lense system.

to rough handling, as an M70 with Alaskan in G&H mount was dropped 30 inches and lit on the ocular end of the glass. As I zeroed it that morning, I checked up. The blow had left it 12 inches low at 100." He gave that as an extreme example, naturally, and I know darn well it wasn't his rifle, or his hand that dropped it.

We have two general types of mounts, side and top. The latter may either "bridge" the receiver like the Redfield Junior or be in two-piece style, like the new Griffin & Howe top mount that is made practically on a toolroom basis. The side mount can give the lowest position, closest to the receiver, but top mounts can be lighter.

Either can be made quick on-or-off, for use of the scope or for use of the irons, as need requires. One of our earliest side mounts, the Niedner, employed big, coin-slot thumbscrews fore and aft to attach the mount to the base that was fixed permanently to the left side of the receiver. It wasn't fast. The Griffin & Howe locked on with a single lever, later with the double-lever system which it still has in this *side mount* variety. That is fast, and more firm. A late, light side mount from Kruzell Distributing Co., 211-R Sams

Bldg., Bay City, Michigan, uses a vertical pin with plunger release at the front of the permanent base. It is fast, and its strength has been reported OK. Ackley's snap-in mount is a top, one of those that are detachable. "On or off in three seconds" is the description.

Redfield Dualite two-piece mount.

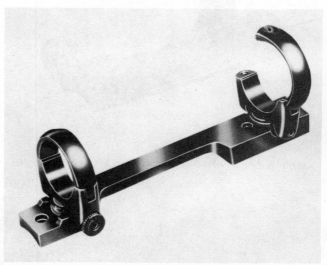

Leupold & Stevens Adjusto-Mount has hinged, not split, rings.

Leupold & Stevens Detacho-Mount for quick change from glass to iron sights. Peep sight appears in rear mount, at the left of this picture.

These are only samples, picked pretty much at random. The advertising and commentary literature of mounts is nearly as large as that covering the scopes.

The Pachmayr Lo-Swing and the Weaver Pivot are examples of mounts that swing aside quickly to clear

Stith mount for Savage 99.

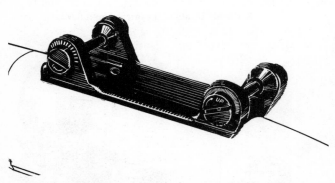

Bausch & Lomb solid-type mount base for 760 Remington.

the deck for use of iron sights. If there's an audible click when they bring the scope into battery, that ordinarily does no harm: the glass is for long shots, or for any shots we can take with it. But if the swing-off is noisy, that could be bad: the game may be close, unaware of the shooter's nearness, and scope or atmospheric conditions no good for glassing.

Lots of us hate to use an open rear sight even in an emergency. The Little Blue Peep, the Mykrom, and the Williams Ace-in-the-Hole are examples of a way out. They go on the scope mounts.

The Kesselring See-Em-Under mount is hollowed through, to let us use peep or open sights when the scope is still in place. Some of us remember target-scope blocks, concaved on top as is usual for sporting-rifle use, that let us see the sights under the glass. Squint? I'll say we did! The other day I saw a Weaver Pivot that would have done a little better if the gun factory had been prophetic, prescient or something and had settled on a lower iron-sight line in designing that rifle model! Used to be that your scope always rode above any standard irons you chose, and you made like a giraffe to use it. Side mount, or drilled top. That could still pay off in a time of danger. Who wants to study a grizzly's or buffalo's teeth for cavities when he's that close? Shucks, that near, the scope would blur, anyway.

We want to look through the middle of the scope for cross-hairs intersection or the top of the post.

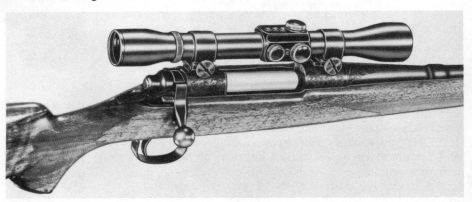

Coin-slot screw system anchors Weaver detachable top mount. Scope is Weaver KV, 2¾ to 5x variable power.

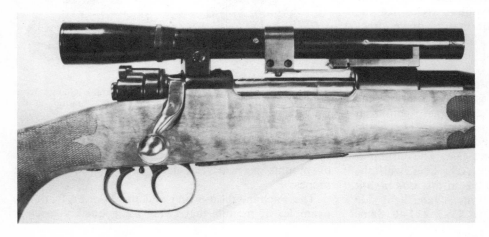

Ackley Snap-In mount is quick on-or-off, light but strong.

With windage and elevation both in the mount, we can. But internal adjustment scopes have plenty of admirers. A good gunsmith can do wonders. Crosshairs should be a straight-up plus sign, and a post upright, not slanted. The Buehler base is an example of being obliging. Two screws in the rear part help to line up if the factory sent out the rifle with a cock-eyed receiver. Recent Weaver K-series and Koll-morgen scopes have self-aligning reticles that don't appear to move when you make adjustments.

And we certainly do want to see the full field of the scope, or nearly that much, whether we fire from prone with our face *reasonably* close to the breech, or from offhand, and perhaps downhill. A good hunting scope has obliging *lateral* eye relief: we don't

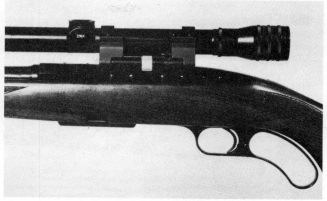

Pachmayr Lo-Swing mount.

have to get exactly behind it, as with iron sights of any sort. It also has good *length* of eye relief, back and forth—couple of inches or so. The big-game scope is used mostly in offhand. If the mount design and

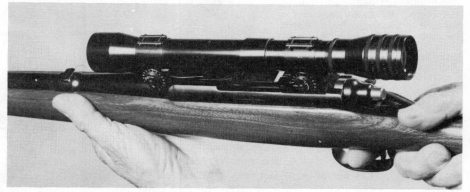

Stith Master mount.

Another view of Stith Master.

Left-hand view of Ackley mount.

This .300 Weatherby Magnum rifle and its 4x Weatherby Imperial glass use the Buehler mount.

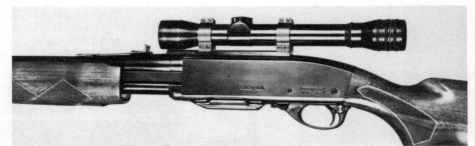

Stith dovetail mount for Remington 740 or 760 allows good rear or forward positioning. Note varying locations of the scope bands or rings. Tightening the lower screws gives firm hold for heavy scopes and grip against heavy recoil even from light rifles.

the wind and el turrets (if any) on the scope tube allow positioning for full field only when we shoot prone, they just aren't the team to buy. Though many fine offhand smallbore target shots shove their heads forward almost to the dislocation point (seems so, at least), this is not the way to develop a quick, accurate, game-shooting style. Some shooting of this kind almost resembles shotgun work, and a good shotgun is *comfortable*.

And the shotgun cheeks up right. You look over the barrels, not along them, without stretching your neck or squashing your face into a vast concave. The rifle stock needs the same sort of fit, to make pointing become instinctive—after some practice. There isn't always time to remember to accommodate ourselves to an ill-fitting stock.

Sights Need Care

They need care afield and in storage. Irons can get along with less than the glass, usually, though they don't respond to abuse. Canvas gun cases generally have leather reinforcements to protect front and receiver peep sights, and a tang sight is folded in storage. Rust doesn't help iron sights. It can't hurt ivory, but oil can. Excessive scrubbing wears off blueing and is tough on the magnesium fluoride coating (that dainty, light blue) of good lenses.

The hunting field is no place to try to repair, and then readjust, either iron sights or scopes. Though a combination set is good insurance, it just might happen that we'd need quite badly the kind that had been knocked out, metal or glass.

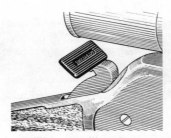

← ELEVATION SET SCREW

Williams Ace-in-the-Hole auxiliary peep sight.

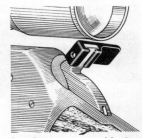

Williams auxiliary hammer extension lets a scope ride low over the receiver of a Marlin lever action.

Excessive heat—on a top shelf in the attic during summer is a glorious example—is bad for scopes. Many are temporarily ruined by such storage, must go back to the factory. Now we have a new kind of lens cement that doesn't run under pretty high temperatures, but it isn't yet in general use and probably won't be for years.

Outdoor weather can put a scope out of action. Going into excessive cold may do it, for a few minutes, unless the tube is gas-filled, as with nitrogen. Bringing a very cold scope and rifle into a warm room makes them both sweat: better leave 'em outside or use a cold corner, which sometimes works.

WHEN WE fire a rifle we don't want to give our attention to anything but the safety of the background, the sight picture on the target, and timing the trigger squeeze to make the let-off coincide with perfect alignment. Those three details are enough!

We should be aware of the gun's balance, length, weight, stock fit and action type, if at all aware of them, only in a pleased, subconscious way. Then we can say that the rifle "comes up right and feels right."

BALANCE

There are two kinds, handling or carrying balance, and shooting balance. Not by any means are they always the same.

We might add a third kind, store balance. First-off, we're dazzled by the sight of the glossy new model— or the fascinating oldtimer, rich in romance of the past—that we spot in the showcase. Immediately our critical faculties, our guard, are lowered. Pretty soon we have that gun in our hands and we're at the physical or emotional top. The rifle feels wonderful, and "Great grief," we think, "how I could shoot that rifle!"

We aren't tired from a long trail (or trail-less country) or from an exacting session at target. Illusions have their place in getting us through the world with happiness at the masthead, but they don't serve as a compass needle.*

Handling or Carrying Balance

These are hard to define. We could say that amidships, the teeterpoint when the rifle is laid over a straightedge, is the natural and only place to grip the gun when we carry it at trail. If that point lies *about* midway between the natural and easy front and rear hand-grasps when we bring the rifle to our shoulder, then we have handling balance between our mitts. It's much like that of an upland shotgun—side-by-side double for this child's choice—that really fits.

But there's more, and I think it's indefinable, and personal to each of us. Giving personal examples may not help, but here they are. One was an old Remington 12A .22 pump, 22-inch round barrel, straight-grip shotgun stock with hard-rubber buttplate. It weighed less than five pounds, but entirely aside from that feather-puff effect it still had it, the balance, the aliveness. Another is the 64 Winchester in .30-30 or .32 Special, not the .25-35 or .219 with their thicker barrel walls, though they're steadier. Another was the 52 sporter that the Niedner shop stocked and barreled for me, and for a fourth there'd be one of Tom Florich's Springfield sporters, one that looked custom without a snitch of checkering on the walnut. There are others, some of them heavier than any of

CHAPTER 24

GUN FIT

these that have come to the typewriter keys, but no matter.

Shooting Balance

Here again we have at least two kinds, and they're personal. They depend somewhat on the shape of the stock and its pistol grip if it has one—the build and feel of the rifle—and mounting any but the shortest and lightest of scopes can make a difference, for good or for grief.

There's the snapshooting balance. Giving figures may help, though balance always is hard to define. At least we know when we have it and when we haven't!

The game may be standing or moving, the rifle still or swung ahead. I used to think that a balance point four or five inches ahead of the trigger was right for me when I had to mount the gun, aim, and get off the shot rather fast. Such balance makes the piece come up and point in a flash. Later I found that 6, 7 or almost 8 inches ahead of the trig was better, for me. The muzzle settled into steadiness much sooner and on running shots there was more deliberation—which I needed and still need!—and less liability of over-correction of aim ahead, behind, below or above, to hit the point in space where I hoped the game would run into the bullet. It was fully as easy, too, to keep up the swing, not stop it, through and beyond the instant of firing.

Four-position target shooting style corresponds to some kinds of varmint, small- and big-game hunting. An eight- or nine-inch balance point suits many in offhand, the hard-scoring position that wins matches

---

* Sometime. if you've never read it, look up Kipling's short poem "in the Matter of One Compass." Model of 1892, but not yet outdated.

325

because it separates the workers from those who don't put in lots of time at dry and live practice. Some would want more muzzle-weight, and a prone-only rifle can use that more with profit. Bench-resters like some barrels that would make prone shooting a severe muscular strain, and it's natural and right that they should use them.

A four-position rifle can have an aliveness as well as steadying out-front weight in its balance. Example: an M-2 Springfield .22 that went 9 pounds, 6¼ ounces without sling on Harry Thomas' scales, which were checked periodically by a state inspector! But now only a few position shooters would accept an M-2. It's too barrel-light for competition, though for training it's as good as ever.

LENGTH

Some like a short rifle; so we have bull-pups as well as carbines. In jungle or even in heavy temperate-climate brush a yardlong gun will take shots that a musket never could.

Twice I've fouled a barrel in brush and lost the chance to shoot, one of those times with a 20-incher. I've used and liked barrels as long as 26 inches on a high-power bolt action, 28 on a small bore, and 30 on a single shot, and one or two barrels as short as 18. A borrowed .44-40 had a heavy 14-inch octagon barrel; that was before Federal law made it a "firearm" and out of my class.

These experiences may mean nothing. There are more important matters to consider than gun length—fit, weight, and balance. A long barrel generally contributes to steadiness, unless it's too heavy, and with iron sights it is (for me) quicker to align accurately. But for smallbore target quite a few excellent shots like a short, heavy barrel in offhand. It holds well for them and still has enough sight radius with the type of irons they use when matches call for those sights.

WEIGHT

Here we consider weight—as well as we can—apart from balance and/or muzzle steadiness. The hunting rifle is to be carried unless a car or some other vehicle does most of the walking for us, and it mustn't be burdensome toward the end of the day, when some of the best opportunities come. Balance has much to do with a gun's apparent weight—some feel lighter, or heavier, than they are—and the mid-section we grasp at the trail carry can be comfortable, or too great a stretch for the hand. In open and fairly level country a sling eases the load.

A well balanced 6¾- or 7-pound rifle seems light enough for me all day, and I shoot it better than a 6-pounder, other details being as equal as I could hope to have them. My father used an eight-pound Remington single shot for most of his deer hunting, in his later years changing to an Extra Light Weight .30-30 Winchester with dense wood in its stock. I think it weighed about 7½ pounds. When I was

younger it seemed just right to me. Maybe it would now. These are woods rifles. In open country, maybe hilly, but not mountainous, we'd carry a pound or more extra.

There's no sense in lugging too heavy a gun, to demonstrate our strength, or in floating along with a pinweight, to prove that we can hold a walking-stick like a match rifle. Usually it takes some years to find out the ideal, individual weight, and some country is quite a bit rougher than others! But do remember that a hunting rifle feels lighter in the store than it does after a few miles in your shoes. About the same reasoning goes for a target rifle.

BUTTSTOCK FIT

American factory-made stocks vary from about 13- to 13½-inch length, and drop dimensions might be as little, or as "straight," as 1½ inches at comb, 2½ at heel. We measure length from the forward edge of the trigger's curve to the middle of the buttplate, and drops are taken from the line of sight, irons or glass. With the latter they usually run much greater on a sporting rifle, though not always from the shooter's choice.

These dimensions mean little except that if *all* were correct the rifleman might pride himself on being a strictly average, normal man—if that helped him any! Probably we all have seen a short-armed, heavy-chested man, possibly rather tall, too, handicapped with a "standard"-length stock. When wearing a heavy, old-fashioned mackinaw coat he'd be next door to helpless. A long stock is an abomination when shooting must be done fast or not at all except in a grandfather's story, and it can make off-the-shoulder bolt operation not only slow but even impossible. Shorten it by the once-and-be-done-with-it method and recoil may be too heavy, or the front sling swivel too close for comfortable hand-reach up the forestock. But cut by degrees that stock may end as short as 12¾ inches—just an arbitrary figure—and fit the shooter perfectly. Few of us need rifle stocks longer than 14 inches when we wear winter clothing.

Comb drop is more important than heel drop, but not much. Our cheek must lie comfortably, easily, pressed against the comb for good shooting and to help us steady the piece into aim after working the bolt hard and fast. The Monte Carlo comb seems to be about 95 percent popular just now for scoped rifles. Generally it raises the point of the comb at least one-quarter inch above the iron-sight comb height—and needs to. The Monte may slope up or down toward the front, and with rifles of any considerable recoil, say that of an 8½-pound .270, it had better slope down. That saves us from jawbone and dental buffet, which is hard to take. We learn to accept recoil on the shoulder as a matter of course.

Thickness adds to a comb's apparent height and head support, but it should taper toward the front (as most do) for the same reason that a Monte should slope forward and down. The ideal comb, like all the rest of the rifle, is built for its owner, who should have considerable shooting experience to know what he really needs. It's obvious that a thin face needs a thicker and/or higher comb than a full, rounded one. Custom stocks are expensive, but ordered in the ripeness of time they pay off. Meanwhile, there are cheek pads, home-made wood inlets, and other dodges. One is the offset scope mount made primarily for top-ejecting lever actions. Since I shoot right-handed, I'd want one that hung the glass over to the right, like the Echo 18 DC for Winchester 64 or 94. I'd have to *press* my face against the comb to aim; so I'd have a thicker comb to compensate for the higher sight line of the scope.

The pistol grip is almost universal on modern American rifles. It helps in holding the butt to the shoulder a little better, probably, than a repeater's finger lever loop or a Stevens, Winchester, or other lever-action single shot's graceful trigger guard extension does. If the pistol grip is a bit large for our hand it helps us to take up heavy recoil, and most small- and bigbore target shots like it large for sure control in slow fire. For other kinds of shooting it can and perhaps should be smaller. The Wundhammer* swell, properly located in making or ordering, fills the hollow of your hand. It curves up to a rounded peak perhaps 3/8 inch above the stock's surface, and it's a real help. Some think that an all-round, not just partially checkered grip helps take up recoil. Walnut checkering isn't like that on an old Colt New Service Target .44 Special's backstrap, which can cut your hand like a little rasp after you've fired a few rounds from that sixgun.

For prone target a close-up pistol grip helps in hard holding and lets the trigger finger move back more nearly parallel with the others. Target-shooting influence has made some of our sporter grips too close, awkward for an offhand snapshot, awkward, some of them, in almost any position. Roughly, more than three inches from trigger curve to point of grip is sporter, three inches or less, target. But these dimensions mean little if the actual swell of the grip starts too soon, or starts so late that the pistol grip is not much more than a lump, back there on the stock.

Those who shoot with their thumb across the stock may need a much deeper than standard flute or undercut of the comb. Don't be afraid to give it plenty if you'll shoot with gloves on when it's cold.

Now for drop at heel. An inch more than comb drop is about standard for a sporter, sometimes less than half that difference for a rifle stocked for a high-mounted target scope. So we come to the matter

*Ludwig Wundhammer was one of the first of our custom gunsmiths to remodel Springfield and other bolt-action rifles in the early 1900s style of efficiency and beauty that persists until today without many radical changes to improve either quality. They were big-game sporters.

of leverage. A Monte Carlo stock with extremely low heel and high comb has leverage. No wonder the comb, even though it's slanted down, up front, at least tries to rise and smite our chops. Such a stock, not overdone, can come up beautifully, giving us an instant view through the hunting scope, but with practice a different kind of stock will do as well and be more comfortable because it hasn't the leverage of a bore line so high above the heel. Maybe it will be even better looking. Stocks on our best smallbore target rifles give the *starting* idea. So do those on our only factory-made bigbore target rifles, the M70 is in that classification. From these as starting models an efficient and rather good-looking sporter scope stock can be built. Most hunting scopes, at least for big game, lie closer to the bore than target scopes do, and that's a help in our planning.

The buttplate finishes the buttstock, and to make weight *or* balance suit us we can choose between steel and thick, soft rubber, and the lightness of aluminum, plastic, hard rubber, and horn. A slight rounded swell at the heel helps to hold the rifle to our shoulder when we work the action, and a not too sharp or narrow toe gives comfort much appreciated in prone if recoil amounts to considerably more than a tap.

Reasonable down-pitch of the buttplate also makes the rifle stick better when we work its action off-shoulder, and target shots like more than most hunters do—three inches or so down. You measure as with a shotgun: stand the smoothbore up to a wall, its butt flat on the floor, and take the distance from muzzle to wall. This works with a smooth, double-barrel hammerless shotgun, but most of our rifles are much more angular at the breech, and the best method I know of is to use common sense and never start. If a shotgun has no pitch, its barrel stands straight up and down when its butt is level on the floor. That's all right for a lot of trapshooters; some even prefer a slight upward pitch. If the rifle's pitch is right (for the individual) in offhand it's one of those factors that make for instantaneous alignment. Too much down-pitch lowers the muzzle; not enough raises it. In target, mostly prone, a lot of down-pitch certainly helps, and I don't remember one of this sort so extreme that it was useless for me in hunting.

FORESTOCK FIT

Target-rifle influence brought the wide, rounded, semi-beavertail forestock into modern sporter styling. On a bolt action, with its wide mid-section, it can be beautiful, tapering down forward to the tip. But a sudden bulge of wood ahead of the receiver can be ugly on any rifle, and ungainly as a brick (to quote Oscar Hammond) if it comes at or near the balance point where our hand goes at trail carry. Advantages are the protection of the hand from being fried on a hot barrel, hardly liable in hunting, and a better leveling of the rifle, for some of us, in both slow and rapid fire. The forestock should fit the individual hand, not

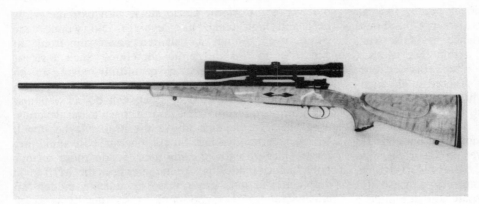

A 6 mm. Lynx wildcat caliber varmint or open-country deer or antelope rifle, Mauser action, barreled, chambered, and stocked by Chet Carmichael of Southwest Gun Accessories, Tucson, Arizona, and fitted with a big, bright Kollmorgen 6x Bear Cub scope, necessarily mounted high to clear barrel and breech. Note the stock's high heel and its good, thick cheekpiece and comb to pillow the shooter's face. Pistol grip curve is set back so that the second finger couldn't possibly be bruised by the trigger guard when the rifle recoils. The short, compact Lynx case is a necked-down and blown-out .250 Savage.

This custom rifle, too—by Pachmayr of Los Angeles—has a high heel. Some who object to the lines or the behavior of a Monte Carlo comb might like the type of stock on this rifle and on Carmichael's Lynx. They are typical of a class, and other specimens may be found illustrated in the chapter on custom rifles.

Top view of the Pachmayr rifle, showing inlay work and the shape of the heavy, comfortable cheekpiece. Since human faces vary in outline from long oval to practically buckshot round, the size, shape, and height of a comb, with or without either cheekpiece or Monte Carlo, are some of the stock details that ought to suit the *individual*.

a manufacturer's idea of what is one for all and all for one, and we must remember that a shooting glove on the hand makes a difference. Lots of targeteers want a full beavertail at least 2¼ or 2½ inches wide to help them prevent canting the rifle.

Semi-beavertail cross-sections vary from nearly round to the popular pear shaped, to an almost or actual U. Except in a strong cross-wind or when operating an action we seldom *grip* the forestock. We develop our own preferences as to forestock size and shape, and these ideals vary for different kinds of shooting. For quick snap work we may choose, for instance, a rather narrow one.

The slide handle or movable forestock of most pump action rifles is entirely or just a little too far out for proper hold in the good Army offhand, elbow free from the ribs and the hand just beyond the rifle's balance point. But a longer reach helps us to direct the muzzle in crossing or angling shots at running game and the pump gun is mostly for woods use, though some have fine accuracy for long shots. If the carrying point lies between receiver and slide handle we may have some slight discomfort, but at least there is no tiring finger-stretch.

Pulling back on the slide handle as the shot is fired makes the action break open rather disconcertingly, though safely unless we have a .22 and a hangfire.

Bigbores usually are fitted with a recoil lock to prevent this happening. But then, that sort of sweat and strain isn't the marksman's method.

The pump gun's shooting sling, if any, is attached to steel ahead of the forestock. It may or may not affect elevation zero or cramp the forward hand in firing position. Personally, I should be glad of even a light support of the sling in any fairly deliberate shooting, and the leather comes in handy for some kinds of carry, decidedly so when both hands are busy with other things.

About 17 inches ahead of the trigger is the correct location for a forward sling swivel, but people are different and rifles are, too. Some hold farther out than others, and though I'm short-armed I like a long forward reach in a low, steady sitting position. The M70 distance of about 16½ inches is a bit short for me then, but the cutting of my stock to one-quarter inch under standard helps to account for that—just to be real fussy over microscopic details. With a heavy winter hunting coat I find the fit just about perfect, by way of the added thickness of perhaps .18275 inch! The reach of the M52 target rifle with standard 13⅛-inch stock is slightly more comfortable for me, though I narrowed the butt considerably, thus in effect shortening the stock by letting it seat more deeply into the hollow between shoulder and collar-bone. We have to work out these things for ourselves.

A long, sling-comfortable forestock may look odd on a 20- or 22-inch-barreled rifle, but let her! Barrel band, sweated-on lug, or other sling swivel anchorage ahead of the wood is too liable to result in different elevation zeros, sometimes with, sometimes without, the pull of a sling.

Snobble forestock tips are back in popularity and never did disappear completely. That little swell or lip is decorative, though some like a rounded tip as well, with a slightly swept-back upper surface, next to the barrel. The fine old single shots, inexpensive or costly, the Winchester '95 in sporting rifle model, and most Savage 99s had a snobble. It's a neat way of finishing off a light-weight forestock, and if there is no sling it helps as a forward edge to the hand-grasp in some shooting positions we use afield. If the rifle is light-barreled, check it for possible elevation changes as the hand goes 'way out front or close back.

ACTION TYPE

This has a great influence on the ideal rifle fit. The obliging autoloader can be disregarded, as an action. Well made, well cared for, and given good ammunition, it perks. But the combination of a long lever-throw and heavy clothes calls for a shorter stock, and so does bolt operation, for most of us. This is a personal matter that it's certainly advisable to settle in advance, by trial when we're dressed for the outdoors!

Action length—rather, that part from barrel breech to trigger—varies from the shade over two inches of a close-coupled single shot to the 7½ plus or minus of a bolt gun, let's say. It affects rifle length and balance, and the mounting of target or hunting scopes.

Some big actions make a breech-heavy rifle—the Winchester '95 and Remington 8 autoloader being classic examples—if stock and barrel are fairly light. The action of the future, if we gaze into the crystal ball, probably will be much lighter. Almost certainly it will be shorter, with improved powders to make ammunition more compact. The .308 is a footprint along the way.

But the action's chief influence on gun fit is the answer to the question, "How do you like it?" We may like all types, just as we may like all dogs, regardless of breed or no-breed, shape, size, fur coverall styling, age and condition. Great people they are!

Back to this book. Some actions become more familiar to us than others, though each has its place and purpose. Familiarity—and that in a sense is gun fit—lets us do our best. It gives us pleasure, too.

CARE pays off in reliability. It also pays—though this comment may be only for the true gun-crank's acceptance—in the double satisfaction of keeping equipment in beautiful shape, and of just doing it. Some of the pleasantest conversations in camp have been punctuated by the faint click of cleaning rods and the tap of a set-down bottle of bore dope. We relived the past and created the imagined future, and there was no hurry, no urgency of any kind. At the last a bolt would snick home, a striker or hammer be lowered carefully, and a pleased, almost grandfatherly proud look light the face of the rifle's owner. "Harry, you know this old smokepole of mine . . . ."

THE BORE

Disregard the lazy Land of Oz viewpoint—only the Wizard worked there, and we're told that he was a whiz—and two schools of thought remain. You can scrub the accuracy out of a bore. A well-cared-for barrel always shoots best.

Non-corrosive priming, smokeless powder, and plain lead, uncoated but lubricated bullets leave a protective film in the bore. Even salt-heavy seaside air may best be foiled by it. Many smallbore match shots leave their rifles uncleaned, inside, all through a season. They might occasionally "brush out the lead," and I've seen pistol shots, who ought to know better, whisk a dry bristle brush down and back through the bore, wiping out some of the ammunition residue's protection.

Bench-resters usually shoot jacketed bullets, and some have found to their conviction that cleaning after every string of shots improves accuracy. Switching to a different kind of jacket metal can temporarily destroy varmint-hunting precision, too. A metal jacket doesn't, in any event, leave the protective film that greased lead does, and for storage safety, I think, a brief wipe-out and an oiling are the least advisable care, though not always necessary in extremely dry or cold climates. Cleaning doesn't seem mandatory during a two- or three-day stay in camp, but please note the word "seem." It doesn't mean "become."

Long-established custom tells us to clean from the breech. Some long-established rifle models and some newer ones won't permit that, As for accuracy, breech wear from a cleaning rod can be as serious as muzzle wear, and if the wear amounts to anything it's simpler to have the muzzle cut off a fraction of an inch and trued up than to have the breech shortened, with rechambering and setting-back jobs involved.

It pays to use a smooth cleaning rod, not a rasp. Polished steel is good, and a perfectionist may want to complete the polishing of some of them. The Parker-Hale celluloid-covered steel rod does well, for the brass section up front is almost too short ever to contact the barrel surface. Since it's more flexible than a plain steel rod of equal diameter, it may rub the bore harder when tight patches are forced through.

CHAPTER 25

CARE OF RIFLES AND AMMUNITION

Still, I like mine, for it's given a bit over 20 years' service at home, in camps, and on canoe trips. One-piece and hard to stow away, it doesn't go back-packing. Then a necessarily much less rigid jointed rod replaces it. The American-made Pachmayr has a plastic coating over its spring steel core.

Brass and hickory are in bad repute. If they aren't kept clean and smooth they can pick up grit and carry it into the bore. But then, any wiping-rod should be taken care of.

With modern ammunition, almost any bore-cleaning solvent will do. There are many, and buying a bottle in March helps to relieve spring fever. Plain household ammonia, now that Winchester Crystal Cleaner (the little bottle with the knockout smell) is gone with the tide, is fine for dissolving copper fouling. I use it on general principles about twice a year. Actually, auto crank-case oil, No. 10, or 20 if you want more body, does most cleaning, lubricating, and preserving jobs. Government bore cleaner is excellent, but not as a preservative.

Jacket fouling, even yet, can pile up and affect accuracy. A brass wire brush usually gets it out; if not, ammonia should, or one of the commercial cleaners. Some of the latter have at least brief protective qualities, too, and we just mustn't spill am-

Typical jointed and solid or one-piece rifle rods by Marble.

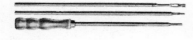

A standard type of brass rifle brush, also a nonfreeze oil for the action, Marble brand.

monia on blued outer surfaces. It makes 'em grow pale.

Lead fouling gives way to a brush, and a barrel badly coated with it shouldn't be fired with a high-intensity, jacketed-bullet load, for reasons of safety. The same precaution goes for a barrel fouled with black-powder residue, so easily scrubbed out with water, hot or cold.

Outing flannel, once-laundered unbleached muslin, or almost any strong yet absorbent clean cloth serves for bore-cleaning patches. They shouldn't be uniform in size. The first should be undersize, not to stick in the dirty bore, and the last still smaller, to carry in plenty of preservative oil or grease. If a patch does get stuck, run oil down the rod and down the other end of the barrel, let the thing stand a half hour, and then the jammed rod should move out, one way or the other, without much trouble and with no damage. Sometimes you have to tap a rod out, with great care.

As cleaning progresses, we need tighter patches if the bore is to be scrubbed more than just anointed. Heavy oil or grease should be wiped out before firing, though some rifles, with some bullets—lead or jacketed—are obliging and print the first shot from a lightly oiled barrel right in the pattern that succeeding shots would make. Others throw the first shot wild, even if we use a thin oil, lightly applied. Heavy application of grease or even oil can make a barrel unsafe to use when it's like that. Extreme cold increases the hazard, with most of them.

We develop our own methods of easy, efficient cleaning, gentle on the bore. It isn't necessary to sit up until 3 a.m. to get the last gray trace out. Long before that, the stuff is harmless—lead or powder residue. But inspect the groove corners of a black-powder rifle to make sure that they're really clean.

Getting a patch into the chamber and bore of a front-locked bolt action is troublesome at first. Most of us use a button-tipped rod. The Belding & Mull sprouts a needle on which the patch can be impaled,

and it's quite all right except for muzzle-end cleaning, the only way with many rifles. That needle would be rough on the bolt-face, for these rods are of good, hard, durable steel. (I never saw one bent.) With the plain button tip, balance the patch on your little finger and poke it up against the chamber. Then a short grip on the rod lets you center it, after a bit of off-centering practice. A slotted tip is fine for revolver chambers, and it's usable on rifles.

The best way to get in and clean the chamber of a rifle like the Winchester 64 and Remington 760—for examples—is to use either the Garand's "combination tool" with a patch wrapped around its wire brush, or a wire-handled bristle brush bent to make insertion easy. This too holds a patch well. A chamber ought to be cleaned at least occasionally.

Bolt actions, double-barrels, old single shots, most takedown repeaters, old or new, and some other rifles give us a free, fair inspection squint through the bore from either end. For others, and for these too, there·are the Boreskope, a few old Winchester barrel reflectors floating around, and narrow strips of mirror to stick in the breech for a look. A flashlight helps in such doings.

Perhaps the naked eye can see all the grief the mind will welcome, but there are bore lights for sharper inspection. At one extreme of price is the economical little Gun Bore Light, from Tulsa, Okla. Its curved lucite rod lets you direct the beam. The Zeiss-Kollmorgen Borescope (Kollmorgen Optical Co., Northampton, Mass., imports it) costs nearly $200. Its tiny lamp uses a flashlight battery, and a rheostat controls the voltage, or you can tap into home current and use the regulator to vary light strength. Full power doesn't often give best results. It comes for various calibers, but the sizes are rather elastic in use.

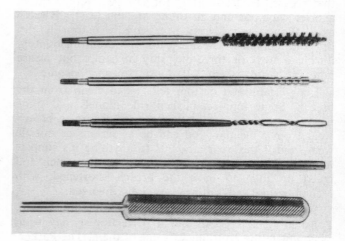

Belding & Mull rod tips, and the handle. From top: the brush; the button tip with needle to center the cloth patch; the double-slotted tip for cleaning or oiling; the push tip for forcing a lead slug through the bore, to calibrate it; the revolving handle (common to most rods) that lets patch or brush turn with the rifling, B&M rods are of stainless steel, polished. The double-slot and push tip are extras, supplied on order.

THE ACTION

One of the big advantages of the modern bolt action is that you can remove and strip the bolt of its striker to clean and oil it at intervals, or right away after a ducking in a puddle, big or little. Some, like the Remington 721-722, want a penny or a washer as a tool, though a non-strategic metal button might do. The inside of the bolt cylinder should be kept clean, and oiled just a little. Too much oil in an open-breech, non-hammerless action sprays back when a consequential charge is fired, and that can be more than unpleasant if we don't wear glasses. Once or twice a year, if the rifle is lucky and gets much use, it should be dismounted for cleaning and lubrication, thorough except when the factory advises us to leave certain parts alone, the 52C trigger mechanism, for instance.

Extreme cold has furnished alibis for lost shots—gun froze up—but we can guard against it. Herter's Silicone lubricant is described as effective down to —30° F., and Fred Ness' Palma Compound to 70 below. Palma is a cleaner, too, and Ness is one of the men who is remembered with gratitude and affection for his work in the "Dope Bag" department of the *Rifleman*. Now they have other men there, and always this service has been a great help to shooters needing advice, or an explanation of some queer phenomenon. Sorry for the digression, but it seemed to be called for just out of decency.

Powdered graphite is an old standard lubricant for the Arctic, and so is no lube at all. Our servicemen on the far and lonely northern frontier know plenty, too. If you know one up there he'd like to hear from you, and if he's a gun-crank, too, your letters (note the plural) sure as hell will be extra welcome. OK, no more digressions.

Screw-head slots appreciate a non-tapered screwdriver blade that fits them right down to the bottom. Cloth wrapping a misfit blade doesn't help much. The aim in setting up gun screws is not to demonstrate virility but to set 'em up to hold—though we watch them carefully. Linseed oil is a sealer for the chronic looseners.

Stock screws *can* be over-tightened. If by kind fortune they set up and give good shooting with their slots north and south (straight up and down with the length of the gun) or east and west, the location is easy to remember and check. Some I have to write down, lazy though I am. Seasonal humidity of course makes some difference.

We can learn to do some gunsmithing on our own. The cost may be a few ruined parts, depending on luck, natural aptitude, and skill acquired in other mechanical lines. But I'd hate to see private gunsmiths give up and go into industry, wouldn't you? There are excellent books on the subject and the hobby is fascinating. It helps us to appreciate a fine rifle, maybe to make one.

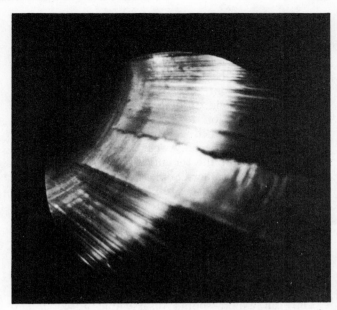

This photograph, taken through a TG-2 Borescope by Kollmorgen, shows the condition of a rifle's lands and grooves. Infernal, this picture, but it's truthful.

THE WOODWORK

Scarred and scabby varnished stocks don't look creditable. Naturally some business rifles have them. But refinishing a stock is fun, and there's much gratification in seeing the grain become more prominent and—almost always, to a normally pixilated rifleman's mind—plumb beautiful. There are far more efficient finishes than linseed oil to waterproof a stock, though *enough* coats of that stuff do pretty well.

Waterproofing the steel-contacting parts—barrel groove, action inlet, and so forth—can prevent the warping that affects accuracy and zero. Here there's no need for beauty, and varnish does well. Most stocks have no such protection, it almost seems.

THE SIGHTS

Sights probably come to more grief at home or afield than any other part of the rifle. They needn't. In careful hunting, irons are pretty safe, and scope sights, except those of target design, are now almost as durable, some perhaps more so. But spiderweb cross-hairs can be knocked out by a rather light tap, depending partly on how they're attached, and nylons seem to be stronger. The former is the only kind of sight I ever broke, as far as I remember. But I've been lucky as well as reasonably careful. Spare sights are worth their weight in the kit-bag for really hard trips, though most explorers seem to have got by without them, all over the still-wild parts of the world.

Perhaps the most durable rear aperture sight is the tang peep, folded when no shot is expected. But it takes little time to raise a Lyman, and a Marble Flexible can be just as noiseless to bring into battery. The thumb presses gently as the rifle barrel is slightly lowered—if your Marble is very old and needs a new spring—and eases the sight up. If there's no need for quiet, the Marble is almost instantaneous.

Sights shouldn't be neglected in the overall oiling, though we skip the lenses of a scope, naturally, and the ivory of a front bead or an open rear sight's inletted ivory triangle or diamond. A case or a fitted box gives protection to the scope at home, and a holster for a detached hunting scope afield certainly has its uses still, especially when we're aboard a horse.

Lens covers for the mounted glass help to keep it usable in wet weather. Some are transparent, some opaque but made to snap off at a touch. We can get a blurry but usable look-through by quickly wiping the ocular lens with our thumb; the objective, if we hunt with muzzle down, should stay dry enough.

Be particular about the mounting of the scope. Loose lenses can cause great errors, and pressure of mount rings can loosen them or a reticle. A wrongly mounted scope is the least durable afield.

Only an expert should disassemble a scope, and that goes for some receiver and tang sights, too. For cleaning outside lens surfaces a camel's-hair brush is probably best, but perfectly clean tissue or linen will do. We always blow hard on the glass, first, to dislodge any loose dirt—or grit. The "hard coating" of magnesium fluoride on some scopes and binoculars really isn't so hard: too vigorous polishing can remove it. Lately there has been improvement in this matter, but that light blue is so darn pretty that it's just as well to treat it rather reverently, or so it seems to me. The wonderful stuff lets us see later in the evening, earlier in the morning, and against sun-glare that would put an uncoated job out to pasture.

THE AMMUNITION

Cartridges, primers, and even sealed powders need dry, cool storage. Loose primers and .22 rimfires with heel bullets are perhaps most liable to deteriorate under the opposite conditions, the .22s because their bullets are seated rather lightly in the cases—compared to centerfires and inside lubricated rimfires like the .22 WRF—and the primers because only those thin paper discs cover their vital compound. Sealed glass jars give protection against extreme dampness, which is rough on black powder, too, weakening it. Using them might be worth the trouble.

Clean ammunition doesn't carry dirt into a barrel, and for that reason it's more likely to function correctly when we need it, perhaps rather badly. Time and again I've suffered at the sight of rimfire .22s with greasy lead bullets being dumped loose into a pocket or even on a cement floor or a dirty mat, indoors. The reason goes back to a Smith & Wesson .22 Perfected or Olympic single shot I used to have, a swell woods gun with its barrel cut to seven inches. The operation left its muzzle off-center, for those barrels were bored on a slant; seems that the earlier model had been made from a centerfire .32 *revolver,* the single shot .22 being interchangeable on the frame. No matter: these barrels were of target accuracy, and no fooling. So was a heavy Lovell or some such varmint barrel I heard of, slightly off-center up front, but highly accurate.

Well, we all worked in the old Maydole hammer factory, rather a gritty place here and there, and before the late Saturday afternoon cleanup in which all hands participated with great joy and relief. When my friends brought the little pistol back from a trip its barrel was scratched to hell-and-gone. Too bad, but tuition charges generally go with education, and I didn't cry —much. Modern wax coating used on many .22s is less of a dirt-catcher than soft grease, but it can do it.

There are all sorts of cartridge belts, short belt loops, and other carriers. To mention one is enough for illustation. The Tack-L-Toter Co., Coon Rapids, Iowa, sells a vinyl resin plastic carrier for .22 rimfires, short to long-rifles. Pocket size, but it holds 52 rounds in the separate compartments, slit on the sides to make removal easy, and the hulls go in right up to their rims. Some grease may be rubbed off—and it would be well to clean the thing occasionally—but I'd prefer less lube to grit or even fuzz. Who wouldn't?

EVERYONE defines that word "useful" for himself. Accessories mentioned here seem to me to qualify as useful, but we all have different backgrounds of experience. Be too bad if we hadn't: what would happen to those sessions at the hardware or sport store, at camp, or any place where the fraternity meets? A vast silence, signifying less than the nothing that sound and fury generate.

BOOKS AND SUCH

All down the calendar, print, reading matter, books, magazines and advertising literature can entertain the rifleman, and usually inform him. So the writers contradict each other? They all have their opinions, we should hope. I used to be choosy and partial; now I read almost anything on the topic, and it's a scarce book that doesn't teach me something new—and believable, too. Whether this stage represents sharpening or softening of the brain I don't know.

The "outdoor magazines," as they're called—hunting and fishing and what-all—have their gun departments, mostly written by prominent men. These authorities, so-called if you like the one in question, give us good service. Each has his following. Probably at least a half dozen have had weighty influence on the shape of factory arms and ammunition in this century, and manufacturers are more attentive to outside suggestions than they were a short generation ago.

A few publications are devoted almost 100 percent to guns and ammo. Here are just four examples, though I've known and liked others.

The American Rifleman is published monthly by the National Rifle Association, 1600 Rhode Island Ave., N. W., Washington 6, D. C., and edited by Walter J. Howe, a shooter of background and achievement. A sizable technical staff answers members' inquiries and conducts tests of new equipment. The *Rifleman* has broadened its coverage since World War II, and wisely, I think. Whether a person's chief interest lies in modern or antique rifles, shotguns, or pistols doesn't matter as much as his being a gun-lover. The main aim of the NRA, as I see it, is to keep us Americans armed, and skilled in the use of arms. "To make America, once again, a nation of riflemen" is a statement of the goal, or part of that goal. Subversive elements that would disarm us don't like the NRA very much. Probably no other organization does anything comparable to its effort to maintain that part of the Constitution that says "The right of the people to keep and bear arms shall not be infringed."

Precision Shooting is a successor to *Shooters' News*. St. Johnsbury, Vt., is the publication office's address, and the editor, P. H. Teachout, has his office at nearby Lyndonville. Bench and position shooters use this monthly magazine as their news exchange medium, and there are technical articles on what makes accuracy that are second to absolutely none that I've found anywhere. Phil Teachout is as crazy about shooting as

CHAPTER 26

USEFUL
ACCESSORIES

you or I; he's a hunter, position shot and bencher. I don't know anyone who works any harder for precision shooting in America, and I don't see how anyone could, and live. He gets results, but you can't weigh 'em on scales. "Intangible' is the word. Leave out intangibles, and life would be a jungle. That was one of the Nazis' mistakes.

Guns comes from 8150 N. Central Park Blvd., Skokie, Ill., and William B. Edwards is its technical editor. He has beefed it up with the solid meat that guncranks demand. But *Guns* has another purpose. Its makeup is aimed at the man in the street, the fellow we might be able to interest in shooting, to share our fun and help "make America, once again . . .'"

Gun Digest comes out once a year, and news-stands and sports stores have it or they're crazy. John Amber edits it and usually is one of the 30 or so contributors. There are "big names" and some you may never have heard of, but they all have something worth writing. It's like getting an over-300-page, double-column book except that there are so many authors and viewpoints represented. The catalogue sections are up to date, and with comments. John Amber is a shooter of the investigative, curious kind, and one of his hobbies is metallic-cartridge single-shot rifles.

Remember, please, that these four publications are typical. There are others, and I haven't even touched on books, which go so well before an open fireplace, or in a dinky little crawl-in tent with a carefully mounted candle for light, and the night life of the woods going on much as usual, hardly a biscuit-toss from its thin

Mossberg spotting scope, drawtube focus, and stand. Dust caps are removed.

walls. For that matter, I knew a man who had read most of Shakespeare while sitting quiet and easy in squirrel country.

TARGET ACCESSORIES

If some of us fell into deep water on our way to the range, we'd likely enough drown. We can tote as much as the rifle's weight, in accessories, and all of them help—or could help—most of us. Here are a few.

Ear-plugs may play a double part: they help to prevent flinching from muzzle blast, and they probably save the acuteness of our hearing, though medical men might not agree on that subject. Rubber, cotton, wax, or mechanical: take your pick, but empty brass cases aren't advised. The Lee sonic ear-valves are of the kind that let conversation in—such important words as range commands, for instance.

Shooting glasses certainly can save our vision if a case bursts, high-power or rim-fire. Big lenses may make you sweat, but they're made big to stop all flying fragments of brass.

About 20 power or a little up is generally useful in a spotting scope, though some have interchangeable eyepieces to let us switch magnification when conditions warrant it. Too much power isn't all-around serviceable. Some makes are Mossberg, Saturn, Bushnell, Unertl, and Bausch & Lomb. A right-angled eyepiece is handiest for some shooters in prone, and in sitting you just look down into it. Take pains in adjusting the stand to make it as easy as possible to see without crawling out of a good position you like to stay in till the string has been fired.

There's little need for quick-detachable sling swivels on the range, for we do *not* hurry when we're there. The 1¼-inch sling is target standard, and fine for a

heavy hunting rifle. A light sporter is comfortable to tote on a ⅞- or 1-inch sling, or on a carrying strap. With the latter you can carry the rifle muzzle-down, strap over the non-shooting shoulder, then whirl it up into a sort of hasty sling hold, without twisting it around your arm for greater security. The Williams "Guide" strap is an example.

For the shooting sling there are "keepers' keepers," like the Albree brand, to prevent the arm loop from loosening. Why some gunslings come with one of the standard leather keepers on the loop, where it belongs, and the other down on the tailpiece, I don't know, except that it'd be natural just outside Buckingham Palace, for looks. Touching each other on the loop, the keepers have some chance to hold the sling high up on your arm in shooting positions. But you *can* use the Army web sling for target, after you're accustomed to it, and that has no keeper at all. A tremendous triceps muscle could help!

The Morgan adjustable recoil pad alters both pitch and drop. Soft rubber, comfortable, and it could help some of us in position shooting. It's a bit like having your own try gun.

Triggers

Almost everyone wants an adjustable-weight, single-stage trigger for target as well as hunting. This doesn't mean that the military type, with takeup before final pull, is no good, and the "as issued" service rifle is prescribed for some most interesting matches. The Timney, Jaeger, Mashburn, Dayton-Traister, and Canjar are representative single-stage, special-job trig-

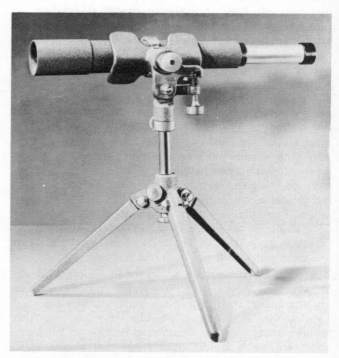

Bausch & Lomb Balscope Junior spotting scope, drawtube focus.

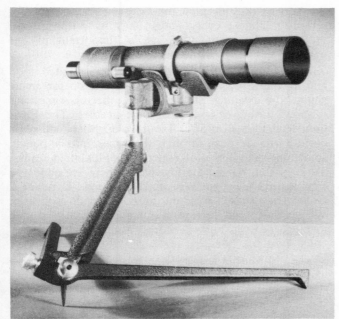

Bausch & Lomb Balscope Senior spotting scope, screw focus.

the hard, hard ground), rifle rests for long prone strings when we're not aiming and firing, glove or mitt for the forward hand, arm cuff for the sling, and maybe a spring "sling tension equalizer" to cut tremor to the minimum—all these can help. A cartridge block lets us keep our mind on making a score, not on how many rounds are yet to be fired, and it should hold a big supply and have a cover to exclude dust. A score-book is for records, not particularly of the scores but of sight settings, temperature, wind, light conditions, make and lot of ammunition, and so on. These details we'd use again for reference *and* study to see what caused what.

A tyro's natural reaction to a list of target accessories is "Do I have to have them all to do any good?"

Maybe most of us could learn from him. Shooting is

Unertl spotting scope. A right-angle eyepiece model also is made for convenience in sitting (look straight down into it) or in prone (turn your head just a trifle).

gers. Canjar also makes a set trigger—push it forward to make it of "hair" weight—and there are others, including some from abroad. Canjar uses a "shoe" on his, to make the unset pull seem lighter.

This is another popular extra for target rifles and pistols. Some arms, like the 52C Winchester, come from the factory with that extra-broad surface. A fully adjustable single-stage trigger can be changed for depth of sear engagement and amount (if any) of overtravel or backlash, as well as for weight, though the first two details, unless they're terrible, might not be important to a good many target shots.

Colonel Townsend Whelen wrote an article for the September, '56 issue of *Precision Shooting* that is most helpful—"Serviceability of Triggers." He mentions the Winchester 70 and the Sako as easy to clean and care for, to leave perfectly dry for extreme cold if we wish to. To remove the oil from a trigger mechanism he suggests Stoddard's Solvent (Esso "Varsol"), and for relubricating to take about −10°F. cold, either Fiendoil, that popular bore cleaner, or "MIL-L-644A, Oil, Lubricating and Preserving, Special" that an NRA member can buy from the Army's Director of Civilian Marksmanship. For 40-below cold he advises "MIL-L-17353, Lubricating Oil, Low Temperature, Special," from the Lehigh Chemical Co., Chestertown, Md.

Any of these precautions is more for the hunter than the targeteer, though I've seen some bitterly cold days on the range and hope to see more, if I can't go when it's warmer. Just so I go.

Other Aids

Ground-cloths, padded shooting coats (to keep the rifle butt at the shoulder and protect the elbows from

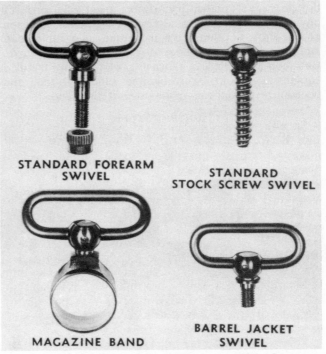

STANDARD FOREARM SWIVEL

STANDARD STOCK SCREW SWIVEL

MAGAZINE BAND

BARREL JACKET SWIVEL

Some typical fixed swivels by Williams Gun Sight Company. The magazine band type slips over the magazine tube, just ahead of the forestock.

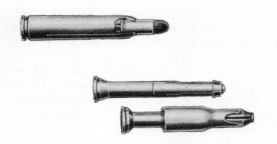

Marble auxiliary cartridge and broken shell extractor. This particular auxiliary is for .30-06, holding a .32 Automatic Colt cartridge, and the extractor is shown off duty, also as ready to haul a .30-30 case casualty out of the chamber.

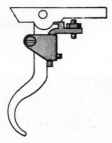

Viggo Miller's inexpensive trigger attachment, from 4340 Charles St., Omaha, removes the military takeup or slack from Enfield, Krag, Mauser, Model 30 Remington, or 1903 Springfield triggers, converting the pull from double- to single-stage.

or should be for all of us Americans. Do we need classifications based on equipment as well as on ability achieved?

That must be the stupidest question of the month, though here's another try: do we need riflemen? It's obvious, though, that a sort of post-graduate division of rifle-shots develops both techniques and equipment, and it's a specialists' school to work into, *if we want to.* But shooting with less expensive, more easily handled equipment should be recognized officially, too, and beginnings have been made toward that end.

HUNTING STUFF

Here too the manufacturers seem to go hog-wild in

the variety of stuff they think up and turn out. But seriously, almost every gadget has its purpose, and the small businessman is just as important to our national economy as the giant corporation.

A weighted thong pull-through with a patch loop and maybe a brush at the other end will do for emergency bore cleaning. Stuff gets into a barrel, sometimes —snow, dust, weed seeds or pine needles. The Flex-Gun Rod Co., Box 561, Trout Lake, Mich., makes a curl-up rod or push-through that goes into a pouch, something like the old Winchester Flexible Cleaner. To keep stuff out, in the first place, there are neoprene caps, as made by the Woodford Mfg. Co., Lyndhurst, Ohio. They stretch over the muzzle and do no harm. We get increased pressures, sometimes heavy enuogh to bulge or even burst a barrel, when something goes down *into* the bore.

The old Marble firm at Gladstone, Mich., must have had some woods-loafers in the family. Their broken-shell extractor has saved nice days for hunters. If we shoot a rear-locked rifle and reload our brass we may get a head separation: the sides of the case grip the chamber walls and the head goes back with the spring of a loosely breeched action, and the result is s-t-r-e-t-c-h. With a rimmed case a rupture from this cause is seldom serious to our eyes or face, but the front section of brass stays in the chamber unless we have the means to get it out. In rare instances a case neck is carried up into or clear through the rifled bore.

The auxiliary cartridge made by Marble is typical of quite a tribe that lets us fire pistol ammunition (or .22 Hornet, in some makes of adapter) in high-power rifles. The Marble has the now almost universal firing pin, hit by the rifle's own striker. The old Winchester supplemental chamber was a straight-through tube with no firing pin of its own. Possibly it was easier on the rifle's striker, but the pistol bullet had to take a long hop through the smoothbore tube to get into the rifling.

Marble makes other things for the hunter, some of which he'd be glad to have if he were bushed and had to lie out overnight. Compass, knife, little axe, and

This fine Griffin & Howe 722-.222 Remington is fitted with a Canjar set trigger, unset in this photo. When it is set, the "hair trigger" stands forward from the center of the trigger proper, easy to see—and clean and so easy to release! It can be unset without firing the rifle. This sort of trigger is particularly indicated for precision target work when a set trigger is allowed, and for long-range varmint shooting. The rifle has a G&H detachable floorplate, and the Kollmorgen 6x scope is held in the new G&H quick-detachable top mounts.

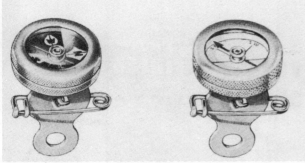

Pin-on compasses, made by Marble Arms, and more compact than their early type, seldom get lost or broken. To read them you just stand still and look down. The dial on the left is floating or revolving; the other is stationary.

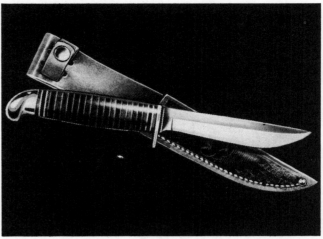

Marble's Sportsman knife has a narrow 4-inch blade and is a good representative specimen of the type that's big and heavy enough for almost all outdoor needs.

waterproof matchbox—but don't use up those matches in smoking! Some food, some kindling if the woods are soaked and there's no birch, fat spruce or other standby, a flashlight, and an extra shirt or sweater—such things come to mind. A stub of candle weighs not much more than five .22 short cartridges and it *could* start the all-night campfire if you shield the beginning from rain. We can carry enough to tough it out if we must, and still go light and happy. The experience can be delightful if we're ready for it.

Muzzle Brakes

Popular use of these devices to reduce recoil started with the general acceptance of the Lyman Cutts compensator for shotguns. A muzzle brake lets us carry a much lighter rifle, with endurable recoil, than one that has no such shock absorber. Featherweights are in fashion not only now; they always have been, and legitimately so for certain purposes.

The present tendency is to streamline the brakes to improve the rifle's appearance and, for some of us, to make it less muzzle-heavy. The Pendleton is made to fit the muzzle, and the Christy ramp brake, threaded to the barrel as most of these devices are, though cutting of the barrel itself can do it, has its own front sight on the ramp. So it's out front, not several inches from the muzzle. One of the newer makes, the Sorenson, is home-attached by a screw collet. Since this one is open at the top, not finned along the sides, it doesn't reduce the backward thrust (recoil, as we generally know it) as much as some others do. Its purpose is to reduce the upchuck of the muzzle, make it easier and quicker to pull down into the line of aim once more, quicker to see the effect of our shot, too. It gives less muzzle blast than the average brake, though the long-established Sha-Cul always was noted for lack of blast.

Muzzle blast is as definite a part of the recoil effect we feel as the backward drive of the buttplate and the thrust of a stock comb that's wrongly designed for our personal use. To some of us the blast is more distracting, more destructive of markmanship. If the brake is of the usual type that slams the racket back at us, an extremely short overall barrel length, includ-

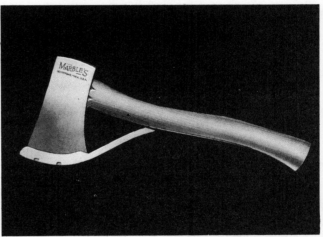

This sort of pocket axe needs no holster. Marble made, it has a lead-lined edge guard that can—and had better—be folded back into the handle before chopping starts.

ing the brake, isn't going to help so much. Conversely, a long barrel actually assists in reducing the recoil we feel, by its very length, irrespective of any weight it may add. This is not given as argument in favor of long barrels; we choose what we want for the kind of country we hunt, and to suit our tastes.

Soft rubber recoil pads help most of us when we fire heavy charges in a light rifle. Some shooters think that their resilience gives the butt a runing start before it hits us, and this may be so. There are two other possible disadvantages to the pad. It is definitely not light in weight, and it can catch on our clothing when we try to mount the gun fast. Sometimes a shotgun pad is dressed up nicely with leather facing to make it less sticky against the clothes. For hunting in rocky country it couldn't be expected to have a long life span.

Safeties

Few safety catches except the top tang or the fairly large side type, pivoted or sliding, are as quick to thumb as an exposed hammer. Some of us do find the Mauser or Springfield type wing at the rear of the bolt just as handy unless a low-mounted scope stands over it. But many excellent factory rifles have a safe that must be "learned." That takes practice, and the safety may never be a really good job to use.

The Fischer safe for the Mauser, from Modern Gun Shop, 2522 Chicago Drive, S. W., Grand Rapids 9, Mich., is on the side. It doesn't affect any special trigger mechanism; it will work with any trigger. A

This Williams stock-finishing kit is representative of a good many that are offered. It should do for several stocks.

For a half century or so the Marble waterproof match box has needed few if any changes. In size and capacity it's like a 10-gauge shell. The knurled outer surface is for a scratcher when the woods are dripping wet, and the lanyard swivel— if it's *used*—assures us of having matches on land or on or in water.

special Fischer model has a bolt-lock button; the standard one doesn't lock the bolt handle down.

The Jaeger M1 for the Mauser is a thumb lever, right or left hand as chosen, and the M2 is a handy wing type safe for scoped Mausers, Springfields, Krags, and 54 Winchesters. The Doc Line make `is another special Mauser safety, of the sliding type.

A cross-button safety in the trigger guard is unhandy for some hunters, especially when they wear gloves. A tang safe for the Remington 572 .22 and the 740 and 760 high powers comes from Triangle Gun Co., Baldwin, Mich., and a similar type, for a few other rifles too, from the J. Dewey Gun Co., East Hampton, Conn. A different solution is simply to make the cross-button a great deal bigger. First popular on shot-

guns, it's now available for rifles also. The Williams Gunsight Company's "Giant Head" is made and advertised right along.

These are only a few of the custom safety jobs, and new ones can be expected to come up at any time.

Cases and Scabbards

In the drift and sift of wind-driven, powdery snow an Arctic hunter or explorer may carry his rifle in his hand or on the sled, cased up, until the moment before firing. He needs a case from which the rifle can be drawn or slid in a hurry, just as the mounted man demands a saddle scabbard or boot that not only protects the gun from being spilled but also allows a quick grab-out. In an all-day rain the canoeist welcomes a rig that gives protection and handiness, and he must strap it to a thwart or a seat in case of an upset into the drink.

But the average hunter wants a case to use on the way to camp, in camp, and when packing out. The worst kind is the old-fashioned flannel-lined canvas, a terror to dry after a wetting, and wool fleece lining can be bad enough, though at least it gives protection against roughhandling. A plain, heavy, unlined canvas case, leather reinforced at muzzle and breech, certainly is serviceable, and not bulky, either. It won't attract moisture, as flannel does. Thin, light, waterproof cases are splendid in damp countries, and they can be folded to pocket size.

For home storage anything from vaporized paper bags through nylon-fur, wool, and what-have-you lining, to hard, stiff leather or wood cases and on to cabinets protected by Dampp-Chaser or the old-time chunk of gum camphor can be used as space and whim decide. The main idea is to look at the guns from time to time, check 'em over. Friends don't like, to be forgotten except when we make use of them!

Williams Giant Head safety on 760 Remington slide action.

BINOCULARS

Most spotting scopes except some of the drawtube type are long and rather heavy. A rifle scope can be unhandy for glassing possible hideouts of game, and the swing of the rifle liable to give us away at short ranges. So the binocular and monocular have their uses, out hunting.

For lightness, wide field, and plenty of light the 6x30 (6-power, 30-mm. objectives) binoc is a favorite, the heavier 7x35 still more so, at present. The 8x30 has lightness but not quite the bright definition of the other two. Actual differences are small.

Similar to the 7x35 in size and weight is the 9x35, really a mountain or plains glass. At a distance, in fairly good light, it just about equals the brilliant and much heavier and bulkier 7x50, the sailor's binocular. The 9x35 is no night glass, but it's better than none at all in dim light.

There are other combinations of power and brilliance, and we trade either quality for the other as we like, remembering that a companionable, much-used and profited-by glass rides our neck on a shortened strap, quick to raise, more comfortable because less bunglesome than one in the long-strap, belly-busting carry. I found a 4x20 Zeiss an excellent little woods binoc with good illumination—divide power into objective and you get the same dividend as with the 6x30 or 7x35. Somewhat similar little glasses are still available, and for brightness the power must be low. The temptation is to use too much.

A monocular doesn't give the depth and distance-judging effect of a double-barrel glass, but it's compact and useful. Though it never rode my chest as comfortably as a binoc, the 8x30 Zeiss I once had did well as a varmint glass before I used scoped rifles to any great extent. The only binocular I have or want now is the 9x35 Bausch & Lomb. Just one to take care of and stay familiar with.

It pays to get a name brand, I suppose, and they are made here, in Germany, in England, in Japan, and I don't know where else. It pays most of all to try before we buy.

MISCELLANEA

Dictionary says I can use that mouthful of word. This catch-all could go on indefinitely, still sticking to "useful accessories," but a few little hints are enough, then a bigger one at the last.

Soft-point bullets get messed up in most box magazines from recoil—we can't do much about them in a tube mag. For the Springfield, Mauser, Enfield and Winchester there's a typical and proved bullet-point protector. It comes from I. J. Sullivan, Culdesac, Idaho.

For headspace gauges L. E. Wilson is famous, and there are other good makers, such as Forster and H. & M. Tool Company. Whether a gauge is to check the headspace of a match .22 rimfire for accurate shooting or of a powerful bigbore, for safety, it's either reassuring or informative, and with good luck, both. Gunsmiths use them right along.

The bench-rest action stiffener from Bellows & Son, Box 132, Wilcox, Pa., is, I believe, a rather new one. It sounds good: heavy steel sleeve 13 inches long, sweated on. The length permits scope base positioning on it, and it doesn't touch a free-floating barrel.

We do well to judge the value of any rifle accessory by asking ourselves whether its cost, weight

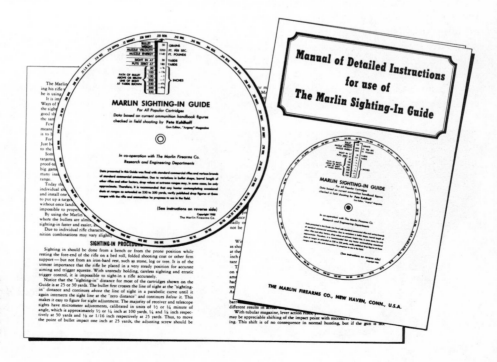

Marlin's plastic Sighting-In Guide gives practical trajectory information for zero settings, overhold or underhold, with twenty different rifle cartridges, some with more than one weight of bullet. Calibers run from .22 long-rifle high velocity to .358 Winchester.

(except for bench), ease and sureness in learning to use it, and its frequency of use make it worth while. Some streamline a rifle that is to be carried a good deal, and some do the opposite. We go to the range or the hunting grounds to enjoy ourselves, not to nurse a flock of gadgets. No, that's wrong: some of us enjoy piddling with them, and if we want to, that's our inalienable right.

H E LOCKED the car, put his shotgun together, and tossed it to his shoulder several times before we started for the woodlot, that morning of opening day. I wondered whether that was all the practice he'd taken since the last year's season had closed.

Shotgun shooting becomes almost instinctive from long practice, dry or with live ammunition, and so, in different ways, do all the forms of rifle shooting. From habit we grow accustomed to doing a certain job in a definite way, and that way can be right or wrong in the matters of efficiency, sureness and ease.

Watch a good bench-rester, prone shot or snapshooter go through the movements preparatory to firing and you see the smoothness and certainty of habit, no lost motions. The first two do settle down rather slowly, but their movements are calculated. They know what they're doing; there are no frustrated twists and squirms. They accommodate themselves to the bench and stool, or to the ground. The snapshooter's rear or forward knee may bend or straighten, his body lean or crouch or stretch upright, but these things are done instinctively, to give him the balance, the base for easy swing, maybe to open a road over or under obstacles that could stop or deflect his bullet.

Trigger squeeze to suit the occasion, and aiming too, become familiar through long practice. It takes time to learn a rifle.

RIGHT AT HOME

We can become right at home with a rifle sooner if we get in lots of practice right at home, and we stay that way by keeping up the practice. This can be fun, and varied, too, for their are several grindstones on which to whet our skill.

Position

Position drill could come first, and like the others it isn't only for the beginner. Offhand shots practice it several times a week, with benefit. We have learned from a really good, experienced shot or from a book or manual,* how to assume the positions. In time they become comfortable and steady.**

But watch yourself, not to get into bad habits, such as failing to hold the supporting elbow almost directly under the forestock in prone. Every so often it pays most of us to have other shooters check our positions.

---

*Townsend Whelen's *Ultimate in Rifle Precision* (for bench-resters) and *Hunting Rifle,* Edward C. Crossman's *Military and Sporting Rifle Shooting,* the Sporting Arms and Ammunition Manufacturers' Institute's *Handbook on Smallbore Rifle Shooting,* and inexpensive NRA manuals, including the little *Junior Rifle Handbook* for the kids—these are some of them.

**Yes, they do. I learned to sit on the side of my foot, kneeling, and like it, when I was just past fifty. Hurt? Of course it did at first, but before spring came I could hold that position indefinitely. I'd almost expected a dislocation or fracture—first-off, you feel like a turkey being disjointed—but time proved me to have been grossly pessimistic.

CHAPTER 27

HOME, RANGE AND FIELD PRACTICE

Going through a course of fire like the Camp Perry instruction once every few years is a wonderful refresher.

Aiming and Gun Fit

Since the act of aiming is simple, it can become casual. Rifle sights are for precise alignment. Lineup may have to be fast, and it should never waste time, for even in slow prone there is the process of trigger squeeze to go through, and a poky shot wears himself out in just holding the rifle.

A little bullseye on the wall of your bedroom can take a lot of dry firing, and here comes up the question: why do we use a round bullseye for almost all rifle shooting but bench? So far it seems to be the best: we can hold a flat-top or even a round bead front sight under it, or quarter it with scope cross-hairs. Sure, it doesn't look like game, and for that matter, dry practice on animal outlines in a bedroom does us nearly as much good as live practice does outdoors on such silhouettes, for we can get a lot more of it. The thing is to do plenty, and few of us overdo it.

Slow, careful alignment on (or under) the target stuck on the wall in time is supplemented, not replaced, by tossing the rifle up and aiming fast. Both ways, we get to know the feel of our rifle. If it's properly made for us, or we for it, the sights are almost on target, after we've learned, as soon as the butt hits our shoulder.

Working the Action

For our first hunting rifle we're apt to choose one that seems easy and natural to function. If we aren't experienced, the quality of speed may loom up as all-important: fire-power still seems to consist of volume more than accuracy. Later we learn better, and practice can make even the bolt action fast enough in off-the-shoulder operation. This takes time—and the ability to appreciate the need for it.

I knew a seasoned old guide who habitually lowered his lever action .30-30 to hip level to work it when he needed a second shot, fast. Not much sense in that, but few of us knew better then.

It isn't hard to develop speed in functioning, and with some rifles it's best to use dummy cartridges. They work differently with brass from the way they do empty. Be sure that the cartridges *are* dummies, with fired primers or none at all, to make identification easy.

Trigger Squeeze

Most modern rifles can be dry-fired, snapped, indefinitely, without danger of breaking a firing pin, or of marring the edge of a rimfire's chamber. Dummies with dead primers can be used with old rifles, or for reassurance with new ones, and some hammer guns can be fitted with rubber plugs to protect their firing pins.

In dry-firing we can call our shots as easily as with live ammunition. "That's a 9 at 3 o'clock," close to the 10-ring but a bit right. Here, as usual, honesty pays off! No one can call a shot that he's flinched.

Good pistol shots usually take to the difficult off-hand rifle act because they've mastered trigger squeeze. "The Bullseye Pistol" fires No. 6 shot—take 6 from 17, the rule goes, and you get .11-inch diameter—and snaps them out accurately enough to hit its quarter-inch black bull right along at eight feet, if the rubber band propellant is adjusted correctly. That pin-weight gun with its long, spongy trigger pull is a great trainer: you never know when it'll fire; so it's silly to flinch. Firing it is about as noisy as breaking a matchstick and the pellet is unlikely to break any window glass. Close-up it can ruin a light bulb—I just tried that, to find out!—and it could destroy an eye. But who wants a gun that can be handled carelessly?

Live Firing—If

Some of us live where we can fire .22 rimfires or round-ball squib loads down cellar or in the garage. There's no sense, and there's much unjustified risk, in doing this illegally. If we're found out and punished, another black mark goes up against shooting in general, and it's liable to be publicized.

But when it's OK we can get more from it than amusement and relaxation, though there's plenty of those. Every shot fired, indoors or out, should be the best we can do at that moment. When we're tired, we'd better quit.

Indoors or out, this is fun. Firing in rough weather has its points, for not all match or hunting days are perfect.

Rifle Clubs

Congenial people are a big part of living, and one place where we find them is on the range. Sometimes the practice and competition we get there seem to be almost by-products.

Senior Clubs. Almost any senior club has an indoor range, and a lucky or enterprising and impossible-to-discourage outfit may have an outdoor range, too. If 200 yards is its limit, the hunter and target shot can still learn plenty there with .22 or with bigbore, provided the latter is allowed. We learn a little about range estimation, just looking over the distances, and much about wind's effects on bullets. Windage tables help, but different handloads and different abilities in "reading" the wind, its force and direction, vary a great deal. It comes down to the basic "Learn *your* rifle" foundation.

A 300-yard range is enough for most hunters' practice. For one thing, it teaches us how hard it is to hit the equivalent of a vital spot, at the very least 19 times out of 20, with the advantages of knowing exactly what the range is and of firing from a good position. Rapid fire is commonly practiced outdoors, at least with bigbore, and it teaches us action functioning *and* the quick settling back into steadiness after we've fired and reloaded.

Competition, inside or inter-club, is keen, and shooting under pressure is great preparation for more important shooting—big match or any game. Not that hunting ever should be competitive: the game supply can't stand much more of that, and we lose our deepest enjoyment in hunting when we value, say, newspaper publicity, more than the sport itself. Sportsmanship is hard to define—and a lot of people aren't interested in it. Stewart White once called it doing a thing for the pleasure that lies in it, not for any rewards. He was precisely right: that's the way to pleasure.

Junior Clubs. Any rifleman learns from coaching. It reminds him of the principles of marksmanship. Occasionally new angles come up, too.

Coaching junior clubs is one of the most rewarding things I ever did. Age difference need be no bar to friendship. Sometimes a kid is pathetically appreciaciative, and in this generation, too, when they're given all the world on a plate, except for that intangible—adults' time. You see most of the adult emotions in youngsters, usually without effective camouflage. It's like studying the world through the wrong end of a monocular, and you know what a bright, clear little vision that gives you.

Some junior clubs are subsidized and some stand on their own feet. Both ways have advantages unnecessary to discuss. Those that amount to much generally are NRA-affiliated, for kids value the medals, pins

Lee Richards (left) and Kenneth Williams, Cub Scouts, age 10, are members of the Spring Airgun Division of the Tidewater Musketeers. They were the first boys of the Virginia Peninsula to make Expert rating with .18-caliber smoothbore Daisy airguns. *Courtesy Roy S. Tinney.*

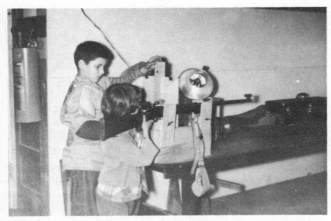

Tidewater Musketeers discuss technique. Stephen Cook shows Ann Chambers why bullets don't always hit the bullseye. "Your sighting is wrong," he explains. "This is the correct way to aim a rifle." Thus are the youngsters taught to handle firearms with precision, and with safety to themselves and others. Safety rules are strictly enforced; no carelessness is permitted. *Courtesy Roy S. Tinney.*

and brassards in a refreshingly unsophisticated way. Affiliation doesn't cost much, and there are the DCM supplies and loan of rifles. In general it's by no means the lack of cash that limits the number of junior clubs. It's the lack of men and women to take the plunge—and keep up their own attendance—as instructors. (The kids had best do at least 90 percent of the paper work.) If folks realized how deep and abiding the rewards are, there'd be no difficulty.

Over at Hampton, Tidewater Virginia, Judge Roy S. Tinney has had as busy and happy an experience with junior shooters as anyone I know of. He starts them at age X, "Sub-Juniors (11 or younger)" in his "sneeze gun," spring-powered, smoothbore airgun, and his .22 rimfire divisions, and he goes right on up. Some matches include parents, for instance, and there are lots of matches. Novelty events, such as "Miss-and-

you're-out" matches at thumb-tacks, competition on paper man targets, and so on are seeded through to maintain interest.

The Judge at once realized the value of the Canadian Civilian Association of Marksmen (Box 635, Station B, Montreal, Quebec) 15-yard target with large scoring rings for beginners, and competition limited to light, usually inexpensive rifles. Naturally he appreciates fine equipment—and the greater value of shooting that's made easy, accessible and safe for everyone who has the slightest itch to try it. His photographs show something of the job he has put over, and notice how *interested* all those people look! That study of the tiny ones at the Winter device, for instance, is absolutely fascinating, *and you could get similar results if you'd wade in and try.*

His people go about as far up the ladder as aptitude and unlimited opportunity let them, and he has helped make his part of the Old Dominion as gun-conscious and gun-favoring as any place we'd be likely to find. (He would be quick to say that he has *only* helped.) This happened in a densely populated area. I call this work 100 percent American and as sickening to the anti-gun legislators as any development could be. People in that part of Tidewater appreciate firearms because they're no dreadful unknown quantity. They're the means to a way of living and to the retention of that way.

Offhand, that difficult position, pays off 95 percent of the time in a four-position match, in hunting, or in shooting for keeps. Here is the Judge's description of a certain kind of event the people out there shoot at times:

"Penny-in-the-Hat is an old English game, so

Front view of the Winter Sighting Device used by all branches of the armed services. This one is on the indoor range at Langley Aeronautical Laboratory. Besides teaching the optics of marksmanship it reveals defective vision that should be corrected. One of the Junior Musketeers has defective vision; yet he won the individual high-over-all small-bore rifle trophy awarded in 1955 by the Virginia State Rifle and Revolver Association. Note that both rifles' bolts are open, as they should be, always, except on the firing line after the command "Load" or "Commence firing" has sounded. *Courtesy Roy S. Tinney.*

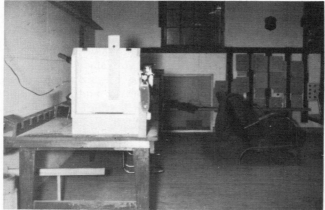

Rear view of the Winter Sighting Device. *Courtesy Roy S. Tinney.*

Schuetzen offhand by one of Judge Tinney's riflemen using a palmrest for the forward hold. *Courtesy Roy S. Tinney.*

named because the score was kept by tossing pennies in a hat. On our indoor range we use the eleven-bull official NRA match target and place a white thumb-tack in the center of each of the bullseyes to save a trip to the butts each time a direct hit is scored. Two wooden bowls replace the hat and we use poker chips instead of the big copper pennies. All firing is done in the standing offhand position. Grazing the tack is scored as a miss; it must be eliminated. A difficult shot that will 'prove the hold' and measure the skill of the best smallbore shots. A time limit is set, usually one hour.

"The shooters draw lots and fire in that rotation. If the first shooter knocks out the tack his score is one point and one direct hit. He retires and the next shooter comes to the firing-line. Each time a tack is missed its value is increased one point. Should shooters two, three, four, five and six miss that tack and the seventh one knock it out of the target, his or her score is six points and one direct hit.

"As each shooter comes to the firing-line the scorer takes a poker chip out of the left hand bowl and places it in the one to the right. The number of chips in that bowl indicates the value of the next direct hit. Occasionally there will be as many as twenty-odd chips in the right hand bowl. The high value of his shot causes the shooter to feel the pressure experienced during a hotly contested match, and the comments of the 'gallery' often induce an attack of buck fever."

Did you notice how he held back the climax, the meat of the story, for the last sentence?

Shooting for Everyone

Sometimes a component part of "everyone" likes to shoot alone, without companionship or competition. That's fine—and the only way—for certain people, and attempts to drive them into the fold may be no less than persecution. Then too, some of our keenest testing is likely to be fired when we're alone or with just one companion. But most Americans are as gregarious as the bison on our nickel, though *he* in real life was

too gregarious for his own good when the Sharps and Remington rifles went out west.

"Shooting for everyone" is a goal, not yet a reality. Switzerland approaches it, and she hasn't been invaded since smokeless powder added concealment to the rifleman's precision.

The Canadian Civilian Association's system, usually modified in allowing the use of the gunsling and in other and minor ways, is one that we could follow with profit. It has been followed to some extent. Phil Teachout, *Precision Shooting's* editor at Lyndonville, Vermont, has worked hard to promote it. The light, easily handled rifle and the less difficult than standard targets make the change from tin cans to paper less disillusioning to the still casual shooter, and paper does show exactly where you hit, and what to do in order to improve.

Canadian or "Sporting Rifle" shooting is an all-the-family game. That's one of the greatest things in its favor. Grades of qualification mark progress and

Spotting and scoring Penny-in-the-Hat. Bowls of poker chips stand under the spotting scopes. Judge Tinney's photograph proves that riflery is an absorbing game for any and all Americans—or as near as could be to all—that are given a chance at it. He's caught that rapt, expectant look. *Courtesy Roy S. Tinney.*

the sport is "official" without appearing too formal. Certainly it's a long step in a smart direction.

Sometimes a club goes at it in a quite different way, the aim being identical, to popularize shooting by demonstrating how safe, interesting and enjoyable it can be. Paying a dollar per shot at a turkey match is a slow, expensive way of learning marksmanship, though the competitive spirit and the concentration are certainly present! There are better avenues of introduction.

Mr. C. F. Robbins of Selinsgrove, Pennsylvania, was instrumental in his club's part at a Harrisburg sportsmen's show, the first big one held in that area. "No one knew what would happen," he wrote— but just read on.

"Seven and one-half pound [maximum weight limit] rifle with metallic sights fired on a crow target at fifty feet, ten shots, ten minutes, junior and senior class; offhand, twelve targets, 50 cent entry fee; and good prizes. I believe our heaviest entry for the afternoon and evening session ran over 400. The show people are offering us three times the space for next year. It was the best drawing card in the show. We ran it the first three days and the junior program on standard targets, 10 offhand and 10 prone, the last two days."

Since his club obviously made money, one might say that they'd commercialized the sport. I don't think so. People at the show were in a holiday mood, ready to spend, and ready to receive new impressions. A lot of them must have known almost nothing about rifle shooting when they came through the gates.

Here was an exhibit, a "concession" if you like, but "the best drawing card in the show." Many hesitant parents, completely uninformed about shooting, must have realized at that fair that it can be safe as well as thrilling. The lead-edged holes in the targets showed some of the difficulties, the challenge of shooting, *but the targets weren't too small.* The 50-yard crow— there are smaller ones, too, but the nearly life-size would be right at a fair—has a 10-ring, or oval, 1x3¾ inches, and who'd notice the X-rings of 7/16 inch, at chest center and eye? "Oh, the brave bulls!" to face those Pennsylvanians, a shooting breed, lots of them, though no one but a hero of romance *inherits* marksmanship.

Well, the complete scoring area is 8¼ inches long. Miss a standard (and beloved) NRA target 10 times in 10 shots offhand, not hard to do, and only a few come crowding back for more. Most of them would fade away like ghosts at sunrise and steer clear of that part of the fair for the rest of the day.

Maybe they'd keep away from shooting for the rest of their lives.

FIELD PRACTICE

All the four standard target positions—prone, sit, kneel and offhand—are handy in hunting as opportunity offers. Unconventional positions, too, can make the difference between a miss or a tragic, crippling, lost-game hit and a clean kill. We take those positions as we can: log or rock or rolled-up coat rest, our (flesh and blood) forearm steadied against a tree, a sprawl that may combine kneel and sit, our feet propped against the thwart of a canoe, our back against a tree, and so on.

Rifle recoil must be remembered before assuming some of these positions. If it's too great or if the body is ill-poised, don't try. Results can be the (perhaps) comic ducking of an overboard spill, or severe bruises, even a fracture. The back position, for instance, with the rifle barrel held in a V between the raised legs and the butt in the hollow of the shoulder or even in the cup of the left hand, behind the head, can be more than uncomfortable when a stiff charge lets go. It does let us hold steadily without a sling. For this position, the butt-in-shoulder form, some of the black-powder target rifles had their vernier peep sights mountable at the heel of the stock.

Snapshooting

That's the general name for firing at a moving target, or a still one that must be taken right away or never.

It's best to try the latter way first, in practice, for thus we learn command of the rifle—quick mounting and sight alignment, and the speeded trigger press that is not a yank. Single shots begin it, followed much later by magazine fire. All these are timed, but speed means not one hundredth as much as accuracy that's capable of killing hits. Military-style rapid fire with .22 or bigbore is a fine trainer, but offhand should be included.

After a while we go to moving targets. Some clubs build a running-deer setup, which is splendid even if the deer runs like a mouse, without bounding. The lone shooter—in absolutely safe back-country, wilderness by choice—can roll a keg downhill, and it'll bounce plenty! With an assistant—whose safety he values—other methods can be worked out to make a target move.

Just as with the shotgun, there are three methods of firing a rifle at moving targets. The snapshooter gets off his shot in a flash, at the place where he expects his target to arrive simultaneously with the bullet. He doesn't swing the rifle, and probably his method is the hardest of all to make even fairly reliable. But people are different.

The swing-through method is fast. It starts behind the target, passes it, and ends with the bark of the rifle at what seems to be the appropriate time. Even in fairly thick woods this method is practicable, sometimes. The swing doesn't stop until after the bullet has gone, and there's some tendency to over-swing.

The sustained lead is somewhat similar. It starts, or tries to, with the correct lead and ends after the shot. The swing has a chance to get well under way, and this technique is good for a cool shooter. The other kind has a very tough time on moving targets.

Probably all of these methods should be practiced, for any could be right on a certain occasion, though the first, the snapshot, takes the most skill, I think. It comes nearest to demanding a "gift" for shooting. We know that that gift is a good 90 percent practice, the rest genius. We also know, or we should, that shooting a rifle at moving game is a sort of last resort, not a show-off stunt. Thing to do, when it's at all possible, is to get ourselves a standing shot and a sure kill.

Wind and Range

The field-practice shooter goes out in all sorts of weather, all the year 'round, and has unlimited opportunities to study wind and range. His only limitation is safety: there must be no ricochets unless he's in a wilderness. Such country abounds in large parts of the West. East, we have to look for it. When we're there in a dry season, the spout of dust tells where our bullet hits, making wind and range study that much quicker and easier. It takes a lot of shooting.

So the varmint supply might not hold out, and we must leave seed for next year and for following generations of humans. No matter if few of the preceding ones thought of us! Varmints are game, to us riflemen.

There's as much marksmanship training in trying to bust a bare spot of earth, a clump of grass, or a chunk of shale—we're using high-velocity, quick-breakup bullets, anyway—as there is in breaking a woodchuck's neck. It's as difficult to clip a dandelion as to hit him in the eye. I've done a good bit of such shooting, taking as my aiming point a spot some two feet to the side of a chuck, not in front of his face, for that might blind him, and letting off my shot with the greatest care. That improved my marksmanship and afforded some challenge to the next chuck hunter who came along!

My friend Bradley Upton, out in Solano, New Mexico, practices field shooting all through the year, and you can try almost any sized rock at any range in his country, with no fear of consequences if you use common sense. This constant shooting makes Brad deadly in deer season. He's owned, learned and mastered many different rifles, but as a rule he does nearly all of his shooting, for a long time, with just one. Occasionally, jackrabbits are pests out there, and he's a really fine running shot. But he doesn't shoot at a running deer from choice. He's particular about adequate power for the game in question, and as a matter of course he handloads. Instead of going to the 50,000-pounds-pressure levels he gets a case that's big enough to start with and doesn't need to be strained!

Seeing Game

Brad saw the ears of that muley over 200 yards away because he knew what to look for. A trained eye picks up game because it's so different from its background. We can get practice almost anywhere off concrete and asphalt, in the tall grass of a neglected dooryard that we pass by, for instance, where a cat may be lying.

No daytime trip through the country by car, bus or train need be monotonous—if someone else is driving. A big-city park is a charm to walk in, with its birds and squirrels, not all of whom are anxious to be seen. Even a bush beside the house or a square yard of lawn is a hunting ground. Insects live there, and some have "protective coloration," as the old and much debated term went. The walking stick, leaf or fern has life, intelligent life, and looks so different from his background that the trained eye sees him before he moves. There's seldom much time to be wasted if we can only get outdoors.

B ERT SHAY told of a friend of his, a southpaw being struck in the eye by an empty from a .22 auto-rifle. "He didn't make much of it," Bert observed, "but unless an autoloader has bottom ejection like the M24 Rem a left-hander has no business with one."

That was an unusual accident, for which the victim couldn't be held at fault. Most .22 auto-rifles, at least the good ones, fling their empty fired cases straight out to the right, to the right and forward, or straight down like those 24 and 241 Remingtons and the Browning from which they came. The Garand may hurl a magazineful of .30 caliber brass in a complete semicircle, but unlike the .45 Colt auto—and once in a great while the Luger—it rarely if ever aims them at our face.

It's just possible that the man in this story let his forward hand, the right, partly cover the ejection port and thus deflect the empty as it hopped out. Or the rifle could have been defective. Another practically unforeseeable accident, unlikely with the .22 rimfire powders used now, is an injury to the face or the eye when we fire into a strong wind. This "12 o'clock" wind can carry a half-burned powder kernel straight back, and still hot.

ACCIDENTS ARE PREVENTABLE

That .22 auto mishap, fortunately a slight one, was a freak. *But over 99 percent of gun accidents are preventable.* This percentage is due to carelessness, being too eager, ignorance, stupidity, or plain lack of consideration for others—or for oneself!

Since metallic cartridges and standardized dimensions of ammunition and arms came in, the material itself has rarely been at fault when it was used with reasonable intelligence. And today most of the old, weak rifles—a few of which were unsafe even with the ammunition of their times—have been retired. Some, of course, are used by people who understand them, and that's a quite different matter. In general, we can trust modern arms of standard manufacture, those described in this book, as examples.

THE CRIMINALS

Then who is at fault? Every year we have a great many gun accidents and most of them are publicized. They're *news*. Each one gives anti-gun legislators or voters material for their use.

The answer is all too obvious. It's as broad as the side of a house on an L of the road that is hit time and again by motorists who aren't fit to drive. It's the careless or the uninformed who pile up the casualty lists. There are more of them now because there are so many more hunters than—why, than just a few years past. We still have free hunting, not the restricted, undemocratic, European kind, but we deserve to have it only as long as we're considerate.

CHAPTER 28

GUN
SAFETY

JUNIOR HUNTER TRAINING

Start with the kids. That was the idea that sparked the New York State legislature, in 1949, to rule that youngsters under 17, who never had held a hunting license, must undergo training before they'd be eligible to buy their first one.

Of course the NRA was behind this. The *Rifleman* reported a breakdown of casualties into their causes, mistaken for game, line-of-fire accidents, and so on. Better than any other group the Association knew what is needed for prevention, and it still stands ready and eager to advise any individual or outfit how to get started on this life-saving project.

About a dozen states now have this will-to-help. Some of them use their school curricula for the purpose. In fact, no state is without NRA-certified instructors. The examination set up for instructor candidates isn't difficult because it's based on common sense!

When you explain that trained Junior Hunters have been, by actual record, nineteen times as safe as those that were just let loose—see the story, "A Good Beginning," in the September, '55, *Rifleman*—people are likely to listen to you.

Note that word "Beginning." One of its implications is lighted up by the fact that in 1952 New York raised the age limit to 21. In time, we hope, all hunters will have to take instruction and pass an exam on it before they can buy their first license.

"CLASS WILL COME TO ORDER"

Fay Mundt and I were a team, up in York State, and Art Plummer had taught us. Art travels thousands of miles a year on this job, locally, and out to the State Conservation Camps where our Country's flag flies, sunup to sundown, and beneath it some fortunate kids learn what they should about the outdoors and how to treat it. They learn for themselves and to pass on to their friends. Does Art get paid for his work? Naw, we're all volunteers. We don't cost the State much.

Fay and I would have from one to a couple of dozen boys and girls at a session. Did they want to learn? Most of them did, and they all *had to*.

Briefly, we taught them gun handling, responsibility for the bullet or shot that can't be called back like a dog on a wrong trail, field courtesy, and regard for private property rights. We had a lot to do in the four hours, with forty-five minutes off at the last for the written exam and the post-mortem on it.

Specifically, "What can you do to a gun to make it safe to let the muzzle point at a person?" Answer: "Nothing." Or "What should you do if your companion won't pay attention to safety rules?" Answer: "Reason with him, and if that's no go, get out while you're still alive."

We'd explain and demonstrate the safe field, boat, or car carries, protective colors of clothing (not forgetting the color-blind, and what deep shade does to red), fence crossing, getting into or out of a vehicle, fields of fire when a group is hunting, and so on. They'd demonstrate, too. For example, each one had to come up, with his rifle or shotgun, name its caliber or gauge, and its make. Some wouldn't know the make, dreadful to relate; so they'd sneak a look at the barrel, and did they get a ribbing from the other kids? Then they'd show how to operate the gun, or sometimes have to be shown.

They'd get more of this on the firing line, for we'd give them a little shooting.

"Load and fire." The kid would slip or fumble a load in, raise the piece and aim. And then, "Hold it!" came the next command. "Now unload." We wanted to see if he could do it safely, and with muzzle-awareness. Then we'd let him go ahead and fire a few rounds, not many, for you can't do a great deal about marksmanship in a small slice of a morning. But some instructors give this training as an extra, optional course, and that's the most, unless a junior club is possible.

We did stress the idea of being calm and rather deliberate, for safety above all, and for better field results, too. And all through our instruction we'd seed in comment on guns and ammo and hunting, what is and what isn't and how to. Though the course is required study, a lot of them found it interesting and said so. That's the way to teach anyone, even a Ph. D. candidate.

Occasionally I've met some of these kids afield, later on. Always it seemed that our time hadn't been wasted.

HUNTER HAZARDS

But not all hunters are so carefully trained. Parents who could do it often fall down badly, just not being interested, and the legal requirement for gun training is not nearly as well-spread over the U. S. A. as it is for driving a car. We still have to look out for hunters in general, like drivers in general, as potential killers.

Here are some of the things that don't-care hunters do: shoot at a sound, no need to look for game or to be sure the thing *is* game; shoot at a deer you're packing out; shoot at anything that moves against the light, as on a hilltop; shoot across highways and over the tops of hills; crawl over a fence or through brush with a gun cocked and ready; let the muzzle swing any old way when loading, unloading or just holding a gun.

Sometimes they hurt themselves, and that's bad enough. Helping a wounded man out of the woods is no pleasant experience, though it's certainly memorable. Nearly always the self-inflicted grief is preventable, and we can be thankful when someone else too isn't involved.

GUN AND AMMUNITION HAZARDS

The shooter is seldom injured by his own gun because it or the factory ammunition *made for it* is defective. Trouble generally comes to someone else, nearby or perhaps so far off that he isn't even seen. The old low velocity .22 long-rifle cartridge was credited with a range of from 1300 to 1400 yards with 17.80 degrees elevation. (There are only 1760 yards in a mile.) This round, a low starting point chosen as an example, obviously has a respectable reach. To be *respected,* literally.

But a gun, like a child, should be kept clean and properly fed. We might add "loved," too. A few handloaders have met sorrow as a result, usually, of asking too much from their firearm. Here are a few of the factors that alone or in combination with others can raise pressures above the safe working level for rifles of a certain class, or an *individual* rifle of that class:

Excess weight of bullet or powder.

Unduly hot primer, or the wrong primer for the load, maybe too thin and weak in cup construction.

Oversize flash-hole in the primer pocket; thick brass that reduces powder capacity, too deep seating of bullet that has the same effect, or, in some instances, long loading of the bullet that seals off the planned-for escape of a fractional part of the gas ahead of the bullet, to ease pressure.

Finer grained or otherwise faster powder than is necessary to give efficiency with the bullet used.

Heat: of the weather; of a cartridge placed in a hot chamber and left there beyond the normal aiming and firing time.

Rusted, rough or undersized bore and rifling; extremely tight chamber; chamber or case giving excess headspace.

Faster than standard rifling twist, higher than standard rifling lands, more than the usual number of lands if they are of standard height, which those in the Marlin Multi-Groove system, for instance, are not.

Oil in chamber, unless the rifle has practically zero headspace with no tolerance for maximum-length standard cartridges.

Excessive oil or grease in the bore, and worse if it's congealed by cold. Many shooters hunt with a dry bore, or one recently fouled.

Any other barrel obstruction.

Unduly hard lead bullet or hard jacket or core of a jacketed bullet.

Oversize bullet or one with extreme bearing length. The latter factor, in good, standard custom bullets like some of the Hornady line, for instance, ordinarily can be disregarded, but borrowing a bullet from another cartridge design can make trouble: .303 Savage in .30-30, for instance.

Bullet constructed for much lower velocities. It might be just possible to blow the core out of a bullet with open or soft point and weak base, leaving the jacket stuck in the barrel. The long-discontinued Winchester .30 Luger hollow point with unjacketed base could have been a candidate.

At high .30-06 velocity, let's say, the full-jacketed Luger should be safe, though its core could melt out and send accuracy down the drain; yet if it held together it might be a fair short-range varmint bullet, expanding rather well. Even the old 5.5 mm. Velo Dog full-patched 45-grain would rivet in wood when fired at only about 2800 f. s. from the .218 Bee.

Extremely thick jacket, hard or soft.

Soft cases. These rare ones do not increase pressure, but they can let even somewhat below normal pressures give most serious trouble when they burst in a rifle that isn't truly gas-proof.

Wrong cartridge. This can be somewhat like a soft case in its effects. An 8x57 mm. Mauser in a .30-06 rifle that will accept it, or a .303 Savage in a .303 British, is obviously too short. The 8 normally wrecks any but a very strong action. The Savage *may* only swell, not even allow serious gas escape to the rear.

* * * *

"Watch that muzzle" and "Be sure of your target before you shoot" are close to all-inclusive advice. Always know where the muzzle points and always make sure that the lead will come to rest in a safe place, not ricochet to hurt others or bounce back, as from perpendicular steel or rock, to hurt us.

Add "Know your gun and its ammunition" and you've just about got it made.

We'd better have it made, for our own good and for the good of the sport. We still have a generous lot of free hunting, for landowners as a class have been awfully kind. We do not expect them to undergo personal risk for our pleasure.

Do we?

F OR PERHAPS three seconds there was a spasm of clickety-clicks as the .303s arched out of the Savage 99. "Guess she'll work all right now," said the gunsmith, and the group of loafers, wall-proppers, unsubstantial citizens—perfectly delightful men, to a small boy—nodded wise agreement.

It was safe for them to do so, for Jess Brooks had done the job and pronounced the verdict. He was a good small-town gunsmith, and when you've said that you've given high praise. But most of all he was a man who understood men with the boy and boys with the man in them. "I remember him as if it were yesterday."*

We kids climbed the stairs to his shop on any valid excuse, a bike to be repaired, a pound of airgun shot weighed into one of those Bull Durham sacks that Jess—and his friends—emptied so fast, a box of .22s if we were old enough to have a rifle. Though we could get all these services and goods elsewhere, we went to the placed marked GUN SHOP in letters a foot high. Down below was a harness shop that smelled just wonderful—oil and leather—and that was all you could say for it. But Jess' domain was full of wonders, to stare at or, as a rare privilege, to touch. You stayed as long as you dared, maybe a half-hour or so, and went away in a daze.

For Jess, though he was a kind man, was busy. Perhaps we sensed, too, that he was that rare specimen, an individual, the kind that Walt Whitman went lyrical about. And such a man has deep, inscrutable thoughts, hasn't he? and needs some inner privacy. Jess could be abstracted, withdrawn, wrapped in the mysteries of his trade.

Any gunsmith, employed or on his own, is pretty apt to be an individual. The profession isn't lucrative, and it calls for almost unbelievable versatility, long hours, and a rush season when a man can scarcely catch time to turn around, spit out a butt, and tramp on it. But men become gunsmiths from choice, because they love guns. In spite of dire threats of going into a factory and a forty-hour week with breaks, the good ones almost always hang on.

In their domain they are kings, and deserve to be. They aren't to be pushed around, and they don't know deference to a long checkbook or a big name. They live in their own world of self-respect.

No one with sense tries to hurry an artist. He waits. If we all took our work in, six months or so from hunting season, the gunsmith would have a better life of it. But he knows human nature as few others do, so he doesn't expect that. He's only thankful, and surprised, when we show a little fore-handedness.

His harvest season is comparatively short, and short indeed for the racks of work he must get

*Sometimes I think it'd be worth a shot of amnesia to have the pleasure of reading *Treasure Island* again, *and* for the first time. Quote is from the first page.

CHAPTER 29

GUNSMITHS
AND
THEIR WAYS

through. So sometimes he makes promises that he isn't sure-to-gosh he can keep. But he does try, about ten times as hard as we do.

One of my friends has had—or did till recently—work waiting for three years at a shop. But this story is about good gunsmiths, not the other kind, and a good one isn't irresponsible. (Yes, we all know about the old master, Harry Pope. Try to hurry him and he'd give you your gun and show you the door.) He makes the best estimate he can and tries to meet the date. I've often had work come out in a few days or weeks, and sometimes in a few minutes, but that wasn't in late summer or fall.

The gunsmith is responsible, too, about the safety of his work. If a customer's idea is unsound he'll say so, and he'll explain why in complete, clear fashion—and this when time is of the essence to him. He refuses to perform a job that includes risk to the shooter. Insist though you may, he still refuses. Then, if you know no better, you take your work to an irresponsible man.

When you get to know him—the good one—fairly well, he'll make suggestions if any are needed. Almost certainly he's a shooter of considerably varied experience, and he learns from contact with other shooters, and from reading, too, like any other professional man. In the matters of handiness, durability, accuracy and so on his advice is to be considered carefully. It's easy to dry up that wellspring, for like most specialists of the better sort, he's sensitive to ignorance!

You get to know him by slow degrees, as you get to know a woodsman or a saddle-horse or a bird-dog. When we go to his shop for a loaf and a talk with the attendants of the inner sanctum—not much at first with the smith, for he's busy and his words come rarely, like pearls—we don't go to show what we know. We go to listen and learn, and we do *not* sound off our own conflicting opinions. The time for friendly arguments comes after we've made friends at that place. As a rule, we're on trial for quite a while.

That is one way to get into the inner sanctum. Another is to keep out of the way. A man hurrying to wait on a customer up front or to fetch a tool or gauge from out back doesn't care to half-sidestep and say "Excuse me."

The following letter from a gunsmith, not to be named, explains some of the difficulties in the business under present conditions. It shows why a rather extensive job, done at the best, could seem to the uninitiated to be exorbitant in price.

"At best, the stockmaking business is a rough row to hoe, and most of the stockmakers have to watch their finances pretty closely. In fact, the gunsmithing trade is probably the hardest of all mechanical trades to make a go at, especially during these times of high wages. Almost anything else, including digging ditches, pays more than they can get in the gunsmith business.

"This is especially brought home to anyone who is trying to employ men in the gun business as we did from [dates deleted]. It was practically impossible to find a man who could produce a profit over his wages, and the majority could not even produce their wages.

"Of course some of these men would have been better on their own, but most of them have the attitude nowadays that there are only forty hours in a week and not more than five days; so when they go out on their own it takes a very short time for them to fold up and go back to work, usually in some other line.

"In the gun business we have both extremes, namely the perfectionists and the butchers. For some unknown reason we very seldom find a man who is well adjusted in the business and especially one who can do the whole job, that is, do a good job on metal and wood.

"The perfectionist is always confronted with the problem of not being able to produce enough to live; the butcher is usually a good producer, but his quality ruins his business.

"Gunsmiths of the Harry Pope variety can no longer exist in this modern world; so we have to strike a happy medium between production and perfection."

None of us would want to see the profession of gunsmithing outdated by mass production. We'd lose interesting, informative contacts and the convenience and pleasure of having work done just as we want it—when we're willing to pay—without the quality-killing pressure of a set time limit. Our country would lose a source of skilled, imaginative, resourceful men in the mechanical line, and she hasn't too many of that kind, and hardly could have.

Abstracted, withdrawn, wrapped in the mysteries of his trade, Charles Canoll turns down a barrel blank on his engine lathe. "Nuts!" Charlie would say. "It's simple. Harry's writing got away with him." And Paul Matthews, the rifleman who took this picture, would agree.

MANY well-to-do big game hunters employ the services of a guide. That is not a roundabout way of saying that they "hire a guide"; it's walking around a bush *not* to say it, for the guide is no hired man, in the old-fashioned sense. He's a specialist, an adviser, and a good many other things too. You don't buy such a man, or even buy his services: you pay for his cooperation and help. Much more may be given you, and with generosity. Almost always that depends on you.

His wage may equal that of a skilled manual worker, or be considerably higher. Seldom is it excessive when we think of what he does for us and the responsibility he carries. Naturally we are speaking only of good guides.

His top-priority job would seem to be showing us the game and getting us a fair shot at it if we're inexperienced in hunting or new to his sort of country. His professional success depends on doing those things because most hunters think no farther. They want their game and if they don't get it they'll try someone and somewhere else next time. So he does his best, and not many of us would have as good success without him. In few countries, though, can shots be guaranteed. They can't be guaranteed anywhere unless the hunter cooperates.

Sometimes part of a guide's job is to cook and clean up and cut wood. At any rate, he tries to keep us comfortable, in good health—and safe. Having one of the party lost and bushed overnight would be an absolute horror to a guide. As a matter of course all hands turn out to find a lost man, but the guide is anxious to prevent that from happening in the first place. If he gets half the cooperation he gives, it almost never does. The woods or mountains are no place for a bullhead or a "Johnny Know-All," but some get there just the same.

Ordinarily he knows the country like the sights of his rifle, and nothing short of a blanket fog is liable to turn him around, if *that* does. It is true that some guides have become so well liked that they have accompanied their hunter friends to strange and far-off fields. But such men know how to read the lie of land and they take off with caution, even though they may not appear to.

Always in the background of the guide's awareness is the regard for our safety. He literally saves life again and again by his forethought—though he doesn't appear to. This alertness, common sense, being prepared for the "unexpected"—call it what you like—becomes a habit. A guide is a hard man to befuddle or even surprise. About the only risk he takes lies in the behavior of a certain kind of client, and that risk he tries to reduce to a minimum. Although he's most tactful as a rule—some guides do have a certain saltiness as part of their stock in trade, and usually it's relished—he's as safety-conscious of firearms as of any wilderness perils. And rarely indeed is the wilderness, even in

CHAPTER 30

GUIDES
ARE
SPECIALISTS

her most fractious moods, perilous to men like him or to others who think ahead.

A lot of experienced hunters who don't "need" a guide—and a few really don't, for there's a difference! —would be unhappy without one, and generally a particular one. They value his companionship. There's the entertainment, the dry, hard-sense humor; there are the encouragement and the optimistic slant that almost anyone needs once in a while; and there's the friendship.

He's appreciative, for he's downright human, no machine. Take the haversack, the shoulder-slung, hip-bopping sack that one of his clients had given in good faith to Henry. It was a beautiful thing, fine brown canvas with leather-reinforced bottom. I haven't seen one as good for years. Henry didn't *need* it; he had pockets for lunch, matches, compass, extra cartridges and the rest. But he carried it for a good many Octobers and Novembers, witch-hopple snatching at it and the bulgy thing scuffing his left arm as he walked, just because it was the gift from a friend and therefore he was no-end proud of it.

Like most good woodsmen, Henry believed in having plenty of ammunition, fifteen to eighteen rounds, perhaps. Not that he expected to need them for himself, but sometimes a man who knows the country might have to answer those desperate threes belted off skyward by a lost one, to encourage him by announcing that help was on the way!

Just a little more about what the typical good guide is like, though he's as "different" and as much of an individual as the gunsmith.

Above all, he doesn't bluff, nor does he go for that quality in others, and he's shrewd in sizing them up. That's part of his efficiency. His own success depends on his clients' success in the field, and he tries not to ask too much of their patience, self-restraint, strength, or marksmanship. He does *not* enjoy tracking up wounded game, and naturally he's a conservationist: the game supply is important to him. In addition, he's apt to be humane in his outlook, for he has had plenty and too much opportunity to read the signs of what a hopelessly disabled animal sometimes goes through before death stamps its ticket and lets it through the gate.

Since he's a hunter of ability, he rarely is in a hurry about anything. He's likely to be a bit conservative, too, about some matters. Fact, for instance. He answers your questions about the outdoors as best he can, and he's a mine of information about what goes on there and how to live there comfortably—and, of course, safely. Seldom does he make positive statements: there are too many exceptions in the unregimented world of nature, and he's seen enough of it to realize how little any of us know.

He isn't often an experimenter in equipment. Instead, he tends to stick to the proved and familiar. The small caliber, high velocity rifle and the autoloader had to be demonstrated as efficient before many guides would accept either of them. You still find a few that have low regard for them—for their own use, that is.

Not many years back, one I knew still stuck to his Model '95 Winchester lever-gun in .30-06 caliber, and he guided in New York's Adirondack forest. Out there, a 200-pound buck is rather large and a black bear is either a scarcely expected by-product or the reward of a special and carefully planned hunt. That country's hogsback ridges, witch-hopple tangles and spongy beaver meadows can make the going hard, and a guide does an awful lot of walking. The '95 in 06 weighs about nine pounds. "Makes my arm ache, sometimes," he admitted, "but I like it."

In it he uses a moose load, and a slow one at that, the heavily constructed 220-grain soft point, hardly the bullet for quick or even sure expansion on a white-tail. "Did you ever have one stay in a deer?" I asked him. "No," he agreed, he never did. But it got through the brush pretty well when it had to. (And of course he was a good rifle shot, just about impossible to rattle, and he could place his bullet.) Being a bit of a conservative, he liked plenty of power and penetration in reserve for any need, and he didn't particularly care to see a whole shoulder, for instance, turned into hamburger by a lighter and faster bullet. To him, game was essentially more for the table than for the wall-mounted head, that is. I'm quite sure he wouldn't have recommended the 220 grain to any beginner.

Reading this over, I wonder if it will be taken as a song of praise or the prose of weighed facts. It is certainly meant to be the latter. Guides detest ballyhoo (except as a source of amusement), so do I, and I presume you do, too. This composite sketch is as accurate as I can make it.

UNCLE VOLNEY was able to make only one trip to our Green Pond camp, a good piece back off the Stillwater Road, but I think he enjoyed it as much as any of us did. He was certainly great to have along. I liked him as a small kid likes a man who's always cheerful and who puts up with his everlasting wanting to know the why and the how. So did the others act like that, but they'd been with us for a good many October fortnights, and they belonged. Uncle V. had to be proved.

He proved up all right, and now I can see that he did it by other ways than just being pleasant and good-natured.

Since he had no rifle of his own he carried Father's .50-95 Model '76 Winchester, which I began using on woodchucks a few years afterwards, and did it pull me round-shouldered! It weighed about nine pounds, a lot of rifle for the Adirondack hills and brush, and it must have been the heaviest gun that ever went to that camp, except maybe Uncle Lester's 12-gauge Remington with the full-length .38-55 liner poked through the left barrel.

Father had bought the .50 years before, to hunt Florida alligators and Montana mule deer; so he hadn't carried it much afoot. But I guess Uncle Volney liked it, and it really was a fine old rifle.

He was careful of it—watched the muzzle and kept the big hammer at half cock just as a matter of course—but I mean he handled the rifle as if it were precious. It was, too, like any gun you can trust.

He never complained about its weight. He'd peg along quiet and easy, but I guess his pipe tasted extra good when he sat down for the hour or so it would take Henry and Oren, and maybe one of us kids helping them, to make a drive. A middle-aged smoker such as he was can savor tobacco, and he was woods-wise and terribly careful of fire. He never smoked on the trail.

It was getting along toward the end of the trip and still Uncle V. hadn't laid the Lymans on a deer. You'd think the old Winchester would have grown pretty heavy by that time, and his spirits, too, because he'd looked forward to that trip for a long while. But he was as cheerful as ever in the cabin or at lunch breaks by a little fire in a safe place, scraped and drowned, beside one of those brooks with that clean, cold water, browned a bit by leaf-mold, that tastes like no other drink on earth. Along with the rest of the crowd, he took his luck as it came.

He played his part as well as he could. If a deer had ever gone by, he'd almost certainly have seen it, for he sat like a stone and watched like a hawk. But they just didn't come his way. They went by other watchers, or doubled back past the drivers, or slid off to the side.

Then one morning there was a terrific boom, obviously black powder and not the .40-50 that Father had hunted with for well over a quarter-century. No second blast came. It sounded like venison.

CHAPTER 31

HUNTING PARTIES AND THE LONE SCOUT

Oren got up that way first and bellowed out, "Did you get him?" Not much need to be quiet after the .50 had sounded off.

"I guess so," said Uncle Volney, slowly and with relish. "He lays right over there."

The big, solid bullet had broken the buck's neck, and he was a good-sized one—eight or ten points; I don't remember. So Uncle V. was happy, and everyone else, too. He'd earned his deer. But then, he would have been happy, anyway, just to have had the trip. What he took home in the baggage car was just an extra dividend.

Later years, all of us wished he could be there again. He belonged.

Probably most of our big-game hunters go in parties, and there are some great advantages in doing so. It's safer under the more or less crowded conditions so common out east, for great care is taken—or should be—to know where each member is stationed or what driving route he's to take. If anything does go wrong, help can get in at least fairly soon.

It gives the less experienced hunters a better chance than if they were off on their lone, and the spirit of cooperation is a help in itself. The captain—professional guide or one of the old hands at the game—normally exercises a good deal of judgment in trying to give everyone a fair chance, and certain stands that are thought to be especially good don't always go to the same fellows—or at least they shouldn't! Just you

357

get a team really working together and everyone's happy and hopeful.

There's the fun, too, the companionship, and some lasting friendships have been built in camp and out under the sky. You get to know a man there.

To some of us, three's a crowd, and nothing else can compare with having just one companion along, one you know from a good many seasons. With this sort of buddy you don't have to worry. You might with a new one, for there are two absolute essentials to a hunting pair-up.

Each must know, all the time, where the other is, and never fire in his direction. Some country is too thick for this sort of hunting; it's safer to separate and meet at about a time and exactly a place agreed on. The other essential is that we shouldn't expect our friend to spook game our way; we do our own looking and listening just as if we were alone.

A few of us have the gift of being pretty good company for ourselves, and though we like hunting with our friends, our deepest enjoyment afield comes in being absolutely alone. When my father was a young man he was taught by a guide, one I never met, but he certainly was a legend in our house, and deserved to be. No one had a better time than Father did, with the party in camp, or in reliving it afterwards, but he always hoped to get in a day or two by himself. Sometimes that wasn't possible, for he knew the country

as well as the guides did, and they depended on him to help them see that the others got their deer to take home. And if my brother or I were still in camp when that had been looked after, he'd take us one at a time to teach what he could about still-hunting. (Of course he saw that we had Theodore Van Dyke's old classic to read, *The Still-Hunter*.) Father always planned to let the guides get in some of this lone hunting, for he knew they wanted their winter deer-meat, and knew, too, that they liked to have some time in the woods by themselves before the season closed down.

There is a great deal of satisfaction in being on your own, and an extra pleasure when you're successful and get your game, big or small, completely unaided. A lot of hunters go it alone, one set of tracks out and back home.

But I don't think that the beginner is quite safe in real wilderness, and in heavily hunted areas anyone is probably better off with a friend along. They look out for each other. However, there *are* hunting countries between the extremes of wilderness and ten-acre wood-lot, and using as much common sense there as we do in driving or ·in city walking we're almost certainly just as safe.

If the reader can tell from this chapter which sort of hunting I prefer, lone or party, it would be helpful. I don't know, myself!

Main camp, Buffalo River, Wyoming. First-rate wapiti country. Mule deer, sheep, and grizzly are less common inhabitants of this area, and the rare Shiras moose is also to be seen. *Thomas C. Florich Photo.*

SHE TAKES one trip, or many. That depends on whether she goes as an equal, or as background or gallery for Himself.

Time was, a woman seldom accompanied a hunting party. But there were always some who did, and a few hunted on their own, and do yet. But now it's become fairly common, and a good thing for the sport, too.

You note the pictures of man-and-wife hunting teams and can hardly miss seeing the happiness they reflect. Age doesn't seem to matter: the fifties and beyond are no bar; young couples start cementing the span of their married lives in the hunting field, and on the target ranges as well.

Perhaps even more afield than in practice or competition on black-and-white paper there's evident the complete and so welcome change from day-to-day routine. Out there, life is simple. It shakes down to basic realities. Some of the hardest workers, people of real though perhaps unrecognized achievement, enjoy outdoor interludes the most.

Some women don't care to kill game. Native instincts lie deep, and to both preserve and take life seems contradictory. Yet Nature herself does both, and so deep is her hold in other ways that most of us relish an outing to natural, unspoiled scenes. A good many women enjoy a hunting trip to wild and beautiful places—the two adjectives are, after all, synonymous—and never lift a gun.

But there is this thought about killing, even though logic may not alter feeling, and in the rightness of things it shouldn't always be expected to. Game is going to be killed, and the feeling one has when it's dispatched cleanly and humanely is that at least decency has triumphed. The bullet could have done a lot worse, and disease, starvation or predators could have, too.

Your girl will know what sort of clothing she wants, light and easy, but warm enough, and with that indispensable, indefinable touch of chic. And she'll have pretty sound ideas about footgear, that base that makes or ruins a trip, though some town-bound folk fail to realize that the human foot goes up a shoe size after a few miles over rough country. But she may find it difficult to choose the rifle, and she must have the right one, for she wants her kills to be clean. A wounded and lost animal can sour her on hunting, and so can a slovenly kill. In either wretched event she'd be justified in her feeling.

Killing power is far less important than our ability to use the amount of it we have between our hands. Her marksmanship training with the rifle should go through the same stages that ours would if we had the chance to do it all over again, and knew as much as we know now.

TRAINING

Here's one system of training. It may seem slow, but it *has* worked.

CHAPTER 32

WHEN SHE GOES, TOO

Begin with the .22 rimfire, and a light one, too. Five or six pounds aren't much, but that weight and the way it must be handled, the second-nature familiarity with it that she needs, are new to her. Sight and sling this rifle so that she can aim it precisely, hold it steadily, and, after learning about sight picture and trigger squeeze, make good 50-foot groups with it. The gun should have decently adjustable sights so that she can learn the principles of elevation and windage and apply them, for and by herself, as soon as her groups shrink to an inch in size. Laying them on the high-scoring rings will give her confidence, and learning to keep them there will teach her what uniformity means in rifle shooting.

Although she'll always be grateful to the little gun for what it taught her, and always will have some use for it, the pinweight can go only so far as a trainer. A heavier .22, from seven even to nine pounds, or at any rate as heavy as the varmint or big-game rifle she'll carry, opens a most instructive secondary school after primary's over. It's steady to hold, and if not too heavy it can take so much of the wobble out of offhand that she'll get along much faster in that difficult but 95 percent useful position.

Or she can go directly to the centerfire. If hand-loaded ammunition is available in the quantities she'll need, this second rifle can be the one she'll use in hunting big game or varmints. Report, recoil and power can start low and work up by degrees. If hand-

359

loading is out, a Hornet, a Bee or even a .222 could be Rifle No. 2. They aren't noisy and they have almost no recoil, but they are fast and accurate and obviously businesslike. For varmints, they're adequate in most shooting at the ranges a beginner should tackle, to be sure of making clean kills. But don't let any sort of hunting come too soon, and the reasons for that are plain.

Almost any rifle more powerful than those three or the .220 Swift needs a recoil pad for her use, at least in the beginning. The gun must be stocked for her comfort, too. The jab of an over-long stock or the bruise of a too-high Monte Carlo comb can destroy the good works of weeks of careful training and faithful practice. "Faithful"? Well, maybe, though it's fun in itself, and to see the improvement is even better.

With the start of the .222 or equivalent shooting, and perhaps with the Bee or Hornet, she should have the chance to use ear-plugs. Usually one in the left ear —for a right-hander—is enough. That one takes the worst of the salute. Noise can be so disconcerting that it ruins the effect of the good lessons in hold, aim and trigger squeeze that have gone before. Women are liable to be more sensitive to ear-ringing blasts than men are, or at least I've noticed it right along on the target ranges.

By this time, if not before, she's graduated to a variety of targets. The conventional black-and-white ringed paper is easy to aim on, simplifies sight adjustment, and tells us how well we are doing. But neutral-colored targets and silhouettes look more like game, and they can be partly hidden to add realism. Later, if you can, use a moving target, though she must understand that such shooting at rifle game is in a sense a last resort for all but the most expert. However, it does become necessary if the first bullet that lands doesn't disable the animal.

A running deer silhouette is fine, but only a few rifle clubs yet have one. Various other means can be used—in absolutely safe country—and firing at a bit of wood sliding down fast water is excellent practice, where and when we can get it safely. Not many places! It shows exactly where the bullets strike, and only incoming waves are at all liable to route them back toward the shooter.

Even at stationary targets she can get in good practice under a time limit. It teaches her to shoulder and cheek the rifle quickly and smoothly, pick up the sights fast, and press the trigger softly but without hesitation. Single shots come first. Later, rapid fire can be timed, the gun held at the shoulder during reloading, and three shots in a string are enough. This is not a military course of fire; it's for hunting. Your girl, coming to the sport with a fresh, open and mature mind, will see at once that accuracy *is* fire power, with volume or speed the most minor factors. She will approach the sport with confidence, ability and knowledge.

THE RIFLE

Women (and some men) have sense enough to realize that the most simple mechanisms are the best for a hunting rifle. The mind should be on the game, or on marksmanship, rather than on the musket. Most women in their daily work do a great many things automatically, smoothly, efficiently, by second nature. Furthermore, a woman has a sensitiveness to beauty of line, to symmetry and flow. Therefore and to wit she should have a decisive voice in choosing her own rifle. And may Diana look down from her silver chair, the crescent moon, and shield her from a hand-me-down!

Weight

Weight of the rifle? That's for individual choice. There should certainly have been some field trips with the .22 or .22s before she selects the centerfire. And shooting at safe inanimate targets on those safaris is part of her ideal training because they look at least somewhat like game.

Except in the roughest or most tangled country a sling helps in carrying, but not much. The drag is still there. It's only transferred, and she will want to carry her own rifle, all the time, because this is a man's game and she's going to play it as well as a man, not asking favors.

Apparent weight depends a lot on balance, and the mid-section of a rifle grasped in trail carry shouldn't feel like a stick of cordwood. If it does, it tires the fingers, then the hand, then the whole arm. The final result could be an application to the local library or bookstore for a copy of that book Ed Zern wrote, *To Hell with Hunting!*

Caliber

Name almost any rifle cartridge except perhaps a few of the heaviest bigbore, black or nitro powder lot, or the modern extreme magnums, and some woman, somewhere, must have used and liked it in the hunting field. A woman can handle about as much *reasonable* recoil as a man, though it takes either one a fair while to learn to be supple and ride it out instead of fighting it. Maybe she learns this simple technique faster; it sometimes seems so.

But with good rifle shooting we need less power, just as in upland hunting with a shotgun an experienced gunner can go to a smaller bore because the gun is lighter and faster, and the bird hasn't got as far away before he fires. We have figured on the training sessions' having given her more shooting experience and skill than the average hunter—can't call him "rifleman"—gets in ten years.

The .257 Roberts is quite a favorite for a lady's deer or antelope rifle, and it deserves to be. With the right bullets and the right shooting it has power enough, and moderate report accompanies its moderate velocities. Among a good, comfortable-sized raft of other choices is the .300 Savage, which comes in some reasonably light, easily grasped and carried rifles, and when more power is needed, the .270, 7x57 mm.,* .308 and .30-06 have been considerable favorites. A few women have used the .375 Magnum with success and complete satisfaction, and some have liked still more powerful calibers.

The main point is for her never to be overgunned, and this holds for us men, too. Almost always it's the shooting, not the metal thrown, that does good work. But times have changed since the .25-35 was considered ideal for the woman who, like Diana, would hunt the stag. I say this regretfully; the .25-35 is one of my old favorites and I still love it. But your girl is not to run any risk of being let down by inadequate power. You would hardly expect her to drive you home from the commuting station in an old bus that could barely wheeze up the grades. The little, "inadequate" cartridges are for the experts if they want them, and only for experts who can pick their shots or not fire.

AFIELD

You may not have to teach her to see game as well as you do unless you're really experienced and have developed the hunter's selective and rejective eye. Most women are observant, and especially so in strange places. (You can prove this up, if you haven't taken her out to dinner in weeks heaped upon months, by

_____
*The 7x57 is underloaded by our factories because so many old Spanish Mausers are still around. Even so, its long 175-grain bullet has great sectional density for penetration on heavy game, though it usually expands pretty well on deer. Handloading widens its usefulness and, when properly done, increases its power safely.

taking her out this evening.) It's their nature to be observant, and when they're interested they surely aren't preoccupied! A shrug of the shoulders and the old, familiar world is sloughed away. Is it as easy for us to leave the shop or the office, completely?

Buck fever? I don't know, but it seems less liable to affect her than a man. She's not so terribly over-anxious, so desperate to succeed. Though I can't define or pinpoint the damn thing, it seems to me that there's a little, smiling corner of her mind that asks, with devastating humor, "Just how important is this 'serious' matter? I'll do what I can, and anyhow, tomorrow's another day and a new chance."

How will she fit in with the rest of the party? Just fine! Guides, as a rule, show an old-world courtesy—and mean it—toward a woman who acts like a lady. And other hunters envy the man whose wife accompanies him because she wants to. "That guy's sure got what it takes. Gets his wife to come up here and slosh around in the snow and the swamps, and like it!"

But let him be modest. That last isn't necessarily so. Women are human, and our civilization isn't yet so stuffy that some of us, regardless of our sex, don't enjoy getting back to basics. Hunting country is interesting, downright beautiful, and down-to-earth, too. Coming to it fresh and unaccustomed, she sees in it some delights, savors some pleasures, that we grew up with and came to take for granted. The edge of _her_ appreciation is still sharp. It could be a whetstone to ours, to scramble a couple of metaphors.

Still and all, it's a great compliment for her to want to go. For her to enjoy it—and she probably will—is better yet.

IF ANYONE believes he is about to learn how to be a "woil' champeen" he can just keep turning pages because I'm not one and I'm not about to become one. I have watched with envy and care some of this Country's finest shots. It has been my sad duty to report to myself that I was not up to their brand of competitive skill and will never approach it. Their story is not mine and I do not speak for them.

My vice is a simple one. I like to shoot. If it burns powder and if it looks as if it will stay together for the next shot, I'll try it. With such a philosophy I've managed to burn a variety of powders in a variety of weapons. At best I guess my qualifications could be summed up as those of a duffer with enough vocabulary to sound as though I understand ballistics. Actually my only hope at this time is that I know enough about guns and their usage to know what I don't know.

On the matter of advice to the beginner, poor soul, he gets so much from well intentioned shooters like me that his biggest job turns out to be listening instead of doing. But I can't resist putting in my two cents.

This material is not presented to tell you where to put your elbows, feet and fingers, or how to manipulate them when they are positioned. There's an abundance of good material on these topics. I have a nodding acquaintance with some of it, and it ranges from *circa* 1790 to the present proposed U. S. Army "Trainfire." Almost all these systems get you there. As a practical matter I suggest that you get the booklets published by the NRA, or Army Field Manual 23-5 from the Superintendent of Documents in Washington. The NRA and U. S. Army marksmanship systems rarely contradict each other, and if you know either you are at home on any range in the United States. The advantages are too obvious to discuss.

Far more important than the book you use is your coach. Learning a manual art from the written word is not easy, and the most valuable asset a beginner can have is one coach, a good one, teaching one system. If your book and the coach differ, get the coach's book, if you must have a book. Whatever you do, don't go around shopping techniques from system to system before you have mastered any one system. They often appear contradictory, and sometimes they are.

For example, trigger-squeeze can be taught on the basis of not knowing when the rifle is going to fire. This is one of the better ways to *teach* it, but it is not the only way. Actually it is simply not true, once you have learned to shoot. Riflemen know when their rifle is going to go off because if they didn't the most valuable asset a rifle could have would be a creepy pull. How many trained riflemen do you know with such a pull on one of their pet rifles? There are many ways to learn how to squeeze the trigger, but you can use only one at a time; so stick to one system, no matter which it is, until you have learned the rudiments of shooting and have attained some proficiency. Remember, shooting is a manipulative skill which fuses a num-

CHAPTER 33

MARKSMANSHIP CRITIQUE

By Thomas C. Florich, Jr.

ber of individual motions into an apparently single movement. You're not a shooter until this movement has become a conditioned reflex. Like hitting a golf ball or a baseball, for teaching purposes the apparently single movement may be broken down into component moves, but in practice this must be a unified single action from start to finish. That's the real reason for the coach. You just cannot see yourself make the mistakes every beginner makes.

Now what is this word "system"? The best example I can think of is Field Manual 23-5. That's a system! Few indeed are the publications available that assume you know nothing and presume to teach you everything you need to know. Although its style of writing is not exactly racy, the material is complete, really complete. Both the German and British military marksmanship courses are good, too, and there are many more, all with individual and often differing viewpoints. A number of excellent treatises by shooters of national and international stature outline the methods they consider best.

Unfortunately there is no magical incantation that transforms a man into a marksman, and none of these systems is gospel. Or at least they aren't gospel once you have learned to shoot using any one of them initially. I automatically think of two pistol shots who rank among the top of their generation. One was a strict "as issued" man using a revolver as it came out of the box except for a possible smoothing of the action. The other had no compunctions about extreme modifications, on occasion going so far that about the only thing that wasn't changed was the caliber! Grips, trigger shoes, wide-spur hammers, short actions, fancy sights: you name it and he had it. They both were tops.

I can recollect having the world by the tail as a kid with my kneeling position. Being limber, I could sit on the side of my foot, and my low kneeling position gave me scores that equaled my sitting scores. After I broke my leg the ankle was too stiff to fold under my butt, and I had to sit on my heel in the high kneeling position. It isn't as steady and it cost me points, but I was still doing all right. Later, at Fort Benning, I was informed that my kneeling position was poor. This was not news to me; so I was delighted to take a crack at their version. It really would have made no difference if I hadn't liked the new position, for this was the doctrine and the only kneeling position. It called for the toe of the right foot being back, the weight of the body being thrown on the left leg, and then sitting back on your heel with the right ankle at an angle. This was uncomfortable but I managed, and if I had just started shooting I'd have got by with such a position. But I am not convinced that that position is the best kneeling. There are many positions and techniques and no manual can outline all the variations needed to take care of the peculiarities of individual conformation. If you have learned one you have a basis for evaluation and can select the best of the alternatives offered by the various systems.

Another moral can be drawn from my modest adventures in the kneeling position from age 12 to age 23. These system changes often reflect no more than style changes. Yet at any given time many people think there is no other way to shoot. Personally, if I thought I'd get better scores I'd become a staunch supporter of the old back position. As a matter of fact, sooner or later I'm going to take a crack at it. The scores they shot at 1,000 yards during the 1870s when using it aren't to be scorned today. I watched the two leading contenders shoot for the National Collegiate Championship, and when they'd finished, no one ascribed the difference in their scores to the fact that one used the NRA hip-rest offhand and the other the standard military position, in those days with or without sling. Today—or was it yesterday?—a sling is mandatory in military offhand.

Having been educated in the normal military and NRA doctrine of the moment, I was profoundly shocked at a club match a few years back. A seventy-year-old member appeared with a well-kept Model 1895 Winchester, lay down at 100 yards, and fired a five-shot group for sighting. The only thing correct in his prone position, by my schooling, was his stomach. It was on the ground. Other than that he had broken every rule in the book, and I thought I ought to help the old boy out. Fortunately some kind god told me to shut my mouth. The five shots measured 1¾ inches

extreme and he used iron sights, and no sling. Watching the old man perform shook up my thinking, and a tour of duty in the Infantry rocked many more of my convictions.

Most shooting is artificial. The practical applications at best can be considered no more than tenuous derivations of the popular forms of firing. Put your hand in the hat and pull out Bench Rest, Smallbore, Olympic, or the ordinary Standard American Revolver Course types. For the most part they can be characterized as employing artificial positions, cadences, weapons and targets. Mind you, this is not derogatory, but expository. I am no more opposed to Bench Rest or Olympic than I am to golf or baseball. I like to play, myself, and most of my shooting is just that—playing. It should be understood that these games are games. Certainly an Olympic competitor is 'way ahead of a beginner.

But it's also a long way from set triggers, palm rests, and all day long to fire 40 shots each, prone, kneeling and standing, to flipping over in a slit trench to pot a young Asiatic pulling the pin on a grenade. Bench Rest shooting goes further from reality in both equipment and technique. Rifles weighing 20 pounds and stocks with forearms four inches across that couldn't possibly be held are the rule, and the most successful shooter is usually the one who has eliminated human error as much as possible. Normally this is accomplished by *not holding* the rifle. In other words the bench-rest shooter aspires to equipment and techniques that simulate an artillery gun carriage. Bench Rest is as far from Olympic as golf is from tennis. Each requires highly specialized equipment and the utmost refinement of technique.

This tirade applies to a greater or less degree to most of the commonly accepted forms of shooting. I am not mocking them, or opposed to them. The difficulty comes in with human psychology. We all tend to over-simplification and most of us think "Shootin' is shootin'" and a good shot is a good shot. The results of such lack of discrimination vary from pathetic comedy and some danger in the hunting fields to Colonel Blimpism and horrible tragedy for police and soldiers.

Aside from having a gun in your hand, I find, there's little in common between the conditioned reflexes needed to puncture on command a well illuminated Police L target standing still 25 yards away and the trained reactions required to puncture a half concealed punk 15 feet away in a dark alley, who happens to be shooting at *you*. Yet today the biggest police force in the world uses the Police L. They may use helicopters, speed-boats, cars, two-way radios, micro-chemistry laboratories and closed circuit television, but at this writing the good old Police L appears to be better intrenched than the pension system. I don't think that a year goes by without a policeman dying because his marksmanship was inadequate.

To see the evils of the bullseye target attitude, cast an eye on the current U. S. military rifle and the courses set up to teach recruits to use it. Good target shooting requires sights adjustable to fine graduations with the honors going hands down to a peep sight, and the finer the peep the better. What does a military rifle need? First, it should be able to be dropped on a hard floor without impairment of its functioning ability. Second, it should be able to be cleaned after complete immersion in mud by a couple of fast passes with a toothbrush, the indispensable tool carried by every American soldier. Third, it should be simple enough to· be readily used by a trained moron. This is not a poor joke, but a serious training problem. They raised the minimum mental standards to a 70 I. Q. in our Army a while back, and I understand the generally accepted I. Q. level for a moron classification is 70 and lower. A person of normal intelligence should get the idea in a few minutes. I speak freely, since I have been trained.

Well, what have we got? A peep sight with minute clicks for windage and elevation, employing a mechanism so complex that disassembly is forbidden to all except Ordnance personnel. Normally that's not a dissuasive factor to me, but after looking over a diagram of this rear sight assembly I decided I probably couldn't get the damn thing back together again, and I never have stripped one. You will find a few mechanically adept men in every outfit who can strip that Rube Goldberg contraption, but they are in a very small and elite minority. I've seen Ordnance repair trucks run out of spare rear-sight assemblies before lunch, two days in a row on a Fort Benning range. Under field conditions the ever-practical G I simply screws the peep right down to the bottom and forgets about it until the next inspection, at which time he removes the accumulated dirt with the all-purpose toothbrush. The pity of this situation is that under combat conditions a very high proportion of the peeps will be found all the way down, as usual.

Take the peep on that sight. The aperture is too big and the overall diameter too small for really close target holding, and for snapshooting the aperture is too small and the overall too big. Why you need minutes of angle adjustments in a service rifle whose accuracy standard is three to four minutes, I'll never know. And the whole mess is the result of being bullseye-happy.

If a composite of the man behind the gun were drawn it would develop like this: he has never shot a rifle before; things like trajectory curves, sight radius, windage allowance and minutes of angle mean nothing; he couldn't care less. To him they are just more useless facts foisted upon him by the Army, and he's not interested. There is a good deal of truth in that.

The open rear sight on a German Mauser service rifle is extremely simple and sturdy. Oddly enough, I have never seen one set for 100 meters and fired with service ammunition that was not on a smallbore target at 100 yards. It has no fine adjustments or fancy mechanism and is much better off without them. You really don't have to explain how to use that sight; it is almost self-apparent. Now I'm not implying that it is semi-useless, either. Very creditable scores were made in International competition at 300 meters with those sights, and after 50 years the thing is still a widely used military rear sight. Today in the "dangerous game" fields the open sight is the overwhelming favorite of people who bet their lives on their marksmanship.

The truth of the matter is that this Nation's shooters, including the Army, have become enamored of formalized target shooting and have allowed the arbitrary standards of a game to dominate the needs of a practical profession. Result: the Army spends endless hours in trying to teach what isn't necessary to use, what isn't needed, to people who aren't interested.

The most incongruous part of this situation is that there are soldiers in the Army who should know about minutes of angle, trajectory curves and battle sight settings. To every Infantry platoon a scope-sighted Garand is issued for sniping, but most of the time there is no one who can use it for what it was designed to do. Today there is no sniping school or special training for snipers in our Army, and a real sniper must be a great deal more than just an expert rifleman. The British Army very wisely has a sniping section attached to each infantry battalion headquarters and these men are graduates of a sniping school where a rigorously selective volunteer system is the basis for admission. These snipers are detailed out to the line companies where needed, and they perform invaluable work.

To date, the most promising forward step is the so-called transition courses where silhouette targets are used. The basic requirements are there, hitting neutral colored targets exposed for short intervals, some moving, and at unknown ranges. The round black bullseye is a fiction; it exists nowhere in real life. It is a means of zeroing and scoring and no more. Even more of an abomination is the six o'clock hold. Hours are spent in teaching a recruit to hold his front sight at six o'clock, at the bottom of the bull. But this is more than a fiction; it is a matter of taste. On any target range today you will find shooters using a center hold. As a matter of fact, for years the whole U. S. Navy taught and used the center hold. To non-shooters—and the majority of recruits never have handled a rifle before—this six o'clock business is very confusing. Why impose a matter of taste upon men who have much to learn in so little time? And why not give them a more realistic target, even for preliminary familiarization and zeroing? Your old National Match shooter loved the D 200 and 300 yard rapid fire silhouette, even though it wasn't perfect. My own preference is for a full length silhouette similar to what I believe was the old E target used for squad firing problems at

Camp Perry in the 1930s. It should have scoring rings based on center holding; that's where you're going to hold when the chips are down.

When a recruit can go through his entire training without firing a shot at a bullseye, real progress will have been made and an unnecessary, confusing step eliminated. He is introduced to a game with rules entirely different from those of the real game he is going to have to be ready to play, combat. Today, training for the real game is treated as a sort of icing on the cake, mentioned in a few words here and there, and provided by some transition course shooting.

Formalized positions and the use of the loop sling are other examples of the "rules of the game" approach. If half the time devoted to tangling yourself up in a sling and placing your elbows and knees just so were devoted to realistic shooting, a far more effective combat soldier would result. How many veterans that you know used a loop sling and formal position when they were playing for keeps?

Roll some oil-drums down a hill and see how many hits you can get. Shoot from a slit trench, a parapet, or a bunker firing slit. Instead of learning the proper sight picture for a six o'clock hold under a bullseye, try hitting pop-up silhouettes at 10 feet, from the hip, so very useful in turning corners in trenches or in hostile towns. Above all, train to keep shooting until you get a hit. When your target is shooting back, potential future targets are of no moment! Conservation of ammo for the future is fine, but the real business at hand is survival NOW. Put scoring on a time and number of hits basis rather than on a number of shots fired basis.

It is not my intention to criticize U. S. Army marksmanship training as such. Since most of us are familiar with it, it serves as a common ground for illustrating current thinking on basic marksmanship training. My main point is that in practical shooting—hunting, soldiering, defense, or police—the necessary elements are either treated as a post graduate gloss or ignored altogether. Instead, people spend their time learning a game that has only a vague connection with the logical application. The basic standard of performance in the shooting world of today is premised on a bullseye score, and that's wrong except when you're playing a game. Now don't misconstrue this. I'm not giving license to that old routine, "He's a crack shot on game, but he can't hit a target." That's baloney, too. If you can hit a neutral colored moving target you can certainly hit a clearly defined motionless one. However, the difference between a smallbore shot and a fellow who shoots smallbore is about one minute of angle. This is poles apart from the chap who can throw a rifle to his shoulder and get a hit on an area approximately 12 inches square when it's moving right along, and do all this in two or three seconds. The moral of this story is to prepare for the type of shooting you like but don't think "Shootin' is shootin'." Good scores

on the smallbore range all year offer no excuse for taking the lever action off the wall, come November 1st, with the assumption that you're a well-prepared game shot. Hitting the X-ring and hitting a deer are different sports, a twain that ain't never gonna meet.

In a discussion of marksmanship, why talk about equipment? That question has puzzled me for years. Almost universally the question is not "How long has John Q. Champion been shooting? What kind of position does he use? How does he practice and how often?" but rather "What kind of rifle did he use?" Shooters are extremely equipment-minded. Now as a sport or a game—or a matter of life or death—it's obvious that the weapon is important. However, the question is not "What is the best weapon available for the enterprise in mind?" but rather "What weapon that will do the job *can I use best?*"

Perhaps a short aside is in order on monetary matters. The most expensive always has tremendous drawing power. People just gravitate toward a $500 shotgun like cats to cream, but for the occasional shooter who for the past ten years has owned Uncle Gawge's trusty old double (price $25 from a mail-order house 40 years ago), the biggest mistake would be to buy the $500 beauty. It will take Mr. Occasional Shooter five years at three boxes of shells a year (his annual consumption) to learn to use his $500 divinity as well as he can now use Uncle's old gaspipe.

Along other lines, the difference of 100 percent in price is the cost of being able to shoot a smallbore rifle capable of minute-of-angle accuracy rather than just 10-ring accuracy. Factually, there are not too many of us able to use that extra bit, and it really is just a bit, too, until you're a first-class shot, and then it's the most important thing in the world.

Right now, for somewhere between $25 and $50 you can buy any one of six different models of domestic or foreign used service rifles, by mail. They are capable of accuracy and performance in the field that will be exceeded only by rifles costing several times those amounts. Then you'll have to shop around or load your own to find ammunition that will beat the three- or four-minute normal standards in a high-grade premium rifle.

Thorsten Veblen used the phrase "conspicuous consumption," and "Main Street" is not the only place where it is practiced. The man who has $100 to spend and plunks down $97 on a new rifle and $3 on a box of cartridges will impress his neighbors and be applauded by the deer. If he had spent $40 on a rifle, $30 on good sights, and the remainder on ammunition to practice with, the deer would laugh a whole lot less —and who eats neighbors?

To resume this "best gun" business. If you plan a trip for big game the .375 H&H Magnum is a most impressive weapon. As a matter of fact, the .375 is a beautiful game cartridge, capable of very fine accuracy and giving excellent knockdown power and penetration. It will also knock your hat right off unless you are used to the heavy recoil. Oh, I know. "It's just a big slow push." Well, some of these big slow pushes have given me a fat lip as well as a swollen finger that was banged by the rear of the trigger guard. We won't mention the mild bangs on the forehead from scopes when a rifle wasn't grasped as firmly as it should have been. It is my honest conviction that most people who initially equip themselves with a heavy caliber rifle are buying a handicap. Sure, it makes a bigger wound channel and leaves a better blood trail, but if the game had been hit right with a 6.5 Mannlicher you'd be skinning it instead of following the excellent blood trail left by an elk shot in the hindquarters because you flinched before that cannon went off.

That brings us to the nugget of my proposition. It is readily admitted that you don't notice recoil when you shoot at game, but you don't notice the flinch you brought with you from the time you fired at a target, either. That flinch is the biggest single handicap to good shooting that I know of. The insidious thing is that it can exist without your knowledge, and what's worse, if you do know about it and try to cure it, the cure can be a partial one where sometimes you flinch and sometimes you don't.

What's the answer? It is more than practice. It is starting with a light caliber and building your good habits on it. And lots and lots of beginners flinch on a .22. As you go into heavier calibers you gradually find your limit and have good habits to fall back on rather than bad habits to break. My personal feeling is that when I go beyond a .30-06 I am going uphill. I can use a .35 Whelen nicely but I don't use it more than necessary. For me, more than a .375 H&H is too much. These 12-pound double .470s—the kind that "handle like a shotgun" because they're so beautifully balanced—they push me so far back and their muzzles climb so high up in the air that I honestly feel I could get off a second shot from a bolt action of reasonable caliber in about the same time, and I am talking about aimed shots, based purely on using the wasted recovery time from the excessive recoil in bolt manipulation of the lighter rifle.

Actual recoil is an unalterable mathematical rela-

tionship of rifle weight to bullet and powder weight multiplied by velocity. Although you can't change this you can either mitigate or aggravate it by stock dimensions. A well-fitting straight stock will deliver the blow in the best way possible. Two of the worst examples I know in stocking are the old "rifle" stocks with the narrow, curved buttplate and too much drop, and the German service Mauser with the top of the buttplate angled. An old-style .30-30 carbine and an 8-mm. sporter with a "rifle" buttplate cut me up something fierce with those thin stocks. Well stocked, they aren't bad at all, and you can develop a nasty flinch from a sore shoulder regardless of the caliber. So it makes sense to pay attention to stocking.

As to light rifles, I love 'em—and leave 'em. There is a perfectly beautiful 8-mm. G-33-40 Mauser carbine with a first-class stock and a good scope on the rack at home, and it weighs seven pounds complete with sling. It stays on the rack. I carry a Springfield sporter that weighs two full pounds more, and those two pounds mean a lot towards the end of a day. I do it for one simple reason. Quite honestly, I cannot shoot as fast or as accurately with the lighter rifle. I overhandle it. Now you may say that by the end of the day when I'm tired I'll appreciate the light rifle and I'll have slowed up so much that it will be the better one. Sounds good, but within normal limits the heavier rifle is still the better one for me, because muscle fatigue means tremor, and that little weight slows down my tremor. Also a seven-pound 8-mm. with a 236-grain bullet has noticeable recoil, just about what a .35 Whelen with a 275-grain bullet gives you when it weighs in at 9½ pounds. As in any art, "Know thyself."

The best approach I can advise for a tyro is a coach and a .22. Until you are proficient with a .22 you are not a shooter at all. Once the basic proficiency is there, it is an easy step to the hunting or service rifle with your then conditioned reflexes. But unless you are interested only in smallbore, get up off your stomach. Prone is one of the least-used positions in any form of practical marksmanship.

THERE was never a more interesting time than the present in the history of the American rifle. And perhaps there was never a more critical time.

It's interesting and it's promising because we have so many varieties in styling and price, and even in caliber—counting the wildcats, though the factory line has been whittled almost to a minimum. New developments in the rifle and its accessories push up over the horizon almost if not quite every month, and most of them have at least a little something different.

These newcomers could confuse the tyro, perhaps, but not the old hand. Take the still fairly recent 6-mm. cartridges of modern vintage, the .243 and .244. Even if the oldtimer were not a 6 mm wildcat fan and hadn't followed those developments with much attention, he'd have been able to size up a .243 or .244 as soon as he'd seen and handled a specimen pulled out of a factory box. "Shoots flat, ought to be accurate even in a light sporter since it doesn't pack an awful lot of powder and lead, good varmint load because the wind couldn't push it around like a Swift or a Varminter, ought to kill deer or antelope because the bullet's got pretty fair weight as well as lots of speed."

But this is a critical time, too, for us riflemen. An unprecedented number of hunters goes afield, in game seasons and even in the off times of varmint shooting, with the result that the accident toll grows and grows. It's exactly like having more cars on the highway, and we certainly have those!

No one in his senses tries to do away with cars, to set us back to the buggy and phaeton and carryall age. Cars are a necessity, even to get us to the edge of that blessed country where they can't navigate! People earn their living by and in automobiles.

But guns are a luxury, and from this true reasoning it's only a short, though false, step to say that they aren't a necessity. "The police will take care of you, and as for wild animals, the conservation personnel is perfectly able to hold them in check."

We know better! We haven't forgotten who made and kept America strong, chiefly the citizen-soldier, from the Lexington and Concord battles of April 19, 1775, right down to the present. Sure, they had courage, like that which the street fighters in Budapest demonstrated to the world—the free world, that is—in 1956. Also they had the ownership of firearms and the right to learn to use them. With those advantages, the blood price is not so high.

There are well-intentioned citizens who would disarm us, starting with the pistol and taking the rifle and shotgun next. They are the pawns of the subversives, those who would take not only our arms but also our freedom. The statement that "Guns are dangerous" is a powerful weapon, worn shiny with use but still effective if we let it be.

CHAPTER 34

THE FUTURE OF THE RIFLE IN AMERICA

For a generation and more the National Rifle Association has been the private gun-owner's chief counter-weapon. It has been accepted as a sensible, down-to-earth adviser of legislators, not of all, but of many. Its recommendations are being accepted with the good faith in which they are offered, for there are wise as well as unwise laws that control the ownership or use of firearms.

The NRA keeps its members advised of proposed legislation in their states. Less than ten years ago a bill came up in a certain legislature to prohibit the sporting use of centerfire rifles except during the brief big-game season. There is good varmint hunting in that state, and many NRA members, too. Enough of them wrote to their congressmen, and the bill was killed.

And there's the junior hunter instruction, NRA sponsored. It parallels the driver education and examination systems that are a matter of course in so many state motor-vehicle departments. Where it is enforced it has cut the accident rate no less than sensationally. If every new hunter, regardless of his or her age, were obliged to go through the training and prove mastery of it in an exam, we'd have taken the next, the logical, and maybe the essential step toward keeping our guns and our hunting privileges, not only for ourselves but also for those who'll come after us.

THE GAME OUTLOOK

Unlike some other peoples, we Americans did wake up in time. Many of us are old enough to have seen the turning-point, and still young enough to hunt and camp and if necessary lean-to it out overnight. It didn't come in a day or a year or a decade, and it didn't start simultaneously from east to west coast or from the Canadian to the Mexican line.

But wildlife students, sportsmen, and far-seeing folk in general read the warnings, and our game was saved. At least the tide was turned. In many areas there is more game now than there was twenty, thirty, or forty years ago. Sensible legislation, stricter enforcement, and more whole-hearted cooperation of hunters and of sportsmen's associations did it, and they can keep on doing it. In the final shakedown it's people, individuals like you and me.

This is a prosperous age, and travel has become an accustomed and easy thing. Our deepest wildernesses can be penetrated, and always there are some of us riflemen who value such exploration even more highly than the actual hunting—to say nothing of the final act, the shooting—of the game we find in those places. More than ever before, too, our hunters are visiting the African and Asian continents, with little left for boots or boat to explore than the farthest reaches of South American jungles.

There are the pocket wildernesses, too, for those who get a good many free days in a year, but rarely more than two or three at a stretch. It isn't at all uncommon to visit old haunts and find more small game there than there was ten or twenty years ago. Good farmer-sportsman relationships open such close-to-home country, and many of the distinctions between the town and country way of living are melting away, to the improvement of mutual understanding and friendliness.

Game is one of our greatest national assets, and that fact isn't hard to understand, but the so-called varmints are in a bad way for survival. And they're game, too, as well as interesting wildlife that no one with sense would want to see become extinct. Government poisoning campaigns in the West, with that slow, torturesome killer, 10-80, at least wrote the lesson for those who *could* read. When coyotes were wiped out in certain sections, Nature's balance was upset and other "undesirable" species had their chance to multiply—and some were really pests. There were innocent 10-80 victims, too, such as birds, for carrion is pretty common wildlife food in semi-desert countries. In the East the problem is the varmint hunter who tries to pile up a record of kills. The woodchuck may have better self-defense than the bison had, but not much. He can be wiped out, and he has been in some sections.

On vacations of a week or so, a canoe can take us to rarely visited summer jungles or swamps that are impassable on foot, places where we see or hear no other human all day long, though at times the grind and whine of traffic may drift in. Forest streams in New York's Adirondacks, for instance, can float us (with a due slice of wading or portaging) to country so lonely and wild that we are, most seriously, on our own. An ankle caught between submerged boulders could be sprained or broken, and then we'd have bought, perhaps, full measure of disaster. But a woodsman doesn't take chances; so he generally comes home safe.

THE TARGET OUTLOOK

Just with the rifle alone, not using shotgun or pistol, the target shooter can have a lifetime of varied fun.

Red Desert Wyoming, after a rain. Antelope abound in the flats and mule deer use the wooded slopes of the mountains. *Thomas C. Florich Photo*.

In fact, he'll probably specialize in prone, four-position, bench, or maybe muzzle-loader.

Target thrives on the spirit of competition, though there's no surer way to wreck the enjoyment, the game supply in the broad picture, and perhaps a friendship that we thought was everlasting, than to apply this spirit to hunting. Competition can be as narrow as you like—and you-and-me matches are fun indeed—or as broad as Camp Perry's individual or team events, or International, if you can reach that honor. Calibers, distances, number of shots, positions, even the sights used, all offer wide latitude. It is a great sport, and every hour you put into it makes you a better rifleman for your own good, or for Uncle's if he ever needs you.

Is it losing its popularity because it's too monotonous, too regimented? There have been rumors to that effect.

Now it is obvious that any organized sport must have definite rules, and if it can have definite ratings of achievement, too, as shooting does, so much the better. The National Rifle Association is the largest organization to help us achieve this definiteness, but never think that it doesn't favor, too, shooting (safe shooting) for everyone. It wants more people to be drawn into the sport, whether or not they become members of the Association, and to make shooting attractive to more different kinds of people is one of its most earnest purposes.

But here are November 1956, figures on NRA classified shooters, those who've fired often enough in registered or approved tournaments to earn classified ratings: 1954, 36,114; 1955, 37,298; 1956, 41,614. These are dyed-in-the-groundcloth competitors who spend time and money to attend big events. They're a small proportion of club members, junior and senior.

In general the interest is in three branches: smallbore, bigbore, and pistol. Records prove that the interest isn't perishing!

A certain type of shooting may show a decline. This happened to outdoor prone smallbore. Thirty caliber is mainly three- or four-position, not just prone. Introducing four-position outdoor smallbore competition at the 1956 National Matches at Camp Perry was in line with the general shift of interest. If a type of competition in which you're interested happens to slump, don't say that the whole shooting game is going to pot. Look around and see what goes in other parts of the pasture. The general program is far broader and more generally interesting than ever before, and more shooters are active, too.

For concrete proof of the game's vitality, visit a junior rifle club some night! What, none in your locality? First make sure; then write the NRA—1600 Rhode Island Ave., N. W., Washington 6, D. C.—and they'll tell you. The next move is a longer stride, but I wouldn't call it difficult. Start one.

Anyone interested enough in shooting to read or dip through this book should get in on the fun that our most national of all sports provides.

So it costs too much and it isn't thrilling in the sensational way? Competition can give it the kick, all right, even if nothing goes bust or rings a bell when you squeeze off a good one. Sure, plinking is fun, and it can be fine training, at tin cans, candy wafers, or thumbtacks—look back, if you will, to Judge Tinney's contribution in Chapter 27. *He* knows how to combine fun and games and variety with riflery.

Any tight match is thrill enough for the shooters. The gallery? Yes, we have a hard time drawing that in formal, or informal, rifle shooting, and do we really want it? What we do want is riflery for everyone, and our sport is one that everyone can play. The gallery is potential shooters.

The cost? Oh yes. What did you pay for that TV set? I see. For about half that you could have bought a bang-up good .22 rimfire match rifle, new or critically selected second-hand, and if you treat it right it won't ever need a new tube as long as you live! I never saw anyone laughed off the range because his rifle was cheap, provided he really wanted to learn.

And there's the Sporting Rifle program, where you *have* to use a little, light .22, and 90 per cent of them are really inexpensive. Some able minds are working on this problem, how to put the program across with the thrill, the simplicity, and still the accepted, official recognition of qualifications and insignia. They are not publicity seekers, but people of faith. They know, and you and I must in all fairness and logic agree, that *we have got to have something of this sort.* It carries on the work that the thousands of junior clubs are doing; it's fun for all the family, and it's active, not a mere blotting-up of transient impressions. Sporting Rifle takes the embarrassment and reluctance out of the too rare Parents' Nights we put on at junior clubs. It has been approved by the NRA, as we had thought that it would be.

AMMUNITION

Now we assume the big black robe, the peaky hat, and the false whiskers, to go prophetic. None of us can guess what improvements in materiel are coming, and only a fool tries. At least, that's one view of such rashness.

Mass production is going to do some remarkable favors for us riflemen. Now you can start to laugh, for the other night down at the range, after the kids had finished and gone home, I dumped five .22 *longs* into the 50-foot target, from 50 feet. The gun was a standard match model, 16-inch twist for long-rifle ammo, much too fast for the .22 short bullet that's loaded into the long.

The score was 48x50 and I could scarcely believe it. With better centering over the 10-ring it might have been a 49. Though I'm not a good holder, I'm not bad enough to have made this grouping entirely by accident: the stuff was shooting close to where I held. A few years ago, that couldn't have happened. At least I'd tried years before, and failed. Later trial brought a 49, with the off-shot called by the firer.

The long never was a premium load for accuracy and there's no reason why a factory should try to make it good. No exacting shooter buys it except as a gag. The point is that modern chemistry and precision machinery are so good that they *can't* turn out bad ammunition. There are exceptions to that sweeping statement, but you see the point.

Chemistry will give us better powders, excellent though those are that we have now. Western ball powder, compact, accurate in results, and reportedly much cooler than the older line, is only a beginning. Research is working all the time to give us better primers to light off our powders, even though we have splendid primers now, as the steady setting up of new bench-rest records proves. Perhaps in the future there will be no primer to introduce even that slight variable: the dream of electric ignition is an old one.

So far, metallurgists have found nothing better than cartridge brass for our cases. It has reasonable strength, and the spring-back toward former dimensions that makes possible both bullet seating and the extraction of the fired case. No steel is quite as good for the purpose; it is still only a substitute.

Ammunition of the future will be compact. Compare the short .458 with the 3¼-inch-cased .45-120-550 black-powder Sharps and then look farther ahead. The .308 was a beginning, with new powders almost certain to come up, in time, that can and must use cases of still lower capacity to give the fullest efficiency. Bullets will be of smaller caliber, lighter, and necessarily faster. There must be some downward limit, for we need ranging power and wind-bucking ability, and mass as well as velocity to kill our game.

The all-range expanding bullet may be a possibility. For it hasn't, I think, been achieved. True, we do have those that will expand on a solid hit 'way out where velocity is lowered, and still not fly to pieces close-up. But will they expand on a gut shot at some crazy long range, or be so quick in breakup that ricochets off summer meadows are impossible, and yet stop the biggest game in the world from tossing or trampling us if we aim and fire correctly?

Ridiculous? An impossibility? I'm not sure. We cannot know the full possibilities of future design and materials that will make better all-round hunting bullets. We can only guess, but a really good guess is certainly worth a trial. Factory or custom made, these trial specimens are packaged for sale. No one can deny that some of them have been an improvement upon earlier types.

RIFLES

New sporting-rifle models have been common in this decade of the 1950s, still far from ended, just as they were in the first ten years of this century. A few of them have been really new.

Actions

Sometimes the question has been raised: Isn't the bolt action becoming obsolete, with its four-motion reloading? (Four blended into two, for the expert, of course: a wrench that flows smoothly into a pull, and a push with a slap-down at the end.) It could be on the way out, but so far it is, *in general,* unrivaled in strength, stiffness and consequent accuracy, long-haul durability, power of loading and extraction, and the simple dismounting that means so much after a wetting or a dust-storm.

The .22 Mossberg Model 342, just announced, is a hammerless bolt action. Like its twin, the 352 autoloader, it has flowing lines. Their actions are long, and the 342 bolt lies too far ahead for handiness, but they are apparently gas-proof, and reasonably weatherproof, too.

The autoloader has been improved in accuracy and in its ability to handle powerful hunting ammunition, though in simplicity and foolproof ruggedness few can equal the early blowback systems of 1903 and 1905. Now there are streamlined models, and some have been built with considerable attention to balance and handling qualities. Whether the semi-auto becomes the almost completely accepted hunting rifle of the future or is banned by state or even federal laws depends to some extent on how its users behave themselves. There's an old and rather deep-seated distrust of "automatics."

Would a slide action be handier if the reloading motions were reversed—forward and back instead of back and forward? Some have been made on this principle, although they certainly are museum specimens now. It would seem natural, under the push of recoil, to let the outstretched hand go forward, then pull it back as we recovered. This system would place the sliding forestock close to the rifle's balance point, where most good riflemen hold in offhand.

What about takedowns? Will we have those in which the barrel and forestock come off with no receiver parts attached, so handy for packing and cleaning, and will they be capable of giving the accuracy of a solid frame rifle of similar type and quality? Will we have once again—for the old Winchester repeaters and the various fine single shots are scarce items—takedowns with interchangeable barrels of different calibers, and modern high-intensity calibers, too? Would the problems of correct headspace, durability and long maintained accuracy be solved? And if we had all this, who would want such a burgeoning battery, even with only one stock fit and trigger pull to learn? Certainly not those who see advantages in using one or two good calibers, with two or three good loads apiece, to become familiar with in matters of windage and elevation, not only on measured ranges but also where distances are guessed at. And not those who favor certain actions for certain kinds of hunting, or of hunting country.

Barrels

Even in the last ten years or so, definite strides forward have been taken in the manufacture of sporting and target rifle barrels. It's natural to suppose that we are at the beginning of a new era, and perhaps we are.

The undeniably great demand for light weight combined with great power in a big-game rifle has been answered, in some cases, by barrels that would have looked actually unsafe to earlier generations of riflemen. The Featherweight Winchester 70 in .308, for instance, stepped down abruptly just ahead of the receiver ring, at first appeared to some of us as if it had been used by mistake! It appeared to be about right for a carbine using the mild old .30-30 cartridge. Yet it has plenty of strength and in spite of its expected whippiness gives excellent hunting accuracy. Later it was bored out to .358, with good results, and much slimmer custom barrels for still more powerful cartridges are doing all right, within natural limits.

There are such potentialities in alloyed steel it seems unlikely that an entirely different metal need be used to save weight in sporting-rifle barrels. Already steel can give us barrels that are entirely too light for reasonably steady holding.

Military requirements in weight can be quite different; sooner or later the infantry soldier has to crawl, walk or run, and plenty. So a 6¾- to 7-pound semi-auto rifle to replace the Garand M-1 could have its points. A candidate has been made with aluminum alloy barrel lined with stainless steel, some aluminum action parts, and stock of featherweight fiberglass and plastic foam. It is natural that sporters of this type will follow, and be easy to ridicule at the start. One might even suggest that a pink chiffon sling would be suitable for such an arm. That would be an early laugh. The last laugh might be at our stupidity in ever having lugged all-steel barrels and wooden stocks.

But a different metal or alloy may be found to resist longer the erosion of extremely high velocities, and we're only at the beginning of such speeds. Much has been done already. The stainless steels are one example, the chrome-plated bores another. At this point we hardly know how much we've accomplished, since so few of the latest specimens have been shot to destruction, or even could have been, before something new and a little different would come up!

Obviously a smooth, hard, and relatively non-porous inside finish resists erosion better than the opposite. It is less prone to rust, too, though rust from atmospheric conditions is a much less dangerous enemy now that practically all ammunition is non-corrosive.

One way of producing such a finish was described in the August, '56 issue of *Precision Shooting*. It is the Appel Process, Inc., of Detroit, by Dr. Gerhard Appel, formerly a German citizen. The barrel is formed over a grooved mandrel, which suggests a technique of muzzle-loading rifle manufacture but instead is most modern.

It is cold forging. The dies that open and close on the outside of the smooth-bored barrel blank work at the rate of 2,000 times a minute. They do not strike; they press. This cold working improves tensile and yield (load-supporting) strengths, and it is directed straight toward the center of the barrel, not at an angle or tangent. So the finish is hard, and it is said to be less porous than that of a machined or lapped barrel. This seems reasonable, and accuracy as well as long barrel life ought to be one of the advantages of barrels made in this manner.

If barrel cleaning were truly unnecessary because the bore never picked up bits of bullet material—which can, it's generally admitted, detract from the finest accuracy—we'd have longer barrel life for that reason alone. Cleaning rods and brushes do cause wear. Pushing out primer and powder residue, and nothing more, could hardly be called cleaning. One patch should do it if the barrel were perfect.

Grooveless oval and double-oval bores have been tried, with disappointment. They were easy to clean, and nothing else was gained. Grooves have been cut with rounded driving edges, but if this is overdone there's a tendency for the bullet to ride up on the lands. Marlin's Micro-Groove system, 16 narrow, shallow grooves, is not in itself new, for all sorts of experiments have been made through the centuries, but it is not an experiment. It's an accepted commercial method. The low rifling lands have less tendency to draw fins across the edge of the base of the fired bullet—not that fins need ruin accuracy if they are uniform all around the circumference. If a rifle landed all its bullets side-on at 100 yards and put 'em all in the same hole we'd have accuracy, and what a time the bench-rest scorers would have in measuring *that* group! Uniformity is synonymous with accuracy. With less deep working of the Marlin steel there would seem to be less liability of slight variations, and that is what rifle-makers naturally want in the parts that contribute to good shooting.

The growing use of the button or swaged rifling process isn't due only to the fact that it can save time. Pressing the grooves into a barrel *can* result in a smoother finish than cutting them gives. That, at least, is the contention of the button process proponents who speak up to justify their method.

Exactness is the thing. Harry Pope got it by almost infinite patience and skill. It is possible that the machine can replace the man, though the man must devise, make and operate the machine.

Stocks

The sub-machine or burp gun (German Kar. 44, 7.92 shorty, for instance) might resemble the generally accepted rifle of the future in stocking. The stock is up in line with the barrel, taking the thrust of recoil almost directly back to the shooter's shoulder instead of upward, too, levering the muzzle toward the sky. A fine principle: saves time in getting off a second shot . . .

At that point I knocked off work to avoid an attack of mental nausea. I went upstairs, took down a rifle that Tom Shelhamer had stocked for me a good few years ago, also a couple of factory-stocked single shots, Remington and Winchester, that of course are a great deal older. I looked them over in that dreamy way, ran my hands along their smooth and graceful curves. The oldtimers were stocked for looks and for a now completely outmoded technique of firing. The Shelhamer was stocked for looks, too—all three of them have that—and for modern techniques. Not even yet is it in any significant way out of date.

Efficiency and beauty are hard to combine in a rifle stock, but they can be combined. The former is the first goal sought. After the experimenters have done their work—and let us give them the credit and the gratitude they deserve—the refiners come along and try to give us beauty. So far, they have succeeded.

But what is beauty? The dictionary definition is cagey: it doesn't pin it down. And who could? Maybe the word "taste" would be better, for there's a multitude of tastes.

The 1957 Colt—.243 and .30-06 on F. N. Mauser action—didn't interest me chiefly because Colt was making rifles again but because of its stock design. It seems a canny, business-wise choice, almost midway between extremes and conservatives as made today. Colt offers scopes too, in 2½ and 4 power, complete with top mounts. At this writing the rifle hasn't been standardized.

SIGHTS

In the nature of scientific development, variable-power scopes are not far from the "mewling and puking" stage of infancy. It is not even absolutely certain that the majority of shooters would care to pay a premium to get one, for much is to be said for the old, familiar sight picture, always the same. Some of us who have switched back and forth between square and round, red and gold and ivory and black front sight beads or tips will vouch for that statement, though others fit themselves easily and for-the-day to any of them, or to any decent type of scope reticle, or even to any type of rifle action, provided they're familiar with them all.

But improvement in vari-power and in mono-power scopes will go on, limited only by the laws of optics, and helped by such auxiliaries as the coating of lenses with magnesium fluoride to cut reflection and glare and—rather contradictorily, it seems—to increase luminosity when we need it. Engineering advances will make scopes even more available to people of limited means. There may be another figure as legendary as Weaver became by doing just that in depression days.

I can imagine no better scope reticles, for distinctly different jobs, than our present cross-hairs, straight or tapered flat-top post, and dot, but maybe you or someone else can. Perhaps an instantly adjustable size of reticle will become possible and practical, though I don't expect to see one even if I live long and right enough to become venerable.

It seems a sure bet that iron sights will hang on because they can be both inexpensive and durable, and the rough, stamped-out variety of open sight will endure, worse luck! But if scopes entirely displace irons we'll have to have really foolproof mounts, something like the integral mount that Tom Florich once spoke of, just as a gag, which affords a hole to poke the scope into. "There! Now let's see you get busted."

THE INDIVIDUAL

Riflemen are individuals, at least while riding that hobby. We like what we like and want what we want.

Though mass production has its obvious virtues, it can give the real rifle-crank only a start. Precise, individual workmanship always will count, and there will be more tools available to the home worker. Even in the last fifteen years the battery of small, one-man-operated, accurate tools has increased amazingly, and many sell at previously unheard-of low prices, considering the relative values of our U. S. dollar. Experimenters do practical field research for the big manufacturing companies, whether or not they are paid or publicly recognized for what they contribute.

With all our effort toward new and improved developments it is unlikely that any of them will suddenly scrap what we have in that line. For here comes in the human element! The 1895 .30-30 deer cartridge is still the biggest seller in its line, though the reasons are obvious, all of us must admit, and some of them aren't to its credit. The proved and the familiar have a mighty appeal.

We learn much from the old in developing the new, and often the new is suspiciously familiar in many details. Sometimes all that the old needs, in order to win its place in a fine new world, is time in which to have dropped out for a short rest in oblivion. So our rifle of the future is likely to be no great stranger, but what of the rifleman?

May he be as exacting as we are and not pushed around by forces that look bigger than he is. Being particular about our weapon helps to make us intelligent in using it. It's our free-time friend, and one of our guarantees of freedom.

THAT CHAPTER heading may be inaccurate. Our appreciation of good things we've had for a long time tends to grow dull.

Probably you've had the experience of lifting an old rifle from the rack—a rifle that hadn't been used, lately, as much as it deserved—and appreciating it afresh. It was better than you'd remembered.

So let me do that to my concept of the NRA, recalling the ways in which it serves us riflemen, and all our Country, in fact. It is, after all, the National Rifle Association of America. How does it help us? "Let me count the ways."

Membership brings us *The American Rifleman* each month. It's authoritative in facts, though varied in viewpoints, just as we guncranks are in our chin sessions. There is no other magazine quite like it for us, so comprehensive; so exact, too, as some others are.

If we want an individual answer to a shooting problem we get it from one of the technical staff who is particularly well fitted to give it. One such letter that I received, years ago, gave me minute specifications for the first rifle stock built to fit me. The shop was in Michigan, I was in Pennsylvania, and I had no time to trot back and forth for personal fittings. Yet the stock was right for me in every respect.

Then there's the Director of Civilian Marksmanship, the Army's "DCM" through which we members can buy at greatly reduced cost such items as M-1 rifles, .22 long-rifle, .45 Auto and .30-06 ammo, bullets, powders, large size rifle and pistol primers, targets, bore cleaner and oil, when they're available—and they usually are. All are of top grade; they have to be.

Being a member gives us definite standing, just as club enrollment makes that club official. Thus the way is opened to official participation in matches in which there are definite, recognized awards for achievement. The NRA includes about 300,000 individual members and 7,000 clubs, and the United States Olympic Association has put it in the saddle to govern the rifle and pistol branches of our International competition. In the matter of world prestige, are any other branches quite as significant?

The NRA is for firearms handling and hunting safety, and for the advancement of marksmanship. It works hard for these things, and not without positive and increasing results. The reason to be thankful for those results is obvious. By membership we contribute concrete help; we don't just say, "Indeed, those are laudable objectives"! Taking part as an NRA-certified instructor is more active help, and the satisfaction, the downright human interest and the fun are unbelievable —until you've tried it.

All those benefits are of the material sort compared to others that are less tangible though actually more real. The intangible is hard to explain, but let me try.

Of course the NRA is 100 percent American. It

CHAPTER 35

THE N. R. A. --

AN

APPRECIATION

stands—stands right up and fights, when necessary— for our country.

Now this thing is easy to explain, the Constitutional "right of the people to keep and bear arms." You and I, in whatever state or territory we live, almost certainly owe some of our freedom, the retention of that right, to the NRA. The Association fights *unwise* gun legislation, both through its committees and through its individual or banded-together members. At times it seems like a never-ending war, but we're winning. Without the NRA we'd lose. Certainly there are subversives who would disarm us to make possible the overthrow of our Government. Equally certain it is, alas, that many well-meaning citizens believe them.

Education and logical persuasion must go on, or we'll lose our guns. Yes, it *could* happen here. Remember when England begged us for arms, for anything that would shoot, with cross-channel invasion looming up after the Dunkirk miracle, back in 1940? Years before that, it had become almost impossible for the average "middle" or "lower class" Briton to own a firearm.

But there's more, and I'll try to express it, this thing that thousands of us NRA members feel. Did you ever know the warm, present reassurance of a familiar rifle, pistol or shotgun as the timeless, unconsidered seconds of danger ticked away? Or the long-haul confidence of owning a weapon with which you could, if it ever became necessary, do battle to good effect in protecting yourself, your family, or our country? Almost certainly you've had one or the other fortress of strength.

That is how I feel about the NRA and about a certain rifle in my rack. One is intangible, the other hard and clean and bright where bright should gleam. Yet the first is equally real, for it reminds me—every day, almost—that there are millions of us Americans who would make Concord and Lexington live again if the hour struck and we could get an invader into our sights.

Lt. Charles Tait took this photograph for the Winchester (Va.) *Evening Star,* and it was published with the story of the first award of certificates, medals, pins, and brassards at a Parents' Night of the club. Using it saves the "thousand words" I could happily expend in telling what the NRA means to just this one age bracket of rifle-shooters. Bolts are open for safety, as you can see by looking at the lower left. Instruction partner Bob Wolfe is making the presentations.